THE RESTORATION

THE RESTORATION

A Political and Religious History of
England and Wales
1658–1667

RONALD HUTTON

CLARENDON PRESS · OXFORD
1985

Oxford University Press, Walton Street, Oxford OX2 6 DP

London New York Toronto
Delhi Bombay Calcutta Madras Karachi
Kuala Lumpur Singapore Hong Kong Tokyo
Nairobi Dar es Salaam Cape Town
Melbourne Auckland
and associated companies in
Beirut Berlin Ibadan Mexico City Nicosia

Oxford is a trade mark of Oxford University Press

Published in the United States
by Oxford University Press, New York

British Library Cataloguing in Publication Data
Hutton, Ronald
The Restoration: a political and religious history of England and Wales, 1658-1667.
1. Great Britain—History—Commonwealth and Protectorate, 1649-1660.
2. Great Britain—History—1660-1714
I. Title
942.06   DA425
ISBN 0-19-822698-5

Set by Joshua Associates, Oxford
Printed in Great Britain
at the University Press, Oxford
by David Stanford
Printer to the University

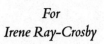

For
Irene Ray-Crosby

Preface

⌒◠⌒

IN the course of the research for, and preparation of, this book, I have contracted a number of considerable debts of gratitude to individuals and to institutions. Of the persons concerned, Dr Blair Worden has been the most intimately involved with the work from beginning to end, in some cases quite unconsciously. It was conceived when I was working as his research assistant upon his edition of Ludlow's *A Voyce from the Watchtower* in 1976, and its final shape formed in my mind during discussions of the period with him around Christmas 1979. When it was being written, he read through most of the script and offered his criticisms. Dr John Morrill also played an invaluable part in stimulating my ideas of the issues concerned, by a number of discussions over the years, and read the entire script in detail, making hundreds of suggestions for it. Last, my own colleague at Bristol, Dr John Guy, was of great assistance in advising me upon certain problems concerning archives and the procedure of research, and in turn read and commented upon the whole work. Between them, these three friends and scholars have possibly doubled the quality of this book, exerting an influence over it far greater than I have provided for any of theirs. The blemishes in the final result are naturally my own responsibility.

In the course of 1982 I presented some of the main themes of the book for debate at the seminars chaired by Mr Keith Thomas at Oxford, by Blair Worden and Dr Anne Whiteman in the same university, by John Morrill at Cambridge, by John Guy at Bristol, and by Drs Roseveare, Miller, and Lockyer at the Institute of Historical Research. Some of the comments made were very valuable and my gratitude is due both to these hosts and to all who contributed. One consequence was the acquaintance of certain graduate students researching into the period, notably Messrs Andrew Coleby and Paul Seward who were then at Oxford University, and discussions with them have been every bit as helpful as many of those with older colleagues.

A different sort of debt is owed to those institutions which supported much of the research itself. Had the President and Fellows of Magdalen College, Oxford, not elected me to a Prize Fellowship in 1979, it is inconceivable that this book could have been produced in less than twice the time it has actually taken. They also made a most generous extra grant to cover the costs of most of the necessary travel through the record repositories of south and west England and of Wales. The British Academy awarded me another large sum to make possible the work in the north and east, and the University of Bristol made a number of small grants to assist specific journeys during the winter seasons. Last, the American Leadership Studies Group was of considerable help in supporting the research in central archives. The total cost of the travelling required has been colossal, and had any of these bodies been less generous then the scope of the book would have been proportionately more restricted. Research plays the same part in the life of a modern historian as war in that of an early modern monarchy: it may bring glory but it always produces strain, and without considerable native resources powerful allies are essential.

Last, I take great pleasure in thanking the staff of those particular archives where I received assistance beyond that either expected or formally required, ranging from the provision of information by letter to the production of documents or their call-numbers in readiness for the visit, to an overt interest in the subject of the research, to the willingness (in one case) to waive formal practice and to admit me to the store itself simply because staff shortage had left the remaining personnel incapable of providing manuscripts at more than a very slow pace. They represent, between all these favours, the record offices of Cornwall, Clwyd, Cumbria (Carlisle), Essex, Leicestershire, North Yorkshire, Bristol, Wiltshire, Somerset and Hampshire, Duke Humfrey's Library in the Bodleian, Miss Margaret Condon of the Public Record Office, and the archivist of the Marquis of Bath. May they be an example, and a shame, to some of the others. I also thank the Marquis of Bath, the Earl of Dartmouth, and the Countess of Sutherland, for their permission to inspect the papers of their ancestors.

Finally, as the book was being eased into the press, I received great benefit from a final round of criticisms made by Professor Austin Woolrych and from much practical advice tendered by Dr Ivon Asquith of the Oxford University Press. If historical research is a solitary activity, its public expression is certainly a co-operative venture.

Contents

Illustrations

❧

The author and publisher gratefully acknowledge permission to reproduce these illustrations from the following: the Cromwell Museum, Huntingdon (nos. 1 and 2); the British Library (no. 3); the National Portrait Gallery (nos. 4, 6, 8, and 9); Dr Williams's Trust (no. 5); Her Majesty the Queen (no. 7); the Master and Fellows of Magdalene College, Cambridge (no. 10); the Museum of London (no. 11); and the National Maritime Museum, London (no. 12).

Particular gratitude is owed to Her Majesty the Queen, to the Museum of London, and to the British Library, for freely granting reproduction rights.

Introduction

DURING the last twenty years our knowledge of the English Civil War and the political changes which followed it has been immeasurably increased, both by major works and by monographs. By contrast, only a few monographs have been devoted to the period immediately succeeding. At the same time, nobody has questioned the traditional belief that the Restoration Settlement marks the culmination of the dramatic series of events commencing in 1640, and the year 1660 is still generally treated as the watershed of the seventeenth century in England. Thus the history of the English Revolution now reads like a marvellous story with the last chapter missing, and we cannot claim to possess any perspective upon the century as a whole.

This problem both inspired the writing of the present book and prescribed the form it has taken. It was conceived eight years ago, as a provincial history of the Restoration Settlement, complementing and revising the accepted picture of central politics in the manner of much of the recent work upon the earlier period. What rendered such a project impracticable was the fact, soon very obvious, that there existed no picture of central politics to be treated in this manner. The first six decades of the century were made familiar by the great narratives of Gardiner and Firth, the last two by Macaulay. For the period 1658-60, there was only Godfrey Davies's volume, which was really a series of monographs strung together, and for the 1660s the authority was David Ogg, whose preoccupations tended to be with a slightly later period and who wrote in less detail than the other pioneers of narrative.

The purpose of this book has therefore altered, to one of 'clearing the ground' for all future work in the period of the Stuart Restoration. On the one hand, it seeks to provide a detailed narrative history of England from the death of Cromwell to the fall of Clarendon, to illustrate the process by which the political and religious world of the Protectorate was transformed into that of the Restoration monarchy. It suggests answers to the traditional questions about this process, and lists the known sources for them more comprehensively than has been done hitherto. On the other hand, it is intended to identify areas for further investigation and the material upon which this might be based, and to create new debates. Some of this process will undoubtedly be unconscious, as this book will highlight aspects of the epoch simply by failing to notice or to take adequate account of them, as the result of preoccupation with other problems. If the work has an overall aim, it is to provoke interest in its subject.

The central theme is the formation and implementation of national policy, and the interplay of central and local interests in this process. In pursuit of it, I have visited every public archive in England and most in Wales, in addition to several private collections. This programme of research has produced a quantity and a variety of evidence unavailable to the older narrative historians, but also a narrowing of focus. There has been no attempt to provide a detailed account of Scottish or Irish affairs, or of the making of foreign policy, and these topics are dealt with only as they impinge upon domestic English and Welsh events, employing the existing secondary sources for them. A preliminary investigation of the primary material revealed that proper treatment of these matters would require three times the period of research, and four times the expense, of the existing work. When this additional scholarship had been completed, after a decade and a half, much of the earlier research upon internal English affairs would have been made redundant.

The balance of the book is not what a reader is likely to expect from the dates 1658-1667 in the title, for over half of it is devoted to the first four years of this span. Such a division resulted from the nature of the material: both the issues and the events of public life were much more numerous in the earlier period than the later, and generated considerably more surviving evidence. Over the whole period, I have attempted to treat these issues and events afresh, rereading the known sources and adding to them whenever possible. Very rarely have I incorporated the work of a predecessor wholesale into my own, even when the previous study has taken the form of a detailed monograph.

One last consideration determined the nature of this book: the belief that it should be accessible to the widest possible audience. This has resulted in the treatment of matters familiar to professional colleagues in the same detail as those of more interest to them, the transference of archival information and academic debate to end-notes, and the employment of a dramatic style when dealing with colourful events. In an age in which academics are brutally reminded of their dependence upon public funds, it would seem particularly appropriate to serve the interests of the public directly whenever there is an opportunity to do so.

PART ONE

SEPTEMBER 1658[1]

In early September 1658 a letter[2] crossed the North Sea. Had it been discovered by the English authorities at its port of embarkation, it ought to have aroused immediate suspicion. Most of it was in code, it was unsigned, and the subscription was simply to 'Mr Tompson', without an address. In fact its destination was Hochstrade, a town on the northern frontier of the Spanish Netherlands, with some fine houses plundered bare by the king of Spain's cavalry.[3] Lodged in one of these was the recipient, Sir Edward Hyde, a fat, petulant man in middle age who held the office of Lord Chancellor of England. In reality Hyde had not seen England for over twelve years. His main duty was to gather information for and present advice to his master, Charles II, England's uncrowned and exiled King. This particular letter carried one of the most significant pieces of information Hyde had ever received. Oliver Cromwell, the effective ruler of his country and mortal enemy of his cause, was dead.

Almost exactly seven years before, Cromwell's soldiers had destroyed the King's last army at Worcester and hunted Charles out of England after a series of terrifying and humiliating adventures. Till that moment Charles or his father had always commanded the allegiance of large forces somewhere in their three kingdoms. Every time decisive defeat occurred in one, fresh adherents appeared in another. After Worcester, the royalists were left helpless throughout the British Isles. Three separate civil wars, spanning almost a decade and claiming uncounted thousands of lives, had ended in their utter prostration. Their monarch and his ministers henceforth depended upon the charity of foreign states, while at home they could carry on the struggle only with futile small-scale risings.

Even in this extremity of penury and frustration the court possessed certain strengths which brought comfort at times to its members.[4] Its monarch was twenty-eight, healthy, intelligent and determined to continue the fight for his throne. He had two brothers, James, Duke of York and Henry, Duke of Gloucester, who could succeed him. To Hyde, Charles seemed to possess most of the vices of youth, notably lechery, laziness and extravagance. Nevertheless he appeared to have acquired the cardinal virtue of loyalty. The factional warfare which had riven the court in the early years of exile was long over. Nobody believed that they could win office and favour there by denouncing an existing minister. The Queen Mother, who had attempted to tie the royal cause to that of Roman Catholicism, had been left to sulk on the fringe of her nephew's court, in France. After much wandering, Charles had been resident for almost three years in the Spanish Netherlands, whose sovereign demanded only a secret promise of toleration for English Catholics. His ministers were men like Hyde, whose record testified consistently to a belief in the episcopal Church of England and in constitutional monarchy.

Nor was the situation in England altogether conducive to despair. Cromwell had found royalist conspiracy a hydra-headed monster. Few, indeed, of the men who had followed Charles I in the field were still active for his son on their native soil. Many were dead or driven abroad. Many more, including the greatest nobles, had been crushed by fines and failure, and bent their influence towards discouraging further sacrifice. Yet new men had come forward to replace them, younger sons eager for profit and adventure, or men who had fought Charles I only to turn to his son in revulsion from his execution and the attendant revolution. Royalist conspiracy had lost much in coherence as a result and something in sagacity, but it had continued. The last plot, for which Cromwell's government had exacted five more lives, had been exposed only a few months previously. Such constant alarms had irritated Cromwell, at first inclined to conciliate royalists, into a policy of political apartheid. For over a year every substantial man who had ever been active for either king was ordered to pay a tenth of his income to support militia to watch him. Gentry opinion, expressed in parliament, had ended this in 1657, but royalists in general remained excluded from office and political life. Their leaders were dragged into preventive detention at each new rumour of a rising. Individuals who had defected long before and proved their new loyalty rose high in Cromwell's regime, but they were few. The counties and cities of England and Wales were left in the extraordinary condition whereby a section of their natural leaders, in some cases the majority, were disqualified from leading.

Local life itself carried on much as before the wars and revolution.[5] Proceedings in law courts were now conducted in English and recorded in a normal hand, but despite repeated talk of reform virtually the same judicial machinery dispensed virtually the same law.[6] Justices of the Peace administered the old system of poor relief, often with greater efficiency.[7] When commoners destroyed forest enclosures or fen drainage works which harmed their interests, the central government acted against them as Charles I had done.[8] Trade and industry proceeded within traditional restrictions.[9] Urban corporations continued to solicit additional privileges from Whitehall, and in most towns the structure of politics was unaltered. The wars and revolution had removed many corporation members, and in several cases Cromwell's government intervened to bolster the power of a particular set of men. But on the whole these changes represented a redistribution of power within an existing élite.[10] Such examples of continuity from a pre-war world testify both to the relative conservatism of the new regimes and to the resilience of the English provinces, in absorbing national changes and adapting them to local needs.

For all this, many local communities were afflicted with a malaise of which the political exclusion of royalist gentry was only a part. Even in Cumberland and Westmorland, an area in which over half the gentry had supported the kings' cause, there should have remained a large minority of old families eligible and willing to work for the republic. Yet most of these withdrew from public life of their own accord.[11] It was the same story all over Wales and in most of the English counties for which studies exist.[12] For local officers, Cromwell's regime depended upon a mixed bag of men from all literate social groups. There were exceptions to this rule: in Sussex and the West Country a number of traditional leaders continued to serve,[13] and there and in other counties greater gentry had begun to drift back into office.[14] But, unless this tendency were sustained and increased, the central government would remain bereft of the support of the majority of the most wealthy, respected and politically conscious members of society.

To such men, this particular government possessed two considerable defects, quite irrespective of its origins and legitimacy, which made active co-operation with it so difficult. The first was that it maintained a standing army. At the time of his death, Cromwell had in pay in England twelve regiments of horse, twelve of foot and one of dragoons, plus several garrisons. In addition, English resources had to contribute to the upkeep of the armies holding down Scotland and Ireland and to smaller forces serving overseas. The total size of the land forces was about 40,000 men.[15] The navy had also been considerably increased since the time of Charles I. All this power had made Cromwell invincible. It had also ensured that the taxation of the civil war years, of a regularity and weight utterly unknown in pre-war England, was to remain indefinitely. Most of this was provided by the 'assessment', the levy on property, which the constables of one Leicestershire village could describe concisely as 'the Army tax'.[16] A large part of the remainder was yielded by the excise duty on commodities. Like all the levies of this regime, these were collected with slow but steady efficiency.[17] Since accepting the supreme power, Cromwell had made considerable reductions in both the army and the assessment, but these were never enough to satisfy the men elected to his Parliaments and persuade them to endorse some adequate provision for the remaining armed forces.

The crux of this problem was that the army was offensive to these men not merely as a burden but in itself. Its implications for central politics and the national religion will be discussed below: here it is important to note its impact at a local level. At the outbreak of the civil wars, fear and distrust of armed men in general was the most common sentiment displayed by provincials. This was justified in the event, and the demands of the rival armies in the ruinous struggles that followed and the responses of the civilians have earned the phrase 'the other civil war'. After the battle of Worcester, old divisions in local society began to close, and former royalist and parliamentarian gentry to share a social life. Yet the soldiers remained, and their occasional insolence and unruliness was a far more palpable threat to order than the royalists. Relations between soldiers and civilians were cordial in some places, but a constant undercurrent of hostility was more common.[18]

This problem was linked to the second great issue dividing rulers from ruled, that of religion. Cromwell, so often accused of inconsistency, has generally been considered to have pursued one goal clearly and with conviction: the creation of a broadly-based national church, with toleration of radical Protestant groups outside it who were prepared to keep the peace. In this manner, he hoped to permit the individual Protestant conscience protection from its enemies, whom he identified as Catholics and episcopalians. He would also guarantee the peace between the various radical Protestant groups, allowing them to develop and test ideas and eventually to sink old differences. Thus, the Church of England would be rebuilt from the bottom upwards by a natural process of revelation and discussion. Thus his accession to power had been followed by the appointment of a central commission of clergy and laymen to examine candidates for the ministry and of local boards to eject those who had proved unworthy of their benefices. Learning, good character, loyalty to the regime and the basic tenets of Protestant Christianity comprised the entire test. After four years of this system it appeared that Cromwell's dream was becoming a reality. Voluntary associations of beneficed and independent ministers had been instituted in fourteen counties to provide joint action and a common framework for ordination and discipline. Thus men who ten years before would have denounced each other's existence were now working together. Likewise, the most outrageous radical intellectuals had been contained. In the heady days after the revolution, men had preached communal ownership of property and the non-existence of sin, but these voices were now silent, or at least unpublished. All this represented a considerable achievement.[19] To understand why, despite this, influential men were not merely dissatisfied but increasingly alarmed by religious developments, it is necessary to examine the great spectrum of contemporary belief.

Huddled at one extreme were the groups of Roman Catholics. Their misfortunes, already long-standing before the wars, had been increased by their identification with the royalist cause. Whether this existed in practice is a matter of statistical standpoint. On the one hand, it appears that in no county did the majority of the Catholic community give active support to the kings.[20] On the other, most Lancashire royalists were Catholic, and the number of Catholic officers in the northern royalist army, in particular, was out of all proportion to the percentage of Catholics in society as a whole.[21] After the wars such men received the punishment reserved for the most obdurate Protestant royalists, of complete loss of estate, while even papists who had remained neutral received the brunt of pre-war prejudice in the shape of loss of two-thirds of their property. Most seem to have recovered their lands by the hard means of repurchase, but even then they had to pay a double share of the national assessment and the fines levied upon Catholics who failed to attend Protestant worship, enforced with a novel stringency. In the year before Cromwell's death, the latter were exacted from 222 Catholics in Sussex alone. Yet, paradoxically, his rule had represented a period of relative peace for these communities. The other anxieties of the country had diverted attention from them to a degree which seems to have allowed them a freedom of worship, and definitely allowed them a freedom of movement, hitherto unknown. It was beginning to be an irony that in some respects the cause which almost none of them had supported was granting them a better existence than had the king for whom so many of them had suffered.[22]

The woes of the Catholics were generations old. By contrast the ruin of their enemies, the Protestant bishops, was spectacularly recent. The revolution which had swept away the monarchy had also taken bishops, deans, cathedral chapters, the traditional festivals and the pre-war Book of Common Prayer. The dilapidated bulks of the former cathedrals and episcopal palaces loomed over English cities as symbols of the defeat of the old order. Nearly a fifth of all clergy had been permanently deprived of their livings, more for the faults of trying to steer a middle course during the wars, or for displeasing their parishioners, than for royalism. Reappointment to new livings was possible, and frequent, for those willing to express loyalty to the new regimes. For those who were not, who would include the true royalists and episcopalians, the law was severe. Not only were they forbidden to hold the private services permitted to more radical Protestants, but they could not enjoy the patronage of sympathetic families by taking posts as private tutors. Their natural leaders, the deposed bishops, appeared content with their retirement and were dying without being replaced.

Nevertheless, just as a lopped tree may sprout healthily from its lower branches, so parts of the proscribed church still showed vigour. No more than the monarchy had it been destroyed by widespread popular feeling: it had been sacrificed, rather, to provide land to pay for the wars, and to propitiate presbyterian Scottish allies and Londoners and a radical army. Nor were the laws against its more obdurate former members commonly enforced. Cromwell's regime preferred to restrict persecution to a formality and local magistrates were happy to concur with this. In such an atmosphere many beneficed clergy still used the Prayer Book, their former colleagues roosted in gentry houses and ministered to the faithful in private, and episcopalian apologists published their beliefs, all with virtual impunity.[23]

A little further along the spectrum of belief were the presbyterians, those men who had hoped to replace episcopal authority with local *classes* of godly clergy and laity whose representatives would determine national policy in synods. Twelve years before, the Westminster Assembly of Divines had prescribed such a system, and a Directory of Worship to replace the Prayer Book. But then men of more liberal views had taken control of the army, the army had taken control of the government, and the new *classes* found themselves deprived of the powers of coercion necessary to enforce any discipline. Some still remained, mainly in London, Lancashire and Derbyshire, slowly decaying like the flotsam they were.[24] The men who had recommended the form of church which Cromwell adopted were those described as 'independents' or 'of the congregational way'. They demanded, and obtained, freedom from interference by the secular magistrate while imposing stringent moral qualifications upon their own congregations: to such men, worship was a voluntary act by true believers. Some preferred to gather the faithful outside the national church, others accepted benefices in it. Some opposed Cromwell's regime upon political grounds, while others had allied with it to achieve the system of Triers and Ejectors and toleration of independent churches which had been erected. In the country the 'independent' ministers were relatively few and concentrated mainly in the south-east, but their influence among army officers, of whom Cromwell had been the greatest, had made them the most effective party of churchmen during the past ten years.[25]

These men straddled the two great traditions of Christian belief: that which demanded a formal church which would prescribe the way to salvation for all, and that which considered salvation only possible to an elect few gathering around pastors whom they had chosen. The latter was represented in England by a number of sects. The most important, and longest-established, were the varieties of baptist, represented by many congregations in the country and strongest in London and the army. The most dramatic were the Fifth Monarchy Men, who believed in the anticipation of the Second Coming by a violent remodelling of society. Like the baptists, they were strongest in the London area but had groups elsewhere. Scattered across town and country were still an uncounted number of tiny sects which had sprung up in the war years. All these gathered churches were described by outsiders with the general label of 'anabaptists'. They had neither a common theology nor a common practice of religion, disagreeing over adult baptism, predestination, ordination and admission of newcomers. They also disputed the importance of dress, whether oaths were permissible, whether one could raise a hat to a mortal, whether days and months could be called by their traditional, pagan, names, and other matters including loyalty to the present government. They could unite to campaign for the substitution of a system of voluntary choice and maintenance of ministers by congregations for the parochial system with its tithes and patrons. Even in total, their numbers must have represented only a fraction of society, but the number of sectaries in the army was one prop of the toleration of dissenting groups maintained by Cromwell's regime.[26]

Taking all these beliefs together, the picture of religion in 1658 was disquieting enough to many. The religious life of the provinces had been badly disturbed. During the first and longest war, the royalists had deprived many clergy in turn, and Parliament had often given these better livings instead of restoring them. Added to natural turnover, it is probable that deprivation had resulted in the majority of livings having changed ministers in the past fifteen years, and many would have been untended for a period. In Wales, where poverty and a language barrier discouraged newcomers, seven hundred parishes had been emptied of clergy. To promote godliness, government committees had divided up many large and unwieldy rural benefices, thereby angering their gentry patrons who had taken the tithes and paid the vicars a pittance.[27]

Yet, by 1658 the process of reconstruction should have been well under way. The new provincial associations united moderate episcopalians, presbyterians, independents and a few baptists. The last three groups were represented in the national Triers of prospective ministers. The Fifth Monarchy Men were in decline; the year before their most violent members had been arrested, thanks to Cromwell's excellent spy system, in the act of hoisting the banner of Judah and taking up arms in London. The civil war sects still expanding were the most respectable, the baptists, and some of these were becoming organised in their own associations, providing a sense of communal responsibility. Most parishes were held by men who had expressed no strong doctrinal views. Many of the ministers ejected during the war had been reappointed. The same London committees which divided large parishes united small and impoverished livings, augmented stipends and did much work towards a more effective national ministry.[28] The vacuum

created by the wars and by Cromwell's policy should have vanished naturally, had not something alien rushed into it. But the crucial problem was that
something new and terrifying had—the Quakers.[29]

The commons of England had usually manifested a healthy disposition to
self-help in economic matters when their social superiors deserted them. It
was hardly surprising that they should do the same in religious affairs, and
that at a time when the national church was dislocated men should fall back
upon personal revelation. This was the situation in which the sects had
spread, and in which the writings of medieval mystics, manuals for contem-
plation, were reprinted in London. The most intense response, however,
came not from the capital, traditional power-house of new ideas, but from
the rural North, famed for conservatism and Catholicism. There, between
1650 and 1653, demobilised soldiers, young radicals from university and
wandering evangelists touched off a movement of extraordinary dynamism,
which sucked in large numbers of sectaries and independent congregations
as it spread. It was not itself a sect, as it intended to win all mankind. It
insisted aggressively upon points which sects had raised more modestly and
often with scruples. Clergy of any description it denounced as ungodly, and
to pay tithes was therefore to serve Antichrist: thus any formal church had to
be dismantled. Fine clothes were blasphemous, and only God merited the
honour of having men bareheaded before him, so most of the outward
marks of the social order were to be removed. Oaths, which underpinned the
legal and political system, were forbidden by Christ. The old names of days
and months, being pagan, had to be discarded, and the only correct gram-
matical form of personal address was 'thou', commonly reserved for social
inferiors. All sacraments and rituals were superfluous and so, in the final
analysis, was Scripture, for the deity could speak directly and intimately to
every human being. These ideas had travelled across the country in six years,
their preachers drawing enormous crowds. If they continued to win converts
at this rate, they would take all the English and Welsh in one generation.

Cromwell's ideal of toleration had been inspired by the needs of the relatively pacific and well-behaved independents and baptists, who set limits to
the possibility of proselytism in a profane world. These he would defend
against Fifth Monarchists, who were direct political dangers, episcopalians
and Catholics, whom he saw as hypocrites seeking power under the guise of
religion, and blasphemers. The new movement, which avoided taking the
name for itself as it aimed at universality, had no interest in high politics. Its
leaders were clearly men of impressive integrity and piety. But it was
certainly neither pacific nor well-behaved. Its members really did quake,
falling into trances and ecstasies. They also went naked or in fantastic dress,
tramped the land whipping up enthusiasm in others, and entered churches

to abuse the ministers. Cromwell had reluctantly issued an ordinance against the latter habit in 1655, only to face a major scandal the next year, when the Quaker leader James Naylor was arrested for entering Bristol in the manner of Christ entering Jerusalem. The House of Commons had spent two weeks, when it might have been working to support the army or to settle the nation, discussing whether he should be hanged, flogged, branded, mutilated, imprisoned or merely rebuked. In the end he was not hanged, but suffered every other punishment. The whole affair was intensely galling to Cromwell: not only was he left high and dry during the whole debate, but his own officers, military and civil, were divided by it.[30] To appease the Commons and the mood of the country as expressed in a flood of petitions, he accepted the judgement on Naylor, and a Vagrancy Act, Sabbatarian Act and Church Attendance Act which all exposed Quakers to prosecution. He endorsed a definition of toleration of minority religious groups which excluded the new movement, and the principle of a national confession of faith to be required of the parish clergy. Yet since then Cromwell had not taken the necessary steps to obtain such a confession. He had quietly weeded out Quakers from the army and local office, but far from putting the weight of the government against them, he had intervened to protect them in individual cases. Local magistrates did gaol many, and in places where the minister was popular mobs accorded Quaker evangelists the treatment normally reserved for malefactors, suspected witches and unwanted aliens. For all this, because of the uneasy favour of the central authority, the new movement continued to swell in numbers and its meetings in size. In one respect it was a healing force, for fear of it was an important reason for the growing rapport between different kinds of churchman. But this was in itself a redrawing of battle lines, a preparation for a conflict which was presaged in local skirmishes all over the country.

The Cromwellian regime's expense, its militarism and its religious policy could therefore all be counted against it. In addition, it had to face the tensions generated by the external pressure of a foreign war. Barely had the battle of Worcester left the British Isles in domestic peace than the new rulers had flexed their muscles against the Dutch, and so created two years of naval war and trade embargo to follow nine of civil strife. Cromwell's accession to power had ended these, only to produce a fresh effort. To remain at peace in a world in which Protestants were persecuted and the interests of individual Englishmen disregarded, would have seemed to him a failure of duty. It was not a question of whether he picked a fight, but with whom. He chose Spain, the most intolerantly Catholic power and a traditional enemy. It was also arguably the strongest and most dangerous foreign state at that moment, and possessed a temptingly rich and extended empire in the New World.

Furthermore, an attack on it promised an understanding with Spain's great rival, France, removing the possibility that the two great monarchies would combine to restore the Stuarts. All this was rational enough. The decision, however, contained two great miscalculations: that the war would be popular at home and that it would yield such rich and rapid gains as to pay for itself.

The immediate beneficiary was the exiled Charles II, who gained his alliance with Spain and his refuge in the Netherlands. Cromwell's own bad planning resulted in defeat for the force he had sent against Hispaniola. As a consolation prize it presented him with Jamaica, but this turned out to be more of a booby prize as the island was not rich and required great efforts to hold it. It was in any case more than counterbalanced by the loss of most of the valuable trade with Spain itself, and indeed much foreign trade in general as Spanish privateers swarmed off English coasts. After two more years in which his fleet failed to capture more booty than covered a fraction of its own costs, Cromwell formally allied with France to make some headway against the common enemy on land. This had borne fruit less than three months before his death, in the capture and annexation to England of Dunkirk, from which he could put pressure in future on either France or Spain. But all the while the privateer raids continued, commerce languished and the total cost of the war increased.[31]

All these factors could disturb the government and pose it difficult problems for the future. But none was immediately dangerous. The army completely controlled the homeland; the navy ensured safety from invasion. Whatever grudges gentry might harbour, royalist rebellion represented to most of them a far greater threat to order than government policy. Cromwell had purged and quarrelled with his Parliaments, but at least he had continued to call them and to legislate and tax in partnership with them. Both the rights to elect and to stand for election were open to men with any past political record other than one of royalism. The regime had won acquiescence, if not popularity. But it harboured one weakness, which was both dangerous and increasing. It has been said that financial matters are traditionally a cold douche to governments. For that of the dying Cromwell, they represented more of an approaching tidal wave.

Despite the weight of its demands upon the country, Parliament had ended the Great Civil War in debt and with troops only partially paid. Its survival, and victory in two further civil wars, was made possible by expedients such as the sale of the Crown and bishops' lands. Confiscated royalist and Catholic estates and continued heavy taxation had enabled governments to get through the Dutch war with an increased debt and their credit ruined. Cromwell's bickering with his first Parliament had left him with a revenue falling short of expenditure by £400,000 per annum. Upon this had been hurled the weight of his Spanish war. The grants coaxed out of his second Parliament had been, again, inadequate. Since then the war had continued and the acquisition of Dunkirk had added another permanent expense. At his death, Cromwell's government was two million pounds in debt and had no opportunity to borrow further. The shortfall of the regular account ensured that each month the pay of the armed forces would slide further into arrears. Indeed, as the grants made by Parliament were due to expire in the following year, there would come a time when almost no money would be available at all, and government would collapse.[32] Its survival would depend upon the skill of Cromwell's ruling team, under its new leader, in obtaining fresh resources from its subjects.

At first sight, Cromwell appeared to be leaving a government bound more firmly by dynastic ties than those of most of his royal predecessors. His elder surviving son, Richard, was at the centre of the court. His younger son, Henry, governed Ireland. The two most influential men in the army, Charles Fleetwood and John Desborough, were his son-in-law and brother-in-law respectively. Another son-in-law, Viscount Fauconberg, was increasingly active in central politics. Scotland and the navy were in the keeping of two able men, George Monck and Edward Mountagu, who had owed their rapid promotion entirely to his favour. His military officers had almost all risen by merit; his civilian officials were likewise competent and experienced. One of the latter, John Thurloe, was one of the best administrators England has known, his speciality being the gathering of intelligence. It was, in all, a formidable body of men. It was also bitterly divided.

Oliver Cromwell had not made the English Revolution. Nor had he devised the form of government over which he had come to preside. Propelling him, and all English history for ten years, had been the army originally raised by the Long Parliament to win the Great Civil War.[33] In the aftermath of that war its officers had come to share three aims which they clung to during the decade that followed: regular Parliaments elected upon a reformed franchise with a redistribution of seats, an improved legal system and a broad state church with toleration of separatist groups. To secure these they had purged the Long Parliament and obtained the death of Charles I. When even the purged Parliament had failed to satisfy them they had pressed Cromwell to expel it until he had agreed with them and done so. Sitting, with regimental representatives, in their Council of Officers, they had then conceived a nominated Parliament as the obvious means to obtain their ends, and chosen one. Eventually a section of them had sabotaged this, to substitute an alternative scheme, the Protectorate, whereby Parliaments would be elected but would share the legislative power with a Lord Protector and a Council on which the military was strongly represented. Protector and Council would wield the executive power alone. Other provisions of this scheme fulfilled or promised to fulfil the reforms for which the army had long worked. The man whom they had invited to accept the Protectorship had of course been their Commander-in-Chief, whose skill had brought them constant victory in battle and who shared their instincts, Cromwell. Through all these changes he, and they, had been sustained by a confidence born of victory. Their triumphs had been not merely unbroken but notable for an appalling loss to the enemy and almost none to themselves. They appeared to have discovered the secret of living by the sword without perishing by it. Nothing quite like them had been known since the fall of Rome, an army which formed a separate estate within the realm and dominated it. Within this physical strength, however, they possessed an ideological limitation which posed severe problems. They believed, like every Englishman of the age, that ultimate authority must rest in a Parliament. Yet every Parliament, even purged to a radical minority, had shown suspicion of them and their ideals.

In the course of these changes, Cromwell and his supporters had steadily multiplied varieties of enemy. Pride's Purge and the subsequent regicide had alienated many men who had fought the king precisely to preserve a constitutional monarchy. The most extreme radicals had felt betrayed when these events had not been followed by the fundamental changes they advocated. The expulsion of the purged remnant of the Long Parliament had sent into opposition the republican MPs who had led it. The institution of the Protectorate had scandalised men who believed in complete parliamentary sovereignty. The Fifth Monarchists and some independent preachers had turned hostile on realising that their theocracy was not to be adopted. Yet however many foes prowled around the pallisade of the early Protectorate, the new government had remained relatively united and secure for three years. The opposition represented too many viewpoints to achieve coherence, and against all of it could be set the army. This was no straightforward matter, for at most of the successive crises the army officers had shown the same volatility which had destroyed their former masters. Yet Cromwell and his commanders had managed to contain it, dismissing in the process a growing number of their own former comrades-in-arms.[34] Once out of arms the latter, like other malcontents, were watched by Thurloe's superb spy system and arrested if deemed dangerous. The treason laws which guarded the Protectorate were reserved for royalists: former allies were confined in remote fortresses, untried, to permit them unlimited time for a change of heart. The government could achieve this in part because of the speed and determination with which it acted. But, in the main, its strength had lain in the fact that it still embodied enough of the soldiers' ideals to retain the loyalty of most. Then, the year before Cromwell's death, this strength had been shaken, and the unity of his own circle destroyed.

The force that had achieved this had come in the first instance from the periphery of the realm. It had begun with a young Anglo-Irishman, Roger Boyle, Lord Broghill. His father was one of history's most formidable social climbers, who had risen from obscurity to be Earl of Cork over the property rights of a few thousand native Irishmen. His brother was to become a great scientist. It was a talented family, and Cromwell, who recognised talent, had taken pains to woo Broghill from royalism and into his service. Having succeeded, he had sent him north in 1655 to persuade a nation to follow his example. Scotland had been reconquered after a protracted royalist rebellion, and Broghill's task was to make it more contented and less exhausting. By paying heed to local practice and law, by drawing Scottish gentry into government, by going, in fact, against much of the spirit of the English Revolution and of the English army, he had succeeded.[35]

Both his person and his policies were respected by the Commander-in-Chief in Ireland, Cromwell's own son Henry. Henry Cromwell had been too young to fight in the civil wars and share their passions. He had grown up in the confusion of their aftermath, and become as inspired by the ideal of orderly government as his father's comrades had been by that of godly reformation. Given Ireland, in the year in which Broghill went to Scotland, he set to work to stabilise it with methods that became the same, and brought the same success. His achievement was, moreover, even more a counter-revolution, for in the process he first alienated and then deliberately excluded the sectaries who were so influential in the English army. These had been the proponents of reform in Ireland, and also the associates of his predecessor Fleetwood, one of the leaders of the soldiery in England and his own brother-in-law.[36]

This process reached the centre of the realm in February 1657, when Broghill and a mixture of moderate gentry and civilian government ministers led a majority of the House of Commons in proposing a constitution to replace that devised by the army officers.[37] It represented a return to a traditional model of government, investing authority in a monarch, a House of Lords, a House of Commons and a national church bound by a common doctrine. This offer appealed to more than one element in Cromwell's personality: the country squire's liking for the old order, the politician's taste for flexible, undogmatic policy-making, the ageing statesman's longing for an enduring settlement. His generals, however, were appalled. The new constitution was the work of civilians, who knew nothing of the joy of battle and the religious exaltation which had been the spirit of their cause. The same House of Commons had only just abolished the military's scheme of a tax on royalists, with several sharp reflections upon the army. Thus the soldiers' Commander-in-Chief seemed to be on the point of being taken over by a faction hostile to their interests. Against this anger and fear Cromwell put the full force of his personality, in an effort to win rational debate of the proposal. After nearly three months of discussion some of his commanders were reassured, but the most important, Fleetwood, Desborough and Lambert, were obstinate. A petition against monarchy had been raised in the army for presentation to Parliament, and many of the gathered churches, independent and baptist, sent Cromwell appeals to the same end.

The Lord Protector settled for a compromise. He refused the title of King but accepted some trappings of royalty such as robe and sceptre. He accepted an Upper House of Parliament, but nominated to it so many soldiers that it replaced the Council as a mouthpiece for the army. He conceded much in principle and nothing in practice to make the national church more formal and powerful and to halt Quaker proselytism. This solution seemed at first a qualified success. Fleetwood, Desborough and most of the senior army officers accepted it, though Lambert, the most brilliant, did not and was dismissed. The civilians who had proposed monarchy also accepted it, but with such a bad grace that they clearly did not regard it as a satisfactory settlement. Then, when the new constitution was tried out in early 1658, disaster had come. Though royalists were still officially excluded from the Commons, the government was now disqualified from purging that body. Republican opponents of the Protectorate took their seats and fanned the dislike of many civilian MPs for the Upper House Cromwell had chosen. This debate automatically jammed legislation. Worse, the hostile republicans bombarded the army with pamphlets, and drew up a petition to Parliament which joined the cause of parliamentary sovereignty with that of the soldiers. One of its clauses was a request for religious toleration, the old ideal of the army. Another asked that no soldier should be dismissed other than by a formal court martial, striking at Cromwell's control.

The Protector lost his temper, and perhaps his nerve. He forestalled the petition, and threw away any chance of obtaining the vital vote of money, by dissolving Parliament. He then made a personal appeal to a meeting of officers, winning the applause of all save the captains of his own horse regiment, some of his oldest and closest followers. These firmly but vaguely insisted that the new constitution threatened liberty, and were discharged. Fleetwood rallied the rest of the English army behind Cromwell, and Monck and Henry Cromwell did the same in Scotland and Ireland. The crisis had passed, leaving the Lord Protector presiding over an unworkable constitution and facing eventual financial bankruptcy. The scale of the defeat, followed by the deaths of a son-in-law, a daughter, and an old friend, seemed to numb him. As the summer of 1658 drew on, his voice vanished from public affairs, his handwriting faltered and became that of an old man. What seemed at first a moral affliction grew into a physical one. The centre of the Protectorate was caving in, revealing the rifts now existing among the men who ringed it.

On one side stood Fleetwood and Desborough.[38] Both were younger sons of gentry, and had emerged from insignificance with the coming of war. Both had fought in as many campaigns as Cromwell, and for the same cause. Both had little sympathy for a national church, and none for royalists. Charles Fleetwood was a man of profound personal piety. He may, in fact, have the distinction of having mentioned the name of God more frequently in his correspondence than any other English soldier. As a colonel he had filled his regiment with sectaries, and his patronage of baptists in Ireland has been mentioned. Yet the fire expected of a holy warrior was missing. Cromwell, in a tense moment, called him a milksop, and throughout his career he manifested a diffidence which shaded into weakness. This was probably the secret of his popularity with the army, for while it was impossible to deny his godliness it was almost as difficult to suspect him of personal ambition. By contrast, when the voice of John Desborough appears in history it is always uncompromising and generally raised in anger. He had been an Ironside, one of the original officers of Cromwell's own regiment, and the image of the 'plain, russet-coated captain' whom Cromwell had held up as an ideal. Throughout his life he defended two interests, that of religious radicals and that of the army. Having achieved power, he was growing into an early prototype of Colonel Blimp.

Ranged against them were Lord Broghill and Viscount Fauconberg. Both were born into noble and royalist families. If they manifested any sense of religion it was only as a prop of the social and political order. Fauconberg, like Broghill, was a proponent of revived monarchy and a friend and adviser of Henry Cromwell. He was developing the dislike which all three now shared for Fleetwood and Desborough to a pitch which approached hysteria. It was fortunate, indeed, that most of the Protector's advisers, now reconstituted as a Privy Council, were not as ready to recognise a growing conflict as these men. Nevertheless, a natural rift was opening between the two great military officers and the civilian ministers.[39] The one person who might have been expected to bridge it was the one member of the Privy Council who was neither a minister nor a veteran soldier and had held rigidly aloof from the kingship controversy, the Protector's eldest son, Richard.[40]

In speaking of Richard at this period, contemporaries tended to stress his youth. This was not strictly necessary, as he was nearly thirty-two in a ruling set in which nobody, including his father, was over sixty. His brother Henry and Fauconberg were both younger than him, the naval commander Mountagu a year older, Broghill and Fleetwood only a few years more than that. The impression of a stripling was conveyed, rather, by his utter inexperience of public life. Richard's education as soldier or statesman had been sacrificed to Cromwell's desire, almost certainly sincere, to appear a public servant devoid of ambition. Thus, while his father had been grilling royalists alive on the church steeple at Drogheda, Richard had been left in the English countryside to read improving books. His marriage had been contracted with the daughter of an unimportant squire. As Cromwell became Protector Richard remained in obscurity, censured by his father for laziness and extravagance.[41] With the kingship crisis, and the realisation that some trappings of monarchy might be an asset after all, the Protector had suddenly pulled his heir into public life and loaded him with honours, though still with no responsibilities. The succession to the Protectorate was still officially determined by the Protector's nomination, but diplomats, civilian government ministers and local worthies alike now regarded Richard as a Crown prince.[42] Never in English history has any person approached supreme power with such little practical preparation. Undoubtedly this dissociation from past events could count as an advantage, lifting him above the mutual animosities of other candidates for his father's position. yet it had not equipped him for the part of a perfect arbitrator. In general, his ignorance of the army and his affection for his brother tended to class him with the civilian, or 'reactionary', faction. In particular, Desborough resented him.[43]

During the spring and early summer of 1658, the impasse at which government had arrived was the subject of repeated discussion by councils of army officers, the Privy Council, and special committees of advisers appointed by Cromwell.[44] Fauconberg believed that the obvious means of winning over Parliament was for the Protector to reverse his decision and take the crown. Somebody else, almost certainly Desborough,[45] proposed a new arbitrary tax upon the royalists. Most of the Privy Council preferred to woo Parliament, but a means of doing so could not be agreed upon. A committee of the Council discussed making the office of Protector hereditary, but although a majority favoured this, it was decided to appease the minority who objected and do nothing. As one inconclusive debate succeeded another, the financial position worsened and the Protector's health collapsed. For a long time his illness, a low fever, was not considered serious. Six days before his father died, Richard had believed that recovery was approaching.[46] Three days before, Cromwell had still named no successor.[47] What he himself felt then about the state of his realm, or the prospects of his heir, nobody will ever know. For, as his last night drew on, and as a terrible wind began to rise about the corridors of Whitehall, the dying Protector had addressed not his followers, nor his son, but his God.[48]

PART TWO

THE END OF THE ENGLISH REPUBLIC[1]

∽⚬∽

I

The Fall of the Protectorate

CROMWELL died in the afternoon of 3 September. By evening it was accepted that he had named Richard as his successor. Whether he ever did so is unprovable.[2] What is certain, and what mattered, was that this was recognised by the majority of the Privy Council and communicated by them to Fleetwood. He took the news to the army officers meeting in London, who accepted it in turn. The following day Richard was sworn in and proclaimed in the capital, and copies of the proclamation were sent into the provinces to be published at large.[3]

In his letter to Henry Cromwell announcing these events,[4] Thurloe added that the populace were in deep mourning for Cromwell. If this was ever more than a piece of tact on the part of a faithful servant, no evidence bears it out. After dark somebody threw dirt at the dead Protector's escutcheon on the gate of Somerset House, where he lay in state.[5] A West Riding blacksmith came up with the idea that now Cromwell was dead there was no more law, and was promptly hauled before a magistrate.[6] In general, the English seem to have corresponded to the parishioners of an Essex clergyman who wrote in his diary 'Cromwell died, people not much minding it'.[7] The government itself might have been forgiven for having something more pressing on its mind: the country's reaction to a new ruler. This soon became apparent. In London some sectarian preachers grumbled, and republican enemies met, but no opposition materialised.[8] On the contrary, the provinces responded, positively, with a near unanimity unknown for at least eighteen years. In town after town Richard was proclaimed with the full civic junketings of bells, bonfires, gunshots and parades.[9] The only hostile response came at Oxford, where some students pelted the soldiers attending the ceremony,[10] a demonstration almost certainly against the military rather than the new ruler. Then addresses of congratulation began to come in, till by the end of the year the City of London and at least twenty-eight counties, twenty-four towns and five groups of ministers, from presbyterians to baptists, had congratulated Richard on his accession.[11] There were some notable gaps: most of Wales was silent, as was Kent, both areas where the gentry seem to have been particularly discontented.[12] The second city, Bristol, sent no address and provided a niggardly show for the proclamation.[13] None of the English county addresses appear to have survived, to demonstrate how large a section of the community they represented. But, at the very least, it had been demonstrated that most of the men who held local power were prepared to hail the new ruler with enthusiasm.

There is not a scrap of evidence in either central or local archives that this response was anything but spontaneous.[14] One can only surmise that it was Richard's lack of any political taint, his dissociation from the wartime parties, the regicide and the army, which had caught the imagination as a symbol of better things to come. Each address combined this sentiment with the promoters' own interests. The Sussex gentry asked for action against Quakers, the radical set who ran Caernarfonshire for the maintenance of godly religion, the citizens of Nottingham for firm control of the army. The process was self-perpetuating, as local leaders came to fear that by failing to represent their loyalty they would weaken any claim to favours from the government.[15] The deputations who carried the addresses to Richard began to record something significant in their reception, that the new Protector had the capacity to win men. It was perhaps not difficult to send the burghers of Leicester home with the feeling that the young Cromwell had a particular affection for their town.[16] But when a canny and experienced politician like Bulstrode Whitelocke, who presented the Buckinghamshire address, pronounced himself impressed, the achievement was notable.[17] There could be no doubt that the change of leader had enhanced, rather than weakened, the regime's standing in the country. By December a royalist correspondent of Lord Chancellor Hyde could report, with bitter disappointment, that England had never been so quiet.[18] The observation, though just, overlooked one major development. Even while the addresses came in, the new Protector was working his way through a crisis. His opponent was not, after all, the country which he had come to rule, but the instrument by which his father had ruled it, the army.

Six months before, when discontent had surfaced so dramatically in Oliver Cromwell's horse regiment, Fleetwood, Monck and Henry Cromwell had rallied support to the Protector by promoting loyal addresses from their respective armies. This effort Fleetwood and Henry repeated at the succession of Richard, while Mountagu obtained an avowal from the fleet, the troops in Flanders sent their own and Monck searched for disloyalty in the Scottish forces.[19] Among these military addresses, that from the officers in England stood out. Unlike the others, it was no simple offer of obedience but made conditions, that Richard promote 'the concernments of the godly', choosing only pious officers, officials and ministers, reforming manners and protecting peaceful religious minorities. It overtly associated the army with the Protector and Privy Council in the work of government, claiming for the military a constitutional status to which it had pretended through previous changes.[20] It contained the expression 'the Good Old Cause', which had an ominous pedigree. Probably coined by a republican enemy of the Protectorate two years before,[21] it had been flung in Oliver Cromwell's face by the officers who had challenged him in the spring. What the Cause stood for was not absolutely clear, but it was plain what it stood against: the reactionary tendencies in government with which Cromwell had compromised in 1657. Yet, in this address the expression was itself made subject to this compromise, for Richard was urged to promote the Cause within the framework of the constitution of 1657.

All reports agree that the man who obtained this document, and led the deputation which presented it on 18 September, was Fleetwood.[22] The officers with whom he was dealing were already restless. Since before Cromwell's death they had been holding prayer-meetings, in the past a prelude to action, and were reported to be murmuring against Richard as an unknown civilian.[23] In view of this, to obtain a loyal address which over two hundred officers were prepared to sign was a considerable achievement and it is hardly surprising that the wording contained provisos. Richard agreed to these with a speech which delighted the soldiers.[24] He had already signed warrants for pay due to individual colonels;[25] now he proceeded to increase the rate of pay for the whole army.[26] All promised well, but in reality the compromise embodied in the address proved subject to the same centrifugal forces as the national constitution, and Fleetwood was caught between them even more than Richard. On the one hand Fauconberg was writing in code to Henry Cromwell that the address was a 'serpent' and armed action was necessary. On the other, some republicans informed Fleetwood that the address was 'parasitical' and at variance with the 'secret engagements' he had made with the officers beforehand, presumably to maintain the achievements of the revolution. A sectarian officer at Plymouth likewise wrote to him, accusing him of increasing the Protector's power till it threatened liberty.[27]

The tension came to a head when Richard bestowed a regiment upon Mountagu, arousing the jealousy of some sectarian junior officers who thought him already amply honoured as the General-at-Sea. In early October they went to Richard to demand that he commission only with the advice of senior officers. He rebuked them sharply, whereupon they framed a petition demanding that he abdicate control over the army. This they showed to Fleetwood and other commanders, who agreed to intercede with Richard. The Protector decided upon a personal appeal of the sort his father had made with success seven months before. He summoned a great meeting of officers on 18 October and delivered a speech carefully drafted with Thurloe's aid, which stressed his fidelity to the army's ideals. It concluded by offering a compromise, to make Fleetwood Lieutenant-General with immediate control of the army while retaining the supreme power, the granting of commissions. This appeared to satisfy most, and Fleetwood commenced his new responsibilities a few days later with a speech urging the army to unity. At the same time the government got some pay through to the men.[28]

Throughout this affair unpleasant rumours had been circulating, and continued to do so in the weeks after its apparent resolution. It was widely believe that Fleetwood and Desborough had themselves inspired the agitation to further their own ambitions. Desborough was said to have set all the sectarian officers against Richard. It was reported that the malcontents were plotting with republican enemies of the Protectorate, while Richard was preparing to recall the force in Flanders to his aid.[29] Whatever the truth of these, it was plain that the tension of October had left Henry Cromwell, Fauconberg and Thurloe still more estranged from the army leaders.[30] It had also opened rifts along less predictable lines. Colonels such as Edward Whalley and William Goffe, who were members of gathered churches and had signed the death warrant of Charles I, had taken Richard's part. Another regicide and veteran soldier, Richard Ingoldsby, had delivered a loyal address to the Protector at the height of the crisis. On the other hand some civilians on the Privy Council shared the desire to limit the Protector's powers.[31] Through this maze of hostilities Richard Cromwell continued to pick his way. He raised his brother to the full power of Lord Lieutenant of Ireland and excepted the Irish army from Fleetwood's new commission, but prevented Henry from intervening personally in the delicate situation in London.[32] He rewarded Goffe and Monck with land, the latter in secret.[33] When the strain prompted Thurloe to offer his resignation, it was refused.[34] Richard conferred with leading officers on means of improving government finances, ordered new uniforms for the soldiers around London and saw that some money was regularly issued to them.[35] He won a loyal address from Desborough's own regiment, which asked only that he appoint godly men and punish Quakers who reviled ministers.[36] When quarrelling and dangerous talk broke out in the officers' prayer meetings in mid-November he made another personal appeal, for unity and trust.[37]

These measures cleared the air sufficiently to stage his father's funeral, and on 23 November the hearse eventually made its procession to Westminster Abbey. To a traveller in the crowd it was imposing enough, a pageant of mourners in medieval hoods, horses caparisoned in black velvet, dark banners and rows of soldiers, all moving to the drums. Others present were less easily pleased. Thurloe was afraid that the army would create a disturbance, and indeed one was provoked although it came to nothing. The royalist Evelyn recorded that 'there were none that cried but dogs', while the soldiers drank and smoked as they marched. None of the splendid trappings had been paid for, nor were likely to be. There were indeed many ironies in the event, apart from the customary one that Cromwell's body itself had been buried two weeks before. What rode upon the hearse was an effigy.[38]

Apart from the funeral, and the soldiers' pay, one other problem had continually presented itself to Richard's Privy Council: the religious question. On the whole, it set itself resolutely to maintain the existing settlement against all opponents. On the one hand it ordered the payment of tithes. On the other it reminded the country that peaceful minority groups should pray unmolested, that ministers were not bound to offer sacraments and that the pre-war Prayer Book was abolished. In London a campaign was launched to stop clandestine use of the Book and to convict Catholic recusants.[39] Policy faltered, as it had always done, over the Quakers. On Richard's accession some of the movement had complained to the Council that their brethren were being molested and imprisoned without due cause. The Council carried out a survey of prisons, and found over a hundred Quakers there, most commonly for non-payment of tithes. As this and most of the charges were valid in law, it could only release a few as an act of grace at Cromwell's funeral and summon the mayor of Arundel for committing some simply for meeting. A section of the Council recommended further pardons, and that the question of hat courtesy be resolved by pulling off their hats as they entered courts, but at this the problem was shelved.[40]

Meanwhile the people of Interregnum England had bickered their way through another autumn. The citizens and garrison of Hull combined to proclaim Richard, but the former were soon back to complaining of the burden of the soldiers.[41] Various individuals were accused of speaking against government or army.[42] Representatives of over a hundred independent churches conferred at the Savoy upon means of producing a common front against sects and Quakers and dissociating themselves from them in the popular mind. The leadership, which included several Triers, was distinguished, but the whole body represented a minority of the independent congregations. It produced a declaration of faith which divided its members both from the sects and the presbyterians, and presented it to Richard Cromwell, who replied with his usual grace and his usual sentiment, for unity. Then the conference dispersed, leaving no discernible impression on the provinces.[43] Another association of ministers, presbyterian and independent, was formed in Essex to resist the challenge of Quakers and sects. An attempt to form another in Herefordshire failed because many clergy there felt that they still owed obedience to the deposed bishops. The philosopher John Durie worked to unite presbyterians, independents and moderate baptists, without success.[44] More presbyterian *classes* dwindled or collapsed, in London and Derbyshire, while the Manchester one was given a case of discipline, its first for years, and ducked it with reference to a committee.[45] Conservative laymen remained more aggressive. Two assize judges were dismissed for encouraging Grand Juries to present ministers for refusing to administer sacraments. Elsewhere, in flagrant disregard of recent laws, clergy were presented for failing to use the abolished pre-war Prayer Book. Essex churchwardens likewise continued automatically to present people for not attending the parish church, while a Gloucestershire rector found his passage to the building barred by parishioners who wanted his ejected predecessor restored.[46]

Despite the sufferings of which the Privy Council had learned, the Quakers continued to increase. In London their meetings grew huge, and attracted the Earls of Newport and Pembroke. They set up a group in Westminster, which members of the army attended. A 'great man' let them meet in Durham Castle, from where they held disputations with ministers. They absorbed members of baptist churches all over southern England. They were arrested for disturbing parish church services in the West Riding and in Kent and beaten up for this in Cumberland. One, or perhaps a sectary imitating their style, entered the Mayor's Court at Norwich and called the magistrates 'limbs of the Beast'. A presbyterian divine appealed to the corporation of London for aid against them, another did the same to the Suffolk JPs, and some gentry and clergy of the West Riding begged action from the Protector. In six counties ministers met to bewail the general decay of discipline.[47]

Only one piece of evidence survives to illustrate Richard's own opinion of the affairs of his new realm. It consists of a solitary message to Henry,[48] that matters were so serious that he dared not commit any comments to paper. He did add that the centre of the problem was the soldiers' arrears. Here he was correct. The bankruptcy foreseen before his father's death had only been hastened by his measures to win acceptance by the army. When the French had refused him the loan no domestic banker would make,[49] all means of escape were cut off save arbitrary taxation, which would destroy any support in the country, and Parliament. If the constitution which had failed the father could be made to work for the son, his government would be saved. Richard's course was as simple, and daunting, as that.

The decision to call Parliament was taken in the Privy Council on 3 December,[50] and the writs went out in the middle of the month. The army at last seemed quiet, even the wary Thurloe finding discontent 'skinned over'.[51] There was rumoured to have been a moment of melodrama in the council on the 6th, produced characteristically by Desborough, who accused Mountagu of conspiring to have him and Fleetwood dismissed and demanded the dismissal of Fauconberg. Richard stood firm and the matter was dropped.[52] The council returned to practical matters, such as a scheme to save money by reducing the size of foot regiments. This foundered, naturally, on the lack of money to disband any men.[53] The government's weaknesses thus remained clear, but it was caught for a time in a circle less vicious than the financial one: the lull between challenges which had encouraged the regime to call a Parliament was almost certainly intensified in turn by the fact that all parties were preparing for the Parliament itself.

It was presumably at that meeting on the 3rd that the Privy Council took one of its strangest decisions, to abolish half of the electoral reforms which had been requested by the army for years and adopted when it established the Protectorate. These had reduced the number of English seats, redistributed the bulk of them from boroughs to counties and admitted representatives of Scotland and Ireland to compensate for the abolition of their constitutional independence. For the new Parliament, the Scots and Irish members were retained. To do otherwise meant either restoring the other parliaments or leaving the other realms under arbitrary rule, encouraging either dangerous independence or dangerous resentment. The English electoral system, however, was returned to its traditional higgledy-piggledy form, with most MPs provided by boroughs concentrated mainly in the south and west of the country. It was all the odder that nobody involved in this decision saw need to account for it. The only contemporary to do so was an enemy,[54] who explained it partly as obedience to the new constitution of 1657 and partly in the hope of rigging elections as borough seats were more easily controlled. Neither idea is satisfactory. The constitution only demanded that elections be by the 'known laws', while the main trouble-makers of the previous session had held borough seats. A radical opponent in London certainly believed that a multitude of boroughs favoured his party.[55] In default of evidence it appears most likely that, given the desperate necessity of winning co-operation from this Parliament, the government hoped that another reversion to old ways would be pleasing to the nation and its representatives.

Certainly the change had disadvantages other than the possibility that it might help enemies win seats. It destroyed another of the army's achievements when the army was already complaining of reaction. By combining the old system with members from other realms it based itself on no one previous constitution, representing another Cromwellian compromise drawing fire from both sides. This hybrid would also be the largest House of

Commons yet convened, posing appalling problems of management. These would combine unpleasantly with a weakness which had played some part in the disaster of the last session. In creating his Upper House, Oliver Cromwell had naturally elevated to it many of his supporters, including Fleetwood, Desborough, Broghill and Fauconberg. Just as naturally, the few opponents he had nominated had refused to serve. Thus most of the government's spokesmen were excluded from the Commons as neatly as by any purge.

The elections were spread over late December and early January and were soon observed to be fierce.[56] The government made considerable preparations for them. Richard replaced eight sheriffs, the returning officers for county elections, interviewed local notables and made Fleetwood and Desborough joint Lords Warden of the Cinque Ports, an office wielding great electoral patronage. Enemies also made great efforts and so did the gentry in general, even in Wales where the majority became active for the first time since the wars. This, like the address to Richard, was at least a healthy sign that many of the nation were now prepared to participate in national affairs. Some electors had a splendid time, such as the freeholders of Worcestershire on whom the victorious members spent £614 in entertainment. The borough of Leominster set out shamelessly to make money. Elsewhere less venial considerations prevailed. In Yorkshire the freeholders shouted against all soldiers, while at the Caernarfonshire elections swords were drawn between the old and new ruling sets. At another extreme, Haverfordwest corporation simply invited a man who had served them well before to do so again.

At last this mêlée produced 549 MPs. Fifty-six of these were from Scotland and Ireland, a bloc of government servants and reliable local men who would strengthen the 'court' representation. In England all the eligible government spokesmen got in, but so did their main republican opponents. Most of the latter had been elected by boroughs, but then so had most of the government men. Soldiers had fared worse than any other group, military governors often failing to win election by the towns they kept secure. The overwhelming bulk of this House of Commons was composed of gentry and urban leaders of no obvious affiliation, dubbed 'conservatives' or 'moderates' by the historians who have studied them at a local level. This was the rule for a pre-war Parliament, another indication of the growing 'normalisation' of politics. What was unusual, apart from the sheer size of the body, was the number of inexperienced and obscure men. About a third had sat in any Parliament before and less than that number would sit in another. It was, all told, one of the biggest corrals of dark horses English politics has ever seen. In guiding them the government's opponents possessed a great advantage: they needed to produce no positive measures. A paralysed and chaotic body would ruin the Protectorate just as effectively as a hostile one.

From four men the government had perhaps more to fear than any others. First was Sir Arthur Hesilrige,[57] who had been one of the Five Members whom Charles I had so dramatically, and fatally, failed to arrest in 1642. Of these he was the only one to survive in politics with the same fierce temper which had drawn the royal anger. During the Great Civil War he and his horse regiment had been celebrated not for their performance as much as for their armour, which was of such prodigious size and weight that it moved even King Charles, one of England's more solemn monarchs, to mirth. This theatrical flamboyance had followed his person into civilian life, where his coach and clothes had been of a magnificence which prompted unkind speculations upon how the people's self-proclaimed servants had been spending the people's money. Yet Sir Arthur was no clown. His skill in debate won respect and attention, and a great following in the purged Long Parliament after the Revolution of early 1649, where he was a leader of the opposition to Cromwell's army and its demands. By the destruction of that Parliament, the army had made a tireless enemy. There is more than his wartime carapace which provokes the comparison between Hesilrige and a rhinoceros. Lacking in positive ideas, he attacked opponents with a savagery without fear and without any sense of compromise. He was a dangerous foe, and a hardly less disturbing ally.

Associated with him was the less spectacular but equally dauntless figure of Thomas Scot.[58] Scot had been of little consequence until the winter of 1648-9, when he had suddenly thrust forward to become the most active man in the Long Parliament during the weeks between Pride's Purge and the regicide. He had signed the death warrant of Charles I. Then, with the return of men such as Hesilrige to the Commons, he had become slightly less prominent. Nevertheless, the fervour which had carried him to the front of the Revolution made him still a notable spokesman of the purged Parliament, before and after its expulsion.

Sir Henry Vane[59] remains one of history's most notable examples of that perennial type, the radical intellectual from a privileged family. In the 1630s, when his father was rising to high office, he was in New England developing what was to become a life-long attachment to religious toleration. A more obviously complicated, and isolated, personality than Hesilrige and Scot, he had something of the modern idea of a revolutionary élite which would guide people into the new age of freedom. As a public man he had been distinguished by ruthlessness, energy and duplicity. He had driven forward the wars against Charles I but had left London at the time of the King's trial. He had been an ally of Oliver Cromwell until the final expulsion of the Long

Parliament but had then chosen to become his enemy. Few men trusted Vane, and fewer understood him, but his undoubted intellect, driven by the conviction of a mystic, could, again, produce a disturbing opponent.

The fourth member of this remarkable alliance was Edmund Ludlow.[60] He had been an MP and Hesilrige had held military commands, but in a basic sense he was a soldier and the other three were politicians. At the opening of the Great Civil War he had enlisted, like Fleetwood, in the bodyguard of Parliament's Lord General. A year later he had commanded a tiny castle which the fortunes of war had left deep in enemy territory. The inevitable siege he turned into one of the epic fights of the decade, surrendering only when his fortress was in ruins, his cause honoured and his fame assured. Years later, he had been a contriver of Pride's Purge and, like Scot, a radical. He had turned against Cromwell not at the expulsion of the Long Parliament but at the establishment of the Protectorate, when the army leaders seemed to him to have succumbed to the temptations of power. He was the pattern of the warrior saint, fiercely religious, utterly honest and utterly fearless.

Personality, belief and political record all divided these men, but they were bound by a common reverence for the sovereignty of a House of the people's representatives, which the Protectorate had destroyed. Associated with them were individuals of equal talent and almost as much reputation, comprising the party known as the 'Commonwealthsmen'. To defeat them, the government made a great effort to manage Parliament without appearing too high-handed.[61] Proceedings opened on 27 January 1659, with a sermon by one of the government's clerical supporters, Thomas Goodwin, calling for unity and tolerance. Richard followed with a speech which, compared with his father's, was a model of clarity and brevity. He stressed the blessings of internal peace and appealed for measures against royalists and for money to pay the armed forces. He spoke with his usual eloquence, standing bareheaded before his audience, and waited patiently while a Quaker delivered a diatribe at the beginning. One of his civilian ministers, Nathaniel Fiennes, then repeated his sentiments in a more flowery fashion. All MPs were then required to swear fidelity to the Protectorate.[62] Three days later Thurloe produced the first government bill, to recognise Richard's title, without warning, in order to catch the Commonwealthsmen off guard. In the ensuing debates he, the Attorney-General, the Solicitor-General and the Speakers repeatedly spoke to expedite proceedings.

It was almost all in vain. Back-bench attendance in this enormous assembly was uncomfortably good, a maximum of 387 members being recorded present, and the majority showed no disposition to be guided. Most of the Commonwealthsmen perjured themselves cheerfully and took the oath to the Protectorate, and their seats. Ludlow simply sat, but when his expulsion was proposed the debate collapsed farcically when it was discovered that a maniac was present in the House under the impression that he was an MP. Thereafter the matter was dropped. Thurloe's ruse in introducing the Bill of Recognition failed to shake the Commonwealthsmen, but gave offence to the rest of the assembly. Hesilrige led his allies in a campaign of filibustering which was not to be equalled until the appearance of the Irish Nationalists under Victoria. The attempts by government spokesmen to conclude debates met with little response, as did a request from Richard himself to turn to the needs of the nation. The House, throughout its existence, found itself staying late and missing meals. The greatest strain fell upon the Speakers, middle-aged men who alone of all the Commons could not leave their place as long as the House was debating. Two collapsed and died in succession. Yet, however appalling the cost in time and energy, progress was made. Most MPs were anxious to show that they were not servants of the regime, but neither were they Commonwealthsmen.

The Bill of Recognition collapsed in deadlock on 14 February, with a vote to recognise Richard, but not till further limitations were set on his powers. The government was said to have decided that to ask for more was pointless, as any bill produced by the Commons would require the Protector's co-operation to become law, producing *de facto* recognition.[63] The Commonwealthsmen now produced the challenge which had driven Oliver Cromwell into the dissolution of the last Parliament, the petition linking the grievances of republicans and soldiers. It was presented to the Commons on 15 February, and met with a hostile reception because it was presented by notable London radicals and sectaries. Inside Parliament at least, it was the greatest anticlimax of the session and proved the conservative temper of most MPs.[64] Shortly after, the government won another victory. Sweden and Denmark had gone to war and England's main commercial rivals, the Dutch, were intervening in the struggle to make permanent their existing supremacy in the valuable Baltic trade. To preserve English interests it was imperative that a fleet be despatched to the area immediately, and Thurloe laid the problem before the Commons. On 24 February they recognised Richard's control of the armed forces, reserving to themselves only the power to decide between peace and war, and the Protector duly sent Mountagu north with a naval force.

By this time the Commons had strayed naturally into debating the existence of Cromwell's Upper House, the question which had paralysed the last Parliament. The Upper House itself had meanwhile been busy with its own legislation, which, as that body never consisted of more than thirty-six men, all connected to the government, went briskly enough. The constitution did not specify its relationship to the Commons so, unlike the old Lords, it

proceeded in isolation to pass acts recognising Richard and outlawing
Charles II. It had concurred in the Commons' one positive resolution, on
the armed forces, but there was no formal co-operation between the two
Houses. A way out of the impasse was apparently found for the government by Arthur Annesley, one of the members from Ireland and, with
Broghill, one of the first of the brilliant line of Anglo-Irishmen who have
contributed so much to English political and cultural life. He, realising the
depth of prejudice against Cromwell's Upper House with its crowd of
soldiers, seems to have persuaded the regime to offer to call to it those
hereditary peers who had been loyal to Parliament in the wars. This proved
immediately attractive to the Commons. The Commonwealthsmen, scenting defeat, now challenged the right to sit of the Scots and Irish MPs, and
used up two weeks on this, only to see these men recognised. On 28 March,
the Commons voted to do business with the Upper House, and by 14 April
was doing so. The new 'lords' had even gained some popularity by discussing the reduction of the hated Excise to a fixed term. The constitution had
begun to work.[65]

It is easy to gain the impression that this achievement had been at the
expense of the vital work of securing funds, but progress had been made very
quietly towards this as well. On the fourth day of the session it was resolved
to gather the necessary figures to determine what was wrong with the
revenue. A fortnight later this had arrived and a committee was set up to
reduce them to a proper balance sheet. In mid-March, while the committee's
work continued, the House began hounding the Excise farmers to bring in
their arrears and so provide ready cash for the forces. The Commons also
found time to set up a committee to recommend more effective measures
against sabbath-breakers, users of the Prayer Book, Catholics and Quakers.
They demonstrated their independence of the government again by ordering the release of certain republicans placed in preventive detention by
Oliver Cromwell. One, the former army officer and Fifth Monarchist
Robert Overton, was given a hero's welcome on his return to London. The
government endorsed these meaures without complaint, to strengthen its
good relations with the Commons.[66] The only group of people who had
suffered absolutely from the House's proceedings in its first two months
were the local communities who had expected their representatives to
further their interests, in the traditional manner, with private bills. The
punishing debates on public affairs had left no time for such measures, which
were to many electors the principal reason for possessing an MP. In mid-
Essex it was called 'the Parliament that most forget'.[67]

Alongside the proceedings at Westminster, government policy continued
to be enacted. The work of rationalising the parochial structure of the

Church claimed much attention, and had now reached distant Caernarfon-shire.[68] The parallel private movement towards conciliation continued also. A presbyterian and an independent divine both preached unity to Parliament as Goodwin had done. The same message came from presbyterian pulpits in the City. In Lancashire presbyterians and independents approached agreement, while notable ministers of both persuasions and from baptist churches corresponded on the same question. The religious world was in flux, independents and baptists dividing and falling into different camps which had the presbyterians in one and the Quakers in the other. The same division was occurring in the political sphere: some baptist churches at this time gave a loyal address to Richard, while others, which had supported his father, handed in the Commonwealthsmen's petition to Parliament.[69] It was also appearing, fatally, in the army.

Oliver Cromwell had not, after all, dissolved the previous Parliament merely, or indeed primarily, from fear of events in the Commons. He was also concerned about the republican agitation in the army. Now, a year later, the Commonwealthsmen also devoted efforts to this, which increased as their influence in the House proved limited. In debate, they were generally careful to praise the soldiers and to speak for their interests. Outside Parliament, they talked to individual officers and printed tracts which linked the ideals of Commonwealthsmen, soldiers and sects, under the label of the Good Old Cause. This was contrasted with the recent development of the Protectorate, portrayed as a conspiracy of those corrupted by power, leading to revived monarchy, religious intolerance and the destruction of the army.[70] Astonishingly, nothing was done by the government to stop dispersal of these,[71] and only one pamphlet seems to have been published to answer the charges they made.[72] Perhaps the Protectorate, censured both in these tracts and in Parliament for arbitrary arrest, wished to avoid aggressive action. Perhaps Thurloe, whose province this was, found that the Commons consumed all his time. Whatever the explanation it was seen as a sign of weakness, which it was.

In his direct dealings with the army, Richard himself showed none of this. At the dangerous moment when the Commonwealthsmen's petition was presented to Parliament, some officers met at Fleetwood's house to discuss giving support to it. Richard, with the energy his father had shown in quelling mutineers, descended on them and warned them that although they were welcome to petition Parliament they must do so in support of the government. The project was dropped, and observers noted the new solidarity between Protector and army in the succeeding weeks.[73] It could not last, as five forces were working against it: the Commonwealthsmen's propaganda, the growing arrears upon the soldiers' pay, the number of remarks made by MPs against the army in the debates on the Upper House, the divisions in the army itself, and the personality of the Protector.

For his intimate advisers Richard turned to neither of the extremes at his court.[74] Fauconberg, having failed to precipitate action against the army leaders, was now complaining loudly to royalist agents. Desborough came up with an equally dangerous scheme to impose taxes through the Upper House, and tried to get that House to vote the abolition of hereditary peerages just as it was about to win recognition by associating itself with hereditary nobles. It is hardly surprising that the Protector turned to the judicious Thurloe, and to Oliver St. John and others associated with the wartime 'middle group',[75] who believed in coaxing a larger assessment out of Parliament. Yet, even before Richard's accession, Thurloe and men like him were regarded by the Desborough set not as a middle ground but as part of a general opposition. The same problem of emphasis governed Richard's own actions. Royalist agents might report that he did everything 'tenderly and prudently' and credit him with saying that 'he had rather starve than displease the people', but his attitude to the army never seemed so fulsome. Moderate presbyterians repeatedly gained the impression that he shared their views with enthusiasm, but no sectary did. The French ambassador, clearly not an interested party, guessed that by private inclinations the Protector was some sort of presbyterian. When Richard delighted and won over an opponent of his father by telling him that he intended to rule through godly men but not through army officers, he may merely have been bidding for support, but it was a dangerous thing to say.[76] Two unfortunate incidents of this sort were to count against him even as matters in Parliament began to go his way.

One was put about, and eventually printed, by the Commonwealthsmen.[77] A cornet of Ingoldsby's regiment was reported to have been summoned before Richard for insubordination, and to have complained of his major as ungodly. Richard is said to have turned to Ingoldsby, with the words 'thou canst neither preach nor pray, but I will believe thee before I will believe twenty of them' and then deprived the cornet of his commission. It may have happened, apparently gained wide currency, and was only as tactless as Henry Cromwell's remark at the same time that independents and baptists, once in power, were just as intolerant as any other denomination.[78] The other story was certainly true, and important. It began in the first week of March with a public quarrel in Westminster Hall between Richard's supporter Colonel Whalley and Colonel Ashfield. Whalley accused Ashfield's set of excluding honest men from their meetings; Ashfield said something against the government. Whalley reported him to the Protector, who summoned Ashfield and ordered him to apologise to Whalley. When

Ashfield refused, Richard instituted proceedings to court-martial him, and carried these on through March although some independent ministers interceded on Ashfield's behalf. The Protector had clearly decided to make an issue of the incident to browbeat the army, though from all accounts Whalley had been the more aggressive party in the quarrel. Fleetwood and Desborough showed a greater restraint, for when the Commonwealthsmen asked them to support Ashfield they replied that Whalley was an old comrade. Then, at the opening of April, it all suddenly blew over.[79] Perhaps Richard was pacified in some manner, perhaps he began to suspect that his victim would be triumphantly acquitted unless he packed the court in an outrageous fashion. This is another of the irritating open questions which hang over his Protectorate.

By this time, with Parliament at last working as a unit, legislation seemed likely. The Commons had proved their conservative, anti-military temper, and the Upper House, where many of the members were Richard's close supporters, might concur with it if the Protector wished this. Tension rose accordingly. The army feared its replacement by a militia.[80] Fleetwood, Desborough and their set were apparently afraid of being caught between the Protector's circle and angry soldiers, and rejected by both. To widen their options, they seem to have entered into tentative contacts with the Commonwealthsmen.[81] Independent ministers took alarm when the Commons' committee on religion talked of replacing the Triers and of imposing a presbyterian confession of faith upon the national Church.[82] The sects got a shock on 5 April, when the House passed a declaration censuring magistrates for their laxity in punishing 'heresies', which accorded ill with the principle of toleration of peaceful minority groups.[83] The Commons themselves were badly shaken on 7 April when their committee on public revenue at last produced its balance sheet. It was certainly clear and concise. The government was now nearly £2½ million in debt, its regular revenue was falling short by nearly £333,000 per annum, and it owed the army nearly £890,000 of arrears.[84]

At some period before the end of March, Richard determined to permit the convention of a formal General Council of officers, of the sort constituted at previous points of national crisis, to frame a petition to Parliament. The grounds for the decision are lost in that same gap in the evidence in which Ashfield's court martial foundered.[85] He is most likely to have seen it as a way of controlling discontent and of using it to put some legitimate pressure on Parliament. The General Council met in the first week of April, and the junior officers immediately showed their temper by electing those members most suspected by the government, including Ashfield, as a committee to frame the petition. These produced a violent document which

Richard's friends, and Fleetwood, managed to have rephrased. The petition which resulted on the 6th asked for two things, measures against royalists now gathering openly and insolently in London, and attention to the army's pay, the soldiers now being reduced to suffering for the lack of it. It was delivered to Richard, who promised all possible support and forwarded it to both Houses with a covering letter on the 8th. On that day the regiment of the late Colonel Pride printed a declaration to Fleetwood of its intent to stand by the Good Old Cause, but by means of the petition. The uneasy semantic compromise of the Protectorate, like its political compromise, still endured.[86]

The House of Commons now produced its decisive political failure. The condition of public finance, revealed by the report, and of the army, revealed by the petition, demanded one solution, a massive increase in direct taxation. This was the most unpopular action that the country's representatives could take. The House, faced with this predicament, began to flounder. It talked of retrenchment by the government, questioned the accuracy of the report and bullied the hapless excise farmers. These replied, apparently with truth, that with the country so depressed by the Spanish war, the public was simply not paying the duty properly.[87] Then, having failed to help the army, the Commons proceeded to offend it. On the 12th they heard the complaints of persons connected with the estate of a royalist conspirator, who had been maltreated by Colonel Boteler in the course of his duties under Cromwell. Their response was to disable Boteler from his civilian office and order his impeachment. Thus, far from persecuting royalists as requested, the House seemed to be punishing the army for action taken in suppression of them. Fleetwood and Desborough, who had performed similar duties, feared for themselves, and even Fauconberg felt that the MPs had behaved stupidly. The next day the officers held a prayer-meeting in an angry mood, with much muttering, while the House forbade its proceedings to be published, heightening a sense of emergency and giving rumour full scope. The day after, it favoured the widow of a notorious royalist by returning his confiscated London mansion to her.[88]

On this day, 14 April, the General Council of the army reconvened. Desborough opened proceedings by proposing that all officers be made to swear an oath applauding the execution of Charles I. Perhaps this was a measure of the fear some soldiers now had of the reactionary propensities of the Commons, that they might be planning to revive monarchy. Perhaps it was an attempt to squeeze out former royalists like Broghill. Broghill, united with the regicides Whalley and Goffe, proposed an oath of loyalty to the Protectorate instead. Both ideas were eventually dropped.[89] Two days later the Commons reminded the world again of their religious views. Some London Quakers presented a petition complaining of the fact that 144 of their fellows were in prison, in twenty-six counties, and offering to change places with the ailing if they could not be released. The MPs replied curtly that they should go home and behave themselves.[90] The next day, the 17th, was a Sunday, when Parliament did not sit. Richard summoned the officers, and spent until evening trying to restore unity to the army and to persuade them to continue co-operation with the Commons.[91] A sympathiser believed that he had succeeded, but Richard evidently did not, for that evening he seems to have determined to precipitate a crisis which would establish his authority for all time.

The government, ten days before, had used the army to put pressure on the Commons. Richard's close allies now apparently decided to reverse the trick. On the following day, the 18th, the Commons reconvened and passed two sets of votes. On the one hand they outlawed the sitting of the General Council of officers without the permission of Protector and Parliament, and demanded that every officer subscribe a declaration against the coercion of Parliament by force, or be dismissed. On the other, they agreed to get to work at once upon satisfying the army's requests, by getting the royalists out of London and finding money for the arrears. The evidence makes it clear that Richard anticipated the resolutions and was ready to use them immediately. Broghill long afterwards claimed to have persuaded him into the plan, while Sir Thomas Clarges credited it to Thurloe and other civilian advisers. It turned out to have an ironic flaw. The government had devoted great efforts to securing recognition of the Upper House. At this crucial moment the new 'lords' failed to prove to be the servants of the regime that both friends and enemies had expected them to be. They included too many men such as Fleetwood who were now suspicious of Richard's circle, and who were able to prevent a decision on the Commons' votes. Thus these lacked the required constitutional concurrence of both Houses.[92]

Richard did not in any case wait for the Upper House to pronounce. He summoned the officers to Whitehall, and as soon as the Commons had voted he told them that as Parliament was now remedying their grievances he was dissolving the General Council and dispersing them to their commands. Desborough protested that the Council controlled the soldiers' discontent, Ashfield said that they dared not face their men without bringing money. Richard answered both sharply, and the officers withdrew in silence. The meeting of their Council scheduled for the 20th did not take place, but its members did not disperse. Richard ordered his Life Guards to stand to arms. The corporation and militia of London sent the Protector addresses expressing support, though some of the militia, and some sectaries, were said to have opposed them. On the evening of the 20th Fleetwood and Desborough

avowed their loyalty to Richard, and were said to have carried away to the
officers his promises of affection.[93]

The next day, the explosion came. With fatal lack of tact, the Commons
began to debate settling the armed forces as a militia, perhaps controlled by
Parliament: the development most feared by the army. That evening Fleetwood, Desborough and other officers came to Richard and demanded that
Parliament be dissolved. He refused, whereupon they withdrew to St. James's
Palace and called the soldiers around London together. This was the test of
strength that Richard and his friends should have been anticipating. In the
autumn a neutral observer had calculated that a third of the regiments in
England supported them.[94] The Fleetwood group had generally been viewed
as a middle party in the army, and it is likely that Richard believed they
would support him in a serious confrontation. Even now, if the expected
third of the English army remained loyal, the rest might waver and dissolve,
or at least be checked till troops arrived from Henry Cromwell or Monck.
The Protector accordingly called a rival rendezvous at Whitehall. Then
came the terrible shock. The junior officers of the colonels loyal to Richard
led their soldiers off to join Fleetwood. Whalley begged his men to follow
him or kill him, and provoked complete indifference. Goffe's subalterns said
later that they had come to believe that their lack of pay was entirely due to
the corruption of Richard's officials. Even some of the Life Guard defected.
Richard's party were left with two hundred unreliable men to face the
thousands gathering at St. James's. Thus they paid the price of failing to
realise how seriously the army in general had felt that their interests had
been abandoned.

When their victory was clear, the officers at St. James's sent a deputation
led by Desborough to repeat their demand for the dissolution of Parliament.
Richard again refused, but his friends were now frightened. Stray soldiers
had broken into the wine cellars of Whitehall and were molesting visitors to
the palace. Desborough threatened to turn out the Commons with or without legal sanction. So, at last, the Protector signed away his Parliament, and
his whole policy. The commission was delivered to the Houses when they
reassembled on the 22nd. The Upper House obeyed, but the Commons
locked their doors and debated resistance. They were, inevitably, unable to
devise any in the face of overwhelming force, and so formally adjourned the
debate. When they had gone, the army locked and guarded the House,
leaving them with no alternative but to disperse to the provinces.[95]

On the day that the MPs began to leave, the 23rd, their inheritors, the
General Council, commenced the government of the country. It obtained
from Richard a proclamation ordering royalists to their homes, of the sort
they had wanted Parliament to produce, and set up a committee of officers

to discuss means of obtaining money. Fleetwood wrote a hypocritical letter
to the Scottish army to persuade it that all was happening according to the
Protector's will.[96] Over the next five days the other obvious problem, of what
to do with Richard and his friends, was debated less formally. It became clear
that there were two military bodies in London, with different views. One
was the General Council, sitting at Fleetwood's great mansion, who were
inclined to continue the Protectorate, though it was said that when Fleetwood proposed that Richard be retained at its head, Desborough disagreed.
The other was the gathering of junior officers, far more numerous, at St.
James's, who were in favour of restoring the purged Long Parliament of the
Commonwealthsmen.[97] It was not difficult to see from where they were
getting their ideas: the shower of tracts directed at the army by the
Commonwealthsmen had now become a hailstorm. In the fortnight after the
dissolution of Richard's Parliament at least twenty-eight were printed, some
being individual polemics and some petitions from partisans in the City, the
originals of which were piled in Westminster Hall. So demoralised were
other political groups that only two pamphlets were produced against them.
The polemics promised a great deal to the soldiers—pay, arrears, religious
liberty, godly government and swift new elections of trustworthy MPs—in
return for the restoration of the purged Commons of 1653. It is not surprising that by 26 April the officers of the unfortunate Goffe's regiment were
themselves agitating in print for this end.[98]

On the 28th the General Council moved forward, by decreeing the
removal of the most resented of the officers who had supported Richard.
Thus Richard himself, Fauconberg, Ingoldsby and some others lost their
now meaningless commissions and retired. Broghill fled back to Ireland. It
was an obvious concurrent step to restore the more popular of the men
whom Oliver Cromwell had dismissed for earlier opposition to the tendencies of his regime, and so the officers of his horse regiment, Lambert, and
some of the commanders deprived at the institution of the Protectorate were
placed in the posts just vacated. For good measure the Commonwealth
leader Hesilrige was restored to his old commission. The appearance of some
of these men in the General Council strengthened the pressure for a restoration of the purged Parliament. At the beginning of May the officers were still
debating the merits of this against those of a Protector ruling with a large
council of the godly, but the sentiments of their subalterns, who directly
controlled the soldiers, left few observers in doubt of the outcome. To
maintain the Protectorate carried a real risk of being abandoned just as
Richard's friends had been. The army leaders accordingly requested a conference with the Commonwealthsmen.[99]

This took place on 4 May, when the officers presented conditions representing a compromise between Protectorate and Commonwealth: an Act of Indemnity for all actions under the Cromwells, an allowance and some honourable position for Richard, reform of law and religion, and government by an elected Commons and a senate which would include army officers. Ludlow later claimed that the Commonwealthsmen agreed only to the Act, payment of Richard's debts, reforming legislation and a temporary senate. The following day the General Council decided to re-admit the purged Parliament on these terms, plus liberty of conscience, a pension and Somerset House for Richard and a period to the sitting of the restored Parliament. On the day after, the 6th, it issued a declaration recalling the Parliament of 1653 in order to uphold the Good Old Cause. This was delivered in the evening to the Speaker of this Parliament, and the next day he led a party of its members into the House, soldiers lining the corridors and applauding.[100]

All this while Richard himself had been at Whitehall, presumably under house arrest, boiling with rage. His first thought, on finding himself slipping from power, was to bring his other armies to his aid. To this end he got letters through to his brother and to Monck, and tried to contact the troops in Flanders and the fleet under Mountagu.[101] However, the last two proved out of reach, and the first two suffered from the same disability as Richard and his friends had in London. The General Council wrote to the Scottish army on 3 May, explaining its actions in terms of the hostility of Richard's Parliament to the Good Old Cause. Monck found that the junior officers in Scotland accepted this with enthusiasm, and had to send to Richard privately expressing his inability to act, and to write to the General Council openly expressing his support. When he heard of the return of the purged Parliament, his officers were, again, so full of approval that he wrote a fulsome letter submitting to its authority. This left only Henry in Ireland, and when his army proved divided over the matter it clearly became impossible to face the other forces alone.[102] In his fury and desperation, Richard now sold his birthright. As the only people who might resist his usurpers now were the royalists, he offered to one of them to recognise Charles II in return for a pension and for offices for his friends.[103] As this, too, turned out to produce no practical aid, there was nothing left to him but submission.

In mid-May the army, holding true to him in their fashion, requested Parliament to pay Richard's debts and award him a pension. On the 24th he found himself faced with Oliver St. John and another of his former advisers, now acting as emissaries of Parliament. These tendered him a paper for signature, in which he promised to retire and live peacefully in return for the payment of those debts which he had contracted in the public service. Richard signed, and the next day was voted his removal expenses. After six weeks more the restored Parliament resolved to pay his debts by selling the furnishings of the palaces which he and his father had inhabited. Henry held out till 14 June, when he wrote a cold letter to the Speaker making his submission and laying down his command. In early July he retired, like his brother, into obscurity in the English countryside. With this, the Protectorate ended.[104]

By this time the misrepresentation of Richard's career had begun. A feature of the fall of a regime in this period was the swarm of hostile tracts which followed its demise, released by its enemies to blacken its reputation and so insure against its revival. The problem in according Richard this treatment was that he had done nothing much wrong. In his brief reign his policies had been popular with the generality and he had been pulled down by the least popular interest, the army. He had attacked no group directly, his personal life had been blameless and his presence charming. He had fallen because of the potential, not the actual, achievement of his rule. Thus the most effective destruction of his reputation was to present him as an innocent weakling, unfit to wield authority and doomed to fall. The republicans dubbed him 'Queen Dick'. The royalists preferred 'Tumble-Down Dick',[105] and this is the tag which passed into the school-books. Crossed with modern sentimentality, it has resulted in a picture of a young man too good for politics, who fell because of his desire to please all and injure none.

Richard Cromwell was not this. He had inherited his father's temper and sense of a call from God. Having taken power he grew to enjoy it, and fought for it ferociously at the end. It is a truism to say that he fell because he lost control of the army, and that this was ultimately because he had never been a soldier, but this requires some qualification. He never really 'had' control of the army, which accepted him only with Fleetwood as an informal, and then as a formal, intermediary. When he believed that he was winning a section of it, he was merely detaching a few officers from their men. In essence, he could only view the army from outside, with no sympathy. In the autumn he had relied on appeals to it. In the spring, when tension was greater and he was growing less patient, he began to mix these with coercion, and fatally overestimated his own power. His father had always seen the soldiers as the centre of the whole great movement which had swept him to office, embodying ideals which held good for all. Richard could only see them as rather irritating servants of society. There the second half of the truism remains. The man who destroyed the Protectorate was Oliver Cromwell, who pushed it into near-bankruptcy, divided its supporters, and elevated as a potential successor a son who had no understanding of the men upon whom he most depended.

2

The Collapse of the Republican Alliance

THE new regime called itself a Parliament, and took to itself not only the legislative and judicial functions associated with that institution, but also the policy-making function of a monarch or Protector and his council. While it delegated executive powers to a smaller body, it retained control of major decisions. Yet this assembly included neither a monarch nor a Protector, nor an Upper House of any complexion, but was about a fifth of what had once been a House of Commons. Some forty-two MPs gathered on 7 May, and thereafter the total number declared eligible to sit was seventy-eight, of whom some never appeared.[1] Each of this handful of men had at least twelve years of parliamentary experience behind him. All were united by a recognition of the purge which had preceded the English Revolution, and by the four succeeding years in which they had wielded supreme authority. They had been placed in power then, as now, by the army. Then, the soldiers had prevented the entry of most of the people's representatives into the House; now they had forced the dissolution of a recently elected Commons. While in power before, this purged Parliament had been unmistakably detested, associated with the destruction of the monarchy and the Lords, high taxation, centralised and arbitrary rule, and a religious policy which allowed sects to proliferate. It represented, in a concentrated form, all that had disturbed more conservative Englishmen about the Protectorate.[2] In its potential for rapid, ruthless and effective government, it possessed extraordinary advantages, but its heritage doomed it to rule in despite of most of its subjects.

There were other factors in their past which ought to have constrained the new masters of England. The army, which had given them power twice, had also deprived them of it in 1653, because they had consistently failed to produce the reforms which the soldiers desired. These MPs had shared the conservative instincts of any Interregnum House of Commons: they had distrusted the army and been utterly unwilling to act as its servants, and they had not been prepared to produce any fundamental electoral, legal or ecclesiastical reformation. Nor had they managed to devise a permanent model of government which would both satisfy the principles of representation and secure the achievements of the Revolution. Now they had been returned to power dependent upon co-operation with the military and with another mandate for reform. Likewise, their previous indulgence of the sects had been due in the main to the army's pressure, while they had come close to establishing presbyterian church government. Now their leaders and propagandists had been bidding for the loyalty of sectaries against the Protectorate. The two men who had published the recent appeals for a Commonwealth were John Canne, a Fifth Monarchist, and Livewell Chapman, whose bookshop of sectarian literature, as well as his charismatic name, suggests his allegiances. The sovereign Parliament had been reinstated on the strength of promises which it had never before shown any disposition to perform.

The restored MPs also had to reckon, immediately, with an articulate and determined set of enemies, the members of their House of Commons who had been the victims of Pride's Purge. Some 213 of these 'secluded' members were still alive, almost three times the number of those admitted to the House. One was Arthur Annesley, who had so recently aided the Protectorate. Another was William Prynne. Prynne was one of the most prolific writers of any age, and also one of the most destructive. On a normal day he would tuck his lean, saturnine features under a cap, which shaded his eyes, and work until light failed, refreshing himself every three hours with a roll and a pot of ale which he consumed as he wrote. His title-pages are unmistakable, the words bowling down to the bottom as though carried by the force of their own invective. Each noun reels beneath the weight of half a dozen hostile adjectives. Prynne was a natural conservative, the exponent of a stable, traditional and sober society. In defence of this ideal, he had launched himself first against long hair, stage-plays, the drinking of healths, and ecclesiastical innovations. His own hair was worn long now, to conceal the fact that in 1637 the King's executioner had removed his ears because the Queen acted in plays and the greatest innovator in the Church was its Archbishop. This experience had given him a permanent hatred of bishops, but not of monarchy. After the defeat of the royalists, republicans and sectaries had become his sworn enemies, as they came to represent the new threat to the traditional order.[3]

On the day that the purged Parliament reassembled, this individual, together with Annesley and other 'secluded' members, went to the House and demanded admission. The soldiers in the lobby, though clearly embarrassed, denied them entry. Prynne returned alone two days later, slipped in and proceeded to denounce the MPs around him. Hesilrige and Vane, failing to subdue him, had the House adjourned for lunch and appealed to the army. Prynne, returning in the afternoon, found himself barred out by soldiers while his erstwhile colleagues inside voted to confirm Pride's Purge. Having treated the military to a harangue, he retired to commence a literary campaign, joined by his friends, to remind the public regularly of the illegality of the new regime.[4]

All these difficulties would have been less ominous had the restored MPs possessed the unity that their numbers, experiences and isolation should have imposed. Instead, they represented a spectrum of opinion. There were, clearly, differences of belief and personality between Hesilrige and Vane, but prominent men like them were all different in kind from the rank and file. The proponents of reform or of action were usually identifiable, while the opponents, who had previously carried the day, tended to be submerged in the mass. One who was not, by virtue of his office, was the Speaker himself, William Lenthall. He had been the figure-head of the Long Parliament all through the wars, carried along by it but protesting, when his voice was heard at all, his dismay of proceedings. He kept his post precisely because he was so unexceptionable. When the army had invited this Parliament to return, he had led it back with obvious reluctance, having been perfectly contented with his new dignity as a member of Cromwell's Upper House.[5] Thirteen men who had sat in the purged Parliament shared his scruples to the extent that they never returned, and were written off by those who did.[6] Many of the latter may have had almost as little enthusiasm for action.

This regime also contained members of forceful personality and genuinely independent mind, with a reciprocated distrust of the Commonwealthsmen. One such was Sir Anthony Ashley Cooper. Cooper was physically small and delicate, a reminder that in politics as in any jungle the largest animals are not necessarily the deadliest. He possessed the remarkable capacity to change sides regularly without giving his contemporaries, or his modern biographers, the impression that he did so for any but excellent motives. A wealthy young Dorset baronet, he had fought for the king and then for Parliament, slaughtering his former comrades with immoderate zest. He had broken with the Commonwealthsmen to become an active supporter of the Protectorate, only to retire without warning into opposition. His reappearance in central politics was unlikely to increase their stability.[7]

The army itself was now also a more complex organism than it might appear. Richard's friends were gone, but the officers restored in their place included men who had opposed the institution of the Protectorate as well as men who had instituted it, implying different concepts of government and society. In particular, the latter group included John Lambert. Lambert had made his name in the Great Civil War as a dashing cavalry leader, had led an army in the Second and had been Cromwell's second-in-command in the Third, when his exploits had arguably outshone his superior's. Thereafter he had been the architect, and heir apparent, of the early Protectorate. He had urged the expulsion of the purged Parliament before Cromwell had agreed, had probably sabotaged the nominated assembly which had followed, had designed the constitution of the early Protectorate and may have drawn up the organisation of Major-Generals which had controlled the provinces under it. In the army he was loved by the common soldiers as none of the other highest officers was. In government, he represented the controlling interest of the military, permitting elected assemblies their place but limiting their powers. In private life, he was an aesthete, cultivating flowers. In religion, he was a neutral, having no firm belief himself and granting the widest possible tolerance to others. He had risen almost in spite of Cromwell, who was never a close friend of his, and their partnership had first frayed over the Spanish war, which Lambert opposed (correctly) as a dangerous error, and then collapsed when Cromwell replaced Lambert's constitution with that of 1657.[8] On being invited back into the General Council, he had instantly become a leader, attending the talks with the Commonwealthsmen, carrying the resolutions to the Speaker and supervising the re-entry of the MPs. Thus the men who had most firmly striven for the unfettered power of the Commons were now in harness with the man who had most successfully fettered them in the soldiers' interests.

This miniature muddle of alliances commenced work with admirable efficiency. Within a week the MPs had discovered which of their surviving fellows were willing to join them. On their first day they appointed two army leaders and five republicans, including Fleetwood, Hesilrige, Vane and Ludlow as a temporary Committee of Safety to take executive action. On the 11th they passed an act to confirm all existing local officers in their positions. On that day the Committee of Safety presented a bill for a Council of State to replace themselves, and such a body, empowered to command the armed forces and to conduct foreign policy, was established on the 19th. It numbered thirty-one members, twenty-one of whom were MPs; Fleetwood, Desborough and Lambert headed the army's representatives and Hesilrige, Vane and Ludlow the Parliament's. When Fleetwood and another officer refused the oath to the Commonwealth that was expected of members, apparently having the sectary's objection to oaths in general, they were allowed to affirm instead. Scot tried to remove two possible opponents at the beginning, the maverick Cooper and the trimmer Whitelocke, by accusing them of corresponding with royalists. Both stood firm, the charge was dropped, and the Council settled down, the air cleared, to work. It did so harder than any Privy Council, sitting early, late and on Sundays.[9] Meanwhile government supporters turned out pamphlets to extol the new regime as a promoter of liberty and honest administration. Its own newspaper, *The Faithful Scout*, had been launched before the return of the MPs and was wound up only after Canne himself displaced the Cromwellian publicist as editor of the official journals.[10]

In the provinces, reactions to the changes took various forms. Surviving private comment is, as usual, very rare. The vicar of Earl's Colne, Essex, thought the army leaders 'a self-seeking, deceitful crew', and noted of the restored Parliament: 'sectaries rejoice, others gaze'. A Manchester presbyterian minister thought it a 'most sad thing that we must be ruled by such as hate us'.[11] Both remarks indicate how firmly the new regime had been linked, in reputation if not in reality, with the sects. Otherwise opinion must be surmised from action. In the Forest of Dean, commoners destroyed enclosures to which they had long objected, while in many places they treated government parks as though they had reverted to wilderness, eating the deer and grazing livestock in them.[12] Both sorts of disturbance had been a feature of the civil wars, demonstrating that many plebeians regarded the changes as a lapse of legitimate government. In early April, when Richard's Parliament seemed to be countenancing a national ministry, two London vestries had campaigned to gather in tithes: these efforts now halted.[13] When the Midsummer Quarter Sessions were held, many prominent justices failed to attend in Devon, Somerset, Essex and Yorkshire, and the gaps in records may conceal the same development elsewhere. It is the more striking in that, in the first two counties, attendance by important gentry had hitherto been better than elsewhere, and increasing. The indictments for seditious words, a feature of legal archives under other regimes, almost vanish—a sign that few thought a grumble against this government worth reporting. Instead, at Gloucester Assizes on 27 July, a man was actually indicted, convicted and sentenced to be burned in the hand for having defamed Richard Cromwell.[14] Municipal records keep a stony silence: there were no bonfires, no bells, and not a drop of wine poured into any conduit. The governing set was overthrown at Colchester, but replaced by men who were less sympathetic to the attitudes associated with the new rulers, and had clearly made national changes an excuse for a local coup.[15] A few boroughs were lucky in having representatives in the new House who still remembered their obligations to the men who had elected them many years before, as Vane did in the case of Hull.[16] These constituencies did not, however, show any more delight than the rest.

On the other hand, in its first three months the restored Parliament received thirty-one loyal addresses from local communities.[17] These differed considerably in kind from those delivered to Richard. There were far fewer of them, almost all were from south-eastern England, and they tended to speak for particular groups within wider communities. They very often asked for reforms, and the same county or town sometimes produced another address later. London itself may be taken as an example. On 9 May the restored Parliament received a petition from some citizens for a purge of the City militia. This was probably the work of the Commonwealthsmen in the Corporation, led by the Lord Mayor, John Ireton, and Alderman Tichbourne, who had already replaced some officers who had supported Richard and his Parliament.[18] On the 10th some Southwark citizens, probably Quakers, requested the release of all imprisoned for religious beliefs. Two days later more Londoners, led by the secretary and political radical Samuel Moyer, handed in a request for the promotion of the Good Old Cause.[19] On 1 June some 'young men' from Southwark requested a senate, religious liberty and the codification of the law.[20] On the 4th Ireton finally coaxed an address from the City Corporation, asking for religious liberty, speedier litigation, less taxation and the City's traditional privileges.[21] In general, these documents were the work of those reformers in English society who, though a minority, were not an unimportant one, as the Quakers alone now numbered thousands. Little is known about most of these groups and the links between them. If more could be uncovered, an important aspect of the Revolution would become clearer.

The addresses were associated with a great commotion in the London press. Under the Protectorate, with a firm government holding a middle course, the literary excitement of the war years had died away. Now the reappearance of the purged Parliament, with what appeared to be a commitment to reform, set to work every writer who desired change. The printing houses of the capital soon appeared like a colony of excited seagulls. One pamphlet bore the title *Let Me Speake Too?* Others could refer to 'this time of general scribbling' or rank overpublication with overtaxation as a national burden.[22] The world of this press is another important and unstudied feature of the period.

Probably the greatest pressure for a single reform was for the abolition of tithes, an issue for many years. The purged Parliament had previously divided over it, and shelved it. The nominated assembly of 1653 quarrelled over it. It had been a platform in some of the elections to Richard's Parliament. Now, apart from its place in the pamphlet literature and in some local addresses, it was the sole object of two great petitions to Parliament, one delivered on 14 June and the other on the 27th. The first was collected in the western counties, the second was general. The process by which they were raised is obscure, though Quakers raised many signatures for the second by touring the north-western counties on horseback. A third petition, produced but not presented in July, was signed by 7,000 Quaker women. Most of the propaganda against tithes did not propose a substitute, envisaging the destruction of the national Church, but some tracts suggested voluntary payment or national or county rates instead.[23]

The other religious development most frequently campaigned for was liberty of conscience, another issue with a long pedigree and one graced with the pen of Milton. Vane now became the most distinguished author of a new set of pamphlets in this cause.[24] Likewise, several Quaker writers hailed the restored Parliament as the regime most likely to embrace the aims of their movement.[25] A Ranter leader of the late 1640s resurfaced to deny the existence of Hell or sin, the claim which had provoked the Blasphemy Act of 1650 and questioned all traditional morality.[26] The most common political demand was for the dismissal of officials who had served the Protectorate, frequently coupled with the insistence that they refund their salaries.[27] Proposals for legal reform ranged from mere restriction of the death penalty and relief of poor debtors to the reduction of all law to a code, the decentralisation of the legal system and the abolition of the legal profession.[28] The registration of land and the abolition or reform of copyhold tenure were other targets.[29] One writer revived the Digger demand of 1649 for settlement of waste-land by the poor and co-operative communities.[30]

This literature provoked a hot reaction from conservative authors. Richard's friends had now recovered sufficiently to accuse the army of treachery and the purged Parliament of tyranny, and to demand the revival of the Protectorate.[31] Prynne came to the defence of tithes, citing precedents from Scripture, law and morality, and had companions in this work.[32] Other men wrote and preached the virtues of the national ministry as upholders of the social and moral order.[33]

There was one group whose views the MPs could not possibly ignore, and whose petition, when it arrived, would be debated clause by clause: the army. The officers, having gained only hazy verbal promises from the Commonwealthsmen before restoration, gave the Parliament five days to settle in and then presented their address.[34] They declared, decisively, against a Protector but asked for a select Senate, with some control over legislation, to represent their interests in the government. They wanted Fleetwood made commander of all the armed forces, and the ministry, universities, schools and all offices purged of the ungodly. They asked a provision for Richard, as said earlier, and an Act of Indemnity for those who had served the Cromwells. They needed their arrears paid. They wanted toleration for all sober Christians who reverenced Scripture and the Trinity, except episcopalians and Catholics. Finally, they desired provision for a new, full, Parliament. These several concerns neatly categorised the preoccupations of the restored MPs during their first three months.

The religious request was easily disposed of on 20 May, when the army's formula was voted almost word for word. It was no novelty, being only the ruling in Cromwell's 1657 constitution, minus the clause for a confession of faith. It left the status of Quakers, who did not consider Scripture essential, as equivocal as ever, together with the question of the national ministry and of tithes. The MPs had already started to deal with these other matters on the 10th, when the Southwark petition concerning prisoners of conscience had been referred to a committee chaired by Vane. This summoned Quakers to give evidence, whom Vane, after initial argument, allowed to wear hats throughout the proceedings. It ran up against all the legal complications which had baffled Richard's Privy Council, but did release a few Quakers from prison and summmon ministers who had raised mobs against them. In the House's debates, Vane was regarded as the champion of the sects: it was he who led the lobby against tithes when the first great petition for abolition arrived on 14 June. The resulting discussion was inconclusive: it was agreed to devise a substitute, but by Speaker Lenthall's casting vote this work was given to a Grand Committee of the House, instead of a small one better suited to produce swift proposals. On 27 June the debate revived on the appearance of the second petition, and ended with a decision to continue tithes unless an alternative could be found, which effectively shelved the matter indefinitely. To press the point, Parliament appended a proclamation directing that tithes should be paid properly now that it had decided for them. Three days later it hit at Quakers again, by resolving to tighten laws protecting ministers from disturbance. The clergy most favoured by the MPs, who were invited to preach to them, were congregational independents who also ministered to Fleetwood's circle and had advised the early Protectorate. On the whole, this Parliament had proceeded no further than it had done before, and ended by confirming Oliver Cromwell's original ecclesiastical policy.[35]

The same pattern recurred, ominously, in finance. On 20 May, the MPs resolved to confirm the Cromwellian assessment and to advance the date of its payment, and passed an Act for this on 18 June. To extinguish some of the soldiers' arrears, they voted to sell Whitehall and Somerset House, but as there were no buyers for these great palaces, no money appeared. The proper payment was ordered of the excise and customs, whereupon the wretched excise farmers, foreseeing another ordeal, resigned. Lord Mayor Ireton managed to persuade London's Common Council, though not its aldermen, to lend the government some money, but at the same time, to please the soldiers around the capital, the MPs increased their pay. The House's revenue committee twice reminded their colleagues of the huge annual deficit and standing debt. Nothing was done in response, this Parliament proving as reluctant to face fiscal realities as Richard's. The soldiers' arrears grew larger, and by June one regiment could ask the House how its men and their families could be as hungry under an honest republic as under a corrupt Protectorate.[36]

The Act of Indemnity was the first measure which required protracted debate, taking almost two months till its passage on 12 July. There was great reluctance to let the Cromwells' leading civilian servants, who were blamed for the supposed 'reactionary' aspects of the later Protectorate, escape punishment. Also attacked were financial officers suspected of peculation and military officers who had carried out some of Cromwell's arbitrary arrests. What saved all was the natural human disposition to forgive other people's enemies. As no victim had incurred the odium of a majority of the House, nobody was eventually excepted from the act. There was one loop-hole, upon which Hesilrige insisted, through which future persecution could be possible, that the terms only covered officers who had received 'necessary' salaries under the Protectorate, leaving the judgement of what constituted an exorbitant one to the current ruler. There were also two qualifications, that the titles of honour conferred by the Cromwells be revoked, and that to gain benefit of the pardon men had to subscribe a declaration of loyalty to the Commonwealth. In practice, however, these were of little importance. Nobody was prosecuted under the 'necessary salary' clause, or for refusing subscription. The Cromwellian lords were often referred to as lords there-after. In another sense continuity had been preserved.[37]

This pattern reappeared in the formal relationship between government and army. At first the Commonwealthsmen worked hard to foster the vital partnership. One of Hesilrige's allies, Henry Neville, sponsored a successful motion to give Fleetwood custody of St. James's Park. The initial Commit-tee of Safety requested the House to invest control of the army in him, Lambert, Desborough, Colonel Berry and Hesilrige. Parliament added Ludlow and Vane to this commission, but this still left the army's own leaders in a majority, providing the practical independence which they had sought under Richard. Then the mood changed during the debates on the army's petition. The House made Fleetwood Commander-in-Chief as requested, but on 6 June resolved that not he but the Speaker should sign commissions, with Parliament's consent. This provided it with an effective veto over the whole personnel of the army, as every officer in it would need legal confirmation of his place. Ludlow and Vane opposed this development as divisive, but Hesilrige and Scot were reverting to their old desire to control the military, and most MPs followed them. The officers, already resentful of being outnumbered on the Council of State, were furious. Desborough informed the world that he would never accept a commission from the Speaker. But here the divisions in the army worked, again, to the advantage of this Parliament. The morning after the Act passed, a friend of Hesilrige's, Colonel Hacker, led his subalterns to receive their commissions, and Ludlow, who had been given a regiment, followed.

Fleetwood then acquiesced, and by late July the leading officers, including Desborough, had submitted to the process.

The remodelling began with the common soldiers themselves, whom the Committee of Safety had invited to submit lists of godly and loyal officers. The Army Commission then drew up the command structure of each regiment for Parliament. Most of the actual changes were made before the commissions arrived in the House, and represented a compromise between junior officers, their superiors, and the Commonwealthsmen. Those friends of Richard who had kept their commissions in April, if only on paper, now lost them, Goffe being dropped by the army itself and Whalley and Boteler by Parliament. Those officers dismissed by Cromwell who had been restored in April were now joined by others of whom the General Council had been more wary, the Fifth Monarchists Overton and Nathaniel Rich and the fierce republican Matthew Alured. The members of that Council themselves, however, all seem to have been confirmed in their respective places, though individual voices were raised in the House against Lambert and Desborough. Several regiments were simply recommissioned entire. The whole process left the army even more divided than before, in the Parliament's interest, and established firmly as the subordinate partner in the alliance it had itself constructed.[38]

Most of the addresses to the restored Parliament, including the army's, had requested a purge of the administration and militia, and this took place. The great civilian officers of the Protectorate were replaced by commissions of MPs. A few of their subordinates were also dismissed, but most continued on taking an oath to the Commonwealth. The regime had less success with the judges, for so many refused this oath that during the summer Assizes four circuits had only a single judge in commission.[39] The work of appointing new commissioners to run the City militia commenced on 9 May, in response to the petition delivered that day. Those for the rest of the country replaced indemnity as the House's main business. The relevant acts were passed between 28 June and 26 July. The men whom they placed in power were a mixture resulting from the varying views and local knowledge of MPs, limited by the material available. In Wales, both the 'moderate' gentry added to the militia of the late Protectorate and the chief supporters of the Cromwells were replaced by obscure figures. The one notable person left in the South Wales commission was Bussy Mansell, assumed to be a loyal republican but in fact corresponding with the royalists. In Sussex, this Parliament had an important representative, Herbert Morley, who simply returned to power his own set dating from 1653, displacing men who were, on the whole, more radical. In Kent it also had the support of notable leaders, but used these on government service, leaving insignificant men, mostly of more conservative beliefs, in power in the county. In Somerset the MP John Pyne led an active and committed republican team back to dominance. The Buckinghamshire, Devon and Cornwall commissions, by contrast, mixed presbyterian gentry, who had staffed most preceding bodies, with a few soldiers and sectaries. The House struck out a Bristol Quaker leader from the proposed commission for that city, but five of his companions stayed on; others of the movement found places in the lists for Westminster and at least nine counties. Eight Fifth Monarchists were also included. Overall, the regime had accepted support wherever it thought it could find it. In the process, it had produced a political reaction in some counties and entrusted others to the most extreme reformers they had known. It is typical of the restored Parliament both that this should have been so and that it was largely the result of accident.[40]

As well as providing for its own protection, the government attempted to keep general order. Like every preceding regime, it denied commoners the right to violent action, ordering the local justices to suppress the riots in Dean.[41] A more complex disturbance, which became national news, occurred at Enfield. Some army officers who had purchased confiscated land proceeded to enclose the attached common land. The villagers, who had used it hitherto, broke holes in the enclosures in May and sent in their cattle, whereupon the purchasers appealed to the Council of State, who ordered the JPs to quell the rioters and sent two troops of horse to ensure that this was done. The soldiers arrested the ringleaders, but a jury acquitted them, whereupon the troopers were left to watch the district. They amused themselves by bullying the locals, until on 11 July these overpowered their principal tormentors, at the cost of one life. A JP then committed the captive soldiers to Newgate, and the villagers stated their case to Parliament and published it in pamphlets. The purchasers sent in a counter-petition to the House. Rumour spread that every aggrieved commoner in the land would now take up arms. The MPs, again, came to the aid of property and order, directing the local JPs to arrest the leaders of this rising and bailing the soldiers. The affair now ended, some private settlement being reached. It had exposed all the problems inherent in the regime's image: while defending the social and legal system, it was also accused of overriding local custom in the name of central government and of defending military usurpers against civilians.[42]

With all these practical preoccupations, it is not surprising that, though the restored Parliament soon voted not to sit longer than one year, it found little time to discuss the form of its successor. The press was bound by no such limitation. Some of its deliberations centred on the army's request for a senate, the proponents arguing that the populace left to itself was too ungodly to be trusted, and the opponents that a second house would breed conflict. Some writers wanted two elected houses, one to propound and the other to resolve. The republic's most distinguished political philosopher, James Harrington, propounded his model of a bicameral, rotating Parliament, elected by equal districts, with a property qualification. A sectary continued the traditional Fifth Monarchist call for a nominated assembly of saints. All these ideas, save the last, found favour with some MPs. Ludlow and Vane agreed with the principle of an independent second House, but Hesilrige's allies did not. The army itself seemed divided, Fleetwood still said to be hankering after a Protectorate, Lambert after an oligarchy and the newly-restored colonels after a Commonwealth or a nominated assembly. Yet all that Parliament could do was to resolve, on two occasions, to consider the whole question.[43]

The restored MPs had, then, produced no reforms. This fact diminished much of the enthusiasm for them among reformers, particularly Quakers.[44] It also, arguably, prevented a serious uprising of scandalised gentry.[45] On the other hand, this Parliament remained associated with radicals. It did, after all, include Vane and his followers, and had restored some sectaries to the army and put others, and Quakers, in control of the militia. The Quakers expected it to remodel commissions of the Peace in the same manner, and made lists of brethren whom they thought suitable for justices and of existing magistrates whom they thought fit to be retained.[46] In Ireland, which under successive regimes had been feared to be a blueprint for future policies in England, Henry Cromwell was replaced with a commission of five noted radicals. These did appoint many Quaker and baptist JPs and, as Henry had predicted, the latter soon strove for dominance over every other group.[47]

In any case, as has been said earlier, the Quakers in particular were so aggressive and successful that mere tolerance on the part of a government appeared to be betrayal to conservatives. Fear of religious radicals now increased to a hysterical pitch. When a huge Fifth Monarchist meeting was held in West Sussex, a royalist agent could write 'We daily expect a massacre.' A philosopher in London wrote to a friend, who had complained of the propaganda of the Quakers, 'we have more cause to fear the sword'. A broadside was scattered in the City warning that Vane and the Fifth Monarchists were about to kill its citizens. Tiverton, in Devon, was thrown into a panic by a similar rumour. When a gale blew stones off the tower of St. Martin's, Oxford, during a service, the congregation believed that the sects had risen. At some summer Quarter Sessions and assizes there was a noticeable increase in indictments for witchcraft, perhaps an index of tension in local communities. At least nine writers devoted tracts to informing readers of the

Quaker menace. Mobs attacked members of the movement in at least eight southern English towns, usually for disturbing services.[48]

The religious life of England was in a melting-pot which was now being stirred with terrifying speed. In Worcestershire a presbyterian minister, who had long worked for unity, found that the baptists with whom he had spoken of association now withdrew, hoping to achieve supreme power like their fellows in Ireland. The Lancashire presbyterian and independent clergy signed their long-prospected agreement on qualifications for the ministry. Quakers developed their organisation to a new level of sophistication. Groups across southern England met to construct associations with regular gatherings and common funds and records. In the north, where such bodies already existed, their meetings increased in number and frequency. The independent ministers patronised by Fleetwood and Parliament, trying to achieve closer union with their fellows in the country, wrote to other gathered churches asking for their views on public affairs. The only recorded answer is from Yarmouth's congregation, which wanted the retention of tithes and the exclusion of Quakers from all office. In general, the sects and independent churches tended rather to fragment further. Not the least offensive aspect of sectarian teaching to many was the prominent role played in it by women. In Exeter this rebounded upon one Fifth Monarchist preacher who, having given women an equal right to speak in his church, found himself denounced in print by two of them who took a dislike to his running of it.[49]

At the centre, every commentator realised that the partnership between Parliament and army was become strained. The officers had been forced to pass under the yoke of taking commissions from the Speaker. They had suspected, as with Richard's Parliament, that the new militia was intended to replace them. They were watching as their men's arrears of pay grew. They felt kept at the mercy of the MPs by the dormant 'necessary' salaries clause in the Act of Indemnity, which seemed to them a breach of faith. They were offended, as with other Parliaments, by hostile expressions used about them by MPs in the House. Some pamphlets made a deliberate policy of rubbing salt in their wounds, railing against individual officers, crowing over the humiliation of the army by the House and warning the common soldiers to contrast their miserly pay with the landed wealth of some of their superiors. Others, more ingenuously, complained of the heavy taxation that the soldiers caused and requested a reduction of both. Observers agreed that the main force keeping officers and MPs together was a mutual awareness of the trouble brewing up in the provinces.[50]

This trepidation was perfectly justified. As the summer of 1659 passed its meridian, the various sources of tension in England and Wales were becoming inflamed to a point at which large-scale violence was only a matter of time. On the first of August, it came.

All through the winter and spring, the letters had continued to pass between Sir Edward Hyde and his monarch, and their contacts in England. From all the disappointments of two decades there survived three separate groups of supporters to whom the exiled king might look to lend aid to a royalist rising.[51] First in length of service was the 'Sealed Knot, representing the men who had followed Charles I in the Great Civil War. With the loss or retirement of so many leaders, this was run by men who were almost all younger sons of nobles, having less to lose than their fathers and elder brothers. Even so, having been formed to co-ordinate conspiracy, the Knot had, despite its splendid name and modern reputation, spent most of its career discouraging risings as futile. One of its members, Sir Richard Willis, had almost certainly become a double agent, passing information to Thurloe, rendering this group now worse than useless. The second set was a handful of men who had fought on the other side in the first war and later changed allegiance. This defection had been made in spirit by a great many, but few had translated it into action. The most dashing of those who had was Edward Massey, who demonstrated the same courage and skill in eluding capture that he had once shown against the army of Charles I. Third was the Action Party, those diehards, converts and youngsters who had come forward to compensate for the caution of the Sealed Knot. It was this group which had kept royalist conspiracy alive for the past years, supplying most of the recent martyrs in the process. The Knot contained not a single magnate, but the Action Party was socially even less prestigious, most being gentry or merchants. The most highly-born, and most active, survivor was John Mordaunt, younger brother of the Earl of Peterborough. Mordaunt had been involved in the last plot, in early 1658, and had been arrested and tried for treason. The tribunal which sentenced most of his companions to death acquitted him only by a single vote. Mordaunt heard the verdict, was released—and went straight back to plotting. A fanatic could do as much, but this man seemed to love peril for its own sake. He was, unquestionably, dangerous, to the enemies he opposed and the friends whom he tempted after him.

As Richard's Parliament debated the Upper House, King Charles made Mordaunt a viscount and put him to work rebuilding an active royalist leadership. The process soon encountered some opposition from royalists themselves. The Sealed Knot, as before, saw Mordaunt as a rash upstart. Some younger royalists led by Viscount Falkland were jealous of his new importance. The circle of exiles round the King's brother James, Duke of York, were jealous of Hyde and his colleagues, and therefore their connections in

England were wary of any venture which Hyde sponsored. On the other hand, Mordaunt succeeded in attracting a new and very promising number of men, former Parliamentarians who had refused to support the Revolution but remained passive during the succeeding conspiracies. These had retained the local power and self-confidence which many royalists had lost, and were not under the government's suspicion. Nevertheless, many of them, while professing interest in the royal cause, were at the same moment working to establish the Protectorate in Richard's Parliament. Perhaps they were, as some professed, trying to serve the King there. Perhaps this was a form of double insurance. Perhaps, most likely, they were simply devoted to a traditional form of society, which they would accept from a Protector if he defended it. Whatever the truth for each individual, the army's coup and the restoration of a Commonwealth provided their decision. Mordaunt's obscure talks now acquired a great momentum.

Even as he sponsored lay followers to work for a monarchical state, so Chancellor Hyde was working through loyal clerics to preserve an episcopalian Church. In May, when the sects were saluting the restored Parliament and the royalist Evelyn could consider the national ministry doomed, Sir Edward and his monarch set about strengthening their ecclesiastical adherents. Two clerical agents were sent to England, to have the surviving bishops consecrate the most talented junior royalist churchmen to fill vacant sees, and to form an alliance with presbyterian ministers.[52]

By 16 June Mordaunt could report that the programme of revolt was ready. It consisted of a multiplicity of local risings, intended to divide the opposing army and destroy it in detail, or to hold it up in one region while the rebels in others united in overwhelming force. The leaders of these outbreaks were to be a remarkable mixture of old royalists, former parliamentarians, men who had been children during the wars, men who had remained aloof in them, and the occasional friend of Richard Cromwell, such as Fauconberg. The Sealed Knot and the Falkland set had been persuaded to co-operate. This span of support testified to the unpopularity of the restored Parliament. It contained, however, relatively few men of great ability, reputation or rank, and its very size led to indiscretion. The initial talks had been sufficient to produce the rumours which had frightened the army in April and got royalists ordered to their homes, as described. The new Council of State, appointed in May, made the detection of conspiracy its main business, and cut much of the ground from the new rebellion even as it was planned, by seizing arms and arresting leaders intended for it.

On 9 July the conspirators fixed the date of the enterprise, for 1 August. The King had given promises of pardon for everybody who co-operated, except for regicides, who would be given time to emigrate. At the same time, the Council of State decided to increase the strength of all regiments, send more soldiers to key points in the provinces and instruct the corporations of Bristol and Gloucester to raise volunteers. The Sealed Knot, scenting disaster, now withdrew from the plan, taking the East Anglian leaders with them. Few last-minute recruits came forward in their place, though one was the Cromwells' friend Richard Ingoldsby, who offered help if a restored King made the fallen Protector Commander-in-Chief. Nevertheless, the other conspirators held to their plan. As the Knot had feared, the Council of State had warning of some of it three days before the vital date. It used this interval to fire letters into the provinces, warning all local officers to be on their guard and raise more men.[53]

On the 1st the most ambitious royalist revolt since the end of the wars was launched, only to repeat in most areas the muddles and failures of the smaller plots. Mordaunt himself in Surrey and the Falkland group in Oxfordshire were seized with panic at the last moment and cancelled their particular risings. The leaders in the north-east, south-west and Midlands followed their example. In the Severn valley they rose with small parties and were overpowered. There was, however, one unfamiliar success in Cheshire, where the rebels swiftly obtained control of the whole county save Chester Castle, together with the adjacent part of Lancashire. This was possible because the rising there perfectly harnessed the tensions created by the new regime. Presbyterian ministers, unusually strong in the area, raised recruits by predicting a Quaker uprising. Many Chester aldermen, having failed earlier to dislodge the set which had dominated the corporation under the Cromwells, seized the opportunity to do so by violence. Most important, the local leader, Sir George Booth, was unusually effective. He was an experienced soldier, having held Nantwich for the Long Parliament through the great siege of 1644. He had some prominence in national life, being one of the 'secluded' members of 1648 and having only recently sat in Richard's Commons. He was also a local magnate, head of one of the great traditional factions of Cheshire politics. So impressive was his influence that he led out not only many gentry but the militia itself. His declared aims in rising were studiously moderate: to secure readmission of the secluded members and thereby to call a new, free Parliament. He refused to work with Catholics and never suggested that the King should be recalled without terms of the sort that he and his party had once tried to impose on Charles I. Such a man would never have risen against the Protectorate. He did not expect to be the sole leader of this rising to draw an army into the field. It was not his fault that the greatest revolt of the decade would go down in history as 'Booth's Rebellion'.[54]

The republicans responded with all the formidable energy of which they were capable in their own defence. On the 2nd the MPs passed an act renewing the powers of the wartime committees for sequestration of royalists' estates. They discussed settling the lands of rebels upon those of their tenants who stayed loyal. On the 9th they proclaimed Booth and his chief accomplices traitors, and exonerated a colonel who had commandeered horses without payment to mount some of his regiment. On 31 July the Council of State had summoned home the three regiments left in the field in Flanders. In the first four days of August it ordered the immediate transportation of 1,500 men from the Irish army to Wales, decided on the raising of no fewer than fourteen more in England and called out all the new militia. On the fifth it instructed Desborough to command in the west, while the best soldier of all the army, Lambert, went against Booth with five regiments. Lambert left London two days later. One of the regiments allocated to him refused to move until it was given some pay, but cash was found for it and it duly marched.[55]

Meanwhile, Booth's success had encouraged some further action against the government. Sir Thomas Myddleton, once the Long Parliament's commander in North Wales, proclaimed the King in Denbighshire, and another group occupied Derby. Fauconberg in Yorkshire and other leaders in Nottinghamshire and Leicestershire called out their friends, while presbyterian clergy, as in Booth's area, preached support. Only in Nottinghamshire, however, did these rebels get into a party, and the militia broke them up. Mordaunt spurred his allies in the London area into action, but they too were arrested. In the City, where it had been rumoured that a petition on behalf of the secluded members had been canvassed in July, there was talk of another, for a free Parliament. Many presbyterian ministers in the capital refused to publish the proclamation declaring Booth a traitor. The government sent guards to the Guildhall, while Lord Mayor Ireton doubled the watch and refused to call a Common Council. So the Londoners did nothing but murmur. In the far north-west the presbyterian clergy received appeals from their fellows with Booth, but waited on events.[56]

Lambert was held up in the Midlands by the need to collect all the units allocated to him. Booth was therefore left undisturbed for nearly three weeks, in which he did virtually nothing. There was indeed little that he could do. He had about a thousand men under arms, not a large body compared with those that his enemies could concentrate elsewhere. A witness described it as 'made up of fire and snow', so conflicting were the views of its members on Church and State.[57] Perhaps it could have raised more men by advancing south through the Marches, but it is likely to have lost others as it left home ground. Perhaps it could have taken shelter in fortresses, but no relief would have come in the inevitable sieges. Sir

George's growing desperation was reflected in a fresh declaration which he issued as Lambert approached, offering the army its arrears and the sects their freedom, in patent contradiction of his previous attitudes. On the 19th Lambert was upon him, with over four times his numbers. Booth chose a strong position at Winnington Bridge, in hedges facing his enemy across a river, but Lambert's regulars pushed past these obstacles with perfect discipline and the rebels then fled. In the next week, the fortresses they had occupied all surrendered. Lambert had kept his soldiers restrained after the battle and granted the garrisons generous terms, so the whole rebellion cost about thirty lives. Booth himself, disguised as a woman, got as far as Buckinghamshire before an innkeeper wondered why his lady guest required a razor and reported the fact. On the 24th he was committed to the Tower charged with treason. As every leader of an English rebellion for the past ten years had been executed if captured, his position was most unpleasant.[58]

On 7 September the Council dismissed the militia. On the same day Mordaunt, who had evaded capture and been hiding in London, left England feeling that God was against his cause. Every active leader of the rising was either a refugee or in prison, with many innocent royalists arrested on suspicion. The Sealed Knot was collapsing, permanently, under the accusations of treachery now levelled at Willis. Evelyn attributed the defeat to the sin of allying with former parliamentarians, a view which he soon published and which boded ill for any future alliance. Even the deposed bishops were so cowed that they would consecrate no new colleagues, and Hyde's efforts in this respect also came to nothing. The royal court was placed under fresh siege by its creditors. Charles himself abandoned it, going south towards the Pyrenees, where the Kings of France and Spain were meeting to conclude the war in which Cromwell had participated. Despairing of his countrymen, he had some faint hope that these potentates would lend him troops with which to crush the Protestant English republic.[59] That republic had proved more resilient than its enemies had believed. It had rallied to itself a significant number of civilians, as the performance of some county militias and partisan groups had demonstrated. It had the support of an army which had once again proved its quality. Unpopular it might be with the majority of articulate Englishmen, but it appeared indestructible.

Indeed, supreme by land, it was now equally secure by sea. In May, with Mountagu and most of the English fleet lying off Denmark, the MPs had gathered the remaining ships into a force to protect the Channel. This was placed under John Lawson, an experienced seaman, a baptist, and a noted republican. The administration of the navy was vested in a commission headed by Vane, and representatives were sent to attend Mountagu and conduct diplomacy with the Baltic powers. Mountagu himself had fought hard for Parliament as a teenager in the Great Civil War, but he had subsequently retired. His friend and kinsman, Cromwell, had pulled him back into public life in 1653, and made him one of the great figures of the Protectorate. He thus had no connection whatsoever with the Commonwealthsmen, and they had reason to suspect his loyalty. When he heard of the restoration of the purged Parliament, in late May, he offered submission to it in a letter which reads warmly enough now, but seemed to the MPs to lack the fulsome quality they desired. Their instincts were probably right, and the unwelcome company of the republic's diplomats soon confirmed his distaste for the new regime. In July the exiled King sent him an agent to offer high office and an earldom, and Mountagu seemed to respond favourably. In August, claiming that the fleet needed victuals, he set sail for England, sending ahead an ambiguous message to his steward to talk to his friends and tenants. All this represents slight circumstantial evidence that he was considering joining the rebellion, but whatever the truth, all was over when he returned. He made a satisfactory report to the Council of State on 10 September, but on the 20th wrote a touching letter to Richard Cromwell in retirement, giving an account as if to a head of state. Then he likewise withdrew into the country, leaving his ships to the government.[60]

The process of reward and punishment was now in progress. Lambert was voted £1,000, and lesser figures were given lesser sums. Otherwise, repression took up most of the MPs' time. On 27 August they passed an act ordering the sequestration of the estates of all involved in the rebellion, vesting central control of the county committees which did the work in a panel headed by Samuel Moyer, a notable London radical. The local committees got slowly to work, and within six weeks had secured the lands of many persons, including Myddleton and Mordaunt. Mordaunt, Massey, and four other fugitives, had prices set on their heads. Myddleton's castle was condemned to demolition. On 23 September the Council ordered a review of JPs with the intention of dismissing those who had proved dilatory during the risings. It proceeded throughout the month with the work of releasing prisoners against whom nothing could be proved and adding others to the list, headed by Booth, of those charged with treason. The set which had ruled Chester under the Cromwells, and opposed Booth, now petitioned the MPs to reduce the size of the corporation to include only themselves, but the House went much further and deprived the city of its charter, and county status, altogether. It attempted a similar coup by interfering in the annual election of London's Lord Mayor, ordering the corporation to re-elect the invaluable Ireton. The Common Council, however, was determined to prevent this and petitioned the MPs for its ancient privileges. A debate ensued in which the cautious Lenthall and the fiery republican Henry Marten united to lead a majority against the Fifth Monarchist Colonel Rich, in favour of conciliation. They left the election free, but reserved the right to vet the victor. The mild Thomas Allin was duly elected, and approved, and the corporation feasted both MPs and army leaders as a gesture of gratitude.[61]

Outside Chester and London, the local records register the victory of the Commonwealth as little as they had its inception. The MPs annulled the charter Cromwell had given Salisbury, restoring the former one and with it the former dominant faction, which included two of the House's present members. As at Colchester, however, this gave power to men apparently of a more, not less, conservative stamp. At Dover the proponents of godly reform got into office, but at Newcastle they resigned, and Norwich chose a man noted for moderate views as sheriff. The other towns for which studies exist show no changes, and those which are unstudied contain nothing dramatic in their records. The Ipswich city fathers were concerned to gain control of the town's militia, a matter which had also worried those of London, but this does not seem to have been a general grievance and it earned no sympathy from the purged Parliament, which trusted to its chosen commissioners.[62]

As usual, the records of religious life register the strongest reaction. Fear of the radicals had remained through the period of the risings. Rebels in Worcestershire and Gloucestershire, as well as in Booth's area, were raised by talk of an impending massacre by Quakers. A Norfolk man questioned about the weapons in his house replied, apparently with honesty, that they were there to protect him from the sects. The official newspaper denied a rumour that a Quaker had murdered a Somerset minister. In reality, the emergency certainly did strengthen the co-operation between government and sects. Observers agreed that the latter, and the independent churches, supplied many enthusiastic recruits to the new regiments being formed, and to an extra volunteer force raised in London under that patron of sectaries, Vane. The Quakers divided over the question: in Westmorland some stood aloof from the conflict, while others aided the republic's militia.[63]

Under pressure of events the religious kaleidoscope shifted again. In Lancashire, the rapport between presbyterians and independents was shattered by Booth's rebellion, which divided that community with great bitterness. In Worcestershire, however, a presbyterian divine was moved to open correspondence with an episcopalian leader to discuss unity against the sects, whom he believed Booth's defeat had encouraged. In London, leading presbyterians, independents and baptists met to form a front against the Quakers. The Quakers themselves continued their campaign with high morale; two of their leaders held a public disputation with a divine at Cambridge University. In Worcestershire, Essex, Flintshire and Yorkshire, ministers went in fear of being railed at by them. At York an army colonel expressed sympathy for a Quaker meeting, after it had been mobbed when a visiting Quaker evangelist had disturbed a sermon in the Minster. The mayor offered to release a woman gaoled for challenging a preaching minister, if the evangelist would only take her out of town, but he refused. At Liverpool Lambert's soldiers attended Quaker meetings; at Manchester they gave members of the movement the keys of the town hall for their gathering, and they protected them in Cheshire.[64] One good reason for the undoubted decline in mobbings of Quakers, without a decline in the anxiety they inspired, was the large number of troops sympathetic to them now scattered through the provinces.

The regime's victory emboldened the radicals to renew their demands for law reform, the abolition of tithes and freedom of conscience. Milton himself joined the literary war on tithes.[65] Such was the demoralisation of conservatives that these demands went unanswered, even Prynne's pen falling silent. Significantly, the main conflict in the press was now between the republicans themselves, over the permanent form of the Commonwealth. On the one hand were the Fifth Monarchists, who unleashed a pack of tracts calling for rule by the godly few and reformation of law and Church on Mosaic lines.[66] On 17 September some sectaries presented a petition to the House for these ends.[67] On the other side were those writers, led by James Harrington, who believed in elected Parliaments, bound by some device to prevent a counter-revolution.[68]

The aspect of policy which received least attention from pamphleteers, but loomed large as ever in practice, was finance. Upon the assessment fell now not only the burden of the veteran English army, which it had never adequately supported, but of the newly-formed regiments, those recalled from Ireland and Flanders, the militia, and the fleet brought back by Mountagu, which had to be paid off. The total expense of the standing army had almost doubled, and its units, and those returned from abroad, were now scattered through the provinces, exposing many householders to the ordeal of quartering underpaid soldiers.[69] The militia was dismissed, as has been said, but in Devon and Cornwall this remained a paper resolution as it could not be paid off. In Staffordshire and Suffolk matters went a stage further, and the men kidnapped the militia commissioners as security for their wages. The sole surviving set of militia accounts, for Leicestershire, shows that the levies there took two months to get their money.[70] The new regiments were also reported to be destined for disbandment, but there are no records of this process.[71]

Despite these obstacles, some money was found for soldiers, militiamen and sailors. Most seems to have been obtained by demanding the whole remaining sum of the assessment immediately. Ready cash was always short in the provinces, and the sums squeezed out of them now left tenants unable to pay their dues to landlords.[72] Some relief was given in the matter of quarters by means of reshuffling. Thus Rye, tired of providing free hospitality to a foot company, complained to its influential MP, Morley, and the soldiers were dumped on Sandwich instead.[73] But these measures were clearly inadequate, and on 18 August the House at last took the vital step of deciding to raise the assessment. It eventually agreed to double it, and a bill for this duly progressed. It was about to pass in mid-September when it suddenly stuck. Political events had overtaken it.[74]

The MPs' attitude to their radical allies remained ambivalent. They repeatedly decided to discuss the legal system, but never did so. They exonerated two former enragés, reversing their own former judgement against the famous London reformer John Lilburne, and releasing the Quaker James Naylor, who had caused such a storm in Cromwell's second Parliament, on the petition of a friend. Lilburne, however, was dead, and Naylor, whose punishment had been carried out all too effectively, was dying, so that neither gesture had any practical effect upon politics. On the other hand, the House dismissed the healthy and active John Canne from the editorship of the government newspaper, perhaps because his press had turned out an embarrassing number of the reformers' pamphlets. He was replaced by Cromwell's editor, Marchamont Nedham, a talented time-server who had just turned his coat again, with a tract defending the Commonwealth.[75]

What probably lay behind these contrasting actions was the rivalry of factions among the MPs, which became clearer during the debates on the future form of government, a subject to which they were now paying sustained attention. Four days were devoted to it in August, despite the emergency of that month, and on 3 September the ideological rifts in the House suddenly became general news. On that day the Hesilrige set proposed an affirmation of loyalty to the Commonwealth to be taken by all militiamen. Vane almost came to blows with Sir Arthur over this, and his opposition was shared by the army leaders. Their anger derived, apparently, from a feeling that men should not be committed in advance to something which had not yet taken its final shape.[76] The House eventually dropped the idea, and on the 8th appointed a committee representing all its leaders to agree upon the permanent shape of the republic. This soon reproduced the division in the wider body, Vane being suspected of promoting the sectaries' petition for a government of saints and Hesilrige laying Harrington's model before the committee, though he expressed doubt about the notion of rotation. Neville, Harrington's friend, naturally agreed with this blueprint, and so, it was said, did Fleetwood. Just as naturally, Vane and Lambert, who both tended to favour rule by élites, drew together. They agreed likewise upon the need for the widest possible toleration, which gave them the support of most of the sects and the army, and also of a party of Catholics led by Sir Henry Howard. The natural distaste of most of the MPs for fundamental reforms, however, counted against this party, and on 27 September the committee on the form of government voted against wider toleration. On 3 October the question of a blueprint was postponed, as the House resolved to fill its many vacant places with suitable MPs without giving way to any new body. Then the same crisis which had halted the finance bill stopped further discussion.[77]

The force behind this was the personality of John Lambert. Alone of all the leading men of the regime, he was at once a first-rate soldier, statesman and administrator. In a republic which embodied the concept of the dispersal of power, he represented a concentration of talent which seemed distinctly out of harmony to observers. His past record could only enhance suspicion. Now, on his triumph over Booth, gossip about his ambitions acquired a new intensity.[78] At this delicate time, on 16 September, the officers of the force he had led to victory convened at Derby, to complain of the lack of interest shown by the MPs in some of the matters the army had requested in May. They concluded by drawing up a petition to the House, accusing it of dilatoriness and ingratitude and demanding godly reforms, a senate, and a proper command structure for the army, with its leaders all to be made generals and no officer to be dismissed without court martial. This was signed and then sent out to the other units for agreement. Lambert was not present at the meeting, and the degree of his involvement, and that of the other army leaders, in the petition, remains a mystery. The junior officers had certainly acted without their commanders before, in the 1640s, and the provocative tone of the document was at variance with the other addresses produced earlier and later in the year by the whole army: it may well have represented a genuine initiative by the soldiers at Derby.[79]

On the 22nd a copy somehow came into the hands of Hesilrige. Sir Arthur was never the man to miss an opportunity to dramatise a situation. He dashed to the House, ordered the doors closed, and read the petition as though he were disclosing a dangerous conspiracy. The MPs' traditional distrust of the soldiery flared up with fresh violence, and it was proposed to send Lambert to the Tower. Vane, however, spoke eloquently for unity and Fleetwood defended his colleagues. Even Hesilrige came to join them, against his usual allies Neville and Scot, in urging moderation. On the 23rd it was decided only to order Fleetwood to admonish the army, and to refuse the request about the command structure.[80]

Nevertheless, the MPs were now more suspicious, and the army more aggrieved, than ever. The former suspended their new assessment bill, to threaten the troops with starvation in the long term, recalled all their absent colleagues, and decided to seek reconciliation with the City, as described. Lambert returned to London on the day that the House reached a decision on the petition, and agreed to accept this after a stormy meeting with the other military leaders. He then strengthened his links with Vane's circle, as described, and was seen with Thurloe, that adviser of past Protectors. Part of his force had been ordered back to the capital: other parts now followed without orders, slipping along in small parties.[81] Fleetwood, working for conciliation, called some officers to his house on the 27th and asked them to draft a loyal address for the General Council of officers to tender to Parliament. The army's blood, however, was now up, and when the General Council convened in Somerset House chapel, it discussed demanding the revocation of the Speaker's hated power over commissions. The minority present who were friends of the MPs played the role of Richard Cromwell's friends in April, of moderating the clauses. None the less, the gathering decided, by 230 votes to 3, on a document which remained very aggressive and which Desborough duly delivered on 5 October. It began by defending Lambert's officers and demanding censure of MPs who had vilified the army. It then repeated the old requests for arrears and for no dismissal without court martial.[82]

The House was in a conciliatory mood, having voted the previous day to devote half the proceeds of sequestration and of the sale of state forests to the arrears. It now received the new petition with some courtesy and resolved to debate it at length. There was never a chance that any request save that concerning arrears would be granted, but the MPs seemed to be producing a formula which possessed a little tact. Then distrust overpowered them, as the officers grumbled and rumours spread through the capital that the military were talking of dissolving this Parliament as they had done in 1653. On the 11th the MPs suddenly passed an act in one sitting, declaring it treason to levy a tax not imposed by a Parliament, an attempt to keep the army without money if they were expelled. The same statute revoked Cromwell's grants, laying the officers open to expropriation, though at the last moment a clause was inserted preserving the Act of Indemnity. Then, the next day, one of the colonels who supported them, John Okey, brought the members a letter signed by Lambert, Desborough, Berry, Ashfield and five other important officers, directed to units in the provinces and requesting subscription to the petition. This was in fact an attempt by the army leaders to muster support for further pressure on the House, but the MPs read it as an attempt to unite the army for an attack. Their nerve broke and they resolved to strike first. By a huge majority they expelled all the signatories from the army and placed it under a commission on which Fleetwood was to sit with Hesilrige, Morley,

Ludlow and three other supposedly loyal officers. They then called up
Morley's foot regiment, and that of another trusted colonel, Moss, to reinforce the House's Horse Guards.[83]

Like Richard Cromwell's circle, Hesilrige's had taken steps to have soldiers
to hand. In 1653 they had lacked any means to resist Cromwell: they believed
that they had such means against Lambert. Near the capital were not only the
regiments of Morley and Moss, but also of Okey and Hesilrige's friend
Hacker, and all were summoned. What followed that night was indeed a
repetition, not of the coup six years before, but of that six months previously.
Like Richard Cromwell, Sir Arthur made the simple, fatal, error of judging a
regiment by its colonel, and the more complex mistake of failing to convince
the soldiers in general that the government had their ideological and
material interests at heart. When Lambert and his comrades, learning of
their dismissal, called the troops round London to their aid, most came.
Okey and Hacker were left stranded by their men just as Richard's colonels
had been.

By the morning of the 13th Morley's and Moss's regiments, and the Parliament's Horse Guards, were surrounded at Westminster by Lambert's
soldiers. Some MPs got into the House before the cordon closed, but most
did not. Some of the latter appealed to the City, but the Common Council
refused to assist. Then Lambert led his men forward. At the gate of Scotland
Yard he found the Horse Guards barring the way. In a gesture worthy of
Napoleon, he walked forward alone and ordered the commander to dis-
mount. The man hesitated, and then did so, and his men joined Lambert's
ranks. Many of Moss's soldiers followed, and soon Morley's men were the
principal defenders of the House, and wavering. Speaker Lenthall, trying to
get in, showed unwonted spirit by informing the hostile soldiers that he was
their true commander. He earned the reply that they had not seen him at
Winnington Bridge, and Lambert brusquely ordered him home. At 4 a.m.,
Hesilrige, Scot and Morley capitulated, declaring through the Council of
State at Whitehall that the House's defenders should disperse to quarters. As
Morley's men marched out of Westminster Hall they gave Lambert an
ovation. The opposing troops entered, and, twenty-two weeks after it had
unlocked the House of Commons, the army fastened it again.[84]

The officers had not planned for this development: it was an automatic
reaction of self-defence, and they had no substitute ready for the purged
Parliament. Their confusion was plain during the succeeding week, as the
Council of Officers and the Council of State both continued to sit. On the
14th the former completed their victory by suspending the commissions of
those officers who had supported the MPs. On the 17th the latter divided
permanently over the question of negotiation with the army, and Hesilrige,

who opposed this, withdrew to leave the proponents, such as Vane, to commence discussions. The Council of Officers, noting the obduracy of Hesilrige and his faction, decided that a restoration of the purged Parliament was out of the question and that a new government would have to be made. The next day, they began with themselves, by declaring Fleetwood Commander-in-Chief, Lambert his deputy as Major-General, and Desborough and Monck Generals of the Horse and Foot respectively. They appointed the first three, with Berry, Vane and Ludlow, to form a committee to nominate officers, and gave Fleetwood the authority to commission them. Finally, they gave themselves the right of no dismissal without court martial and so at last turned the army into a self-governing corporation. Messengers were sent to Monck in Scotland and to Ludlow, who had left in July to command the Irish army, to explain what had happened.[85]

On the 20th they turned to the national government, and decided to form a Committee of Safety, representing a mixture of parties and with a majority of civilians, to run the present government and consider the next. The remainder of the Council of State debated for two days and then chose ten men from themselves to sit upon the new body. The General Council accepted these and added thirteen more. The result was hardly a mixture of parties, consisting of ten colonels, including all the army leaders, and thirteen civilian collaborators. The latter did, however, vary considerably in their political and religious instincts, from the inevitable Vane to a man like Bulstrode Whitelocke, who had consistently opposed legal reform and wide religious toleration, but never declined the opportunity of office. In general, this Committee of Safety contained more members of Whitelocke's kind, the respectable ballast which had filled up Cromwell's Council and then the restored Parliament's before adding their weight to this body. Despite the lobbying of sectaries and Quakers, it was no more a group of reformers than the preceding executives.

On the 25th the Council of State sat for the last time, and the commission for the new Committee was drawn up. Then the bomb-shell burst. A letter arrived from General Monck, in Scotland, condemning the work of the General Council and declaring, with his troops, for the expelled MPs. For the first time in its history, a large section of the army had turned against the rest. The Fourth Civil War seemed about to begin.[86]

3

The Breaking of the English Army

❧

GEORGE Monck was descended, at many removes, from a bastard son of Edward IV. For practical purposes, it was more important that he was the fourth of ten children of an impoverished Devonshire squire, obliged to find a profession or trade for his living. He had chosen that of arms, and had fought successively for the English, French and Dutch against the Spanish, for the English against the Scots and the Irish, and for Charles I against the Long Parliament. This last had earned him three years in the Tower as a prisoner of war, resulting in some reconsideration which led to his serving the Long Parliament against the Irish. Cromwell had then noticed his qualities, as he had those of the other former royalist Broghill, and obtained him high command in the army which beat Charles II in the Third Civil War. Since then he had alternated as commander of the army in Scotland and as a general-at-sea, positions which he owed, again, to Cromwell's favour and had justified with great accomplishments. He was now fifty-eight years old, forty-two of which he had spent as a soldier.[1]

The dashing Lambert had been a cavalry commander. Monck, as appropriately, had risen through the infantry. There was much about him—the heavy, swarthy jowls, the coarse humour, the savage anger, the obstinate bravery—which reminds one of a bull. While Lambert planted tulips for recreation, Monck chewed tobacco and shared drinking bouts. He guffawed to hear his wife, who had been his laundress in the Tower, described as 'our dirty Bessie'. As a commander, he had been characterised by luck, courage and ruthlessness. Apart from having the extraordinary fortune of Cromwell's patronage, he had repeatedly come through fierce battles unhurt. When his co-general was killed beside him during a naval fight, he merely dropped his coat over the corpse and carried on. When a mob of unpaid sailors had menaced him in a London street, he had drawn his sword and routed them. He had sunk Dutch warships rather than be burdened with prizes and devastated Scottish countryside to demoralise royalist rebels.

At Richard Cromwell's accession, Monck sent him not only the formal congratulations of his army but a private letter of advice, advocating means of strengthening the Protectorate.[2] There is thus no reason to doubt the later assertions of his friends that he had bowed to necessity in abandoning

Richard at his fall. It is none the less of interest that he chose to put his career above old loyalties. He was soon in trouble with the restored Parliament notwithstanding, for writing to its Speaker to protest at the changes proposed by the Army Commission in his officer corps. The MPs, quick to smell disloyalty in a servant inherited from the Cromwells, debated the letter angrily and agreed upon a cold reply directing him to submit to their judgement.[3] Eventually every regiment in Scotland was altered, five drastically, though as a gesture of conciliation Monck's own horse and foot suffered slight changes. The general owed his survival at all to the fact that Scotland, like England, was on the brink of revolt, that he was working hard to keep it quiet, and that to replace him would make dislocation, and an explosion, very likely.[4]

In July the King wrote him an appeal for support, as he had to Mountagu. This was entrusted to Monck's royalist cousin, Sir John Grenville, who employed as carrier the general's own brother Nicholas, a presbyterian clergyman with royalist sympathies. In August, Nicholas Monck carried out his mission, and was said later to have reported that George was 'more inclinable to the Parliament than to the army but yet more inclinable to a free (Parliament) than either'. In another version of his report, it was said that the general had refused the letter but expressed sorrow at Booth's defeat. Many years later, three friends of his who were present insisted separately that he actually formed a plan to join Booth, which was kept secret to protect the participants after Booth's defeat scotched it.[5] Whatever the precise truth, all through the period of the risings George Monck was busy arresting royalists and holding down Scotland, which proves him a master of duplicity.[6] Yet, after Parliament's victory he was sufficiently depressed to offer his resignation to the Speaker, which, arriving as it did when the trouble between the House and the English army was brewing, was refused. Only one of his posthumous apologists claimed that the gesture was anything but sincere.[7]

In the conflict between House and army Monck dissociated himself from the latter as soon as trouble began. When the officers at Derby sent him a copy of their petition he ordered his army to ignore it, and reported this action loyally to Parliament. His friend Clarges believed this to be the cause of the MPs' decision to deal so bluntly with Lambert and his colleagues, though it is unlikely to have done more than encourage their mistaken faith in their supporters in the English army.[8] When the news reached Monck of the expulsion of the Parliament, on 17 October, he decided immediately, and without advice, to oppose it. His army was scattered in bases across the country, and many of its field officers were away in London. Most of the men whom the government had dismissed were still in Scotland and most of their replacements, who tended to support the English army leaders, had not yet arrived. Monck therefore had the opportunity for a coup of his own, gathering his most trusted subordinates and using them to win over the various units separately, arresting those officers expected to make difficulty. In each case junior men, and those recently dismissed, were promoted into the posts of those absent or confined, giving them a stake in the achievement. It was all carried out successfully, but left the new leaders unsure of the reactions of their men if put to a test. By the 20th Monck felt confident enough to send to London the formal declaration which produced its sensation five days later.[9]

This, then, is the accepted sequence of events which begs, resoundingly, the question of Monck's motives. Three answers have been suggested. The first, propounded by his posthumous apologists and accepted by his most recent biographer,[10] is that he was entering upon the first stage of a plan to restore Charles II. The problem with this is that it credits Monck, hitherto a practical and pragmatic man, with a project requiring the coincidence of a great many eventualities. On the other hand, there can be no doubt from his past history that he had no reason to love the purged Parliament. It seems extremely likely that he did intend to join Booth. In his letter to Richard Cromwell he had recommended Sir George as a man of excellent views. The minimum import of his brother's remarks to the royalists after the rising was that Monck sympathised with the principles for which Booth had risen, and one of the accounts of the conspiracy to join Sir George is minutely circumstantial.[11] It includes the very Monck-like touch of a decision to await the result of Winnington Bridge. Booth, after all, stood only for a free Parliament, which was likely, if it restored the King, to do so upon strict terms. However, this in itself presents the problem of why Monck proceeded so cautiously in August and then acted immediately, and alone, in October. The English army followed their coup, as shall be seen, by discussing the replacement of the purged Parliament with forms of government of which George Monck apparently thought better. Yet he never gave them a chance.

The second theory is that he acted from dislike of the usurpation of government by the military. This was the case he made at the time, and has been accepted by modern historians of the period.[12] Certainly there had been a natural animosity between him and Lambert in Cromwell's time,[13] and he had no love for the whole set now in control of England. He had, after all, nothing in common with them save Cromwell's favour, having been on the opposite side in the Great Civil War and abroad during the Revolution. But he had supported his colleagues when they ejected Parliaments in 1653, 1654 and April 1659, and in general this interpretation suffers from the same weaknesses noted in the first. Nor, as the English army had just incorporated him into their new command structure, need he have felt any personal threat from it.

There is, however, the third possible explanation, hitherto only proposed in passing by a writer principally preoccupied with different interests.[14] This is that Monck fell prey to the 'Quaker terror' of the summer. His letter of advice to Richard Cromwell had given first priority to the achievement of a conservative religious settlement, for which work he recommended the most distinguished presbyterian clergy and laymen. Instead, in the course of 1659, the Quakers appeared as aggressive and successful in Scotland as in England. In the words of one diarist, they 'aboundit and drew themselssis in companyis throw the cuntrie without controlment'.[15] The new officers imposed upon Monck included notable sectaries. His feelings showed when one man spoke at table against the ministry, and Monck berated him with fury. One of his chaplains now urged the Church's danger to him repeatedly, while his wife formally declared herself a presbyterian.[16] The purged Parliament had become a bulwark against the religious radicals, while Lambert became identified with them. In early October, Mordaunt could write 'if Lambert succeeds, the Church of England must of necessity fall'.[17] Then came the coup, and Lambert did succeed. To a correspondent who admonished him for his stand, Monck replied that he had risked everything to save the country from the 'fanatical party', who blasphemed against Christ. He told the Irish army to trust neither 'Cavaliers nor Anabaptists'.[18] Such a reason fits both words and deeds precisely. It would explain the precipitate urgency of his reaction to the coup. If correct, it is yet another example in this period of religious feeling determining individual political action.

His colleagues in London were completely baffled by his reaction and returned futile appeals to solidarity and to the justice of their case against their ungrateful masters.[19] Then they were faced with the problem of how to act if Monck remained defiant. Booth had raised about 1,000 hasty levies. Monck could field at least six times that number, from thirteen regiments of trained regular soldiers. He was much further away, across more difficult country, and the campaigning season was over. This was unlikely to be an easy war.[20]

It was all the more essential, then, that the new government be established swiftly. On 26 October the Committee of Safety was formally commissioned by the General Council and convened. Five days later it issued a proclamation continuing all civil officers in their posts, while the fourteen most prominent members were named as a subcommittee to consider the future government. On the 28th the Committee decided to send a force against Monck, and by the next day it was known that Lambert was to command it, taking all the soldiers around London except two foot regiments and eight troops of horse. For the next five days the capital was full of drums and trumpets as the units departed; Lambert himself left on 3 November, having

obtained as a conciliatory gesture the release of six royalists held on suspicion.[21] During the month after the coup, the army printed at least six statements of its case, ranging from simple pleas of self-defence to a claim for its
representative role as the people in arms, upholding and renewing states.[22] It
also established its own newspaper, *The Loyal Scout*.

All this activity, of course, concealed much division. Of the twenty-three
members of the Committee of Safety, only twelve can be identified as having
ever taken their seats.[23] Ludlow, returned from Ireland, refused to sit but
acted as an informal adviser, trying to reconcile army and Commonwealthsmen. Whitelocke claimed later to have been persuaded to sit by Fleetwood
and Desborough, to stop radicals like Vane overturning the laws. Vane himself greeted Sir Archibald Johnston, a member of rigid presbyterian views,
with the observation that the recent events heralded the Millennium. He
received the reply that they were, rather, God's punishment of pride. The
Committee commenced its career with bitter quarrelling.[24] In the army,
Fleetwood was said to resent his eclipse by Lambert. The former's unimpor-
tance during the coup had left him, more clearly than ever, a mere figure-
head. The Venetian ambassador thought him a man of 'unexampled
frigidity', his rival one of 'spirit'. The 'rationalists' mocked him for his piety.
That Lambert, and not he, was chosen to command the expedition against
Monck was taken as a sign that real fighting was intended.[25]

The first constitutional settlement presented to the new government was
the revival of the Protectorate, which appeared so likely that Richard
Cromwell was escorted to London by a party of horse. The Committee,
however, rejected it by a few votes, reputedly because the army still regarded
him as an apostate. Fleetwood at least secured an undertaking to pay his debts
from public funds, which the purged Parliament, despite its vote, had not
done. The idea of elevating another Protector was said to have been opposed
by the junior officers, who associated the whole institution with reaction.[26]
Likewise these men objected, this time ineffectually, to the lack of sectaries
on the Committee. The army united, however, behind the idea of a nominated Senate to represent their interests, though whether this was to act
alone or with an elected House was left open.[27]

On 1 November Vane laid a model of government before the subcommittee on the constitution, which was bitterly opposed by Johnston because
of the religious toleration it granted. The other members hovered between
them over the question for the rest of the month. Likewise, when the junior
officers urged the abolition of tithes and of the Court of Chancery, their
superiors refused for fear of offending too many people at once. The General
Council debated compounding for tithes and creating a skeleton national
clergy salaried by the state, but again did nothing.[28] On the 11th the

Committee of Safety ordered the commissioning of persons to administer the Treasury, but this paper progress was more than balanced on the 16th when the judges' commissions expired. Only two had remained active since the coup and these now retired, leaving the new government to wonder how it could provide its subjects with litigation. The subcommittee on the constitution was twice formally reconvened, without bringing itself any closer to unity.[29]

The campaign against Monck was conducted on much the same theoretical level. Monck himself had nothing to gain from a swift attack as Robert Lilburne, the commander in northern England, had declared solidarity with the soldiers at London and secured Carlisle and Newcastle, the routes out of Scotland.[30] Monck's army was proving unstable as feared: in the first month after his stand against the generals in England, ninety-seven of his officers deserted, while some garrisons sent letters refusing to concur with him.[31] He had money for his men, having recently received a grant from the Council of State and just gathered the Scottish assessment, without having to share it with new levies or militia as the army in England had done.[32] He and his confidants had therefore every reason to play for time, and to this end they held a council of war on 3 November at which it was decided to treat. Three representatives were commissioned to ask for the restoration of the Parliament and the preservation of the national Church, and an armistice during the talks. The officers in England were happy to comply. Lambert needed time to gather a force large enough for an offensive, and his existing one seemed as unsteady as his opponent's. Many of the soldiers in it had expressed reluctance to march against their own colleagues, and the General Council had dismissed officers, especially in the regiment which had been Hacker's, just as Monck had done. To force the remainder onto the offensive when their enemy was offering peace would have been very difficult. Lilburne and Lambert accordingly both gave Monck's emissaries safe conduct, and they were welcomed at London.[33]

Monck used his breathing-space effectively, imposing a declaration of support for his actions upon the units in Scotland and arresting the officers and discharging the common soldiers who refused it. Even some who subscribed were dismissed on suspicion. The gaps in the officer corps were filled from the ranks, and the ranks filled by recruiting. Slowly a new army, in both personnel and attitudes, was formed.[34] Monck had the post searched for hostile propaganda, and to catechise his troops he printed two newspapers and at least two pamphlets. These combined arguments for the constitutional justice of their cause with vilification of the sects.[35] From Yorkshire arrived the encouraging news that the English army's first commander, Lord Fairfax, long retired, was prepared to rise against Lambert and that some of the latter's own force would assist.[36] To encourage the same response in London, Monck wrote to the Common Council on the 12th, asking for aid against a military tyranny.[37] He met representatives of the Scottish gentry on the 15th and obtained an agreement to remain quiet while he invaded England to assert 'the ancient constitution'. On the same day, however, exceeding both the letter and the spirit of their instructions, his commissioners in London signed a treaty, by which both he and Lambert would disperse their armies and representatives of the forces in all three realms would meet in London on 6 December to settle a republican government. This created fury and consternation among Monck and his intimates when it arrived on about 22 November. Just before then, Lambert at last advanced to Newcastle with 8,000 men and more to follow.[38] If all had been well for the new government elsewhere, Monck would have been in a very dangerous position. But it was not.

Of all the political changes of the period, the army's coup produced the least reaction in the country. It was, after all, a squabble between two unpopular groups of men, with similar policies, over power. There were no loyal addresses sent in to the General Council from anybody. One, reputedly the voice of the friends of the Good Old Cause in northern England, was sent to Monck urging him to compliance, but this may have spoken for no more than the army's propagandists.[39] There seems to have been little enthusiasm for the officers' cause in outlying garrisons. At Hull the Fifth Monarchist Overton now commanded, and declared neutrality as neither Monck nor Lambert seemed sufficiently godly. Other governors, more concerned with pay and supplies than politics, felt that the centre had forgotten them. The Irish army acquiesced in the events at London with obvious regret.[40] The English radicals, understandably in view of the lack of reform by both regimes, were divided. In Somerset John Pyne bewailed the fact that nobody seemed to advance 'the true Good Old Cause'. At London the more moderate baptists supported the Parliament and an agreement with the presbyterians, while their stricter colleagues favoured the army. Milton thought that the officers' behaviour was 'scarce to be exampled among any Barbarians'. Quakers argued about whether to aid the soldiers, while Fifth Monarchist writers likewise expressed different views upon the quarrel.[41] The publishing team which had worked for the Parliament in the spring, Chapman and Canne, tended now to further conciliation;[42] leaders of the independent clergy, and former officers such as Whalley and Goffe, did likewise. In North Wales militia commissioners co-operated actively with the army; in Northumberland they raised men for Monck.[43] Amid all this confusion, pamphlets calling for reform became much rarer.

In wider national life there was much continuity as usual. The justices still held the Michaelmas Quarter Sessions, and the magistrates and corporations of towns still met. Despite the absence of judges, the sheriff of Durham still ordered the arrest of four men on a private suit pending in the central courts.[44] A conservative press revived in the capital to profit from its opponents' dissensions, Prynne renewing his pleas for monarchy, Lords and 'secluded' members and new tracts being published against Quakers.[45] Mobbings of the latter recommenced, at London and Newark, and their opponents continued to apply legal sanctions against them, men from eight different parishes in Somerset alone being gaoled for withholding tithes in October and November. The Committee of Safety itself upheld the prosecution of an Oxfordshire man for this offence.[46] A different sort of continuity was provided by the central sequestration commission, which continued to urge the seizure of property of the recent rebels, although the authority which had empowered it had gone. This disability decreased public respect for some county committees, and others proved unwilling to act. Most, however, were afflicted with a considerable practical problem, that as most of those involved in the rebellion had never risen it was difficult to convict them; this accounted for much of the lack of interest and ineffectualness of many local sequestrators. The central commission certainly replaced dilatory local representatives with more active men; in Booth's area, where rebellion had surfaced, the local committee stripped houses, and made men glad of Sundays when it did not work. Most of the actual business of seizing property was carried out under the Committee of Safety and, given the problem of conviction, was by no means as negligible as has been thought.[47]

For all this, the new regime retained a taint of extreme radicalism. The division in the London sects was typical: the hardliners were the army's supporters. In Durham the cousins Robert and Thomas Lilburne had fought through the civil wars and applauded the Revolution together, but now disagreed. Robert, a patron of the sects, was the army's local champion, while Thomas, who wanted a national Church, supported Parliament.[48] At Brecon Fifth Monarchist militiamen showed enthusiasm for the coup of October, and were encouraged by it in a sustained campaign to intimidate the corporation into accepting a radical bailiff. The Committee of Safety, to oblige supporters, confirmed this achievement, so appearing both undemocratic and a tool of sectaries.[49] More Quakers seem to have been actively associated with this government than any other, despite the strictures of the movement's spokesmen. Some achieved positions of trust in Lambert's army, while others armed in Denbighshire and seized the horses of gentry to mount themselves and so patrol the countryside.[50] Clearly some men took the views of the junior officers more seriously than those of their superiors. Nor did the protestations of the latter, that they had set up a civilian government, count for much in practice. Some troopers arrived at a Nottinghamshire hall to demand arrears of the assessment from the owner. He, a man of unusual presence, turned them away and complained to Fleetwood that they had replaced the legal collectors. Fleetwood apologised and ordered their colonel to punish them; the colonel promised to do so, and all that happened was that the soldiers reappeared in the district to gather the money, laughing about the whole affair.[51]

Overall, however, the provinces initially accorded this government the same grudging compliance given to others since the outbreak of the wars. Nevertheless, opposition did slowly materialise—not at the periphery but in the capital itself, which a military regime should have held most securely. It was a compound of economic, political and religious pressures and of that elusive but important factor in history, a change of generations. Since the Great Civil War the City, while containing many religious and political radicals, had generally been a conservative force. It was preached to by some of the most respected presbyterian clergy and by ministers who had been dispossessed of parishes by the Long Parliament and had found refuge in lectureships. In 1647 it had risen against the army and the supporters of religious independency; its corporation had shown more affection for the Protectorate than the preceding Commonwealth, and the restoration of the latter had, as said, met with a cool reception.[52] Now economic hardship was being coupled with political disaffection. The formal war with Spain had been suspended since Cromwell's death because of the urgency of domestic affairs, but privateers continued to prey on English shipping. In March 1659, they had almost halted trade with Ireland, and made fishing boats reluctant to put out of eastern ports. The Baltic war choked much commerce with that region. By the winter of 1659/60 house rents in the City were said to have fallen by a tenth since Cromwell's time, its merchants were unwilling to invest, the Yorkshire cloth trade was described as ruined, and Norwich had a serious poverty problem. Everywhere prices were rising and business falling off.[53] Yet the Londoners who most actively sought a political solution to this turned out not to be the merchants, nor the artisans, but the youth, particularly the apprentices. Having fewest possessions, they had least to lose from direct action. These City apprentices had long represented a self-conscious and self-confident social group, as every respectable citizen who had run into a mob of them on Shrove Tuesday would know to his, or her, cost. They were also traditionally active in politics, having been the shock troops of the crowds which had given violent support to parliamentary leaders in the 1640s.[54] This generation of young men had grown up during the 1650s, a world in which the army appeared an unpleasant authoritarian force, and knew nothing of the causes for which the officers had fought. Unlike earlier apprentices, they were to take action, initially, as a force by themselves rather than as a part of a wider movement within the City. As such, they were to represent the first boulder which starts an avalanche.

Trouble in London began soon after the coup when, the militia being divided, the Committee of Safety entrusted peace keeping to the sects. The Common Council reponded by discussing the need for a free Parliament. The Committee forbade the Lord Mayor's Show for fear of a riot, only to rescind the order on a protest from the aldermen. In the event, the only disorder was created by Quakers, one of whom denounced the Show for its pomp, while another smashed the beautiful statues in the gardens of White-hall.[55] The Committee now determined upon a positive effort to win over the Londoners. On the 4th Fleetwood agreed to replace sectaries with regular soldiers to guard the City, and four days later he, Desborough and White-locke came to the Guildhall to promise a settlement to please all parties and the preservation of the national Church, appealing for unity. They were answered by the Mayor, who requested a free Parliament, by the mob, who shouted for one as they left, and by the Common Council, which voted for one the next day.[56] Then Monck's commissioners arrived, and the City held its peace, awaiting the outcome of the talks. The Committee, despite its promises, placed the militia in the hands of the baptists, who were its only dependable supporters. The soldiers became even less popular with the citizens as they began to accompany collectors attempting to extract the remains of the assessment. The troops' lack of pay was now bad enough, and their reputation unpleasant enough, for the goldsmith-bankers to hide their funds for fear of being plundered. Yet discontent remained muted through mid-November. It was in this lull that some youths began to canvass a petition complaining of the decay of trade, and asking for a free Parliament or the restoration of the purged one, and the preservation of the national ministry, as the remedy to all ills.[57]

Meanwhile the hostile republicans were preparing their counterstrokes. Having spent up to six years in opposition to the Cromwells, they returned to this posture with ease. Hesilrige, Scot and their allies on the Council of State continued to meet, secretly, in London, joined by Okey, Alured, Morley and others of their supporters in the army. With them was the enigmatic Sir Anthony Ashley Cooper, who had retired to Dorset before the recent rebellion as though intending to join it, yet remained passive there and then returned to the Council on summons. After the October coup, he turned against the army with determination and a new energy. Such passages of indecision, followed by a new and absolute commitment, were the stations of his peculiar political pilgrimage.[58] These men acted first through the easiest medium, of print, producing a set of tracts against the army which stressed the illegality of its proceedings. Together with the writings of Monck's clients, and of the proponents of a free Parliament, these represented a considerable body of literature, which gave the Committee of Safety much anxiety.[59] They appeared, however, to produce no great upsurge of sympathy for the purged Parliament. Instead the Londoners talked of a freely-elected assembly, while Fleetwood ordered Hesilrige out of town in mid-November.[60]

Sir Arthur and his circle turned this necessity into a virtue, most of them dispersing into the provinces and urging the inhabitants to go on tax-strike to starve the army into submission. By the end of the month their allies in Berkshire, Wiltshire and Hampshire, counties where Marten, Neville and others of the set had influence, had declared for this tactic.[61] The next step was to acquire a military base in the area, and open a second front to take the pressure off Monck. Portsmouth was the strongest garrison, governed by Nathaniel Whetham, one of the officers commissioned since the purged Parliament's restoration. He thus had little connection with the generals at London and his men were known to be angry because the generals had diverted the pay due to Portsmouth to the soldiers in the capital. The garrison appeared, in short, ripe for defection, and it was. On 3 December Hesilrige, Morley and another MP entered the town, and were welcomed secretly by Whetham, as had been arranged. The next day the untrustworthy officers were secured, and the rest declared for the purged Parliament.[62]

On the bitterly cold day that this news reached London, the young men's petition achieved its result, in bloodshed. Through late November, while the corporation held to its formal policy of waiting on events, informal tension grew. Citizens began to resist the soldiers who came for the assessment. When Monck's inflammatory letter reached the Common Council it produced a furore. The two active members of the Committee who were present, Ireton and Alderman Tichbourne, 'swelled for anger like two toads', and Ireton's cautious successor as Lord Mayor, Allin, dissolved the assembly. When it reconvened a few days later, it formally refused the government a loan.[63] Then, on 1 December, the apprentices' petition became public news. It had been subscribed at a house in Cannon Street, reputedly by 20,000 hands. The Committee of Safety reacted swiftly, by drafting a proclamation forbidding its presentation to the Common Council. On the 5th the two documents were carried through the streets at once, the petition to the Guildhall, where it was tactfully referred to a committee, and the proclamation to the Exchange, to be announced by the leader of a troop of horse. The youths, gathering together, treated the latter to a hail of stones, tiles and pieces of ice, and the generals sent in more soldiers to restore order. What followed is familiar enough in living memory from the streets of Ulster and the campuses of America. The troops endured a renewed pelting until their patience broke and they fired into the crowd, killing and wounding several. This ended the riot, but not the issue, for the next day a coroner formally pronounced the dead youths murdered, and the Grand Jury prepared to indict the officers.[64]

Meanwhile, Monck was still desperately spinning out time. To the treaty signed by his representatives, he and his officers returned the opaque reply that the terms were inadequate, and that further talks were needed at Newcastle. To the angry comments made by the generals in England upon his letter to the Common Council, he replied that this had been a defensive reponse to the northward advance of Lambert's troops. He then moved his whole army forward himself, to the border at Berwick, claiming that this would facilitate the exchange of messages. This manœuvre indicated the depth of faith he now had in his remodelled officer corps, and his readiness for an engagement when necessary. All these tactics were successful, his opponents deciding, though suspiciously, to comply. Those in London placed all hopes in a speedy settlement of a new form of government there. Lambert's officers acquiesced for the probable reason that they were still unready for battle, the physical condition of their troops now becoming more alarming than the ideological. Lambert had brought no money with him, expecting that, and supplies, to arrive from London later. Instead, the difficulties of gathering taxes there left the soldiers in the capital themselves unprovided, let alone those in the field. Lambert's force was left to take free quarter, and grew correspondingly uncomfortable and unpopular. The question of the soldiers' pay, which had helped bring down two governments in six months, was now working against their own officers. On the other hand, despite all Monck's efforts, he was still losing men by defection, so that Lambert may well have thought fit to wait till the supplies, for which he was writing furiously, arrived, being reinforced in the meantime from his enemy's army. If these were his reasons, they were mistaken, for his appeals went unsatisfied while Monck's force at last stabilised. On 8 December the latter made another advance, to Coldstream on the Tweed. Here he and his men settled down to wait again, shivering and scratching in the town's smoky hovels, but consoled by a splendid military position, regular pay, and the increasing plight of the enemy.[65]

The General Council of officers at London now made a great effort to tackle all its growing problems. It detached a force to besiege Portsmouth. To pacify both Monck and the City, it bypassed the Committee of Safety and set about deciding a form of government itself. Rejecting plans for a Protectorate, a nominated assembly or a restoration of the purged House, it decided on the 10th to call a new Parliament. This was to have two Houses, one elected to placate the country and one chosen by the army to represent its interests. On the 13th it drew up a declaration to this effect, promising in addition liberty of conscience and a new executive council, independent of the legislature; this effectively reproduced the existing military and civilian leaders, with the addition of two Fifth Monarchists. Then, remembering constitutional niceties, it handed over the package for formal proclamation by the Committee of Safety. This fixed 24 January as the date for the Parliament's convention and published the document the next day. The City continued through this period to operate on two levels. Its corporation, recognising the physical power of the military, made representations to the officers requesting the removal of the soldiers and compensation for the families of the dead youths. When the Common Council received a petition from mature citizens, seconding the demand for a free Parliament, it returned this with a request not to print the paper. Meanwhile the apprentices shouted for vengeance and took shots at the soldiers from the roofs. A rumour spread that the sects would massacre the other citizens, which some baptist leaders then formally disclaimed. Shops were closed and most trading ceased.[66]

Then, on the day that the government drew up the resolution for a Parliament, it lost control of the sea. The only fleet still active was that in the Channel under John Lawson, the purged Parliament's nominee. On hearing of the October coup, he and his captains had expressed sorrow but remained passive. Now they acted, swayed either by the appeals of Hesilrige and Morley from Portsmouth, by fear of anarchy, or by dislike of the constitution, that of 1657 with several Protectors in place of one, which the General Council was proposing. On the 13th they declared for the purged Parliament, appending the hope that this would produce godly and responsible government, with freedom of worship and the remedy of specific grievances of seamen. To press the point, on the 16th they sailed into the Thames as far as Gravesend and closed the river.[67] The blow must have been trebly demoralising to the General Council: it was on their doorstep, they had no military answer to it, and it destroyed the satisfaction consequent upon a genuine achievement in smoothing out relations with the City. There the apprentices had come now to appear more of a threat to order than the soldiers, particularly as the latter were now prepared to call a Parliament. The youths were left to rage as the corporation exchanged courteous messages with the government and invited the troops to patrol the streets. Even the London Quakers condemned the young men as trouble-makers.[68]

Events now moved swiftly to a conclusion. On the 20th the City corporation, afraid that it might appear too compliant with the army's wishes, declared that it was determined upon a free Parliament, not a restoration of the purged one. The Lord Mayor stated his dislike of the proposed executive committee. The government, ironically, proved itself more inclined to be swayed by the City in its desperate need for support. The Committee of Safety threw away the last vestiges of a reform programme, a redistribution of parliamentary seats which Vane, now absent treating with Lawson, had secured the week before. It jettisoned with this most of the qualifications intended to obtain loyal and godly MPs, only retaining the exclusion of royalists. The General Council, for its part, dropped the idea of the executive committee, insisting only upon a senate. The next day the City held its municipal elections, and produced a Common Council even more firmly in favour of a free Parliament than the last. Simultaneously, the news arrived that that the force sent to blockade Portsmouth, tired of this uncomfortable task and perhaps moved by ideological considerations, had mutinied and joined the garrison. Some of Berry's horse regiment had already done so, and Hesilrige now had an army large enough to march on London. The news threw the Committee and the General Council into panic, and resulted in the recall of the writs prepared to call their Parliament without any positive political initiative in their place. The following day the officers debated the merits of a free Parliament against those of a purged one, and agreed, not upon either, but upon a declaration of fundamental beliefs. These proved to consist of liberty of worship for all save episcopalians and Catholics, which a free Parliament was unlikely to accept, and republican government with a separation of executive and legislature, which the purged House would certainly reject. The document was a futile statement of principle, the Last Will and Testament of the Council of Officers, the body which had determined most English politics for twelve years. The next day its members dispersed to their regiments, to salvage what they could of their soldiers' loyalty.[69]

This turned out to be very little. A royalist agent at this time could consider the army and suggest that the true Good Old Cause was money.[70] The remark had some justice, as it had been repeatedly demonstrated that the soldiers would not (naturally enough) feel much affection for a regime which failed to provide for their material needs. The Committee of Safety had just proved less adequate in this respect than any preceding government. But it was equally clear that when the junior officers and privates had chosen to support one set of men against another, the precipitating reason had been ideological, and in this case the same set of factors may well have operated. The soldiers were now not only receiving scarcely any money at all, but they were being put to uncongenial duties, fighting boys or their own comrades, while their leaders slowly sold the Good Old Cause. Having failed to produce reforms, the General Council had been creating a Parliament which, with its lack of electoral safeguards, was likely to reverse the existing reforms, where the purged one had merely failed to provide more. The basic charge of the Hesilrige set against the senior officers, that they were concerned with nothing but their own ambitions, could have seemed plausible.

Thus, as the Council dispersed, the units around London were already starting to shout for the purged Parliament. Lambert had sent Desborough's own horse regiment south to assist its colonel, but on arrival these troopers merely joined the agitation. Lenthall, Scot, Cooper and other leaders of the purged House ordered the soldiers round London to muster under Okey and his colleagues, and on the next day, which would have been Christmas Eve had that feast not been abolished, most obeyed. They were marched down Chancery Lane to Lenthall's house to make a formal submission, after which the Speaker dispersed them to their posts and proceeded himself to receive the obedience of the Tower garrison. It only remained now to send to Fleetwood for the keys to the House of Commons. That individual had been melting slowly in the past week into a confusion of prayers, tears and hopes that Lambert would return. Now he delivered the keys as ordered, and passed out of public life with the comment that God had spat in their faces.[71] It was not an unreasonable statement. Since his youth he had been content to trust to providence and its apparent instrument, his army, drifting through successive changes on the current of the latter's moods. Now it had deposited him, for ever, upon a sandbank.

Desborough, always more resilient, retired into the provinces, but sent in his own gruff submission within five days.[72] All over the southern two-thirds of the country events were following those in London. In early December the weight of occupying troops had kept the provinces quieter than the capital. Many municipal leaders must have felt like those of Southampton, who complained that 'the Civil Magistrate hath not any power or capacity left in them'.[73] The city fathers of Bristol and Gloucester were lending the unpaid troops money to keep them from plunder, while at Exeter the garrison extracted their own levy directly from the householders. The latter also put up with being disarmed by some sectaries to ensure that they did not resist the army. Only at Taunton was there a disturbance, in mid-December, when the army's sympathisers attempted a similar operation and were beaten into the castle by furious citizens.[74] With the collapse of the General Council in London, however, widespread disorder broke out. Garrisons and units of soldiers declared for the purged Parliament in succession, with corporations sometimes following suit. Isolated fortresses and individuals or small groups within the soldiery dissented, but were soon overcome by their fellows.[75] In some counties the militia declared for the purged House; in others, where it did not, the House's members and their allies raised irregular forces to establish control, a means by which partisans had secured areas since the beginning of the civil wars. A practised survivor like Bussy Mansell in Glamorganshire mustered his force under Fleetwood's authority and then proclaimed the purged Parliament at its head. All these men encountered little resistance from the army's few supporters, who were demoralised by the defection of the regiments themselves. They did find, however, that bodies of armed men were gathering, either for self-defence or self-enrichment, which favoured neither party. In Staffordshire nearly a thousand irregulars played 'Have at all'. In Oxfordshire a major raised 1,200 men but declared for nobody, while bands of robbers made the roads unsafe.[76] If there was a time in 1659 which justified the term 'anarchy', so often misapplied to the whole year, this was it. Yet within two weeks these anomalous groups had dispersed under Parliament's strengthening grip, and in another week the Epiphany Quarter Sessions were being held. Compared with the havoc of the civil wars, the disruptions of the later Interregnum were slight.

The further outposts of the army conformed to this pattern. On 26 December the Speaker received the congratulations of the Dunkirk garrison and, two days before, news had reached London of a coup in Ireland. The soldiers there had been growing restless since November, with local mutinies in favour of Monck and general discomfiture among the officers. On the day that Lawson declared for the Parliament an alliance of discontented colonels, former supporters of Richard Cromwell and leading Protestant settlers, seized the government at Dublin. This was followed by risings of prominent Protestant gentry in the provinces in favour of the conspirators, and declarations of the junior army officers for their cause. Within a week most of that realm had offered its obedience to the House.[77]

The last force to forsake the authority of the generals was that commanded by the best of them, Lambert. It had been Monck's great contribution to their downfall to keep this man, the finest soldier and statesman of his party, and its most loyal troops with him, tied down far from the capital until the government there had collapsed. By mid-winter Lambert was paralysed, unable to turn his back upon Monck and unfit to attack him. The army at Newcastle were said now to be short of shoes and stockings. Monck was able to suspend negotiations with the excuse that they would now have to take the views of the Portsmouth garrison and of Lawson into account. On 27 December Lambert and his officers decided that the situation in the capital was serious enough to risk turning away from Monck and marching south to retrieve the situation there. Robert Lilburne was sent ahead to secure York, and some Quakers sent out orders to their brethren to assemble to assist him. News of this forced Lord Fairfax, who had promised Monck aid, to rise ahead of plan, on the 30th. He gathered together his old gentry companions of the Great Civil War, some of Lilburne's own regiment, which defected under its major, and the brigade brought over from Ireland in the summer. When this composite force summoned York, and the citizens rose, Lilburne agreed to admit all who would sign a declaration of loyalty to the commonwealth. The test was enough to divide Fairfax's followers, as only the soldiers would sign, but they secured the city for the Parliament quite effectively by themselves.[78]

On 2 January, hearing that his enemy had definitely moved south, Monck advanced into England on his heels, sending a party ahead to secure Newcastle. In fact Lambert never brought his army nearer to London than Northallerton, for it fell apart on the first stage of its march. The Speaker had sent a letter instructing the regiments to disperse to quarters; now either the men disowned their senior officers and obeyed, or their commanders themselves decided that further resistance was hopeless. The thousands of men who had surrounded Lambert at Newcastle dwindled in three days to a few hundred, leaving him and his colonels to sue for the Parliament's mercy. His garrisons declared for the MPs as complete groups, or arrested their officers and did so, aided by the citizens who welcomed Monck as a liberator from a particularly oppressive military rule. Monck himself made his way cautiously south, accepting the surrender of fortresses, removing local collaborators with Lambert from power, and supervising the dispersal of the latter's soldiers. When he reached York on the 11th his work was substantially over, and he halted.[79] Complete victory was his, without having fought an action from beginning to end.

On the 29th Hesilrige had arrived in the House from Portsmouth, in riding dress, very cheerful.[80] He had every reason to be, for after ten years he and his party had at last obtained real control of the army of England. After twelve, the power in politics seemed genuinely to lie with civilians again.

4

The Road to Restoration

⌒〰⌒

As the first month of 1660 passed, the English Commonwealth was busy with a new cycle of retribution and reward. The former, either because of compassion towards former comrades of the Revolution, or of fear of the soldiers' feelings, was light. Hesilrige, who had done so much to oppose the Committee of Safety, now worked hard for clemency towards its defeated members. He succeeded in having the leading officers, including Lambert, granted life and property, but not liberty. They were kept under threat of arrest, and ordered to stay out of London. He failed to save Vane and another MP from expulsion, and a third from suspension, from the House, but he did receive Ludlow warmly and secure the vote of a hearing for him and the commissioners arrested at Dublin. For the trimmer Whitelocke he had no time, and this individual retired in fear of punishment. In this manner Sir Arthur and his set attempted to retain the services of their former allies against Cromwell, and did obtain mercy for all their recent opponents.[1]

Nevertheless, to consolidate the Parliament's victory, the army was subjected to the most extensive purge in its history. The treatment that Monck had meted out to his own units in Scotland he now accorded to those which had followed Lambert, while the MPs gave this their blessing and dealt with the regiments in the south themselves. After the fall of the Protectorate an observer had estimated that 160 officers had been removed, while the General Council had suspended twenty in October. Now a full three-eighths of the entire corps were replaced, including half the field officers and two-thirds of the captains, while many of the survivors were given different posts. By the same policy, of breaking the formidable unity hitherto displayed by the army, half the new appointments were given to men unfamiliar to the unit concerned.[2] To ensure security while this process was carried out, the MPs ordered Monck to bring his loyal troops to London.[3] At the same time the fundamental enemies of the Commonwealth were treated with a rigour which was spared those who had merely disputed the authority of Parliament within it. The sale was ordered of the property of Booth and his adherents, and the central sequestration commission began prodding its local representatives, who had stopped work during the confusion of late December, into renewed action. Likewise a bill was ordered to harass the Catholics.[4] The republic was to be guarded upon all sides.

Monck was naturally the main beneficiary of the rewards. In November the Hesilrige group, claiming the authority of the old Council of State, had appointed him acting Commander-in-Chief of the armed forces. The Parliament now promised him lands worth £1,000 a year, the custody of St. James's Park and the honour of *custos rotulorum* of his native Devon. His chaplain was made a Fellow of Eton and his brother-in-law made Commissary-General. Lawson was voted land worth £500 a year. Okey and the other loyal officers were, of course, restored to their commands; Morley was made Lieutenant of the Tower, Cooper and Lenthall's son became colonels, and the rest of the other military commands were granted to men who had helped to secure the counties at the generals' collapse. Almost half the Council of State was replaced, Monck and Lawson giving lustre to a list of relatively insignificant newcomers. Nor were the common soldiers forgotten. On receiving their submission Lenthall had promised them money, and the bill for an increased assessment, suspended in September, was now passed.[5]

These changes in personnel represented a decisive shift in ideology, although, as in the summer, the purged Parliament was doing no more than accepting support where it believed this to lie. Just as the generals, despite their efforts, had been identified by many with radicalism, so their defeat was the final blow to the cause of further reform. Its main proponent in the House, Vane, had been expelled, and his supporters there had been sent with him or cowed. Only one MP, that renegade aristocrat the Earl of Pembroke, now even spoke for broad religious toleration.[6] The army was stripped of most of the surviving officers who had brought about the Revolution. Whalley and Goffe had compromised themselves by urging Monck to reach agreement with the General Council, but more conservative supporters of Richard Cromwell were now restored to their commissions. Ingoldsby, who had become a royalist conspirator, was only denied a colonelcy by two votes. Men were recommissioned who had been dismissed in 1647-8 for opposing the course of events which led to the Revolution. The field officers still included the Fifth Monarchists Rich and Overton, and the fiercely republican Okey and Alured, but the Commander-in-Chief was now the Church's defender Monck.[7] The leading independent clergy had also entreated Monck to comply with the generals, and were no longer invited to preach to the House, which discussed replacing the Triers.[8] The Common Council ejected most of the religious separatists from the City militia, and it may be presumed that Monck followed the same course in his purging of the northern trained bands. He put two 'secluded' members in charge of Newcastle and Northumberland.[9] The judges who had resigned in the summer, rather than swear loyalty to the Commonwealth, were reinstated without being put to any test. Canne was left as editor of one of the newspapers permitted by the new government, but the other four were the work of the flexible Nedham and two clients of Monck, Henry Muddiman and Giles Drury.[10] As so often, the other realms mirrored changes in England in an exaggerated form. Before his departure Monck had admitted the Scottish gentry to a greater degree of power in local defence and administration than they had enjoyed since their conquest, so extending Broghill's policy. The coup in Ireland had swept away the sectaries favoured by Ludlow and returned to authority, among other relatively conservative leaders, Broghill himself.[11]

Practical consequences of this tendency were soon apparent. When the Parliament issued a manifesto on 23 January, it upheld the existing liberty of conscience, but also tithes and the existing laws. On the 14th many leading London baptists printed a declaration stressing their pacifism and obedience to the regular magistrate. A large number of new tracts against religious radicals appeared. In Lancashire soldiers had protected Quakers in the summer: they now attacked them themselves. When a baptist preacher inveighed against the recent changes in Balliol College chapel, the Vice-Chancellor threw him out.[12] Many MPs failed to return to the purged House on its second restoration, so that the maximum number now recorded present was fifty-five. Nevertheless it was as divided as before, but with a significant difference. Whereas in the summer Hesilrige had opposed Vane to prevent reforms, now he and his set found themselves attacked by MPs who were regarded as more moderate or conservative. It was the latter who ensured the expulsion of Vane. They also opposed a proposal of Hesilrige's circle that the House be required to abjure the royal line of Stuart. Their leaders were Cooper, whose behaviour during Booth's rising had been equivocal, and Morley, who had considered turning royalist in November. Their stand against the abjuration was joined by members of the new Council of State who were not MPs, such as Fairfax who had never actively supported Pride's Purge or its consequences. Their arguments were based on the general moral objections to oaths, but the split was unmistakably one between the true Commonwealthsmen and those who had qualms about the republic. Thus the powerful unity achieved against the army was already lost, and even the negative task of securing the existing Commonwealth was bedevilled. The House did press ahead with measures to this end, expelling the 'secluded' members altogether and voting to fill itself up with fresh elections, without withdrawing its promise to dissolve in June. The question of how to qualify suitable candidates, however, naturally both posed practical problems and worsened the existing tensions among MPs.[13]

Hesilrige's position was rendered still less comfortable by the perennial weakness of the Commonwealthsmen, their lack of support in the country. The City had indeed now gone over from coolness towards the purged Parliament to outright rejection of it. As under the generals, the Lord Mayor and aldermen showed willingness to compromise, perhaps because of their exposed position and perhaps because of their investment in the Commonwealth, represented by the confiscated lands several had bought at the Revolution.[14] But they, like the Commonwealthsmen, had to reckon with citizens who had almost obtained a free Parliament, apprentices whose fellows had died for one, and a new Common Council which had been elected to press for one. At the purged Parliament's reappearance, the latter reacted with fury, and drafted a petition to the MPs to readmit their 'secluded' colleagues. These, led as usual by Prynne and Annesley, made another formal attempt to enter the House and, on being barred out again by soldiers, Prynne recommenced a furious literary campaign for readmission.[15] Lord Mayor Allin and the aldermen formally submitted to the purged MPs, but the Common Council voted once more for a free Parliament and remodelled the City militia by itself. When Hesilrige paraded soldiers through the streets, the apprentices hurled insults at them. Ropes were hung at the doors of Aldermen Ireton and Tichbourne.[16] To this campaign of vilification, the press now presented a potent image. In May a royalist correspondent had referred to the purged House as 'the Rump'.[17] The term had grown in use among his party, and after the second restoration of this House Prynne had finally published it. Less educated pamphleteers rapidly exploited its full noisome potential, most commonly in rhyme, and so the Parliament of the English Revolution acquired its enduring label.[18] Panegyrics are forgotten within weeks; abuse outlives centuries.

In the remarkably cohesive society of seventeenth-century England, contacts between capital and provinces could remain strong even in times of political confusion: under the Committee of Safety, gentry in Caernarfonshire were eagerly passing around a copy of Monck's letter to the City corporation.[19] It is correspondingly difficult to say whether the example of London encouraged the provinces to resistance in January 1660, or vice versa. The purged Parliament had the army, and irregular forces led by its partisans, to enforce its will upon the country.[20] Its expectation of sources of local support is revealed by the commissioners appointed to collect the new assessment, which, while reproducing many of the names in the Militia Acts in July, included a greater number of prosperous gentry and men noted for 'moderate' views. Those of Worcestershire had the highest average income of any Interregnum commissioners in the county.[21] Despite this the provinces were more discontented than ever. The usual problem of too many soldiers for too little money remained: including Monck's army there were now about 34,000 regulars in England, plus the republican irregulars, and the new assessment would not be collected for weeks.[22] Frequent disorder was created by unpaid soldiers, such as plundering in Gloucestershire and bullying of countrymen in Somerset.[23] Only in Derbyshire do the Quarter Sessions seem to have been cancelled altogether, but attendance by justices declined still further in most counties except the western, where they became platforms for protest. Urban corporations tended to meet less frequently. In Taunton and Bath, where the Parliament had influential representatives, there were bells and bonfires for its return,[24] but apparently nowhere else. Sectaries tried to capture a Cornish castle, an attempt was made to suborn the garrison of Cardiff, and the Quakers there discussed taking up arms,[25] but in general the religious radicals were quiescent. The restored government had rather to face a peaceful but considerable challenge from conservatives who were determined to press the defeat of the reformers into full-scale reaction.

The process began in Cornwall on 27 December when, at the collapse of the army's supporters, many gentry who had supported the Long Parliament up to Pride's Purge met to consider the state of the county. After four days they declared for a free Parliament. When the Devon Epiphany Quarter Sessions opened at Exeter, the apprentices there took up the cry. The mayor quelled their tumult, but a group of gentry, all wartime parliamentarians and religious presbyterians, framed a petition for the readmission of the 'secluded' MPs. Another of these was drawn up at the Sessions at Gloucester, this time with the mayor's support, but crushed by the governor, one of the purged House. In Kent a mixture of former royalists and parliamentarians, members of the pre-war county élite, decided to declare for the secluded MPs in December and did so in early January, only to be arrested by another military representative of the purged House, who now governed Dover. Many Northamptonshire magnates met in the first days of January, men of the same political record and religious views as those who composed the western petitions, and in the middle of the month these declared for a free Parliament in turn. Agents were sent into neighbouring counties to ask support, and Richard Temple, an ambitious young Buckinghamshire squire, responded with energy in his own locality. Royalists encouraged the movement by writing tracts and carrying messages.[26]

The army which had held Scotland began its march from York to London on 16 January. It needed nearly three weeks to get there, wading through snow, subsisting in quarters where the army of England had consumed most of the available supplies, and sleeping in straw provided by urban corporations.[27] A foot regiment was left at York to watch the North, leaving four others, and three of horse, some 5,800 men, for the capital.[28] At their head moved the two George Moncks: the man who had fought for many masters and had abandoned Richard Cromwell to keep his own post, and the man who upheld the national Church. Both personalities were plain to observers, and the warring factions of the country sent representatives to him *en route*. In the House, only the Commonwealthsman Henry Marten protested at the general's removal of radical officers, the rest of the MPs choosing to approve his work and to believe his loyal letters.[29] They sent two of Hesilrige's allies, Scot and Luke Robinson, to accompany him south. Lenthall, however, on behalf of the more 'moderate' MPs, may have sent to him in secret, warning him against Hesilrige's party.[30] The men who were agitating for a free Parliament noted his views on the Church, which so much accorded with theirs, and hoped that he would share their political objectives as well.[31] The 'secluded' members and the City Corporation sent emissaries, and of eight county declarations for a free Parliament or for the 'secluded' MPs produced during Monck's march, five were presented to him by way of petition. The London apprentices and the citizens of Hull added their appeals.[32]

Initially the general's reactions seemed faintly equivocal. He gave a 'secluded' member 'some hopes' in private. Lenthall's messenger found him devoted both to a Commonwealth and to a presbyterian Church, and Monck wrote to Oliver Cromwell's old friend St. John expressing equal hostility to royalists and sectaries. Certainly he was constrained by the facts that most of his officers were offended by the deputations requesting a free Parliament, and that he was usually watched by Scot and Robinson.[33] However, he soon dispelled most doubts about his attitude to the 'secluded' members by publishing a personal declaration that to readmit them would be unacceptable to the army and would cause violent disturbances in the nation. He concluded with the observation that the present Parliament, by filling itself with fresh elections, would become 'free' naturally.[34] The statement could not have been blunter or more practical, and given Monck's good relations with the purged Parliament was not tactically necessary. His posthumous apologists, significantly, gloss over it. Instead they stress the only letter written by the general and his officers to the House during their march, requesting that the units of the English army quartered around London, which outnumbered their own, be scattered into the provinces until the delicate business of remodelling their officer corps was complete. The apologists claimed this to be a device to deprive the Parliament of military protection, but the reason given was practical enough. The House certainly saw the sense of it, and obliged.[35]

Removing the soldiers in question, still underpaid and deprived of their familiar leaders, was not easy. Many units refused to leave London till they had some cash in hand, and although the Exchequer was emptied for them, individual MPs still had to borrow on private credit to make up an acceptable sum. Yet when some apprentices took the opportunity to start a riot for a free Parliament, the mutinous troops overpowered and disarmed them: the army of England was still republican. As its units dispersed, on 2 February, Monck's army marched into Whitehall, impressing observers with its air of discipline but watched by the crowds in cold silence, broken by the occasional shout for a free Parliament.[36] The new soldiers settled in Westminster, and came across the local Quakers meeting in Palace Yard. These they immediately beat up, saying that they had come to rid England of sectaries. It was a faithful reflection of Monck's propaganda, but the injured men complained to Parliament and the general disclaimed responsibility.[37] On the 6th Monck himself attended the House to receive its thanks. He did so with ostentatious respect, refusing a chair and remaining bareheaded, but his reply was a clear political admonition. It commenced with his now familiar warning against both royalists and 'fanatics', which he developed into an explicit insistence upon the need to win over moderate men. To this end, he urged the abandonment of the controversial oath against the Stuarts, and the acceleration of the business of filling up the House with fresh elections.[38] With these words he ranged himself alongside the Cooper-Morley bloc, against the Commonwealthsmen. In part this can be seen as a political choice, as both the 'moderate' MPs and their 'secluded' colleagues had repeatedly laboured to convince him of the jealousy of Hesilrige's set and their suspicion of all soldiers.[39] But its sentiments were entirely consistent with the advice he had given Richard Cromwell, with his actions in Scotland, and with all the attitudes he had adopted hitherto.

The campaign to vilify the purged House and to replace it continued, meanwhile, with undiminished force. 'Kiss my Parliament' replaced a more familiar obscenity among London children, and a picture was hung on the Exchange 'of a great pair of buttocks shitting of a turd into Lawson's mouth' with the caption 'The Thanks of the Parliament'.[40] The Common Council voted for a tax strike till the purged House capitulated, with many violent speeches.[41] In the provinces the appearance of the thousands of soldiers dispersed from the capital intensified dislike of the government. The great agitation among urban youth, which had begun in November with the Cannon Street petition, now spread to Gloucester, where the apprentices planned a riot, and Bristol, where they produced one on the approach of a regiment from London.[42] Some citizens of Bristol and Canterbury raised petitions for a free Parliament, and some gentry, freeholders, townsmen and clergy in perhaps five more counties, declared for this or for the 'secluded' members. Most of these concurred with the tactic of a tax strike. At least one such declaration was sent down by Londoners for subscription, but the numbers who subscribed it on arrival were considerable.[43]

Against this movement, despite its own divisions, the government turned the formidable energy it had shown against Booth and his allies. The Council of State ordered troops in some counties to suppress all meetings, and the City magistrates to stop the hostile pamphlets. The House renewed the powers of its sequestration commissioners and ordered the arrest of the chief promoters of the provincial petitions. On the 9th the Council finally asked the MPs to use Monck's army to cow London. They instructed him to march in, impose order, destroy all the City's defences and arrest eleven leaders of the agitation. They resolved on the dissolution of the Common Council, to be replaced by one elected within stringent qualifications, and produced a bill to put the militia under their own supporters. Meanwhile they continued with the positive business of recruiting new colleagues, debating the extent of the franchise in the forthcoming elections.[44]

The Long Parliament had faced an equally determined challenge from the City in 1647, and a much more serious one from the provinces in 1648. The army had crushed both. During the early part of 1660, its purged remnant never lost its grip on the counties, where the same army made violent protest impossible. Moreover, it retained the support of collaborators in many local communities, particularly the urban corporations which displayed little enthusiasm for the campaign for a free Parliament. The Leicester city fathers dissociated themselves from the county petition presented to Monck. The mayor of Bristol crushed the apprentices' riot there and the council declined to approve their cause. In London the radical minority produced a loyal address to the House, delivered by Praise-God Barebone, the lay pastor of a separatist church after whom the nominated assembly of 1653 has taken its popular name. The other citizens looked 'mighty blank' when faced with Monck's army. Scotland remained quiet.[45] The threatened tax strike never materialised, for the arrears of the old assessment continued to trickle in, even from London, as they had through all the previous commotions.[46] Hesilrige's faction dominated the Council of State and had the clear support of the House for a policy of repression. They should have been in a stronger position than during the conservative challenges of the late 1640s. In fact they suffered from a fatal weakness: the army concentrated at the centre was not the traditional one, but George Monck's.

Neither Monck nor the officer corps he had created possessed any emotional sympathy with the cause they were now expected to defend. They were openly hostile to the religious ideals of men like Barebone. They had not shared in the Revolution and one of them, Colonel Clobery, was a secret royalist. A representative of the Irish army was with them, declaiming against the House for failing to prosecute Ludlow. Lenthall, Cooper, and other members of the 'moderate' faction with whom the general had identified himself urged him privately to conciliate, not to offend, the City. Before the House ordered him to punish it, he had already told Clobery that he found the government unacceptable as it stood. On receiving the MPs' direct orders, he continued to walk a political tightrope. First he arrested the citizens named as ringleaders, destroyed the chains stretched across the streets, and required the Lord Mayor and aldermen to recognise the purged Parliament. Then, after conferences with his officers and some of the 'moderates', he wrote to the House suggesting that, as a conciliatory gesture, the City's gates be preserved. The result was to widen the breach in affection between him and the Commonwealthsmen, who led the House into ordering him, curtly, to proceed as instructed.

The same pattern was now reproduced with greater intensity. Monck obeyed the order, on the 10th, and then returned to Whitehall to confer with his officers. They expressed their dismay at developments, and the general's wife, his brother-in-law and Morley, all concurred in this sentiment. As Morley commanded the Tower, all the soldiers in the capital would support an alternative policy, and next morning Monck and his chief officers initiated one, sending a letter to the House which turned the general's previous advice into a direction. Having expressed dislike of the policy of repression, of the address presented by Barebone, and of the private contacts maintained by Hesilrige's set with Ludlow, Lambert and Vane, they instructed the MPs to issue the writs for new elections within a week and to dissolve altogether once the House was filled. Then, as a physical expression of their feelings, they moved their soldiers to quarters in the City. There followed the night of 'the Roasting of the Rump', possibly the greatest expression of popular rejoicing London has ever known. The corporation welcomed Monck, while the citizens gave his soldiers money and drinks in the streets. The bells rang for hours, and bonfires were kindled in such profusion that Pepys could count thirty-one from the Strand Bridge. Over them were roasted the rumps of cattle, sheep and poultry, which were then swung from poles or torn to pieces. Pickpockets made record takings in the boisterous crowds. The windows of Barebone's house were broken and citizens who had opposed resistance to the House were pursued. Meanwhile, the MPs had received the letter and returned the cool and polite reply that they were indeed busy with the matter of the elections. Then, as night came, Hesilrige whipped them into one of those suicidal rages which had been their downfall in October, and perhaps in 1653. They concluded proceedings by depriving Monck of his post as Commander-in-Chief, and vesting the supreme military power in a commission of five, of which he was a member but not one of the quorum. Either because the 'moderates' had completely lost hope of persuading the House into a gentler course, or because they were glad to see the general still more aggrieved with the Commonwealthsmen, this measure was passed without a division. It merely welded Monck's personal ambitions to his political and social instincts.[47]

In considering the forces behind these events, it is necessary to remove three traditional distortions from the picture. First is the assumption that Monck's public attitudes underwent a striking change in early February 1660. As has been suggested, from the moment that he arrived in London he made his preferred policy clear: what altered, with some warning, was his treatment of the House when it failed to honour the advice. Indeed, this policy, to stabilise the country by gaining the middle ground, was that which he had implemented in Scotland and recommended in England in previous years. This becomes still plainer if the second distortion is removed: the assumption that his opposition to the General Council in October derived principally from a wish either to save the purged House or to restore the King. As has been suggested, this stand probably resulted from an urgent desire to save the Church, his actions in February from a broader conception of the country's needs. He supported the House as a bulwark in the first case and abandoned it as an obstruction in the second. But there has also been too much emphasis on Monck himself in the events of 9-11 February, and not enough on his officers. All accounts agree that they were more firmly opposed to repression than their leader, and made this plain to him. Their motivation is at least as important as his, for without them he could hardly have acted. It seems reasonable to suppose that the whole corps, including its commander, shared neither the past experiences nor the ideals of the Commonwealthsmen, and therefore failed to support their policies.

London's joy raised echoes in the provinces. Bonfires flamed down the western hills from Wiltshire to Cornwall. Rumps were roasted at Queen's College, Oxford, and hurled at the windows of the firmly republican Warden of All Souls. The apprentices of Gloucester and Bristol rioted for a completely free Parliament and there were celebrations at Yarmouth and in Herefordshire and Devon. Outside the capital, however, the old army still ruled, and the last five disturbances were all crushed by it. Only in York was rejoicing encouraged by the military, because that city was held by part of Monck's force.[48] The soldiers, nevertheless, could not prevent the demoralisation of the Commonwealth's civilian officers. None of the local sequestration committees responded to the new act intended to hasten their work. In Kent fifteen out of the eighty-seven assessment commissioners met to commence the levy. In Somerset six of the commission met, only to witness one of them declare the Parliament's authority illegal and be arrested by the local republican irregulars.[49] New declarations for the 'secluded' members were sent to Monck by gentry in Oxfordshire, Lincolnshire, Yorkshire and three other counties. The first was the work of Viscount Falkland's group, the royalist conspirators of the previous summer, while the third was subscribed by Monck's ally against Lambert, Lord Fairfax, and his former companion in the Cromwells' favour, Viscount Fauconberg. The Middlesex Grand Jury formally indicted Okey and Alured for having kept the 'secluded' MPs from the House in late December.[50] In Ireland Broghill's army of Munster and the officers at Dublin issued appeals on behalf of the 'secluded' members, and rid themselves of republican colleagues.[51]

In the capital the events of 11 February were followed by ten days of political limbo, produced by Monck's insistence on freedom of manœuvre between the competing factions. He welcomed the Lord Mayor and aldermen to his quarters and the citizens continued to make his soldiers drunk, but he forbade the Common Council to meet. He sent letters to Hesilrige's group expressing the most fulsome affection for a Commonwealth, and received even Ludlow warmly and with the same sentiments, but refused the Council's entreaties to return to Whitehall. Those who had urged him to deal strongly with the Commonwealthsmen were puzzled and irritated by his amicable exchanges with them. They in turn, with the possible exception of Ludlow, were inclined to trust the general's words, and to reconcile him by pressing ahead towards the elections as he had directed. The House completed the preparations on the 18th, and apparently provided for a Parliament as 'free' as those of the Protectorate, save for the minority of 'reserved' seats occupied by the existing MPs. While royalists and Catholics were excluded as usual, both 'secluded' members and the promoters of the recent petitions were eligible to stand, a convincing adoption of the policy of conciliation urged by Monck and his officers. Likewise, the oath against the Stuarts was watered down to a promise, and Vane and Lambert were ordered out of town. The general encouraged the tendency further by initiating two conferences between the sitting and the 'secluded' MPs, designed to achieve unity. He may have intended these to be a prelude to the readmission of the 'secluded' members. He may have been spinning out time till he had disarmed the City radicals and prepared his officers for this change of policy. When he told Ludlow that he would not readmit the 'secluded' MPs, and informed the Falkland set that they must await the consequences of the elections, he may have been insincere. But if that was the case, it is difficult to explain the letter which he wrote to Fairfax and the Yorkshire gentry on the 18th, pointing out that as the 'secluded' members were able to stand for election it was superfluous to readmit them. Why, if Monck was playing a deep game, did he waste time upon a letter which probably did not arrive until after his tactics had changed?

Two days later, they had indeed changed, and several factors may account for this. After initial promise, the talks between the two sets of MPs had resolved nothing, Hesilrige storming out of the last. Monck was under constant pressure from his wife, brother-in-law, chaplain, Colonel Clobery and another trusted officer, Colonel Knight, to readmit the 'secluded' members. He had become friendly with the leading London presbyterian clergy, who added their voices to this. It was urged also by the 'moderates' in the House, and Speaker Lenthall held up the writs for the new elections by refusing to sign the warrant for them. The case for readmission was based upon the assurance that, once in, the 'secluded' members would do nothing but prepare the House for dissolution. Such a prospect may well have come to seem simpler to the general than the business of new elections to obtain the same end. It would also hasten the provision of money for his troops, and he may in addition have resented the fact that nothing was done by the existing House to restore his position as Commander-in-Chief.

On 20 February, if not before, he and his officers decided to permit the readmission, on stiff terms. The following morning these were dictated to a group of the MPs at Whitehall. Monck had apparently insisted to the 'secluded' men that he be given supreme military power and the republican Lawson be retained as Vice-Admiral. Now he warned them of the destructive effects of a restored monarchy, and directed them to preserve the republic, with a presbyterian Church permitting toleration of separatist groups. He obtained their consent to a speedy dissolution and permitted them to proceed to the House, where his soldiers let them through. The Hesilrige set were taken completely by surprise, and came to the general in fury, but he spoke soothingly, explained that he intended only to stabilise the Commonwealth, and advised them to continue to participate in the work of the House.[52]

Despite these words, and whatever the future of the republic, the period when the Commonwealthsmen had dominated political life was now over. In all three periods of power, the purged Parliament had depended for survival upon the soldiers at its doors. It had attempted repeatedly to gain some proper control over these men, and always failed. Armies created it, readopted it, and then discarded it whenever it proved an inadequate tool. Circumstances were now to ensure that this third demise was final.

Like many another group of politicians, the men restored to power in February 1660 had been united more by events than by principles. They had all supported the parliamentarian cause in the Great Civil War, and failed to dissent from the vote to continue negotiations with Charles I which had provoked the army into Pride's Purge, but their individual reasons for both stands were naturally varied. Before the purge most had supported presbyterian church government, but some would probably have preferred modified episcopacy and some were willing to tolerate separatist groups.[53] After it, some had offered support to the King, some had given it to the Protectorate, and most had done neither. Overall they were a more conservative group than the purged Parliament, but their ideological overlap with that body was symbolised by the retention of Lenthall as Speaker and the election of Cooper, Morley, St. John and three other members of the old Council of State to a new Council on 23 February.[54] Two of Oliver Cromwell's protégés who had been suspected of disloyalty by the Commonwealthsmen, Mountagu and Richard Norton, were appointed to that body. Prynne, though cheered into the House, was either considered too intemperate or too pedantic for it, but Annesley, more shrewd and less flamboyant, was easily elected. Most of the new Council were substantial gentry who represented the range of religious and political opinion among the 'secluded' MPs. What all these men had in common was a distaste for the narrowly-based republic of the Commonwealthsmen.

This fact was at least sufficient to guarantee them immediate popularity. The news of the readmission spread out from London amid a great clamour of church bells and a flaring of bonfires.[55] The urban corporations, who had tended to remain loyal to the purged Parliament, now acquiesced in its demise, though at Bristol a clear hesitation and division is apparent from the records which may be concealed in those of other municipalities. The Hull council registered the change easily enough by petitioning the larger House for reforms similar to those once requested of the purged one.[56] The most open hostility to the readmission was exhibited by the units of the army of England who, from their new quarters in the provinces, frequently repressed popular celebrations of the event, even when these were orderly and without royalist overtones.[57] The continuing strength of republican feeling among these soldiers, though now scattered and under unfamiliar officers, represented Monck's greatest anxiety upon acceding to the pleas of the 'secluded' members. To cope with it, as the members returned to the House, Monck and his officers in London dispatched copies of a letter to the troops elsewhere, explaining that the readmission had been made only to gain a proper representative, under firm qualifications to secure the Commonwealth, pay the soldiers and confirm the confiscated lands of Crown and Church to their purchasers.[58] Regiments commanded by men who favoured the event rapidly made declarations of concurrence to set others an example of loyalty.[59] To strengthen his grip on the army, Monck formed a special guard for himself and re-employed two of Oliver Cromwell's favourites who had been dismissed at Richard's fall and become secret royalists, Ingoldsby and Charles Howard. Their reappearance completed the return to public life of those, like Monck himself, who had embodied the 'reactionary' tendencies in the later Protectorate.[60] As a complement to this work, the new Council of State ordered the irregular forces led by the purged Parliament's more zealous local supporters to disband.[61]

There were three men still officers in the army of England who were celebrated for their fidelity to a Commonwealth, and of whose reactions Monck had most reason to beware: Okey, Rich and Overton. Thanks to the general's proposals to disperse the English units, these colonels were at opposite ends of the provinces, in Bristol, Suffolk and Hull respectively. Okey's regiment was scattered over counties far from him; Rich's was also dismembered, and Overton's garrison was penned into a corner by the regiment Monck had left at York. Using this advantage, the general dealt with each man in detail. To win Okey's compliance, he sent an officer of proved republican sentiment, armed with a declaration by Lawson, the Commonwealth's favourite seaman, in support of the readmission. The colonel was convinced, and came to London alone as Monck requested.[62] Rich, by contrast, began calling his regiment together on hearing the news from London, and the general launched at him his own guards, accompanied by Ingoldsby who had formerly commanded Rich's men. The latter offered no resistance, and their colonel was forced to come to the capital to surrender his commission, leaving his officers to be purged.[63] Overton hesitated for a few days, and then he and his subalterns wrote a letter to the commanders at York expressing alarm at the course of events. The recipients, Monck's men, forwarded it immediately to the general, who ordered them to advance on Hull and sent messengers to persuade Overton to come to London. These emissaries were chosen with his usual cunning, one being the Cromwellian governor of Hull, who would be popular with the garrison, and the other being Alured, the staunch republican colonel restored by the purged Parliament. This man had for some reason been converted to Monck's policy in London, and presented arguments for it to Overton. The latter gave way under all this pressure, and did depart for the capital, where he was dismissed from the army. Monck replaced him with neither Alured nor Cromwell's governor, but with the most trusted of his own officers from York. Soldiers from the York detachment were placed in the castle; the garrison's officer corps was remodelled and the local militia, who had been sympathetic to Overton, disbanded. The citizens rang bells for eight hours to celebrate these changes.[64] Elsewhere in the country individual officers in regiments or garrisons expressed disquiet at the readmission and were discharged. Monck employed the brigade sent from Ireland in the summer, which had particularly effective new officers, on a tour of North Wales and its March to purge the garrisons, which were still commanded by men put in by Lambert after Booth's rebellion. Key fortresses in the south were placed under governors associated with the re-admitted members, and an irregular force was raised to keep South Wales quiet in the same interest.[65] Lambert himself was summoned by the new Council of State and, when he expostulated at this treatment, committed to the Tower for being unable to pay impossibly high securities.[66]

Among the civilian population, the only dismay at the readmission was displayed by the Revolution's main beneficiaries, the religious radicals, or 'fanatics' in Monck's parlance, a term which he had made fashionable amongst their enemies. A group of sectaries were reported to have attempted to seize Shrewsbury, while their co-religionists were restless at Bristol, York and Carlisle.[67] Attacks upon them increased once more in proportion to fear of them: houses of baptists and Fifth Monarchists were plundered in North Wales and Quakers were mobbed in South Wales, Bristol and Gloucester, in each case with the connivance of the new army officers.[68] Always less involved in politics than any other religious group, the Quakers remained favourite targets of conservatives because of their extreme ideas and con-tinued public preaching. Monck pursued a considerable double policy towards the radical groups. On the one hand, his personal detestation of them, and his determination to render them impotent, remained. When a Hertfordshire magnate warned him that local baptists were stirring, he replied savagely that he desired nothing better than an excuse to fight them, and sent soldiers to seize their weapons.[69] Yet he was also careful not to provoke them into armed opposition if this could be avoided, for he released London baptists who claimed to have been arrested without cause by the militia, and answered Quaker appeals by ordering the whole army to leave their meetings in peace.[70]

Thus, by manipulating his resources with the skill of a chess grandmaster, Monck ensured the immediate survival of the enlarged House. Its eventual fate, however, depended upon whether the readmitted members would prove more adept than any other Interregnum MPs in gratifying the wishes of their military sponsors. Initially, it appeared that this would be so, for during the first two weeks of its existence the enlarged House made Monck Commander-in-Chief and appointed him automatically to the new Council of State. It confirmed the heavy new assessment to pay the army, patronised the presbyterian ministers favoured by the general, resolved to dissolve by 15 March and prepared a bill for this purpose. Its readmitted members behaved towards their colleagues with the restraint Monck had recommended, releasing the republicans' prisoners, including Booth and the recent leaders of the agitation for a free Parliament, but clapping up only Lambert in their place. To gratify the City, the House confirmed the existing Common Council in office, ordered the reconstruction of the gates and approved all the militia officers, including several royalists, recommended by the corporation. The latter, in turn, made Monck commander of the militia and, after much haggling, lent the government £27,000, a trifling sum in comparison to its needs, but enough ready cash to keep the soldiers around London paid. The livery companies began to feast the general in succession. The citizens lit bonfires to celebrate the readmission, smashed Barebone's new window-panes and thereafter became peaceful.[71]

For all this, political excitement increased rather than diminished. Speculation was rife about the form of government which might succeed the Commonwealth, the elevation of Monck as Protector, the restoration of Richard Cromwell and the recall of the King, all being regarded as possible.[72] The press represented the two extreme voices of republican and royalist. Milton, alone of the former, wrote positively for a Commonwealth, embodied in a permanent House of Commonwealthsmen, as the only guarantee of liberty.[73] The others preferred to vilify the King, and their most celebrated achievement in this regard was *Newes from Brussels*, apparently written by Nedham and printed by Livewell Chapman, who also published Milton's tract.[74] Calculated to provoke the greatest possible fear of a royal restoration, it purported to be an intercepted letter from one of Charles's courtiers, gloating over the vengeance intended by the King upon all who had opposed him or his father. This was a shrewd blow, in that the several royalist tracts of the period argued for monarchy, and sometimes for episcopacy, not in terms of the actual conditions of a restoration but of the theoretical merits of traditional government.[75] On the other hand, religious and political radicals, individually and collectively, were subjected to a campaign of slander and mockery which may well represent the most vulgar collection of writing in English poetical literature.[76] The various verses upon the theme of the Rump, in particular, though none of sufficient wit to be worthy of quotation, should be a valuable source of information for historians of early modern sanitary arrangements. Both aspects of conservative publication were translated into action, a City minister preaching for the King and several using the old Prayer Book openly, while youths assaulted Hesilrige in Westminster Hall.[77]

The enlarged House contained within it all of the warring views. The Commonwealthsmen, after initial demoralisation, decided to take Monck's advice and continue to sit. Ludlow and Scot apparently discussed gathering the soldiers in the provinces to attack the capital, but Hesilrige and their other friends preferred to work through Parliament. As many of the 'secluded' members failed to return to the House, and its average attendance was still only 111, as opposed to 44 before the readmission, the republicans had some potential both for obstruction and persuasion. They commenced deftly on 25 February with a bill to present Monck with Hampton Court Palace, a material stake in the Commonwealth. Among the 'moderate' faction of the purged House, Cooper was later said to have spoken firmly for some form of republic, while St. John wanted to restore Richard Cromwell. Belief in the latter's prospects was enhanced on the 27th, when Scot was replaced as Secretary of State with two men, one of no consequence but the other that pillar of the Protectorate, John Thurloe. A clause against Kings and Protectors was excised from Monck's commission but retained in the act empowering the Council of State. Amid such uncertainty and division, MPs began to reconsider the wisdom of a speedy dissolution.[78] Doubts about the value of the readmission were soon expressed by men who had welcomed it: 'Rump Major begins to smell as rank as Rump Minor' was the comment of one such by 1 March.[79] Most ominously, the capital began to fill with officers from the regiments elsewhere, in defiance of the enlarged House's orders against this.[80] They were soon joined by Okey, as the price of Monck's success in bringing this man under his eye, and gathered around Monck in a kind of resurrected General Council.

The inevitable crisis came in the second week of March. On the 2nd the MPs struck the reference to the Commonwealth from the instructions to their committee on revenue, implying that the form of government was debatable. Prynne, with his wonderful lack of tact, spoke in favour of monarchy. The following day the House released three royalist peers confined since the Third Civil War, and on the 5th it ordered the republication of the Solemn League and Covenant of 1643, which proposed the settlement of a national Church without bishops. They associated with it the Westminster Confession of 1646, stripped of its disciplinary clauses, signifying that presbyterian doctrine was to be recommended to, but not enforced upon, the clergy. This was all consonant with Monck's religious demands. However, the Covenant contained a promise to defend monarchy, which was not excised, and to drive the point home another MP, Edward Stephens, made a speech commending that institution and was applauded. The House began placing the militia under men noted for their past distaste for a republic. On the 7th some army officers led by Okey responded by drawing up a remonstrance requiring the MPs to declare against King and Lords. They were almost certainly encouraged by the Commonwealthsmen, who now launched a great effort in the House to defeat the bills for the militia and for dissolution.

Monck survived this collision, which had toppled Richard Cromwell, because most of the army was now dispersed across the provinces under unfamiliar officers, while the soldiers closest at hand had been catechised in principles opposite to those with which Canne and Chapman had bombarded the regiments a year before. In these circumstances he could employ successfully the advantages, his personal influence and a party among the colonels, which he shared with Richard but which had not availed the latter. When the officers gathered at St. James's to discuss Okey's remonstrance, he advised against it, seconding an eloquent speech by his brother-in-law Clarges. Their arguments apparently turned upon the point that to put pressure on the House was to delay dissolution and the election of a better representative, and to endanger the supply of pay to the army. Monck did, however, express personal devotion to a republic and set up a conference between officers and MPs, on the evening of the 8th, to remove suspicions. As he did so, Prynne, Annesley and Stephens led a majority of the House in pushing the bills forward over the objections of the Commonwealthsmen. At the conference that evening the soldiers requested measures to protect themselves in the event of a change of regime, such as indemnity for past actions, secure possession of the lands they had gained from the Revolution and their arrears of pay. The MPs, who included Annesley and other men of moderate views, replied that such legislation was far better undertaken by the full Parliament to come, but also did their utmost to soothe the soldiers' fears. This interchange must have had some conciliatory effect, but what decisively crippled Okey's initiative seems to have been the number of his fellow-officers who, from desire for a royalist restoration, a broader foundation for the republic, or the effective payment of their men, declined to support him. The next day Monck ordered most of the military men back to their commands, apparently with success.[81]

Perhaps spurred on by this confrontation, the House completed its work in a week. Five measures provided the tolerant presbyterian Church settlement Monck had wanted.[82] A new set of Triers was empowered to select ministers, consisting of the most celebrated presbyterian clergy with a few 'of the congregational way' who had not supported the Committees of Safety. The Council of State was required to repair the Church in Wales, persuading patrons to fill vacant benefices and restoring clergy ejected after the Revolution, if they seemed worthy. The division of the country into presbyterian *classes* was to proceed, but all existing ministers were confirmed in their livings and separatists were allowed to meet. The latter had to pay tithes, however, and Catholics were to be harried under the existing laws. All this created no controversy, and was probably not very different from what the purged House had intended in January.

It was otherwise with the Militia Act, which was passed on 12 March.

Somebody, suspected to be the Commonwealthsmen, then stopped its progress through the printing press, while some army officers expressed their alarm at the measure to Monck. The latter actually agreed to write to the MPs requesting its suspension, but on the day of dissolution they sent Prynne and two others to ensure immediate publication, and Annesley and two others to allay the general's fears (if indeed his letter had been more than an empty gesture). Both missions were successful, and Monck in turn somehow calmed the officers.[83] The new commissions reflected on the whole the views of some Warwickshire gentry, who informed an MP that their main desire was to have a militia led by men of substance again.[84] The commissioners of six counties now included as many titled men as the act of July 1659 had empowered in the entire country. Control of the provinces had passed to those of their natural rulers who had not fought for the Kings, with some who had, some men who had risen to influence under the Protectorate and a few complete newcomers. The Commonwealthsmen were usually retained in counties where they possessed natural authority, though now outnumbered by gentry of more conservative political opinion. Those who were displaced were the men of lesser social status, soldiers or civilians, who had staffed Interregnum local administration in default of the magnates. Where several important gentry had always continued to serve, as in Devon, the result was a change of emphasis. Where very few had, as in Wales, it was a counter-revolution. Two political checks were placed upon the commissioners: they were required to testify to the justice of the war against Charles I and the sanctity of a professional religious ministry, and the Council was to vet all their officers.[85]

The greatest tension was naturally created by the bill for dissolution. On 9 March Annesley persuaded the House to issue the warrant for the writs for elections with a republican formula, opposing Prynne and Stephens who wanted it done in the King's name. On the 13th, however, the MPs abolished the declaration of fidelity to the Commonwealth required of new members, though they did exclude Catholics and Quakers from voting, and former royalists and their sons, unless clearly repentant, from standing, in the forthcoming hustings. A proposal by the Commonwealthsmen to deprive royalists of the franchise was defeated. The loss of the declaration apparently created another flurry among the army officers, which Monck again somehow argued down. Two days later, the republicans lost another trick, by only seven votes, when it was decided to make the general Steward of Hampton Court and give him £20,000 rather than full ownership of the palace. Rumour was rife that officers would attempt a coup or that the MPs would fail to dissolve, but on the 16th, a day later than proposed, the vital act passed. At the last moment, a proviso was inserted expressing sympathy for the right of the peers who had fought Charles I to sit in their own House, a blow at the Commonwealth's principle of complete sovereignty of the Commons. Monck had been sufficiently sensitive on this point to keep the House of Lords locked and guarded for two weeks. The MPs almost followed this with an even more provocative declaration against the regicide, but this was dropped after an emotional exchange in which Scot, remembering the greatest days of his political life, declared that he wanted his part in the event recorded on his tomb. At this the chamber emptied.[86] The Long Parliament was at an end, nineteen years and four months after it had first met. The previous evening an unknown man had drawn a premature conclusion from events by climbing a ladder outside the Exchange and painting out the inscription *Exit Tyrannus, Regum ultimus*, which had replaced the statue of Charles I at the Revolution. The watching crowd kindled bonfires and drank royalist toasts, and the incident featured as prominently in news-letters as the dissolution itself.[87]

There was much justification for this reaction. Monck had made the achievement which had eluded Oliver Cromwell, of securing the active co-operation of a large proportion of the country's natural leaders. This was the consequence of the fact that he had done what Richard Cromwell could not and his father would not do: he managed the army in the interests of Parliament instead of vice versa. Six times in seven years MPs had failed to satisfy the military and been ordered home, till events provided a general and officers who were capable of sponsoring policies acceptable to the members and ready to do so. On the other hand, despite the efforts of Prynne and Stephens, this House of Commons had operated with greater circumspection than the others. It is easy to see why it alarmed some officers but satisfied others, including Monck. It had worked within the terms of readmission, settling the Church, leaving the legislation of the Revolution intact and dissolving to make way for a full Parliament. Its measures had fulfilled the general's principle of spurning both royalists and radicals. The sort of men qualified for the next Commons were roughly the same as those eligible for the Protectorate's, for that which the General Council almost called in December, and for that almost recruited by the purged Parliament in February. What was now missing was any constitutional check upon them, whether a Protector, Council, Upper House, senate, oath or declaration. Gone also were the military men, religious radicals and middling gentry who had staffed the local commissions for the central government while the Parliaments debated. The only limitation upon the men now invited into central and local power was that they must have sworn support for a professional ministry and for constitutional restraints upon monarchy. This made either the unconditional restoration dreamed of by royalist plotters or the republican oligarchy of the Commonwealthsmen very unlikely. What government would be established depended upon three groups of men: the electorate as a whole, the King and his advisers, and the republicans. One would have to choose, one to negotiate and one to fight.

Charles II and his ministers had spent the winter in their customary uncomfortable fashion, receiving information, laying plots and evading creditors. The news of the October coup had brought the King back to Brussels and Viscount Mordaunt to London, while some of the exiles came up with the idea that Charles should marry Lambert's daughter. Monck they generally took at face value as the purged Parliament's champion, and its return was a heavy blow, compounded for Mordaunt by the personal problem that the English royalists were inclined to blame him for the disaster of August and disinclined to follow him any longer.[88] Nevertheless, another network of local leaders designed to promote the King's interests had been formed by early February, only for the exiles to receive the dreary news that Monck seemed to be crushing the City to secure the Commonwealthsmen in power. Then came in quick succession the almost incredible tidings of the general's change of tactics and of the readmission.[89] There began to dawn upon the exiled royalists the wonderful possibility of a peaceful restoration, and upon the royalist conspirators in England the appalling possibility that this would take place without their aid. Both began to probe gently towards the key men of the decaying republic, attempting to make the personal contacts necessary to purchase their support.

It was soon obvious that the group of men whose loyalty was most easily vouched for would also drive the hardest bargain. These were the surviving leaders of the party in the Long Parliament who had striven to preserve the monarchy in 1648, and so provoked Pride's Purge and the abolition of the House of Lords: the Earls of Northumberland, Manchester, Bedford and Clare, William Pierrepoint, John Crew, Denzil Holles and Sir Harbottle Grimston. The last four all sat upon the new Council of State, and their faction dominated it. Their ideal had remained unaltered for twelve years, of a monarchy strictly bounded and balanced by Parliament, and surrounded by advisers who would defend this settlement. Some of them had hoped to erect it around the Cromwells, but since November 1659 they had been agreed upon the restoration of Charles Stuart, constricted by the terms they had tried to rivet upon his father.[90] Mordaunt gave them the convenient nickname of the 'Presbyterian Knot'.[91]

Some who had been worse enemies made easier conquests. William Lenthall, who had presided over the Commonwealth, came dashing to Lady Mordaunt as soon as the Long Parliament dissolved, avowing unconditional loyalty.[92] St John and Thurloe remained hostile to the Stuarts, and apparently loyal to Richard Cromwell,[93] but his cause was for ever doomed by the loss of its main military man, Edward Mountagu. Mountagu had originally been appointed a General-at-Sea by Oliver Cromwell to check the republican officers in the Fleet. On 2 March the readmitted MPs reappointed him for precisely the same purpose. At this period observers considered him one of the Cromwellian faction, though from his private conversations with his young secretary, Samuel Pepys, he seems to have been reserving his opinions. Their drift became clearer at the time of the dissolution, when he disassociated himself from St. John and became close to the 'Presbyterian Knot', to which he was personally connected through his wife, a daughter of John Crew.[94] In early April, when he was with the Fleet, he received a royalist agent carrying a letter from Charles requesting support. This he acknowledged in writing, with protestations of loyalty, and so, while making no public avowal, linked himself to the King's cause.[95]

The adherence of *politiques* such as Lenthall and Mountagu both testified to the growing likelihood of a restoration and made it yet more likely. This double effect was true with proportionately increased force of the greatest *politique* of all, George Monck. With him, it was not a problem of how contact could be made, for an avenue was clear, but whether he would repond to it. On his march towards London the general had summoned a kinsman from Devon, William Morice, to join him there. Morice was one of the 'secluded' members, had sat in Richard's Parliament and been named by the purged one to a militia commission; he was a gentleman experienced in public affairs but neither prominent nor credited with strong political views. If Monck's chaplain is to be believed, the general was reminded of this cousin's existence by a tract Morice had written against the principle of independent churches. Once in London, he became one of Monck's closest companions and added to the chorus of pleas for the readmission.[96] The two men had another Devon relative of more uncompromising political record, Sir John Grenville, son of a paladin of Charles I who fell in the Great Civil War. Sir John was as devotedly royalist as his father but more cautious, one of those quiet, clever, affable men who rise easily to positions of trust. It was he who had been given the King's letter to Monck the previous summer, and passed it to the general's brother for delivery. Now he undertook to deliver a second royal appeal in person.

By the beginning of March at the latest, it must have been obvious to George Monck that the policy he had initiated was making a royal restoration likely. Before the 10th, when still speaking publicly for a Commonwealth, he was reported to have told a friend privately that he would submit to the next Parliament if it wanted King and Lords.[97] He must have been prepared for this eventuality when he allowed that Parliament to be called under such light qualifications. There is no evidence that he contemplated setting himself up as Protector and, perhaps more important, none that his friends and close supporters considered this. Lambert had designed the Protectorate to permit the country a relatively free Parliament while preserving the existing reforms and making others possible. Monck and his allies were not concerned with reform so much as with achieving a disciplined and united England, and the tendency of events made a royal restoration upon suitable terms the most obvious means to this end. It did, however, present the general with the tactical problem of making a personal bargain with a monarch whose army he had helped to destroy at Dunbar ten years before, and whose adherents he had chased around Scotland since. These considerations must have run through his mind as the Long Parliament moved towards dissolution and Sir John Grenville appeared among the crowd at his receptions in St. James's Palace.

Soon after the Parliament ended, the vital interview took place, arranged by Morice.[98] Alone with Sir John, Monck accepted his letter and commission to treat, together with spectacular verbal promises of high office. To these he replied with the account of his actions accepted by his admirers ever since, that his consistent object had been the King's restoration. A few days later, with the greatest courtesy, he dictated his terms, which were concerned, in contrast to those projected by the 'Presbyterian Knot', with the material requirements of his army rather than constitutional balances. They were simply the demands made by the officers to the MPs at the conference on 8 March: indemnity, arrears, confirmation of titles to former Church and Crown lands and a degree of religious toleration. He added that it would improve the King's reputation if he moved to territory less associated with Catholicism and absolutism than that of Spain. Carrying these messages in his head, Grenville left for Brussels. In his absence, Monck agreed with the 'Presbyterian Knot' upon the desirability of a royal restoration, but refused to support the making of a treaty with Charles before Parliament met, which some of them wished.[99] This was a typically astute political move, for if the Parliament proved republican, or the King tactless, then the general could back safely out of a restoration. At the same time, if the King did return, he would be all the more grateful to Monck for resisting restraints upon his authority. As usual, Monck was preserving the greatest possible space for manœuvre.

Charles and his ministers had naturally been giving thought to the terms that they themselves would offer. The previous September, in a desperate attempt to rally support in the wake of Booth's defeat, they had appealed to the civilian community in general, offering pardon to all but seven regicides, abolition of most taxation and therefore the disbanding of the army, and the repurchase of the Crown lands. As a guarantee against royal absolutism, they promised a free Parliament at once, and the convention of regular successors under the Triennial Act of 1641.[100] Just before Grenville brought Monck's message, they seem to have been considering the reference of any settlement to the new Parliament, upon the perfectly reasonable and cynical grounds that, as it was not called by a King, the terms it made could be renegotiated with a more regular, and tractable, successor. The only reservation was to exclude the regicides from pardon.[101] Then Sir John arrived, and having spent years projecting a restoration involving the defeat and destruction of the English republic's army, the King found himself negotiating with that army. Into this business he admitted only his most intimate advisers, the three men who had been his chief confidants and ministers for nearly a decade: the Chancellor, Hyde, the surviving Secretary of State, Sir Edward Nicholas, and James Butler, Marquis of Ormonde, who had led the royalists of Ireland. All agreed that Monck's point about the royal residence was a good one, and having informed the Spanish that he intended to visit his sister, Charles moved his little court to Breda, in the territory of the impeccably republican and Protestant Dutch. There he and his three advisers debated a means of circumventing Monck's terms, by which they were no more willing to be bound than by others. The solution was to incorporate these in their original plan, by referring the specific problems of indemnity, lands and arrears to the forthcoming Parliament. In one clause only, which unlike the others was devised by one man alone, Sir Edward Hyde, was this rule made ambiguous: religious toleration, probably the most explosive issue, was immediately promised to all peaceful Christians, with the invitation to Parliament to confirm it after 'mature deliberation'. This, then, was the Declaration of Breda, signed on 4 April, copied five times and enclosed in separate letters to Lords, Commons, Army, Fleet and City. With these was wrapped a commission for Monck as Commander-in-Chief and an invitation to him to choose a Secretary of State to complement Nicholas, and a written promise to Grenville of an earldom, court office and a large sum of money in the event of a restoration. Sir John collected the whole package, and crossed back to England quietly on the 8th.[102]

Meanwhile, Monck was preparing the army for another stage in its re-indoctrination. That this was needed is evinced by the addresses sent up by the outlying regiments, in response to the letter from the officers at London of 21 February, which, while accepting the readmission, tended to stress ominously that section of the letter which predicted the strengthening of the Commonwealth. Nor were these units receiving much money even now, for the records of urban corporations refer to loans of the sort they had often made to soldiers to cover gaps in pay.[103] To manage these men, the general's prime weapon remained the replacement of individual commanders, a steady process of attrition. The hapless Okey was rewarded for his trust in Monck's earlier protestations by being deprived of his commission before 28 March and replaced with Edward Rossiter, who had conspired to rise with Booth. A detachment of the new militia supervised the transfer of power, in case of resistance. Hesilrige was left in formal possession of his horse regiment, but this was effectively put into the hands of a new lieutenant-colonel. Not all disaffection was uncovered among the soldiers in the provinces, for twenty-three of Monck's own guards were cashiered.[104] As a balance, however, Colonels Alured, Thomas Saunders and John Streater, who had been stripped of their commissions by Oliver Cromwell for their fidelity to a Commonwealth and only returned to power with the purged Parliament, now showed a surprising acquiescence in the trend of affairs. So did Hacker, who had been identified with Hesilrige's set in the previous twelve months. None of these men left memoirs or diaries. Had they done so, candidly, much of the history of the Interregnum might have been written around them.

The government's attempts to preserve control of the troops were made in the face of an increasingly desperate republican resistance, embodied in agitators who moved among the soldiers and the tracts which they dispersed. Their case was stark enough, that a royal restoration was becoming possible and that this would mean the end of the army and of all the achievements for which it had fought.[105] Against them, the Council of State hurled itself with all the fury which Richard Cromwell's government through caution or over-confidence, had not shown. On 24 March it offered a reward for information leading to their apprehension, while Monck put one of his trusted colonels, Knight, at the head of a flying party of horse instructed to tour billets in search of them. Soon five were in custody. Nedham was dismissed and all the official newspapers put in the reliable hands of Dury and Muddiman, and Chapman, the great republican publisher, was arrested.[106] A series of tracts was printed for the troops, denouncing the attempts to suborn them, and Monck circulated an appeal to stand with him for the nation's privileges and liberties.[107] To assuage their material needs, the Council coaxed a further loan from the City corporation.[108] By the last week of March, Monck and his intimates were bold, or anxious, enough to apply a test to the whole army of England, an engagement subscribed by every officer to eschew meetings and to submit to whatever the forthcoming Parliament might decide. It was discussed first with Clarges, Annesley, Cooper, Howard and Knight, and subscribed by the regiments of the last two officers and of Monck himself. Copies were next dispersed to the other units around London and to the general's trusted colonels in Yorkshire. On 9 April, signed by all the officers of these, it was formally presented to Monck at St. James's and copied to the regiments scattered through the provinces.[109]

Beside all this, Mountagu's taming of the navy was an inconspicuous affair. This was partly because of the relatively small number of men involved, and partly because the role of the sailors was generally muted, their intervention in December being exceptional. But the key factor was that, against all expectation, Vice-Admiral Lawson proved as responsive to the government as Alured and Hacker, and for reasons as mysterious. He welcomed Mountagu to his fleet on 23 March, and when some captains murmured against Monck's actions six days later, both commanders rebuked and dispersed them. In mid-April, Lawson was rewarded with a new commission from the Council and a letter from the King. This left the obdurate republicans leaderless, and Mountagu dealt with them individually. It was a gentle process, some captains being called before the Council for examination and one sent off on convoy duty. No actual dismissals are recorded. For all this, the operation was important and effective. If warships blockaded the Thames now, it would not be for the Commonwealth.[110]

At the same time, the Council was working against civilian opponents. The day after the dissolution, it ordered all disbanded soldiers and old royalists out of the City and outlawed all political meetings, save the elections.[111] In the next fortnight, it worked hard to pass the new militia officers, and searched the houses of London sectaries again. It called Hesilrige, Scot, Barebone, Desborough and other republicans before it to sign an engagement to keep the peace, and sent Berry, who apparently refused, to prison. Hyde's agents were, by contrast, allowed to move freely, one being examined and released on a promise to behave with discretion.[112] The domestic royalists, however, did provoke concern both in the Council and the exiled court, for as the hopes of the more foolish rose, so did their tempers, manifested in threats of vengeance against their late persecutors. Monck summed up this situation in one of his neat phrases, by commenting that he had fanatics on one side and 'frantics' on the other.[113] The corporation of Yarmouth, believing that civilians were gaining control of the military, threatened the garrison for going about its duties.[114] The Council wrote to individual militia commissioners, reminding them not to appoint old royalists to their forces, and were apparently heeded, but in South Wales the former parliamentarians themselves behaved so high-handedly towards suspected republicans that the government disbanded them.[115] The greatest 'frantic' of all turned out to be a chaplain of the late King, Matthew Griffiths, who, propelled by blind loyalty or misplaced opportunism, preached a sermon in Mercers' Chapel, London, which defended the absolute power of kings and predicted punishment for those who had opposed Charles I. He then had this printed with a political tract on the same lines and dedicated both to Monck. The little book sold five hundred copies in a day, and its author was rewarded by being locked up on the Council's orders, together with another royalist divine who had preached in similar terms.[116] The exiles were if anything even more furious with him, and begged their supporters not merely to be passive but to make conciliatory gestures.[117] These were being undertaken before the royal warnings arrived, in the form of declarations by men who had supported Charles I in eight counties and the London area, promising to submit to the decisions of the new Parliament and forswearing any revenge upon old enemies. The impressive number of nobles and gentry who subscribed to these must have done much to counteract the effect produced by the two clergymen.[118]

Royalist propaganda in general continued in the same volume as before, but with a changing emphasis. The abuse of radicals remained constant, but the more positive literature adapted to cope with the increasing likelihood of a restoration and the challenge presented by *Newes from Brussels*. Arguments for monarchy were partially replaced by assertions of the mild intentions and pleasing personality of this monarch, a genre which achieved its masterpiece at the hands of Sir Samuel Tuke in late April. Readers of Tuke learned that Charles II was handsome, graceful, serious, learned, shrewd, just, brave, generous and (here a barely perceptible qualification) had been of good morals for some time.[119] To all this the republicans, apparently sensing the popular mood, attempted little reply: they concentrated upon provoking the army to mutiny. The exception was Milton, who, unwilling or unable to the end to notice how little a part reason had played in the whole course of the Great Rebellion, published two more apologies for the Commonwealth.[120]

The opinion of the country was revealed by the elections.[121] That for the City itself may stand as typical: from a field of up to forty candidates, the four who were most clearly royalist took the seats without a division. They included Aldermen John Robinson, who had concealed Mordaunt during the winter, and Richard Browne, a 'secluded' member who had conspired to rise with Booth and returned to the House after the readmission with a beard grown long in months of hiding. Booth himself was returned for Cheshire with a fellow-rebel, and Myddleton for Denbighshire. Massey ignored Monck's instructions to him to lie low, and was elected at Gloucester after a riot when the garrison tried to arrest him and the citizens came to his rescue. Men associated with the taming of the armed forces were generally successful: Monck and Mountagu were both elected in two places, and Howard, Rossiter, Ingoldsby, Clobery, Knight and Clarges got in. So did Monck's other associates Morice and Broghill, and most of the men who had led the agitation for this free Parliament. In addition, the qualifications for members were widely and spontaneously ignored, and at least sixty-one were either wartime royalists or their sons, only a few of whom could be said to have shown any active loyalty to subsequent regimes. Strikingly, these captured over a quarter of the prestigious and heavily-contested county seats. A common attitude to their position may be represented by a letter to one of them in Somerset from another gentleman, informing him that his candidature was illegal, but would have to be accepted if the community ardently desired it. They did, and he was elected for the county, causing the republican Whetham to write despairingly to Monck offering to recognise him as Protector if he would only prevent a restoration. The republicans themselves fared atrociously. Two hundred gentry rode into Leicester, one of Hesilrige's former seats, and told the corporation that they would spend no more money there if Sir Arthur were elected. He seems, however, not even to have stood, and the same is true of Vane and most of the former military leaders. Lambert, from prison, did try for a borough but was defeated. Luke Robinson, Ludlow and Scot were elected for towns where they possessed personal influence, but the last two results were challenged by opponents who expected the new House to overturn the decisions. Lenthall, despite his own pliability and Monck's support, was not forgiven for his position as the head of the purged Parliament and failed to enter the new one. Cooper and Morley, two leaders of the 'moderates' in that House, were successful, but St. John and others of that faction who had opposed the drift towards restoration were not. The leaders of the 'secluded' members were re-elected, but when they were opposed by men of less qualified royalism, as happened to Grimston in Essex, they lost and had to stand again elsewhere. The crowd at the Surrey election shouted 'No Rumpers, no Presbyterians that will put bad conditions on the King', and the great majority of returns faithfully reflected this sentiment.

None the less, when describing any general election before modern times, there is a danger of exaggerating the importance of national issues. Although contemporaries certainly considered that this one was fiercely fought, more evidence of individual results ought to have survived if contests were the rule. It is likely that the majority of seats were taken without a poll. Nor were contests, of course, invariably concerned with ideology: the Mountagus and the Bernards struggled for Huntingdon as usual, and gentry of similar political views collided like billiard balls all over Yorkshire in the effort to settle into a seat. As in the case of the Militia Act, a separate issue of 'natural leadership' was embroiled with the one of form of government. It is notable that Kent and its boroughs, so often in the past a refuge of servants of the central regime, now returned a set of local worthies. Mountagu, the only exception, was elected at Dover because the corporation wanted to employ his influence to regain a sum owed to it by the navy. Nor did the electors always approach their duty in the manner of arbiters of their country's destiny: a traveller in the Severn valley found borough after borough merrily drunk upon the candidates' entertainment. Although the new House was socially more substantial than Richard Cromwell's, nearly half of it were still men who had sat in no previous Parliament, and most of it is difficult to categorise in terms of a previous political record.

Having said all this, the fact remains that contemporaries agreed that the election as a whole was fought over the issue of monarchy, and decided it. The new House simply did not look like those elected under the Protectorate, upon similar qualifications: the Commonwealthsmen and Cromwell's army officers were gone, and in their place were royalists and their sons. Contemporaries were also unanimous in believing that the new men were royalist in sentiment, and this proved correct. The records leave a strong impression that boroughs which normally passed tranquilly through elections were now contested, such as remote Haverfordwest where the 'fanatics' worked hard for their candidate. After the reservations have been made, it does seem that unlike those of the Protectorate Parliaments but like that of the Long, the election of the Convention Parliament of 1660 was in a real sense dominated by national affairs. What remains archaic about it is the lack of even rudimentary party organisation of the sort which the Commonwealthsmen had put together for Richard's Parliament and which Cooper was to develop to a more than rudimentary degree for the Exclusion Parliaments twenty years later. This did not mean that the mood of the nation was any less effectively expressed. In April 1660 England was a democracy.

When the ten regiments gave Monck their declaration of submission to the people's will, there seemed to be no longer any danger to that will. Across the land and around its coasts, the general and his allies had spun a web in which the republicans were held fast. Any agitation of a strand would bring immediate destruction upon them. Their leaders had been driven from the government and the officer corps of the armed forces, and were losing any hope of a party in the legislature. They had failed to rouse the soldiers in the provinces, and a hostile army was concentrated around Monck at the capital. The new militia was now arrayed against them and would be reinforced in a crisis by gentry volunteers. Such was the prospect on 9 April. The following night, Lambert slid down a rope into a boat on the Thames, and the web broke.

John Lambert had clearly lost none of his force of character, for it seems that he had persuaded the maid who tended his chamber in the Tower to don his nightcap, sleep in his bed and so prevent any alarm until morning. It was also a sign of how much some republicans valued him that they had contrived his escape,[122] and of how the government feared him that it reacted with frantic energy. The Council offered £100 for his apprehension, and informed the army that payment of its arrears was only a matter of time. Presumably because of the City's new loan, money was getting through at least to favoured units in good quantity, and it was possible to disband Mills's regiment, which had been noted for loyalty to the purged Parliament, with arrears satisfied in full.[123] Monck issued another appeal to the army, and instructed his favourite colonels to tender the declaration of 9 April to their common soldiers, calling them together without informing them of the reason in advance and discharging any who refused to sign. He disbanded not only Mills's men, but also the garrison of St. Michael's Mount which had been governed by a noted local radical. The Tower was filled with the general's own regiment, and his soldiers or the militia searched the houses of religious separatists again in London and the provinces and secured various former military and civilian supporters of the Commonwealth. In Caernarfonshire the new militia commission neatly expressed the change of regime by arresting the old one.[124] On about the 18th, the government received intelligence that Lambert was about to gather forces in the Midlands. The Council accordingly warned the local governors, while Monck sent Streater to hold Coventry and Ingoldsby, Howard and Rossiter to scour the region with mobile forces, and ordered the remainder of the army around the capital to muster.[125]

These measures, and those of March, were rewarded to the extent that the former republican leaders remained remarkably quiet. Hesilrige seemed shattered by the defeats of early March. All his fire had gone, and after a period in which he received friends with his head in his hands, repeating that they were ruined, he went home to the country. Monck promised him life and fortune if he kept the peace and (here a curious dour jest) gave the general two pence, and Sir Arthur trusted this.[126] There is no trace of any more activity from Scot, Vane, Fleetwood, Desborough, Ashfield and most of the former army leaders. Whalley and Goffe, Richard's old supporters, refused to follow Ingoldsby and Mountagu into royalism but tamely promised to attend the Council when Lambert escaped.[127] Only Ludlow, Okey and three other former colonels seem to have been prepared to support the latter. Presumably some of their former comrades had been demoralised like Hesilrige, or were too painfully aware of the government's strength and its particular interest in them. But there is also the suspicion that some, like Lawson and Alured, were becoming reconciled to the prospect of restoration itself. Nicholas Lechmere had been a high civilian servant of the Protectorate, and had fallen with it. In March 1660 he contacted Mordaunt, whom he had helped to acquit at his trial in 1658, to ask for a pardon if the King returned. This was all practical enough, but it is interesting to note that his diary acquired thereafter a fervently royalist tone, as though he was trying to brainwash himself into his new allegiance.[128] At a slightly humbler level, Pepys noted on 19 March that the secretary to the Admiralty Commission spoke against a restoration, but by 4 April was remarking that Charles II was said to be an admirable man.[129] A particularly amazing, and perhaps disgusting, case is that of John Canne. For nearly thirty years this individual had written, printed and preached for the cause of radical reform, and endured prison and exile for it. Yet now he launched two fresh newspapers, which supported the government as firmly as the official press.[130]

When all this is considered, it is striking, and significant, how much active opposition to the government Lambert's escape actually did let loose. Soldiers from at least six horse regiments, scattered around the Midlands and Yorkshire, rode off to join him. One major reported to Monck with embarrassment that he had sent out a troop to find him, only to hear that it had defected as soon as it did so. The infantry lacked the mobility to do this, and had always been less politically active, but disaffection appeared in the garrisons of York and Hull; the 'fanatics' in Warwick Castle shut out Monck's governor and those of Red Castle, Montgomeryshire, declared for Lambert. Agitators reappeared in many units, and numerous soldiers refused the declaration of submission to Parliament, and were dismissed. Risings by civilian republicans occurred in Somerset, Nottinghamshire and Leicestershire, and were said to have been prevented in five more counties. Some of these may have been mere rumour, but it is noteworthy that nobody reported a plot in Wiltshire, where Ludlow was busy preparing a rebellion and suborning the militia. Most of this resistance was the work of relatively unimportant men. The most serious rising was the Nottinghamshire one, which left the government's supporters afraid to do more than hold the county town. At its head was Nicholas Lockyer, one of the original 'agitators' of 1647, who had resurfaced in March among the men arrested for suborning soldiers. Released on parole, he broke this when Lambert escaped, to entice away troopers from his old regiment at Nottingham, and it was this stiffening of regulars which made the local insurrection so formidable. Lack of information may well conceal other examples of radical continuity among second rank leaders. The civilian rebels were described as sectaries, but possess the usual obscurity of provincial republicans. It was said that Quakers had sold whole estates to equip the rebellion, but there is no local evidence for this.[131] Taken as a whole, and set in its unpropitious context, the scale of resistance was considerable enough to reinforce two points made before: the ingrained republicanism of the old army of England and the existence of a sizeable minority of dedicated local supporters upon whom a permanent Commonwealth might have been based.

Lambert's plan was to hold a muster in the centre of England on Easter Day, the 22nd, and to move down to Oxford to link up with rebels from the south and west. For the initial rendezvous he showed his usual vivid imagination and chose Edgehill, where the first battle of the civil wars, and of the Good Old Cause, had been fought nearly eighteen years before. The idea had the usual flaw of nation-wide conspiracies, that to publicise it widely enough to gain many adherents inevitably meant warning the government. So it fell out. On that Easter morning at Edgehill, Lambert and Okey met a few hundred men, but before more could arrive Ingoldsby and Streater were upon them. The former had fewer regular soldiers, though a reinforcement of armed civilians, and decided to parley. What they offered was the restoration of Richard Cromwell. It was exactly a year since Richard had fallen, bringing down Ingoldsby and raising his present opponents, and the irony was obvious. From Ingoldsby it provoked only derision and the order to attack, whereupon Lambert's tiny army defected or fled. The great soldier's unvarying sense of style now finally undid him, for he was mounted on a splendid Arab horse better suited to a race-track than ploughed fields. As he floundered in one of these, Ingoldsby came up with pistol drawn, on a humbler and sturdier mount, and offered him death or surrender. After pathetic appeals for freedom, Lambert yielded. The following day he was brought into London, exposed to the catcalls of the militia and the additional humiliation of being forced to stand beneath the Tyburn gallows. Then the Tower closed around him once more.

The magic of his name was demonstrated afresh by the speed with which the risings now collapsed. Ludlow called off that in Wiltshire. The troopers making for Edgehill either shambled back to their units in hope of pardon or were hunted down with the civilian rebels. Warwick Castle seems to have capitulated immediately, and Red Castle was reduced by a party under Thomas Pury, son of another former stalwart of the Commonwealth. The whole episode had provided Monck with another purge of the army, which he followed up by dismissing Alured and Hacker, although they had remained faithful, simply because their men had not. Hesilrige, whose son had been out with Lambert, anticipated the inevitable command by resigning his now worthless commissions. His horse regiment was given to Fauconberg. Mountagu inherited Alured's.[132] The moral of Lambert's Last Stand was clear: the republic was over, because men like Ingoldsby, who had signed away the old King's life, Monck, who had destroyed the present King's soldiers, Pury, whose father had voted for a Commonwealth, and Streater, who had printed defences of one, were now determined to end it.

The obsequies commenced with the gathering of the Convention Parliament on 25 April. It was likely to determine the fate of three nations, for Scotland was still entirely passive and although the leaders in Ireland had convened a national assembly, this waited upon English events.[133] At the readmission in February, Monck had requested that the new Parliament be elected according to the reforms of 1654, another gesture of continuity with the republic. This had been ignored, and in the tense days before the dissolution he did not press the point. As a result the Convention was even more an imperial body, for it included no representatives from the other realms, although the executive in London retained absolute control of Scotland and nominal mastery of Ireland. For this crucial meeting, the 'Presbyterian Knot' made great preparations. In early April they leafed through draft treaties from the 1640s to compile a set of terms for a limited monarchy. The former Cromwellian Thurloe and the maverick Cooper were won over to this plan. To manage Parliament, despite the strongly royalist propensities of the many MPs who had either fought for or did not remember Charles I, they resolved to control the Speaker of the Commons, expel MPs who contravened prescribed qualifications, and confine membership of the Lords to their own party. For these tactics they appeared to have obtained the co-operation of Monck. It was a formidable programme, contrived by experienced politicians, but the royalists had detailed warning of it from Annesley, who deftly won favour with the King by spying upon his colleagues.[134]

On the 15th the 'Presbyterian' plan went into action. They reached the House of Commons swiftly, and elected Grimston as Speaker as soon as it was quorate. At the same time the peers of this party occupied the Lords, made Manchester their Speaker, resolved to admit a total of sixteen men of compatible views, and sent a formal message to the other House. There Luke Robinson challenged their right to sit, but Heneage Finch, one of the new men, spoke of the need to heal the nation and was acclaimed, and the Lords recognised. The 'Presbyterian Knot' were now entrenched according to plan, and would have to be defeated if the old and new royalists were to have much share in the Restoration Settlement. The weapon selected for this purpose, apparently by Mordaunt, consisted of the young lords, who had come of age during the Interregnum, had a hereditary right to enter the House, and although not tainted by wartime royalism were expected, like the young MPs, to be royalist in sympathy. To keep them, or anybody else, out, the 'Presbyterian' lords depended on Monck's soldiers. The general's response was characteristic: to warn the young lords away for two days, and to observe the mood of the Commons in this interval. Their opinion was made plain on the 26th, when they discussed the danger that the existing Lords would jeopardise a restoration and were reassured by the argument that the young peers, once admitted, would not. That evening the general informed the latter that they could sit the following day, and so they did, swamping the 'Presbyterians'. By that day it was becoming obvious that the majority of the Lower House had no intention of challenging the rights of its royalist members and Monck was not going to prompt them. The 'Presbyterian Knot' felt as deep a sense of betrayal by him as the Commonwealthsmen had done, and to as little effect. The likelihood of a restoration with constitutional limitations was gone.[135]

One of the various extraordinary features of the Convention was that, alone of English Parliaments, it had opened without any sort of pep talk from the government. Monck was the obvious man to give one, but his whole strategy was based upon following, and not directing, the MPs' opinions. These were made absolutely clear on the 27th, when a man petitioned for the post of serjeant-at-arms. Instantly Finch was on his feet, holding that the office could not be disposed of by an incomplete Parliament, lacking a King, and thus released a volley of loyal speeches. The House resolved to adjourn for three days to permit due reflection and, as observers surmised, to await a move from Charles. Indeed, the 'speech from the throne' to launch the Sessions was at hand, in the Declaration of Breda, and on the 29th Sir John Grenville formally presented it to the Council. Both Speakers were primed to receive their copies, and letters, and when the Houses reassembled on May Day, Grenville delivered them to be read. In the Commons, Morice and Finch led a chorus of gratitude and the MPs prepared to confer with the Lords. The latter were soon ready with a declaration that, according to 'fundamental laws', the English government was by King, Lords and Commons, and with this the Lower House voted agreement.[136] All the questions of settlement, compensation and vengeance remained, together with the long-term policies these would engender. But one thing was decided in that moment: the republic was gone.

5

Conclusions

༄

AT the close of his pioneering study of the period 1658-60, Godfrey Davies suggested six main reasons for the Restoration: the constant unpopularity of the army and of godly reform, the divisions of the republican leaders, the waning of ideological fervour among the soldiers, the lack of interest of the reformers in social evils, the corruption of 'Puritanism' by power, and the death of Cromwell who alone had sustained the Interregnum for so long. As the preceding chapter has reworked and supplemented the sources upon which that book was based, it seems fitting to reconsider its conclusions in turn.

The first, the unpopularity of the republican regimes, must survive any revisionary study. The direct cause of the Restoration was that the enfranchised public mandated a Parliament to produce one, after fierce agitation against the existing regime. The point can, indeed, be extended, in that the origins of this agitation lay among the ordinary citizens of London and that this can be cited as one of the various points in English history at which plebeians played a significant independent part in politics. To push it still further, and remember that apprentices launched the London campaign and the riots in other towns, it seems justified to represent the movement as a genuine case, before the present day, of an intervention by youth in national affairs. Three riders, however, must be attached to these considerations. The first is a commonplace, that active disaffection for a republic only became widespread when it was demonstrated that Cromwells could not replace Stuarts at the head of a revived traditional order, and when the republicans divided. Second, it is perhaps a little artificial to isolate this as an example of political action by commoners. Ordinary men, after all, filled the army and determined the fate of governments when they chose to listen to one set of officers rather than another. They also produced the Quaker movement, attended the gathered churches and comprised the mobs which attacked religious radicals. Obscure figures precipitated the fall of the republic, and also led much of the last attempt to save it. Third, the theme of the loss of youth to the Good Old Cause is a major one which extends beyond the apprentices to Henry Cromwell, Mordaunt, and the young MPs and peers who determined the course of the Convention. The vital ten years which lay between these men and even those in their late thirties, like Fleetwood and Ludlow, would represent the difference between those who had known (or imagined) the threat of royal tyranny and those who knew only the chaos of war, the confusion of the Interregnum Church and the rule of Cromwell's army. It is a concept which explains much, but should not be made absolute. After all, early Quaker leaders were generally young men and, like the royal-ist conspirators, younger sons.[1] Dissatisfaction with Interregnum politics and society did not necessarily drive youths to be reactionaries.

Against all this must be set the main argument of the present chapter, that public opinion only mattered because it was permitted to do so. The English radicals in 1647-8, or the French in 1793, or the Russian in periods between 1918 and 1941, were equally unpopular. The army produced the English republic, maintained it, and eventually destroyed it because its leaders decided to let the civilians have their way instead of repressing them as usual. The vicar of St. Lawrence at South Walsham, Norfolk, had his priorities correct when he greeted the Restoration by writing 'Blessed be God and General George Munke' among his lists of baptisms. If there was a moment at which the republic became doomed, it was when the purged Parliament invited Monck's army to London. But this raises the question of how a man of Monck's views was in a position to intervene so decisively in English affairs, and the answer is because Oliver Cromwell put him there. Far from keeping closed natural divisions in the army which gaped open at his death, Cromwell created division by his consistent policy of promoting men of dif-ferent political and religious instincts simply on the strength of their rela-tionship to himself. He ensured that power became concentrated in a network of relatives and favourites which only he held together. The restored Commonwealth spared only Monck of all his more 'reactionary' clients, and that single omission proved fatal. To this important extent the Restoration did not happen because Cromwell had died, but because he had lived.

This in turn, however, draws attention to the great complementary issue, that Monck only gained his opportunity because of the divisions of the leaders in England. A powerful case could be made for the fall of the republic as a tragedy of errors: Richard had to please Parliament to pay the army, but the former inevitably provoked the latter to mutiny; the junior officers forced their commanders to accept the purged Parliament on the strength of promises made by republican propagandists; the majority of that Parliament were never inclined to keep those promises, and provoked the army to another mutiny; Monck's stand drew off the army's natural leader and so paralysed his government till its enemies took heart and its supporters lost it; Monck then took over, and came to consider the Commonwealth not worth saving. By this reading, a republican settlement was never achieved because there was always an emergency going on to distract attention.

What is incomplete about such a portrait is that it underplays the clash of ideology which runs through all the events. The Revolution was partly the vengeance of a victorious and battle-maddened army, and partly political action carried out by religious separatists to guarantee their survival. This interpenetrating alliance of soldiers and sectary in defence of the republic remained, as has been seen, valid till the end. Most of the divisions between republican leaders, and between the republic and the majority of its subjects, were based upon a conflict of saints and non-saints, between men whose first instinct was for a personal union with God and men whose first instinct was for the preservation of an orderly society. This separated the factions at Richard's court. It divided Vane from Hesilrige, Lambert's supporters from Monck, and a regicide like Ludlow from one like Ingoldsby. It was the leaven of saints that kept the republic buoyant: it sank as soon as they were removed from power. This interpretation is not, of course, flawless. Whalley and Goffe attended gathered churches but supported Richard (though not, like the rest of his faction, the Restoration). Lambert was apparently irreligious but a patron of the religious (unless he was, as some have thought, a secret Catholic). The flexibility of Lawson and Canne poses further questions, but the generalisation still has more merit than most.

The problem with it as it stands is that it tends to portray the later republic as a static entity, the separatists struggling to retain their freedom against the conservatives. In fact it was a centrifuge, the forces of reaction being opposed, and inflamed, by a drive towards further reform. The radical pamphleteering of 1659 showed as much vigour as that ten years before, and possessed in the Quaker movement a base which the earlier reformers had apparently lacked, covering almost all the country and representing both town and countryside. The junior officers showed strong support for it. The resources for a second English Revolution were present.

The crucial thing, of course, is that the republic's leaders chose instead to cling to a contracting middle ground, by attempting no more than a defence of earlier achievements. In part this was a caution born of insecurity, as they faced the challenges of Booth and then Monck. In part it was a personal hardening of arteries: in 1643-5, Cromwell and Ireton had opposed their senior officers to obtain a more vigorous war effort and a measure of toleration, in 1648-9 they found themselves damping down the reforming enthusiasm of their junior officers and in 1659 the latter, now the commanders, were restraining their subordinates in turn. But it was also a reflection of the disintegration of 'Puritanism', not corrupted by power but torn apart by the forces noted above. The saints of the 1640s had been overtaken on the road to the new Jerusalem, by the Quakers. There is an air of limpness, of intangibility, about many of the republicans of 1659 in comparison with their earlier selves. The fervour and determination of their words and deeds in the previous period is now breathed by the Quaker tracts. There are various moments which can claim the title of the Thermidor of the English Revolution, but in the ideological context Naylor's Case may stand out as the one. There is something a little absurd about the picture of Vane, one of the few leaders to embrace the cause of further reform, berating a Quaker for wearing his hat before a committee, but it also has a tragic significance. The later republicans were men who had suffered the demoralising experience of being taken in the rear by a fresh enemy equipped with their own weapons.

Under such pressure, which squeezed much of the spirit from their cause, they were left with the substance, the institutions they had created. The Commonwealthsmen believed that all would somehow be well if the country were controlled by a sovereign House of republicans. The officers believed the same of the army. The result was that their preoccupations tended to reduce to the single one of retaining and perpetuating power. The purged Parliament never showed great interest in further reform, and the one issue which united it was its own survival. The army had been the force behind the existing reforms, and its junior officers wanted more, but its commanders' petitions to Protector or Parliament were concerned primarily with the material needs and political influence of the soldiers. From this perspective it is no coincidence that so much of the history of the later republic revolves around Lambert, the breaker of foes, darling of soldiers, maker of constitutions: the man of power personified. Nor, that it was ended by Monck, who strove for something more. Yet even in its caretaker role, the republic could still inspire defenders. It did not die naturally, but was murdered with great skill and effort.

Finally, it may be said that the radicals of seventeenth-century England worked within the context of a very successful society. Secular reform was directed to improving the system in detail rather than altering it in essentials: when a Quaker could complain of a magistrate that he had arrested him under a defective warrant, an October Revolution was not very likely. Perhaps this was a failure of imagination, but a society which possessed Parliaments, poor laws and juries, in which the government attacked depopulating enclosures and the magistrates pursued grain hoarders, where the rich and titled were (in theory) taxed more heavily, was not, for its age, that bad. This sentiment could operate against republican governments, as is illustrated by the addition of their leaders to representative assemblies and civilian rule, which contradicted the realities of their position. But it was also a source of strength, for the same instinct kept many Englishmen paying taxes and turning for justice to even an unpopular regime. The thousands who lay in the mass graves at Edgehill, Marston Moor and Newbury were there because the government had ordered them to kill each other.

PART THREE

THE RESTORATION SETTLEMENTS[1]

⟨◦ᵂᵂᵂ◦⟩

For over a century, the term 'Restoration Settlement' has been used to denote the legislation of 1660-2. Yet it is a misnomer, for there were two settlements in these years, of different character and produced by different groups of men working in different circumstances. In this section each will be treated measure by measure, returning to a chronological progression only when recounting the passage from one settlement to the next.

I

The First Settlement

Almost a month elapsed between the King's legal restoration and his arrival in London. On 8 May, he was proclaimed there; on the 23rd he and his court embarked on Mountagu's flagship, and two days later he stepped ashore at Dover and embraced Monck. On the 29th he entered London in a gorgeous procession of soldiers, militiamen and gentry. The citizens found themselves cheering a tall young man with glossy dark hair and a thin moustache, tired almost beyond speaking.[2] By this moment, the first Restoration Settlement had been three weeks in the making, propelled by fear.

Little of this anxiety was inspired by the republicans. It was true that local representatives of the fallen regime sometimes menaced people celebrating the Restoration, that the garrison of Deal Castle did the same and that murmurings were still reported in some regiments.[3] The events of April, however, had revealed the government's strength, and the army was now well paid, as on 2 May the City corporation, for once, offered twice the loan requested of it.[4] During May the isolation of the republicans was further illustrated by the intensity of popular rejoicing. Churchwardens' accounts almost invariably record the ringing of bells at the King's return, and contemporary observers concur upon the fervour of celebration in both town and country. When Clarges passed through Deal carrying the army's compliments to Charles, the townspeople strewed herbs before him. London was in festival for three days after the royal entry, while the corporation of

Norwich had to halt the merry-making after the proclamation when it had continued undiminished for nearly a week. Melton Mowbray kept its bonfires burning for seventy-two hours, while Oxford appeared 'perfectly mad'.[5] Maypoles, prohibited by the Long Parliament, featured prominently in the festivities, a reminder that the reforms of the 1640s had been an attack upon the traditional culture of many commoners as well as a catalyst for the radical notions of others. That culture was now being restored with the old political system, and the joy of the experience left indelible impressions upon the English folk-memory. At Castleton, Derbyshire, a man dressed as Charles II still rides through the streets every 29th of May, leading a flower-bearing procession. At Aston-on-Clun, Shropshire, a tree is decorated with flags, while the villagers of Wishford Magna, Wiltshire, parade with oak branches. Within living memory Oxfordshire schoolboys were thrashed with nettles if they did not wear an oak apple on this day, to commemorate the tree in which Charles hid in 1651. No English political event other than the arrest of Guy Fawkes has inspired such enduring enthusiasm as the Stuart Restoration.

It was precisely this hysterical excitement which was worrying the government. The drunken misbehaviour consequent upon the celebration became the subject of two successive proclamations. In many places, men denied the authority of local officers on the grounds that they had not been appointed by a king. Commoners despoiled former Crown lands of timber, either pretending royal authority to do so or insisting that until the King resumed ownership these estates were open to all. The villagers of Enfield destroyed the enclosures of the Chase once more. Goods were frequently seized on the pretence that they had been taken from royal palaces.[6] Ministers intruded into the livings of ejected clergy suffered abuse and assault, while meetings of gathered churches were harassed in London, Gloucestershire, Carmarthenshire and Lincolnshire.[7] Quakers were attacked in fifteen counties during May and early June,[8] while, as in the previous summer, mobbings of religious radicals were accompanied by a marked increase in prosecutions for witchcraft.[9] A swift legal settlement to accompany the King's return must have appeared the only alternative to near-anarchy.

On his arrival, Charles's duty was to form an administration which would assist the work of settlement and enforce its provisions. In theory, his freedom of choice was absolute. During May the 'Presbyterian Knot' had attempted to obtain some parliamentary control over the men who served the King, to compensate for the failure of its plans for limitation of royal power. To this end, Parliament was persuaded to invest Hyde's office of Lord Chancellor in a commission led by the Earl of Manchester, while Sir Walter Earle proposed to the Commons that the two Houses choose all the royal ministers. The project, like that for wider constitutional checks, foundered upon the royalist sentiment of the Convention Parliament and the defection of men initially associated with Manchester's group. Charles made his support for Hyde clear, and Annesley took up Sir Edward's cause, joined by Howard and by Cooper, who suddenly informed the King that he had been a secret royalist for six years and was an admirer of the Chancellor.[10] In practice, also, Charles had a wide field from which to select advisers. The Council and armed forces were still controlled by men who had fought against him and his father, while the Commons, as has been said, consisted mainly of men associated with neither of the two wartime parties. In late May the Lords agreed to extend the principle of restoration to Charles's old followers, and invited back those members of the 1642 House who had been royalist during the Great Civil War. Together with the sons of royalist peers, they comprised a majority.[11] At the King's arrival, therefore, executive and legislature were divided neatly between the wartime parties and neutral or new men.

Charles took the obvious step, and appointed a mixed Privy Council of sixteen royalists (including Hyde, Nicholas and Ormonde), four former supporters of Cromwell (Monck, Mountagu, Cooper and Howard), and eight men who had been wartime parliamentarians but opposed subsequent regimes (including Annesley, Morice, Holles and the Earl of Northumberland).[12] Likewise, the great ministerial and household offices were divided between eight royalists, five of their old enemies, and one newcomer, Finch. Hyde and Nicholas retained their old posts as Lord Chancellor and Secretary of State, while Morice became the other Secretary on Monck's nomination. Monck was made Captain-General of the army, Master of Horse and Lord Lieutenant of Ireland. Lord Robartes, of the 'Presbyterian Knot', became his Lord Deputy, and Lord Privy Seal. Ormonde, resigning Ireland to them, was made Lord Steward, with Northumberland as Lord High Constable. Manchester was Lord Chamberlain to balance a royalist Lord Great Chamberlain. Montagu became Master of the Wardrobe, and Vice-Admiral to the King's brother James, Duke of York, who took control of the navy. Finch was made Solicitor-General, and a royalist lawyer, Geoffrey Palmer, Attorney-General. The financial offices were at first put in commission, but after ten months one of Charles I's wartime Councillors, the Earl of Southampton, was made Lord Treasurer. The subordinate post of Chancellor of the Exchequer was offered to a wartime parliamentarian, Crew, but on his refusal passed to Cooper, who despite his republican past happened to be Southampton's son-in-law.[13]

It was a government which not only symbolised the reunion of the nation but mixed social prestige with natural ability in the best tradition of previous royal administrations. Charles proved an energetic leader, attending most Council meetings and applying himself to business in a manner which met even Hyde's high standards.[14] Like other rulers, he found it convenient to form an inner ring to discuss the most important matters, consisting of Hyde, Nicholas, Ormonde, Southampton, Monck and Morice.[15] Within this, one man soon emerged as the most important: Hyde, who succeeded in making the transition from exile while preserving his place as the King's closest adviser. His post of Chancellor not only gave him great resources of patronage, but carried with it the Speakership of the Lords, who accepted him after some grumbling. In June a committee of Councillors was asked to draft a royal message to the Commons; in July Hyde drafted one to the Lords single-handed. The King and he exchanged private notes at Council meetings, in which he took the tone of a strict but kindly uncle. Charles advised petitioners to apply to him rather than to other ministers, and they did, in thousands. By 1662 the age's most durable sycophant, Dryden, could address the King as the heaven and Hyde as the earth.[16]

The trappings of monarchy were restored with the person. Tenants and squatters were evicted from former royal palaces and a hunt commenced for their original furnishings.[17] To substantiate the semi-divine nature of kingship, Charles spent two June days touching nearly a thousand sufferers from scrofula, who were presented with gold pendants and assurances of miraculous recovery.[18] The court ceremonial of Charles I was resumed.[19] All was not, however, as in the old King's time, for Greenwich and Eltham Palaces were ruined beyond repair and many treasures, including most of the Crown Jewels and the great collection of paintings, were never returned. Nor, despite the reappearance of so many great offices, was the structure of administration entirely untouched by the republican experiment. In November and December, permanent commissions of Trade and the Plantations were set up, which were not committees of the Council of the Caroline sort, but mixed advisory bodies of Councillors and merchants, such as the Commonwealth had found useful.[20] Although the Duke of York was made Lord High Admiral, the navy was run from day to day by a board of experts after the manner of the republic's commission, staffed with a mixture of former royalists and parliamentarians.[21] The new government was almost as much a hybrid in its form as in its personnel.

The same principle was observed in staffing other central offices. In the course of the summer the King restored the two surviving royalist judges and reappointed four from the Commonwealth and eight from the Protectorate, using the formula of tenure during good behaviour (instead of royal pleasure) wrung from Charles I by Parliament in 1641.[22] Monck placed half the army regiments and perhaps half of the garrisons under old royalist commanders. The unit which had once been Cromwell's Ironsides was accorded the honour of being given to the Duke of York.[23] Simultaneously the King put the militia of each English county, and of Wales, under the leading local magnate, according to custom, irrespective of his Civil War record. Where the dominant family had died out, opportunity was taken to elevate a man who had worked for the Restoration: hence Mordaunt, Howard, Grenville, Monck and Fauconberg all became Lords-Lieutenant of the counties in which they owned land. The Deputy-Lieutenants and officers chosen subsequently had as mixed a political past as the Convention Parliament and Privy Council, and the government instructed them to levy according to the rates prescribed by the Militia Act of March.[24]

As a complement to this work, the leading gentry were restored to civil power by the reissue of commissions of the peace. The results varied from Anglesey, where not a single Interregnum justice was re-employed, to Devon, where over half survived. In most counties the majority of the bench were changed, and many of the replacements were young men from important families rather than members of pre-war and wartime commissions. To this extent it was a genuine reunion of local communities, but the precise identity of the bench was determined by personal connections. Thus heirs of royalist families represented in pre-war commissions were sometimes left out if they lacked allies at court, and justices who had served the republic were re-employed if they had some: the exceptional continuity in the Devon commission was due partly to the influence of Monck and Morice.[25] The new sheriffs possessed the same mixed record as the Deputy-Lieutenants.[26] In most counties, a few local families who had risen during the Interregnum retained their position in county society, as did the occasional complete outsider, such as John Birch in Herefordshire and John Carter in Denbighshire, who had originally been imposed upon the locality as military governor. Favour at court was not sufficient to obtain a man office in a county where he had inadequate local support: thus Cooper failed to become Lord-Lieutenant of Wiltshire and Howard to become governor of Carlisle, in the face of gentry hostility.[27] Individual minor officials who had been deprived for royalism were restored on petition,[28] but there was no systematic replacement of bailiffs and constables of the sort that had occurred in 1648-9.

To one group of commoners, however, the principle of restoration made great changes: those royalist soldiers who had been crippled during the wars. During the Interregnum they had been ignored while their parliamentarian counterparts had been cared for in a central institution at Ely House or by local rates. In the course of 1660-2 this anomaly was corrected, and most counties seem to have provided pensions or grants to impoverished or maimed men who had fought for the Kings. Though the inmates of Ely

House were dispersed into the provinces, the crippled parliamentarians were in most places treated as before. There were, however, exceptions, such as Devon where their pensions were stopped, Wiltshire where they required confirmation by a justice, and Norfolk where they were continued only to conscripts.[29] These were ominous signs that to some gentry even-handedness signified not a division of benefits, but their transfer from those who had enjoyed them hitherto to those who had not.

The government attempted to secure the restoration of royalists in corporate bodies by indirect means. In at least three borough councils, radical leaders either resigned or failed to obtain re-election in the spring of 1660.[30] In at least five more, they resigned on the King's return or were dismissed by their fellows on the grounds that their original election had been irregular.[31] Their replacements, however, were not royalists but members of other factions of the 1650s, though at least six other assemblies did restore individual officers and members deprived for supporting the Kings.[32] Corporations in general spent large sums on celebrating Charles's proclamation, made fulsome addresses and expensive presents to him and restored their fee-farm rents to the royal coffers, but the men who did all this were almost always those who had run their communities during the Interregnum. The government's response to this situation was for the King to write to six of the largest councils during the autumn, requiring them to restore their expelled royalists and to remove their replacements, in the name of national unity. They were also urged to administer the Oaths of Allegiance and Supremacy to all members, which would displace not only the disloyal but those sectaries who objected to oaths in general. Occasionally Charles recommended a royalist for an office.[33] This policy still left a majority of the republic's city fathers in power, but as it was implemented there were hints of retribution to come. Hyde, in private, spoke not of reconciliation but of the need to do things 'by degrees'.[34] In Kent, the government had some direct influence through the persons of the Lord Warden of the Cinque Ports, now the Duke of York, and the governor of Dover. During the winter these men and the King between them ordered five corporations not merely to restore royalists, but to dismiss men who had petitioned for Charles I's trial, or been elected since then, or seemed disaffected.[35]

The same pattern appeared in dealings with those different corporate bodies, the universities. Cambridge's parliamentarian Chancellor, Manchester, had removed its royalist fellows during the Great Civil War, while Oxford had suffered a more intensive purge by a commission after the end of the war and the removal of its royalist Chancellor, the Marquis of Hertford. The House of Lords commenced the reversal of both processes during May 1660, by restoring Manchester and Hertford to their posts and granting restitution to some of those deprived at Oxford.[36] During the summer Manchester wrote to colleges requesting the restoration of those men whom he had previously removed who now wished to return. They occupied vacancies, if any existed, and displaced those elected in their stead if none did. By this process, generally an amicable one, some colleges were left with a majority of former royalists, while others retained all of their intruded fellows.[37]

At Oxford, by contrast, great bitterness and public interest was created. Some existing heads of houses responded to the Lords' orders to restore royalists by petitioning the Commons for aid. After a sharp debate, in which Holles and Annesley spoke for the petition and Finch against it, it was referred to a committee.[38] The Lords riposted by asking the King to commission a Visitation to adjudicate between claims in the university. This, composed of Privy Councillors, bishops and members of colleges whose titles were not in doubt, was named on 13 July, and empowered not only to restore royalists and remove their replacements, but to deprive the 'scandalous', though the King urged it to behave moderately. In the course of two months it ejected fifty fellows and heads of houses, most to make way for the old royalists. One of those deprived, Seth Ward, went on to high office, and two received new livings, but the others, like those removed at Cambridge, were not re-employed. The presence of university members among the Visitors, who in practice did most of the work, was of obvious tactical value but contrary to the university's statutes. Those deprived sometimes departed with obvious reluctance, and one Fellow of Lincoln had to be dragged from his rooms by soldiers. Nevertheless, the Convention Parliament gave retrospective confirmation to the changes in December, and their net result was a situation similar to that at Cambridge, whereby noted radicals had been removed altogether but some colleges retained most of their Interregnum fellowship. As a gesture of unity and loyalty, the university unanimously elected Hyde to the Chancellorship when Hertford died in the autumn.[39]

Thus far government policy towards the great centres of learning had been a successful exercise in arbitration. Yet, as with the municipal corporations, there were indications of more aggressive action to come. During the summer, Charles imposed new heads upon Merton and King's, each time ignoring the existing one and in the latter case breaching the Fellows' right of election. When, in the winter, he made his nominee at Merton a bishop and forced another stranger on the college, the Fellows locked the gate on their new Warden, only to submit in time.[40] These institutions were the first in England to discover how heavy the hand of the restored Stuarts could be.

All these settlements, from Privy Councillors to mutilated soldiers, consisted of redistributions of benefits within a class. It is time now to consider whether the Restoration brought about a redistribution of power between classes, as two specific studies have suggested. One is of Bedford corporation, in which the freemen won equal representation with burgesses in 1650, only to be deprived of these concessions in August 1660.[41] The other is of the Worcestershire Grand Jury, which before the wars and during the Interregnum contained many freeholders and a few gentry, but after the Restoration was chosen only from gentry and a few of the wealthiest farmers.[42] If these cases are typical of their kind, then the return to power of the traditional rulers was accompanied by a tendency towards oligarchy. But they are not. The constitutions of most corporations remained unaltered in 1660, while the Commons' committee on elections decided several cases, in which freemen and burgesses disputed the power to elect MPs, in favour of the freemen. The burgesses of King's Lynn conceded it independently. Likewise in other counties where excellent sessions records survive,[43] the Grand Juries seem to have been drawn from the same sort of men before and after the Restoration, though it must be said that the Worcestershire one was usually prominent in the affairs of the county. On the other hand, the Quarter Sessions of the 1660s were not entirely like those of the 1630s. Techniques of administration which were developed during the Interregnum in some counties, such as the decision of petitioners' claims by the whole bench and more flexible arrangements for rating, were retained.[44] Combined with the return to high attendances by JPs from Michaelmas 1660, and the greater popular respect shown for them than during the Interregnum, this must have made for more efficiency. Like the central administration, the local government of the Restoration incorporated both personnel and methods from the republic.

The legal procedure of the first settlement carried on alongside the changes in personnel,[45] and to both government and Parliament the most important part of this was the Bill of Indemnity and Oblivion.[46] The King sent three messages to hasten it and both Houses gave it priority over other business. Designed to be the great gesture to reunite the country, it had from the first an air of ceremonial artificiality in that its principal victims were not the leaders of the republic as such, but the men who had sat in the regicide court of 1649. These ranged from individuals who had played a great part in subsequent governments to some who had been, and remained, relatively obscure. In his declaration of September 1659, Charles had offered pardon to all but seven of them, and when the bill was introduced on 9 May, Monck proposed five exceptions. On the 14th the Commons fixed the number at seven. The act which received the royal assent on 29 August put thirty-three men at immediate risk of their lives, but this still represented considerable restraint in the Convention, as over sixty individuals had been exposed to death in the various drafts which had been debated.

Much of the measure's relative moderation was due to the tendency of the two Houses to reject each other's victims. The Lords persuaded the Commons to punish twenty men, including Lenthall, Berry, Pyne, St. John, Whitelocke, Fleetwood, Desborough and Alderman Ireton, with nothing worse than disqualification from office. In return, they agreed to impose the same light penalty on members of the tribunals which had sentenced royalists to death. The Lower House believed that nineteen regicides who had surrendered, including Marten and Robert Lilburne, should be shown mercy, and the peers did not. Their executions were therefore made dependent upon a separate act of Parliament, which the Convention never introduced. Lambert and Vane were exposed to death, as the Lords wished, but reprieved by the King as the Commons desired. Hesilrige's life, which the Lords sought, was saved at the insistence of Monck, who thus kept his promise at the last. Both Houses agreed upon the deaths of those regicides who had sought to avoid capture and stretched this to include Scot, who had surrendered in Brussels. Eleven men within this definition were in custody, while twenty-two others, including Ludlow, Okey, Whalley and Goffe, had escaped abroad.

As with the selection of JPs, the identity of the victims within each category was determined by their personal connections as well as their records. The close-knit nature of the English ruling class, which had made the civil wars so tragic, now assisted the process of granting indemnity as many republicans proved to have friends, relatives or men who owed them gratitude, sitting in the Convention. Colonel Hutchinson, a regicide who had expressed no joy in the Restoration, escaped with life and liberty through the efforts of friends from both wartime parties. A similar alliance probably saved Milton and certainly defended Whitelocke, who bought himself an additional royalist connection by paying a man heavily for an introduction to the King. The Privy Council resolved to safeguard the life of the regicide William Heveningham out of respect for his grandfather-in-law, a royalist earl. Even Ludlow found allies in Speaker Grimston and Ormonde. Animosities proved as complex and personal as loyalties, and between them make nonsense of any attempt to identify parties in these debates. Generally, Prynne proved as vindictive in life as he was violent in print, and a few of the new men in the Commons pressed for severity. Booth, Holles, Annesley and Cooper tended to defend individuals, and the government members in the Lower House argued for moderation in most cases while pursuing their particular enemies. Little information survives upon the Lords' debates, though Hyde appears in other sources as greedy and unforgiving. He failed to seal the pardon of his former friend Whitelocke until he received £250, and objected to that of Hutchinson. Charles himself, in his rare moments of personal comment, seems relatively mild. When a mob hanged an effigy of Cromwell outside Whitehall, he had this removed, and he granted Whitelocke a courteous conversation, ending with the advice to retire into the country.[47]

During the Convention's recess in October, all the regicides in custody were tried and condemned, and all but one of the eleven immediately vulnerable were hanged, drawn and quartered. Like the Interregnum High Courts, the tribunal included many men who were not professional judges, in this case mixing former royalists and parliamentarians to emphasise reconciliation yet again. Unlike the High Courts, it left the verdicts to a jury, according to common law, though the procedure breached custom by requiring only one witness for each act of treason. Those executed went to their deaths with courage and piety. Scot, defiant to the last, had to be prevented from justifying the regicide on the scaffold, but this was not, after all, recorded on his tomb, for he was never entombed. His quarters, boiled to preserve them longer, decorated the City gates with those of his colleagues. One old soldier was still sufficiently alive as his naked body was sliced open to sit up and strike the executioner. A moment later his heart was displayed to the cheering crowd. Another's butchered carcass was towed past the spectators, the head fixed to the top 'bloody yet pale, ghastly'.[48] The regicide itself had been a solemn and tragic ritual: these men died amidst the atmosphere of a bear-baiting.

When the Convention reconvened in November, its appetite for revenge proved only to have been whetted. The result was an Act of Attainder convicting the fugitive regicides and confiscating their property, along with that of their colleagues who had died before the Restoration. The most important of these men were Cromwell himself, Henry Ireton, who had led the army into Pride's Purge, and John Bradshaw, the President of the regicide court. The Convention resolved to mark the twelfth anniversary of the regicide by having them taken from their tombs in Westminster Abbey and hanged in their shrouds, before their skulls were impaled in Westminster Hall beside some of the trophies of October. This was done, and the crowd at Tyburn was entertained by the sight of the three corpses suspended in varying stages of decomposition, while apprentices cut off their toes. The other distinguished parliamentarian and republican dead were officially sacrosanct, but the Dean of Westminster none the less disinterred all those remaining in the Abbey and threw them into a pit.[49]

All this, however, evaded the point that for many royalists the crucial issue in the Act of Indemnity was not one of life but of lucre. It was not a question of sharing a judicial bench or a race-meeting with an old opponent, but of seeing him continue to enjoy the profits of one's plundered goods and cattle, while one continued in the financial difficulties that resulted.[50] The Act entirely ignored this grievance, which would do much to explain the famous accusation, scattered in Whitehall in June, that it was an Act of Indemnity for the King's enemies and Oblivion for his friends.[51]

Was it either? The problem of indemnity must be treated again below, in the context of the second settlement, but certain factors were already obvious before the end of 1660 which were to be constant features of the matter. First, the act was an almost complete formal success in that there seems to have been only one prosecution under it (in Dorset in 1663) for berating somebody for his wartime record.[52] Second, those former enemies of the King who had assisted the Restoration continued to enjoy honours and offices. The aristocratic dynasties which Cooper and Howard founded on the proceeds survive to this day. The most fortunate regicide was Ingoldsby, who for his service in capturing Lambert was permitted to clear his name with one of history's most preposterous lies, that his firm signature on the death-warrant was produced by Cromwell, holding his hand. Equipped with the thanks of the Convention, he was made a Knight of the Bath at Charles's coronation.[53] Royal favour, however, was not always sufficient to obtain a former republican a reward. This has been illustrated already in the case of local offices, and was made obvious by the Commons in December, when they rejected a royal request to confirm Lawson in the land granted to him the previous January.[54] Henry Cromwell, through the influence of Ormonde, Monck and Broghill, succeeded in retaining much of the land he had acquired during his years of power, but Yarmouth corporation, which had made him its High Steward, still stripped him of the office and erased references to him from its books.[55] Third, those men who had advanced money to the Interregnum governments now forfeited both principal and interest. The most important casualty of this was the late Protector Richard himself. In October 1659, when his restoration was discussed, he had attempted to reassert himself in national affairs, writing to Oxford University to remind it that he was still its Chancellor. In April 1660 he renounced all hope of power, resigned this office and wrote to Monck begging for help. His public debts, which the purged Parliament had assumed, had never in fact been paid, and his creditors were pursuing him. No assistance came, and in June Richard fled England, to commence a life of utter obscurity, in which he would eventually survive every other public figure of his Protectorate.[56]

The fourth factor was the most important, that the most effective means of gaining vengeance upon an enemy for old sufferings was to denounce or harass him for disloyalty to the restored monarchy. Charles himself provided the context for this when he twice told the Convention that the Act of Indemnity was intended only for past deeds, and that the government would proceed vigorously against sedition.[57] During the first years after the Restoration, the State Papers and judicial records fill with accusations spanning the social hierarchy. Given the evidence already provided for a significant minority of republicans in the country, there is no reason to doubt that many were genuine. Anyone who had been an enthusiastic supporter of the preceding regimes found the summer of 1660 a bad time to get drunk. But some denunciations were exposed as fraudulent,[58] and some were directed at general sceptics, such as the Wiltshire man who spoke against the King, but also against magistrates of any kind, and 'took a piss' in church.[58] It is impossible to quantify each category. Just as the authorities in Devon, where most Interregnum JPs survived, behaved most callously towards parliamentarian soldiers, so some justices who had been most assiduous in detecting disloyalty to the Protectorate proved just as energetic in searching out the King's enemies.[60] Some former leaders, such as Fleetwood, escaped this process. His last contact with the central government was in January, when he requested Monck, touchingly, to care for Richard Cromwell.[61] After this he retired to the countryside, only molested once when somebody seized a horse of his.[62] Desborough was less lucky, being arrested in Essex and brought into London for questioning, to the jeers of youths.[63] His fate was the more common among the notable republicans, and even some parliamentarians who had declined to support the republic were searched and abused by militiamen.[64]

During the summer, the government treated the provincial denunciations and arrests delicately, ordering a proper investigation of the facts behind the more serious and releasing many of the republicans taken into custody.[65] In December, however, it increased tension by publicising the so-called 'White's Plot', said to be a plan by former soldiers to seize the capital.[66] This seems to have been an official panic resulting from rumours of the genuine Venner's Rising to come, mixed with fear of the large numbers of disbanded soldiers in London, some of whom were selling arms. Overton, Rich, Desborough and over fifty former officers were arrested, and even Monck's town house was searched on Manchester's orders. No real evidence was uncovered, and no trials resulted, but Hyde still told the Convention that a great conspiracy had been uncovered. It seems that, having seen the early leaders of the Long Parliament reinforce support for themselves with revelations of Catholic and ultra-royalist plots, and Cromwell appeal to his Parliaments with details of royalist conspiracy, the new regime could not resist this tactic.

The other question, of royal ingratitude, was a major theme of comment at the Restoration and after. Within a month of his return, royalists were accusing the King of granting favours only to their old enemies, and the Venetian ambassador believed this to be correct.[67] In 1661 a royalist who had obtained an office, James Howell, wrote *A Cordial for the Cavaliers*, arguing against this complaint as erroneous. A royalist who had not, Roger L'Estrange, produced *A Caveat to the Cavaliers* by way of scalding reply, claiming that rebels now kept their spoil, while the only beggars were the King's old friends. This image became a theme for heart-rending ballads.

In Howell's favour, it is easy to find numerous cases of generosity by Charles to his traditional supporters. On his return he insisted, against the wishes of the Convention and of Monck, that peers created by himself or his father since 1642 be allowed into the Lords.[68] He went on to confer two more peerages promised by his father during the wars.[69] Royalists obtained slightly more places in the government than any other group, and received many more of the baronetcies and knighthoods at the Restoration than their old opponents.[70] In the three years after his return, Charles rewarded at least 159 former royalist army officers[71] and at least thirty families of followers now deceased.[72] At least seventy royalists received Crown land, as grants or as leases on easy terms,[73] and so many were given pensions that Lord Treasurer Southampton begged the King to be less benevolent.[74] Charles also repaid fifty-four men who had lent money to his father, from his personal income.[75] If Charles I had won Edgehill, the booty would hardly have been greater.

Moreover, individual charges of royal ingratitude collapse on scrutiny. The poet Abraham Cowley, a former royalist agent, was certainly ignored at the Restoration, and complained of this, but he had abandoned his cause to write praises of Cromwell.[76] When another agent, Samuel Morland, considered himself neglected, this meant that he expected the Garter as well as the ordinary knighthood and pension which he did receive.[77] A Yorkshire royalist, Sir Philip Monckton, stated that he received no reward for seven years but was in fact given three posts in that time.[78] L'Estrange himself got office the year after his tract. The royalist put in charge of the Post Office was censured for re-employing most of Thurloe's staff, and replied that most of those ejected for loyalty were dead and the record of the new applicants suspect.[79] There seems no reason to doubt Hyde's comment that in general the most importunate were the least deserving.[80] So many gentry crowded into London to hunt places that prices there soared, and even their servants followed in the hope of employment at Court.[81] It was a gold-rush atmosphere, with disappointment inevitable for most.

When all this is said, some truth remains in the complaints. The circumstances of the Restoration demanded that rewards be given to many non–royalists, and the greatest beneficiaries were the military men who had made it possible, Monck and Mountagu. The former became Duke of Albemarle, the latter Earl of Sandwich. Both received huge grants of Crown land and Monck was given a palace. Their principal officers and clients received gratitude in turn, and where, as in the cases of Clarges and Pepys, the office conferred had a royalist claimant, the latter had to give way.[82] A project to found a new order of knighthood, the Royal Oak, for the most distinguished of the King's old adherents was mysteriously dropped, presumably to avoid offence to former parliamentarians.[83] Most of the new knights and baronets were newcomers to politics, the rising men of the shires whose support the government had to confirm. Furthermore, the crowds of impecunious royalists were not a myth, for in 1663 over five thousand needy former officers were identified.[84] Charles was able to reward only 9 per cent of the men who had suffered for his cause in Lancashire and 11 per cent in Yorkshire.[85] The problem was one of means not intentions, but a problem it was.

If indemnity seemed an obvious contribution to the stabilisation of the realm, the removal of the army seemed another. To raise the huge sum necessary to pay it off, the Commons decided on 12 June to impose a poll tax, by which each individual paid a fixed sum appropriate to his rank in society. This device was apparently adopted to provide slight relief to property owners, who were still bearing the full weight of the 'assessments' imposed to keep the armed forces in their normal pay. In the nick of time, six days before the recess, the Lords pointed out that the new tax was unlikely to produce enough, and an additional assessment was rushed through after all. A central commission was chosen from both Houses to employ the money sent up by local commissions of collectors, and claimed later to have written over 1,500 letters to remind the latter of the urgency and importance of their task.[86] For all these efforts, problems soon arose, particularly concerning the collection of the poll tax in the capital. Social status was less clear there than in the provinces, and the commissioners for the City were at a loss as to how to determine it for some time.[87] The corporation objected to the sums eventually required and would only grant a loan against the assessment, at the King's personal request.[88] As feared, the poll tax produced much too little and in its winter session, after some recrimination, the Convention had to impose yet another assessment.[89]

Nevertheless, the task was accomplished. Sufficient sums came in to disband most of the army during the autumn and to complete the task, and pay off twenty-five warships as well, by January.[90] Arrears were guaranteed to those officers who were removed in the summer to make way for royalists, and to all soldiers who did not refuse the Oath of Allegiance to Charles. They seem to have been paid in full; the King provided an additional donative, and Monck's officers set an example to their men by holding a cheerful farewell dinner. The regiments around London laid down arms with good humour.[91] In view of all this it is remarkable that some soldiers chose, for political or religious reasons, to refuse the oath and forfeit their pay. Others in outlying units grew restless at the prospect of disbanding and the local militia was raised to watch them.[92] Even after so many purges, the ghost of the Good Old Cause still walked parts of the institution which had embodied it.

In two important respects the actual consequences of the whole operation differed from the spirit in which it was carried out. First, the disbanded men suffered the fate of the republicans officially accorded indemnity. In his speech at the Convention's recess, Hyde praised the soldiers and promised them royal favour in civilian life, while an act was passed to continue a series of measures of the 1640s which absolved former members of the army from the apprenticeship laws, to assist them into new employment.[93] In the event, the dispersal through country and capital of so many men trained to arms and formally imbued with republican principles was an inevitable source of tension. They had been allowed to keep their swords, and some were rumoured to have smuggled away other weapons.[94] By publicising 'White's Plot', the government increased suspicion of them, and in April it issued the first of successive proclamations ordering all former members of the armies of the Long Parliament or Protectorate to leave London unless granted individual permits.[95] Their old enemies were allowed to move freely.

Nor was the pre-war military situation restored. Soon after his return, Charles told the Spanish ambassador that he intended to have an army supported by his private resources. If the proposal was serious it was not practicable, but to protect himself against republican plots he did retain 3,574 guards, far more than any previous monarch had kept.[96] One troop of horse and one foot regiment of these were Monck's own, preserved from disbanding, and the fame of the latter, named the Coldstream Guards after his headquarters in December 1659, has obscured the general character of the force. Most of it consisted of fresh men officered by royalists, and likewise, by May, only one small fort out of twenty permanent garrisons was not commanded by men who had fought for the Kings.[97] Charles II, unlike his father in 1642, now had his fortresses and magazines kept by followers of proved loyalty.

Thus, in its first session the Convention dealt with two major aspects of settlement. For a third, the fate of lands confiscated from Crown, bishops, deans and chapters, it failed to provide a measure, though it established a principle. The purchasers of these lands included many soldiers, London merchants and gentry, and some former tenants.[98] Together, they constituted a formidable enough interest for Monck, in January 1660, to declare them a considerable obstacle to a royal restoration.[99] In his 1659 declaration Charles had offered some unspecified compensation to them, and in May 1660 Monck proposed that this should consist of long leases on easy terms.[100] Throughout the summer various purchasers held meetings to strengthen their chances of obtaining these by co-ordinated efforts, expressed in addresses to King and Parliament.[101] Monck's last speech to the Commons, on departing to the Lords, was a request for special attention to the issue.[102]

As always, the Convention proved more royalist than expected. On 22 June a bill which seems to have guaranteed long leases to purchasers was introduced, only to be defeated. Monck's client, Howard, was among the tellers against it, suggesting that this faction was abandoning the interests of purchasers in general. On the same day the Commons agreed that the widowed Queen's jointure, which was owed to her under a treaty with her native France, had to be restored entire. The following day Finch introduced a different bill for confirmation or compensation of buyers, and on 11 July, upon the motion of a former royalist agent Sir Job Charlton, the Crown lands were exempted from its restrictions. The Lords followed this up by voting the King into all his possessions. The Lower House neither concurred with nor challenged this, but continued to the end of the session with desultory discussion of the Church lands. No statute resulted, but resolutions were passed that churchmen should augment the stipends of vicars dependent upon impropriate tithes in any lands to be leased; various categories of republicans should forfeit their purchases outright; other purchasers should receive their money minus their profits, but plus some interest and the value of improvements; old tenants should have an option on the lease; and a commission should be empowered to supervise the process. 'Party' divisions are again difficult to detect in these deliberations: a wartime parliamentarian and a royalist conspirator united to propose the augmentation clause, while Prynne and Stephens proposed harsher treatment of those who had bought Crown land than did Finch and Palmer.[103]

As soon as the principle of repossession had been conceded, King and churchmen seized the initiative. Nine days after the Lords' vote, the Surveyor-General began to resume control of Crown lands and to negotiate with those who had bought them.[104] Although granted representation in 1641, Durham was traditionally a County palatine, returning no MPs. The purchasers in it were not men of influence in 1660, and Charles felt able to move swiftly. On 30 July he ordered the seizure of both royal and ecclesiastical land in the county.[105] Nearer the capital more caution was required, as was proved by John Cosin, Dean of Peterborough, who called his chapter together in early August and granted several leases.[106] He provoked a resolution of the Commons that no Church land be leased till the bill to regulate this was passed, and a furious letter from Hyde urging him to be tactful. Charles overruled the resolution, but insisted that augmentation of vicarages be a feature of future transactions.[107] Cosin's lessees themselves emerged from the affair well pleased; far from damping down the tendency to let land, these events encouraged gentry elsewhere to press churchmen for the same favour.[108] At the same time some of the most important purchasers were placated with leases: thus Cosin ensured that Lord Mayor Allin and St. John retained their acquisitions at low rents.[109] The problem was starting to solve itself piecemeal, and the Convention's recess left it entirely in royal hands. Both Crown and Church immediately began leasing on a large scale, and on 7 October Charles commissioned a body of peers and MPs to arbitrate in case of disputes, as the Commons had planned.[110]

In the settlement of his own property, Charles kept faith with Monck's army, though not as comprehensively as the general had wished. Any officer who had been at Coldstream, and some other military purchasers who had aided the Restoration, were allowed to receive rents up to March 1661 and thereafter became tenants paying nominal rents or were given what they had not yet recouped from their outlay. Other soldiers who had taken the Oath of Allegiance were permitted the rent due in September 1660, and existing or former tenants were given an option on the lease before any but the favoured officers.[111] The King ordered churchmen to favour purchasers and old tenants in sealing their leases,[112] and named individual purchasers for particularly good treatment.[113] Just as soldiers dismissed during the purges forfeited their Crown land outright, so regicides lost all their purchases to the former owners and other notable republicans were dispossessed of the Church land they had bought. In some cases this was effected brutally: Whitelocke's daughter's family were thrown out of the episcopal manor of Fulham by soldiers who plundered their personal goods.[114] On the other hand, royal favour was not always enough to protect a purchaser. Colonel Birch was supported by the King, Hyde and Monck in his desire to lease an episcopal palace he had bought, yet he required a twelve-year lawsuit to do so because the new bishop was an old enemy.[115]

The southern dioceses settled most of their lands before the end of 1660, while some in the north did not commence the work until the next year, but all seem to have worked according to Charles's general recommendations. Fines were usually kept low and rents unrevised. Old tenants tended to be given priority over purchasers, but many of the latter received leases and those ejected were paid compensation according to the Commons' plan. Augmentations of vicarages were made.[116] During the winter session of the Convention, enough purchasers remained unsatisfied to petition the

Commons for a general right to leases. A bill on Church lands was produced, which may have required a universal award to parish clergy from the wealth of deans and chapters, but it was never completed.[117] Thereafter the whole issue slipped from parliamentary history, to disintegrate in individual settlements. Most were peaceful, the royal commission not being required at all in two dioceses and being called in to settle only a few disputes in each of the others. These it resolved according to their separate circumstances, using the guide-lines established by the Commons in August. The factor which did most to remove bitterness from the whole business was almost certainly that after ten years the majority of purchasers had recouped their outlay.[118] This much now seems clear: the great question that remains is how much the sale and repossession of the Crown and Church lands resulted in an alteration in their tenantry. The only study which as yet touches on this, of the estates of the Archbishop of York, suggests that the effect was marginal.[119]

With the land settlement as with indemnity, the private individual was sacrificed to the greater good. After the confiscations of public land, many royalists had suffered deprivation to pay for the Commonwealth's wars. A large number of these, varying from almost half in the south-east, to two-thirds in the north of England, had rapidly regained some of this property either by direct repurchase or the efforts of friends. In 1660 eleven of the most important regained all their estates by private act of Parliament or orders of the Lords. The remainder were provided for in the Commons' August bill on Church land, which proposed for them a simple restoration of property without compensation or penalty. The failure of this abandoned them to the tedious and expensive business of regaining their estates by lawsuit, as the sales were excepted from the Act of Indemnity. All but a small percentage succeeded, but the process must have irritated men who watched their old masters, sacred and secular, resume their wealth with relative ease. Even less content would have been the far greater number of royalists who had sold land or undergone hardship in order to pay composition fines or the decimation tax. The Earl of Derby introduced two private bills in the Lords to regain lands which he claimed to have parted with in the belief that they would be held in trust for him. Both failed, the first because of a general feeling in the Commons that such voluntary sales should not be overthrown, and the second, which offered compensation to the purchasers, for lack of time. To such men, as to those who had lost goods to plunderers, the First Restoration Settlement offered no redress. The result was privation rather than ruin, and as a group the royalist gentry survived. This was the ominous fact: the Restoration had left them both powerful and with reason for resentment.[120]

The religious question presented an unusual emotive problem which transcended any pattern of rewards, penalties and compensations.[121] Nevertheless, in mid-1660 there were several reasons why the settlement of a national Church of flexible principle and practice could be expected. As has been said, during the Interregnum various groups of churchmen had drawn closer together to meet the challenge of the gathered churches and Quakers, and expressed this in the many local associations. Even before this, episcopacy had only been abolished after hesitation and for political and financial reasons. The wartime royalists had offered to reduce the institution to its 'primitive' form, operating with the assistance of presbyters. From 1656, a group of ministers led by John Gauden began working for this model, and in early 1660 one of the most respected of all the beneficed clerical writers of the decade, Richard Baxter of Kidderminster, declared his support for it.[122] Few of the trappings of prelatical episcopacy still existed. Hereford Cathedral had been partly demolished and Lichfield was choked with a fallen roof, while Canterbury was a shell. Durham had been used as a prison, St. Paul's as a stable and shopping precinct, and St. Asaph as an ox-byre and wine-shop. Three of the palaces of the Bishop of Winchester had been destroyed, while that of Exeter was now a sugar-factory, that of Salisbury a tavern, and that of Chester a gaol.[123] Fourteen sees were vacant, and only three were occupied by men who had been associated with the policies of Archbishop Laud. Surviving traces of parish religion suggest confusion and deprivation: a sample of churchwardens' accounts for the late 1640s record the retention of the illegal Prayer Book in over a third of cases (without proving its use), while the Directory which the presbyterians had produced to replace it appeared in less than a quarter. Nearly half of these parishes, therefore, possessed neither the old nor the new forms of service. At Easter 1660 over a third of a larger sample of parishes failed to take communion, according to the reforms of the 1640s which were intended to remove the old feasts, but the rest did.[124] It could be expected that a revived traditional Church, which embodied some of the reforms and tolerated others in individual parishes, would be well received at all levels of society.

In March Hyde commenced the process of achieving this by sending one of the clerical royalist exiles, George Morley, to persuade the leading presbyterian ministers to accept episcopacy. He found many of them willing to accept a limited form, and to confer with moderate episcopalians, though he found the restraint upon bishops which most of them wanted, too considerable for his own beliefs. In May they conceded the use of the Prayer Book, providing that individuals could omit passages of it. Baxter, the great apostle of reconciliation, had come to London, and Henry Hammond, the greatest writer among the obdurate episcopalians, had died.[125] (The Convention

House of Commons) was immediately observed to contain men of both persuasions, and its most favoured preacher was Gauden.[126] On his return,
Charles chose a Privy Council of laymen associated with both clerical camps,
and accepted a set of chaplains to match. Most of the episcopalian clergy who
had rejected the Interregnum Church now preached reconciliation, while
their old opponents divided. After the City corporation proved hostile to a
petition against episcopacy, the majority of presbyterian leaders professed
willingness to accept bishops if they were elected and advised by presbyters,
as well as the Prayer Book, if it were revised by a joint conference and if three
ceremonies were made optional.[127] Within a month of the Restoration,
therefore, the way to compromise seemed open.

It should be stressed that in their reaction to this situation, both government and Convention operated according to principles which governed
their conduct of other parts of the 1660 settlement. It was accepted that
royalist clergy, like all other royalists, should resume the positions from
which they had been ejected. It was also necessary to preserve order in the
provinces, and to remove republicans from positions of influence. All these
ends were accomplished in an act passed at the end of the first session, which
confirmed the security of all parish clergy who were not baptists, had not
preached against the King and did not occupy the livings of royalists requiring restoration.[128] The royalist clergy did well by it, for six-sevenths of those
alive and unbeneficed were restored or promoted to a better living.[129] On the
other side, 845 ministers were definitely ejected in the two years after the
Restoration, the large majority for suspect political attitudes rather than title
to benefice. Despite this, at least 161 were reappointed elsewhere and only
134 were noted as continuing to preach illegally, suggesting something corroborated by individual case-studies: parishioners and patrons were taking
the opportunity to get rid of unwanted incumbents on false pretences. Even
men who had a good political record and title were displaced by fraudulent
claimants put up by enemies. In the last resort, a minister depended upon the
loyalty of his parish and the power of his protectors, such as Hyde who intervened to save at least three individuals. This would explain the very small
degree of disturbance with which the changes occurred.[130]

If the Commons' eventual treatment of the religious issue was consistent
with their other measures, it nevertheless produced a unique bitterness in
debate and a division into recognisable ideological factions. On one extreme
were men like Prynne and Stephens, pressing for a parliamentary settlement
of the Church as close as possible to that proposed by the presbyterians in the
1640s. On the other was a set of episcopalians, either royalists or new men,
who wanted one equivalent to the pre-war situation. The government
members tended to unite behind the proposition that an assembly of

churchmen should resolve the question, which not merely promised wide-spread acceptance of the result, but strengthened the monarchy by giving it the role of arbitrator. After two heated discussions in July, which lasted into the night—and in one of which the candles lighting the chamber were blown out to disrupt proceedings—this was conceded. The Prynne group were left to concentrate upon the settlement of ministers in livings; the departure of many episcopalians to attend the harvest and the moderate speeches of most government members prevented the passage of a statute permitting a more extensive purge. The Lords did not seek to obtain one, and Hyde, in his speech at the recess, praised the act which had been passed, while calling for action against ministers who now preached sedition.[131]

In late August, when the rival clergy were showing signs of impatience, the government began to move towards settlement, by encouraging the bishops to discuss the presbyterian proposals and by inviting men from both groups to the vacant sees, just as it was filling the parochial livings in the royal gift. This was a precise equivalent to the settlement of secular offices and the same policy was to be followed, with success, in reconstructing the Scottish Church. In England, however, it was checked by the refusal of all the presbyterian leaders except Edward Reynolds, who had always been the most willing to compromise, to accept the episcopal office. Their motive remains mysterious, though it seems likely that the spontaneous revival of deans and chapters, to be described, had already made the institution insufficiently 'primitive' for their taste. Charles had to make do with appointing the widest spectrum of churchmen remaining, from Gauden who had served the Inter-regnum Church, to Cosin who had closely supported Archbishop Laud. Most of the appointees, like most of the surviving bishops, were wartime royalists who had done neither of those things. Morley was one, and another was Gilbert Sheldon, to whom was given the vital see of London.[132] Sheldon, though devout as any and eloquent as most, was neither a theologian nor a pastor but an organiser of men, a holy bureaucrat rather than a holy warrior. At this time his record and his words alike suggested that these gifts would be employed in the cause of moderation.[133] Canterbury itself was given to William Juxon, who had been Charles I's Lord Treasurer and attendant on the scaffold and had occupied the see of London since 1634, but was now too feeble to be more than a figure-head.

Nor did the clerical conference turn out quite as hoped. Charles instructed Hyde to draft a 'treaty' acceptable to both groups, and he carried out this work with enthusiasm, but the result offended the presbyterians with the fervour with which it praised the episcopalian conception of the Church, while proposing that it should not be enforced on individuals. Although the ensuing discussions were held at Hyde's London residence, he was replaced as a mediator by Annesley and Holles, whose previous sympathies had been presbyterian. The result was the Worcester House Declaration of 25 October, an interim settlement close to the presbyterian model of June, which required bishops to ordain and censure with the assistance of presbyters and left clergy to use as much of the Prayer Book as they wished. This was, however, a more artificial achievement than it appeared, for it was imposed upon the churchmen by the decisions of Holles and Annesley and represented no genuine agreement.[134] When the Convention met again, Prynne's group attempted to have it made the basis of a parliamentary settlement, but were eventually defeated by 36 votes. Both the advantages which they had enjoyed in August were gone, for the episcopalians were present in strength and the government members held to the principle that the Church was properly the business of King and clergy. Prynne's set was at first more successful in salvaging something of the 1640s movement for godly reform; bills to preserve the Sabbath, prevent profanity and endow poor vicarages were sent to the Lords, but there they remained unfinished for lack of interest.[135]

If the behaviour of the clerical leaders now boded ill for a comprehensive Church, the action of laymen in the provinces was still more ominous. The episcopalian MPs who had gone home during the first session had not been idle there and did not lack supporters. The London petition against episcopacy in June was countered by seven from the counties, most of which called for the entire pre-war Church.[136] In September and October, ministers in at least thirteen counties were prosecuted under the old statute enjoining use of the Prayer Book.[137] None are known to have been sentenced and the cases reveal a pattern of localised harassment, but together with the petitions they suggest that most of the gentry actively concerned with the Church were now fiercely episcopalian. Furthermore, it was becoming obvious that the distaste of the young for the republican achievement extended to the more moderate earlier reforms. The young MPs in the Convention, like the young JPs commissioned in 1660, generally pressed for bishops and the Prayer Book. In part this may be ascribed to the shock of the sectarian and Quaker evangelism, which could have convinced gentry of the merits of a religion which stressed hierarchy, order and ceremony. But to many who had grown up since the fall of Laud, the ceremonies of the old Church also appeared novel and glamorous in themselves. A young Oxford Fellow who had grown a long beard under Cromwell, to suggest patriarchal dignity, was now seen swaggering about in a surplice, while crowds came to those college chapels which installed organs, to enjoy the music. At Cambridge, a student who had promised his father never to attend episcopalian ceremonies wrote him a 'saucy letter', ridiculing his old-fashioned ideas.[138]

If the issue of comprehension threatened to divide the government from many gentry, that of toleration compounded this danger. The gathered churches presented only a minor problem in this regard, as their close association with the republic made it easy to arrest their leaders and disperse their meetings on grounds of political security alone, in which case the Privy Council only required a proper hearing for the accused. In the summer and autumn of 1660, separatists suffered this treatment in Wales, the Marches and the Midlands, while groups elsewhere ceased to keep records or bewailed the loss of membership and the baptist associations disintegrated. One of the lay preachers arrested, John Bunyan of Bedford, was to employ his time in captivity more memorably than the others.[139] The Quakers were a more delicate matter, for their leaders had held aloof from the preceding regimes, hailed the King on his return as their natural leader,[140] and made several personal approaches to him for protection. These interviews were a considerable success: the Quakers thought Charles a man 'of sober countenance', were allowed to retain their hats before him and were promised security for their meetings. He seems to have found them entertaining,[141] but was as good as his word, for seven hundred Quakers were released on his orders. In November he set up a committee of the Privy Council to find grounds for liberating more, and the following month he promised a Quaker before the Council that their meetings would be protected and that they would not be punished for failing to attend church or remove hats.[142]

These good intentions were bedevilled by a number of difficulties. First, as shown earlier, some Quakers had assisted Lambert. These were now under suspicion with the sectaries and their innocent fellows suffered with them.[143] Second, the tactics employed by Quaker missionaries remained offensive to many, ministers still being interrupted during services while two women had ridden through Canterbury with a flaming torch.[144] Their tracts continued to prophesy destruction for the ungodly in a furious language which left the reader uncertain as to whether the retribution was to be at divine or human hands.[145] Bristol citizens, Dorset villagers and Kentish gentry alike found them genuinely frightening.[146] But third, many gentry and commoners found their teachings distasteful or ridiculous, and had been longing to repress them for years whether they behaved tactfully or not.

As a result, Charles's enthusiasm for toleration left him almost alone among the new rulers of England. His ministers were visibly embarrassed by his interviews with Quakers.[147] Hyde inserted an irrelevant passage criticising the Quaker mode of language into his speech at the Convention's recess, and attacked enemies of the Church in general in his one at the dissolution. The Commons wanted religious radicals to pay double taxes, while the Lords encouraged the dispersal of separatist meetings.[148] A Westmorland

Quaker thought the gentry 'like so many hungry eagles'.[149] The chief weapon employed by these men was the Oath of Allegiance, which Quakers could no more take than any other oath. Using this as proof of disloyalty, justices imprisoned them in at least thirteen counties, from Cumberland to Dorset, between August and September. This proved insufficient for some, who at Oxford in October disinterred the fearsome medieval writ of praemunire, whereby a man who refused to swear loyalty to the King could be locked up indefinitely and forfeit all property. Quakers were now entering prisons faster than Charles could free them.[150]

The last part of the First Restoration Settlement, and the main business of the winter session, consisted of the attempt to provide the government with a regular revenue. In part, this was the successful culmination, made possible by the shock of the Interregnum, of sixty years of attempts to replace the ancient feudal dues of the Crown with something more popular. It was also a matter of practical necessity, for both the remaining principal sources of government income, customs receipts and land rents, were badly depleted, the former by economic recession and the latter by generosity to former purchasers and supporters. The revenue of regicides' estates was swallowed up by the need to provide for the Duke of York.

The stabilisation of the country took precedence over this work, and although a Commons' committee upon it was set up on 3 May, nothing important was achieved till July when the Convention revised the customs rates (a task hitherto carried out by the government) to increase duties upon imported manufactures. This was intended to shift a burden onto the foreign producer from the native consumer, who was relieved by the abolition of the republican excise, which was extended only until Christmas. In September the Commons decided that the yearly revenue of the government should be £1,200,000, an estimate apparently based upon the normal expenditure of Charles I with an allowance of 8 per cent for inflation, and that over a third of this needed to be made up. Voting the King a lump sum in the interim, the Convention went into recess.

Its work in the winter concentrated upon the problem of supplying the deficit. It initially expected to do this by a much reduced extension of the republican assessment, but this project encountered growing opposition from back-benchers who argued, on behalf of landowners, for relief from direct taxation, as well as contesting the apportionment of the tax to individual counties. As a substitute, they proposed an excise on alcoholic drinks, which promised both to be lucrative and to discourage vice. The government members divided over this, Finch and Cooper coming slowly to support the excise, while Annesley argued that it was a levy inflicted upon the common people in the interests of the landed. On 21 November the scheme was adopted by two votes, and it duly became embodied in an act. While MPs had questioned its ethics, nobody seems to have doubted that it would be financially adequate, and in his speech at the dissolution Hyde called it 'a noble revenue'. This was to prove the most considerable mistake that the Convention Parliament had made.[151]

During his first six months as a *de facto* monarch, Charles himself had created a universally favourable impression, appearing industrious, patient, charming, courteous, healthy and athletic.[152] His only perceptible fault, his tenderness towards Quakers, could be excused as a superabundance of the princely virtue of mercy. He was, however, the head of a family which in the same period exhibited some of the human weaknesses from which he appeared free. In addition to his two brothers, he possessed two sisters, Mary, who had married the Prince of Orange, and Henrietta, a child still in the keeping of their mother, the widowed Queen Henrietta Maria. In the autumn of 1660 they, and the country, were disturbed by a succession of disasters which were to shape the future course of the restored monarchy.

These began on 13 September when the King's younger brother, the Duke of Gloucester, suddenly died, either from complications resulting from smallpox or from the attentions of his doctors. He had seemed a sweet-tempered youth, and his demise shocked the country and caused Charles profound grief.[153] The arrival of their sister Mary from the Netherlands on the 25th may have assuaged the King's sorrow in some measure,[154] but tragedy was now followed by scandal. In early October, Hyde's daughter Anne was discovered to be heavily pregnant, named the Duke of York as the father and claimed that they had been secretly married. York denied this, while Charles and his sister were appalled by the notion of the heir apparent marrying a commoner and Hyde was determined not to lose royal favour. Henrietta Maria arrived swiftly from France to prevent any danger of such a misalliance, while some of the Duke's friends attempted to poison his mind further against Anne. There was talk of the matter being raised in the Commons when the Convention regathered, to avoid which Charles made Hyde a baron, in order to secure him the privileges of a peer.

What rescued Anne's cause, despite such powerful opposition, was that she had spoken the truth and had reliable witnesses to this. During November Charles came to accept the fact, and a month later the opposition of the Queen and the Princess of Orange collapsed. In the latter case the reason was mortal, for Mary died on Christmas Eve of a rapid and mysterious fever. Henrietta Maria was broken-hearted at the loss of a second child within four months, and also now under pressure from the government of her native

France, which saw an opportunity to win favour with the English King by healing his family quarrel. The Duke, miserable and confused, came to speak to Hyde once more and to recognise his new-born son, and when the Queen returned to France in early January, Anne Hyde was recognised by all as the Duchess of York.[155]

These developments had three considerable consequences. The Duke, having been distinguished hitherto by his handsome features and physical courage, was revealed as deficient both in intelligence and integrity. Hyde's position as the King's favourite minister was enhanced by a connection with the royal family, but attracted greater envy and resentment in proportion. The death of one brother, and the discredit of the other, made the question of the King's own marriage, and the heir which it ought to produce, of some urgency. Around the problem was to be written the political history of late seventeenth-century England.

The year 1660, the Convention Parliament, and the First Restoration Settlement ended together. Their most obvious beneficiary had been Charles. He had regained and secured his throne without any of the constitutional concessions required of his father during the war years. He had resumed his lands and assumed the role of an arbiter between former rival parties, drawing upon the loyalty and talent of men from each. This position, however, remained under a dual challenge. On the one hand was the danger of republican conspiracy. On the other was a large number of gentry who desired a settlement of vengeance and punishment. In the first six months after his return, the King had room to manoeuvre between these difficulties. Three events were now to reduce this.

The first was the disappearance of the army, which both removed a check upon the proponents of revenge and multiplied the fears of plotting. The second was Venner's Rising. Thomas Venner was a London cooper and the leader of one of those gathered churches which bore the label of Fifth Monarchy Men. He embodied with exceptional fervour the single belief that marked this sect off from all others: that the reign of Christ upon earth could be produced immediately by an armed rebellion of saints. In 1657 he had attempted this with a small company, only to be captured at their point of rendezvous, because of the excellence of Thurloe's spy network, and committed to prison for a time. Apparently inspired by the speeches of the regicides on the scaffold, he decided in the winter of 1660 to try again, and this time his plans slipped through the intelligence system of the newly-settled monarchy. Enough was rumoured to cause the government acute anxiety, but it struck at the wrong target, the former army officers, and when Venner's church rose on the evening of 6 January,

1. Richard Cromwell

2. George Monck, Duke of Albemarle from 1660

3. The Execution of the Regicides, 1660

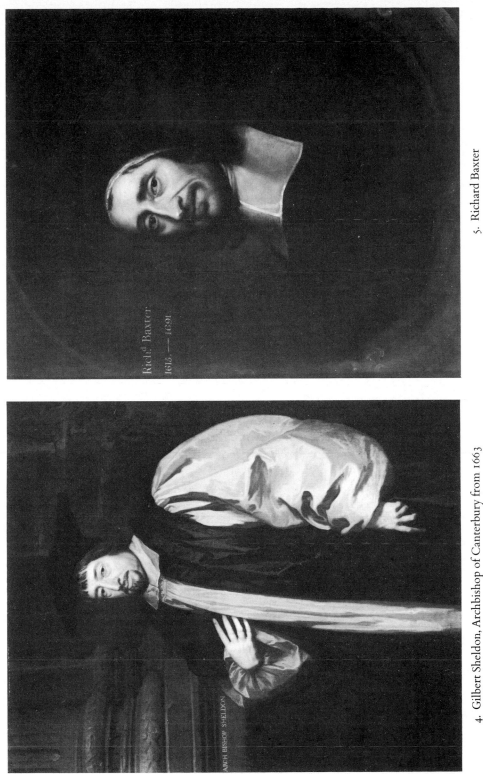

Rich.ᵈ Baxter
1615. — 1691

5. Richard Baxter

ARCH BISHOP SHELDON

4. Gilbert Sheldon, Archbishop of Canterbury from 1663

6. Catherine of Braganza

7. Barbara Villiers, Countess of Castlemaine from 1661

8. Sir Edward Hyde, Earl of Clarendon from 1661

9. Sir Henry Bennet, Lord Arlington from 1665

Multituds flying from London by water in boats & barges.

Flying by land.

Burying the dead with a bell before them. Searchers.

Carts full of dead to bury.

10. The Plague of 1665

11. The Great Fire of London

12. The Four Days' Battle, 1666

the King was absent escorting his mother to her ship and London was un-patrolled.

The rebels seem to have numbered about thirty-five in all, who between them intended to seize successively the capital, the country and the world. In the event, they occupied St. Paul's until the gathering of trained bands and armed volunteers caused them to withdraw to a wood near Highgate. Three nights later, they broke back into the City and were killed or overpowered in a series of fierce fights with the militia and royal guards. Twenty survivors were tried, and the heads of fourteen of these, including Venner who remained entirely unrepentant, were sent to decorate London Bridge.[156]

The truth of the affair was so fantastic that the government, quite naturally, failed at first to understand it and believed that Venner had repre-sented, like the royalist risings of the 1650s, only a corner of a nation-wide conspiracy. The news, spreading out from London to alarm the provinces, was closely followed by a royal proclamation forbidding unauthorised meetings for any purpose and by directives to the militia to arrest all suspected persons and search houses.[157] For those men who wished to per-secute separatist groups and former republicans, a dream had come true. In many counties, the trained bands were supplemented by irregular troops of armed gentry who carried out the royal instructions with enthusiasm and sometimes without legal warrants.[158] Within six weeks at least 4,688 Quakers were in prison,[159] and the sufferings of the gathered churches were probably as great in proportion to their numbers.[160] Former republicans without obvious religious affiliations, and ministers removed since the Restoration, were also targets;[161] in London soldiers, searching for arms, plundered men who had never shown any sort of radicalism.[162] Bodies of Quakers, baptists and congregational ministers rapidly issued declarations condemning Venner and professing loyalty to the government,[163] without perceptible effect. The Quaker one represented the famous Peace Testimony of the movement, the basis of its later absolute commitment to pacifism, but its impact at the time was weakened by the fact that several leaders failed to subscribe to it.[164]

The government slowly realised that Venner had led only a tiny group and that the reaction posed a threat to order in itself. On 17 January Charles proclaimed against the searching of houses without warrant, and on the 25th the council ordered the release of most Quakers confined in the capital. The Lord Mayor, however, was now Sir Richard Browne, the former parliamen-tarian general turned royalist conspirator and an enemy of religious non-conformists, who protested so vehemently that the order was rescinded. Likewise the Lord-Lieutenant of Wales was unable to persuade his deputies in Caernarfonshire to set free their prisoners. The appalling overcrowding of the prisons at length produced a royal order, on 4 March, requiring the release of most Quakers, but permitting the retention in custody of their leaders.[165] This procedure was, in general, followed with the prisoners during the following two months, magistrates keeping in custody those whom they disliked most.[166] Nevertheless, the temper of some gentry remained unmoderated, for at the Lent Assizes and Easter Quarter Sessions in eight counties more Quakers were committed for refusing the Oath of Allegiance, and sixteen suffered the penalty of praemunire.[167] Venner had produced two enduring consequences, both ominous: the decision to retain the unprecedentedly large force of royal guards,[168] and an intensified fear of rebellion in general and of religious radicals in particular.

The third event which weakened the proponents of conciliation was the London election in March, one of the earliest for the Parliament called to succeed the Convention. The City's new bishop, Sheldon, though still treating leading presbyterian clergy with respect, was enforcing a narrow interpretation of the Worcester House Declaration. London had always been the greatest stronghold of presbyterianism, and its citizens were further irritated by the poll tax and the new excise on alcohol. As a result, four firmly anti-episcopalian MPs were returned at a hustings where the crowd shouted 'No Bishops! No Lord Bishops!' Furthermore, some of the more extreme City presbyterians wrote to allies in the provinces, encouraging them to mount a similar campaign. The government was infuriated by this attempt to overturn its policy, and reacted swiftly. On the one hand, it commissioned the conference of leading clergy of both persuasions, which had been projected at Worcester House to achieve a lasting compromise. On the other, it ordered the arrest of the men who had urged a general effort against episcopacy, and instructed the Earl of Warwick, patron of the Essex presbyterians, to stay away from the county election. The episode made presbyterians appear the principal obstacles to the royal will and to a conciliatory religious settlement, and awoke memories of the popular demonstrations in London which had preceded the civil wars.[169]

An inevitable reaction against men who had held a monopoly of power; the discontent of individuals who felt that the policies of 1660 had been contrary to their own or the public interest; the three events described above. All these factors in combination amply account for the 'Cavalier Parliament' elected in March and April. Nearly half of its number *were* 'cavaliers', in the sense of men who had been fined for royalism, or their sons, or conspirators of the 1650s.[170] The majority of the returns were of men who had risen to prominence since the wars, and like the young gentry in the Convention, many of whom were themselves re-elected, these were generally episcopalian. Lord Wharton, a champion of presbyterian clergy, considered that much less than a third of the new Commons consisted of either 'friends' or 'moderate men'.[171]

Some details survive of the means by which this was achieved in individual constituencies. The government intervened directly where it was able, notably at Oxford University where Hyde used his position as Chancellor to secure the return of his own son and of Finch, and in the Cinque Ports which were supplied with York's clients. The number of influential offices given to royalists and episcopalians had some effect, such as in the Isle of Wight where its captain, the Earl of Portland, nominated one of the members for Newport, and at Dover where the governor, a scourge of local radicals, was returned. Royalist magnates such as the Earl of Derby used their natural influence energetically; of the defeated episcopalian candidates at London, Lord Mayor Browne was elected by a pocket borough of the Seymour family, while Sir John Robinson was brought in later through a Cinque Port. By contrast, the former supporters of presbyterianism in government and provinces often seem curiously passive, raising the possibility that the King may have warned off more of such men than Warwick alone. Nevertheless, many of the results were clearly produced by an independent choice by the electors of men with a royalist past or episcopalian views. A number of references survive to contests in which 'presbyterians', 'independents' or 'fanatics' worked hard but were defeated by the drift of public opinion. Former leaders of the 'Presbyterian Knot' lost at least three county elections. Fairfax himself failing in Yorkshire. At Northampton and York, the corporations wanted representatives associated with the presbyterians, only to be challenged successfully by the freemen who preferred episcopalian gentry. As with the elections to the Convention Parliament, in the last analysis public opinion was the decisive factor.[172]

The government was obviously pleased with a result which guaranteed both monarchy and episcopacy, and the coronation of Charles upon St. George's Day was invested with even more than the usual symbolic significance of such an occasion. Historical precedent was studied and developed to produce royal pageantry of breath-taking splendour, while London citizens paid for a supplementary display to illustrate the blessings of episcopacy. The union of Church and King was represented by the ceremony itself, Archbishop Juxon placing the crown upon Charles's head and Bishop Morley preaching. The nobility competed for position and in ostentation. Northumberland and Ormonde quarrelled over precedence and Monck, now Duke of Abemarle, was affronted by the Duke of Buckingham. Buckingham's robes were said to have cost £30,000, Hyde 'shone like a diamond' and an onlooker wondered how so many ostrich feathers could have been found in England.[173] All over the country, bells were rung and municipal corporations provided wine, music and parades.[174] A Flintshire minister recorded the local festivity with the cryptic words 'King crowned, great joy, much sin, the Lord pardon. T'was a very wet evening, which prevented something of God's dishonour.'[175]

To remind the nation that his restoration had represented a reunion of parties as well as a triumph of ideals, Charles headed his coronation honours list with a set of new peerages, divided between five wartime royalists, six of their old opponents and a new man. Crew and Holles were made barons, Cooper became Lord Ashley, Booth Lord Delamere, Annesley the Earl of Anglesey, Sir John Grenville the Earl of Bath, and Howard the Earl of Carlisle. Hyde refused a dukedom for fear of jealousy,[176] but accepted the lesser title, by which he has generally been known to history, of Earl of Clarendon.

Less than three weeks later the Cavalier Parliament opened, and its Commons elected as Speaker the government favourite, Sir Edward Turner. The King welcomed the Houses with a speech commending the Act of Indemnity, followed by Clarendon who praised the character of the Commons and asked them to confirm the work of the Convention, to honour the spirit of the Declaration of Breda, to improve the royal revenue and to repress the seditious, but relieve the peaceful nonconformist.[177] They gave thanks for this with every sign of pleasure, and then set to work instead upon two destructive tasks. One was to obliterate most of the constitutional reforms of 1641-54. The other was to replace the First Restoration Settlement.

The Second Settlement

⟨⟨⟨∗∗⟩⟩⟩

THE most obvious feature of the attack upon the achievement of 1641-54 was the destruction of the measures which had produced reforms. In its first session the Parliament ordered the public burning of the Solemn League and Covenant, and of four other documents from the period 1644-54. The statute of 1642 which excluded bishops from the Lords was repealed. An act was passed declaring control of the militia to be vested in the King, followed by another to reverse the attainder of Charles I's great minister Strafford, upon the grounds that this had been obtained by the threat of mob violence. Thus the two great issues which had divided Crown and Parliament before the wars were decided in the monarch's favour, and the security of his person was further increased by an extension of the law of treason to cover attempts to coerce the King and both the spoken and written word. Much of this activity provoked some opposition in the Commons, Prynne speaking against the bishops, and the presbyterians from London proposing that the rights of the subject be increased as well as the safety of the ruler. The immolation of the Covenant, a text held sacred by the more rigid presbyterians, was considered by many to be a violation of the principle of reconciliation, and was opposed by 103 MPs. It was probably the first issue to produce an open division in Charles's government, for Morice acted as teller against it while Clarendon and the other Privy Councillors in the Lords seem to have let that House endorse it without a struggle. Nevertheless, all these measures were achieved with relative ease and speed.[1]

What they emphatically did *not* represent was the final victory of King over Parliament after twenty years of conflict. The Cavalier Parliament did not restore the monarchy of Charles I, but retained those subsequent reforms which benefited its members as a class, an estate or an institution. Thus they explicitly excluded the Court of High Commission and the Canons of 1640 from restoration, thereby denying the bishops the power they had wielded under Laud. The repeal of the Triennial Act, and the revival of Star Chamber and the Council of the North, were discussed but not pursued.[2] Alone of the old prerogative courts, the Council of Wales was resurrected, as it had been the least unpopular and not the subject of legislation.[3] The immediate reason for declaring the King's formal power over the militia was to indemnify its officers for the many actions committed by them since the Restoration under the authority of royal directions. In January 1662 the government asked Parliament for the means to support a new standing army under the Duke of York, and was obliged instead to be satisfied with the right to levy £70,000 per year to keep the militia standing in case of an emergency, with the further limitation that this power would lapse in 1665. The same act which provided for this also safeguarded the rights of subjects more explicitly, reduced the scale of charges for the militia, and resolved all the confusion between the responsibilities of justices and Deputy-Lieutenants, parish and private arms, and the assessments of estates in different hundreds, which had debilitated the trained bands for over a hundred years.[4]

While thus securing themselves against pressure from above, the members of this Parliament took care to erect barriers against pressure from below, in a set of measures designed to ensure that the tactics employed in 1640-1 to whip up popular feeling could not be repeated. It was made illegal to call the King a Catholic, to subscribe to a petition requesting an alteration in the law without the approval of magistrates or a Grand Jury, or to present one accompanied by more than ten persons. Finally, after a lengthy dispute between the Houses over the privileges of peers, an act was passed which required the registration of all books and presses, the submission of bonds by printers and the censorship of all printed works by a panel of the most important government ministers and churchmen.[5]

This measure to restrain the press illustrates, on closer inspection, how delicate was the relationship between the Crown and this Parliament, even during the latter's first sessions and over an issue in which they had common interests. Since the King's return, the production of literature regarded by many as seditious or offensive had been a common complaint, and both executive and legislature had acted upon it. In July 1660, the Privy Council deprived Canne, for all his time-serving, of his newspapers, and gave a monopoly of the writing and printing of news-books to the reliable Muddiman and Dury. Over them in turn, the King seems to have set the man who had run the royalist newspaper of the civil war, John Berkenhead, and in February 1662 he employed that embittered cavalier, Roger L'Estrange, to hunt down seditious pamphlets.[6] The Council ordered the arrest of those responsible for a succession of tracts which had complained of the consequences of the Restoration,[7] and in 1660 and 1661, while the press was still nominally free, the printer who published most of Bunyan's early works was seized four times.[8] In the same period, the Lords sent another printer to the Tower, the mayor of Chester confiscated Quaker pamphlets, the corporation of Sherborne burned those of baptists and the city fathers of Exeter those of presbyterians.[9] A formal system of licensing would greatly facilitate such repression, and the Cavalier Parliament provided it in an entirely typical manner. It entrusted the work to the greatest officers of Church and State, but limited the effect of the act to two years, thereby leaving the executive utterly dependent upon Parliament for a renewal of those powers.

The effects of the statute were profound. It did not entirely prevent the production and dissemination of the literature which it was designed to curb, for unlicensed tracts, particularly by Quakers, continued to appear. What it destroyed was the atmosphere of free debate, the sense of a plurality of possible futures, the discussion of fundamental issues from all points of view, the hope that governments might be converted by force of argument, which had made most of the two previous decades so exciting and disturbing. The pamphlet collection of the London bookseller George Thomason, which today represents the principal source for the controversies of the civil wars and Interregnum, peters out at the end of 1661 as though he no longer considered the work of continuing it worthwhile. The Restoration government newspapers illustrate the truth that power corrupts style as well as persons, containing progressively less news and providing that in a dour tone which lacks all the wit and fire of Berkenhead's wartime press. If they had an overall aim, it was to foster a lack of interest in public affairs. It cannot be a coincidence that the two enduring literary masterpieces of the 1660s came from the pens of a sectary held in Bedford gaol and of a blind and impoverished republican living in obscurity in the capital.[10] The final irony is clear. English people of subsequent generations have lived in a political and religious world which was substantially created at the Restoration, but have turned for delight and edification to men who had been among the principal victims of the event.

The one part of the First Restoration Settlement which the government was more anxious to alter than the Cavalier Parliament was the financial provision. Clarendon had closed the Convention by praising this, and opened the new Parliament by asking to have it improved. In the brief interval, it had already become obvious that none of the sources of royal revenue were producing as much as expected. The profits which were received were depleted by the repayment of the Convention's own debts and some of those accrued by the King and his father before the Restoration, for neither of which additional supplies had been made. Despite the Chancellor's appeal, the presence in the House of Sir Philip Warwick, one of the principal financial officers, and the lack of competing concerns of the urgency of those which had distracted the Convention, the new MPs proceeded even more slowly in the matter than their predecessors. It was certainly not a propitious time to burden the country with further exactions, for trade had not yet revived and prices rose more in 1661, as constant rain ruined the harvest.[11] But the sheer lack of attention given to the problem for much of the time suggests that they were simply more interested in other things.

During the first session, the Commons did nothing but collect information and produce bills for a voluntary subscription to the King, collected by county commissioners, and to hasten the arrears of all previous taxes. The former measure was proposed by presbyterians in the House, which automatically diminished the enthusiasm of the majority for making large donations, and neither, when enacted, raised very much.[12] At the beginning of the second session, in November, Charles made a personal request for a better supply, and earned a grant of £1,260,000 by the effective means of an 'assessment' to balance his accounts until a permanent provision was agreed upon. A means for the latter, however, was not decided before the recess, and nothing more was done about it in the third session until March, when the King made another speech complaining of this neglect. At that moment, the Commons decided to remove the annual deficit by the crude direct taxation of a levy imposed upon each hearth and stove in a house. The origins of the proposal remain obscure, and it was argued in the Commons that the new tax was both an imposition upon a necessity and would affect relatively poor people. Perhaps to decrease its inevitable unpopularity, the MPs determined upon a means of collection certain to reduce the yield considerably, whereby householders themselves certified the number of their hearths and paid over the levy to local constables, who forwarded both the certificates and the money through the JPs to the Exchequer. Despite this ominous detail, Charles thanked Parliament for its generosity at the close of the session when the levy became law.[13]

In financial as in political affairs, the MPs had attempted to find a medium between serving the Crown and protecting its members and the public. The fiscal measures which they and the Convention produced were certainly more adventurous than those of any previous Stuart Parliaments, and for this the royal gratitude expressed to each was deserved. The essential problem was that neither King nor Country were to behave responsibly in this matter.

If the Hearth Tax represented an addition by monarch and legislature to the text of the first settlement, the Corporation Act of 1661 was a connivance by both in a breach of its spirit. In 1660 the government had usually been content with the restoration of royalist members of urban councils and the removal of their replacements, though signs of a harsher policy had appeared at times. During the early part of 1661 the royal temper became frayed by the reluctance of some corporations either to restore royalists or to accept the

King's nominees for offices, and also by the number of noisy quarrels which broke out in municipalities.[14] It is not surprising that as soon as the election results for the new Parliament were known, and the government felt secure, a full-scale assertion of royal authority commenced, based on the fact that most towns were governed under charters conferred by Interregnum regimes which were open to challenge. In April a writ of *quo warranto* was issued against Bristol's corporation, which had been one of the most obstinate in its failure to grant royalists restitution. This was dropped after delicate negotiations at court which cost the council £584, but the new charter was nevertheless made conditional on the removal of all those 'unduly elected'. As a result, within six months, three out of the forty-three members of the corporation of 1659 remained in office.[15] On 7 May the Privy Council decided that the King would claim the nomination of the first aldermen, recorders and clerks when issuing all new charters, and restrict the parliamentary franchise to the corporation. In June Attorney-General Palmer and a judge recommended that he nominate the entire council since the existing one was full of 'usurpers' from the Interregnum.[16]

On 19 June, however, the Commons introduced a bill whereby municipalities would be purged by commissioners chosen by Parliament. It is easy to imagine that many gentry resented the fact that supporters of the republic retained power in the towns, while they had lost it in the shires, and also that they should perceive an opportunity of gaining personal influence in the urban centres, many of which contained parliamentary seats, by dislodging these men in favour of others. In the first nine months of 1661 some of them attempted this by informal means at Leeds, Christchurch, Wallingford and Bath, only to be foiled in each case by the government.[17] Other men must have believed in preserving the policy of reconciliation upon which the Restoration had been based, and some in the House were personally endangered by the proposal, such as Prynne who had been a target of the intrigue at Bath. The battle between the two sides was fierce, and the bill only survived by five votes. When it reached the Lords, Prynne took up the pen which had been uncharacteristically idle since his return to active parliamentary politics, to publish an appeal to the peers. They ignored it, but the Commons subjected him to a formal rebuke which reduced this man, who had presented his face to the executioner's knife without flinching, to tears of humiliation. To compound this, the House published the whole affair. It bore no lasting malice, for Prynne was soon appointed to committees again, but he had been broken. Henceforth he turned to antiquarian works, and with the removal of his passionate voice another link with the former age was gone.[18]

Now the bill encountered the opposition of the King, who persuaded the

Lords to rewrite it completely, removing the proposed commissions and instead awarding him the powers he had aimed at since May. Three amendments were made in these to make them palatable to the Commons: he now asked to choose future mayors from a list of six names presented by a corporation, dropped the clause about the franchise, and permitted county justices to exercise authority in local towns. These efforts failed, for the MPs rejected the entire package with the objections that it would give the Crown too much power and would fail to achieve their wish for a purge. The recess intervened, and during it Charles treated corporations as though he intended his plan to operate, and exacted from London itself the right to remove a few aldermen at will, as the price of a new charter.[19] At the opening of the second session, however, either weakened by its financial plight or finding the Lords wavering, the government backed down and offered an acceptable compromise, whereby the original bill was restored with the King selecting the commissioners. The men he chose were royalists and episcopalians of the sort who made up most of the Commons and whom the latter must themselves have intended. Thus the Crown had won a portion of the form and lost all the substance.[20]

The commissioners operated from April 1662 until the expiry of their powers the following March, most of their work being done in the late summer. The results varied according to region. Most of the boroughs of the north, Wales and the east Midlands were gently treated, only a few men being replaced in each and the process often representing a transfer of power within the existing élite. Elsewhere, the same was true of those which were tiny and intimate, such as Stratford-upon-Avon or Bere Alston, or where the Interregnum leaders had already lost power, as at London, Bristol, Great Yarmouth, Worcester and Eye, or which were important enough to be dealt with by a commission of their own members, like Coventry and Southampton. The others lost a majority of their corporation members, and the damage was greater in that proportionately more of the most important, the mayors and aldermen, were removed. All members were required to sign a declaration against the Covenant and to take an oath against the principle of resistance to the King, but the commissioners had power to displace even those who signed and swore, and usually did. Acceptance of the tests represented instead a partial insurance against being regarded as a suspected person thereafter, and subjected to search and arrest at moments of tension. The essentially negative nature of the whole operation is illustrated by the difficulty frequently encountered in finding replacements for those discharged; the commissioners were reduced to appointing obscure citizens or strangers from outside the town, or simply leaving places vacant for years, unless, as at Ludlow and Liverpool, they installed themselves as members. All told, it was a partisan purge unprecedented in English municipal history, far exceeding anything during the wars and Revolution. Some of the men who had been removed returned quietly to office in later years with the connivance of the corporations concerned; others were re-elected by defiant freemen, only to fall again before the barriers of the oath and declaration, and also the sacrament of the revived episcopalian Church, which remained as tests for all future members. Most were consigned to personal bitterness and public impotence.[21]

The process still presents some puzzles. One is the fact that much of the House which pushed the act through had itself been elected by the corporation members who were to be its victims. County seats, and those in which the freemen had imposed their wishes on the council, would account for a good many of the MPs who desired a purge, but not all. It is probable that urban leaders chose these royalists and episcopalians in an attempt to complete that rehabilitation in the restored monarchical state which their representatives in the event prevented, and also that these MPs had offered their constituencies the most faithful service in their anxiety to be elected. Certainly, it appears that many boroughs did not realise what they were getting. Then there is the geographical variation in the intensity of the purges, which had no obvious correspondence either to former royalist territory, western towns suffering badly but not those of Wales or Yorkshire, or to areas where gentry had been most markedly alienated from Interregnum regimes. It is possible that one is in fact plotting a map of presbyterianism and congregational independency, but this does not conform perfectly to the known distribution of these beliefs. Such a problem is linked to another and greater one, that recent historians[22] have tended to discount the role of ideology in provincial urban politics during the civil wars and Revolution, emphasising instead the effect of traditional rivalries, the influence of key individuals and the fortunes of war. The fact that corporations in general celebrated the Restoration with enthusiasm, surrendered their fee-farms to the King and sent him gifts would seem to project this view comfortably into the 1660s. Yet in 1662, hundreds of their leaders preferred to sacrifice office and expose themselves to harassment, rather than accept a political oath and a religious declaration. It would be helpful if we could demonstrate that the declaration was a greater obstacle than the oath but, maddeningly, the records do not reveal this. The historian is left to wonder how ideology entered urban politics during the 1650s, or to reconsider the prevailing orthodoxy concerning the previous decade.

The number of occasions on which the Cavalier House of Commons checked royal power during its early sessions was balanced by the government's successful defence of the legislation of the First Restoration Settlement. This was vulnerable as a whole because the Convention, never called by a King, could be deemed an illegal assembly. Before the Restoration, as has been noted, this seems to have been seen as an advantage by Charles's advisers, who had feared that they would be made to accept unpalatable legislation as the price of his return. Instead, ironically, they found themselves protecting statutes which had turned out to be in the royal interest.

For the government, now as before, the most important of these was the Act of Indemnity, and the King's speech to the new Parliament had stressed his desire to preserve it. Over six weeks later, he had to repeat his views sharply, as the bill to confirm it had been held up by furious debate and a proviso to exclude more men had been proposed. This intervention succeeded in easing the measure up into the more compliant Lords. The MPs had to be satisfied with punishing men whom the original act had left vulnerable to further legislation, consisting of those who had sat in the regicide court without signing the death warrant, the regicides who had surrendered in 1660, and Lambert and Vane. The first category were abandoned to the Commons' rage and suffered the loss of their property, while those still alive were sentenced to imprisonment, relieved by being dragged around London on hurdles once a year.[23] The men who had surrendered, however, were protected by the personal wish of Charles, who passed Clarendon a note indicating that he was 'weary of hanging' and requesting that the bill prepared by the Commons for their execution be 'left to sleep' in the Lords.[24]

In the end, the Act of Indemnity claimed four more lives. Three were those of regicides who had fled abroad and were lured into a trap in Holland, to be shipped to London and executed in April 1662. Among them was the great republican Colonel Okey.[25] The fourth life was Vane's, which was taken, as others had been spared, upon a royal whim. In the same month in which Okey perished, the government responded belatedly to repeated requests by the Commons for the trial of both Sir Henry and of Lambert. This not only involved the revocation of the reprieve granted to both in 1660, but was awkward in legal terms, for neither was a regicide and their actions had amounted only to those of many men who had been indemnified: their real crime was to have proved themselves more able, and therefore dangerous. Lambert chose to face realities, expressed contrition to the court and thereby obtained the King's mercy. Vane, by constrast, defended himself with furious indignation, and so revealed in Charles a capacity for vindictiveness which had hitherto lain dormant. A royal letter sped to Clarendon insisting upon Sir Henry's death, which was duly obtained by keeping the jury without food or drink. His execution, though by the courtly means of beheading appropriate to his family's importance, was arranged with finely calculated malice, taking place upon the anniversary of Naseby, on the spot on Tower Hill where Strafford had died, with musicians under the scaffold to drown his final speech. He spoke none the less, as he offered his neck, with perfect courage. Significantly, whereas the City had exulted over the agonising demise of the regicides in 1660, now it spoke only in praise of Vane's deportment and in criticism of the manner in which he had been destroyed. By overplaying its hand, the monarchy had turned a symbol of treason and schism into one of dignity and law.[26]

The Convention's act for the settlement of ministers provoked both a more determined attack by the Commons and a greater effort in its defence by the government. A bill to replace it, with a measure which would displace more clergy surviving from the Interregnum and exact financial penalties from others, made a closely-argued passage through the Lower House, only to be rejected by the Lords in February 1660 because Clarendon mobilised against it the full array of government supporters there, including Sheldon and the bishops. Some MPs threatened Charles with a suspension of the work of improving royal finances until the statute was passed, but he stood firm and the House withdrew from the prospect of such open confrontation.[27] A less dramatic, but equally effective, process ensured the survival of the land settlement. In 1662 Parliament did extend this slightly to restore advowsons and impropriate tithes signed away by royalists in lieu of composition fines. The judges were unable to decide whether this constituted a breach of the Act of Indemnity, but the measure was allowed through, for reasons to be discussed, and caused no stir. Indeed, some royalists seem already to have reclaimed these assets informally.[28] What did produce anxiety, and threatened to produce widespread disturbance, were three private bills introduced by royalists to reclaim land they had sold to pay fines, or to recoup profits made out of their confiscated estates during the Interregnum. One, representing another attempt by the Earl of Derby to achieve the compulsory repurchase of certain of his lands, passed both Houses despite an official protest entered by Clarendon and the government peers. Charles destroyed it by taking one of the most drastic steps open to a monarch, of refusing his assent.[29]

In the arena of parliamentary politics, therefore, the government championed both the letter and the sentiments of the Act of Indemnity. On closer inspection, its position loses much of the disinterested generosity which filled the speeches of its members and appears to contrast so nobly with the attitude of the Commons. For one thing, reprieve did not mean release, and the men saved by Charles were left to die in prison. Lambert, the man of action, may have come to envy Vane his fate, during the twenty-two years of life which remained to him, penned in island fortresses. His existence may

have been eased latterly by the fact that his mind gave way. The final achievement of Monck's efforts on behalf of Hesilrige was that Sir Arthur died in the
Tower instead of upon the scaffold, in the winter after the Restoration, both
flesh and spirit apparently broken by the shock of that event. In April a
proclamation was prepared which announced the King's intention of
excepting twelve more men from indemnity, at will, though this was not
issued and there is no evidence of who had proposed and opposed it.[30]

Furthermore, as with 'White's Plot', the government could foster fear
while it preached reconciliation. This process became easier in the course of
1661 when, to avoid being taken by surprise again as they had by Venner, the
Secretaries of State constructed a system of spies which covered the country.[31]
It was naturally most active in London, and towards the end of the year
turned up there the so-called 'Wildman Plot'. All that can be established of
the truth behind this is that a group of former republican soldiers, politicians
and writers had taken to meeting and discussing current affairs. In early
winter they were arrested, and Clarendon informed Parliament that these
men had been at the centre of a conspiracy intended to seize key towns and
topple the government. It was upon this that the latter based its appeal for a
standing army, which, as has been seen, came to nothing. So, also, did the
examination of the accused, and none were tried, but neither were they
released, being sent to join the regicides in remote prisons. Among them was
James Harrington, the republic's great political philosopher, who had been
arrested with his latest treatise lying unfinished on his desk. Unlike Lambert,
he was freed after some years, but not until his mind had also collapsed. The
most pleasant interpretation which can be placed upon the episode is that the
Privy Council believed that it had found a genuine conspiracy and exploited
it, unscrupulously, to further its political ends and to remove potential opponents.[32] Some former republicans retained their liberty by discreet presents
to those in power, the best-documented case being that of Whitelocke,
whom Clarendon treated for years as a sheep to be sheared repeatedly of
property and money.[33] Others, like Desborough, found peace only by fleeing
abroad. It is difficult either to avoid pitying these men, or to refute the observation of Pepys, that when in power the republicans had treated their own
enemies no better.[34]

The lesser supporters of the fallen regimes were persecuted by local
justices and militia officers, who submitted them to repeated interrogation
and searches for arms. One former captain who had followed Lambert
underwent this process five times in the two years after the Restoration,
while an ex-colonel was finally released from bonds for good behaviour in
1687.[35] Much of this work was undertaken in genuine fear of risings and
encouraged by the Privy Council; after Venner's escapade the need for it

appeared obvious.[36] Other actions, however, were clearly intended to obtain vengeance for the past rather than security in the present, and were directed by royalists against their enemies of the 1640s as well as of the 1650s. One example of these consisted of lawsuits lodged against former sequestrators and county committee-men in defiance of the Act of Indemnity, at least eight of which are recorded.[37] It is hard to imagine that any of these met with the approval of the government, but there survives, in the Public Record Office, a document dated in June 1662 which appears to consist of returns to an Exchequer Special Commission of Enquiry into the losses of Norfolk royalists during the wars.[38] It was presumably intended to relieve the victims rather than to punish the perpetrators, but fits into no obvious context and represents at present a disturbing enigma.

A less scrupulous, and more effective, way of attacking a wartime enemy who had not actively supported the republic was to implicate him in a conspiracy. At the same time, in late 1661, that the government used the Wildman affair for its own convenience, some provincial gentry produced a separate plot scare, in circumstances which arouse even greater suspicion. A Worcestershire royalist, Sir John Packington, claimed to have come by some letters dropped by a stranger in a local lane, which represented the exchanges of participants in an imminent rising. Those named were local presbyterians, including the only one of these to have become a national figure, Richard Baxter. The result of this, combined with the revelations in London, was a nation-wide panic in which scores of suspects were rounded up. Baxter himself was protected by royal favour and by the fact that only his surname, a not uncommon one, had appeared in the letters, but the lesser men implicated were kept in custody for months without trial by the Deputy-Lieutenants. One of the victims, long after, published the accusation that Packington had written his 'evidence' himself. No refutation of this appeared, and the circumstantial evidence in favour of it is considerable. Shortly afterwards, similar letters were 'discovered' in Herefordshire, but the men named in them were some whom it suited the government to conciliate, and their captors were severely reprimanded.[39]

Lesser offences than treason could be foisted upon old enemies with satisfying results. In Somerset, the formerly royalist Deputy-Lieutenants had a grudge against William Strode, a wartime parliamentarian and an outspoken presbyterian. They charged him successively with defying proper authority (he had protested against over-assessment for the militia), sedition (for his views on bishops) and questioning the royal prerogative (he had protested against his arbitrary arrest). The Privy Council had no interest in Strode, and ordered him to apologise to his tormentors on his knees, after which he was left in peace.[40]

A further qualification of the notion of a vengeful Commons facing a benevolent government is the fact that the former also took positive steps to remove some of the bitterness of former royalists. A bill intended to enable them to take loans at a tiny rate of interest was not completed by the Lords, but two associated statutes were. One regularised, and encouraged, the existing provision of local relief for maimed and needy men from the Kings' armies. The other apportioned £60,000 of the assessment granted to Charles in the second session to be divided among impoverished former royalist officers. This project proved better upon paper than in practice. So many claimants pressed forward that further legislation was required, to clarify procedure in detecting the genuinely loyal and needy. Even when this work was done, the number of worthy cases were so numerous that an equal division of the money would have left each man with less than £12.[41]

Nevertheless, after this time the grievances of Cavaliers became a less strident theme in public and private affairs. The Commons' efforts to satisfy them must have played some part in this, and so did their continued employment by the King, as fresh posts at his disposal fell vacant. It is extremely likely, however, that this material compensation may have been less important for many old royalists than the emotional satisfaction of observing the punishment inflicted upon their former opponents. The Corporation Act represented a part of this process, but most of it was contained in the religious legislation of the Second Restoration Settlement.

During 1661 the government's basic aim in religious affairs remained what it had been in the previous year: to become accepted as an arbiter and a protector by all parties. Clarendon had opened the Cavalier Parliament by speaking on behalf of peaceful nonconformists. In the same month, the conference between leading presbyterians and episcopalians, which Charles had commissioned in March, opened at the Savoy, and a royal proclamation forbade the imprisonment of Quakers for refusing oaths.[42] Even those older enemies of the national Church for whom neither the royalist, parliamentarian nor republican parties had proposed toleration, the Catholics, enjoyed royal favour. Charles's life had arguably been saved by them after the Battle of Worcester, and soon after his restoration he told their clergy that the penal laws against them would be laxly enforced. At the Worcester House Conference, he opposed an attempt by Baxter to obtain an explicit clause against them in the Declaration.[43] In one year almost every aspect of this programme was to be destroyed.

The Catholics' hopes were disposed of most easily, and gently. The essence of their case was that the efforts made by so many of them for the royalist case rendered ridiculous the laws against them, which were based on the premise that they were natural traitors. This was not an argument likely to carry weight with the Commons of 1660, which included so many men who had been of the opposing party and had censured the followers of Rome for seeking to manipulate Charles I for their own ends; indeed it had manifested hostility to them at every opportunity. The Upper House, with its twenty-five Catholic members[44] and royalist majority, had been markedly more sympathetic,[45] and the election of 1661 had now returned many MPs who had fought and suffered alongside the Pope's adherents. There was thus good reason to believe that the Cavalier Parliament would prove receptive to a plea for the removal of the laws against the latter: one was duly made to the Lords in the first session, delivered by Sir Samuel Tuke, the Catholic royalist who had written the celebrated eulogy of Charles II. The response at first promised limited success, for although the peers proved unwilling to alter most of the penal legislation, they did resolve to modify that against secular priests. At the recess, however, no bill had yet been produced for this purpose, and thereafter the project was quietly dropped.[46] A factor had come into play which had hitherto been missing from the process of settlement: a division among government supporters, following not the lines of the wartime parties, but those of previous factions among the royalists themselves.

During the Great Civil War, Clarendon and his allies had pursued the goal of a negotiated peace, which would confirm the traditional powers of the Crown within the restrictions placed upon them in 1640-1. In this they found themselves opposed, and eventually eclipsed by, men who worked for an absolute victory which would enable the King to impose whatever terms he wished. Of these the most influential had been George, Lord Digby, who had subsequently succeeded his father as Earl of Bristol. Physically, this man was a huge cherub, with puffy cheeks and a mop of blond hair, and his personality was just as baroque. All his life he remained the proponent of the bold stroke, the (briefly) calculated risk, the unorthodox solution. His energy was imposing, his enthusiasm infectious and his judgement invariably wrong. In isolation he was a comical nuisance, but when given power he could be deadly. His advice had almost certainly provoked the attempt upon the Five Members, which helped to precipitate the Great Civil War, and produced the Battle of Naseby, which lost that war for the King. In the late 1650s he had urged Charles II to become a Roman Catholic to secure foreign aid, the one course which would have made the Restoration virtually impossible. Always entirely convinced by his own reasoning, Bristol had made the conversion himself, only to endure not only the rejection of his policy but dismissal from his office of Secretary of State, which was subsequently given to Morice.[47]

Unfortunately for his contemporaries, this Earl was never vanquished for long. When the Restoration occurred, he crossed to England soon after the royal party and drew attention to himself with a notable speech in favour of the Bill of Indemnity. By winter he had returned, if not to office, to royal favour, and his flamboyant, shallow, exciting personality became one of the focal points of the court.[48] Clarendon, whom he had displaced from power nearly twenty years before, reacted with an almost childish spite, using his own new authority as Chancellor of Oxford University to dismiss Bristol from its Stewardship.[49] It was apparently this feud which became interwoven with the attempts of the Catholics to obtain relief and foiled them, for Bristol pushed forward to champion his co-religionists' cause. Clarendon always regarded Catholics with some suspicion and distaste, and the brazen new confidence of those at court, allied with his old enemy, seems to have cost them his support. The reappearance of the bishops in the Lords, increasing the potential opposition, and the fissuring of the Catholic lobby in a new round of quarrels between secular and regular clergy, may have completed the demise of the project for relief.[50]

Nevertheless, in practice if not in law, the sufferings of the Roman Catholic community appeared to be over. Some provincial commoners still expressed hostility to it,[51] but magistrates almost all chose to let the laws against both Catholic recusants and clergy become dormant.[52] The government encouraged this clemency, and when Bishop Cosin harassed a recusant in his new see of Durham, he was rebuked by Sheldon himself on behalf of the Privy Council.[53] To this extent, the Penderells had done service to their religion, as well as to their monarchy, when they assisted the latter into the tree at Boscobel.

This said, it must be added that the peace now enjoyed by the traditional victims of Anglican orthodoxy was probably due not only to their royalism, but to the preoccupation of the defenders of that orthodoxy with the other end of the religious spectrum. The King's May proclamation on behalf of the Quakers procured the release of many, but in the succeeding eight months more were imprisoned in nineteen counties, from Devon and Kent to Durham and the end of Wales. Officers of royal garrisons joined local magistrates in this work, and the only change effected by Charles's attitude was that the captives were now convicted more frequently for meeting for seditious purposes than for refusing oaths. In London itself, Lord Mayor Browne gaoled fifty-seven, seizing any whom he met in the street who would not doff their hats to him.[54] This persecution, however, cannot be perfectly understood unless it is stressed that the aggression of the early years of the movement was not yet spent. A Cheshire parson could still be halted in mid-sermon by two Quakers equipped with a candle, with which they proposed to burn an offending text, while Browne's hostility could hardly have been moderated when he was presented with a tract of exhortation addressed to the 'so-called Lord Mayor'.[55] The established order could still feel itself under attack.

The gathered churches continued to pay heavily for Venner's folly: they were raided and their leaders were secured. In London the new Lieutenant of the Tower, Robinson, employed the garrison in this sport.[56] One lay preacher paid for the hauteur with which he responded to examination by being convicted of treasonable words. His head was set on a stake before his meeting-house.[57]

The attitude of the Cavalier Parliament was that of the intolerant provincial gentry. When the King absolved Quakers from oaths, the Commons responded with a bill to punish all religious radicals for refusing them. The Quaker leaders themselves may have provoked this by publishing an appeal to both Houses which, with more integrity than common sense, cited the righteousness of their beliefs, rather than the propriety of their political behaviour, as an argument against persecution. When they appeared before the Lords in person, to solicit opposition to the Commons' bill, they enraged the peers so much that the House set up its own committee to discuss measures against them. Any hope that the government would come to the rescue was destroyed by Clarendon, whose fundamental conservatism seems to have been outraged by their principles and behaviour. Writing to his Vice-Chancellor at Oxford, he described them as 'a sort of people upon whom tenderness and lenity do not at all prevail', and he drove the bill against them through the Lords in the third session. As in the case of the Catholics, the Chancellor now seems to have felt himself sufficiently indispensable to his royal master to flout the latter's own wishes. His fellow ministers, Nicholas and Southampton, supported Clarendon in his attitude to 'fanatics', and it is likely, from their respective past records, that most of the Privy Council did so.[58]

Some of the Lords argued for moderation, particularly Bishop Gauden who held that severity would stiffen resistance, but to little effect. A baptist petition to the Upper House, which shrewdly appealed to the Declaration of Breda and stressed the signatories' utter subservience, seems to have caused it to restrict the measure to Quakers alone, but the Commons refused to accept this. The act that resulted was directed at anybody who refused the Oath of Allegiance and held or attended a meeting, and the penalties stiffened through fines and imprisonment to transportation for the third offence. If enforced strictly, it was a means of annihilation, rather than correction.[59]

As with any statute, the results depended upon the differing beliefs and personalities of local magistrates. In the fifteen months after its passage, this one was enforced extensively in Cheshire, Lancashire, Westmorland, Wiltshire,

Somerset, Oxfordshire, London, Devon and Worcestershire, and more sparsely in twenty-two other counties. Clarendon urged its implementation at Oxford, while in the capital Browne and Robinson had two hundred Quakers in gaol by August; two of their greatest leaders died of the diseases soon rife in the swarming cells. There, and wherever else, the persecution was intense, sectaries suffered also.[60] The King continued to make efforts to achieve greater toleration, such as a proclamation in August for the release of those Quakers awaiting trial in the metropolis who were not leaders,[61] but he was thwarted virtually upon all sides. The Commons and his greatest ministers had made their attitude clear, some assize judges encouraged prosecutions, and the government press, run by Berkenhead, portrayed religious radicals as criminals and fools and applauded the act against them. For their part, Quakers continued to display that marvellous lack of tact that was a concomitant of their zeal and supplied Berkenhead with ammunition. Some refused to sign a promise to abstain from plotting before the Privy Council, on the grounds that it imposed upon their rights as free men. Two women poured blood upon the altar of St. Paul's, and Browne received another tract warning him of his impending destruction.[62]

No true picture can be obtained of the sufferings of the Quakers, in the period immediately after the passage of the statute against them, unless it is stressed that this was but one of several instruments employed by their persecutors. In a number of places the new law was used to intimidate the rank and file, but their leaders were picked off by praemunire, which was inflicted upon at least eighty Quakers in the years 1662-4. It was, however, used with some delicacy. The accused were often allowed several months to alter their opinions before sentence was passed; some were released after a few years, and only three lost their property.[63] Alongside them, many of their fellows were prosecuted for non-payment of tithes, either by ministers or lay impropriators, as they had been since their first appearance and were to be for another century. The consequences varied from the confiscation of a portion of a man's harvest or household goods (often to a value greatly in excess of the debt) to imprisonment till payment was made. The latter penalty acted as a steady process of attrition upon the active membership of local groups.[64]

In most counties, the recusancy statutes produced originally against Catholics were enforced against religious radicals after 1661, and 203 Quakers fell foul of them in Cheshire alone between 1662 and 1665. Here again, some restraint was shown, for the lower rate of fines decreed by law was usually imposed, though conscientious defendants often went to prison rather than pay these.[65] The revival of the church courts exposed radicals to the penalty of excommunication for recusancy, non-baptism of children, working on Sunday and other offences, which, when made the basis of an appeal by the Church to a secular magistrate, could land the accused in gaol until he or she conformed. The ecclesiastical courts of the Restoration period, however, compared with those of the pre-Reformation Church, and perhaps of Laud, do give an impression of barking much more effectively than they could bite. In 1662-4 at least eighty Quakers suffered in secular courts as a result of the clergy's writs, but during the same period 134 were excommunicated in Essex alone.[66] The absence of a Court of High Commission had thrown churchmen more than ever upon the mercy of the local JP, at a time when they had an unprecedented number of enemies.

Put together, all these cases reveal that the Second Restoration Settlement produced a pattern of localised persecution, severe in places, but mild compared with that which had followed Venner's rising, or that which was to come. Magistrates who wanted to extirpate religious nonconformity were continually frustrated by colleagues, constables and juries who were less worried by it.[67] Those arrested were usually released after a number of weeks, and nobody was transported. One Quaker was literally delivered by his piety, for his loud prayers so disturbed the justices at their play on the bowling-green near the gaol that they decided to discharge him.[68] A fellow-believer in York Castle in October 1662 could write that he was one of 110 held there, but add that, in most of the county, meetings were undisturbed.[69] Quaker leaders could still tour gatherings of the faithful throughout the country in 1663 without suffering more than the threat of arrest.[70] Yet the turning-point of the movement had been reached. Until now enemies had been individual and the central government, republican or royal, had been sympathetic and able to intervene. Hopes of an ultimate victory, of a nation of Friends, seemed tenable. Now the position was reversed, and safety lay only in the moderation of individual and local men. The energy of the evangelists was turning inward, upon the task of maintaining the spirits and numbers of existing converts. The Lamb's War, which they had declared ten years before, had been lost.

While providing a weapon against dissenters who rejected the established Church, the champions of orthodoxy took pains to rid that Church itself of aberrant opinions. The Act of Uniformity which they employed for this purpose has ever since represented the best-known part of the Second Restoration Settlement, has to some extent distracted attention from the other measures, and has been the subject of some of the best recent research. In treatment of it here, it must be stressed that this act functioned as a part of the whole settlement, and, as with the associated legislation, closely reflected developments in the provinces.

In the summer of 1660 the last presbyterian *classes* dissolved, as part of the acceptance by most of their leaders of modified episcopacy.[71] Simultaneously, episcopalians in many areas commenced a restoration of the traditional Church without tarrying for whatever hybrid the churchmen might produce. A nation-wide sample of churchwardens' accounts[72] shows that nearly half of these parishes bought the pre-war Prayer Book in the eighteen months after the Restoration, most of them doing so during the first year, despite the constant expectation that this book would be replaced. The figure is more impressive still when it is noted that rural communities, which were frequently more conservative, and counties such as Dorset, where episcopalianism was unusually aggressive, show few entries for this purchase. The suspicion, reinforced by the surviving Interregnum inventories, is that there, existing Prayer Books were simply being dusted down and re-used, if indeed they required dusting. By contrast, only just over a quarter of the City's churches whose accounts survive bought the old liturgy, and the inventories of 1659 there contain only one surviving copy. This information both reinforces the traditional picture of the capital's presbyterianism and adds a background to the activities of the provincials who attempted to force local clergy to use the Prayer Book. In the eighteen months after the Worcester House Declaration, and in defiance of it, ministers were indicted for not using the book in eighteen counties, often by their humbler parishioners.[73] The old religion was in effect returning with the maypoles.

Upon this base the former hierarchy was reconstructed. Part of this process was literal, consisting of the repair of cathedrals, chapter houses and palaces. It was slow and expensive work, the restoration of Winchester Cathedral alone consuming £8,517 in the first two years after the King's return. Much of the money was provided by the windfall of entry fines resulting from the land settlement, but the amount naturally varied with the wealth of the see, so that the Dean and Chapter of Winchester could employ an 'army' of workmen from their revenues, while those of Chester had to borrow heavily to make any substantial repairs. Some older bishops apparently enriched themselves, while some of their new colleagues devoted their private wealth to the task of rebuilding. In some dioceses laymen also contributed generously to it. From this uneven progress, it seems possible to generalise that, although embellishments such as organs were often still missing, all the cathedrals save those of Lichfield and Rochester were in good repair by the end of 1662. It is an achievement which testifies to the high morale and energy of most of the higher clergy in the period.[74]

The latter is true also of the revival of diocesan machinery. Although Charles, at the Restoration, had made clear his attachment to bishops, he had been significantly silent upon the future of deans and chapters, and Ussher's influential model for 'primitive' episcopacy dispensed with them. Two-thirds of their former representatives had died. Yet the survivors included men of the spirit of Cosin, and they seized the initiative in other respects than that of their former lands. In July and August the Chapters of Peterborough, Canterbury and Exeter had reconvened, without arousing local hostility, and the King took advantage of this to fill up the cathedral clergy with a mixture of former royalists, members of the Interregnum Church and new men, as part of his general policy of reconciliation and usually without reference to the views of bishops or deans.[75]

At the same period visitations and disciplinary procedures resurfaced, carried up by the same current of clerical and popular enthusiasm. The Archdeacon of Essex recommenced his act book a month after the King returned, upon the page following that on which it had ended in 1641, and before the end of 1660 archidiaconal visitations were proceeding in Leicestershire. Although the church courts were formally recognised by the Cavalier Parliament only in July 1661, those of Chichester, York and Chester had been in action for over six months and that of Canterbury for nearly a year. Their revival testifies to the value of these institutions to early modern life, as providers of cheap and swift probate and a means of arbitration between minister and community and within a community itself. All the initial business in each Consistory Court concerned wills, but tithe disputes followed rapidly and marital and moral suits came after these. By April 1661 the Chester court was employing its corrective powers behind the same range of judgements, from divorces to church dues, that it had known under Laud. These did not achieve the same in practice as in theory, for, as in the case of excommunication of Quakers, effective results depended upon the attitude of local laymen. Initially, indeed, many citations were ignored. Nor did some courts revive until some time after the statute of 1661, that of the Carlisle Consistory not till January 1663.[76] In the revival of the old Church, as in other aspects of the Restoration, such as the agitation for a free Parliament and the purging of corporations, it is remarkable how much the initiative was taken by the south of England, while the supposedly royalist and conservative north remained passive or worked for conciliation.

The restored or newly appointed bishops wielded their powers according to their individual dispositions. Reynolds and Gauden ordained in collaboration with presbyters as the Worcester House Declaration requested, but the others apparently did not. Sanderson of Lincoln and Walton of Chester put direct pressure upon ministers who did not use the Prayer Book, but Henchman of Salisbury preferred to encourage those who did, while Ironside of Bristol was so impressed by one nonconformist parson whom he interviewed that he bid him go in peace. Morley presented a drunkard who heckled him at Worcester with a smile and five shillings, but did all he could to drive

Baxter from the area. Cosin splashed his way into his diocese across the Tees, gripped the sword which had reputedly killed the Sockburn dragon and ruled like his palatine predecessors, entertaining two hundred neighbours at Christmas and ignoring the fact that parliamentary representation had been granted to Durham under the republic. In every recorded case, the bishops entered their cathedral cities accompanied by enthusiastic citizens and gentry. All were immediately busy with institution and ordination, as clergy pressed to confirm their livings. Sanderson was faced with so many requests for ordination that he performed this duty before his own formal consecration and upon the day of that ceremony, and on one occasion dealt with sixty-seven applicants.[77]

As in all other matters, from its first weeks the attitude of the Cavalier Commons was that of the intolerant episcopalian provincials. The latter presented clergymen for failing to use the Prayer Book, the MPs commenced a bill compelling them to do so. The Commons welcomed bishops back to the Upper House as provincials cheered them into their sees. This stance relieved the episcopalian clergy of any need to make concessions, and when the Savoy Conference opened their commissioners offered none. They made the occasion instead an opportunity for their younger members to display polemical skills, and naturally nothing was resolved.[78] At the same time, an episcopalian press, led by L'Estrange, was working to destroy the two great claims of their opponents, that the presbyterians had done more to bring about the Restoration, and that the ceremonies in dispute were too trivial to be insisted upon. Both were dealt with by using the presbyterians' wartime actions, when Baxter had preached to Fairfax's army and Calamy justified war against Charles I, to prove them inveterate rebels who seized upon such minor rituals as excuses for further disobedience.[79] Baxter and Morley themselves were soon assailing each other in print over the latter's refusal to let the former preach in his diocese.[80] The government newspapers, which could have been used to preach conciliation, were employed instead by Berkenhead to voice his own hardline episcopalian views. It seems absurd to conclude that, after the repeated illustrations of the importance of the press during the previous decades, the early Restoration government should lack complete control over its own propaganda machine. Yet this appears the only answer, and indeed Berkenhead himself once insisted that the King never read the official journals.[81] Nothing else demonstrates with such force the extraordinary ramshackle nature of the restored monarchy.

In May a more significant clerical meeting than the Savoy Conference occurred: Convocation, the dual assembly of the national Church which sat at York and Canterbury to represent these respective provinces. The elections for it, held concurrently with those for the Cavalier Parliament, produced a body even more episcopalian in character. In London this was achieved by sleight of hand, as Sheldon employed a legal technicality to disqualify the presbyterians who had been returned. Baxter attributed the result in the counties to the fact that ministers who had not been episcopally ordained were denied the vote;[82] but this was only true in certain shires and, in default of any other evidence, it seems possible only to explain the returns lamely as part of the same general reaction which produced the Cavalier Commons. On 10 October Charles resigned the policy of comprehension by entrusting to this Convocation, as the formal representative of the Church, the promised revision of the Prayer Book. In the course of a month six hundred small alterations were made, most apparently under the influence of Bishop Sanderson. These included proposals of the Laudian party in the 1630s and of the presbyterians since, but the finished product was unequivocally unacceptable to the latter, for it enjoined all the ceremonies to which they took exception. On 24 February 1662 the Privy Council formally passed the new book to the Lords, to be the text for the Bill of Uniformity which the Commons had sent up long before.[83]

This did not mean that the government had abandoned the presbyterians: on the contrary, it continued to give them comfort and support. Its linkman in this work was Clarendon, who met and corresponded with their leaders continually. Tactics alone had changed, from the comprehension of both parties within the one settlement to the dispensation of loyal nonconformists from the settlement which had been made. Accordingly, as soon as the Lords had received the new Prayer Book, Clarendon proposed an amendment to the Bill of Uniformity, enabling the King to relieve clergy from observation of the specific clauses which the presbyterians found repugnant. Behind this he arrayed the full set of government peers and several bishops, including Sheldon and Morley. This was the means by which the Commons' attempt to amend the 1660 settlement of ministers had been defeated a month before. It sufficed to have the proviso adopted in the Upper House, despite the opposition of Bristol, who seems to have disliked it simply because it was introduced by his rival, and despite the fact that the Lords as a body showed no enthusiasm for toleration and made other details of the bill more severe. An obvious effort was now mounted to persuade the Commons to concur, including the King's assent to the Quaker Act, renewed work by the Lords on the bill to restore advowsons to royalists, and the appointment of Clarendon and Sheldon as managers of the first conference between the Houses upon the proviso.

All was in vain. As with the Corporation Act, the Commons refused point-blank to grant the King the powers he desired, with such feeling that no vote was taken on the question. Indeed, by only six votes did the MPs accept the revised Prayer Book without inspecting it first. They had swallowed defeat by the government over two major issues in the past year, indemnity and the settlement of ministers, and determined that this time the Crown should yield. And yield it did. The act that was passed on 19 May provided for the deprivation of every minister who, by St. Bartholomew's Day (24 August), did not testify to his acceptance of the entire Prayer Book and denounce the Covenant and the principle of resistance to royal authority. Almost concurrently, Convocation instructed congregations to observe a greater ceremony and sobriety, standing for hymns, kneeling for prayers, bowing at Christ's name and removing hats in church.[84]

The government, however, did not yet consider itself beaten. Its capitulation in May was probably from fear that the Lords would waver, but it may even then have been considering the dangerous notion that the monarch could dispense individuals under his prerogative, the lack of parliamentary confirmation notwithstanding. When Charles assented to the act, Clarendon urged Parliament to permit the King to decide upon whom it would be enforced, and defiantly reiterated the phrase 'tender consciences' which had appeared in the Declaration of Breda and which the Commons had condemned in the exchanges over the bill. Within two weeks potential nonconformists were being invited to expect royal protection, and when the act came into force Charles called a conference of advisers at Hampton Court to discuss such action. Clarendon and Manchester supported the plan, but it was foiled by Sheldon, who, on behalf of most of the bishops, absolutely refused to co-operate. The breach in his erstwhile supporters forced Charles to drop the project, and the act remained unqualified.[85] It was a turning-point not only in the history of the Church but in the career of Sheldon himself. After his unpopularity had been displayed in the London election, he had been withdrawn slightly from public view and permitted to play no great part in the coronation. Royal favour towards him seems to have revived with his willingness to support government policy in the Lords in early 1662. Now he had suddenly reversed his alliances, and called in public opinion to defend his concept of religion against the King himself. It was a manœuvre he was to repeat with equal success during the next thirteen years, and in doing so he would shape the nature of his Church for at least the next hundred. By identifying episcopacy with the wishes of the ruling class, against opponents either royal or plebeian, he was to alter James I's famous equation to another, more fundamental and durable: 'No bishops, no gentlemen'.

The act resulted in the expulsion of at least 961 parish clergymen, about a tenth of the total in England and Wales, and several factors made the loss more dramatic than this figure might suggest. First, some counties were naturally worse affected than others, London being the most severely damaged with over a third of its ministers gone, while Sussex lost a quarter and Devon, Leicestershire and Essex one-fifth.[86] Second, the degree of dislocation was still worse when the expulsions in 1660-1 are taken into account, together with the further 129 clergy who were ejected at some uncertain date between the Restoration and 'Black Bartholomew'. Together with natural wastage, this process meant that three-quarters of the parishes of Cheshire and Leicestershire, two well researched examples, changed hands in the three years after Charles returned.[87] Third, the men lost at Bartholomew included some of the Church's ablest and most eloquent representatives and, unlike those deprived earlier, were almost all ejected because of questions of conscience rather than of title or political past. They were certainly much more numerous than the bishops had anticipated, and the latter were unable to fulfil their boast of obtaining able replacements immediately. In no diocese does it seem to have required less than an average of two months to fill a vacancy, and although most were disposed of within six, some remained for years. Some bishops, Sheldon in particular, were forced to put temporary readers into the empty livings to provide a service.[88]

At least the quality of the new clergy who eventually were instituted was not as bad as their predecessors liked to think.[89] They included almost as many graduates, and in some dioceses a quarter of them had held livings in the Interregnum Church.[90] The difficulty they presented as a group was not, indeed, their personal capacity, but whether they would prove the champions of orthodoxy which they were intended to do.

In the autumn of 1662 the bishops went on visitation of their sees, to expose the surviving weaknesses in the Church and commence the work of repair in detail. Their progresses were carefully stage-managed, troops of armed gentry escorting them through areas with a reputation for disaffection.[91] The articles of enquiry which they addressed to churchwardens varied significantly between the individual prelates.[92] Wren of Ely, now the last of Laud's bishops still active, was correspondingly the only one to stress the Laudian preoccupation with railing the altar, for which the existing churchwardens' accounts and vestry minutes suggest little popular enthusiasm at the Restoration. Cosin stressed ritual; Nicholson of Gloucester was interested in catechism and Lloyd of Llandaff in episcopal re-ordination, while Reynolds and Gauden were generally less inquisitorial and precise than most. The surviving replies represent our best illustration of the state of the Church at this moment. In Buckinghamshire 79 of 183 parishes had no surplice, and 25 no Prayer Book. Of 266 parishes in the diocese of Salisbury, 105 lacked a surplice and 25 a prayer book. Seventy West Sussex parishes included 23 without a surplice. Matters were worse further north. In the Stow archdeaconry of Lincolnshire and the whole province of York, the majority had no surplice and no books of homilies or canons, and over a third had no Prayer Book, while many churches were in ruin and many churchwardens failed even to reply. Between a fifth and a quarter of all these places complained of nonconformity among parishioners, and hanging over every set of returns was the question of the honesty of those who declared that all was well.[93] The whole situation represented anything but conformity, yet was not such a bad basis for the achievement of it. When the defective parishes are located on a map, it is remarkable how many of them appear along the major roads formerly used by armies and commissioners, bearing out the episcopalians' assertion that their condition derived from the unhealed physical and spiritual damage of the wars rather than antipathy to the old Church. Time would now show whether this was true.

What had been sacrificed in the drive for uniformity were those further reforms which many had long deemed necessary. The restoration of seques-tered clergy to livings had quietly undone most of the work of uniting parishes achieved during the Interregnum, which provided one good answer to the long-standing problems of clerical poverty, pluralism and non-residence. The return of impropriated tithes to royalists was at the expense of the clergy to whom they had been allocated. Bishops indeed augmented vicarages for which they held the impropriated tithes, as the King had ordered in 1660,[94] but the legislation for general augmentation had failed. So, crushed by the weight of other business, did a bill against pluralism, a plan of Convocation for the improvement of ecclesiastical courts, and a project of Gauden's for the rationalisation of dioceses.[95] Not only had a great chance to overhaul the Church been missed, but those measures taken to solve its economic problems in the previous two decades had been destroyed.

The whole story raises at least two major problems. First, why did Charles and Clarendon persist in trying to help former enemies when a resolutely loyal legislature and the armed forces relieved them of any need to do so? Indeed, they reached the point of jeopardising the support of traditional friends. One reason may have been fear of rebellion. As St. Bartholomew's Day approached, and the Corporation and Quaker Acts were also being put into effect, rumours of an impending rising poured into Whitehall. The government destroyed the City gates, just as the purged Parliament had done. It also demolished the walls of four towns with strong presbyterian populations, garrisoned two more, added three foot regiments to the stand-ing army and kept the militia in arms all autumn. It also kept its intelligence network busy,[96] a precaution which ironically may have produced the very phenomenon that it was intended to prevent, for it seems that two spies now took the easy step from agent to *agent provocateur* and, having located a hand-ful of disaffected London artists, apparently religious separatists, encouraged them to plan a rising. The result had the inevitability of classical tragedy: the agents reported in November, their dupes were arrested, were shown the rack and confessed, and four more heads joined the impressive collection already rotting on London Bridge. With that perfect circularity common in a process of repression, the affair, called 'the Tong Plot', reinforced the government's belief in the danger of conspiracy. The newspapers broadcast this view, and prosecutions under the Quaker Act intensified in the capital and in those areas which possessed intolerant magistrates.[97]

But *raison d'état* could also have motivated royal policy. A loyal establishment and nonconformists who were dependent on, and grateful for, government protection would mean almost complete security for the monarchy. To balance factions against each other in order to achieve freedom of action is also a habit of rulers. A case study which supports this view is that of Oxford University, an institution over which Charles, as patron of colleges, and Clarendon, as Chancellor, exercised unusual power. There the royal habit of trampling the feelings of college fellows, begun at the Restoration, continued. Magdalen, both in its financial contributions and in its sufferings during the parliamentarian purge, had been the most royalist college in the kingdom. Yet when the King imposed an outsider on it as President in late 1661 and its Fellows complained, they received a rebuke of despotic rudeness. The university in general was displeased by the fact that it was used as a government pocket borough for parliamentary elections and by the number of degrees squeezed out of it for royal clients. Clarendon obtained from Sheldon the money for the beautiful ceremonial centre which bears the latter's name, but he also commandeered buildings to house government and Parliament themselves when needed. Charles retained the services of Interregnum professors who were prepared to transfer their loyalty, and appointed gifted new men to chairs, but too often kept the latter employed at court, to the neglect of their classes.[98] In brief, the university was used as a machine to render maximum service to the state, and it may be argued that this was a blueprint for the intended fate of the Church.

Having said this, it would still perhaps be unwise to rule out the operation, in the last analysis, of personal predilections. Everyone who knew Charles personally remarked upon his lack of profound religious feeling, his love of order and yet also of the exotic, his genial temperament which altered to savage anger if he felt that he was being insulted or coerced. Such foibles alone can account for his benevolence towards Quakers. No real evidence exists either to prove or disprove the old accusation that he possessed a long-term plan to assist the Catholics and sponsored toleration in general merely for their sake. To associate, in the minds of the orthodox, amelioration of their condition with freedom for all nonconformists would not seem the wisest method of achieving the former end. As for Clarendon, he had spent his youth in a circle which believed in the reconciliation of all men who accepted the basic tenets of the English Church, and during the 1640s had worked for religious unity and condemned clerical bigotry in general.[99] His behaviour in 1660-2 was of a piece.

The other great problem is how the Act of Uniformity was enforced, with no other disturbance than a scuffle in one, or perhaps two, London churches.[100] Again, the solutions appear varied. First, the measures of government and gentry to anticipate rebellion were extensive enough to make resistance very difficult. Second, the obvious sympathy of the government for the presbyterians held out the hope that loyalty and quietism might secure relief for them in time, if not immediately. In this sense, royal policy made a positive contribution to the peace of the country, even while it created tension at Westminster. The leaders of the ejected clergy, furthermore, were men who had for a decade made loyalism and conciliation their political creed and could not be transformed easily into rebels. No more than thirty-five became afterconformists (at least from the time that hesitation became impossible in each diocese), yet only about an eighth carried on an active ministry in the first decade after 1662, and only a small proportion of these did so immediately. Some became chaplains to Annesley, Fairfax, Herbert, Morley, Booth and other laymen who had formerly patronised their party, and more became schoolmasters. Most seem to have retired to practise household religion and await better times. As a group, they were both more rigidly principled and more passive than those deprived as a result of the First Restoration Settlement.[101] The United Reformed Churches may date their inception from 'Black Bartholomew', but this was the result of the efforts of only a fraction of those who suffered that day.

3

Conclusions

∽⌇∾

THE remainder of this book will be devoted to the question of what the Restoration Settlements actually settled. Here a related question will be posed: whose victory did they represent? Who had effectively *won* in 1662? The reply most often given in recent years is that the King did, and that the Restoration represented the ultimate triumph of the royalist cause. The legal issue which had provoked the Great Civil War, the question of who controlled the militia, had been decided as Charles I had wished. None of the constitutional checks which the parliamentarians had sought to impose upon the monarchy from 1642 till 1660 had taken hold, and now the very notion of resisting the Crown was made the grounds for loss of office. According to this school of thought, the monarchy emerged from the Interregnum stronger than before, and only the Glorious Revolution prevented it from growing stronger still.

There is much truth in this, particularly in the renewed stress which it places upon the importance of the reign of James II. It is also arguable that had the royal army won the Battle of Edgehill, a settlement would have resulted somewhat similar to that of 1661–2. In a sense Milton's worst fears had been realised: once restored, the monarchy had reached for more power almost instinctively, like a plant seeking the light, both by acquiring further constitutional rights and by levelling all parties beneath itself. Yet qualifications are needed. For one thing, it is very likely that had Charles I won the Civil War after 1643, when his army and court were dominated by men dedicated only to serving his wishes, the result would have been an infinitely more despotic government than that of the Restoration. Parliament's victory in that war was in this sense a permanent achievement. For another, it may be doubted whether Charles II felt much like a victor in September 1662. His religious policy, his request for a standing army in the provinces and his attempt to increase his control of corporations had all been rejected. He had become the first English monarch since the Middle Ages to be successfully defied by his leading churchmen. The freedom he had won in 1660 had been lost, and important measures forced upon him by a faction. His direct power over the community was truncated by the permanent abolition of the prerogative courts, and his ability to wage war and to censor the press depended upon the goodwill of Parliaments. The Church and the local magistrates could, in effect, afford to preach non-resistance because they had resisted the royal will perfectly well without recourse to arms.

If, then, Charles had obtained at best an equivocal success, had the true victors been the royalists themselves? Their official war aims had consisted of the preservation of the monarchy within its powers of December 1641, the defence of episcopacy, the Prayer Book and a ceremonial religion, the punishment of separatists and the right of the King to employ men such as Clarendon, Southampton, Ormonde and Nicholas as his advisers. All these were actually achieved in 1660-2, the Covenant burned and the corporations purged of most of their surviving members who had actively supported the parliamentarian cause. From this perspective, it appears as though the King's party had triumphed in the end, despite the King himself. Again, however, the limitations must be stated. If the royalists had won the wars, they would not have had to share the Privy Council with Manchester, Saye and Robartes, and the county bench, the militia and the honours lists with lesser parliamentarians. They would have been the ones who were enjoying the proceeds of plunder, while their opponents laboured to regain estates or recoup the money spent in fines. As has been emphasised, the sense of injustice harboured by many of the King's traditional followers had provided much of the bitterness which had informed the second settlement.

Indeed, an ironic case could be made for both settlements as a confirmation of the victory of John Pym and the original parliamentarian party. Most of the reforms of 1640-1 had been confirmed, and England now had a King who ruled as Pym's set had wished, with the advice of a Privy Council and bench of bishops representing a number of parties. The overhaul of the royal finances for which Pym had striven had now taken place, while the feared subversion of the government by Catholics had not. The Convention had revised the Book of Rates, unprecedentedly, on the government's behalf, while the Cavalier Parliament, in granting its voluntary subscription, had denied that this was a precedent for a forced loan like that of 1627. Above all, the monarch was still bound by the Triennial Act to summon regular Parliaments, and his need to satisfy them was reinforced by the temporary nature of the press law. Pym's body now lay in an unmarked pit in Westminster, but his spirit survived in much of the early Restoration polity.

At this point, a negative conclusion seems to be emerging: that in politics there are no absolute victors in the long term and that national life is ultimately the produce of all who set their hands to it. But perhaps a different approach to the Second Restoration Settlement may yield a more positive result. This would involve drawing attention to two portions of that settlement which lie beyond the immediate concern of this book. The first is the Poor Law of 1662, which considerably strengthened the powers of justices over their localities by permitting them to deport to their home parishes any newcomers who had occupied a tenement worth less than £10 per annum. The second is a statute of 1661 which imposed a penalty for hunting deer on any land without the permission of its owner, the first of the succession of game laws which were to make the following century such a fearsome time for poachers.[1] Both were measures whereby the ruling class reinforced its privileges and its control over the community. Precisely the same comment could be extended to cover the whole settlement.

It has long been noted that two of the greatest developments of the Tudor and early Stuart period consisted, at all levels, of an increase in the power and formality of government and the subordination of the Church to the laity. It could be argued that the Second Restoration Settlement represented a further stage in these processes, and one at which the landowning classes seized initiative in them from the Crown. The Corporation Act occupies a place in the long sequence of 'invasions' by gentry of urban centres and the parliamentary seats they contained, transforming the municipalities of the Middle Ages into the pocket boroughs of Hanoverian England. Under the Tudors, laymen had replaced clerics as government ministers and bureaucrats, and engorged much of the Church's land and patronage. Now the alliance between the gentry and the episcopalian Church, with the former in the role of protector, left magnates safe from clerical pretensions, whether of evangelists or of prelates allied with a monarch. Bereft of both the prerogative courts of his ancestors and the powerful army of his republican predecessors, Charles II in 1662 was essentially the president of a federation of communities run by their landowners, who operated a uniform judicial, administrative and political system. The 'county' gentry, as a group, gained absolutely from the Restoration, and its settlements comprised, in sum, a dress rehearsal for the social and political system which was to exist under the Hanoverians.

Two caveats must be added to this assertion. First, it is the sort of observation which is only provided by hindsight. The men who made the settlement of 1661-2 were concerned with the short-term ends of reducing the country to order, after what had been to them a period of chaos, and of punishing old enemies so far as they were able. The preambles of their statutes, and their propagandists, argued for the restoration of the old order and their innovations were intended to erect safeguards for this against the forces, royal and proletarian, which had produced its temporary ruin. Nor

would the gentry who had favoured presbyterianism have felt any more ela-
tion at the result than the Tory gentry felt under George I. Second, the transition from the Restoration to the Hanoverian state was to be difficult,
bloody, and very far from inevitable. The King in 1662 was not George I but
Charles II, to whom much of the Second Restoration Settlement was not a
mandate to be obeyed, but a defeat to be avenged.

PART FOUR

THE TESTING OF THE REGIME

❧

I

The Years of Doubt

IT is normal for new regimes to undergo a period of initial popularity which becomes tempered with time. Few, however, have fallen in the estimation of their subjects as dramatically as the restored monarchy did. The hysterical rejoicing of 1660 has been described. In 1663 Annesley could write anxiously of the hostility of the Londoners, while in Southwark the King's arms were torn down.[1] In the same year Prynne, who had worked so hard for the Restoration, believed that only betrayal had followed, and that true liberty was as remote as ever.[2] In 1660 Charles was regarded as a paragon, uniting an able and creative Privy Council. In 1663 a courtier, a beneficiary of the regime, could comment that 'the King has abandoned himself to his lust and his ministers to their passions against one another'. The same man could compare the behaviour of the Cavalier Parliament, which had opened two years before with fulsomely loyal speeches, to that of the Long Parliament in 1640-2.[3] Part of this transformation may be ascribed to the tensions generated by the Second Restoration Settlement, but other factors contributed concurrently to it. These, and the consequences of all, must now be considered.

The first was an aspect of the period familiar to many today who have never heard of the Act of Uniformity: the decline in public morals. It must be stressed that Interregnum England was far from sober and virtuous. In 1659 a writer could describe London as a city of taverns, where topers of both sexes caroused and danced. In polite society it was considered witty to get drunk, while the ladies were addicted to gambling.[4] Young nobles duelled, sometimes fatally, while one of them wrote upon his mistress's chamber-pot the exquisite compliment:

> 'Narcisse, se mirant en l'onde,
> vit la plus belle chose du monde.'

(Narcissus, looking at himself in the water,
saw the most lovely thing in the world.)[5]

The 1650s had also seen an unprecedented increase in erotic literature, often by writers from families associated with godly reform; it was one result of the contemporary freedom of the press, but perhaps also a symptom of the general disorientation of an age which produced Ranters and Quakers. For those who wished to put their reading to practical effect, a guide to the capital's prostitutes was published in 1658.[6] Nor was libertinism absent from the ruling circle, to judge from Mountagu's homely advice to Pepys that for a man to recognise his bastards was to 'shit in his hat and then clap it on his head'.[7] What changed after 1660 was that scandals became more spectacularly public and that the ruler himself was at the centre of one of the greatest.

In June 1663 a group of young gentlemen dined at a tavern in Bow Street, and one, Sir Charles Sedley, went out on a balcony to preach a mock sermon. The crowd which gathered proved hostile; both parties pelted each other until the watch arrived, and Sedley was subsequently fined, gaoled, and then bound over. These are the certain facts of the story. When it reached Pepys, Sedley was supposed to have preached stark naked, with obscene postures. Fifty miles further, in Oxford, it was said that the entire dinner party had undressed. By the time it got to Flintshire, the dinner itself had been served by six nude women. The significance of the event is twofold: it illustrates the relish with which such gossip was conveyed (and still is, to judge by the number of modern writers who recount the more lurid versions of this one uncritically)[8], and Sedley was a member of the royal court.

In September 1661 the incidence of syphilis in that court was already a matter for complaint.[9] In January 1663 the new French ambassador thought Charles's society innocent and dull compared with that of the Sun King, but by August he was sufficiently impressed to dub the spa of Tunbridge Wells, whither the courtiers had migrated, 'L'Eaux de Scandale'.[10] Much of the 'scandale' was recorded by Pepys, including the particularly vivid item that a lady-in-waiting had given birth to a bastard at a royal ball.[11] It would indeed have been puzzling if the Frenchman had not come to feel at home, for the tastes that Charles II brought back from exile turned out to be those of the country which had allied most closely with his enemies, France. In conformity with these, he insisted that female parts upon the public stage, hitherto played in England by boys, should be taken by their natural performers. A Mrs Norris, who played Desdemona, became the first actress in this country in 1660, and her successors soon spread across the land, arousing both horror and delight. The court displayed only the latter, finding the theatres a new source of bedfellows.[12] The royalist Evelyn had his first doubts about the restored monarchy when he attended the Chapel Royal and found violins accompanying the organ, again in emulation of the Louvre.[13] French tutors became the fashion among the aristocracy, as did long wigs, face-paint, muffs and perfume. An observer at Oxford expected to find the ladies in these when the court arrived in 1663, but was taken aback when the royal Horse Guards appeared in them.[14] The second most distinguished lecher in this society, and the nation, was the heir apparent, James of York. To comfort himself after his enforced marriage, he was soon taking advantage of the shortcomings of other unions, and contrary to popular belief his early conquests at least were considered beauties. One earl in December 1662 packed off his countess to the provinces, out of the ducal reach, as soon as James had been seen in conversation with her.[15]

The most distinguished lecher of all sat on the throne. Not for one and a half centuries, since the youth of Henry VIII, had an English king kept mistresses, but Charles II compensated nobly for the omission. His *affaires* commenced near the beginning of his exile, and if there is any truth in Pepys's assertion that there had been over seventeen before the Restoration, then they were generally discreetly managed. There was, however, a resounding exception: the first, with Lucy Walter, which had given him a son. Lucy, like most of Charles's great passions, combined a powerful personality with a feeble sense of tact. On the collapse of the liaison she had advertised her woes to the English, until her providentially early death had enabled her child to be committed to obscurity, as the fosterling of a royalist peer, Lord Crofts. This episode had concluded a comfortable two years before the Restoration, and it might have been hoped that the burdens of active kingship would increase Charles's sobriety of life. As he sailed from Breda this possibility was already doomed. He had met Barbara Palmer.

She was born Barbara Villiers, a branch of the greatest family of adventurers in the century, the leader of whom, the first Duke of Buckingham, had founded his fortunes in a royal bed precisely as his kinswoman was to do. She was the daughter of a royalist viscount who had died of his wounds; the consequent financial problems in her childhood may have been responsible for her enduring appetite for wealth. Her other notable appetite was whetted at the age of fifteen, when she became the mistress of the aristocratic rake who had inscribed the chamber-pot. She was soon married, to an honourable young royalist squire, Roger Palmer, who took her with him in May 1660 when he conveyed a gift of money to the King at Breda. She was now a ravishing nineteen, with auburn hair and deep blue eyes. On his return Charles took care to see more of the Palmers, and by the spring of 1661 gossips began to have suspicions, which were certainties by the autumn. At that time Roger Palmer was created Earl of Castlemaine in the Irish peerage, an honour which he had clearly earned by proxy. Receiving his other title, of

Europe's most celebrated cuckold, with fury, he subsequently left the country. His wife remained, and her position was public and unpopular enough by mid-1662 for a ballad against the Hearth Tax to refer casually to it and express the hope that she would become a magdalen.[16]

One foundation of this was the possibility that she represented a last gigantic wild oat sown before Charles's own marriage. Like most royal unions, this depended upon the selection of princesses whom foreign policy made available, and in this case, according to Clarendon, the field was further narrowed by the King's concern that his French mother would never bless a union with a Protestant. None the less, the matter was settled within a year of the Restoration. In July 1660 Charles concluded Cromwell's war with Spain, an obvious piece of gratitude to his recent hosts. A month later the rebel King of Portugal, till recently a subject of King Philip of Spain and now struggling for survival against the latter's armies, offered Charles his daughter Catherine with the richest dowry ever brought by an English queen. It consisted of Tangier, Bombay, trading privileges in the Portuguese tropical empire and £1½ million, in return for which he asked for soldiers to defend himself. Manchester apparently carried this offer to Charles, who put it to his 'inner ring' of Councillors at Clarendon's house and obtained a favourable response.

Now factional politics intervened, for the ever-busy Bristol got wind of the project. The Earl had a fondness for the Spanish, with whom he had spent much of his exile, and saw an opportunity to advance his position by becoming the successful sponsor of a rival candidate. He and King Philip's ambassador argued for the daughter of an Italian client of Spain, with a dowry provided by the latter. Charles hesitated, Clarendon dutifully followed suit, the Portuguese were treated coldly and Bristol set out for Italy. Louis XIV now intervened to prevent any strengthening of his traditional enemy Philip, by offering to support the alliance with Portugal to the extent of paying the English troops sent there. Coupled with doubts as to whether the Spanish could find money to match that offered by Lisbon, and whether they would be prepared to write off the territory taken from them by Cromwell, this was decisive. The alliance was approved by the Privy Council, with Clarendon showing particular enthusiasm, announced when the Cavalier Parliament met, and formally concluded in June. England, France and Portugal had all gained; Bristol had suffered another humiliation, and King Philip had reason to curse the years he had spent preserving Charles.[17]

Catherine of Braganza had been reared in a convent, and spoke no English. Her olive-tinted features were pleasant rather than pretty, and she brought with her 'six frights, who called themselves maids-of-honour'. What she did not bring, though she failed to arrive until May 1662, was more than half the promised money, and she brought some of that in goods, not cash. On disembarking into an English summer, she promptly caught a cold. Incredibly, the wedding night was a success, the King writing rapturously to his ministers of it and all observers in these first days agreeing upon the patent happiness of the couple.[18] This adds colour to the belief of Charles's apologists that his next move, to instal Barbara as his bride's lady of the bed-chamber, was motivated solely by the need to reward yet another loyal subject for more than usually important past services.

This move ended the honeymoon atmosphere, for Catherine had been apprised of Lady Castlemaine's record and refused point-blank to accept her. Much of Charles's fondness for his bride seems to have derived from her initial docility. Her defiance produced much the same reaction from him as Vane's, which occurred simultaneously in mid-June, and the consequences of this in turn provoked the same public disapproval. By July the rift was complete, and notorious. Charles had returned in soul and almost certainly in body to his mistress, and Clarendon, his mediator with the presbyterians, was employed upon the parallel errand of mediating with his wife. The Chancellor performed this with the fidelity with which he followed his master's other direct instructions, while Charles applied the crueller pressure of dismissing Catherine's beloved maidservants. The wretched young woman conceded defeat and received her rival in August, but this belated surrender merely added contempt to her husband's hostile feelings towards her. In the winter of 1662-3, Barbara was at the apogee of her power, the King being utterly devoted to her and courtiers competing for her patronage.[19]

The Queen's misfortunes were still not complete, for one remained to come which was to have dramatic consequences for the future of her new country. By winter it had become clear that, despite enthusiastic efforts by Charles after the wedding, and more sporadic attempts thereafter, she had failed in her primary duty of becoming pregnant. The King's virility had recently been proved afresh by the birth of his first child by Barbara. His response to the problem was to elevate the earlier fruit of his indiscretion, the boy called James who had been entrusted to Lord Crofts. There is no reason to suppose that guilt or pity inspired this change of policy after years of lack of interest; in default of evidence one can only ascribe it tentatively to a desire to parade a further proof of potency before the world, or a hazy design of securing the succession in the event of the death of his brother. The final irony of York's marriage had been that the baby which produced it had expired after a few months. Young James was noticed in his father's coach in September 1662, was created Duke of Monmouth, with precedence over all non-royal peers, in the following February and was married to the nation's richest heiress in April. Immediately rumours began to circulate that Charles had secretly married Lucy Walter. The King's brother, mother and mistress were all irritated, but the latter had the cunning to make a fuss of the boy to confirm her position.[20]

The two individual victims of this sequence of events were the unhappy, isolated and exiled Catherine, and Clarendon, whose enthusiasm for the marriage treaty was now linked by gossip with his daughter's marriage, to suggest that he had obtained a barren queen to strengthen his family's hold on the country. The main casualty, however, was the King's reputation. By late 1662 an ambassador could quote the Londoners as saying that their monarch only 'hunts and lusts', and other observers confirmed this opinion with less concision.[21] It is an irony, and perhaps a distasteful one, that later ages which have prided themselves on a stricter morality than Charles's one have frequently shown him more indulgence than his subjects.

The second factor in the government's growing unpopularity was the sale of Dunkirk, Cromwell's greatest foreign acquisition. The motive for this was simple: its upkeep cost £321,000 per annum at a time when the public revenue was deficient and had just been further burdened by the acquisition of Tangier and Bombay. It was not easily defensible and had been of no obvious value to trade, and its sale would both reduce regular expenditure and provide a sum to balance the overall account. It is possible to believe Clarendon's later insistence that he had derived the initial idea for it from Lord Treasurer Southampton, particularly as he had told the Cavalier Parliament, at its recess in May 1662, that Dunkirk was a jewel in his master's crown. Nevertheless, the records make it clear that once he had been given the plan, Clarendon made it his own in a further effort to win royal gratitude. As the port lay between French and Spanish territory and Spain's revenue was consumed by the Portuguese war, the obvious customer was Louis XIV. He duly bought it for 5 million *livres* after fierce bargaining lasting from June to October. Charles and Clarendon persuaded the Privy Council into approval, perhaps with the aid of French bribes. To reassure English merchants, the French monarch declared that Dunkirk would never again be made a haven for privateers, and to satisfy Clarendon he sent an official letter thanking the Chancellor for his invaluable work in producing agreement. The transfer was made in November, and the huge garrison either disbanded, shipped to Tangier or loaned to the French and Portuguese.[22]

The response when the news broke was infinitely worse than the government expected. The merchant community had no faith in Louis's promise, while Londoners in general, who had shown no fervent pleasure in the town's capture, were furious at its loss. In part this seems to have derived from a general sense that a conquest obtained at heavy cost should have been preserved; but it also drew upon an intense popular Francophobia which reflected both traditional rivalries and the fact that the French embassy possessed an old right of asylum for criminals.[23] Bristol's faction alerted Charles to the fact that Spain had been further provoked, while no alliance had been made with France to compensate. As Clarendon had so carefully advertised his responsibility for the affair, he naturally drew the ensuing anger upon himself.[24]

Cromwell's other conquest remained English almost by default: in Jamaica, the garrison and settlers held their own against heat, mosquitoes, pirates, Spaniards and escaped slaves. In time it was to become the richest and most important portion of the British West Indies, with all their exciting and disturbing consequences for English life. This fact sufficed to earn Cromwell a place in late Victorian children's works upon Makers of the Empire. It may now be argued that the complexion of Brixton is the most tangible enduring achievement of the Protectorate.

These two developments were linked with a third: the appearance of hostile factions within the government, produced not by the division of the Privy Council of 1660 but by the intrusion of new personalities into high politics. The title 'Ministry of Clarendon', so often applied to the period 1660-7, is really only appropriate to its first two years, as by the end of 1662 the Chancellor was already no longer in control of policy. The newcomers had taken over.

Although Charles retained the services of his mixed Privy Council of 1660, he felt no affection for the non-royalists within it except for Monck, who looked after military affairs impeccably without any further interest in high politics. He found men such as Annesley and Cooper less amenable than his older advisers[25] and so tended to remain dependent upon these, particularly, as has been shown, upon Clarendon. The latter in turn was supported and comforted by the other ministers of the exile, Nicholas and Ormonde. This pattern became intensified as 1661 progressed, the King's *affaire* with Barbara developed, his interest in daily government fell off, and Clarendon's utility as a work-horse became ever more obvious. The latter's central position in the government initiatives of 1662 has been noted, and was rewarded with grants of land, while his younger son became Master of the Robes.[26] Dryden's eulogy has been quoted; four separate urban corporations elected the Chancellor as their High Steward.[27]

Nevertheless, Clarendon had notable deficiencies as a servant. For one thing he was a work-horse who frequently went lame, his portly body being confined to bed by attacks of gout. These had incapacitated him during important periods such as the King's stay at Breda and the second session of the Cavalier Parliament. For another, he was capable of ignoring the King's views when they conflicted with his own, as they had over Catholics and Quakers. When they did not, he could be remarkably unsuccessful, and all the policies for which he worked in 1661-2 either failed or produced unfortunate results and left him disliked by the public. But his fundamental fault was one of character: his new responsibilities reinforced an already considerable tendency to self-importance and self-righteousness. His private notes to the King had the tone of a kind but strict schoolmaster. At times he treated the Privy Council like a lecture hall and determined business as though he and not Charles had overall control. For the King's private pleasures he had no sympathy and no approval.[28] In brief, he was not a natural companion to Charles, and was accordingly vulnerable to those who were.

This was precisely the weakness which Bristol was equipped to exploit. The charm and irresponsibility which made the earl so dangerous in politics were considerable assets in private life, and his social entertainments were noted for their brilliance. His personal interest at these, predictably, was in the gambling. The alliance which developed between him and Barbara was entirely understandable, both being flamboyant adventurers and enemies of Clarendon, who detested the countess and all she stood for so much that in his memoirs he could not bring himself to call her by name. Another addition to Bristol's faction was the Queen Mother, who returned to England in 1662 and had in common with him both Catholicism and a long-standing hatred of the Chancellor. Thus far, the combination was not sufficient to menace the latter. Charles used the one for pleasure as he did the other for business, and indeed may have found Clarendon more tolerable because of the balance thus created.[29] Bristol's set, however, became extremely potent when it acquired Sir Henry Bennet.

Bennet was a royalist of impeccable record. His upper nose was covered with a black plaster which concealed (or, as some said, advertised) the scar left by a parliamentarian sword. He had spent the time of Charles's residence in Spanish territory performing the crucial role of the King's representative in Madrid, and acquired there a taste for rich clothes and ponderous dignity, the last of which must have been enhanced by the frown imposed upon his face by frequent headaches. On his return after the Restoration he was made Keeper of the Privy Purse, which he regarded as a step to high office. He was intelligent, industrious, and spoke more languages than the existing Privy Council possessed between them. It is Clarendon's treatment of this man, more than anything else, which reveals his inadequacy as man and politician. The two had been friendly in exile, and had in common devotion to the monarchy and a basic seriousness of mind. Yet the Chancellor used his newly acquired power not to gratify Bennet but to block his advancement to every post he coveted, including that of ambassador to Paris which would have removed him from the country. This infantile jealousy had the inevitable effect of pushing him into the welcoming arms of Bristol's faction, and by the autumn of 1662 Charles was sufficiently impressed by its arguments, and disenchanted with Clarendon's achievement, to give that faction power.[30]

In the late summer Bennet set out for the King his advice upon the fittest means to stabilise the country, which had been urgently sought because of the rumours of impending risings coming in. This was twofold: to keep the militia standing to overawe the disaffected, and to reconcile them not by a dispensation under the prerogative, but by the less controversial means of promising to open the next parliamentary session with a request for greater religious toleration.[31] The first part of this was followed in the autumn and the second in the winter, and in the interim Bennet was brought into the government. In September he replaced Clarendon in the informal post of arbitrator between the King and his wife,[32] and in October he replaced Nicholas in the formal one of Secretary of State. Nicholas seems to have been selected for sacrifice partly because of his age, which was nearing seventy, and partly because of his unassuming and obedient nature. Indeed, he went quietly enough once he had been assured of a golden handshake of £10,000, and the retention of his place on the Council and the considerable per-quisites given to himself and his family since the Restoration.[33] Bennet proved an excellent employee, commencing the systematic docketing and filing of correspondence in the Secretary's office and insisting on clearly written dispatches. The court resounded with rumours that the dismissals of Clarendon and other older ministers would follow,[34] but this was specifically not Charles's intention. He did begin calling meetings of advisers at his mother's mansion instead of at the Chancellor's, and his private notes with the latter almost ceased, but he instructed Bennet to treat Clarendon and his allies as partners, which Sir Henry scrupulously did.[35] The King had not replaced his sources of advice, but had multiplied their number.

In late December Bennet's second recommendation was implemented and extended, in the drafting of a declaration of Charles's intention to ask Parliament in the next session for the power to dispense from the Act of Uniformity he had failed to obtain in the last, and so honour the promise of toleration in the Declaration of Breda. It also expressed his desire to have the removal of laws against Catholics recommenced and completed.[36] This was published in mid-January, by which time the policy proposed in it had already been spectacularly enacted in the case of Edmund Calamy, one of the most distinguished of the City clergy ejected at Bartholomew. Entering his old church with the encouragement of several Privy Councillors, he had preached a sermon, for which Sheldon had promptly secured his arrest, which was followed by his equally swift liberation by the government. This was accompanied by the release of most of the sectaries and Quakers imprisoned in the capital.[37] The whole initiative appears to have represented an unhappy combination of three different preoccupations: Bristol's, with the relief of Catholics, Bennet's, with the security of the state, and that of the former parliamentarians and republicans on the Council, perhaps led by Cooper (Lord Ashley since the coronation), with the succour of the presbyterian clergy. Charles alone shared all these, and by late January he seems to have been the only man involved who was not seriously worried about Parliament's response.[38]

For one thing, the government would face it bereft of support it had enjoyed in 1662. Sheldon was carrying out his threat of August and leading most bishops in encouraging MPs to fight for uniformity,[39] while observers had doubts about the reliability of Clarendon himself. Ormonde had departed to resume his old work of running Ireland in July, and Nicholas's replacement had left the Chancellor bereft of his trusted friends. From November he had been incapacitated by an unusually prolonged agony of gout, and left ignorant of the deliberations which had produced the declaration. Bennet had brought it to him for approval, which he gave only with severe qualifications, and the French ambassador noted that Clarendon's tribulations had only further embittered his feelings towards Sir Henry. He added with satisfaction that both factions were now applying to him for support against each other.[40]

For another thing, the whole policy was absurdly provocative. The arguments for the royal dispensing power had all been deployed a year before, and rejected absolutely by the Commons. Now they were merely reiterated. In addition, the Act of Uniformity had been breached by royal command in the case of Calamy, before Parliament had pronounced upon the declaration. Worse, the issue of Protestant nonconformity had been yoked with the different one of Catholic relief, itself extremely delicate. Charles had turned Bennet's expedient for preventing rebellion into a programme likely to produce furious constitutional opposition. Clarendon had every reason to dislike it, but then he had sponsored, in August, the project of using prerogative powers. Both he and Bennet suffered the weakness of being principal servants of a king who wanted services which ran counter to political realities.

One other theme ran through the King's worsening relations with his subjects: the fact that the Second Restoration Settlement, like the first, had not succeeded in providing for the government's financial needs. This did not mean that Englishmen did not feel over-taxed. Since the Restoration they had been required to produce huge sums to pay off the army and then to cope with the existing shortfall in public revenue. The new permanent impositions of the excise on alcohol and the Hearth Tax affected all levels of society. Trade remained depressed because markets lost during the recent wars and domestic instability could not be swiftly regained. The bad harvest of 1661 had pushed up food prices.[41]

Popular impatience was reflected by a growing official concern with resistance to taxation. In July 1661 the Commons produced a scheme for improving the yield of existing impositions, including the farming of excise collection, investigations by MPs and JPs into means by which this collection might be improved, and a survey by MPs for maritime boroughs of the extent and nature of evasion of customs duties.[42] The last produced the swiftest results, revealing that watermen and seamen in estuaries were colluding to avoid payment, while mobs sometimes rescued those goods which officers did confiscate.[43] In the autumn of 1662, the excise was duly farmed out to commissioners in each county recommended by the justices, and their efforts to recoup their payments to the Crown provoked, or revealed, constant obstruction in the collection of this levy. Brewers hid their barrels, subcommissioners took bribes to overlook them, and where officers encountered open resistance, the parish constables often declined to assist them and magistrates discharged offenders who were arrested.[44] The Hearth Tax provoked a furious outcry in the capital,[45]despite the marvellous potential for evasion contained in the principle of self-assessment, which was exploited to the full. The King informed the Corporation of London, without amusement, that some citizens were actually returning themselves as dead, and all over the country less spectacular forms of fraud were normal and collection was slow. In Kent, not the most remote or backward county, it was discovered that many householders were too illiterate to return the requisite information.[46]

On the other hand, the most irresponsible individual in the fiscal system was the King himself. In the penury of exile he had preferred to evade creditors rather than to increase frugality, and on his restoration he clearly viewed England as a cornucopia, much in the fashion that his grandfather had done on his arrival from Scotland. Clarendon later asserted that Charles wanted a court more magnificent than his predecessors', while Pepys wrote in 1661 that his own work on the Navy Board was crippled by lack of funds as the King was only interested in new ways of spending money. Much of it would have gone on rewards to loyal followers rather than mere high living, but the increasingly bad reputation of the court fostered a popular impression of corruption and profligacy. By August 1662 it was a proverb in London that 'The bishops get all, the courtiers spend all, the citizens pay for all, the King neglects all, and the Devil take all', and the provinces echoed this sentiment. Ironically, it was the sober and thrifty Clarendon who was blamed, as most royal grants were supposed to be controlled by him through his office of Lord Chancellor.[47]

Thus a genuine inadequacy of government revenue was being disguised by, and the prospects of its reform vitiated by, an equally genuine royal extravagance. These two pressures consumed not only all the grants made since the Restoration, but the great windfalls of the Portuguese dowry and the proceeds of Dunkirk, news of which would have made the public even less inclined to view their monarch as being in want. By December 1662 the Treasury was almost empty,[48] and it was obvious that Charles would have to ask Parliament for further assistance in the next session. Thus the government was seeking to impose an unpopular religious policy upon the Commons at a moment when it depended upon their goodwill for its financial survival.

The fourth session of the Cavalier Parliament opened on 18 February 1663,[49] with a great effort by Charles to secure the success of his policy. He greeted both Houses with a speech reiterating his desire to dispense peaceful non-conformists and to relieve royalist Catholics, though he also promised not to give the latter office and asked for legislation to prevent the growth of Catholicism.[50] He instructed Clarendon and Bennet to call a meeting of their respective friends and clients in the Commons to ensure a concerted effort there.[51] He talked of marrying Clarendon's son to Bristol's daughter to reconcile the factions.[52] As before, the government's attempt to obtain sanction for the dispensing power was launched in the more compliant Lords, being introduced by Charles's brother James on the 23rd in the form of a bill according the King this power in the case of peaceful Protestants. It proceeded rapidly to the committee stage.[53]

The inevitable disaster followed swiftly. Far from thanking the King for his speech as usual, the Commons resolved to debate it on the 25th, and the courtiers could raise only thirty votes between them against this decision.[54] The House went on to reject the project for dispensation without a division, and reply formally to Charles that toleration would endanger, not produce, domestic peace. Soon after, it resolved that Calamy's release could not be justified in law, and on 6 March it began work on a bill intended not only to prevent the spread of Catholicism as the King had asked (by exiling converts) but to facilitate prosecution of existing recusants by ordering regular reports by churchwardens and the punishment of justices who failed to act upon them. It went on to propose an invitation to Charles to banish all Catholic priests.[55] Throughout these weeks, and those preceding and succeeding, pulpit and press resounded with denunciations of dissenters and Papists (sometimes preached to the King's own face) and Berkenhead threw the official newspapers behind this campaign.[56] In the provinces, tenants of the nation's most illustrious Catholic, the Queen Mother, refused to pay her rent.[57] Nor did royal policy provoke a great swell of gratitude from Protestant nonconformists themselves, for although a deputation of independent ministers attended Charles to give thanks, the presbyterian clergy were offended by the favour shown to Catholics.[58] This sentiment extended into the Privy Council, for two days before Parliament met Morice committed to prison a priest captured in Holborn. The sub-committee of the Lords set up to consider the bill for dispensation amended it to exclude the followers of Rome from its provisions and to impose harsher penalties for failure to attend the established Church.[59]

On 12 March Clarendon made his long-awaited return from his sick-bed to the Lords. In the preceding weeks he seems to have drafted a reply to the Commons' statement, defending his monarch's right to dispense,[60] and the government must have been anticipating the moment when he would use his eloquence and influence to assist the Toleration Bill: indeed, debate of the measure may have been adjourned six days simply to await his reappearance. If so, the result was a surprise, for either from a desire to win favour with the episcopalians to compensate for his declining influence at court, or from despair of the success of the measure, he neither supported nor opposed it. His abstinence was decisive. The bill was dropped, and Charles, for the first time, showed open anger with his Chancellor.[61] Now the disappointment of the Protestant dissenters was followed by that of the Catholics. Bristol had been arguing their case in the Lords, and when the Commons' proposal for a royal proclamation to exile priests came up, the peers were persuaded to water this down to a petition to the King to turn out only the most tactless of the Roman clergy. Clarendon, struggling to mend his relations with Charles, made a strong speech in favour of royalist Catholics and the more moderate of their priests, only to lose such support as he had won among the episcopalians without significantly regaining the friendship of his monarch. All was in vain, for the Commons insisted upon their wishes and on 2 April Charles surrendered upon this issue also and duly made the desired proclamation.[62] By June, the triumphant Commons had sent to the Lords not only their bill against Catholics but another to impose upon vestry members the tests already enforced upon clergy, and a third to extend the penalties of the Quaker Act to all Protestant dissenters who were caught at a religious meeting.[63]

The principal comfort to the government in this resounding humiliation may have been the hope that the Commons would be disposed after their victory to deal generously with the public revenue. In mid-March Charles had drawn their attention to this, and obtained a committee, chaired by one of his own officials, to look into the matter. One of his principal financial officials, Sir Philip Warwick, explained to this that the entire annual revenue was still only £978,000 per annum, while the most stringent economies could not reduce expenditure below £1,085,000. In reality, this paper deliberately concealed the true extent of the problem, in order to conceal the extent of royal mismanagement. A private report which Warwick made simultaneously to Charles stated it honestly: that the King was currently spending twice his receipts. Unhappily for the government, the bulk of the Commons committee clearly suspected their monarch of irresponsibility, for having commenced an investigation to substantiate Warwick's figures, they extended this within days to inquire how and to whom Charles had granted land since his return.[64]

In April this attitude to the court expressed itself in a direct attack upon the alleged habit of royal officials of selling junior offices, which was believed, with more passion than evidence,[65] to be both a symptom and a cause of the presumed corruption in public life. In May a bill to establish a commission of enquiry into the complaint was produced and extended to cover all existing grants of office as well as those to come. A further extension, to investigate the sale of honours was prevented by only one vote. In the same week another provocative bill was ordered, to assign public expenditure to particular branches of revenue to reduce the likelihood of misappropriation.

In early June, however, an event occurred which promised a more sympathetic attitude: the revenue committee reported on the state of the public income, revising Warwick's figures upward to £1,025,000, but agreeing that all sources were producing less than expected and that the new Hearth Tax was the biggest disappointment of all. Charles decided to risk following this up with a firm message, accused the Commons of neglecting the public good by proceeding so slowly with the revenue and promised to account for the expenditure of the previous grant. His tone almost provoked the MPs to defiance, for they resolved to supply him by only forty-eight votes in a House of nearly three hundred. Thereafter the bills concerning offices and assignation of the revenue were dropped, and three statutes were passed to augment the royal income, but this display of loyalty was rather less effective than it appeared. Influenced by a concern for their own pockets and those of their constituents, perhaps by persisting distrust of the court and perhaps by the narrow gap between the maximum actual income and the minimum potential expenditure of which they had been informed, the Commons were giving very feeble assistance. One statute permitted the excise farmers to search cellars, while ignoring the problem of local indifference or hostility to the result. A second permitted constables to search houses suspected of making false returns of hearths, and assumed that they would have the courage or ill-will to inform upon their neighbours. The last ordered a direct supply to remove the accumulated deficit upon the public account, but chose the old method of the subsidy, whereby the levy was based upon a percentage of each taxpayer's presumed wealth. In the 1620s two war efforts had collapsed because of the evasion which this system made possible, and it had been replaced by the much more effective 'assessment' which required a fixed sum from each county. Members of the government predicted that the result would be a fiscal disaster, and in the end this grant produced less than the voluntary subscription of 1661. To illustrate why this was so it may suffice to cite the case of Bristol, where the aldermen were assessed at less than one-hundredth of their true wealth.[66]

To comprehend the actions and attitudes of the Cavalier Commons during this session, it is important to stress how much they represented a continuity with those of the previous three. As before, the MPs were carrying out with great determination a programme suited to the tastes of royalist episcopalian gentry, and if their attitude to the government was more hostile this was because the King had proved more of a nuisance to them than previously. Their work in the session had a momentum of its own, independent of royal action: indeed, the renewed persecution of Catholics and the provision of a minimum subsistence for the central government, at the lowest possible cost to the taxpayer, were the only aspects of it that the King could specifically be said to have provoked. They produced measures to improve the militia and the relief of indigent royalists, and to halt the current decline of agrarian rents, together with several bills to aid individual communities and interests. They discussed imposing the tests in the Act of Uniformity on office-holders and ordered a bill to purge offices of all but formerly 'loyal' persons and episcopalians. As before, also, their actions were extensions of developments in the provinces. The self-confident royalism of the House was echoed regularly in the counties, most spectacularly at Taunton. This town had held an annual festival in May to commemorate its relief from a royalist siege in 1645, which was terminated abruptly in 1663 by a party of militia horse who informed the citizens that they would be ridden down if they repeated such a disloyal celebration.[67] The bill against dissenting conventicles was longed for by intolerant gentry and bishops who required some clear law against the followers of those ejected clergy who remained active. As things stood, they were trying to use a somewhat limited statute of Elizabeth against religious meetings, or indicting their captives for riotous assembly. The defence of a peaceful gathering against the latter charge was obvious and employed with notable success at Abingdon where a jury returned a verdict of not guilty, although sent out three times by the furious magistrates.[68]

Bennet, in May 1663, considered that the government had 'fallen into an unhappy middle of leaving the presbyterians and other dissenters totally disobliged, and not secure to us the affection of our own party, so as to be able to support, with power or money, the persecution they engage us in against others.[69] This situation was not to endure. Just as a set of factors had combined to emasculate the monarchy at this period, so a different set were now to operate to produce a new policy, and a stronger regime.

Charles II, in the short period of his effective reign, had revealed himself to be as capable of pursuing rash political schemes as his father had been. There was, however, a difference: with his father's fate to contemplate, the son was less inclined to defy a formidable and determined opposition. So it was in 1663. For the presbyterians he had no personal affection. He had been humiliated by their Scottish counterparts in 1650 and had disparaged them privately to Clarendon since the Restoration. In early 1663, when he was promising them relief, he was also laughing at the satirical portrait of them in Samuel Butler's *Hudibras*.[70] With the Catholics it was different, for he owed them personal gratitude, had friends among them, and told the French ambassador in April 1663 that he thought 'no other creed matches so well with the absolute dignity of kings' than Catholicism. He added, however, that he would persecute even this if he were forced to.[71]

It was this sense of realities which allowed him to keep a working relationship with the Commons during that year. In private he was known to be furious at the rejection of his religious policy, and when Clarendon failed him in March he requested the retired republican lawyer Whitelocke to draft a defence of his power to dispense under his prerogative.[72] His own replies to the House, however, were at first tactfully evasive and then conceded all that it wished. At the end of the session, on 27 July, he thanked it for the money he had received without any qualifications, promised retrenchment, affected dismay at the failure of the bills against Catholics and dissenters to reach completion in the Lords, and promised to bring in substitutes in the next session and to enforce the existing laws severely in the interim. If his voice lacked sincerity this would not have been apparent, for he always made speeches by reading without feeling from a paper in his lap.[73] Far from punishing Sheldon for his opposition, he admitted him to the Privy Council and when Juxon at last expired in May he raised this champion of intolerant episcopalianism to the summit of his Church as Archbishop of

Canterbury.[74] Berkenhead was deprived of control over the government newspapers in August, but replaced not by a spokesman for toleration but by the Prynne of the Cavaliers, L'Estrange, who marked his accession to power by halving the size of the journals and publishing an editorial expressing his contempt for the ordinary reader.[75] To please the Commons further, a royalist was put in charge of the Post Office, the section of government most fully staffed by men inherited from previous regimes, with instructions to dismiss all who had been zealous parliamentarians or republicans.[76]

This policy was a cosmetic one. Charles's speech at the prorogation barely concealed the fact that the bills against Catholics and conventicles had perished quietly in the Lords and that this would not have been the case had the government genuinely willed otherwise. The request of the Commons on that day, for royal proclamations to urge the enforcement of the existing laws instead, was ignored. Two weeks later, Clarendon and Annesley (now Earl of Anglesey) were already discussing the possibility of relieving loyal nonconformists once more.[77] Although the Privy Council now left most religious radicals to their fate, it did intervene in May to stop some Buckinghamshire magistrates who were stretching the Elizabethan statute against conventicles to permit themselves to hang some local baptists.[78] Quakers and sects in the capital were in any case enjoying relative peace under a tolerant Lord Mayor. Nevertheless, the monarch had shown a remarkable superficial docility to the Commons' wishes, and reversed his formal policy under the pressure of these without a serious struggle. Protestant dissenters were left no better off for his intervention on their behalf, and Catholics fared considerably worse, for the pleas made for them only enraged intolerant magistrates into breaking the unofficial amnesty which had existed since the Restoration and campaigning to exact recusancy fines.[79]

Furthermore, Charles kept his promise to make economies at court, to such effect that in the late summer he reduced his household expenditure by two-thirds. Some of this was achieved by abolishing courses at table, but most by laying off servants and attendants or depriving them of wages. The process, driven on by Lord Treasurer Southampton and by Bennet, was obviously unpopular with those who lost profit or prestige by it, and Clarendon and Anglesey protested on their behalf. The benefit to the government's solvency, and the potential benefit to its reputation were nevertheless obvious.[80]

In the same period the factional warfare at court, which had so debilitated the regime, was resolved. During the early summer, this had been hotter than ever, Clarendon's downfall being sought not only by Bristol and Bennet, but by Ashley, who had apparently not forgiven the Chancellor for the loss of the Toleration Bill.[81] What resolved it, and restored stability, was that Bristol now ruined himself with a thoroughness probably beyond the capacity of an enemy. The process by which he achieved this originated in the problems of the man who had led the agitation for a free Parliament in Buckinghamshire in 1660, Richard Temple. Temple had been too young to take part in the wars, but possessed a passionate interest in politics propelled by the fact that he was burdened with £12,000 worth of inherited debts, which could be most swiftly paid off with the fruits of office. At the Restoration he failed to obtain these despite his services and the friendship of Morice, perhaps because he annoyed Charles with his sheer importunity. All that he received was a knighthood, which could not satisfy creditors,[82] and by 1663 he was desperate enough to exploit the difficulties between King and Commons. Approaching Bristol, he offered his influence in the House to secure the success of Charles's policies, and was accepted. After the ensuing catastrophe, he decided upon the easier course of making himself such a nuisance to the government that it would buy him off, and accordingly became a leader of the campaign against sale of office and was a teller for the minority in the vote to supply the King. Charles, far from being impelled to gratify him, decided to destroy him in June by informing the Commons of his offer to manage them. The tactic rebounded, for Sir Richard denied the charge and the House demanded the name of Charles's informant.

By now the King's irritation with Temple was beginning to spill over to include Bristol, who had been Sir Richard's contact at court. Royal favour flowed back proportionately towards Clarendon, whose establishment as a local magnate was completed with the post of Lord Lieutenant of Oxfordshire. Bennet, like a true courtier, drew apart from his erstwhile ally and showed affection for the Chancellor again, and Castlemaine turned Bristol from her door. On 26 June, with or without the earl's consent, Charles named him to the Commons. From this moment Bristol decided to win popular support sufficient to round upon the government and force out his rivals. On 1 July he attended the Commons and cleared both his name and Temple's by insisting that a misunderstanding had occurred. When the MPs had finished laughing at his theatrical delivery, they closed the affair. Next, he arranged to impeach Clarendon in the Lords, in alliance with those peers who blamed the Chancellor for the failure of the Toleration Bill. His list of charges included every popular libel against Clarendon, including that he had arranged the sale of Dunkirk for a huge bribe and obtained a barren Queen to strengthen his daughter's position, and Bristol deliberately courted the Londoners. They, in return, made this Catholic courtier their hero.

The attack upon Clarendon occupied the Lords from 10 to 14 July, and represented the last and greatest fiasco of Bristol's public career. Few of his anticipated supporters spoke for the impeachment and some, like Ashley, sensed the course of affairs and commended the Chancellor. The latter was supported actively by certain royalist peers and bishops who disliked Bristol; the judges ruled that the charges were inadequate, and the fury of Charles, who bitterly resented the attempt to coerce him, was plain. Bristol's passage to the Tower was certain as soon as the impeachment failed, and the earl escaped it only by going into hiding. The King not merely issued a formal proclamation for his arrest but, with exquisite irony, had him proceeded against as a Catholic recusant.[83] When representations were made to Charles on his behalf nine months later they were rejected absolutely,[84] and the earl had to remain living obscurely for years.

The affair cleared the air at court, as henceforth Clarendon and Bennet gradually accepted that they would have to live and work together. Charles never returned to his dependence upon the former, for apart from retaining Bennet he immediately elevated in Bristol's place another member of the earl's faction, a young man of devotedly royalist background called Sir Charles Berkeley. On the day that Bristol's charges failed, Berkeley was made a viscount, and henceforth the King's affection for him was plain to all commentators. His private life was less reputable than Bristol's (indeed Pepys recorded more scandalous stories about him than any other individual courtier) but unlike the earl he had no interest in politics. Leaving these to the royal ministers, he preferred to remain the boon companion of Charles's pleasures, and so reinforced the new stability of government.[85]

As Bristol sank from view, so Castlemaine's absolute dominance of the King's sexual affections vanished. In mid-1663 Charles fell in love again, if one may so dignify the emotion. His object of desire was a virgin of about sixteen years, Frances Stuart, daughter of a Scottish Catholic royalist. Sent to court in 1662, her remarkable elfin beauty soon created comment, and by early 1663 Barbara was making a special friend of her in a desperate effort to reinforce the King's interest in her own company. This ruse failed, for in June Charles's passion for Frances was open and he was quarrelling with Castlemaine. Throughout summer and autumn Bennet and other courtiers attempted to use the new favourite to strengthen their own influence with him. What halted this natural course of events was the personality of Frances herself. The evidence remains equivocal as to whether she was at this period a clever and virtuous woman or a feather-headed innocent,[86] but the upshot was clear: she refused absolutely to surrender her virginity to the King or to take political affairs seriously. Barbara's utility, and survival at court, were thereby assured. At the same time, Catherine of Braganza regained some of her husband's affections through a wholly fortuitous piece of good fortune: she almost died. Having spent the late summer being carried from spa to spa in an attempt to cure her infertility, she contracted a fever on her return to

Whitehall so severe that her end was expected. This she approached with such touching affection for Charles that he wept passionately at her side. The reconciliation survived her recovery, and henceforth the royal affections were divided between the three women, two of whom declined to meddle in public affairs.[87] The area available to political intrigue in court life was thus further circumscribed.

A pattern was now becoming clear in the relations of Charles II with other human beings. He had proved himself capable of employing a ministry of mutually antipathetic men and of forgiving them if, like Clarendon, Bennet and Ashley, they were closely associated with unsuccessful policies. These are qualities generally praised in a ruler by historians. Furthermore he could pardon people, like Clarendon at other moments, Sheldon, and La Belle Stuart after her fashion, who had thwarted his will but remained too useful or powerful to be punished. In the same manner Temple, for all the offence he had caused, was left undisturbed once the Commons had rallied to him. What set Vane, Queen Catherine (in 1662) and Bristol apart was that they had crossed Charles without possessing any such compensating advantages. This was the lesson: the full vindictive anger of this monarch was reserved for the vulnerable and expendable.

For all these reasons, the regime survived the first half of 1663 without a breakdown in its relations with Parliament, and then remedied several of its own weaknesses. This process was to be greatly reinforced by an external event which drove executive and legislature together. More than at any time since the Restoration, the provinces were about to impinge upon central affairs.

In almost every month since Charles's return, rumours of impending rebellion had reached the Secretaries of State from some part of the country. Not a single one had been authenticated, the actual rising and plot which had occurred both being metropolitan affairs. In 1663 the most insistent reports had been from Durham, in the spring, and from that county and Yorkshire, during August, both accompanied by extensive arrests.[88] The Privy Council ordered the militia elsewhere to search for disaffection and it did so, finding little to report.[89] The northern suspects were released on bonds, and by late summer the kingdom seemed as peaceful as ever before. Charles went on his first progress, to Bath, Bristol and Oxford, returning to the capital in early October to find 'all things as quiet'. When the warnings from Yorkshire recurred a few days later, Bennet commented that 'all circumstances make us conclude it a false alarm'.[90] Anglesey wrote to Ormonde on the 13th: 'Here is speech of plots and insurrections, but your Grace may be assured there will be none, and I wish there were less speech of them."[91] As he penned those words the northern rebellion of 1663 had already occurred.

Or rather, it had almost occurred. What had so disturbed the Deputy-Lieutenants of Yorkshire was the report, insisted upon by one informant after another, that a great rising was planned for the evening of 12 October. Accordingly, the militia of every riding was fully prepared for that date, reinforced by troops of gentry volunteers. Patrolling a rain-sodden landscape on the 13th, they received news of gatherings of armed horsemen in the night and proceeded to round up every individual under suspicion, a procedure followed by the militia of the other northern shires and North Midlands. From the confessions of the captives and the evidence of those who informed against them, a story was pieced together.[92]

Since the spring, a group of men who had been prominent in the middle ranks of the Interregnum army, administration and religious bodies had been working to foment a rebellion across the whole region. This was the design which had been uncovered and interrupted in August, but had then been rescheduled for October and driven on with great energy, mainly because of the dedication of the leaders, but to an extent because a few of those arrested in August had been released only on the condition of becoming *agents-provocateurs*. A large number of men were approached, and in the counties of Yorkshire, Durham and Westmorland some of these agreed to co-operate. They came on the whole from those groups which had been the mainstay of the republic, the ex-soldiers and gathered churches, but included a few presbyterians and (in Westmorland) some Quakers. Socially, they were artisans, small-holders and tenants, with the occasional minor gentleman. They were convinced that they represented but part of a nation-wide rebellion and that former leaders of the parliamentarian and republican causes, such as Fairfax, Manchester, Browne, Ludlow, Lambert and Hutchinson were at the head of this. Their programme consisted of religious liberty and greatly reduced taxation, with local variants to please different groups. What ruined the plan was not merely that its organisers had been infiltrated by spies but that too many people had been canvassed for the secret to be kept. As the 12th arrived, the obvious vigilance of the militia caused many of those who had pledged support to remain dormant, but three musters of rebels were held, in the North and West Ridings and in Westmorland. The largest number recorded at any was thirty-one men, and all dispersed when their weakness became obvious. At the gathering near Leeds the principal agitator had grandiloquently drawn his sword and flung away the scabbard, only to start hunting for it after forty-five minutes when the enterprise was called off.

The elements of pathos and farce present in Venner's Rising were plain in

this one, and the more dominant in that no blood was shed. Yet the consequences were as tragic. Having failed initially to take the northern rebellion
seriously, the government proceeded to punish, publicise and exploit it to the
greatest possible extent. The judges sent north to try the captives resolved to
use the extension of the definition of treason made to kill Vane, to consider
those who had talked of rising as being of equal guilt as those who had risen,
and thereby to secure as many convictions as possible. In a series of hearings
lasting from January till August 1664, forty-four were charged, twenty-six
condemned and all but two of these executed. Their heads, having been
soaked in a tub overnight to drain out the blood, were impaled on poles
around York, Leeds and Appleby. Some remained there for thirteen years.[93]
The government pressed the northern gentry to provide yet more victims
and examinations to demonstrate to the public the danger in which it had
been, and to facilitate this process it promised pardon to those prisoners who
turned King's Evidence. In this manner most of those originally responsible
for the insurrection who had not made their escapes eventually survived, and
in some cases went free, while the rank and file died. It is with satisfaction
that one learns that local gentry managed to delay a royal messenger carrying
a pardon just long enough to hang the man who had led the Westmorland
rising and who had almost purchased his own life with those of his dupes.[94]
Further south, the Privy Council took advantage of the affair to arrest those
surviving republican leaders who were still at liberty in England and could
be considered dangerous. Of these, Henry Neville was released on promising
to go abroad and others freed on oaths and bonds, but some were detained.
The most prominent of the latter was Colonel Hutchinson, the regicide par-
doned by the Convention. The damp in the prison in which he was lodged
soon killed him as efficiently as the executioner's knife would have done.[95]

Despite the tremendous publicity given to the rebellion by L'Estrange's
press, it does not seem to have created much excitement among commoners.
Even in Yorkshire they were inclined to consider it an official fraud invented
to justify persecution, while the Londoners were more interested in the
execution of a notorious burglar.[96] It was otherwise with the upper classes.
On receiving the news from the north, the militia of western and midland
counties had carried out a programme of arrests and interrogations intended
to determine whether the plotting had extended to their areas, with entirely
negative results.[97] Nevertheless, the facts remained that a rebellion had been
organised over a wide region, that insurgents had actually appeared in arms,
that they had included members of every species of Protestant dissent, and
that they had been foiled only by the wariness of the gentry. The case of
magistrates who wanted to prevent conventicles was greatly strengthened,
while their more moderate colleagues were abashed.

This was naturally most true of the north. The original homeland of Quakerism, this had hitherto contained areas, such as the Lancashire–Westmorland border, which were virtual citadels of dissent, the nonconformists there being very numerous and the justices disinclined to disturb them.[98] In Furness in late 1663 resided two of the most distinguished Quaker leaders, George Fox and Margaret Fell, who were noted not only for their influence within the movement but for the favour they had obtained from the King in 1660-1, and who had accordingly escaped molestation. This situation was ended by the rebellion. During the six months following, large groups of dissenters were tried in Lancashire, Westmorland, Durham and Yorkshire, and among them were Fox and Fell. True to their principles, they refused either to swear allegiance or to promise to hold no more meetings and were committed to prison immediately. The militia and volunteers who made the arrests plundered houses like a civil war army occupying enemy territory.[99] The intensity of persecution was rather less elsewhere, but similar trials were still held in twenty-three other counties and in the capital during the same period,[100] and because champions of orthodoxy had recently been elected mayors of Bristol, Reading and Colchester, the gaols of those towns were particularly full.[101] Some Wiltshire militia horsemen, failing to catch any living nonconformists, wrecked a Quaker burial ground instead and then rounded off a day's exercise by brawling with merry-makers at Marlborough Fair.[102] The crusade against dissent in some other places took forms as filled with discipline and piety as this.[103]

When Parliament reassembled on 21 March, the government was ready for it with a programme based upon lessons drawn from the rebellion. Charles commenced his speech by alluding to the event and insisting that the danger of further insurrection remained acute. He then demanded the repeal of the Triennial Act of 1641 which obliged a monarch to call a new Parliament within three years of the dissolution of the last, explaining that the rebels had interpreted it to mean that each Parliament should dissolve after three years and that the present one was therefore invalid. He closed by noting how little the subsidies had augmented his revenue and invited the Commons to deal with the problem of tax evasion, particularly of the levy on hearths. Behind him he now had a united ministry, intent not merely upon working through the clients and friends of its members but through every MP holding a royal office or pension, a list of whom was compiled before the reconvention. Clarendon was ill again for the first weeks of the session, but on his recovery worked so hard for royal policies in the Upper House that he declared himself 'absolutely dazed'.[104]

The Commons repealed the Triennial Act within a week, while the House was still thin and back-benchers still arriving. The opposition doubled in size within this time, and was eloquently led by Temple, who was still trying to bully his way into office, and John Vaughan, a Welsh royalist who had been rewarded at the Restoration but who now commenced a career of opposition to the government for reasons that remain mysterious. Nevertheless, the measure still passed by a comfortable fifty-seven votes, not merely because of the determination of the court interest but because men unconnected with the court genuinely believed that the act had bred tension between King and people and that the rebellion proved this. In the Upper House Lord Wharton, a former parliamentarian and a patron of dissenters, argued that repeal would diminish the prestige of Parliament, but it still went through in three days, *nem. con.* The statute of repeal declared that no more than three years should intervene between Parliaments, but there now remained no mechanism by which this could be achieved if a monarch chose to disregard it. At Newbury the citizens were reported to be infuriated by the change, but they had a grudge against the King because of the unpopular minister whom he had presented to one parish, and elsewhere people seem to have received the news passively.[105]

Next, the MPs attacked the means by which rebellion could be fomented. The prosecutions during the winter had revealed all the more clearly the need for a statute to facilitate the prevention of nonconformist religious meetings, and this was swiftly provided by the revival of the Conventicle Bill which had failed to pass in 1663. It passed now, because the government had abandoned the dissenters. Charles regarded the involvement of Quakers in particular in the northern rising as a betrayal after years in which he had striven to assist their co-religionists. By way of reprisal, he explicitly withdrew his protection from Margaret Fell and turned a deaf ear to Quaker deputations begging for his intervention to halt the new bill. Indeed, he actually prolonged the session to ensure its passage.[106]

The Conventicle Act of 1664 decreed that any person aged over sixteen who attended an unorthodox religious gathering of more than five was to be fined up to £5 for the first offence and £10 for the second. The third incurred a payment of £100 or transportation to the tropical colonies for seven years. Those with no property or a holding worth less than £5 per year were liable to terms of imprisonment for failing to pay fines, and those unable or unwilling to meet the cost of their transportation were to be bound as servants or labourers to wealthy colonists. Not even those who recanted were to be reprieved. The statute provided for the punishment of local officers who failed to enforce it and of High Sheriffs who neglected to arrange the shipment of those condemned to exile, while a single justice sufficed to put it into action. It passed the Commons with even less argument than it had occasioned in 1663, and among those who applauded it was

Vaughan, who had spoken so powerfully for the liberties of Englishmen. In the Lords, Wharton did oppose it, but his colleagues merely added a clause making Quakers and sectaries who refused oaths liable to instant transportation. The only serious debate over it concerned the desire of the peers to preserve their own mansions from a raid by a social inferior, and the only substantial qualification of the provisions was that the statute would expire after four years unless renewed. This may have been a reflection of more moderate opinion, but might equally have represented an attempt, as in the case of the censorship law, to increase the indispensibility of Parliament.[107] Within eight days of reconvention the Commons had also set to work upon the problem of evasion of the Hearth Tax, and this time they tackled it properly. The statute which resulted sliced through the whole web of local loyalty and intimidation, by empowering the King to appoint his own officers to inspect houses. A proviso to secure the public against misbehaviour by these men was rejected by twenty-three votes, and a proposal to exempt poor householders from payment found few supporters.[108] When Charles prorogued Parliament on 17 May he thanked it with absolute sincerity.[109] The rebels who had gathered on that October night had succeeded, spectacularly, in uniting King and Parliament behind the reinforcement of the very policies which their rising had been intended to end.

The most dramatic and obvious consequence of the session was the enforcement of the Conventicle Act. During the first year of its operation, it produced trials in the capital, Bristol, Chester and thirty-one counties, the persecution being most severe in the three cities and in Durham, Somerset, Staffordshire and the shires around London. Conventicles were hunted by the militia, royal soldiers, or constables and justices accompanied by crowds. A total of 230 men and women are recorded as having received the sentence of transportation, almost all from the London area, where first and second offenders were given very light sentences in order to tempt them to incur the maximum penalty as swiftly as possible.[110] The prisons to which captives were committed varied greatly in quality. The best were probably in the capital, such as Newgate where dissenters slept in hammocks and were segregated from common criminals, while the worst were the cold and damp chambers of royal fortresses. County gaols differed in intrinsic comfort, but none were designed to take more than a small number of inmates and the confinement of a complete conventicle overcrowded most to an appalling extent. At Hereford, prisoners had to relieve themselves on the floor, and visitors speaking through the bars could hardly bear the stench. Launceston's lock-up had neither latrine nor chimney, while at Ilchester the captives were driven to remove roof-tiles to admit air, and hung up a mat to gain momentary privacy.[111]

Nonetheless, the full rigour of this law was repeatedly moderated. For one thing, there remains a sizeable minority of counties in which no record of prosecution under the act survives for this first, worst, year. The import of this discovery is diminished by the fact that some shires, such as those of Celtic Wales, simply had few dissenters, while there and elsewhere judicial documents have perished. But Gloucestershire and Norwich are examples of places where nonconformists were numerous and records are excellent, and there is still no trace of the Conventicle Act in 1664-5. In the former it was enforced only once, in Gloucester itself in 1667,[112] while in the latter it seems to have been ignored entirely, and the dissenters met almost unmolested.[113] Local reigns of terror were generally the work of individual magistrates, that in Bristol being propelled entirely by the Mayor, Sir John Knight, who had wept with joy when the act was passed. Despite the penalties which it imposed, such men could still complain of the indifference of colleagues, subordinates and juries. Two Durham justices sent wine to console prisoners committed by fellow magistrates.[114] A Deputy-Lieutenant in Kent reminisced about his mutual school-days with a captured minister.[115] The replacement of the zealous Falkland by the absentee Clarendon as Lord Lieutenant turned the nonconformists of Oxfordshire from some of the most to some of the least harassed in the country. Even royal judges sometimes showed clemency. A former republican among them, Sir Matthew Hale, reduced a fine inflicted upon a presbyterian by a colleague from £100 to £2, while a former royalist, Sir Orlando Bridgeman, devised a declaration of allegiance for Quakers in place of the oath.[116]

Given this situation, it is not unduly surprising to find that many people guilty of three offences were left in prison for varying periods instead of being sentenced to transportation. Of those who were sentenced in this first year, less than a tenth were definitely sent overseas. In part this may have been due to a desire to accumulate large numbers for shipment, but it was also a result of public disapproval. The seamen who were instructed to transport three Bristol Quakers were so impressed by their charges' piety that they refused the task. Those sentenced at Hertford got on to a vessel, but it suffered so many coincidental obstacles to its departure that the crew detected the hand of God at work and liberated them.[117]

The impact of the statute was uneven in another sense, which is perhaps most neatly illustrated by the committals made under it in the City itself.[118] There were 804 of these listed between August 1664 and April 1665, of which five were of presbyterians, five of congregational independents, three of baptists, and all the rest of Quakers. With a slightly less remarkable disparity this is true of most other areas of the country: when the judicial records are compared with those of Quakers, it is found that the latter suffered considerably more than any other variety of dissenter. The reason for this is that they would not run. They insisted upon meeting openly, in their usual places, and accepted arrest and imprisonment as a means of testifying to their faith. Other nonconformists preferred to go underground, a fact that is again well portrayed by records relating to London. The government's intelligence service there was so good that few conventicles could have gone undetected. Agents reported them almost daily in the winter of 1664-5, eight being held regularly in Cannon Street alone. Almost all were of gathered churches of sectaries and independents. Catching them, however, was another matter, for their alarm systems were so good that they generally dispersed before armed men could arrive. If this proved impossible, the pastor and most important members were helped away first, leaving the others to protest their innocence. One prisoner being conducted to a magistrate gave his captors money to let him obey a call of nature, and then vanished completely.[119] The same sort of tactics enabled the Bristol baptists to survive in freedom, while despite an absence of persecution at Bedford in 1664, the independent congregation there prudently ceased to record its activities.[120]

Presbyterian clergy fared in general even better, only eighteen of them being recorded as prosecuted during the first year of the Conventicle Act for offences either definitely or possibly connected with it. Not merely were they sheltered in many places by magnates or large groups of former parishioners, but the surviving diaries of their representatives reveal that prayer-meetings were often cancelled altogether if local champions of conformity became active or strangers arrived.[121] One Lancashire apprentice went regularly from parish church to dissenting conventicle as a sort of spiritual wine-tasting, with little sense of crossing a legal boundary.[122] For such people the experience of 'puritanism during the period of the great persecution' was not a dramatic or an arduous one.

No such statement, however, can be made on behalf of the Quakers. The arrests immediately following the rebellion had left over six hundred of them in prison even before the Conventicle Act took effect,[123] and by the end of 1664 every surviving leader of the movement had been gaoled. In some places virtually every member of the local Quaker group was confined. The reply of these people to the system of persecution was to challenge it directly but passively, evolving techniques of peaceful resistance which presaged, and in some ways surpassed, those used by dissident groups in the present century. The fundamental one was that after members of a meeting had been arrested, the remainder would continue to gather regularly until the raids had been abandoned or every one of them was in prison. This made nonsense of the expectation of magistrates that they could destroy nonconformity by picking off its leaders, and left them with the practical problem of a grossly overcrowded gaol and the moral one of locking up women and adolescents.[124] If a Quaker meeting-place was locked against its *habitués*, they gathered in the street outside. At Colchester the mayor tried to solve all these difficulties by having them savagely beaten each time that they met, by militia horsemen equipped with spiked clubs. After six months the Quakers were still patiently gathering, and what the soldiers had initially regarded as a duty or a sport had become a chore, and an embarrassing one at that. In the seventh month the meetings were left in peace.[125] Where some members of a group had been left at liberty while others had been committed, the former settled a rota to provide the latter with food, drink and other comforts. In areas of little or no persecution, money was collected for those imprisoned, and unable to earn, elsewhere.[126] Secret presses turned out tracts of encouragement, and exhortations also circulated through meetings and gaols in manuscript.[127] Most who suffered had their names and tribulations recorded in rolls of honour,[128] and in 1664 for the first time the suggestion was published that Quakers marry into each other's families to reinforce solidarity.[129] Running through all now was the creed of absolute pacifism, proposed after Venner's Rising and universally endorsed once the northern rebellion had finally exposed the folly of any other course.

All these measures assisted the survival of Quakerism in its homeland, but what ensured this was the disposition of so many Englishmen to live and let live. Had the Conventicle Act of 1664 been strictly enforced, all the heroism and determination described above would have served merely to fill parts of the New World with Quakers. That this did not occur was due to a compound of irreligion, laziness, good nature, good neighbourliness and, perhaps, a growing realisation that the statute had missed its mark. For it had. The religious nonconformists always most closely associated with republicanism and rebellion had been the gathered churches, and these, as said, generally avoided the penalties of the act. It fell heavily instead upon those sections of dissent which had been most harmless in political terms, if most offensive in ecclesiastical matters. If, as the preamble stated, the purpose of the new law was to prevent rebellion, it was in practice worthless.

The sovereign at least showed no concern about the problem. He now regarded the Quakers with the same cold fury as he had his other former protégé, Bristol, and his Privy Council actively encouraged persecution of them.[130] This confirmed the removal of the principal source of friction between government and gentry, while the Crown's other problem, of finance, was easing. Improved harvests, relief from heavy direct taxation and the slow recapture of markets after war and internal dislocation combined to produce growing prosperity in the country at a time when tax collection was becoming slightly more efficient under the impact of successive statutes. Revenue from the customs and excise improved·significantly as the new farmers found it possible to pay their rents, and the King's ministers both put pressure upon local officers to punish defaulters and gave cash rewards to those who obliged. The public debt was still considerable and the annual revenue about £$\frac{1}{4}$ million short of expenditure, but if the increase in income continued it seemed likely that a balance would in time be achieved.[131]

Like a sailing ship before a rising wind, the government began to sense its new power and react to it. Among the municipal charters preserved in the chests of English corporations, those issued in 1663 and 1664 contrast significantly with each other. In the former the pretensions developed by the King soon after the Restoration have been abandoned, and the town's existing constitution and privileges are confirmed without amendment. In most of the latter, the monarch claims the right to approve the appointment of recorders and town clerks. This was complemented by the fact that Charles intervened repeatedly in this year and the next to promote the interests of favoured men in individual corporations.[132] His arm was lengthening again. This is not to say that the regime was more popular, in the strict sense, than before. The King's morals and those of his court remained the subject of frequent gossip and censure, and Clarendon remained the most detested of royal ministers. The Londoners called the great mansion he was building near Westminster 'New Dunkirk', believing that it was paid for by the sale of that port.[133] These opinions, however, were irrelevant to the strength of the Crown as long as it ruled successfully in practical respects.

In the same period Sheldon was continuing the strengthening of the Church. In 1663 he inspected his own patronage resources by having a list made of the names and values of every benefice in his gift as Archbishop,[134] and asked every diocese for details of how its leading churchmen had employed the money received since the Restoration.[135] In 1664 he sponsored a reform of the ecclesiastical courts designed to increase efficiency and eliminate corruption.[136] It is probable, though no more, that he encouraged three more unsuccessful attacks upon clerical poverty in the parliamentary sessions of that year, bills to increase the stipends of curates, to unite urban parishes and to allow the creation of new tithes by landowners.[137] His greatest project, however, which opened a new age in the history of the English Church, was achieved in November. This was to end the system of separate clerical taxation, by which Convocation, sitting parallel with Parliament, voted the King its own supplies of money. In this month, and thereafter, the clergy were included in finance bills devised by the Commons. There is not a hint of evidence in the records that Sheldon acted under pressure from laymen: they indicate instead that he proposed the change to the bishops on his own initiative, and the surviving reply expressed support upon the grounds that it would reduce friction with the laity. This it certainly would, and carried with it a right for churchmen to vote in parliamentary elections, winning the gratitude and favour of candidates.[138] The most feasible explanation for Sheldon's policy is that it was designed to strengthen the alliance with the Commons which he had employed so successfully in 1663, in case it should be necessary once more to defeat royal policy. For his extraordinary political acumen and systematic mind, coupled with his attitude to dissent, it seems no exaggeration to describe Sheldon as the English Torquemada.

During 1664, therefore, it appeared as though the future of secular and sacred government would consist of a steady and peaceful growth of strength at the centre, achieved principally at the expense of religious nonconformists. This was not to be. As provincial events had intervened in central policy the previous year, so now foreign affairs were at last to play a decisive part, with even more dramatic effects.

Since the Norman Conquest every English king who had reigned longer than two years had engaged in warfare against a foreign power. The seventeenth century in Europe was as violent as most of its predecessors, and its first sixty years had included only one of general peace. It was not likely, therefore, that Charles II would remain passive in Continental affairs indefinitely. In the early years of his effective reign his most likely prospective opponent was Spain, which was provoked by his betrayal of its former aid to the point of waging an informal war upon Englishmen in the Mediterranean and West Indies by 1663. His most likely ally was France, with which he had co-operated so cordially over the questions of Portugal and Dunkirk. There was, however, a third power looming across the Channel: the Dutch republic of the United Netherlands. This had in common with the English a Protestant religion and a vested interest in curbing the strength of France and Spain. However, it also happened to be the greatest mercantile nation in Europe, while England was the second greatest. Its fishermen clashed with English counterparts in the North Sea. It had virtually turned the East Indies into a private trading preserve and had commenced the same process on the coasts of India and West Africa. English merchants who ventured into these areas ran the risk of losing their ships and even their lives. The Dutch colony of New Amsterdam represented a smugglers' haven in the midst of England's North American possessions.[139] The hatred and jealousy resulting has left its mark upon our very language. A person may be said to take French leave if a coward, but in general our other great rivals have lent their national name to objects and activities associated with the more delightful human pastimes. By contrast, we are still at times forced to go Dutch, listen to double-Dutch or admit to having taken Dutch courage, and the Oxford English Dictionary contains thirteen other expressions, now obsolete, coupling these neighbours with avarice, parsimony, idiocy and pusillanimity.

This completely natural and spontaneous rivalry led to war as soon as the English possessed a fleet big enough to challenge that of the United Netherlands, which occurred, despite the additional common trait of republicanism, under the Commonwealth established in 1649. The purged Parliament passed a statute to eliminate the Dutch as carriers of English trade, and then allowed the wrangle over the claims of merchants to deteriorate into a full-scale naval conflict which lasted two years. Cromwell concluded this upon fairly favourable terms, including the acquisition of an East Indian island and compensation to certain English merchants for their losses. The private war of the traders then recommenced, producing a new volley of complaints and claims, while the Dutch provoked even more resentment by capturing most of the Spanish markets lost to England by Cromwell's war. The Convention of 1660, while reversing the political policy of the republic, carried on its economic one, by reinforcing the statute concerning the carrying of merchandise. Nevertheless, during the following two years Clarendon conducted patient negotiations over the problem of traders' claims, and established a procedure for compensation.

According to one intelligent contemporary, the Second Anglo-Dutch War 'arose by strange avoidable things ... from several parts and parties'.[140] It seems possible now to identify two great forces behind the failure of diplomacy: a surplus of energy at Charles's court among men grown used to excitement during the turbulence of the past two decades, and the new confidence of his government in 1664. The French ambassador identified as 'the veritable author of this war' the King's brother James, Duke of York, young, martial and underemployed.[141] Associated with him was another prince of more remarkable talents, his half-German cousin known to historians as Rupert of the Rhine. Rupert had been the royalists' best general and then their principal naval commander, and came back to England in 1660 to settle down upon a large pension. It is possible that his tropical voyages inspired him with an idea which became reality a short while after his return: a new chartered company, the Royal African, intended to trade slaves from the western coast of that continent to the American colonies. York was president and Rupert a major shareholder, as was Charles himself, Bennet, and, ominously, the two military men inherited from Cromwell, Albemarle and Sandwich (formerly Monck and Mountagu).

It remains unclear whether the company was aware of how strong the Dutch hold had become on the commerce in which it proposed to deal. If not, it was swiftly informed for its first representatives in West Africa found themselves attacked by their rival and unable to do business with a native population in awe of the latter. Any other English trading consortium would have responded by adding to the perennial chorus of merchant complaint. This one instead fitted out three warships under a former royalist soldier, Robert Holmes, with instructions to protect its interests. These sailed in the autumn of 1663, and in the following eight months Holmes cheerfully interpreted his instructions by capturing a Dutch fort and several ships and loading up with booty.[142] During early 1664, growing still bolder, the shareholders of the Royal African Company set up another, the Corporation of the Royal Fishery, which was intended to operate in the North Sea and again struck at Dutch interests. Simultaneously, the government, acting officially, decided to put an end to the nuisance created by New Amsterdam by granting it to James of York as a personal possession and seizing it. A force did so in the summer, giving it the permanent name of New York in honour of the proprietor.[143] None of these actions, however, were intended to produce war, as Charles and James both expected the Dutch to concede the claims of English merchants to compensation and to a greater share of tropical trade, once confronted with this demonstration of English might.[144] They were encouraged in this by a natural calamity which assailed the United Netherlands throughout 1664, a great epidemic of bubonic plague carried from Smyrna to Holland in a merchant ship. With thousands of its subjects dying, it was believed that the Dutch government would have little appetite for battle.[145]

Charles's man at The Hague was precisely suited to such a policy. This was Sir George Downing, a brother-in-law of Charles Howard who had risen with him in Cromwell's favour and like him made the transition to the restored monarchy with profit. His twin posts of envoy to the United Netherlands and Teller of the Exchequer had been confirmed and the honour of a baronetcy added. Downing's theory of diplomacy was summed up in the phrase 'render tit for tat and force for force', an attitude made easier by his personal envy and dislike of the Dutch. He was an able, creative and plausible man, but perhaps better fitted to be an administrator than an ambassador.[146] It was apparently he who suggested that Parliament be utilised to increase the pressure on the Netherlands during its session of early 1664.[147] The English trading companies were duly encouraged to present their complaints to the Commons, who referred them to a committee chaired by Thomas Clifford, one of the court's most notable spokesmen in the House. On 21 April this reported, provoking a resolution filled with patriotic enthusiasm, that the King be requested to seek redress.[148]

From this moment the possibility of an actual war began to be discussed, in somewhat fanciful fashion. York was thrilled by the prospect of turning his post of Lord High Admiral into an active command, while Albemarle, who had fought the Dutch in the previous war, spoke slightingly of them. The opposing view was put by Clarendon, who feared that such a struggle would make England vulnerable to the Spanish and to rebels, and by Lord Treasurer Southampton, who feared its financial cost. It was shared by York's own secretary William Coventry, a dour, industrious and clever individual from a noble royalist family and one of the rising young men at court. Unhappily, Coventry suffered the moral ailment of the latter breed: whatever he said privately, he encouraged Charles to deal roughly with the Dutch when it was clear that this was what the King wished to do.[149] Considering the actual experience of the First Anglo-Dutch War, it is surprising that a second was considered feasible by men such as Albemarle. Repeated English efforts had failed to destroy either the Dutch navy or their trade. The cost in lives and ships had been considerable, and the financial burden so serious that despite desperate expedients the state had been driven to the verge of bankruptcy and unpaid sailors had rioted in the capital.[150] Since then the enemy had become more united and their leadership more effective, while their warships had been improved. In 1662 they had allied with France, a result of Dutch fear of the English and French designs on the Spanish Netherlands.[151] Time had indeed lent a dangerous enchantment to the memory of the former struggle.

During summer and autumn the English sabre-rattling grew more vigorous. In May Charles decided to parade twelve warships in the Channel, and in August to send them to Guinea under Rupert himself to follow up Holmes's work there.[152] In September the news of the English conquests in America and Africa arrived, sending the Londoners wild with joy. The restored monarchy suddenly seemed to them to be achieving gains as glorious as Cromwell's at almost no cost. Clarendon was rewarded for his efforts to avert war by being rumoured to be in the pay of the Dutch (instead of, as before, the French) and Charles was delighted to enjoy a brief tremendous popularity.[153] In reality his policy had already borne deadly fruit, on 12 August when the leaders of Holland had persuaded or deceived those of the other states into sending their Mediterranean fleet to re-establish Dutch supremacy in African waters.[154] The English did not discover this until mid-October, when Rupert's expedition was only just preparing to sail. By then it was too late for the prince to intercept the rival force, and the report in itself exposed the fallacy of believing that the United Netherlands would capitulate without a struggle. Charles, feeling unable to withdraw now, made two still more threatening moves: he ordered all available naval forces to concentrate around Rupert's ships at

Portsmouth, with York himself taking command, and instructed them to seize Dutch shipping.[155]

Only one factor could still prevent hostilities: money. Charles I's foreign wars had failed for precisely this reason, the Parliaments voting sums according to the ineffective system of 'subsidy' with the result that the war effort and the Crown's relations with the Commons had both collapsed in a welter of misunderstanding and recrimination. This time a promising start was made, when the City Corporation expressed its enthusiasm for a Dutch war by lending the King £100,000 in June and an equal sum in October.[156] These were, however, relatively small amounts compared with what was needed, and only a parliamentary grant could supply that. Accordingly, the government prepared for a new session with the same care and unity as it had met the last. Charles opened it on 24 November, by portraying the Dutch as aggressors and appealing for £800,000 to put out a fleet capable of saving English trade. The following day a back-bencher primed by the court proposed the sum of £2½ million. In the debate that followed not a voice was raised against the war and even inveterate enemies of the government such as Temple and Vaughan felt it expedient to add to the belligerent rhetoric. The latter attempted instead to have a ridiculously inadequate sum voted, but eventually the huge one originally proposed was resolved upon. It was not merely the greatest supply ever made to an English king, but was to remain so till the next century. Three days later the House decided to raise it county by county according to the effective means of the 'assessment', over three years.[157] The MPs thus acted precipitately to preserve their country from foreign enemies, as they had done in the spring to defend it against internal disorder, and in doing so carried out a reform of extraordinary taxation due for about a hundred years. Coventry called the government 'supernaturally successful',[158] while the French ambassador thought the Londoners 'intoxicated' with the prospect of war.[159]

Events now made a stately progress towards calamity. On 18 December a special committee of the Privy Council, including all the leading ministers except Clarendon, decided to issue a general order to their countrymen to prey on Dutch shipping. This they declared to be in lieu of the compensation due to English merchants.[160] Simultaneously, news arrived that the Dutch had swept Holmes's garrisons from the coast of Guinea, and the credit of the Royal African Company was ruined. At the Hague, Downing's blustering proved to have achieved equally little. The Dutch government rejected the English claims, demanded the return of New Amsterdam and was making its own battle fleet ready for the spring.[161] With a terrible shock, the Privy Council realised that a full-scale war was about to commence, and most of it, including the royal brothers, began clamouring for French arbitration.[162]

When Holmes reported back from his expedition he was clapped in the Tower. But it was all too late, neither side possessing room for compromise. Having so assiduously whipped his people into a fury of bellicosity, Charles could not back down, while the leaders of Holland had their own turbulent citizenry to reckon with. The English government decided at length to put a brave face on things and get in their declaration of war first, and so on 4 March two gorgeously apparelled heralds proclaimed it in London. The crowds cheered lustily.[163]

As the proclamation was repeated throughout the provinces, reputedly with the same acclamations,[164] Charles set to work to encourage his principal supporters. He had already entrusted the disposal of captured ships and goods to a commission of nine Privy Councillors rather than to one, to prevent jealousy.[165] Now he gave Berkeley a grander peerage, the Earldom of Falmouth, and raised Bennet at last to the Lords. As 'Lady Bennet' was the nickname of a notorious Westminster procuress, Sir Henry delicately selected a territorial title, of Baron Arlington. At the same time the King appealed to royalist sentiment by creating two new peers and promoting three others for services to that cause during the civil wars and Interregnum.[166] Aristocratic youth volunteered in droves to follow the heir apparent to glory, one adolescent earl doing so simply to avoid the charge of cowardice.[167] A courtier poet, Lord Buckhurst, wrote a song entitled *To All You Ladies Now On Land*, which became the contemporary equivalent of *Over The Hills And Far Away*.

In December a comet had appeared over England, trailing its tail in the night sky for nine weeks. In March a second glimmered its pale and silent course above the country. Such was the confidence of the nation at the time that they were generally greeted with interest and excitement. It was only later in this year, 1665, after what was to follow, that a writer would recall the traditional reputation of such strange visitors, as harbingers of death.[168]

2

The Years of Ordeal

❧

SEVENTEENTH-century naval warfare possessed characteristics which made it a particularly unpleasant experience for all directly concerned in it. For governments, it was extremely expensive. In 1665 a third-rate ship of the line cost over £4,300 to build,[1] and although it could then enjoy an active life of up to three human generations, this depended upon constant supplies of timber, tar, hemp, canvas, cloth, and wadding. In November 1664 Charles II owned a total of 95 ships, but only 61 of these were available for duty in home waters while it was believed that to challenge the Dutch he would need 130.[2] As he could afford to build only eight,[3] the rest would have to be hired from merchants. These were paid a fee for them and the full value of the vessel if sunk, but received no compensation for the wear and tear of service and could not recoup the profits of a normal venture from the price of hire. Such a transaction would not be easy to make, therefore, without coercion. The same applied to the recruitment of sailors, 30,000 of whom would be needed for a fleet the size of that proposed, when the existing navy had only 16,000 in pay.[4] If about £1 million per annum were spent on their wages, each would still receive less than an eighth of the payment for a comparable period in merchant service.[5] In action they would come under bombardment as heavy as any in land warfare, surrounded not by protections of earth or stone, but by timbers which fissured when hit into flying splinters. In a duel between two battleships both could become floating abattoirs. The extra seamen would therefore have to be pressed, in theory a genteel affair whereby the constables in maritime counties served notice to selected individuals, gave them the notorious 'King's shilling' in down payment and sent them to a naval base.[6] They may have gained ironic consolation from the fact that conflicts at sea did not permit the formation of a command post at the rear, so that they resulted in a loss of senior officers unusual on land. There was at least a democracy of horror in them.

The task of organising the English navy had been invested since 1660 in a Treasurer, a Comptroller, a Surveyor and a Clerk, assisted by three 'commissioners' and directly responsible to York, the Lord High Admiral. With the escalation of activity in 1664, two more 'commissioners', one of them Coventry, were appointed.[7] The diary kept by the Clerk, Samuel Pepys, testifies to the bad feeling between individuals of this team and to the personal shortcomings of some, but these details make their corporate achievement in 1665 all the more praiseworthy. They were most successful in finding ships, concentrating a fleet of 107 by April. Owners of suitable merchantmen were offered a sum for the loan of their vessels, which were then taken whether they had accepted or not.[8] Supplies proved a harder matter, as although royal forests provided timber in huge quantities the other materials had to be purchased from private contractors. From the beginning some of these formed agreements to withhold their stocks to force up prices, while wares which reached the shipyards were sometimes quietly resold by workmen in order to supplement their low and irregular pay. In some counties commissioners appointed to collect the 'Royal Aid' voted by Parliament only commenced their work in May,[9] and neither loans made on the security of this nor the profits of captured Dutch shipping were adequate to the navy's needs. Throughout the spring many contractors were paid in promises instead of cash, with the natural result that by May they were refusing further orders.[10]

The greatest problem of all was in getting seamen, despite considerable efforts by the government throughout the winter. All ships were stayed in port to make their crews available for naval service, attempts were made to compile a national register of eligible men, and orders were sent to the vice-admirals of maritime counties to press fixed quotas.[11] These, usually the same magnates who provided Lord-Lieutenants, set the justices and constables to work on the matter, sometimes reinforced by agents from the High Admiral. The result was that in many counties seamen hid or fled over the border, while in others the magistrates scrupled to damage local trade by removing so many of the men who operated it: as so often, they were caught between loyalties to the local and the national community. A solution often adopted was to send landsmen instead, resulting in obvious problems for the navy, for, as one commissioner observed, a fleet could not be run by shepherds. As in most wars of the period, those pressed tended to be the least popular or valuable members of their communities, and a menace as well as a liability to the service they joined. Coventry wrote that 'all are afraid of the new, ragged men'. Recruits, once captured, were sent in small parties, under guard, to the nearest port to be shipped to the bases. Once there, they deserted in large numbers, two hundred vanishing from Portsmouth in four days. A price was set on the heads of those who ran and justices were ordered to catch them, but local records show little trace of such activity. Coventry summed up the situation in another crisp phrase: 'Nothing but hanging will man the fleet.'[12]

Nevertheless, the very intensity of the complaints and recriminations found throughout the papers of the naval officials testifies to the zeal with which they worked, and they were rewarded. By mid-April a fleet had gathered off Harwich which was of at least as good a quality as England had ever sent out before and probably better.[13] It possessed one excellent resource that had been obtained without effort, an officer corps which had learned its trade in the wars of the Commonwealth and Protectorate and the even harder school of royalist privateering. York, Rupert and Sandwich commanded its three squadrons, with Lawson as the former's vice-admiral. Among the captains was the formidable Holmes, whom the vagaries of royal diplomacy had now restored to favour. The petty office of midshipman was turned into a cadet post for gentry volunteers to ensure them training (an innovation which endured to the present) and none of the nobles were given positions of responsibility unless they possessed suitable experience.[14]

On 12 April York called a council of war, which decided to sail for the coast of Holland to challenge the enemy. Accordingly, the English force cruised off the Texel for three weeks but found the Dutch warships unready to emerge and most merchantmen keeping in port. It returned to the Suffolk coast to rest and be supplied, whereupon the United Provinces returned the compliment and sent out the most powerful fleet they had ever collected, capturing a set of English trading ships.[15] There ensued a frantic scramble to regroup among York's captains, who repaired the latest gaps made by desertion in their crews by seizing men from a collier convoy in defiance of a royal proclamation exempting this trade, which supplied London's fuel, from the press. On 1 June they were in a body and on the 3rd they attacked the Dutch off Lowestoft. All day the snarling of the guns was heard as far as Cambridge, London and The Hague. The action consisted of a huge mêlée, groups of ships measuring up to whichever enemy happened to be closest. The English had a slight numerical advantage and slightly larger ships, but their greatest strength was the fact that their captains, whatever their past political record, assisted each other with a readiness lacking among the various components of the opposing fleet. The turning-point came when York and Lawson pounded their way through the enemy's centre, killing the Dutch admiral, whose flagship blew up after a furious bombardment. The Dutch fleet broke and was chased home throughout the following night and day. It had lost at least twenty-six ships, perhaps eight thousand men, and the mastery of the North Atlantic. England had achieved one of its greatest naval victories.[16]

The news inspired fervent rejoicing throughout the country. Most of the surviving churchwardens' accounts record the ringing of bells, and those Londoners who had no firewood for bonfires sacrificed old furniture. Urban corporations competed to supply triumphant pageantry.[17] New loans came in from gentry to the government,[18] while the latter at last acquired a foreign ally, though a minuscule one, in the Bishop of Münster who had designs upon the eastern borders of the Netherlands.[19] The principal reward for the victory was given not to a sea commander but to Coventry, thereby recognising the essential contribution of the naval administration. Gaining a knighthood and a seat on the Privy Council, he had become a force in national politics.[20] The victory had not, however, been entirely without cost, for the English had lost a ship and suffered over seven hundred casualties. One was Lawson, once the republic's favourite seaman, who died of gangrene a short time after. Of the young nobles who had enlisted in the spring four were killed, and among them was the new Earl of Falmouth, the King's dear companion. A cannon-ball had smashed him as he stood next to James of York, spraying the latter with his blood and brains. While his subjects made merry, Charles wept.[21]

The mob in Holland went as mad with rage as the English with joy, and returning admirals were almost torn to pieces. Under these circumstances there was no question of capitulation, and their leaders commenced work immediately upon a new fleet with an improved command system. Louis XIV, still attempting to keep the good will of both countries, persuaded the Netherlands to offer a compromise peace whereby they ceded New Amsterdam in return for control of the East Indies and divided the African coast. The English government refused it outright, the principal opponent of war, Clarendon, explaining candidly that they dared not disappoint subjects who now expected glorious gains.[22] The curse upon the whole conflict was that, contrary to common impressions of seventeenth-century warfare, public opinion played such a powerful part in it.

Having refitted their fleet after Lowestoft, the obvious next task for the English was to sweep Dutch trade from the seas. Despite his heroic leadership in the battle, York was not entrusted with it, for Charles was shaken by his brother's close escape from the death which had removed his friend. Rather than risk a difficult problem of the royal succession, it was decided to keep the heir apparent ashore and make Rupert and Sandwich joint leaders at sea. When Rupert refused to accept a divided authority, Sandwich was given the sole command, and so the principal seaman of Oliver Cromwell achieved the same position under Charles II. He sailed on 6 July with overall responsibility for ninety-five ships, which hunted the waters around the British Isles and Scandinavia. On the 21st, he learned that many Dutch merchantmen, including the rich annual fleet from the East Indies, had taken refuge under the guns of Bergen, a stronghold of the King of Denmark. Sandwich dispatched a squadron under a rear-admiral to blockade them, while an English envoy made a deal with the Danish King to overpower them and divide the profits. This was a neat arrangement, but had one fatal flaw. Sandwich's rear-admiral, knowing of the bargain and having difficulty in keeping his station in a contrary wind, attacked before positive instructions had reached the Danish governor. The latter opened fire from his forts, beating off the English and inflicting over four hundred casualties. It was a painful humiliation, and one which destroyed a promising partnership with the Danes. Among those who witnessed it was a young poet, the Earl of Rochester, who was left to ponder the fragility of life and the pleasures that might be wrung from it.[23]

With their prey now under Danish protection and their own men falling sick, Sandwich and his captains decided to make for home on 4 August. In their absence, the surviving Dutch war fleet hastened to Bergen to convoy the merchantmen upon their final run. Having reached the Suffolk coast, Sandwich found himself immobilised by a breakdown in the victualling system, while only a few landsmen—or boys—were provided by local officers to replace the sick sailors brought ashore. On 30 August he struggled out again and spent the next two weeks chasing the Dutch convoy around the North Sea in a series of terrible storms. More by good luck than any strategy, his ships managed to collide with and capture thirty-two of the enemy before their supplies ran out again. On 12 September they made for the Thames, and, as the remaining Dutch vessels were now safely home and the weather was still bad, they were subsequently dispersed to Chatham and Portsmouth for the winter.[24]

The defeat at Bergen and the escape of so many Dutch traders together made a mockery of the power which victory had appeared to bring the English. None the less, Sandwich's prizes did represent a considerable sum, and one to which the struggling naval administration looked forward with obvious delight.[25] Yet even this achievement was to be tainted. When the captured ships reached the Thames it was found that Sandwich, to strengthen morale among his commanders and, perhaps, to strengthen his private finances and his influence over the fleet, had divided some of their cargo among his flag-officers. A share was due to them, and Charles approved the action, but within days criticism was growing. Sandwich later claimed that £9,000 worth of goods had been taken, but as his own parcel alone realised nearly £5,000, this may fairly be doubted. It emerged that some officers had refused to participate in the action, that those commodities seized had been among the best, and that other goods had been purloined by seamen. MPs, called upon to provide further taxation for the war, believed that the Earl had enriched himself and his cronies at the nation's expense. Some actually declared that it would have been better to have lost the prizes altogether than to have produced such disgrace. Such talk rendered Sandwich vulnerable, but what proved fatal to his position, as to that of most seventeenth-century English leaders, was his possession of opponents at court. He was on cool terms with York and Albemarle, and had recently quarrelled with Coventry, who seems at this point to have used his new influence to persuade the King that the scandal threatened the Crown's relationship with future Parliaments. In November Sandwich was suddenly deprived of his command and sent into polite exile as ambassador to Spain.[26] This was to be the first of a string of sacrifices made by the King to appease his political nation, and a sign of how vulnerable the war had already made the regime.

One development alone was required to make the mood of disenchantment complete, and that occurred in early October, when the Dutch sent out the fleet that they had reconstructed with such effort. It was still smaller than that which Sandwich had brought home, but most of the latter was now laid up under repair and quite incapable of re-emerging. For three weeks the enemy blockaded the Thames, jamming all the seaborne commerce of south-east England, and only the usual problems of weather, supplies and sickness frustrated their leaders in a design of keeping them there longer. It was as though the English had lost, and not triumphed, at Lowestoft.[27]

Behind this irony lay a still more terrible one: that long before this most English people had lost all interest in the war. They were now directly at grips with an opponent which was claiming a hundred times more lives, causing far greater disruption of domestic affairs and had dispossessed the King of his own capital city.

The threat of epidemic disease was a constant factor of early modern English life.[28] Typhus, influenza and a variety of feverish ailments more or less difficult to diagnose at the present day produced regular heavy mortalities, at a local or national level, over the whole period. One infection, however, was dreaded more than all the others: bubonic plague, now known to be carried by the fleas which pasture upon black rats. A few bites from these parasites, if well-infested by the bacilli, poisoned the human system so severely that the victim could expire within two days, covered in blotches. A less complete infection would often result in recovery, but the illness itself was extremely unpleasant as its most obvious symptom consisted of swellings which burst into suppurating sores and gave agony. The suddenness of its appearance, the numbers it killed, the horror of its characteristics and the mystery of its origins and mode of transmission combined to inspire a unique fear. It was to a tiny extent endemic in the English population, the annual bills of mortality for London showing a few deaths from it every year, but at intervals it burst into epidemics. A man in old age at the Restoration could remember seven of these, yet the last was over a decade before, and between 1658 and 1663 Europe as a whole was free of them. Then the fatal ship came from Turkey to Holland.[29]

The sufferings of the Dutch in 1664 were, as has been seen, a matter for pleasure on the part of the English authorities. Before war served to close off trade between the two states, the City Corporation had already established quarantine procedures for shipping, and the winter of 1664-5 produced a severe late frost which discouraged fleas from multiplying. Clandestine trade with Holland, however, clearly continued, for from November plague was troubling Yarmouth, and during April and May rats carrying the infected parasites must have been coming ashore along the Thames.[30] By mid-June over a hundred deaths per week were announced in the bills and the government press was trying to prevent a panic. Then in early July the weekly toll rose over a thousand and most who could afford to leave the capital, including the government, did so.

The King moved to Hampton Court, then to Salisbury, and finally, in September, to Oxford, whither he summoned Parliament and the lawcourts for the following month. The Exchequer was transferred to Nonsuch Palace and the Navy Board to Greenwich, while most of the wealthier Londoners dispersed through the counties bordering the city. A set of the bravest, including the Lord Mayor, remained to care for the remainder of the community. At first the disease was concentrated in the suburbs and in Westminster, areas of cheaper and more overcrowded housing, but during August it spread through the city itself. In mid-September, when Sandwich returned from his campaign, the official weekly death-toll reached 7165, which all observers agreed to be a ridiculous underestimate.[31]

In the course of the summer the churchwardens' accounts of the capital recorded the impedimenta and services consequent upon a plague, which reappear in those of other infected areas, and in the orders of urban corporations. First would usually come padlocks and nails, to close up houses where the infection had appeared and prevent the inhabitants from wandering and spreading it. A red cross and the words 'Lord Have Mercy Upon Us' were inscribed on the front door to deter callers and a watchman with a halberd posted outside to prevent escape. The imprisoned would remain, with rubbish and excrement collecting about them, dependent upon public charity and friendship for food, until as much as a month after the disease had finished its work in the house.[32] As householders were understandably reluctant to report outbreaks in their families, each parish employed people to demand entry and search for them, while others, usually aged women, were paid to inspect corpses and report the cause of death. Another item in the accounts is a sedan chair, with straps to confine the passengers, so that those households which wished to shed their sick could have them carried off to a pest-house, either a shack constructed for the purpose or converted municipal property, where they were concentrated and guarded. No payment for medicines for these people appears in most of the entries.

The City Corporation decreed that the dead be buried at night, to avoid both demoralising the living and infecting them from passing corpses. Parishes therefore paid for carts to transport the bodies, coffins (continually reused) to enclose as many as possible during the journey, handbells to alert householders and watchmen of the carts' approach and candles to illuminate the interior of houses while removing dead. As the toll rose in each parish, individual burial was replaced by interment in communal pits. The church-yards soon rose many feet over their normal level, with bones and planks from old coffins scattered over their surface, and some in the city began to stink horribly. At this point they were abandoned for huge pits dug in the suburbs, where bodies were tipped, in the recurrent phrase of onlookers, 'like faggots'. Premature burial in these was admitted to be a frequent problem, and they possessed in addition a spiritual terror in that the ground was not consecrated and owing to legal technicalities never became so. Mourners were forbidden to attend, and although some ministers offered voluntary prayers upon the rim of the holes, no regular rites were provided. When the plague pit now underneath Broad Street was excavated in 1863, the skeletons were found jumbled indiscriminately, most uncoffined and most in their shoes, prompting unpleasant speculations upon how and where they had died.[33]

The authorities in London were presented with a serious financial prob-lem, of finding the means to relieve those who were shut within their houses and the many more who were left unemployed by the cessation of com-merce. Even the cost of the Bedlam lunatic asylum increased as minds gave way amid such nightmarish scenes as the city now produced. The poor-rate, never so necessary, became difficult to obtain with so many of the richer citizens absent. One partial solution was to bundle sick persons over the parish boundary, another was to sell the property of those who died without heirs. To a great extent, however, the shortfall was remedied by charity, either provided directly or by a national collection ordered by the King to be taken in churches. Bristol, the second city, gave the largest single donation, of £205, but two Gloucestershire villages raised £35 between them. After all this, and while providing individuals with the merest subsistence, there remained a deficit which had to be supplied from municipal funds.[34]

Some commoners profited from the catastrophe. Women employed by the parishes as nurses were believed frequently to smother their charges and rob the bodies. Burial parties were paid quite handsomely, tending naturally to be hardbitten characters who terrified citizens with their swearing. One amused himself by waving the stiffened corpses of children by the leg and advertising them as firewood. When, however, he added necrophilia to his list of perquisites the justices had him flogged and imprisoned for irreverence.[35] The episode is instructive: law and order were maintained throughout all the horror. Both legal records and literary sources indicate that constables still performed their duties and, despite the number of untended houses, that no great increase in crime occurred. The remarkable resilience of Stuart society again served it well.

Contemporaries employed a range of remedies against the disease, some of which deserve more respect than they have till very recently received from historians. The principal one was to isolate infected communities. As the exodus from the capital began, most muncipal corporations and some county benches recorded in their order books decisions to watch the approaches to their communities and stop anyone from a plague-ridden area from entering. Those directions were often enforced with great rigour. A North Riding man who gave shelter to friends from the capital was shut up with them for forty days and watched, at his own expense. Travellers in Lancashire were lodged only in outbuildings, the straw of which was burned when they left. When a man's children fled from London to join him in a Bedfordshire village, the inhabitants forced them to remain outside it in huts. When a boatload of refugees managed to fight their way ashore in Essex, a local man was indicted for assisting them.[36] Such practices, however inhumane, were efficacious. People could carry the deadly fleas upon their persons and in their belongings, and the distribution of the disease was determined by the varying contact of communities with infected areas.

Similarly, contemporaries realised that plague was associated with dirt, and whole folios of corporation order books were devoted to reducing this. Streets were ordered to be cleaned, refuse removed, stray pigs impounded, rats, stray dogs and cats (all of which could carry the fleas) killed. Another favourite tactic was to fumigate buildings, usually with sulphur, a means still employed at present to drive out vermin. Infected houses in London were directed to be treated in this manner, and the Post Office followed the example continuously, staff peering for each other through the smoke.[37] Men who robbed the dead in London were reputed to survive by rubbing their bodies with spiced vinegar, which may well have been a flea-repellent.[38] Certainly the medicinal remedies advertised in the government press now appear laughable, and the shutting up of houses was, as some contemporaries realised,[39] an act of tragic futility. Nevertheless, seventeenth-century English people possessed genuine means of reducing their vulnerability, individually and corporately, to bubonic plague.

Contemporary impressions of London during the worst of the epidemic show a curious discrepancy. In some it is a ghost town, with almost all shops closed, grass growing along Whitehall and corpses lying in the streets. Citizens will not open their doors to friends, and those with errands avoided passing near doorways or other travellers, of whom few indeed are visible. All is silent save for tolling bells, and desolate.[40] In others, it is pandemonium. The churchbells clang incessantly, succeeded at night by the handbells, punctuated with the cry 'Bring Out Your Dead'. Ravings and weepings are heard from the houses and delirious faces appear screaming at windows. The sick stagger in crowds along the streets, because the system of guarding houses had broken down. Vice flourishes even in the pest-houses, as the populace seeks oblivion in pleasure.[41] To different onlookers, tragedy wore different faces.

The tragedy was not, of course, confined to London, but directly involved most of south-eastern England and certain places further off. By late summer plague was reported from certain towns and villages in every county east of, and including, Dorset, Wiltshire, Gloucestershire, Northamptonshire and Cambridgeshire, as well as in Monmouthshire, Staffordshire, Cheshire, Leicestershire, Yorkshire and Durham.[42] The word 'reported' is used here with some emphasis, as in the prevailing atmosphere outbreaks of other infectious diseases may initially have been mistaken for the most dreaded.[43] None the less, contemporaries were usually capable of distinguishing the latter, and most of the evidence is local, and sustained. It reveals that London's experience was duplicated in miniature in many places, and some, relative to the size of their population, may have suffered even more intensely than the capital. Southampton and Yarmouth were so badly afflicted that the King called for collections on their behalf as he had for London, with a similar response, and net effect. Yarmouth lost over 2,500 people, including both its ministers, while at Southampton the corporation was reduced to offering not only money but local offices to men willing to bury the dead. Colchester's epidemic was also particularly devastating, and provoked not only a collection in the county but a poor-rate levied on local hundreds. In Norwich the corporation tried to limit the tolling of bells because of its effect on morale. The Kent Michaelmas Quarter Sessions were postponed. At Fenny Stratford the highway was diverted around the stricken town. The collector of folklore at Winchester in the present day is shown the stump of an old cross upon which country people placed bowls of vinegar, to collect money which the citizens of the plague-ridden community left in exchange for provisions placed nearby. Cambridge University dispersed from July until February 1666, the Master of Peterhouse interrupting his diary of meetings with the words 'Tempus pestis. Miserere o Deus!' One of the Fellows who removed, Isaac Newton, found time in his enforced leisure to contemplate the fall of an apple in an orchard, and the laws that governed it. By ruthless vigilance and good fortune certain towns, such as Oxford and Portsmouth, remained healthy amid counties filled with infected communities. Such centres contributed to the relief of their afflicted neighbours.

As modern pet-owners know, parasites are most active in late summer, and the death-toll of this plague was proportionately worst in every case in August and September. With the colder weather of autumn a general recovery began. During October the official weekly mortality at London fell to just over a thousand, and recovered sufferers, some lame with sores, began to outnumber corpses in the streets. In the following two months it declined to hundreds, and the wealthy began to return. The most important inhabitant, the monarch himself, re-entered Whitehall in February 1666. Although an ominous trickle of plague deaths continued through the winter in the capital and other towns, the land communications networks of the country began slowly to reknit.[44]

In the Catholic German-speaking countries at this period, the cessation of a plague was commonly commemorated by the erection of a baroque column. The Protestant English produced no such monuments, though the site of the mass graves was generally remembered like an unpleasant family secret. The epidemic of 1665 was, after all, the eighth of the century, and it was not quite terminated with the year. Like the Dutch, the disease was expected to resume operations when warm weather returned, and for the government and people of England the winter of 1665-6 represented only a lull in their two parallel struggles.

The demands of these two conflicts may perhaps be expected to have diverted effort from an earlier one, the campaign of orthodoxy against religious and political dissent, but initially at least the reverse was true. The government feared that its domestic opponents would now be encouraged and equipped by the Dutch, and provided with a new freedom of action if local officers became preoccupied with the plague. To prevent this, it urged intensified vigilance and the continuation of the policy of repression which it had supported since the northern rebellion. In March Clarendon wrote to all JPs to this effect on the King's instructions, with the invitation to report the names of colleagues who remained passive.[45] On removing from London, Charles sent his brother James to supervise the northern counties and left his Commander-in-Chief, George Monck, Duke of Albemarle, to guard the stricken capital.

Albemarle had been living quietly for some years, his most notable exploit being to drink an entire dinner-party under the table and walk away, in May 1663.[46] Whether he regarded his grim new responsibility with any pleasure is unknown, but he carried it out energetically. He had at his disposal a strong force of soldiers, whom he quartered in tents in Hyde Park to segregate them from the plague-ridden citizens. Despite this, a third of them still died and many of their officers fled.[47] If this was the experience of the government's servants, its victims could not expect to do better, and nor did they. Over-crowded prisons were ideal breeding-places for plague-fleas, and fifty-two of the Quakers held in Newgate died in the epidemic. Fifty-five of their co-believers had been herded onto a ship in the Thames for transportation under the Conventicle Act, but its captain was arrested for debt. As they were penned below decks awaiting his return, the plague broke in and killed half of them. The remainder sailed eventually, only to be liberated, ironically, by the Dutch, who captured the vessel and returned them to the English shore as valueless prisoners.[48]

From his suite in the almost deserted palace of Whitehall, Albemarle set his hapless soldiers upon a round of searches and examinations. In early August he was rewarded with the discovery of a small group of former republican soldiers who were planning an actual rising on 3 September, the anniversary of Dunbar, Worcester and Cromwell's death. He was, however, cheated of their leader, Robert Danvers, who was rescued by fellow-sectaries who overpowered his guards as they rested at a tavern on the way to the gaol. This was a humiliation likely to provoke the general's testy temper, and as the plague settled yet heavier upon the capital, so did the hand of George Monck. A series of mass arrests began, pulling in fifty more Quakers and many other dissenters, who inevitably added to the list of plague-deaths in prison. The soldiers acted the more willingly in that they blamed the meet-ings of nonconformists for the spread of the epidemic. Yet a month of this activity, and the consequent suffering, failed to recover Danvers or to detect any more of his accomplices. Those already in custody were summed up as 'few worth the hanging', but hanged eight of them eventually were, two being acquitted.[49]

It is a measure of how seriously this obscure little plot disturbed the government that for once the official press failed to publicise and to exag-gerate it. Instead, Charles directed the Lord-Lieutenants urgently to mount guards and hunt for disaffection.[50] His brother accordingly subjected York-shire's nonconformists to their most relentless harrying since the aftermath of the rebellion, gaining experience for his more spectacular work of repression in Scotland two decades later. Dissenting ministers and former republican leaders were summoned, interrogated and often then detained without trial. Many of these perished of a prison epidemic, probably typhus.[51] Inspired by his example, and proximity, the Lord-Lieutenants of the other northern shires followed suit,[52] and similar work was carried out by some of their colleagues in North Wales, the Midlands, East Anglia and the

West.[53] The total number of arrests must have run to over a thousand. Yet none of these prisoners furnished the slightest evidence of a projected rising.

One county which remained in relative peace was Oxfordshire, where Clarendon was Lord-Lieutenant and was in residence at this period. In keeping with his earlier attitudes, the Chancellor acted personally to commit a local Quaker to gaol. But when a justice warned him repeatedly of the activities of presbyterian ministers, there was absolutely no response. This episode lends credence to a hint dropped by a Cornish magnate to the Bishop of Exeter, that Clarendon was quietly discouraging the persecution of presbyterians.[54] Whatever his public utterances, it seems that privately the great minister was still promoting the policy of conciliation with which he had once been openly associated.

Both the justice and the Bishop, on suspecting this of Clarendon, complained to the man whom they regarded, correctly, as the champion of Anglican orthodoxy: Gilbert Sheldon. Through the first two-thirds of 1665 England's pontiff had been continuing the reconstruction of his Church, employing his favourite device, the questionnaire. He requested from each bishop the names and qualifications of all persons ordained in the diocese, then and each year thereafter, the value of all benefices, the number of cases of pluralism, and the number of lecturers, schoolmasters, doctors and non-conforming ministers. He also wished to be informed of all cases of ecclesiastical indiscipline, and employed the same directives to hasten collections for plague-stricken communities, that the Church might be seen to be working for the public good.[55]

Those bishops who made detailed replies drew his attention to a particular problem, the tendency of ejected ministers either to remain in their former parishes or to concentrate in towns. In both cases they could represent a serious rivalry to the established Church. Thus, of sixty-four former clergy in Devon, twenty-seven had remained in their old parishes and sixteen settled in Exeter. Bristol now contained eleven dispossessed ministers. The dangers of this situation must further have been illustrated by a development during the summer: a belief that in plague-infected towns, and the capital in particular, the regular clergy were fleeing and dissenters taking over their empty pulpits. Two pamphlets were published mocking the orthodox churchmen for their cowardice, and one, *A Pulpit To Let*, achieved considerable circulation.[56] Sheldon, who himself remained steadfastly at Lambeth Palace throughout the epidemic, wrote furiously to the Bishop of London on the subject, but received the reply that the accusation was baseless.[57] The truth seems mixed: at least nineteen of London's established churchmen certainly laboured faithfully through the crisis, and eleven of them died in it, but some of their colleagues did take flight and were replaced in a few cases by nonconformists. The same pattern seems to have obtained at Colchester.[58] At any rate, it seems likely that the publicity given to the problem would alone have convinced the archbishop that the situation of the dispossessed clergy required urgent attention.

All the problems of the regime—the war, the plague, the threat of rebellion, the threat of religious nonconformity—mingled in the parliamentary session at Oxford in October. There appeared several reasons for anticipating that this would be as much a success for the government as the previous two. Many MPs failed to make the journey through plague-ridden areas to a small city which was becoming grossly overcrowded. The court took up five colleges by itself, and lodgings for others depended very much on the contacts preserved from their student days.[59] In the event, the highest attendance recorded in the Commons was 160, among whom the court interest must have been disproportionately large, and because of the problem of accommodation and the threat of plague, the session lasted only three weeks. The government opened and conducted it with every external appearance of unity. Falmouth was dead and Arlington, despite his elevation to the peerage, appeared to have settled into the role of a self-effacing and industrious servant. In these circumstances, Clarendon seemed to be regaining something of his old intimacy with Charles. When the latter was presented with the problem of choosing a naval commander to succeed York, he called in the Chancellor to resolve it. During the session the 'Cabinet council' to determine policy was held at Clarendon's lodging, as of old.[60] Meanwhile the government's resources of oratory and administrative ability were both increased by the appearance at court of Downing, who was at last recalled from the Netherlands in September.

Of the issues before Parliament, the plague received the least effective attention. A bill was produced to rationalise the existing practices for its containment, but foundered completely in a squabble over the insistence of the peers that their houses be immune from search and closure, adhered to despite the appeals of government lords for some self-sacrifice.[61] The war was better provided for. Charles opened the session with a brief, frank statement that he could not fight on without another grant of money. Clarendon then enlarged considerably upon both the problems of the revenue and the necessity of the war itself. When the Commons reconvened, Downing was ready with a furious speech against the Dutch, and Sir Philip Warwick with a statement of accounts from the naval administration to substantiate its needs. The result of all this effort was remarkable: within fifteen minutes the House resolved to supply another £1½ million, and when Temple subsequently proposed that this be raised by 'subsidy' not 'assessment' he was disregarded. Downing, who had been impressed, and irritated, by the success of the

Dutch government in getting loans from the general public, was responsible for some clauses in the bill designed to achieve this in England. The receipts from the new tax, and the use made of them by the navy, were to be recorded separately from the rest of the revenue, so that the public could examine on demand precisely how it was spent. Loans upon the security of this tax were welcomed, to yield an interest of 6 per cent and to be repaid in the order in which they were invested, as money arrived. All this was enacted, and the House showed its appreciation of the conduct of the Lowestoft campaign by producing a separate bill to reimburse York for his expenses on it. Only two aspects of the MPs' attitude to the war appeared slightly ominous: the criticism of Sandwich, cited earlier, and a message sent to the King at the end of the session, requesting that the accounts of the navy be ready for inspection once more when Parliament reconvened, and carried by the gadfly Temple.[62]

There was, however, a different sort of disturbing portent connected with the new tax, provided that Clarendon's later memoirs can be trusted on this point. According to these, the King was convinced of the value of Downing's innovations to improve credit in a private interview with him and Coventry. When they were inserted into the bill, they were opposed in Parliament by Finch and Ashley, who objected to the rigidity the new system gave to expenditure and the reduction it made in royal control. To preserve a united front, Charles held a meeting of ministers with Downing in Clarendon's lodging, where it was decided after debate to uphold the reform, but not without a nasty scene in which the Chancellor called Downing a low-born parvenu.[63] If this episode actually occurred as narrated, it speaks well for governmental solidarity that no contemporary source refers to it. An aspect of it, however, is certainly corroborated elsewhere: Clarendon's growing hostility to Coventry and Downing. Just as he had, needlessly, made an enemy of Arlington with his jealousy, so now he was alienating the new set of rising men. Coventry found his attitude particularly absurd as they were both friends and supporters of York, but as the younger man's influence grew and his abilities were proved, the Chancellor's dislike of him waxed in proportion.[64] The taunt to Downing was ironic, for Clarendon himself had risen from origins as undistinguished, if genteel, as Sir George's. Like many an opinionated man, he had outgrown the ability to learn from his errors. This omened well neither for him nor for the stability of the team which now served Charles II.

The Commons dealt with the problem of sedition with the same speed and decision, but this time not, perhaps, as the government would have wished. Clarendon broached the subject in now customary fashion, by exploiting the recent plot scare. He made a quite unproven connection between Danvers conspirators, the republicans in exile and the Dutch, and appealed for measures to produce greater security. Almost certainly what the King hoped for was, as before, an increase in his own powers: he had recently considered a project for a new standing army under his brother, stationed in the North.[65] What he got instead was a bill intended to prohibit any ejected minister from residing within five miles of his old parish or of any corporate town, and from teaching in a school, unless he subscribed an oath that it was unlawful to take up arms against the King and that the signatory would 'not at any time endeavour any alteration of government either in Church or State'. The penalty for breach of this was to be £40, with a possible six months' imprisonment in addition.[66] It was so far from the reality of the 'Danvers Plot', which involved sectaries, and so close to Sheldon's preoccupations in the summer, that a circumstantial case could be made for arguing that the Archbishop drafted it. This has been taken as proved by a letter to him from Clarendon in the previous month, expressing interest in a 'good bill' which he had prepared.[67] There were, however, two other bills in the session which could have been Sheldon's: one for the better recovery of tithes and one (the more likely candidate) to relieve clerical poverty by uniting small urban parishes if the bishop, the corporation and the patrons all consented. This was introduced in both Houses, suggesting powerful pressure behind it, and did become law.[68] There would have been intolerant episcopalians in the Commons who had been made aware of the problem of the dispossessed clergy as Sheldon had been and could have produced the measure against them. Certainly such men proposed a second statute to enforce the same oath upon all office-holders and MPs, but this was opposed as too provocative and divisive, and defeated by six votes.[69]

When the bill against the dissenters reached the Lords, it occasioned a hot debate of which, for once, a good account survives.[70] The measure was opposed by Clarendon, Manchester and Wharton, and most volubly by Lord Treasurer Southampton, who wanted the oath to condemn only revolt and sedition, and nonconforming ministers who attended orthodox church services to be licensed to preach. It was supported by Sheldon and Morley, who condemned dissenters in general as threats to order, and when the argument ended in a vote the majority of peers proved to share this latter view. Again, the Upper House had proved to be in essence no more tolerant than the Lower unless the King pressed it directly to be so, which in this case he apparently did not. So came about the so-called Five Mile Act, the last in the sequence of repressive legislation known for the last hundred and forty years, with preposterous inaccuracy, as the Clarendon Code. Traditionally this has been held to consist of the Corporation, Conventicle and Five Mile Acts and the Act of Uniformity, and the long-neglected Quaker Act deserves to be restored to its place in this company. No individual, including Sheldon, can be portrayed as the driving force behind all of these: they were the work of the episcopalian gentry who formed the majority of MPs in the period and began to frame such laws as soon as they were elected. The Cavalier Commons Code would be a more accurate nickname for the legislation, and although clumsier preserves the alliteration of the Victorian one.

The immediate impact of the Five Mile Act was much less spectacular than that of the rest of the Code, for apparently only one case survives of a prosecution under it during the first year of its existence.[71] There are two reservations to be made to this statement: much of the data, in both quarter sessions and assize records, has perished, and the present author may well have failed to notice other entries among the crabbed Latin of an indictment roll. At least it can be said with confidence that no great set of trials resulted, and on reading the biographies of nonconformist ministers one discovers why: most of the ejected proved, as before, obedient both to their consciences and to the law, and moved house. Sometimes this resulted in considerable discomfort.[72] It is possible that the natural discretion of dissenter archives and a lack of alternative sources conceal the fact that many others took the oath, a suspicion strengthened by the fact that in Devon, where the records are good, thirty of the county's sixty-four dispossessed clergy did so. Some of the remainder, unsuccessfully, offered a declaration of pacifism instead.[73] Twenty-one signed at London, after Finch, Manchester, Sheldon, Morley and Lord Chief Justice Bridgemen had all made private efforts to convince moderate presbyterians that the oath in fact only referred to violent action.[74] The two prelates clearly wanted to interpret its terms at will, generously for men whom they hoped to conciliate to their Church and stringently for those whom they regarded as genuine enemies. A few who fell into this latter class chose to defy the act and to live and preach in hiding.[75] One former minister enjoyed such affection in his old parish that all the inhabitants connived in allowing him to remain there unreported. Others interpreted the statute by measuring the five miles from the actual wall of their old parish church, and one was saved by a justice who insisted that the distance be reckoned round every bend of a lane running between church and house.[76]

The new statute did have one effect upon dissenters that the preceding legislation had lacked: it divided them, over the issue of the oath. Those who took it in London were reviled by the followers of the more rigid clergy, while those who complied in Devon received threats and rebukes from men who refused. In some cases the existing rift between the presbyterians and the gathered churches was widened by the issue, while elsewhere the former split into rival groups.[77] By producing this new instrument of persecution, the episcopalians had ensured that nonconformists would expend against each other much energy which might have been devoted to making common cause against the established Church.

In the autumn of 1665 both Pepys and the Treasurer of the Navy considered it impossible that a fleet could be sent out the following year to fight the Dutch. The principal victualling agent stated that no further orders could be made unless money was provided. In August the workmen at the Portsmouth dockyard had already been dying 'more like dogs than men' of starvation.[78] Yet by May 1666 an English force of seventy-nine ships lay off the Thames ready for action. The story of the naval administration during that winter, even more than in the previous one, is therefore a narrative of triumph over appalling handicaps.

Most of these derived from a crisis in the public revenue: during the financial year from Easter 1665 to Easter 1666, the total income from its three main branches—the customs, excise and Hearth Tax—more than halved, while less than a third of the Royal Aid had come in.[79] Behind this fiscal disaster lay the war and the plague. The former deprived English sea-borne commerce of ships and men, and to facilitate this process all vessels had been kept in port for five months at the opening of hostilities and only allowed to sail thereafter if licensed. As one vice-admiral bluntly put it, fighting and trading could not be carried on together.[80] Furthermore, the English, unlike the Dutch, concentrated their warships instead of detaching some for convoy duty, so that even while they gained the North Sea their merchants were driven from the Mediterranean.[81] But, as during Cromwell's Spanish war, the greatest damage was done by privateers. From June 1665 small privately-owned Dutch craft carrying a few cannon and an armed crew, known as 'capers' or 'pickaroons', hovered off English ports awaiting prizes. Their known movements were anxiously reported in the government press. The cumulative effect of all these problems can be illustrated from a single important example, the coal trade between the Tyne and London. In the spring of 1665 concern for this was already considerable, so that the King forbade impressment of the collier crews and prosecuted men who sold coal at an inflated price. In the next winter many London hearths were unsupplied, while the fuel for them lay at Newcastle for lack of men willing to transport it. In May 1666 the pits were closed and the miners left unemployed.[82]

Meanwhile, the plague had destroyed inland trade even more effectively than the human enemy had closed the ports, only itself diminishing as roads began to seize up naturally with mud and snow. The barriers erected against refugees also halted merchants, and local officers were burdened with a range of responsibilities which distracted their attention from taxation. The commercial centre of the nation, London, was paralysed and over most of the country fairs were cancelled by royal proclamation.[83] The interruption of church courts left heirs unable to prove wills.[84] In counties such as Devon and Cornwall, which remained free of plague, men regarded themselves as besieged by both land and sea.[85]

These blows fell upon a system which had already contained enough inefficiency and obstruction to cause those who operated it grave concern. In June 1665 the government noted that most justices were failing to meet monthly to hear cases concerning the excise, as the statute of 1663 enjoined. When urged to do so, a number of them decided disputes against the excise officers, although the latter were technically correct. Individuals regularly reviled either the impost or its collectors, the most energetic being a Banbury man who posted placards around the town calling on his fellow citizens to refuse payment.[86] Local magistrates likewise abetted those who resisted the Hearth Tax[87] and the Governor of the Isle of Wight, Lord Culpeper, set them an example by flinging into prison an official who asked to inspect the hearths of Carisbrooke Castle. The weakness of the regime at this time is revealed by this incident, for when the island's gentry presented it with a good opportunity to dismiss Culpeper by accusing him of negligence, Clarendon replied privately to them admitting the justice of their charge but explaining that the King feared the upheaval consequent upon replacing the governor.[88] Meanwhile the commissions appointed to collect the Royal Aid in Berkshire and Wiltshire had been incapacitated by internal quarrels.[89]

A measure of delay and frustration was endemic in most seventeenth-century taxation, but in addition this government suffered from a slight disrespect and distrust with which many of its subjects had come to combine undoubted loyalty to it. The taint of corruption which it had acquired by 1663 remained. When some Derbyshire gentlemen decided to lend to the King in May 1665 they were told by friends that royal officials would simply pocket the sum. An acquaintance of Pepys informed him in September that he believed that half the war taxation which reached the government was not spent on the navy. In Essex, at midsummer, a man was indicted for saying that the Hearth Tax 'was granted for nothing (but to) maintain rogues and shags'.[90] How much truth was in these accusations is difficult to determine. In November 1665 Charles directed that a tenth of the money currently obtained from captured shipping be reserved for his privy purse.[91] This was hardly a large proportion, though perhaps in view of the navy's needs it would have been better to have taken none at all. During the first year of the war Pepys almost quadrupled the value of his own estate, but this was probably by manipulating contracts and clients rather than by direct embezzlement.[92] Sir Stephen Fox, the Paymaster of the Guards, who has left excellent financial records,[93] amassed a fortune by acting as broker in complex transactions which benefited the forces in his care considerably. What is certain is that the rest of the royal administration suffered badly from the lack of men of Fox's acumen and precision. Lord Treasurer Southampton was generally recognised to be overdue for retirement, but was kept in post by the influence of Clarendon and York.[94] Naval officials failed to keep dates in their accounts, to list all deliveries to storehouses or to record all tickets issued to seamen in lieu of pay.[97] The details of how this war was paid for and how the taxation for it was spent probably cannot now be determined. Slovenly book-keeping bedevils the historian as it did contemporaries.

It seems equally certain that the character of Charles's court continued to be a political liability. The King himself was fairly responsive to business, attending the Privy Council regularly, though not its important committees.[96] Having commenced the war by believing that he would only need to employ a portion of the Royal Aid upon it, he had learned sufficient realities by October 1665 to inform Parliament that even its additional grant would probably prove inadequate.[97] His weaknesses as a monarch at this period derived not so much from laziness or extravagance as from a desire to balance and conciliate different advisers, which led him to sponsor fiscal reforms while keeping a dotard like Southampton in charge of the Treasury, and in his indulgence of the companions of his pleasures. At a time when some display of austerity would have been tactful, the courtiers provided precisely the opposite. During their stay at Oxford they gambled furiously, Charles's mistress Castlemaine losing £580 in one evening. The ladies took to male clothes as a fresh diversion, and it became a slogan in their society that any serious person should be put in the pillory and whipped. One observer commented drily that though the town was free of plague the court had brought 'the infection of love' there instead.[98] It was generally believed that Charles was postponing his departure until Castlemaine had been delivered of their latest child, the ninth he had produced out of wedlock.[99] Some erudite critic fixed to her chamber door a Latin inscription which translated into plain English as

> The reason why she is not ducked?
> Because by Caesar she is . . . .[100]

It is easy to see why the less cultured Essex villager had doubts about the destination of the Hearth Tax.

The net result of all these factors was that the Navy Board received no money for two months in the autumn of 1665, at precisely the time that the fleet had returned and needed paying off. All that it could do was to give the sick seamen tickets to be exchanged for money when it appeared, and order the rest back to their ships. The men, desperate for a means to support their families, responded by trying to sell their tickets at a discount, by turning to crime or by attacking the naval officials. Reduced to wearing rags, more fell sick and some died in front of the navy office. The windows of the latter were broken and a troop of horse was required to protect it.[101]

This financial collapse was followed by a diplomatic disaster. In September the Bishop of Münster's army invaded the eastern Netherlands and, to the surprise of most observers, made short work of the Dutch troops there. What forced it to retreat three months later was the fact that the Bishop could only pay his soldiers with the assistance of English money, and this was failing to arrive in time because of the crisis in Charles's finances. In the interim the Dutch were reinforced by units from German rulers who had no desire to see Münster grow powerful, and from Louis XIV, who had no desire to see the Dutch utterly defeated and the English over-mighty. The Bishop opened negotiations, and made peace in April 1666. Charles was left destitute of allies, having spent nearly £240,000 upon the profitless partnership with Münster. Meanwhile Louis's last attempt to persuade the English to accept a compromise peace negotiated by himself had failed, and on 16 January he at last honoured his treaty with the Dutch and declared war on England. A sum of French money persuaded the King of Denmark to follow suit in February, while some Dutch dollars obtained the benevolent neutrality of the Swedish monarch.[102] England's trade with the Baltic as well as with the Mediterranean would now be severely disrupted, its Caribbean colonies were exposed to attack, French privateers would appear off its coasts and its battle fleet faced a potential combined enemy force of overwhelming strength.

As so often in human affairs, desperation provoked not despair but extraordinary efforts to survive, and the English government and naval administration devoted the winter to increasing the efficiency with which they could make war. Downing's attempt to improve public credit had been one such reform, and the King subsequently wrote to chartered companies, urban corporations, peers, JPs and the clergy, pressing them to provide loans according to the new system. Sheldon rebuked churchmen who responded feebly.[103] Southampton and Ashley made efforts to recover the arrears of ordinary revenue, including ordering the arrest of sixteen High Sheriffs for negligence in the collection of the Hearth Tax.[104] Pepys, concerned by the frequent problems of victualling during the 1665 campaigns, recommended the appointment of surveyors of victuals in each port to examine and report upon supplies regularly. This was done, and Pepys made Surveyor General to supervise the whole process. He went on to suggest means of improving the efficiency of accounting for pursers' and muster-masters' expenses, which were also adopted. York laid down precise regulations for the keeping of accounts by officers and for the issue of bills promising payment for supplies. At the same time another attempt was made to compile a register of seamen for use by press officers.[105]

Once more efforts produced results. The new parliamentary grant attracted some £300,000 in loans, a significant quantity in the circumstances and one which vindicated Downing's reform. Advances were received from the farmers of regular revenue.[106] Slowly the warships were repaired and supplied. Impressment on the scale of the previous winter does not seem to have been required to man them, perhaps because seamen were forced back by fear of the death penalty for desertion, or attracted by a royal promise of the money already due to them. Nevertheless, slight references have survived to press agents and their gangs at work in south-eastern ports in the spring and clashing with local magistrates. As ever, the naval officials complained constantly of shortages and confusion. The money allocated to them by the government during the spring fell £1¼ million pounds short of their anticipated needs, and during the early summer they received about a third of the money which they deemed necessary to continue their work. As before, much of their achievement was based upon extended credit. Yet the achievement was made.[107]

The retirement of York and Sandwich had left Prince Rupert, alone of the principal flag-officers in 1665, available for active service. Yet when the decision was made to remove Sandwich it was resolved to replace him with a joint command, of Rupert with Albemarle. The latter had led fleets against the Dutch in the republic's war and had made his enthusiasm for a second conflict, and his desire to participate in it, obvious. It was doubtless this which caused him to play a major part in fomenting opinion against Sandwich over the prize goods affair.[108] Why the Prince accepted a partnership with him when he had refused one with the unfortunate Earl is unclear. Perhaps Rupert simply found George Monck a more impressive man. Their formal appointment was made in March, and they joined the fleet in late April as it gathered in the Thames estuary. Within three weeks all was prepared for war.

It had somehow been decided, as in 1665, to concentrate all forces in home waters for a decisive battle instead of detaching squadrons to protect trade or, in this case, to bottle up French warships in harbour. The dangers consequent upon this decision were revealed in mid-May, when Arlington's agents learned of a message from Louis to his allies informing them that his fleet, numbering some twenty to thirty ships, was on its way to join them. At the same time it was known that the Dutch were preparing a powerful force under their best living seaman, Michael de Ruyter. On 13 May the two English commanders decided that Rupert would detach twenty ships and attempt to destroy the French and to return before the Dutch emerged, leaving Albemarle with fifty-six to guard the English coast in the meantime. This strategy required sixteen days for official confirmation, by which time it was known that the Dutch were almost ready. The chance of their conjunction with the French still, however, seemed the greatest danger, and it was resolved that Rupert would make a brief voyage to search for the latter. In fact Louis's message itself had been deceitful, and he was actually keeping back his forces while he observed events. The Dutch, however, believed it as much as their enemies, and the same wind that carried Rupert's squadron away from the main force brought a Dutch fleet of eighty-three ships out of harbour. In attempting to destroy the enemy in detail the English had exposed themselves to the same fate.[109]

Having appreciated the new peril of the situation, the government ordered Rupert, who was arriving at Portsmouth, to rejoin Albemarle. The latter meanwhile called a council of his principal officers at which it was resolved to attack the Dutch immediately, though their own fleet now numbered only sixty. The reason given for the decision was that the enemy could arrive before the Prince and that they could be caught in flank or rear if they tried to reach the safety of the Thames from their existing station off its mouth. Albemarle had, however, denounced Sandwich for excessive caution amounting to cowardice, and the suspicion lingers that he and his commanders feared the same charge. On 1 June, whatever his real motives, he launched his ships into the much more numerous enemy, far out in the North Sea. Both navies demonstrated a capacity for manœuvre in formation which had been missing at Lowestoft, though the English retained a slight superiority of discipline and quality of ship which helped to offset some of their numerical weakness. Nevertheless, numbers gradually told during three successive days of desperate fighting in which the squadrons passed and repassed their enemies attempting to pound them into flight. On the third day, Albemarle's surviving ships were running for home when Rupert at last appeared, and on the fourth the reassembled English fleet rejoined battle. The fighting was as fierce as before, and eventually both the English commanders' flagships were badly disabled, and Albemarle grazed on the thigh by a cannonball which removed his secretary's leg. At evening, running short of ammunition, they made for their bases and their opponents seemed glad enough to let them retire unpursued. Technically it had been a drawn battle, but the Dutch, if the expression can be used of such a tragedy, had clearly won on points. They had lost five ships and nine captains from a total of about 2,800 killed and wounded. The English had lost ten ships, fifteen captains and flag-officers in a total of about 6,000 killed, wounded and captured, and most of their surviving vessels were damaged. Observers noted that some of the English corpses left floating in the water were dressed in their best, Sunday, clothes, for the press gang had seized them at the church door.[110]

Initially, a great victory was reported at Whitehall and the King ordered celebrations. Word spread to the City, which kindled bonfires and rang bells, and then out into the provinces to produce similar festivities. The Cheshire town of Wilmslow rang its bells for most of the night, and many other communities may have responded as exuberantly. When the truth reached Charles he directed the official thanksgiving to continue and his press boasted of success, but the reappearance of the shattered warships caused the real news to filter out at ground level while courtiers communicated it to friends. The celebrations faltered, to be replaced by mourning. This was succeeded in London within another week by fury, as news arrived that the French had seized the English West Indian colony of St. Kitts. England's gains in 1664 were now cancelled out.[111] In the Netherlands the news of the battle was received with frantic and sustained popular joy, and the government made a tremendous financial and administrative effort to follow it up. The Dutch fleet was rapidly refitted and reinforced, and on 23 June it set out again, now eighty-eight warships strong, to ride off the Thames, halt English trade in those waters and consider the possibility of an invasion of the mainland. Had the French king now sent his ships, as his allies begged, the position of the English would have become extremely grave. But Louis had no more desire to see the Dutch over-mighty than their rivals, and continued assiduously to withhold his forces.[112]

Charles and his people were meanwhile behaving as the Dutch had done after Lowestoft: labouring with apparent unity for vengeance. The militia was called out, reinforced by groups of volunteers and three new regiments and sixteen troops of regular horse, paid out of the militia assessments.[113] The King requested a loan from the City Corporation and received an offer of £100,000 immediately. He also appealed to gentry for more, and Sheldon pressed the clergy once again.[114] These efforts produced enough for the labour and materials needed to repair the fleet swiftly in the dockyards along the Thames. In the winter the government had hired forty-one merchant ships, and now a further fifteen were taken up.[115] The greatest problem was with the crews, arising from the fact that a very large number of the existing seamen had clearly decided that never again would they be put through an experience like the Four Days Battle, for on reaching port they slipped ashore and vanished. To remedy the deficiency, an extensive programme of fresh impressment was ordered, and the agents and their gangs operated as far as Chester and Hull. Their captives were herded along under guard, followed by weeping wives, until they lodged at last in the Tower and were then taken by water to the ships. Garrison troops were brought on board to watch them and serve alongside them, and hangings of deserters were provided for their edification. Nevertheless, many sailors succeeded in remaining hidden, and local magistrates and constables were either unwilling or unable to locate their refuges. There appeared to be a serious possibility that some of the warships would be useless for lack of manpower. It was removed by abandoning the formal constraints of the impressment system in and around London, and seizing men at will in the street. Soon few hackney coaches were seen as so many of their drivers were taken. It was believed that a minister who rebuked one press-gang was himself promptly impressed as a chaplain.[116] The final result of all this effort, expense and misery was that by mid-July the English battle fleet, now exactly the number of its opponents, was once more ready to set forth.

It sailed on 19 July, to labour with painful slowness against winds and currents towards the enemy, till on the 25th, St. James's Day, battle was joined to the east of Suffolk. Both fleets employed 'angels', cannon shot chained in pairs to destroy rigging, so that the sea became strewn with spars, and several human limbs. This time, at least, the end was relatively swift. De Ruyter, perturbed from near the beginning by an example of the indiscipline which his navy often displayed and finding the superior weight of the English ships starting to tell once more, broke off the action after six hours. His fleet was chased across the North Sea for thirty-six more, reaching harbour with only two ships lost but the rest severely battered, 1,500 men dead and the morale of the surviving officers destroyed. Rupert and Albemarle had lost one ship and had about 1,100 killed and wounded.[117]

The wind had made the guns audible as far as Whitehall, and when news of the result arrived it produced a fresh round of celebration, naturally most obvious in counties bordering the sea. The militia could stand down, and for a time privateers became scarcer on the coasts.[118] Yet the government and its commanders were aware that if the Dutch had recovered after Lowestoft they could do so all the better after this St. James's Day Fight, in which they had lost less.[119] The English had now to provoke their enemies by some further action, either to treat or to risk another battle in which the Dutch fleet could be more severely depleted. The method adopted by Rupert and Albemarle was to send Holmes, their ruthless employee from the Royal African Company who was now a rear-admiral, to raid the offshore islands of Holland. The expeditionary force made its strike on 8 August, burning a town and an entire merchant fleet found anchored in a harbour, and retiring with the loss of only ten men. 'Holmes's Bonfire', as the incident has gone down in naval history, caused the Dutch about £1 million worth of damage and much fury and sorrow, but did not produce either of the effects hoped from it by the English.[120] Instead the latter, being short of ammunition and water, had to retire towards Suffolk on the 10th.[121]

From this point, the campaigning season wasted away in frustration and anticlimax as that of 1665 had done. On arrival in Southwold Bay the fleet was immobilised for two weeks, not this time by a breakdown in the victualling system but by confusion over the way in which it now operated. Indeed, so helpless did it appear that the leaders of the Netherlands ordered out their own navy once more. Rupert and Albemarle sailed to engage them on the 31st, but De Ruyter, falling ill and having many men in the same condition, avoided battle. The following day an easterly gale blew up and frustrated the attempt of the English to give chase, carrying them instead down to Portsmouth. There, on 6 September, Albemarle was summoned to London for urgent domestic duties. On hearing that he was to be called away from sea warfare to important but peaceful work ashore, tears of sorrow and anger appeared in his eyes.[122] The horror from which his crews fled had become the essence of life to him.

Meanwhile Louis XIV had once again placed his finger delicately upon the scales of war. On observing the new weakness of the Dutch, he had at last ordered his ships to join them, and they were now approaching the Channel, forty strong. The English fleet had eighty ships left effective, still reasonably well-manned as more sailors had been taken at sea from the first collier fleet to make for London since winter, once more despite Charles's orders. Rupert increased his crews still further by sweeping Portsmouth of every seaman his officers could catch, and on 13 September he set sail to achieve the masterstroke which had eluded him in May, of smashing first the French and then the Dutch before they could unite. Instead, the former withdrew to Brest on his approach, and when he rounded on their allies a storm drove them apart. On 2 October he brought his ships into the Thames, almost as battered as a human enemy would have left them.[123] Thus another year's expenditure of energy and blood, even greater than that of the previous, had achieved no final result, and the elements, as in every winter, remained the only absolute masters of the waves.

The seventeenth-century English were fascinated by natural prodigies. The vagaries of their climate, which almost every year produces some extreme, were followed with considerable interest. Deformed births of humans or animals, sudden increases in populations of wildlife, and supernatural apparitions, reported frequently and in vivid detail, all feature regularly in diaries, letters, pamphlets and newspapers. In such an atmosphere the approach of the year 1666, which had the number of the Beast of Revelations, was regarded with particular apprehension. Pastors of some sectarian churches predicted the commencement of the Apocalypse, and in London a range of slightly less spectacular developments were predicted. Even the cynical Sandwich, about to depart for Madrid, was troubled. A prophetess appeared in the North Riding, drawing great crowds, and impressed Fauconberg sufficiently to be permitted to continue her tour.[124]

As summer approached it became obvious that, if for nothing else, 1666 would be notorious for plague. London itself, to the great relief of government and citizens, escaped with only a steady succession of individual cases which added up to an official total of 1,780 for the whole year. It has recently been suggested that the absence of a second great epidemic in the capital was due to the development of rats there who were themselves immune to the plague bacilli and on whom the fleas could feed indefinitely and not be driven in search of other blood by the death of their natural hosts.[125] If this is so, it is curious that the rodent and human populations of Colchester, Southampton, Cambridge and other towns should have been less fortunate, for there a high mortality in 1665 was followed after a winter's lull by another. Many ports along the Thames estuary, and upon the coasts north to Ipswich and south to Dover suffered badly, as did towns and villages all over East Anglia and the east Midlands, and in west Sussex, Hampshire, Wiltshire and Warwickshire. Its distribution was, once again, uneven within infected areas. Ramsey was struck but not nearby Huntingdon. Stowmarket represented a break in the string of plague-ridden towns running through Suffolk. In both years Bristol somehow escaped with only a few cases.[126] Most puzzling of all is the celebrated case of Eyam, the Derbyshire village where plague appeared in October 1665 and wrought havoc in the following summer because of the decision of the inhabitants to remain still and to quarantine themselves in order to avoid carrying it further. It lay far from the nearest source of infection, and the gestation period of the disease does not fit the traditional story that it was brought there in a particular box of clothes from London. The results at least are clear: about half the population of the parish died (an illustration of the maximum potential of the plague), but their self-sacrifice did, indeed, preserve the surrounding counties.[127]

The good health of London's gigantic population in 1666, compared with the preceding year, greatly reduced both the national total of deaths and the number of refugees on the move, which in turn may account for a slightly less extensive geographical distribution for the disease. It also released the wealth of the capital to provide charity for the afflicted areas. The King ordered collections in the City churches for Salisbury, Winchester, Colchester, Rochester and Deal, and provincial towns also made donations. Justices laid rates upon parts of Wiltshire, Hampshire, Kent, Essex, Norfolk and Suffolk to assist infected communities within them, and, despite squabbling over the apportionment of these and attempts to default, contributed significantly to tottering municipal finances. Nevertheless, to many places 1666 brought a pitch of suffering unknown in the previous year. At Portsmouth the graves became so shallow that they were covered in feeding crows. At Winchester the inmates of the pest-house, maddened by pain and neglect, broke out and had to be subdued by the militia. Local JPs mounted guards to seal off Salisbury and Norwich from the surrounding countryside. The latter town spent £8,000 on relieving its confined and unemployed citizens, and a special flying squad was organised to prevent escapes from closed-up houses. Cambridge University was evacuated once more, and the Fellows of Jesus College discussed the problem of how to protect their buildings if nobody remained in them. In the town too few people were left healthy or at liberty to gather the harvest. At Braintree it was noted that the disease killed 97 per cent of those infected.[128] The impression left by this epidemic upon folk-memory was so profound that on two occasions the present author has been told local stories of it in communities which contemporary records show were not touched, although places nearby were. Either the experience of an earlier outbreak had been subsumed in the national memory of this last great plague, or towns which were spared acquired collective feelings of guilt equivalent to those of survivors of the Nazi holocaust.

London at least was relatively at peace in the late summer. Apart from the evaporation of fears of another epidemic, the Dutch had been driven back and business could proceed at a rate which, if below the normal level, kept its citizens far from distress. Some of them must have been slumbering very securely indeed on the early morning of 2 September, when an oven in a bakery in Pudding Lane caught fire and ignited first the building and then neighbouring houses. There was nothing unusual in this. The quantity of timber in most seventeenth-century buildings made them prone to burn, and royal proclamations regularly appealed for relief for settlements which had suffered damage as a result. The primitive equipment of the age—leather water-buckets and hooked poles to pull down thatch—generally sufficed to contain the trouble within a few streets. What made this occasion different was the coincidence of a severe drought, the gale which was sweeping the fleet down the Channel and the proximity to the initial blaze of warehouses full of tallow, oil, spirits and hemp. When the flames, running above the narrow and overhung streets, broke into these stores, the Great Fire of London commenced.[129]

For three successive days it roared westwards, across most of the City and part of the suburbs. St. Paul's, eighty-seven parish churches, 13,200 houses, three markets, the financial centre of England and half of the country's greatest port were destroyed. The streets where apprentices had fought Fleetwood's soldiers, the pulpits from which farewell sermons had been delivered at Black Bartholomew, the livery company halls where Monck had been feasted, all vanished with landmarks of seven centuries of other history. The sound of the conflagration was audible in Oxford, like the rage of a great sea, while smoke darkened the sun. At close quarters the din became deafening, a compound of the tempest of flame, the crash of falling buildings, the clatter of footsteps and carts, and of human voices screaming, cursing and praying. Pavements glowed red, molten lead ran in the gutters and the stones of St. Paul's exploded like grenades. The chains and gates of the City melted and tar and fat ran blazing onto the surface of the Thames. A particularly diligent schoolboy at Westminster was able to read a pocket edition of Terence at night by the illumination of the burning cathedral. At noon on the fourth day the wind mercifully dropped, permitting the process of destruction to be halted at the Temple. Forty-eight hours after this the ground in the burnt area still scorched soles, and the air singed hair; small blazes continued to appear spontaneously for six months. Nevertheless the ruins were soon infested by thieves and respectable citizens avoided traversing them after nightfall.

Compared with the plague, this disaster had certain features which made it slightly less dreadful an experience. It was swift and sudden, it claimed only about a hundred lives, and the entire community could combine to resist it. The King and his brother themselves handled buckets, standing ankle-deep in water from a conduit and throwing guineas to the workmen to encourage them. Manchester and Ashley led the Privy Councillors present in similar activities, and the militia, the Guards, magistrates and nobles all took part in fire-fighting. It was to organise his soldiers for this that Albemarle was recalled from the fleet. Nobody had anything but praise for the government's behaviour. As the flames died, administrative efforts commenced to minimise their impact. Charles appointed new premises for the Exchange and for government offices, named new sites for markets, ordered public buildings to receive the goods of refugees, sent army tents to shelter the homeless and organised the importation of bread for them. The corporation permitted tradesmen to practice from tents and sheds erected upon municipal land and ordered householders to clear the foundations of their ruined property and the streets outside them. It immediately commenced discussions upon rebuilding.[130] Wealthy citizens with housing intact took in friends, relatives and clients who had been less fortunate, and sometimes impoverished strangers also. Many of the poorer homeless erected wood cabins in the burnt area. The provinces sent in a total of £12,794 to provide relief, which although a fraction of the amount needed was still more than had been sent to London in the time of its plague. Nevertheless, unlike the epidemic, the Fire had destroyed wealth directly and imposed a heavy burden on the future. The total cost of its damage is incalculable, though estimates made at or near the time ranged from £7 million to over £10 million. One tobacco merchant lost £20,000 worth of goods, the booksellers £150,000 worth.[131] The destruction of legal papers threatened confusion to business and property not directly affected, and national resources would now have to be consumed in the task of rebuilding. To the economy and the fiscal system based upon it, as to the City and its people, it was a heavy blow.

It also contributed a less tangible problem to the future. The government never had any doubt that it was an unhappy accident,[132] and this has been the verdict of historians. The citizens, however, faced with the problem of how this particular fire had become so potent, decided that it had been the work of conspirators, variously identified as the Dutch, the French, or Catholics serving the latter. The most ridiculous and disgusting incident resulting was in Moorfields, where a woman carrying chicks in her apron was taken for a bearer of fire-balls by a hysterical mob which clubbed her and cut off her breasts. Anybody with a foreign accent or appearance was in danger of being lynched, and Privy Councillors and Guards were forced to divert attention from the Fire to save the lives of sundry immigrants and visitors. Charles appealed to the public both in person and by proclamation to call off the hunt for fire-raisers, and the City magistrates locked up some of the accused for their own protection more than for prosecution.[133]

The rumours of a conspiracy reached the provinces as certain news. The inhabitants of the Yorkshire village of Houlden concluded that the obvious next target of the men who had burned London would be Houlden, and doubled their watch. At Oxford the voice of a swine-herd calling to his pigs was mistaken for an alarm of fire-raising, and produced panic. The people of Warwick almost came to blows with a militia troop which tried to disperse them after the report by an over-excited child of a stranger with a fire-ball had thrown them into tumult. The militia was raised in many other places, and incendiaries were hunted from Newcastle to west Cornwall. In most of the north, the culprits were identified as republicans and sectaries, but elsewhere it was almost always the Roman Catholics who were blamed. At Coventry local officers made strenuous efforts to dispel this impression, and only succeeded in bringing themselves, and the central government, under suspicion of being in league with Papists.[134]

This popular reaction, like the Fire itself, resulted from a set of coincidences. First, the government itself had put incendiaries into the public mind in April, when it tried and executed the Danvers plotters and publicised that it was part of their design to set the City alight.[135] Second, the English commoner's subcutaneous fear of Catholics had re-emerged on the outbreak of war with France, the Catholic monarchy just across the Channel which, with the growing weakness of Spain, was becoming recognised as the most powerful state in Europe. Its co-religionists in England were regarded as a potential fifth column, and in July the citizens of Manchester, a strongly presbyterian town in the county containing most Catholics, were already in acute fear of a rising by the latter.[136] Last, a short while after the Fire a French watch-maker called Robert Hubert, who had settled in London, actually confessed to having started it as part of a conspiracy arranged in Paris. He held to this story with such conviction that he was hanged, and although not known to be a Catholic before, he professed himself one on the scaffold. In reality he was a complete lunatic, seeking notoriety, and it was discovered later that he had been on shipboard, returning from a journey to Sweden, on the night when the blaze broke out. The government remained sceptical of him, but the multitude who had believed in a Papist plot now possessed apparent confirmation of their worst fears.[137] Fresh tensions were added to those active within society, and the government would have to reckon with them.

The year 1666 had still not quite completed its devilry. Exceptionally violent weather had already been experienced in mid-July, when storms had shaken houses at Coventry and unleashed hail-storms around Aldeburgh which killed birds in flight and flattened corn.[138] In October a very bright comet flew low over the Midlands, to be followed, there and in East Anglia, by the worst tempests the people could remember. Many houses were wrecked, churches damaged and trees torn up. So much rain fell that it was feared that the freshly-sown seed would rot in waterlogged soil and a deficiency of crops would be added to the tribulations of the future.[139]

In September a friend of Pepys had comforted him with the thought that the Fire would ensure a continuing sympathy for the government's needs in the impending parliamentary session.[140] He was wrong. The rage of nature during the autumn was matched by a growing political storm at Westminster, which was to bring King and Commons close to a complete impasse for the first time since the Restoration.

Intertwined with political events are always economic developments. The expression 'intertwined with' is chosen with care, as the relationship between the two, far from being invariably a process of cause and effect, is frequently impossible to discern. Yet sometimes the pressure of one upon the other is clear. The continuous economic development of the Tudor and early Stuart period consisted of a rise in population, prices and rents, and historians have regularly linked this with political changes, though notorious disagreements have resulted. By contrast such connections have been made less often for the late seventeenth century, when the population and prices stabilised or slightly decreased, rents fell and an agricultural surplus appeared. Yet one important political consequence of this alteration is clear: the Irish cattle controversy.

The economy of Ireland under the Stuarts was even more pastoral than at the present, and the export of cattle was very important to it. The main customers for these, as for all Irish products, were naturally the English, and they competed with the beasts from English pastures. During the long years of growing demand this was only a minor irritation to those who owned and farmed the latter. By 1663, however, the threat of an agricultural recession was clear, and affecting pasture more than arable land. As men in the grip of fundamental change often do, the members of the Cavalier House of Commons blamed superficialities, and the principal one in this case was Irish cattle. The result was an act which forbade their importation for part of the year. The Irish were naturally horrified, and possessed powerful champions in their Lord-Lieutenant, Ormonde, and Anglesey, who represented them at Whitehall.[141] Charles, because of a general responsibility towards his Irish subjects and a particular affection for Ormonde, sympathised with them, as did Ormonde's old friend Clarendon. Accordingly, when a bill was introduced into the Commons at Oxford in 1665, intended to keep out Irish cattle altogether by imposing a ruinous duty and by limiting their transportation to tiny numbers, it created great excitement. Ominously, its principal exponent was the House's main trouble-maker, Temple. Finch argued himself hoarse against it, and it passed the committee stage by only one vote, but the argument that it would reverse the continuing fall in rents proved so potent that it reached the Lords. There it remained, on the instructions of Charles who declared publicly that he would never assent to it. Nevertheless, the determination displayed by the bill's defenders made it probable that it would be revived in the next session, when a better attendance by backbenchers would increase support for it. Some observers considered that in these circumstances continued opposition by the King would rob him of a supply of taxation.[142]

Other ill portents hung over the reconvention of Parliament. The fact that so much money had been voted by such a poorly-attended House at Oxford carried the danger that those absent would be more inclined to question the result when they reassembled.[143] The result had, of course, been another year of war without a final decision or a tangible gain to set against great losses. Added to this handicap was the continuing reputation of the court as a centre of vice and corruption, which received public expression at three successive by-elections in the second half of 1666 in which a candidate was defeated because of his association with the government. At two of them the crowd shouted 'No courtier!'.[144] The regime had every reason to expect trouble from the Commons, and it did. Sheldon called up the bishops to the Lords to strengthen royal influence in that House.[145]

In the event, an additional factor came into play for which the government had not bargained: the return to central political life of the greatest nobleman in the land, George Villiers, second Duke of Buckingham. The sorrow of Charles I over his murdered favourite, the first Duke, had resulted in the latter's infant son being taken into the royal nursery and reared with the future Charles II and James of York. This privileged upbringing, setting him in a limbo between a prince and a subject, may have spoiled the second George, or he may have been born with defects of character. The latter were as plain in his youth as they are in the satire of Dryden and the anecdotes of Wycherley, based upon his career in middle age: at best irresponsibility and self-indulgence, at worst a fundamental instability. How great a man they flawed is debatable, but he was certainly capable of industry, verbal and physical dexterity and a capacity both to command and to fascinate.

His wartime record had been impeccably royalist, but in exile he had become a leading advocate of alliance with the presbyterian Scots and was suspected of betraying Charles II when the latter attempted to escape from their custody in 1650. During the Worcester campaign, he had made himself a nuisance by demanding a command for which he had no experience and then throwing a tantrum when he did not get it. He had later made peace with the Protectorate and married Fairfax's daughter, thereby becoming regarded by the King's followers as a renegade. At the Restoration he was received at court and subsequently allowed onto the Privy Council, but given no office and, apparently, lacked any influence with Charles.[146] He became instead a prominent but dispensable companion of the King's pleasures, noted for his wit and his aptitude for such tricks as mimicry and building castles of cards, living, in Clarendon's phrase, 'a life more by night than by day'.[147] The frustration he felt in this existence showed in the fact that within three years of the Restoration he had quarrelled violently with Bristol, Sandwich, Rupert and the Earl of Northumberland.[148] In 1663 he retired to his vast Yorkshire estates to play the part of a local magnate and Lord-Lieutenant, with apparent success and popularity.[149] This pattern was broken once, at the beginning of the Dutch war, when he arrived at the fleet expecting a position of responsibility and flew into a rage when he was considered unready for one.[150] In the autumn of 1666 he suddenly threw over the provincial life and returned to Westminster, determined upon Temple's

tactic of forcing his way to power, and equipped with an aristocrat's influence to employ in this task. Part of this consisted of a set of able young allies
in the Commons, most notably Edward Seymour, the son of a Devon
royalist, who had hitherto supported the government with him and now
joined energetically in the business of opposition.[151] The new policy may
have been suggested to him by his current mistress, the Countess of
Shrewsbury, who was one of the most predatory and destructive, as well as
one of the most beautiful, women of their generation. It may equally well
have been an obvious next step in his quest for recognition. Whatever the
reason, the government had acquired a dangerous antagonist.

On 21 September Charles opened the session, by stating that with so
many enemies to fight, now encouraged by the destruction of London, more
taxation would be required to continue the war. The Commons immediately
determined that they would supply this as soon as the government and naval
administration had submitted accounts to show what was required. This
time, however, the House intended to inspect the quality of the accounts, a
step which caused the Navy Board some anxiety because, as has been said,
their books had not been perfectly kept. Nevertheless, the Commons' committee on the matter, which included both supporters and opponents of the
government, proved amenable enough and passed the figures provided. On
11 October it reported back to the House, which resolved the next day to
supply £1,800,000, a more generous sum than that voted at Oxford. Part of
this success was due to the apparent clarity of the accounts, and part to the
eloquence and energy with which Coventry put the navy's case in the
Commons.[152] He also seems to have talked Buckingham out of a project to
impose the death penalty for embezzlement of public money or property.[153]
At the same time, the King attempted to diminish the court's reputation for
extravagance by introducing a new mode of dress which was both inexpen-
sive and patriotic, being made entirely of English textiles.[154]

Thus far the government had done well, but warning signs had appeared.
One was the King's irritation with the Commons because of their inspection
of the accounts,[155] suggesting that he would be extremely sensitive to any
further challenge to his authority. The second was that such a challenge was
already being made. On the day after the royal speech, a new Irish cattle bill
was introduced into the Commons, this time to ban their importation outright. Coventry, gauging the temper of the House, considered it madness for
the government to oppose it, and seems to have persuaded Charles at least to
order no concerted effort against it in the Commons. Finch and Attorney-
General Palmer did oppose, joined by MPs from areas which benefited from
the trade, but after noisy altercations the bill passed by sixty-one votes on 13
October. It contained the particular provocation, supplied by Seymour, of

describing the importation of cattle as 'a common and public nuisance', a term which by legal technicality rendered the King unable to dispense individuals from it under his prerogative powers. When Palmer referred to this fact, the MPs became all the more resolved on the phrase. Its existence strengthened Charles in his resolution that the bill would perish in the Lords.[156]

From now on everything went wrong for him. The Commons, having voted the huge supply for the war, used up three weeks debating how to raise it. At least six different methods were offered, 'each man proposing according to his own inclination, interest or ill-humour', a situation arising from the reluctance of many gentry to pay yet another 'assessment' on property. The court was prepared to accept a general excise of the sort levied under the republic, but this proved unpopular. The shambles ended in unhappy compromise on 8 November when it was voted to raise most of the sum by 'assessment' after all, and the remainder by a tax on legal documents and a poll tax of a more effective variety than before.[157] From this work they took off time to share in the popular animosity against Catholics. In September they appointed a committee to investigate the stories of fire-raising, and on 26 October proposed to the Lords that Charles be asked to banish Catholic priests and order the disarmament and collection of recusancy fines from their followers. The King did so without demur. A suggestion from Prynne, that Catholics, sectaries and foreigners be cleared out of London to house the homeless, was however unsupported.[158]

Meanwhile the Irish cattle bill had bitterly divided the Lords. Buckingham, who was rumoured to have eavesdropped upon the Commons' arguments over it from the Speaker's chamber, led its supporters. He was seconded by one of Charles's own ministers, Ashley, who combined a dislike of Ormonde with an interest in the cattle trade with Scotland and an irrational hatred of all things Irish, the last being a sentiment which probably motivated some of the Commons. Either because of this last reason or for fear of provoking the Commons, Southampton, Manchester and Carlisle also believed that the bill should pass, and Arlington hesitated over the issue. Resolutely opposed to the measure were Clarendon, Anglesey, the bishops and some Catholic peers, the last two groups both bidding for royal favour. The ensuing debates were some of the most bitter that the Upper House had known, and in the thick of them was Ormonde's heir, the Earl of Ossory, a hot-tempered young man whom Charles had admitted to the English house of peers that session, doubtless specifically to argue against this bill. Within three weeks he had to be disciplined twice, once for challenging Buckingham to a duel and once for reminding Ashley of his service to the republic. The words of the Duke which had so provoked him were that all opponents of the bill had either 'Irish estates or Irish understandings', an indication of the tone of the discussion. On 23 November the bill passed by sixteen votes, but with some amendments, the most significant being to substitute a milder expression for the words containing 'nuisance'. The King, being left thereby able to use his dispensing power, could considerably reduce the effect of the statute.[159]

The return of this bill to the Commons disrupted a progress of supply which was already painfully slow because of the complexity of the method chosen for it and of filibustering by the Temple and Seymour groups. On 27 November the House decided by sixteen votes to insist on the word 'nuisance': it intended to give the King no more power over Irish cattle than it had over corporations or dissenters. It then settled down to work slowly through the Lords' other amendments and prepare for confrontation. Nevertheless by 7 December, work on the poll tax bill was almost completed, when a former royalist who had gone unrewarded, William Garraway, proposed a clause setting up a commission to examine the fate of all the taxes voted for the war. In October Coventry had noted Garraway as an able man whose support was worth buying with office. Nothing had been done, and the government now rued the consequence. Eagerly supported by Buckingham's friends, the proposal passed on the 9th. When Charles let his violent displeasure be known, the most he gained was to have the clause removed and incorporated into a separate bill which was sent to the Lords with that for the tax on the 13th. Two days later Charles sent a message appealing for the completion of supply, but three days after this his opponents found a third major issue to divide the Parliament. Mordaunt, the conspirator who had worked so hard for the King, had been rewarded at the Restoration with the posts of Lord-Lieutenant of Surrey and Constable of Windsor Castle. In November the Commons had received a petition accusing him of misconduct in his latter capacity. Now the committee set up on the matter suddenly advised that he be impeached, the first person to suffer this solemn process for over twenty years. This was resolved. Neither the government nor its opponents could persuade their exhausted followers to attend further than that point, and so a recess was called for Christmas.[160]

The King, advised by Clarendon, now strove desperately for a compromise which would concede the substance of the Commons' wishes but preserve royal control, such as had been achieved over the Corporation Act. Just before the recess the Lords were persuaded to substitute for the bill for inspection of public accounts a petition to Charles to appoint such a commission himself. During the recess he did, excluding Buckingham and Ashley but appointing several of their supporters in the Lower House. On reassembling, the peers also proposed to petition the King not to use his dispensing power in the case of Irish cattle. Both ploys failed, the MPs insisting upon both their original bills. When news arrived that the French were moving forces towards the Channel, the Commons discounted it as a story invented by the government. As so often in early Stuart Parliaments, a Lower House which had commenced a session full of loyalty and responsibility had worked itself in a few months into a state of collective obstinacy in which the game of foiling royal manœuvres counted above all else. An outsider such as Evelyn, observing a debate of this House by November, could find something ridiculous in the violence with which it argued trivialities, of which most of the members were quite unconscious. In writing the constitutional history of the seventeenth century, the physical and constitutional environment of Westminster must be taken into account.

In this deadlock, York, Clarendon, Anglesey and Sheldon urged Charles to remain equally unyielding. Arlington was for surrendering anything needed to gain money, without which they would have to make a more resounding surrender to their foreign foes. On 14 January this course was taken and, to the horror of his other advisers, Charles told the Lords to accept the Irish cattle bill with the 'nuisance' phrase intact. The effect on the Commons was minimal: they resolved to remind the peers of the Mordaunt case and other business before proceeding with supply. On the 18th Charles decided on stronger tactics and made a furious speech of complaint to the Houses. This did get the vital bill for the 'assessment' passed a week later despite much opposition, but with another insulting proviso, allocating a sum for seamens' wages as if the government could not be trusted to do so. A still more provocative proposal, to cancel half the grant if the King made peace and pocketed it, was heard but not adopted. Charles now allowed the Parliament two more weeks to attend to the problem of rebuilding London, but he was relieved of the necessity of more concessions and both the accounts bill and Mordaunt's impeachment died in the Lords. On 6 February he pronounced the prorogation.[161]

The new law against importation of cattle was widely evaded, at least sixteen shiploads of Irish beasts being landed in the Dee estuary alone within six weeks during the following summer.[162] Nevertheless, it succeeded in injuring the Irish economy considerably,[163] becoming another illustration of the truth that to most seventeenth-century Englishmen the primary reason for possessing Ireland was simply to prevent it from becoming significant. English agriculture did not, however, greatly benefit. The session made a similarly negative contribution to domestic order, through the medium of the Commons' committee to investigate the causes of the Fire. This was unready to report by the prorogation, and published instead all the 'evidence' it had received in a pamphlet, without comment. Whether this was intended or not, the cumulative effect of so many wild reports of Catholic fire-raisers, laid end to end, must have been to reinforce belief in them among those disposed to it.[164]

The third destructive consequence, which Charles pointed out in his closing speech, was that the long delay in supply made it very difficult to fit out the fleet in time for the summer's campaign. In effect, men motivated primarily by a desire for personal power had almost crippled their country's capacity to fight, by playing with remarkable skill upon the prejudices and anxieties of back-benchers. Under the pressure of their attacks, the government members in both Houses had utterly failed to work together and their followers either fought each other or were 'left to the accident of wind and tide'.[165] If the King were to face the next session with any prospect of success, he had to secure in the interim either a decisive military victory, a diplomatic triumph or a rationalisation of his team of ministers and advisers.

The struggle at Westminster was conducted parallel to an even more desperate one: that of the naval administration to get through another winter of war. All the factors which had produced a financial crisis in late 1665 were still present, some more, and some less, severely. With the appearance of French privateers the condition of seaborne trade had worsened, and customs receipts in the financial year 1666-7 were a third of their already lamentable level in the previous one. The proceeds of prizes came nowhere near compensating the government, and although they provided windfalls for the consumer, such as the cheap French brandy which made Oxford happy in November, overall the prices of foreign commodities trebled. The King's drastic action in throwing open the wool and leather trades to all comers did not prevent textiles from becoming more expensive than at any other time in the late seventeenth century. London began to run out of coal. The brewing and wine-trading businesses were naturally also suffering badly, and therefore the proceeds of the excise continued to decline. Its farmers were said to be going bankrupt daily.[166]

On the other hand, the proceeds of the Hearth Tax recovered considerably. This was the result of improved collection, consequent upon the government's decision to farm the work out in late 1665 as it had been empowered to do the previous year. The farmers were generally local men, sometimes recommended by the justices,[167] but performed their work energetically as they had a financial stake in the result. Having the right to enter houses to ascertain their genuine liability for tax, they used this freely, and became known, and hated, as the 'chimney-lookers'. By the end of 1666 their efficiency was demonstrated not only by the increase in receipts but the fact that householders, finding evasion increasingly difficult, were turning to riot instead. Such tumults, sometimes involving whole communities and abetted by gentry, broke out across the country during that winter and spring. Constables were notoriously disinclined to intervene, and there is a significant absence of prosecutions resulting in most surviving Quarter Sessions records.[168] In November the same House of Commons which had invented the tax and ensured its effective collection was now so worried about its constituents' reaction that it discussed replacing it and the government was happy to concur. No substitute, however, could be agreed.[169]

Thus far the story of Restoration public finance has been told very much from the point of view of the government and its employees, whether ministers or common seamen. It is important, therefore, to stress that defaulting taxpayers were not merely acting from selfishness and lack of patriotism. Early modern governments often required for their wars quantities of taxation which if properly levied did considerable harm to national and local economies. In England in 1666 the Hearth Tax and the 'assessments' were falling upon communities already impoverished close to desperation by the effects of war and plague, and could easily be seen as scourges comparable with these. Thus when an Essex villager called a collector of the new poll tax 'an oppressor of the country',[170] his attitude deserves sympathy. It is the more understandable in that this particular war produced such mystifying results. Each year victories were celebrated, trade fell off further and a fresh burden of taxation was added. Furthermore, despite Charles's order concerning court costume, it had not become any easier for his subjects to approve of and identify with the regime. Pepys heard a rumour in December that the King had paid £30,000 worth of Castlemaine's debts, and diverted £400,000 of war funds to his private pleasures. An unknown woman, a commoner, wrote to Charles to inform him that the people believed that most of the money intended for the armed forces was embezzled and that they were saying 'Give the King the Countess of Castlemaine and he cares not what the nation suffers.' York, the naval hero of the previous year, had been carrying on a public affair with the wife of a friend, who died suddenly in January proclaiming herself poisoned.[171]

It is in this context that one must view the direct taxation granted for the war. So efficient was the system of 'assessment' that 97.4 per cent of the Royal Aid, and 93.4 per cent of the Additional Aid of 1665, were eventually collected.[172] These land taxes fell, it must be remembered, upon an agricultural economy already entering recession before the war. The gentry who voted them were making considerable sacrifices and it is not surprising that they should have been prone to hesitation before granting the third 'assessment' of 1667. The government's problem was one of timing: the taxes simply did not arrive quickly enough. By Easter 1667 about a third of the war supplies voted by then had come in and therefore, as shown, the war had been fought upon loans, which would add their interest to the expense, and unpaid bills. The navy had run up £900,000 worth of these by September 1666. In October 1667 the City of Chester was still fighting the County of Cheshire over their respective assessments for the original grant of 1664, an indication of the kind of situation with which the government had to deal.[173] Thus in late 1666 there was more money entering the public funds than in the previous year, but it was all anticipated several times over. Till Parliament made a further large grant, virtually nobody was willing to lend any more to the state.[174] The poll tax imposed in January was an imaginative fiscal device, being levied on personal goods to take the pressure off real estate, but was never expected to produce more than about £½ million and its complexity presented good opportunities for evasion.[175] The new 'assessment' was the real basis for fresh government credit but, as Charles said, it had come when the season for preparation for war was already passing.

As ever, the principal victims of this situation were the naval seamen. The Treasurer of the Navy could pay off less than a quarter of those who returned with Rupert, and the remainder expressed their anger with more violence than before. From October to January they rioted repeatedly in and around London, and the later outbreaks were so serious that Albemarle had to use soldiers to quell them. They secured nothing except soothing words from Charles and the punishment of ringleaders, and in March Pepys found one sailor dying of hunger in his yard.[176] Meanwhile most of the warships lay unrepaired and unsupplied. To stem the decline of trade, the King sent twenty to escort merchantment to the Mediterranean and issued many licences to other traders to sail, thereby depriving the navy of the option of hiring these vessels.[177] In the same period more of the English West Indian possessions were lost, French forces taking Antigua and Montserrat and the Dutch capturing Surinam. The English troops available for action in the area drowned in a hurricane.[178] On 23 February the Navy Board presented York with a complete statement of their position. They had been able to pay £1,315 of the £150,000 due to suppliers, so secured only four contracts for further supplies. They had paid £140,000 to seamen out of the £930,000 due to them. Unless they received over £½ million immediately, they could not fit out the fleet. They summed up with the sentence 'We are conscious of an utter incapacity to perform what His Majesty and your Royal Highness seem to look for from us.'[179]

As it happened, the winter had also seen developments which promised an honourable way out of the predicament. Philip of Spain, broken by the survival of the rebellious Portuguese, which Charles's marriage had made possible, had died leaving a sickly child heir. Louis XIV was now most anxious to attack the Spanish Netherlands, and there appeared to be a good possibility that in return for England's assistance or benevolent neutrality while he did so, he would end his war with it upon generous terms and force the Dutch to do likewise. In November Charles sent a secret message to him through a Francophile Catholic courtier, the Earl of St. Albans, offering to treat. The French accepted at once. Thus the suspicion harboured of Charles by some MPs, that he was preparing to terminate the war while appealing for money for it, was correct. It was, however, equally true that this very suspicion, and the delay in supply associated, was forcing him to negotiate. In January St. Albans went quietly to Paris, and sent back an offer from Louis to return the West Indian colonies if England promised not to attack France for a year. On 12 February Charles signed this agreement under cover of a letter to his French mother. These moves were kept secret from most of his advisers, his confidant and principal manager in them being Clarendon, whose idea they may possibly have been. At the same time Arlington opened public talks with the Dutch, who agreed to receive ambassadors. Clarendon radiated confidence that a favourable peace was in the making.[180]

In these circumstances it is not surprising that Charles adopted the policy with which he formally instructed York on 6 March, of keeping the first- and second-rate warships laid up and sending out the others to patrol the coasts in small parties. This would save the tremendous cost of preparing a complete fleet for action and would be a more effective means of driving off privateers and preying in turn upon enemy shipping. English harbours would be fortified so strongly as to make an attack on them impossible. If the Dutch put out a fleet, they would be left cruising about aimlessly until they ran out of provisions as the English had done, while the slow attrition of their resources would force them to the peace which now seemed in any case to be approaching.[181]

This was a scheme proposed to the King long before, by Lawson and the Treasurer of the Navy, Sir George Carteret.[182] It seems to have been decided upon in a relative hurry, for in late February and early March members of the Privy Council were still expecting the whole fleet to set forth[183] and York's request for a statement of the Navy Board's circumstances was doubtless intended to that end. Their reply, together with the promising talks with Louis, must have provoked the resolution. Like most important policies of the reign, it was decided in private, and in this case nobody can be clearly identified as the adviser who pressed it upon Charles. Certainly York, Finch, Anglesey and Coventry did not, for they favoured different tactics.[184] The King told the citizens of London three months later that he, York, Rupert, Albemarle and Sheldon had wanted to put out the whole fleet, but had been persuaded by the majority of the Privy Council, but there is no reference in the register of the latter to such a decision, and the contemporary documents do not suggest that a large and formal meeting was called to discuss it. In his memoirs, Clarendon stated that the state of the navy was discussed by a gathering of the most trusted Privy Councillors, senior naval commanders and the Navy Board, and added, baldly, that the resolution was made after this. Pepys, however, does not record any such occasion. Clarendon's memoirs fail to blame anybody for the decision and present its merits, and give rise to the suspicion that he, himself, who was managing the deal with France and had never wanted the war, at the least strongly supported such a course of action. Four months later, however, an observer at court reported him to be calm in the knowledge that he had never done so.[185] The matter is therefore a mystery. All that can reasonably be surmised is that as no individual was ever named as responsible, Charles was telling the truth when he said that most of his advisers were in favour of laying up the fleet. An alternative possibility, that the King himself took up the idea, and that few ventured to disagree with him, is unprovable.

Historical hindsight has provided justification for the policy, whoever was responsible for it: by the time that the war taxation was all in, it only just covered the expenditure upon the war. Had the government sent forth the fleet for a third year, bankruptcy would probably have resulted.[186] As it was, great difficulty was experienced in preparing even the smaller ships required for service. The act for the new 'assessment' offered facilities for creditors, as had that of 1665, with success, but the money as always came in slowly. Bills issued by the navy as promises of payment were selling at a 35 or 40 per cent discount. The suppliers who held them were now themselves often in danger of arrest for debt, while the workmen in the Harwich dockyard almost marched on London. Nevertheless, squadrons were sent out, however defective their equipment and ill-paid their crews, and work was put in progress to strengthen the fortifications of the three great dockyards of Chatham, Portsmouth and Harwich. A series of inspections of other coastal defences produced satisfactory results. 'The Dutch fleet will not attempt anything at land' wrote the head of Arlington's secretariat on 3 May.[187] The secret negotiations with France culminated in agreement in April upon a peace based upon exchange of conquests. Louis promised to persuade the Dutch to accept this and to keep their battle fleet in harbour. An effective armistice appeared to have been concluded.[188] English frigates cleared privateers from parts of their coast, and the Newcastle colliers and the India and Levant merchantmen arrived at London. On 24 May Charles ordered more of his warships to be laid up.[189]

It thus seemed likely that the government would be able to face the next session of Parliament without requesting more taxation or having afforded its members any grounds for criticism. The King had also taken steps to destroy the alliance which had caused him so much trouble in the previous session, by driving its most notable member, Buckingham, from public life. Arlington gathered information that the Duke had been consulting an astrologer in the City. The latter's premises were raided just after Parliament was prorogued, and a letter found, apparently from Buckingham, requesting a horoscope of the King. This was formal treason, and a royal warrant went out for the Duke's arrest. Buckingham, like Bristol, managed to go to ground successfully, but was still stripped of all his offices and rendered almost as impotent as he would have been in the Tower. The astrologer was held there, under great pressure to confirm the Duke's guilt.[190] At Coventry the common people believed that Buckingham was being victimised for his hostility to Catholics, and in other places they viewed him with sympathy: like Bristol, this debauchee interested primarily in his own career had become a hero simply by opposing the court.[191]

This coup was followed by an attempt to eradicate the suspicions upon which the Buckingham group had played. A set of eighteen peers and MPs, including some who had criticised the government and excluding any connected with it, were commissioned to meet after Easter and take the public accounts. The former critics among them transplanted to this new setting the filibustering tactics they had employed in Parliament, by challenging the King's legal right to appoint such a body. Nevertheless, the judges eventually ruled in Charles's favour and by early June the commission was hard at work.[192]

By then, also, the financial administration had enjoyed a tremendous piece of good fortune: the death of Lord Treasurer Southampton on 16 May. He had suffered for years from gallstones or kidney-stones, and his doctors had come up with a new medical remedy which killed him most effectively after days of agony.[193] To replace him Clarendon wanted a conservative and unimaginative nobleman, the Earl of Bridgewater, while some of the younger men in the administration hoped for Coventry. Instead the King, encouraged by York who was impressed by the success of the team which ran the ordnance department, put the Treasury into commission on the 25th. None of his existing ministers were included except Ashley, who was put in by virtue of his office of Chancellor of the Exchequer. His worth in this position had probably been the reason for his survival in royal service after his co-operation with Buckingham, but he made no secret of his contempt for both the notion of the commission and for most of his colleagues in it.[194] The latter included one 'honorific' appointment, Albemarle, but the rest consisted of Coventry and two other men of comparable youth and industry. They immediately requested Downing to keep proper minute-books for them, the first of a succession which were to be kept steadily in the same form till 1870. They then embarked upon a systematic review of what was owed to the state and what it owed in turn. They met four days in every week, ordered Exchequer officials to work longer hours and had a register of all tallies on the Exchequer kept in their office. On the fifth day of their existence they remonstrated with Charles about a jewel he intended to buy, and the following day he agreed to let them vet every warrant issued for payment of public revenue. It was the beginning of the most drastic overhaul that the English fiscal system had ever received, and one that has been recognised as laying the foundations of the modern Treasury.[195]

Even as the foreign war seemed to be running down, so did the domestic struggle between Protestant orthodoxy and dissent. The most obvious gauge of this is the annual number of prosecutions under the Conventicle Act. In 1664, for only six months of which the act was in effect, it was employed in at least twenty-six counties (including those great cities which had county status) and at least ninety-eight people were sentenced to transportation. In 1665 it was enforced in at least thirty-four counties, and produced at least 111 sentences to transportation. The totals for 1666 are twenty-two counties and twenty-one such sentences. In 1667 the act was executed in Gloucester, Richmond in Yorkshire, Newcastle-upon-Tyne, and rural areas of five south-eastern counties, and nobody was banished. At London sustained persecution ended with Albemarle's great sweep in September 1665, though the Tower garrison kept isolated arrests going for eight months more. At Bristol the election of a tolerant mayor in 1666 put an absolute stop to the raids conducted by his predecessors.[196] Slowly, dissent began to recover. In Herefordshire, a county where conventicles were hunted fiercely for the first two years of the act's existence, the Quakers met in perfect peace from early 1666, and recorded their transactions. By late 1666 their gatherings in the capital were as safe as they had been under the republic. In the following year they instituted monthly meetings over most of the country. The Bristol baptists returned to assembling in regular places and began to grow in numbers once more.[197] The Conventicle Act was dying naturally long before it formally expired in 1668.

Many reasons may be suggested for this. One is that the act, in effect, released a flood of anger dammed up within many devotees of orthodoxy by successive regimes which had prevented them from launching a full-scale counter-attack upon the heterodox. It allowed them at last to persecute at will, and to transport or imprison indefinitely those whom they had especially marked down for destruction. After two years many such men may simply have satiated themselves with vengeance. Another reason is that from mid-1665 the same magistrates who might have hunted conventicles had the plague, war-taxation and press-gangs to deal with. The militia and garrison troops were busy preparing for the possibility of a Dutch invasion. Stuart local government could only cope with a limited number of tasks at once, and in this case persecution became the least urgent. A third reason is that dissenters themselves were becoming more adept at evading capture. Thomas Jolly, an ejected Lancashire minister of whom the authorities had particular suspicion, decided to break the Five Mile Act and return to his old parish in 1667. He did so with impunity by preaching from a staircase with a folding door built specially into the foot, which was raised and locked if enemies approached. When a militia troop surprised a conventicle in Worcestershire in that year, the minister immediately flung off gown and wig and escaped while his followers fought the soldiers with determination for some time.[198]

Another factor now working against persecution derived from the fact that it had originally been to a great extent inspired by fear, of the alarming tactics of Quaker evangelists and of the association of sectaries with republican plots. With nonconformists thrown onto the defensive, this fear ebbed. Quakers, providing witness to their faith in courtrooms and prisons, had little inclination to challenge ministers or demonstrate in public places, and such incidents became much rarer.[199] Although reports of plots still came to Arlington and to local justices, all the searches and arrests in the southern provinces since 1660 and in the north since 1664 had failed to substantiate any, and the rumours themselves decreased. In November 1666 a major rebellion broke out among the presbyterians of southern Scotland, which was crushed in battle near Edinburgh.[200] It produced a natural fear that the dissenters of northern England would make common cause with it, and a revival of the project for a northern army under the Duke of York,[201] but the whole region remained perfectly quiet. Indeed, the only disturbance by republicans after the enigmatic 'Danvers Plot' was a skirmish in Yorkshire in July 1667. A former republican governor of Carlisle, accused of having been one of the fomentors of the northern rebellion, had been captured and was being escorted to York for trial. At Darrington he was rescued by twelve masked horsemen, who overpowered his guards and killed one of them. Some were subsequently identified, but all eluded capture.[202] This minute if rather romantic incident would hardly deserve mention did it not stand at the very end of that sequence of violence stretching down from Strafford's death through the civil wars, the royalist rebellions of the 1650s and the republican risings of the early '60s. Thereafter, a lull of over a decade would follow before the mob fury and executions of the Popish Plot and the open warfare of the 1680s.

Another thing now favouring nonconformists was the reversal of the

pattern of the previous twenty years, in which the preoccupation of Protestants with each other diverted their attention from Catholicism. Rena-
scent suspicion of the Pope's adherents closed ranks between the Anglican
orthodox and dissenters in many areas. At Quarter Sessions and Assizes, trials
of conventiclers were replaced by presentations of Catholic recusants,
opening new rifts between those who demanded rigour and those who felt
loyalty or respect for individuals who professed the old religion.[203] Tracts
against Papists began to outnumber those against Protestant opponents.[204]
Detestation of dissent had tended to be more of an upper-class phenomenon
and fear of popery was at this stage more pronounced among the masses, but
the two had in common a sensation of fighting on two fronts. To opponents
of Catholics, as to opponents of nonconformists before 1664, the King
seemed at best a reluctant ally. He had made his personal debt to the Catholic
community clear, he had admitted representatives of it like Bristol and St.
Albans to his personal favour, and all the three women in his life belonged to
it. His queen and Frances Stuart were born so, and Castlemaine had become a
convert in 1663.[205] The latter's motives remain obscure: she may have been
herself attracted by the pomp of the religion, or she may have realised that
Charles, given a free choice, preferred it above others. This last possibility
was precisely the worst fear of a growing number of his subjects.[206]

It is therefore ironic that another source of benefit to dissenters, especially
in the capital, was the return of royal favour, the loss of which had permitted
the Conventicle Act. Charles's new fluctuation in attitude can only be
detected from its effects, his ministers and courtiers making no comment on
it, and is therefore difficult to account for with confidence. Perhaps the
passivity of nonconformists since 1663 left him prone to forgive or to dis-
believe in what he had regarded as their betrayal of him. Perhaps the growing
toleration of nonconformity in practice seemed to represent a shift in gentry
opinion which required following. The Quakers were his first beneficiaries,
in August 1666 when he received an appeal from some of them for the
release of their imprisoned brethren. He told them of his approval and
demonstrated this by liberating George Fox. Assize judges now became
willing to carry other petitions to Charles, and the most respected Westmorland Quaker leader seems to have remained in prison, and died there,
merely because a clerk of the court grudged the money required to get his
appeal to the King.[207]

A consciousness of a softening in both public and royal attitudes must
have encouraged the emergence of a movement among certain higher
churchmen towards a *rapprochement* with the presbyterians. It was heralded
by Bishop Reynolds of Norwich, who had been the sole presbyterian to
accept a see in 1660 and who had been notably gentle towards his former

colleagues in that diocese since. In November 1666 he preached a sermon to the Lords, the essence of which is captured in the sentence 'it is an honour which learned men owe to one another to allow liberty of dissent in matters of mere opinion'. In the course of 1667 two other bishops, of Bristol and Gloucester, became known as supporters of comprehension of the more moderate dissenters within their Church.[208]

Of much greater importance to the vast majority of English people than the Dutch or the dissenters, however, was the resolution of the third struggle, between human being and microbe. The plague died down slowly in its provincial roosts during the winter of 1666-7 and the return of summer brought no fresh epidemic. Instead there were minor outbreaks at Peterborough, Nottingham and Norwich, which faded out by September. The customary small number of cases occurred in London annually until 1670 and then these also ceased.[209] In time the English came to realise that, after three centuries in which it had struck them repeatedly, the disease had gone for ever. The reason for its disappearance remains a mystery, though the latest explanation, that quarantine regulations had at last become effective enough to keep it out of north-west Europe, appears the most cogent.[210] The toll of the last epidemic was grim enough: London had lost between a sixth and a fifth of its people, Colchester and Cambridge about a quarter and Ipswich an eighth.[211]

Nevertheless, the consequences of this mortality appear remarkably intangible. It deserves the title 'Great Plague of London' to the extent that it produced the highest recorded total of deaths of any pestilence in the capital, but two previous epidemics there probably each killed a greater proportion of its inhabitants.[212] Moreover a larger national total of burials was recorded in 1657, when a slow attrition of the population by mysterious fevers achieved more destruction than the plague without producing a panic.[213] The victims of the 1665-7 visitation appear not to have included a single statesman, bishop, magistrate or alderman. It was, as some contemporaries called it, 'the poor's plague',[214] and the poor were easily replaced. Such was the abundance of the population in relation to its resources, and such were the attractions of urban life, that London's vacant housing was filled within a few months and its inhabitants had attained their former numbers two years later. The Fire did more lasting physical damage, as four years were needed to achieve complete or well-advanced rebuilding in half the burnt area, and some of the churches were never replaced.[215] Colchester's cloth production passed its pre-plague level after two years.[216] The decisive impact of the epidemic was not demographic nor economic, but political, in the considerable contribution it made to the government's fiscal problems during the Dutch war and the souring of relations between Crown and people which resulted.

There were no comets in the sky in May 1667. Both Charles and most of his subjects had every reason for optimism and rejoicing as the principal afflictions of the past few years diminished. Rarely has disaster been preceded by quite so many good omens.

The Reckoning

CHARLES consistently underestimated the Dutch. First he believed that they would concede his demands without fighting, then that they would collapse after their first defeat, and now that they would tamely acquiesce in the policies of the French. Certainly he was correct in judging that they had severe problems of unity and that their navy was slightly inferior to his in a straight fight. To compensate, however, they possessed some unusually able leaders, a system of public credit which aroused Downing's envy, and a political nation far more intimately concerned with the profits of foreign trade than that of England. One consequence of the last two attributes can be expressed in simple arithmetic: upon this war the English government was able to spend £5¼ million, their enemies the equivalent of £11 million. The Dutch state still had to borrow heavily, and by the spring of 1667 it was sharing England's difficulty in finding seamen for its fleet. But in a struggle of attrition such as this war had become, it had the resources to persevere.[1] By the third year, it could still launch a battle fleet without throwing its finances into terrible disarray, and the English could not. The leaders of Holland, who dominated the States General, were determined to secure a treaty conducive to the honour and profit of their nation, and to do so, if need be, without the French.

On 4 May the English plenipotentiaries reached Breda to open the great conference with their opponents, and it soon became obvious to the Dutch that their French allies were set upon a genuine compromise affording considerable gains to nobody. The government of the Netherlands decided to deal the English a blow, single-handed, which would force major concessions from them such as the opening of their carrying trade. On the 27th a Dutch force of sixty-four warships put out.[2]

The spectacular achievement which followed may have been considered by the Dutch leaders since 1664, when a report upon the area concerned had reached them. It was carried out with speed and precision. De Ruyter arrived off Kent on 5 June. On the 10th he bombarded Sheerness Fort, which commanded the entrance to the Medway, into surrender, and on the next day sent a reconaissance party upriver. His fleet followed on the 12th, broke the chain across the waterway and reached the stretch near Chatham where the biggest ships of the Royal Navy were moored. Three of these were burned, and the best vessel of the English, *The Royal Charles*, which had carried the King home in 1660 and been the flagship of his commanders since, was towed away as a prize. After an attack on the dockyard, which was foiled by the indiscipline of the troops sent upon it and by the English defence, the Dutch retired. They did so, however, only as far as the mouth of the Thames, where, supplied by sea, they settled down to blockade it indefinitely.[3]

The principal credit for this coup must be given to the Dutch themselves, for the courage and intelligence with which they carried it out, but they were aided by a number of circumstances. The most important of these was the impoverishment and overconfidence of the English government, which resulted in work being uncompleted for lack of money for the workmen and of interest by superiors. The vital fort at Sheerness had been only half built, the one other upriver was undersupplied and the warships had not been taken further up as intended. The garrison troops and dockyard workmen, long neglected, showed little disposition to fight, and only a single officer, a Scot, consented to get himself burned alive defending one of the ships and so afford some consolation to armchair patriots. Next, an unseasonably high tide enabled the leading Dutch ship to bear down upon the chain with sufficient force to break it. Last, there were so many senior English commanders rushed to the spot as the main attack developed, relative to the number of effective troops, that confusion resulted in the defence. Albemarle, the leaders of the Kent militia and of a regular army unit nearby, and three naval commissioners were all present issuing orders which sometimes conflicted.[4]

The English government reacted with all the energy which it ought to have shown earlier, and so prevented this humiliation. Apart from mobilising the militia of Kent, Charles called up that of every other county. He sent Rupert to Woolwich to build batteries and then to supervise the refortification of the Medway, while he himself and York directed the sinking of ships in the Thames and its tributaries to obstruct them. The Prince planted thirty-six cannon at Woolwich and raised powerful gun-emplacements from Sheerness to Chatham. All ships trapped in the Thames were impressed to put together a naval force, and seamen seized to provide crews. To reinforce the militia in case of invasion, an army of 7,000 foot and 2,000 horse was commissioned, and much of it raised within three weeks. Garrisons were also strengthened.[5]

All this work had, of necessity, to be paid for with loans. The King requested £10,000 from the City for the defensive works on the Thames and Medway, and in the obvious emergency he got it. Robinson, who was still an alderman as well as the Tower's commander, acted as intermediary to transfer the money direct to Rupert. There did not, however, remain any in addition to fit out ships or pay seamen.[6] Charles ordered Clarendon to ask the lawyers for advances, and Sheldon to press the clergy once again.[7] The East India Company lent £20,000, more or less under duress.[8] The King also appealed to nobility and gentry, though not apparently with much success as tenants were now often too poor to pay rents.[9] The peers who had been made colonels and captains of the new regular units could at least be expected to employ their private fortunes in raising them. Success in obtaining loans, however, only added to the already colossal public debt. The Dutch had done £20,090 worth of damage at Chatham, quite apart from the value of the four superb warships, and the total cost of the new army came to £45,527.[10] While the Dutch lay off the Thames, the militia of the coastal counties had to remain in arms, but that also had now to be paid, if at all, from central funds. The levy permitted for it by the 1662 act had now been spent during the successive plot and invasion scares since its passage.[11]

The financial cost of the Chatham disaster had to be reckoned beside the damage it had done to the government's reputation. The Dutch had achieved the rewards of a great naval victory without having needed to fight one: they had destroyed the best of the Royal Navy, bottled up most of the remainder, obtained mastery of the British seas and closed the port of London. The official newspaper bravely attempted an impossible task, playing down the losses on the Medway and emphasising the English resistance,[12] but the truth, and worse than the truth, spread faster. All over the country it provoked the same popular response: fury, not against the enemy but against the government. In London this vented itself upon Clarendon, still the ogre of the mob. He was insulted in Westminster Hall and the windows of his newly-finished mansion were broken, the trees outside it cut down and invective scrawled on the walls. The citizens also, however, talked more generally of having been betrayed by Catholics or courtiers, and their suspicions were repeated throughout the provinces with demands for vengeance.[13] While Charles's servants were accused of treachery, the King himself was judged guilty of negligence. In the court and capital it was whispered that on the evening upon which the enemy retired triumphant from Chatham, he and Castlemaine had dined with the Duke of Monmouth, and the party 'were mad in hunting of a poor moth'.[14] It may have been true, and would not have been an unreasonable way of coping with catastrophe. But had he spent the night with his troops on the Medway, he might have escaped some of the tarnish upon his administration. At such moments Charles II failed conspicuously to be a great King.

The growing disrepute of the restored monarchy, like the unpopularity of the republic before it, had by now found its expression in verse. There was, however, a distinction between the cases. The ballads against the purged

Parliament had vilified the entire regime, in the coarsest terms and for the lowest audience. Charles's government attracted a set of pasquinades of considerable wit and sophistication, which advocated its reform rather than its replacement. The first of these was inspired, unintentionally, by Edmund Waller MP, a poet and aspiring public man who hoped to atone for a shifting pattern of loyalties during the previous two decades by celebrating the victory of Lowestoft in verse. He employed the novel and imaginative device of pretending to advise a painter employed upon a great canvas of the event, describing each heroic scene and character of it in detail. The result was a fine panegyric, but by its nature invited parody when a more critical mood developed, as one did during the parliamentary session of 1666. Two anonymous poems were then circulated in manuscript around the capital. *The Second Advice to a Painter* dwelt upon the apparent lack of consequence of the Lowestoft victory, *The Third Advice* upon the division of the fleet in 1666 which resulted in the Four Days Battle. Both were well-informed, and both called for the dismissal of most of the royal ministers. The latter did not lack literary defenders, for the Headmaster of Tonbridge School circulated a reply to The Second Advice impugning the author's motives, and Dryden, climbing patiently towards his eventual post of Laureate, published *Annus Mirabilis*, a celebration of the heroism of the King and his commanders throughout the events of 1666. Neither impress the reader now as effective counters, for the headmaster's poem is simply dull and Dryden's is too full of deliberate conceits and too often cynical in its own tone. It was no accident that his best-remembered poems were to be themselves satires.

The Chatham disaster provoked fresh literary attacks upon the regime, and in greater quantity. Two more *Advices to a Painter* were circulated, blaming the event entirely upon the government, while a third, *Clarendon's Housewarming*, repeated all the traditional slanders against the Chancellor. A prose satire, purporting to advertise new books, concentrated more upon the morals of King and court, and many other libels must have been produced and then perished, as a correspondent of Ormonde complained that they were being daily scattered about the court.[15] The four hostile 'painter' poems and *Clarendon's Housewarming* were rapidly bound together and published, under the name of the courtier-poet Sir John Denham. This was taken at the time, and since, as a guarantee that Denham was not the true author, but the identity of this person, or persons, remains an enigma. The satires appear to have been produced by at least two hands, for the *Fourth* and *Fifth Advices* are notably inferior to the other work, though written in more of a hurry. A Bodleian edition of the pamphlet in which they were all printed contains the handwritten note that they were composed 'for the Company of Poets'. This points to the set of rakes and writers connected to Buckingham, who would have obvious motives in producing them, and such was the suspicion of the Headmaster of Tonbridge. On the other hand, none of these men ever referred to a connection in their memoirs or private correspondence, and L'Estrange and two other men who knew the contemporary literary world well believed Andrew Marvell to be the author. This identification is given some reinforcement by the fact that the Bodleian pamphlet is corrected and annotated in the same hand as are written two of the satires and some poems more certainly attributed to Marvell, which are bound up in a printed edition of the poet's works in the Bodleian collection. However, the writer in this case is apparently somebody working after Marvell's own death, and the contemporary attributions to this poet are all from a period after the 1660s, when he had become a controversial political author. Furthermore, too little is known about his life in this period to answer the crucial question of who his 'Company', if he did work in the context of one, might have been.[16]

For the purposes of the present narrative, the satires have a double importance. First, it is certain that they achieved their purpose of intensifying hostility to Charles's ministry. Even Pepys, who personally admired some of those attacked, found the 'painter' poems hilarious, and the notoriety of these works in their time testifies to their impact.[17] Second, they have continued to deform views of the war ever since, to the extent that the author of the latest textbook upon seventeenth-century English literature can refer to the great triumph of Lowestoft as 'York's supposed victory'.[18]

In this unpleasant predicament, the hardest problem for the government was whether to recall Parliament, as much to associate the political nation with the Crown in this crisis as to gain funds. Crowds at Westminster were shouting for this.[19] The proposal was contested by Clarendon, upon the grounds that it was technically improper to break a period of prorogation and that any supply granted would be gathered too late to assist the present situation. He was supported by York, who was rumoured to have advised his brother to raise money without Parliament and to depend upon the new army to keep order, and by Carteret. All had a personal interest in their arguments, Clarendon and Carteret fearing attack and York displaying loyalty to his father-in-law. The entire remainder of the Privy Council urged the necessity of facing Parliament, and Charles decided by 25 June to recall it for a month later.[20] Nobody was under the illusion that many MPs would fail to share the popular sense of outrage,[21] and the government took steps to reduce its vulnerability to attack without any genuine sacrifices. It had already selected a scapegoat: Peter Pett, the naval commissioner in charge of the Chatham dockyard. Examination revealed that he had done nothing worse than fail to tow the warships upriver and to launch pinnaces as ordered. His real fault, however, was to be the least important and well-connected person with any responsibility for the affair, and he was sent to the Tower on 18 June.[22] By the 26th it was decided to get Carteret out of the way by having him exchange posts with Anglesey, the Treasurer of Ireland. Mordaunt discussed resigning his office at Windsor with financial compensation, and a trading company condemned by the Commons in October as a monopoly offered to give up its charter for a similar consideration.[23]

Buckingham now decided that the moment had come to resurface. Soon after the Chatham incident he sent to Charles offering to assist him in Parliament in return for concessions, and was ignored. The Duke determined next to confront the government directly and so win back freedom of manœuvre, doubting whether it would now dare either to try him or to leave him imprisoned without a hearing. On 28 June he surrendered himself to royal officers after receiving the applause of the crowd from a balcony like a true demagogue. On examination he denied that the incriminating letter to the astrologer was in his hand, and on 14 July, as he expected, the King released him. Charles never, however, forgot either services or injuries easily, and Buckingham was not restored to any of his former offices. He settled down instead at his London mansion, where the General Council of the republican army had once met, to plan further obstruction when Parliament regathered.[24]

Foreign affairs, which had plunged Charles's ministry into such difficulty, now to some extent rescued it. Rather than make damaging concessions to its domestic opponents, it preferred to concede some demands of the foreign foe. In late June Charles's representatives at Breda agreed to permit the Dutch to carry to England any goods which entered the Netherlands by river, and to nullify all the pre-war claims of English merchants. A draft treaty was signed on 1 July and sent to London, where Charles and his principal advisers decided reluctantly that they did not dare to reject it. It received a final conclusion and signature at Breda on the 21st.[25] In the same period the English coastal defences proved strong enough to prevent the Dutch admirals from achieving a second success, despite the pleas of their political leaders for one. On 6 July they tried to sack Harwich, but this time the fort commanding the harbour withstood both naval bombardment and attack by a party landed near it. Thereafter they returned to cruising off the Thames while detachments hunted the south coast, and their presence encouraged privateers to operate in more than usual numbers. Royal naval squadrons sallying from provincial ports did take prizes themselves, but in the circumstances the English could risk little seaborne trade, and the only attempt to harry the main enemy fleet was bungled and ended in hasty retreat. It unfortunately happened on the anniversary of the previous year's great victory, and so was christened, in mockery, the 'St. James's Flight'.[26]

On the same day Parliament reassembled, but the urgent need for it was gone now that peace was almost concluded. This was as well, because the malcontents had appeared in force. The King immediately adjourned the Houses for four days, hoping that the arrival of the treaty for ratification would enable him to dispense with them altogether. Before rising, the Commons showed their mood. Sir Thomas Tomkins was a former royalist who had been rewarded by the restored monarchy but who, like Vaughan, came to oppose its policies either from ambition or genuine distaste. He now complained of the existence of the new standing army, and after a brisk debate the House resolved *nem. con.* to address the King to have it disbanded as soon as peace was made: the rumour about York's advice had been taken seriously. The treaty arrived, as Charles had hoped, and as soon as the Commons reconvened on the 29th they were summoned to attend him. He informed the Houses that peace was made, that the army would be disbanded, that they were therefore dismissed till the end of the original prorogation in October, and that he would pursue some popular policies in the interim. All this was obliging enough, but he also spoke sharply about the Commons' suspicions and failed to thank them for having reassembled. The Speaker 'looked between anger and pity', and most of the members departed in notably bad humour.[27]

The Dutch fleet was less easily disposed of. Its admirals were instructed by their government to keep pressure upon the English until both sides had ratified the treaty, lest Charles have any second thoughts about its terms. In early August they accordingly continued to patrol the south and east coasts, bombarding the forts at Fowey and taking sheep from the Scilly Isles. Not till the 25th did their sails vanish, at last, into the horizon.[28] On the previous day Charles issued the formal proclamations of peace.[29]

The Treaty of Breda consisted of three separate agreements, between the English and their three enemies. That with Denmark was merely a cancellation of hostilities. The peace with France involved some loss, for England had to buy back its West Indian islands with a slice of the North American coast. In addition, Louis had profited enormously from the war in ways not revealed by the formal treaty: he had preserved the two maritime powers as counterweights to each other, fulfilled his obligations to one while obtaining some claim to the gratitude of its rival, and ensured that both would leave him a free hand with Spain. Even as he ratified the peace with England, his armies had commenced a series of dramatic conquests of Spanish territory. He had intervened in the Anglo-Dutch conflict with exquisite skill, and had in a sense emerged with the greatest gains, for the least outlay, of all the participants. But the Dutch also had every reason for satisfaction. Their territorial settlement with the English appeared to be a balanced exchange, for they kept Surinam and resigned New Amsterdam. Their true gains lay in the fact that their enemies gave up claims to compensation for the past losses of their merchants, to territory in the East Indies or to more than two forts on the West African coast. The trade of these two areas was thus to remain more or less a Dutch preserve, and all the major issues which had produced the war, and in which the English mercantile community had an interest, had been decided in favour of the United Netherlands. The latter had even increased their legal share of the carrying trade to England. Unequivocally, the Dutch had won, by sheer financial stamina. At the commencement of their first war with the English, one of their representatives had compared his state to a mountain of gold opposed to a mountain of iron. The remark was intended to express the weakness of the Dutch, but it now held true in the opposite sense. Midas had felled Goliath.

There were no popular celebrations in London when the peace was announced and few in the provinces, though some municipalities provided fireworks and processions.[30] The public were fully aware of the truth that three years of suffering and sacrifice had been for nothing. The tragedy of the war, however, was larger than this, for the great expenditure of life, money and energy by both the principal combatants had left neither much better or worse off. The land ceded by England to France was regained later, and the loss of Surinam was subsequently balanced by the acquisition of what was to become Guyana. It is difficult to imagine that New Amsterdam would not have at some stage been absorbed into the United States as Florida and Louisiana were. The preservation by the Dutch of the tropical markets in dispute did not prevent their later decline, nor England's growth, in power. The most enduring achievement of the whole struggle has been the name 'New York'.

Responsibility for this terrible waste lay with the English, who had been the aggressors, and their King must be accorded a large share of it. He had permitted some of his servants to undertake a course of action certain to lead to confrontation and encouraged bellicose sentiment in his people to the point where he left himself no option other than war. But the English public were themselves culpable. The applause which they had accorded each act of aggression had been the decisive factor in the outbreak of full-scale conflict. They had fully shared their government's expectation that victory could be obtained easily and cheaply, and persisted in it after their leaders had begun to appreciate realities. Ever since February 1665 Charles and his ministers had been in the position of a soldier who continues to assault an impregnable position for fear of being executed if he retreats. There is justice of a kind in the fact that, collectively, they came to share something of the misery of the seamen whom they conscripted.

After the dismissal of Parliament, Lord Chief Justice Bridgeman told a friend that he was disturbed by the obvious exasperation of its members, and felt that the government had every reason to fear their reconvention. Yet he also believed that a fresh prorogation would frustrate them to the point of endangering public order, and that it was better to let them spend their rage at Westminster.[31] This view was shared by the King, and he devoted his two months' grace to a set of measures designed to propitiate them before they regathered. The most dramatic, and celebrated, of these was the fall of Clarendon.

The Earl's troubles had commenced with the death of Southampton, his only remaining friend in the ministry. This was succeeded by the demise of both the sickly children which his daughter had currently given to York, and by the popular fury against him over the Chatham affair. Then, on 9 August, his wife died, and the composure which he had maintained through the previous misfortunes crumbled into obvious grief. He ceased to attend the Privy Council two days before her end and, in the event, never did so again.[32] He seems to have been taken completely by surprise when, within ten days of the funeral, York appeared at Clarendon House to inform him that the King wished him to resign his office of Chancellor before Parliament reassembled. He refused, and on 25 August Charles sent Albemarle for the seals of office, only for Clarendon to decline to surrender them. The following day the news became known throughout the court, and many watched and listened as Clarendon and York visited the King to argue about the decision. Charles ended the interview in anger, but thereafter hesitated until the 30th, when he sent Morice to demand the seals, and this time got them. He gave them to Bridgeman, not as Lord Chancellor but with the lesser title of Lord Keeper. Palmer took over Bridgeman's post, leaving his office of Attorney-General to Finch, who vacated the place of Solicitor-General for Sir Edward Turner, the Speaker of the Commons, who was thus neatly brought into the government.[33]

When writing to Ormonde soon after, Charles described his reason for dismissing Clarendon as 'too big for a letter'. When Pepys asked Coventry for the motives behind the event, he received the reply that they were too many to be fit for discussion.[34] These statements warn the historian from providing simple and obvious explanations. The one given by the King to the Earl himself was that there would certainly be a determined attack upon him when Parliament re-met, ruining any hope of a *rapprochement* between Crown and Commons and, at worse, turning him into another Strafford. Arlington also cited this reason in defending the dismissal to Ormonde, and it was the one generally believed around the court.[35] It is certainly true that if a minister was to be sacrificed, then Clarendon was the obvious choice. His unpopularity had been patent for five years, and the abuse of him by the mob consequent upon the disaster in June had persisted throughout the summer.[36] It was well known that he had advised resistance to the Commons' wishes in the last full session and opposed the recall of Parliament in July. But by itself the explanation is inadequate. Charles had stood by Clarendon when he was attacked during the exile and was to defend Danby and York later in his reign. All the insults to Castlemaine could not shake his loyalty to her, nor did he ever divorce his barren queen. He never dropped somebody brutally until his personal affection for them had been shaken. Furthermore, in the midst of the rage against his Chancellor in June he had demonstrated his support for him by appointing him as Lord-Lieutenant of a second county. Before Parliament met in July he had dined ostentatiously at Clarendon House.[37] His attitude had apparently undergone a swift and dramatic reversal.

In this context it is interesting that the man who claimed openly to have persuaded Charles to his decision was Coventry, and that the only argument which he admitted to Pepys that he had employed was that Clarendon had prevented the King from hearing the advice of others.[38] Coventry wrote to a friend soon after that Charles had agreed that his Chancellor had taken away liberty of debate in the Council, and that he had only endured this because of his brother's affection for him. At many points later in his reign, the King told courtiers that the imperiousness with which Clarendon treated even himself had slowly worn away his regard.[39] This evidence confirms several impressions. The Chancellor's unfortunate manner had clearly not improved with time. He was now almost isolated within the Privy Council, as his old friends had gone and his foolish jealousy had made enemies of the new advisers whom the King had taken. His tendency to sit on the fence regarding delicate issues, doubtless intended to prolong his political life, had further reduced his claims to the support or gratitude of others. This is best illustrated from the dispute over religious toleration. After his fall, two of the bishops who hoped to relieve presbyterians wrote that this process would become much easier now he had gone, while their opponent Sheldon wrote that 'for these divers years I have had little reason to be fond of him'.[40] In December 1664 Charles was already believed at court to find Clarendon tedious but to retain him as an indispensable servant and as York's father-in-law.[41] Both these positive attributes had now been eroded. The King had acquired more industrious and efficient Councillors such as Coventry, and it seems that for a while in August York himself felt that it would be best for the Earl to retire.[42] In view of the serious trouble expected at the meeting of Parliament, this would have been a propitious moment for Coventry to have deployed his arguments. Anglesey, writing at this time, drew the obvious lesson from the last parliamentary session: that what the King needed above all was unanimity in his Privy Council.[43] The elimination of Clarendon was one obvious step towards this.

It would seem appropriate to conclude the discussion there, were it not for the fact that another explanation has been advanced. It appears in the history written by a contemporary who became a Whig bishop, Gilbert Burnet, quite firmly represented as the true precipitating cause of Charles's decision. In the previous March one of the three women in his life since 1663 had dropped out. Frances Stuart had eloped with his second cousin, the Duke of Richmond and Lennox, and married him without royal permission. The union was a genuine love-match, but Frances was rumoured to have told friends that it was contracted so hastily because she was weary of fending off her sovereign's advances. The King was utterly furious, and though he gave retrospective sanction to the wedding he made it clear to both that they had no future at court.[44] Burnet's story, gained from Clarendon's heir, was that Charles came to believe that his Chancellor had encouraged this development from disapproval of his behaviour.[45]

At first sight this looks like a libel invented by the aggrieved family and published by a supporter of a subsequent regime. It is, however, rather difficult to dispose of. Clarendon's opinion of his master's morals was well known. In July it was rumoured that he had abetted Frances's marriage, and Clarendon himself later considered that this belief was a factor in the King's growing hostility to him. In August Charles's anger with 'La Belle Stuart' was still powerful, and it is certainly possible that then Coventry, or another courtier, persuaded him of his Chancellor's involvement.[46] At this stage one is provided with quite enough reasons for Clarendon's fall to fill out the large number to which the King and Coventry referred, and to establish the relative importance of each seems impossible. One general conclusion subsumes all: the Earl had become an increasing political liability with ever diminishing assets as a servant and a decreasing claim upon his master's affections. All that is extraordinary about the matter is that Charles still felt enough for him to hesitate for five days over his dismissal.

The propitiation of Parliament, of course, did not end with this. A royal proclamation ordered due enforcement of the law against Irish cattle.[47] The trading company condemned by the Commons surrendered its patent without compensation, and Mordaunt exchanged his post at Windsor for a pardon.[48] The King ordered all civilian and military officers to take the Oaths of Allegiance and Supremacy, in an effort to weed out Catholics and a number were duly dismissed. He also forbade Catholics the court, instructed magistrates to hunt priests and prohibited any of his subjects from attending mass at ambassadors' chapels.[49] The disbanding of the new army was directed on the day that Parliament dispersed and was substantially completed within a month.[50] To strengthen the government's party in the Lords, Sheldon once again summoned all bishops.[51]

To bid for the support of Protestant dissenters, a bill was drafted to permit use of the Prayer Book without wearing the surplice or including two ceremonies to which presbyterian clergy took exception: in the words of one correspondent, 'to leave the Church a little looser'. It was produced by Thomas Barlow, one of the rising young men within the Church, and submitted to some of the presbyterian clergy in August for their views. These were appreciative. In September the King repeated his gesture of January 1663, when he had liberated a prominent presbyterian minister before launching a campaign on behalf of such men in Parliament, by issuing a special order for the release of an ejected rector imprisoned for preaching in Cornwall. John Birch, a wartime parliamentarian and a patron of such clergy, agreed to introduce the bill into the Commons.[52] In sponsoring a new policy of conciliation, the government possessed one advantage which it had lacked before: a subservient official press. In the autumn of 1665 L'Estrange had been replaced as editor by Monck's original propagandists, Muddiman and Dury, either because Sir Roger's treatment of the war had been inadequate or because of some obscure court intrigue against him.[53] This meant that after five years of control by intolerant episcopalians, the government newspapers were in the hands of self-effacing men prepared to support whatever the King favoured. The change in editors, however, long predated the alteration in the royal attitude to dissent, and indeed the origins of the comprehensive policy are a puzzle. Somehow, the King and some of his ministers had come to believe that Parliament would now accept relief of presbyterians. Yet although the development of support for comprehension is clearly recorded among churchmen, there is no evidence of by whom it was shared in the Privy Council. The new policy preceded any change in Charles's advisers. This, along with the responsibility for the keeping of the fleet in harbour, the authorship of the 'painter' satires and (to a much lesser extent) the reasons for the fall of Clarendon, is another of the enigmas that stud the history of 1667.

Simultaneously the work of the treasury commissioners proceeded, which promised to reduce tension between the government and all future Parliaments by reducing the former's requests for taxation. In the course of the summer they directed all departments to apply to them for permission to spend a sum even if it had been warranted, summoned virtually every local receiver of the Hearth Tax for questioning and interrogated some excise farmers. They warned the King against the custom of granting reversions of public offices, reduced both the independence and the perquisites of the Treasurer of the Navy and discussed extending to the regular revenue the system for attracting loans applied to the last two 'assessments'. One courtier thought them 'a terror', but Pepys found them widely respected and noted that Charles gave them full support.[54] A committee of the Privy Council was set up on 29 July to assist the commission in finding possible economies in government expenditure, and was soon dominated by Coventry.[55] One of the plans soon proposed was for a more efficient use of the peacetime navy, permitting some ships to be sold, and a reduction in the number of its administrators.[56] The government pressed its own servants for loans and raised the rate of interest it offered to 10 per cent to encourage investors in general.[57] Slowly the process of paying off seamen and the owners of hired ships proceeded, though much remained due to them.[58] All these measures, however, were only first steps in a very long process of recovery. They could only make a slight impression upon the public finances before Parliament re-met, and perhaps none upon the associated problem, the false popular belief in large-scale misappropriation of funds. The parliamentary committee for accounts, which might have exposed the latter, had disbanded itself on the shock of the Chatham disaster.[59]

The King also had to strengthen his ministry, particularly as it soon became apparent that shedding Clarendon threatened to create as many problems as it solved. The Earl, far from retiring into private life as Charles had expected, seemed invigorated by his dismissal. He made it clear that he hoped for restitution and intended to participate in the next parliamentary session, and the fear grew that he and his friends would put pressure on the government then as Buckingham had done. An alarming number of courtiers and MPs were expressing doubts about the justice of the King's treatment of him.[60] The most eminent of these was of course York, who dismissed Coventry from the post of his secretary for his part in the affair. Sir William, whose career had long outgrown this particular office, left it cheerfully, but when James also sacked his Privy Purse, Henry Brouncker, for rejoicing at Clarendon's fall, this individual complained to the King and was promised compensation. Relations between the royal brothers came close to a breach, and the irritation provoked in Charles by Clarendon's refusal to resign was warmed to a dangerous anger by his former servant's apparent determination to regain office.[61]

In these circumstances, he bowed to the inevitable and came to terms with Buckingham. On 4 September the Duke was given a long private conversation with him, and eleven days later was restored to all his offices. On the 23rd Buckingham reappeared in the Privy Council, now as a respected adviser of the King, a position emphasised by his waiting upon him that night in the capacity of Gentleman of the Bedchamber.[62] The adherence of the Duke and his allies to the government promised to strengthen the latter in Parliament considerably, but he initially fitted into Charles's team of

Councillors no better than Clarendon had done. For one thing, he bore a grudge against Arlington for the latter's part in his prosecution in February, and the King had to exert considerable pressure to obtain a formal reconciliation between the two.[63] For another, having had no part in the conduct of the war, he was happy to propose that Parliament be obliged with an enquiry into its miscarriages, to the consternation of Charles's other advisers.[64] Third, Buckingham was determined to destroy Clarendon completely, removing the threat that at some later stage (for example, if York suddenly succeeded to the throne) he would return to power and thrust his rivals from it. This he hoped to achieve by an impeachment for treason, but Charles was still unwilling to treat his old servant as an enemy and by the time that Parliament met had consented to no more than that he could be attacked for misdemeanours. Fourth, the Duke naturally hoped for ministerial posts for himself and his friends, and the King was not prepared to grant these until they had proved their value. The vacant office of Lord Chancellor remained both a symbol of Charles's determination to dominate his Councillors and an incentive to them to win his favour.[65]

On 10 October Charles greeted Parliament, and Bridgeman reminded it of all he had done for the Commons' satisfaction. As soon as the MPs commenced the procedure of returning thanks, trouble appeared. Coventry, Palmer and Buckingham's allies proposed that the House single out the dismissal of Clarendon for special gratitude, to commence the process of attack upon him. They were joined by Waller, whom the King had rewarded for his poem on Lowestoft with the post of Provost of Eton, only to see Clarendon, with characteristic pedantry, refuse to seal the grant because by custom it was made only to clergymen. He now repaid the fallen Chancellor by comparing him to Lucifer. They were opposed by a mixture of courtiers and backbenchers, including Birch and Coventry's own brother, who felt the gesture to be improper until Clarendon's guilt had been demonstrated. Only the obvious support of the government for the motion prevented a division and obtained the Lords' concurrence.[66]

In the following two weeks, as though none of Charles's gestures of propitiation had been made, the Commons proceeded to 'fly at all things'.[67] They facilitated the prosecution of Quakers for non-payment of tithes. They allowed a fierce bill for the punishment of Catholic recusants to pass its first reading, though Waller and Vaughan declared it unjust and it was compared to the Spanish Inquisition. They admitted new evidence against Mordaunt and ordered an inquiry into the sale of Dunkirk. They introduced a bill for the taking of public accounts stricter than its predecessor, which Buckingham's friends, who had nothing to lose by it and could gain offices forfeited by its victims, urged on.[68]

Most of the House's energy, however, was devoted to detecting mismanagement of the war. The government had prepared Pett for sacrifice, bringing him out of the Tower for fresh examinations just before the session,[69] but far more than the Chatham affair proved to be at issue. Between 17 and 22 October, eleven other instances of incompetence or corruption were alleged, and the Commons set about investigating them both directly and through a committee, which met with great disorder and vilification. The last vestiges of pride in the Lowestoft victory were erased by dwelling upon an event which nobody seems to have thought significant at the time: that York's fleet had slackened sail during the night of pursuit. It seemed that Brouncker, the man recently dismissed by the Duke, had issued the order on his own initiative for fear of harm to his master. The evidence to confirm this charge was not immediately available, but it became generally assumed that the incident had prevented the destruction of the entire enemy fleet and that the Dutch would not have tried to replace it. Coventry, struggling to defend the record of the naval administration during the war, made one comment which reflected badly on Albemarle. The general, together with Rupert, then criticised Coventry and the Navy Board to the Commons. The members of the board, interrogated by the MPs, gradually began to denounce each other. Even more swiftly and completely than during the previous session, the King's party in Parliament had fallen to pieces.[70]

Two immediate consequences followed for royal policy. First, the comprehension of presbyterians was shelved until a less delicate moment, and the only assistance given to dissenters by the government that autumn was an attempt by the Privy Council to release most of the Quakers still held in local prisons.[71] Second, Charles agreed on 20 October to the impeachment of Clarendon for treason. Such a measure promised both to rally his quarrelling servants and to distract the fury of the Commons. Its articles were drawn up swiftly by Buckingham and his friends, aided by that older enemy of the former Chancellor, Bristol, who chose this moment to offer his services to the King. Charles accepted them with the comment that this earl could win a fortune in any kingdom in three years, and lose it again in three months. The charges they devised consisted of a range of allegations of bribery and injustice, and Seymour duly presented them to the Commons on 26 October. The result was a disappointment to the promoters, for a long wrangle over the propriety of the proceedings ended in the establishment of a committee to settle this point. On 6 November, further progress was made when the committee presented the accusations as a formal set of articles, only for most of these to be rejected over the next five days as falling short of treason. Buckingham's allies were rescued only by the Austrian ambassador, who, desiring to win the support of English politicians against France, told them that Clarendon had betrayed secrets to the French during the war. On being informed of this, the Commons voted the impeachment at last, and sent it to the Lords. There, however, it stuck fast for the rest of the month, as the peers refused to accept it on the grounds that no precise charge had been made. As the ambassador possessed no evidence to substantiate his information, none could be provided and complete deadlock resulted. The tactic of the impeachment had indeed diverted the Commons from the investigation of the war, but had also paralysed Parliament almost completely at a time when Charles had hoped for grants to remove his financial difficulties.

Clarendon was defended in the Lower House not by any 'faction' of traditional followers, but by a collection of individuals prompted by differing motives. Some were government servants such as Warwick, who had respected him as Chancellor for his high standards of conduct. Coventry himself now revealed an integrity as admirable as his administrative ability, by refusing to have his old opponent blamed for miscarriages for which he himself had recently been attacked. Virtually all the members who favoured relief of presbyterians spoke for him, apparently because of his first open and later covert sympathy for their cause. This hypothesis is strengthened by the fact that in the same debates intolerant episcopalians called him an enemy to their Church. In the Lords, the impeachment was supported by Buckingham and his friends, Bristol, the obedient Albemarle, Carlisle and Arlington (though the last was notably reluctant), three bishops and a small number of peers with unknown motives. All the rest, including York, Sheldon and the other bishops, and Anglesey, Ashley and the remaining Privy Councillors, were opposed. Most of this solidarity derived not from feeling for Clarendon, nor for justice, but from a simple desire to protect a fellow peer from the whims of the Commons. The situation was a constitutional absurdity. For the first time a monarch was driving on an impeachment, against one of his own servants, or former servants, and in the process was supporting an assault by the Commons upon his own traditional bulwark of the Lords.[72]

Clarendon himself passed through these events radiating confidence and determination to triumph. He was 'hugely pleased' by the conflict between the two Houses, and when he applied to the King in mid-November for permission to withdraw, this gesture was believed to be insincere and designed only to obtain a reply from which capital could be made. He had by now incurred the same royal fury which had fallen upon Vane, Bristol, the Quakers and Buckingham. The whole affair was a bitter frustration and humiliation for Charles. York had shamed him into denying one of the charges against Clarendon in front of the court. When he had summoned a group of MPs who had opposed the impeachment and rebuked them, one of them had defended freedom of speech to his face. Such specific incidents merely sharpened the emotions provoked by an even more serious division among his Councillors, and an even more complete failure to transact business with Parliament, than before.[73] In some provincial towns, commoners railed against Clarendon and the Lords, without according the King any acclamations for sharing their views.[74] The essence of the tragedy lay in the fact that neither Charles Stuart nor Edward Hyde, for all their long association, had ever completely understood each other's natures.

In the end it was Charles who won, by showing himself prepared to violate every principal of natural justice. In the last week of November it became rumoured that, if the Lords remained obdurate, he would send Parliament into recess, pick a tribunal of peers and have them try, convict and sentence the Earl to death. It was an entirely legal course and one against which its victim would have no effective answer. Clarendon recognised defeat. On the 28th he sat sadly in his gout wheelchair, watching the gates of his mansion in Piccadilly being completed. The magnificent building, seven years in the making and the symbol of his power, was at last entirely ready for occupation. He never saw it again, for the following day he took ship for France, leaving a written vindication of himself for Parliament. The Lords, happy to escape from a difficult position, joined with the Commons in condemning this and banishing him for life. Charles, as one last gesture of grace to the servant he had destroyed, kept Clarendon's sons in favour at court, and in time they made notable careers there.[75]

There remained one last tremendous ironic postscript to the affair. The exiled Earl employed his enforced leisure by completing a great history of public events during the long period of his engagement in them. Composed in a splendid style, it combined original documents, a narrative of occurrences and personal reminiscences to produce an exquisite perversion of the truth which exonerated himself and his friends and excoriated their enemies. It remains his most enduring monument, and has ensured him a fame, and a sympathy, which his political acts alone would never have done. It is an illustration of the truth that just when people think that they have defeated a great adversary completely, they have frequently provided instead the thrust necessary to raise him, or her, to everlasting glory.

4

Conclusions

⟨∾⟩

THE flight of Clarendon has traditionally been regarded as the first major dividing-line in the history of the restored monarchy, around which the King began to take new advisers and so to choose policies which were to lead directly to the dramatic events of the rest of the reign and of its successor. It is therefore the appropriate point in the decade at which to take stock of the impact of the years since the Restoration Settlements upon the polity which those sets of measures had created. With this question is linked a broader one: how the political and religious condition of England and Wales had altered between the first and second of Clarendon's exiles.

In many obvious ways a considerable stabilisation had occurred. The country now possessed a form of central and local government acceptable to the great majority of its inhabitants and a national Church which inspired or compelled the obedience of almost as many. There was no serious threat to the traditional laws and the universities. Plots and revolts had died out, and violence had virtually ceased to be a feature of politics. Where rival leaders had mobilised regiments against each other before, they now denounced each other at court and in Parliament. The penalties of failure had become milder: after all the fury created by defeat in the Dutch war, the only victims were Clarendon, who escaped with life and property, Brouncker, who was eventually expelled from the Commons, Carteret, who lost his office, and the wretched Pett, who failed to regain that of which he had been deprived.

It is also obvious that most of the English and Welsh in 1667 were profoundly dissatisfied with the achievements of the regime of which they approved so much in principle. In part this resulted from accidents of personality and event, but it was also the product of fundamental problems in the state and in society. These were to condition the course of national politics for the next generation, and their eventual resolution created much of the religious and political system that has obtained ever since.

First, a potential doubt had arisen concerning the succession to the throne. Of the three royal brothers of 1658, Charles was married to a barren queen, James to a duchess who had so far produced no heir capable of surviving infancy, and Henry was dead. Charles had·complicated the situation further by making a favourite of his eldest natural son, the Duke of Monmouth, and parading him before the court. In 1662 it was already rumoured that the King had legally married Monmouth's mother. In November 1666 a group of politicians were anxious to advance the young Duke to great power, and a year later they were said to be considering having him made the heir apparent. The two most prominent men associated with these moves were Buckingham and Ashley: the link between Absalom, Achitophel and Zimri had already been made.[1]

Second, although the republic's hated standing army had been almost completely disbanded, there was repeated talk of the monarchy's wish for a successor. The government had applied for one to Parliament in 1662, had talked of raising one in 1665 and 1666, and had actually done so in 1667, to the consternation of the Commons. This force had been paid off, but the number of regular soldiers at the permanent disposal of Charles II was still greater than that employed by his ancestors, and was slowly growing. In late 1663 the total royal land forces already consisted of 8,452 officers and men. In the succeeding years, their size slightly increased, their quality and homogeneity improved as Guards units were employed on garrison duty, and their administration was rationalised.[2] There was little question of the fact that a larger army would be maintained if the monarchy could obtain the financial resources for it. One man was identified in 1665 and 1666 as the obvious leader of such a force, and in 1667 with a proposal to employ troops to impose the government's will upon the nation: the existing heir apparent, James of York.

A third potential source of domestic conflict lay in foreign affairs. Charles had involved himself in a bitter feud with the Dutch which in turn contributed to the growing power of France. He had failed either to appreciate the formidable resilience of the former, nor the fear that the latter, with some reason, was beginning to inspire in his subjects. In the following two decades he and his brother would repeat both these errors, of which the underestimation of the Dutch would be the fatal one. In the 1670s they would ruin his government. In the 1680s they would topple his dynasty.

Popular fear of the French was associated with religious problems. In 1658 many of the English and Welsh were deeply worried by the suspicion of sympathy among their national leaders for religious minority groups in their midst, whom they believed to represent a threat to order. In 1667 the same situation obtained, save that the presumed enemies were now Roman Catholics and not radical Protestants. The anger and fear which swept the country after the Great Fire demonstrated how powerful a source of disturbance hostility to Catholics had already become. As the strength of France was to wax further and Charles was to become more closely associated with the followers of Rome, this insecurity was to remain a potent force in national life.

On the other hand, the Protestant dissenters had not become as innocuous as the Catholics had seemed in the late 1650s. Persecution had certainly made a considerable impact upon them, one aspect of which is illustrated by comparing the churchwardens' presentments for the episcopal and archidiaconal visitations of 1662-3 with those of 1665-7.[3] Each area reveals a similar pattern: in the later period the number of parishes which fail to return a reply, or lack a surplice or Prayer Book, or have a ruinous church, has dwindled to a very few. Attendance at services has also generally increased, and where a small number of adherents to a specific form of dissent are recorded in a parish in the earlier reports, they have frequently vanished or declined still further. However, where a substantial group of organised nonconformists appears in 1662, it is still there and in some cases has increased. Religious dissent was not going to vanish naturally, and the restored Church was never going to enjoy the degree of loyalty commanded by the pre-war one unless further legislation was passed, and enforced, to destroy its rivals.

To a considerable extent the behaviour of dissenters had become less menacing to the orthodox. The connection between the gathered churches and republicanism had almost vanished, and so had Fifth Monarchy beliefs. In May 1666 a general meeting of Quakers, held at London, declared that to clarify and reinforce the witness presented by the movement to humanity, individual guidance by the spirit should henceforth be subject to the corporate approval of elders. This, like the monthly meetings, was part of a process of tighter organisation of Quakerism produced by the need for mutual encouragement consequent upon persecution. It also tended to limit those dramatic individual gestures of challenge which had made the early evangelism so alarming to opponents, and so dynamic. Such techniques were not yet completely abandoned: in 1669 Fox urged his brethren to speak out in churches and markets, and a few cases of denunciation of ministers and of nude or almost nude declamation were recorded thereafter. They appeared, nevertheless, as occasional throw-backs to an earlier age.[4] During the 1660s, also, certain presbyterians began to prepare for the development of a separate church if their comprehension in the national one could not be achieved. In 1666 at Exeter occurred what appears to be the first case of ordination of a new minister by ejected presbyterian clergy.[5]

These changes were conducive to the assimilation of nonconformity into a stable society, but emphatically did not result immediately in the disappearance of it as an issue in secular politics. Twenty-five years after the Restoration, a force composed principally of presbyterians and members of gathered churches fought a pitched battle against the royal army, and the fact that they were supporting a rival king and not a republic did not make their challenge to the established government any less serious. Two years after that a Quaker advised and encouraged the monarch in a religious policy which was greeted with horror by most of the political nation.

Nor, despite the creation of permanent dissent on an unprecedented scale, is it certain that the Restoration Settlements indeed produced a Church of novel conformity. Ralph Josselin's diary is the private record of a minister who remained beneficed by occasional observance of the law. The correction processes of the various church courts seem to show about the same number of citations for inadequate performance of the liturgy in the 1660s as in the 1610s and 1620s. A survey of Canterbury diocese in 1663 revealed much laxity, especially in wearing the surplice, and even newly-appointed clergy were at fault.[6] A powerful circumstantial case can be made for suggesting that the Church of Charles II contained as much casual nonconformity as that of James I.

This situation was assisted by the fact that the King continued to appoint bishops of mixed views. The support of Reynolds, Nicholson and Ironside for comprehension has been mentioned, and in early 1668 this movement acquired an even more energetic advocate in John Wilkins, who replaced a notably intolerant Bishop of Chester. The man who held the see of Lincoln during the mid-1660s, Benjamin Laney, said that 'not he but the law' had produced the drive for uniformity and 'looked through his fingers' at the conduct of his own clergy.[7] Such men were merely the most highly-placed members of an increasingly vocal party within the established Church. By 1665 it was acquiring the name by which it was to go down in history: 'they push hard at the Latitude men, as they call them, some in their pulpits call them sons of Belial, others make the Devil a latitudinarian', wrote an observer of the rigidly orthodox churchmen of Canterbury Cathedral.[8] Three years after the Act of Uniformity, a potential schism existed among episcopalians themselves.

A different serious problem was that of public finance. By late 1667 the restored monarchy owed as much to its creditors as the Protectorate had done at the moment of its fall, despite the repudiation of this earlier debt. Unlike Richard Cromwell, Charles II could remove the immediate cause of his financial crisis, by laying up his fleet and disbanding his new army, without bringing down his regime. Nevertheless, he was left with a regular revenue which had not yet, even under the most favourable circumstances, covered his government's needs, and the two main sources of which, the excise and Hearth Tax, were extremely unpopular. To cope with such a situation demanded an unusual capacity for patience and self-denial. Charles was deficient in both qualities.

All these strains were imposed upon a system of politics which was itself full of anomalies. Parliament had become a feature of government with a regularity unknown before 1640. Under the law, the King was expected to call it at least every three years, a number of statutes of the 1660s were given rapid terms of expiry to reinforce the necessity to do so, and in practice the monarchy's financial and political problems resulted in it being in session in every year of the decade. The Commons repeatedly forced the King to concede their wishes and called the royal administration to account for its wartime expenditure with an unprecedented rigour. Yet the formal power of the monarch remained enormous. He could summon and dismiss Parliament at will and there existed since 1664 no mechanism for calling it independently if he ignored the three-year rule. He could be of any religion, maintain an army of any size if he could afford it, make peace or war at will and dispense individuals from the provisions of a debatable number of parliamentary statutes. His presence in the political system was considered quite essential, and he was credited with powers of physical healing which emphasised his semi-divine nature. The contrast between this potential and the actual weakness of the Crown provoked frustration in Charles and unease in his subjects.

This situation was worsened by divisions among the royal Councillors. Charles, like Richard Cromwell, was forced by events to accept a Privy Council of very different personalities and past records, and his subsequent recruitment of other able men to it multiplied the number of internal rivalries. He made considerable efforts to force his various advisers to co-operate, but the tensions arising from the many difficulties of government in the period repeatedly defeated these attempts. By late 1667 he was not only suffering from the transfer of factional warfare from the Council to Parliament, which had bedevilled his grandfather, but had been forced to give power to men purely because of their influence with the Commons, as his father had done in 1641. Permeating these developments was the collapse of the old royalist party into groups divided by issues and by personalities. Like the Whig party in 1714-20, the very completeness with which it had achieved most of its public ends in 1661-2 contained the source of its disintegration.

Within all the political and religious developments of the 1660s lay the tremendous unifying force which has been present in most of this long narrative: the determination of the English and Welsh gentry that never again would they go through an experience such as the civil wars and Interregnum had been. To this end they fought to have Crown, Church, towns, Catholics, dissenters and vagrants all equally within their control, so that no force could remain within society capable of destroying its stability again.

They would eventually be successful, to the undoubted profit of themselves and, to a considerable extent, of their nation. But it was not to be achieved yet. The framework within which the restored monarchy operated was not that of the early Stuarts. The relationships between clergy and gentry and between King and Parliament had altered. One generation was being succeeded by another and men who survived the transition often did so with very different ideas. But the issues at stake were not resolved. In the period 1638-42, the tensions between executive and legislature, Church and dissenter, and court and country, had developed to the point of bloodshed. They were to remain a cause of this during each decade until 1690. In this sense, whatever had ended in 1660-2, it was not the English Civil War.

References

∽∾∾∽

SINCE the time of my work upon the Royalists, I have to a great extent overcome my distrust of published editions of primary sources. Free use of them has been made in the following notes, though whenever the original documents have been available I have made every effort to check the transcriptions made. The main collection which failed to survive this test was the printed Calendar of State Papers Domestic, which reproduced the contents of the docquet books well enough but provided abridgements of certain other varieties of State Paper which seemed unsuitable, not so much because of error as because of the natural tendency of the editor to cite information which appeared important to her and to exclude that which did not.

When a reference to a piece published in a periodical is repeated soon after its initial appearance, the name of the author and an abridged title of the essay are given. Where the next reference to it appears after some interval, the name of the author and of the periodical and the date of the latter are given to facilitate use.

The following abbreviations have been employed:

AHR	*American Historical Review*
BIHR	*Bulletin of the Institution of Historical Research*
BJRL	*Bulletin of the John Rylands Library*
Bod. L.	Bodleian Library
Brit. L.	British Library
CA	Corporation Archives
CCC	*Calendar of the Proceedings of the Committee for Compounding*
CHJ	*Cambridge Historical Journal*
CJ	The Journals of the House of Commons (printed 1813)
CL	Cathedral Library
CSP	*State Papers Collected by Edward, Earl of Clarendon* (Oxford, 1786)
CSPD	*Calendar of State Papers, Domestic Series*
CSPV	*Calendar of State Papers Venetian*
CTB	W. A. Shaw (ed.), *Calendar of Treasury Books* (1905)
DNB	*Dictionary of National Biography*
Ec. HR	*Economic History Review*
EHR	*English Historical Review*
H	*History*
HJ	*Historical Journal*
HLB	*Huntingdon Library Bulletin*
HLQ	*Huntington Library Quarterly*
HMC	Report of Historical Manuscripts Commission

HR	*Historical Review*
J	*Journal*
JBS	*Journal of British Studies*
JCNWAAHS	*Journal of the Chester and North Wales Architectural, Archaeological and Historic Society*
JMH	*Journal of Modern History*
L	Library
LJ	Journals of the House of Lords
NWL	National Library of Wales
PP	*Past and Present*
PRO	Public Record Office
RO	Record Office
SP	State Papers (held in the RO)
TRHS	*Transactions of the Royal Historical Society*
UL	University Library
VCH	Victoria County History

Where the date of a pamphlet is given within square brackets, this signifies the day or month when it was obtained by the London bookseller George Thomason, who made a habit of collecting as many contemporary publications as possible. A date in parentheses indicates that given upon the publication itself.

I have consulted the following unpublished theses, with great gratitude and profit:

S. F. Black, 'The Judges of Westminster Hall during the Great Rebellion 1640-1660' (Oxford B.Litt., 1970).

J. D. Brearley, 'Discipline and Local Government in the Diocese of Durham 1660-1672' (Durham M.A., 1974).

G. H. Brown, 'The Place of Sir Arthur Hesilrige in English Politics 1659-60' (Oxford B.Litt., 1949).

R. W. Clayton, 'The Political Career of Edward Seymour 1661-1704' (York Ph.D., 1976).

Alan Cole, 'The Quakers in Politics 1652-1660' (Cambridge Ph.D., 1955).

F. D. Dow, 'The English Army and the Government of Scotland 1651-1660' (York Ph.D., 1976).

W. Dumble, 'Government, Religion and Military Affairs in Durham during the Civil War and Interregnum' (Durham M.Litt., 1978).

Thomas W. Evans, 'Hyde and the Convention Parliament of 1660' (London M.A., 1964).

I. Gentles, 'The Debentures Market and the Military Purchasers of Crown Lands' (London Ph.D., 1969).

Anne Hughes, 'Politics, Society and Civil War in Warwickshire 1620-1660'(Liverpool Ph.D., 1979).

A. M. Johnson, 'Buckinghamshire 1640-1660' (Wales M.A., 1963).

—— 'Some Aspects of the Political, Constitutional, Social and Economic History of the City of Chester 1550-1662' (Oxford D.Phil., 1971).

W. G. Johnson, 'Post-Restoration Nonconformity and Plotting' (Manchester M.A., 1967).

M. S. Jones, 'The Political History of the Parliamentary Boroughs of Kent 1642-1662' (London Ph.D., 1967).

K. J. Lindley, 'The Part Played by Catholics in the Civil War in Lancashire and Monmouthshire' (Manchester M.A., 1965).

Derek P. Massarella, 'The Politics of the Army 1647-1660' (York Ph.D., 1977).

H. N. Mukerjee, 'English Constitutional History and Political Ideas from the Death of Cromwell to the Fall of Clarendon' (Oxford B.Litt., 1933).

M. Mullett, 'The Crown and Corporations 1660-89' (Cambridge M.Litt., 1972).

C. B. Phillips, 'The Gentry of Cumberland and Westmorland 1600-1665' (Lancaster Ph.D., 1974).

B. G. Reay, 'Early Quaker Activity and Reactions to It' (Oxford D.Phil., 1980).

Henry Reece, 'The Military Presence in England 1649-1660' (Oxford D.Phil., 1981).

M. K. Roberts, 'Participation and Performance in Devon Local Administration 1649-1670' (Exeter Ph.D., 1980).

H. G. Roseveare, 'The Advancement of the King's Credit 1660-1672' (Cambridge Ph.D., 1962).

R. H. Silcock, 'County Government in Worcestershire 1600-1660' (London Ph.D., 1974).

I. J. Thirsk, 'The Sales of Delinquents' Estates during the Interregnum and the Land Settlement at the Restoration' (London Ph.D.,1950).

E. A. O. Whiteman, 'The Episcopate of Dr. Seth Ward' (Oxford D.Phil., 1951).

Barrie Williams, 'The Church of England and Protestant Nonconformity in Wiltshire 1645-1665' (Bristol M.Litt., 1971).

Richard Williams, 'County and Municipal Government in Cornwall, Devon, Dorset and Somerset 1649-1660' (Bristol Ph.D., 1982).

Notes

⤳✲⤳

Part One

1. The text of this chapter is intended as a very brief summary of the state of England in the last year of Cromwell's life. Its references are taken almost entirely from secondary works and are aimed at the student reader seeking a bibliography for the Protectorate. For the 1650s as a whole, the basic narratives are still Samuel R. Gardiner, *History of the Commonwealth and Protectorate* (1897), 4 vols., and Sir Charles H. Firth, *The Last Years of the Protectorate* (1909), 2 vols. Forthcoming books by Derek Hirst and J. S. Morrill are likely to provide excellent new analyses of the decade, but nothing is likely to supercede the old histories for their mass of factual detail.

2. Bod. L. Clarendon MS 58, ff. 286-7.

3. Edward, Earl of Clarendon, *History of the Rebellion* (Oxford, 1888), xv. 140-2.

4. Charles II still lacks a definitive biography. For his activities in this period the best works appear to be Hester Chapman, *The Tragedy of Charles II* (Bath, 1972) and Richard Ollard, *The Image of the King* (1979). David Underdown, *Royalist Conspiracy in England 1649-1660* (1960) is an excellent narrative of the various plots, with much information on court intrigue. Paul Hardacre, *The Royalists During the Puritan Revolution* (The Hague, 1956) analyses aspects of the experience of the king's supporters in England.

5. Richard Williams's thesis powerfully stresses the element of continuity from the past during the Interregnum. See also M. K. Roberts, 'Local Government Reform in England and Wales during the Interregnum', in Ivan Roots (ed.), *Into Another Mould* (Exeter, 1981) for an important aspect of the question.

6. Donald Veall, *The Popular Movement for Law Reform 1640-1660* (1970).

7. A. Beier, 'Poor Relief in Warwickshire 1630-1660', *PP* 35 (1966), 77-100; J. Walter and K. Wrightson, 'Dearth and the Social Order in Early Modern England', *PP* 71 (1976), 22-42; G. Foster, 'County Government in Yorkshire during the Interregnum', *Northern History* xii (1976), 84-104; J. S. Morrill, *Cheshire 1630-1660* (Oxford, 1974), ch. 6.

8. Buchanan Sharp, *In Contempt of All Authority* (1980); Keith Lindley, *Fenland Riots and the English Revolution* (1982).

9. J. Cooper, 'Social and Economic Policies under the Commonwealth', in G. E. Aylmer (ed.), *The Interregnum* (1972); G. D. Ramsay, 'Industrial *Laisser-Faire* and the Policy of Cromwell' in Ivan Roots (ed.), *Cromwell: A Profile* (1973).

10. J. H. Round, 'Colchester and the Commonwealth', *EHR* xv (1900), 641-64; B. Henderson, 'The Commonwealth Charters', *TRHS* 3rd series vi (1912), 129-62;

C. G. Parsloe, 'The Corporation of Bedford 1647-1664', *TRHS* 4th series xxix (1947), 151-66; L. J. Ashford, *The History of the Borough of High Wycombe* (1960); M. S. Jones, thesis; David Underdown, *Pride's Purge* (Oxford, 1971), 318-27, 332-5; A. M. Johnson, D.Phil. thesis, 340-3; John T. Evans, *Seventeenth-Century Norwich* (Oxford, 1979), 200-18.

11. C. B. Phillips, 'County Committees and Local Government in Cumberland and Westmorland', *Northern History* v (1970), 34-66 and 'The Royalist North', *Northern History* xiv (1978), 175-7.

12. Mary Coate, *Cornwall in the Great Civil War and Interregnum* (Oxford, 1933), 281-98; Alan Everitt, *Suffolk and the Great Rebellion*, Suffolk Records Society (1960), 11-28 and *The Community of Kent and the Great Rebellion* (1966), ch. viii; Forster, 'County Government in Yorkshire', 100-4; Clive Holmes, *Seventeenth-Century Lincolnshire* (Lincoln, 1980), 200-17; A. M. Johnson, M.A. thesis, ch. vi, and 'Wales during the Commonwealth and Protectorate', in D. H. Pennington and K. V. Thomas (eds.), *Puritans and Revolutionaries* (1978); Morrill, *Cheshire*, ch. 7; Silcock, thesis, 280-90.

13. Anthony Fletcher, *A County Community in Peace and War: Sussex 1600-1660* (1975), ch. 14; David Underdown, *Somerset in the Civil War and Interregnum* (Newton Abbot, 1973), 175-88; Roberts, thesis, 1-87; R. Williams, thesis, chs. 1-2.

14. Holmes, *Lincolnshire*, 215-17; David Underdown, 'Settlement in the Counties' in Aylmer (ed.), *The Interregnum*.

15. A detailed analysis is in Reece, thesis, ch. 1.

16. Brit. L. Add. MS 10457 f. 248 (Wimeswould constables' accounts).

17. The great authority on this subject remains Maurice Ashley, *Financial and Commercial Policy under the Cromwellian Protectorate* (3rd edition, 1972). But see now also R. Williams, thesis, ch. 4.

18. This view of the military was presented in Morrill, *Cheshire*, ch. 7, and developed with great detail in Henry Reece's important thesis. Williams's thesis, ch. 6, puts a different case, which is best debated if and when the work of Drs Williams and Reece reaches publication.

19. The main authorities upon the national Church of the Interregnum are still W. A. Shaw, *A History of the English Church during the Civil Wars and the Commonwealth* (1900), vol. ii, and Thomas Richards, *Religious Developments in Wales 1654-1662* (1923). But Claire Cross, 'The Church in England 1646-60' in Aylmer (ed.), *The Interregnum*, is a convenient brief summary and Christopher Hill, *The World Turned Upside Down* (1972), an excellent survey of the extremist thinkers.

20. Lindley, thesis; Phillips, 'Royalist North', 192, which cites related studies.

21. B. G. Blackwood, *The Lancashire Gentry and the Great Rebellion*, Chetham Society 3rd series xxv (1978), 63-5; P. R. Newman, 'Catholic Royalists of Northern England', *Northern History* xv (1979), 88-95.

22. J. C. H. Aveling, *The Handle and the Axe* (1976), 170-8; Fletcher, *Sussex*, 94-104; T. S. Smith, 'The Persecution of Staffordshire Roman Catholic Recusants 1625-1660', *J Ecclesiastical History* 30 (1979), 327-51.

23. I. M. Green, 'The Persecution of "Scandalous" and "Malignant" Parish Clergy during the English Civil War', *EHR* xciv (1979), 507-31; Robert S. Bosher, *The Making of the Restoration Settlement* (1951), ch. 1; P. King, 'The Episcopate during the Civil Wars', *EHR* lxxxiii (1968), 523-37, and 'The Reasons for the Abolition of the Book of Common Prayer', *J Ecclesiastical History* 21 (1970), 227-39; John W. Packer, *The Transformation of Anglicanism 1643-1660* (Manchester, 1969); Valerie Pearl, 'Oliver St. John and the "middle group"', *EHR* lxxxi (1966), 490-519, and 'The "Royal Independents" in the English Civil War', *TRHS* 5th series 18 (1968), 69-96; Victor D. Sutch, *Gilbert Sheldon* (The Hague, 1973), ch. 3; John Morrill, 'The Church in England, 1642-9', in Morrill (ed.), *Reactions to the English Civil War 1642-1649* (1982).

24. Shaw, *History of the Church*, ii; Morrill, 'The Church in England', 95-8.

25. Geoffrey F. Nuttall, *Visible Saints* (1957); Peter Toon, *God's Statesman* (1971), 1-105; S. G. Cook, 'The Congregational Independents and the Cromwellian Constitutions', *Church History* 46 (1977), 335-57; Murray Tolmie, *The Triumph of the Saints* (Cambridge, 1977), chs. 5-8.

26. Louise Fargo Brown, *The Political Activities of the Baptists and Fifth Monarchy Men in England during the Interregnum* (1912); B. S. Capp, *The Fifth Monarchy Men* (1972); Hill, *World Turned Upside Down*; Tolmie, *Saints*, chs. 3-4, 6-8.

27. Cross, 'The Church in England'; Morrill, *Cheshire*, ch. 7; Johnson, 'Wales'.

28. Allan Brockett, *Nonconformity in Exeter 1650-1875* (Manchester, 1962), ch. 1; Green, 'Persecution of "Scandalous" Clergy', 525-30; Shaw, vol. ii; B. White, 'The Organisation of the Particular Baptists', *J Ecclesiastical H* 17 (1966), 209-26, and 'Henry Jessey in the Great Rebellion', in R. B. Knox (ed.), *Reformation, Conformity and Dissent* (1977). R. O'Day and A. Hughes, 'Augmentation and amalgamation' in Rosemary O'Day and Felicity Heal (eds.), *Princes and Paupers in the English Church 1500-1800* (Leicester, 1981) warn against the danger of overstating the achievement of Cromwell's Trustees: they had only a slight effect upon the overall quality of the clergy. Nevertheless, they did represent a systematic attempt to make improvements, and did a great deal of work in absolute, if not comparative, terms.

29. The magnificent propensity of the early Quakers for producing and hoarding records has laid the basis for more intensive studies than for any other religious group: Hugh Barbour, *The Quakers in Puritan England* (1964); William C. Braithwaite, *The Beginnings of Quakerism* (2nd edition, Cambridge 1961); Cole, thesis, and 'The Social Origins of the Early Friends', *J Friends' Hist. Soc.* 48 (1956), 99-118, and 'The Quakers and the English Revolution', *PP* 10 (1956), 39-54; Hill, *World Turned Upside Down*, ch. 10; J. McGregor, 'Ranterism and the Development of Early Quakerism', *J Religious H* 9 (1976-7), 349-63; Reay, thesis, and 'The Quaker Opposition to Tithes', *PP* 86 (1980), 98-120; Richard T. Vann, *The Social Development of English Quakerism 1655-1755* (1969).

30. John Towill Rutt (ed.), *The Diary of Thomas Burton* (1828), i. 24-184; T. Wilson and F. Merli, 'Naylor's Case', *University of Birmingham HJ* 10 (1965), 44-59.

31. This is an over-simplification of a very complex series of choices. Gardiner and

Firth still provide narratives, and M. Prestwich, 'Diplomacy and Trade in the Protectorate', *J Modern History* 22 (1950), 103-21 remains a useful analysis. The most recent important discussions of the subject seem to be R. Crabtree, 'The Idea of a Protestant Foreign Policy' in Roots (ed.), *Cromwell*, and Charles P. Korr, *Cromwell and the New Model Foreign Policy* (1975).

32. Ashley, *Financial and Commercial Policy*, 40-96; H. J. Habakkuk, 'Public Finance and the Sale of Confiscated Property during the Interregnum', *Ec.HR* 2nd ser. 15 (1962-3), 70-88.

33. This is the theme which emerges from Mark A. Kishlansky, *The Rise of the New Model Army* (Cambridge, 1979); Underdown, *Pride's Purge*; A. B. Worden, *The Rump Parliament* (Cambridge, 1974); Austin Woolrych, *Commonwealth to Protectorate* (Oxford, 1982); Massarella, thesis. Yet unless more of Dr Massarella's work is published, and until Ian Gentles's book on the army under the Commonwealth appears, there is little for the reader upon the military men compared with all the books and essays upon the Parliaments they produced.

34. One such crisis is closely studied in B. Taft, 'The Humble Petition of Several Colonels of the Army', *HLQ* 42 (1978-9), 15-41.

35. The most recent biography of Broghill is the rather light *Roger Boyle, First Earl of Orrery* (Knoxville, 1965) by Kathleen M. Lynch. But on his work in Scotland, F. D. Dow, *Cromwellian Scotland* (Edinburgh, 1979) could not be better.

36. T. C. Barnard, *Cromwellian Ireland* (Oxford, 1975) is the perfect counterpart to Dow.

37. For the political events of 1657-8, Firth's seventy-year-old narrative is all we possess. No work comparable with that for the early 1650s has been done. My interpretation of the kingship crisis and its aftermath is based on Firth and his sources, but marries up the new insights of Professor Woolrych's detailed research on 1653-4 with my own on 1658-9. The sequence produced by the process seems a coherent one.

38. Only the *DNB* entries for these men and for Fauconberg below (this under 'Belasyse'), represent anything like biographies. Fauconberg is the most common form of a name also spelt Fauconbridge or Falconbridge. Likewise Desborough is often rendered Desborow or Disbrowe in the sources.

39. Thomas Birch (ed.), *State Papers of John Thurloe* (1742), vii. 56-366, *passim* (letters to and from Henry Cromwell).

40. The biography of Richard is Robert W. Ramsey, *Richard Cromwell* (1935), a rather bland work which is particularly disappointing on Richard's Protectorate.

41. Thomas Carlyle (ed.), *Letters and Speeches of Oliver Cromwell* (2nd ed., 1904), nos. liii, lxxxvii, xcix, c, ci, cxxxii, clxxviii.

42. *CSPD* 1657-8, pp. 266-7 (Lockhart to Fauconberg); Firth, ii. 279-80; *Mercurius Politicus*, 1-8 July 1658 (Richard's visit to Bristol).

43. Thurloe State Papers vii. 56-7 (Henry to Broghill).

44. Firth, ii. 274-80.

45. Who had made the same suggestion in April: Thurloe State Papers vii. 56-7 (as above).

46. The so-called *Old Parliamentary History* (1760), xxi. 223 (Richard to John Dunch).
47. Thurloe State Papers vii. 365–6 (Fauconberg to Henry).
48. (Anon., ?Charles Harvey), *A Collection of Several Passages concerning his late Highness Oliver Cromwell . . .* (1659).

Part Two: Chapter 1

1. The standard text for 1658–60 is Godfrey Davies, *The Restoration of Charles II* (1955). On Richard Cromwell's Protectorate there is Earl M. Hause, *Tumble-Down Dick* (New York, 1972). The main events of the period are summarised neatly by Ivan Roots, *The Great Rebellion 1642–1660* (1966) and J. R. Jones, *Country and Court: England 1658–1714* (1978). The most penetrating recent study, however, is the all too brief sketch provided by Austin Woolrych in his intro-duction to Robert W. Ayers (ed.), *The Complete Prose Works of John Milton*, vol. vii (1980), supplemented and corrected in some details by Reece, thesis, chs. 8–9, and Massarella, thesis, chs. 5–6. The insights of all these authors have contri-buted substantially to the present study, though it reworks their sources and adds others, and differs at moments from all of their texts.
2. Thus I step gingerly over the debate between Earl Hause and Austin Woolrych. Professor Hause (in 'The Nomination of Richard Cromwell', *The Historian* 27 (1965), 185–209, and *Tumble-Down Dick*, ch. 2) has demonstrated that it is impossible to prove that Cromwell nominated his son. Professor Woolrych (in 'Milton and Cromwell', in Michael Lieb and T. Shawcross (eds.), *Achievements of the Left Hand* (Amherst, 1974), 202–8, and his introduction to *Milton*, vii. 5) has demonstrated that it is impossible to prove he did not, and inherently unlikely that he would have chosen anybody else. Between them they cite and analyse every relevant source.
3. Sir Richard Baker, *A Chronicle of the Kings of England* (1670), 653–4 (in reality the *Chronicle* relating to this period is the work not of Baker but of Edward Phillips, relying heavily on the information of Sir Thomas Clarges); *Old Parliamentary History*, xxi. 223–31; Longleat House MS 67a, f. 1 (Privy Council Register); C. H. Firth (ed.), *The Clarke Papers*, Camden Soc. (1899), iii. 161–3; Thurloe, State Papers vii. 372–3. For a copy of the proclamation with covering letter, as received by a corporation, see Gloucestershire RO GBR/BR/3, p. 77 (Gloucester Minute Book).
4. Thurloe, State Papers vii. 373.
5. *Memoirs of Edmund Ludlow* ('Vevay', 1698), 612.
6. *Justice's Notebook of Captain John Pickering*, Thoresby Soc. xv (1909), 279.
7. E. Hockliffe (ed.), *The Diary of the Revd. Ralph Josselin*, Camden Soc. 3rd ser. xv (1908), 125.
8. *Clarke Papers*, iii. 161–3.
9. *A True Catalogue or an Account of the several Places and most Eminent Persons . . . where, and by whom, Richard Cromwell was proclaimed Lord Protector . . .* [28 Sept. 1659] cites twelve such celebrations. Another at Andover is described in Thurloe State

Papers vii. 378 (Tattenhall to Thurloe). Traces of more can be found in the corporation archives of Gloucester, Devizes, Macclesfield, Lincoln and Ipswich.

10. Andrew Clark (ed.), *The Life and Times of Anthony Wood*, Oxford Historical Soc. (1891-2), i. 259.

11. *A True Catalogue* lists most of these, which are reprinted in full in the successive issues of *Mercurius Politicus*. Others are found or noted in Bulstrode Whitelocke, *Memorials of the English Affairs* (Oxford, 1853), iv. 337 (Oxfordshire address); Bod. L. Carte MS 74, f. 203 (Huntingdonshire); *Calendar of Wynn (of Gywydir) Papers* (1926), 351 (Caernarfonshire); Great Yarmouth Assembly Book G, endpiece.

12. See Johnson and Everitt, above.

13. John Latimer, *The Annals of Bristol in the Seventeenth Century* (Bristol, 1900), 283.

14. Royalist and republican enemies later denied this: Baker, *Chronicle*, 654; Ludlow, 614. For an unbiased comment see the French ambassador's dispatch printed in M. Guizot, *The History of Richard Cromwell and the Restoration of Charles II* (translated by A. R. Scoble, 1856), i. 236.

15. See the City of Oxford and the University of Cambridge jumping on the bandwagon, in M. G. Hobson and the Revd H. E. Salter (eds.), *Oxford Council Acts 1626-1665*, Oxford Historical Soc. (1933), 236, and J. Crossley (ed.), *Diary and Correspondence of Dr. John Worthington*, Chetham Soc. xiii (1847), 116.

16. Helen Stocks (ed.), *Records of the Borough of Leicester* (Cambridge, 1923), iv. 450.

17. Whitelocke, *Memorials*, iv. 338.

18. CSP iii. 421 (Rumbold to Hyde).

19. Bod. L. Rawlinson MS A61/3 (Original copy of English army address); *Mercurius Politicus* (23-30 Sept., 7-14 Oct.); Dow, *Cromwellian Scotland*, 233-4; Worcester College, Oxford, Clarke MS 30, f. 190^v.

20. D. Massarella, 'The Politics of the Army and the Quest for Settlement', in Roots (ed.), *Into Another Mould*, 60.

21. Sir Henry Vane, *A Healing Question Propounded and Resolved* (12 May 1656).

22. Thurloe, State Papers vii. 385-6 (Thurloe to Henry), 405-6 (Fleetwood to Henry); *Clarke Papers*, iii. 164 (news-letters); Brit. L. Lansdowne MS 823, f. 104 (Mabbott to Henry).

23. Thurloe, vii. 365-6, 386 (Fauconberg to Henry), 374 (Thurloe to Henry).

24. Lansdowne MS 823, f. 100 (Whalley to Henry). Bod. L. Rawlinson MS A61/1, ff. 45-7 are probably copies of this reply.

25. Like Berry: Sir James Berry and Stephen Lee, *A Cromwellian Major-General* (Oxford, 1938), 206.

26. Guizot, *Richard Cromwell*, i. 238.

27. Thurloe, vii. 406-7, 413-14 (Fauconberg), 460 ('Plymouth fort'); Rawlinson MS A62/2, f. 401 ('The Heads of a Letter').

28. This account appears to reconcile Thurloe, vii. 436, 500 (Fleetwood to Henry), 447-9 (draft speech), 452 (Clarges to Henry); *Clarke Papers*, iii. 165-6 (news-letters); *CSPV* xxxi.254-8; Staffordshire RO D868/4/77-8 (Temple to Leveson).

29. Guizot, i. 246-53; Staffordshire RO D868/4/78; Rawlinson MS A61/1, f. 139 (intercepted paper).

30. Thurloe, vii. 450-1, 462 (Fauconberg to Henry), 454-5 (Henry to Fleetwood), 498, 500 (Fleetwood to Henry), 490-1 (Thurloe to Henry), 513-14 (reply).

31. *Mercurius Politicus* (7-14 Oct.); Rawlinson MS A61/1, f. 139, endorsed on this point by Baker, *Chronicle*, 657.

32. Thurloe, vii. 492-3 (Henry to Richard), 498 (Fleetwood to Henry); Lansdowne MS 823, ff. 116, 138 (Russell to Henry).

33. Thurloe, vii. 504-5 (Richard to Henry); Brit. L. Egerton MS 2618, f. 56 (Clarges to ?).

34. Thurloe, vii. 490-1.

35. *Clarke Papers*, iii. 167-8 (news-letters); Longleat House MS 67a, orders 9 and 30 Nov.; B. G. Charles (ed.), *Records of the Borough of Haverfordwest* (Cardiff, 1967), 159 (council to Assessment commission).

36. *Public Intelligencer* (15-22 Nov.).

37. *Clarke Papers*, iii. 168-70; Guizot, i. 262-4; Worcester College, Oxford, Clarke MS 30, ff. 190^v-2 (speech).

38. *Mercurius Politicus* (18-25 Nov.); Thurloe, vii. 528 (Thurloe to Henry); William Bray (ed.), *Diary and Correspondence of John Evelyn* (n.d.), 228; Sir R. C. Temple and L. M. Anstey (eds.), *The Travels of Peter Mundy*, vol. v, Hakluyt Soc. 2nd ser. lxxviii (1936), 103-4.

39. Robert Steele (ed.), *Tudor and Stuart Proclamations* (Oxford, 1910), i. no. 3102; Sir Gyles Isham (ed.), *The Correspondence of Bishop Brian Duppa and Sir Justinian Isham*, Northamptonshire Record Soc. (1955), 167; Dom Hugh Bowler (ed.), *London Sessions Records*, Catholic Record Soc. xxxiv (1934), 147-52; *CSPD* (1658-9), 194-5; Longleat MS 67a, orders 21 Dec.

40. SP 18/182, 136-9, 183/15-139 *passim*; Longleat MS 67a, orders 3 Dec.

41. Thurloe, vii. 376 (Smith to Thurloe); Hull CA, BB6, p. 249 (Assembly Book).

42. John E. Jeaffreson (ed.), *Middlesex County Records* (1888), iii. 274; Thurloe vii. 388 (Yorkshire information); the Revd J. C. Atkinson (ed.), *North Riding Quarter Sessions Records* (1888), vi. 14.

43. A. G. Matthews, *The Savoy Declaration of Faith and Order* (1959); *Public Intelligencer* (18-25 Oct.); C. H. Firth (ed.), 'A Speech by Richard Cromwell', *EHR* xxiii (1908), 734-6.

44. *The Agreement of the Associated Ministers of . . . Essex* (28 Sept.); Doctor Williams's L. Baxter Letters, i. ff. 96-7 (Durie to Baxter), ii. 137-8 (Beale to Baxter).

45. Shaw, *The Church*, ii. 115-16, 140; the Revd J. C. Cox (ed.), 'Minute Book of the Wirksworth *Classis*', *J Derbyshire Archaeological and Natural History Soc.* 2 (1880), 135-222.

46. SP 18/183/136 (Lincolnshire petition); Steele, *Proclamations*, ii. no. 3102; Essex RO Q/SR 378/24-5; A. G. Matthews, *Calamy Revised* (Oxford, 1934), 201.

47. J. Barclay (ed.), *Letters, etc., of Early Friends* (1811), 59-61 (Burroughs to Howgill, Hubberthorne to Fell); Friends' House L, Caton and Salthouse to Fell), Swarthmore MSS iii. 87 (Curtis to Fox), iv. 197 (Robertson to Fox); Pickering, *Notebook*, 279; Kent RO, Q/SMc/1, Michaelmas 1658; Friends' House L, *A Journal of the Life of John Banks* (1712), 9-10; Francis Blomefield, *An Essay towards a . . . History*

of Norfolk (1806), iii. 401; Edward Reynolds, *Twenty Sermons* (1660); Samuel Slater, *The Protector's Protection* (1659); Joseph Besse, *A Collection of the Sufferings of the People called Quakers* (1753), ii. 98; Doctor Williams's L. MS 12, 78, pp. 1-102 (minutes of meeting); HMC Portland MSS iii. 213 (Woodruffe to Harley).

48. Brit. L. Lansdowne MS 1236, f. 119.

49. Guizot, i. 231-30.

50. Longleat MS 67a.

51. Thurloe, vii. 550, 581 (to Henry); Guizot, i. 274.

52. This is reported by the French ambassador, in Guizot, i. 271-3. It is supported by no other source, but authorities for this month are scarce, and the story is told with such confidence that I repeat it here.

53. Longleat MS 67a (16 Dec.).

54. Ludlow, 616. This change was discussed before Oliver Cromwell's death, when the French ambassador believed it to have been inspired by a desire for greater government control over elections—PRO, PRO/31/3/105/230.

55. Cornwall RO, FS/3/942 (Clark to Bennet).

56. The basic authorities for these elections and their results are G. Davies, 'The Election of Richard Cromwell's Parliament', *EHR* lxiii (1948), 489-501, and G. Nourse, 'Richard Cromwell's House of Commons', *BJRL* lx (1977-8), 95-113. To these can be added the insights of Johnson, 'Wales', 251, and 'Chester', 344; Morrill, *Cheshire*, 293-9; Fletcher, *Sussex*, 315-16; Howell, *Newcastle*, 209; Coate, *Cornwall*, 299-300; Underdown, *Somerset*, 189; Dow, *Scotland*, 237-40; J. Casada, 'Dorset Politics in the Puritan Revolution', *Southern History* 4 (1982), 116-18. I have incorporated material from *Mercurius Politicus* (43 issues, 9 Dec.-6 Jan.); Thurloe, vii. 559 (Clarges to Henry); *Records of Haverfordwest*, 159 (corporation to Upton); HMC 13th report, iv. 392 (agent to Marten); Nottinghamshire RO, DD/SR/221/96/8 (agent to Savile); *Wynn Papers*, 351 (Richard Wynn's affidavit); Latimer, *Bristol*, 285; *Oxford Council Acts*, 237; Josselin's Diary, 126; Brit. L. Add. MS 1570, f. 44 ('Mills' to ?); Hull CA, BB6, p. 277; Brit. L. Add. MS 21425, f. 5 (Ashenden to Baynes).

57. On Sir Arthur in particular there is Brown, thesis. However, he emerges as vividly from the narratives of Anthony Fletcher, *The Outbreak of the English Civil War* (1981); Howell, *Newcastle*; Worden, *The Rump Parliament*; Woolrych, *Commonwealth to Protectorate*.

58. The best study of Scot is in Worden, *The Rump*.

59. Vane has attracted some biographies of more devotion than scholarship. The exception is Violet A. Rowe, *Sir Henry Vane the Younger* (1970).

60. A. B. Worden, in the introduction to his edition of Ludlow's *A Voyce from the Watch Tower*, has shown how much of the Memoirs were rewritten by their editor in the 1690s. Thus, although to an extent Ludlow speaks for himself, he only does so if the personality in the *Voyce* is extrapolated onto the text of the *Memoirs*, an awkward business.

61. The best secondary sources for this Parliament are the later chapters of Hause, *Tumble-Down Dick*, and I. Roots, 'The Tactics of the Commonwealthsmen in

Richard Cromwell's Parliament' in Pennington and Thomas (eds.), *Puritans and Revolutionaries*. For basic primary sources there survive both CJ and the journals of the Upper House printed in HMC House of Lords MSS N.S. iv, and the excellent parliamentary diary of Thomas Burton which is confirmed by all other sources and is cited for Naylor's case, above.

62. CJ vii. 4593; *Old Parliamentary History*, xxi. 265-81; *Clarke Papers*, iii. 176 (news-letter); Burton, iii. 1-11; Guizot, i. 294.

63. CJ 594-603; Burton, iii. 17-287; *Old Parliamentary History* xxi. 282-9 (reprint of Slingsby Bethel, who does not accord in details with other sources, and must be recognised as a propagandist); Thurloe, vii. 603-4 (draft bill), 615-16 (Barwick to Hyde).

64. CJ 604; Burton, iii. 288-96; *The Humble Petition of Many Thousand Citizens to the Parliament* (15 Feb.).

65. CJ 605-21; Burton, iii. 307-574, iv. 7-298; HMC Lords MSS N.S. iv. 4529-52; Brit. L. Lansdowne MS 823, ff. 229, 251, 259 (Annesley to Henry); Old Parliamentary History, xxi. 290-320 (Bethel's narrative); Guizot, i. 345.

66. CJ 597, 607, 614; Burton, iii. 45-6, 307-25, iv. 139-42, 149-63; *Clarke Papers*, iii. 184; *Mercurius Politicus* (24 Feb.-3 Mar.).

67. *Records of Haverfordwest*, 160 (Phillips to corporation); Hull CA Letters 633-4 (Ramsden to corporation); Latimer, *Bristol*, 2895; Josselin's Diary, 126.

68. *Mercurius Politicus* (6-13 Jan.); Wynn Papers, 351 (Williams to Lady Wynn).

69. Toon, *God's Statesman*, 108; Reynolds, *Twenty Sermons*, xiv; George Abernethy jun., 'Richard Baxter and the Cromwellian Church', *HLQ* 24 (1960-1),227-9; *Mercurius Politicus* (10-17 Feb.).

70. The importance of this paper offensive was first noticed by Austin Woolrych, in 'The Good Old Cause and the Fall of the Protectorate', *CHJ* xiii. 2 (1957), 138-44, and his introduction to *Milton*, vii, pursues the theme. I have been unable to add to the examples he cites. The most notorious was *XXV Quæries* (16 Feb.).

71. Bod. L. Clarendon MS 60, ff. 108-9 (Moore to Hyde) notes their open sale with surprise.

72. Charles Marsh, *A Moderate Answer to certain Immoderate Quæries* (24 Feb.).

73. Thurloe, vii. 612 (Fauconberg to Henry); *Clarke Papers*, iii. 182-3 (news-letters); Guizot, i. 304-30; CSP, iii. 425-6 ('Simmons' to Hyde); Bod. L. Clarendon MS 60,ff. 152-3, 199-200 (Slingsby and Moore to Hyde); Lansdowne MS 823, f. 223 (Mabbott to Henry).

74. CSP, iii. 423-5, 440-1 (Mordaunt, Cooper, Broderick, to Hyde); Guizot, i. 345; Lansdowne MS 823, f.259 (Annesley to Henry).

75. Pearl, 'Oliver St. John' and 'Royalist Independents'.

76. Sir George F. Warner (ed.), *The Nicholas Papers*, iv, Camden Soc. 3rd series xxxi (1920), iv. 84-5 (Greene to Nicholas); the Revd W. Stephen (ed.), *Register of the Consultations of the Ministers of Edinburgh* ii, Scottish History Soc. 3rd series xvi (1930), 153-6 (Sharp to Scottish ministers); Matthew Sylvester (ed.), *Reliquiae Baxterianae* (1696), part 1, 101; William Prynne, *The Re-publicans* (1659), 3;

Guizot, i. 252-3; the Revd J. Hutchinson (ed.), Lucy Hutchinson's *Memoirs of Colonel Hutchinson* (1968), 299-300.

77. *A Second Narrative of the Late Parliament* (20 Apr.), 30-1; Ludlow, 633.

78. Barnard, *Ireland*, 108.

79. HMC Leybourne-Popham MSS, 114-15 (Gough, Ashfield, to Monck); Lansdowne MS 823, ff. 245ᵛ, 278 (Morgan, Annesley, to Henry); Ludlow, 634-5.

80. *Nicholas Papers*, iv. 92 (Church to Nicholas); Guizot, i. 347-8; CSP iii. 424-5 (Cooper to Hyde).

81. Ludlow, 633-6. Nehemiah Bourne, in *Clarke Papers*, iii. 210, is often held to be referring to the same incident but may be concerned with contacts made between Commonwealthsmen and lesser officers.

82. Stephen (ed.), *Register*, 158, 163-8 (Sharp to Scots ministers).

83. Ibid. 167, 173; Burton, iv. 328-49; HMC Lords MSS N.S. iv. 560-3; *Old Parliamentary History*, xxi. 321-4 (declaration).

84. CJ 627-31; Burton, iv. 361-448.

85. Ludlow, 636, claims that Fleetwood and Desborough persuaded the Protector into the scheme, to use the Council as a means of increasing their own power. This may well be true, but still begs the question of why he consented and has an air of retrospective taking of credit. Ludlow's whole narrative of the events of Richard's Protectorate, like Baker's *Chronicle*, generally compresses them to a point at which the sequence is distorted.

86. Brit. L. Lansdowne MS 823, f. 291 (Fauconberg to Henry); *Clarke Papers*, iii. 187-8 (two news-letters); Guizot, i. 351-2; *CSPV* xxxii. 6-7; *Old Parliamentary History*, xxi. 340-5 (petition); CJ 632; HMC Lords MSS N.S. iv. 537-8; *To His Excellency the Lord Fleetwood. . . the Humble Address of the late Lord Pride's regiment* (8 Apr.). The most detailed secondary works on the army in April 1659 are G. Davies, 'The Army and the Downfall of Richard Cromwell', *HLB* 7 (1935), 131-67, and the last two chapters of Hause. Professor Davies misunderstands the events of 17-18 April. Professor Hause, I believe, hits the truth, but I am less convinced by his treatment of the crisis of 21 April, and in general his arguments are not easy to follow among a plethora of sources quoted end to end without any rigorous criticism.

87. CJ 631-40; Burton, iv. 361-448.

88. CJ 636, 638-9; Burton, iv. 403-12; Lansdowne MS 823, f. 291 (Fauconberg to Henry); *Clarke Papers*, iii. 189 (news-letter, written like all those for the period in this collection, from Gilbert Mabbott to Monck); *CSPV* xxxii. 8, 13; *Mercurius Politicus* (7-14 Apr.); *Nicholas Papers*, iv. 104-5 (Johnson to Nicholas).

89. Thomas Morrice (ed.), *A Collection of the State Papers of . . . Roger Boyle, the First Earl of Orrery* (1742), 27-9; *Clarke Papers*, iii. 189; Lansdowne MS 823, ff. 291, 299 (Fauconberg, Mabbott, to Henry); Stephen (ed.), *Register*, 173 (Sharp to Scottish ministers).

90. *A Declaration of the Present Sufferings of above 140 Persons . . .* (6 Apr., a misprint); CJ 640; Burton, iv. 439-48.

91. *Mercurius Politicus* (14-21 Apr.); Lansdowne MS 823, f. 295 (Aungier to Henry).

92. CJ 641; Burton, iv. 448-63; Lansdowne MS 823, f. 299 (Mabbott to Henry); *Orrery*, 28-9; Baker, *Chronicle*, 659; HMC Lords MSS iv. 563-5, which refute Thurloe, vii. 657-8 (Clarges to Henry).

93. *Clarke Papers*, iii. 190-2 (two news-letters); Guizot, i. 363-6; *To His Highness Richard . . . the Humble Representation . . . of the Trained Bands of the City of London* (21 Apr.); Thurloe, vii. 662 (Barwick to Hyde); Lansdowne MS 823, ff. 299, 301 (Mabott, Morgan, to Henry).

94. Bod. L. Rawlinson MS A62/1, f. 139 (intercepted letter).

95. I have based this account on the contemporary sources, Guizot, i. 370-5; SP 78/ 114/236-7 (Sir L. B. to Hyde); *Clarke Papers*, iii. 193 (news-letter to Monck); 210-15 (Bourne's relation); Burton, iv. 469-82; HMC Lords MSS N.S. iv. 565. The retrospective memoirs, Ludlow, 639-42, and Baker, *Chronicle*, 659, have been used where they are consistent with these. Whitelocke, *Memorials*, iv. 343, seems inconsistent, and Thurloe, vii. 659-61 (Bamfield to Thurloe) an unlikely rumour. The views of Goffe's men are expressed in *To . . . Parliament. The Humble Petition of the Sentinels in the Regiment.formerly belonging to Major-General Goffe* (10 June).

96. Steele, *Proclamations*, i. no. 3106; Guizot, i. 372-5; *Clarke Papers*, iii. 194 (Fleetwood to Monck).

97. Bod. L. Clarendon MS 60, f. 411, 465 (Slingsby, Cooper, to Hyde); Stephen (ed.), *Register*, 177 (Sharp to Scots ministers).

98. Austin Woolrych, in 'The Good Old Cause' and his introduction to *Milton*, is again the expert on the Commonwealth tracts and lists them. There are references to their effect in *Clarke Papers*, iv. 3-5 (news-letter to Monck) and Guizot, i. 379. The hostile tracts are *The Humble Representation and Remonstrance of Divers Freemen . . .* and *Certain Quæries upon the Dissolving of the Late Parliament* (3 May). Goffe's regiment's declaration appeared as *Remonstrance* of the *Commission Officers of . . . Major-General Goffe's Regiment*.

99. *Clarke Papers*, iii. 195-6 (two news-letters to Monck), iv. 1-2 (resolutions of General Council); Guizot, i. 379; Orrery State Papers, 29; Thurloe, vii. 666-7 (Barwick to Hyde); HMC 3rd Report, 88 (Chapman to Potter); Lansdowne MS 823, f. 308 (Mabbott to Henry); Brit. L. Add. MS 22919 (Thurloe to Downing).

100. CJ 644-6; SP 78/114/248 (Thurloe to Lockhart); *Clarke Papers*, iv. 6-8 (two news-letters to Monck); Guizot, i. 381-3; *Mercurius Politicus* (5-12 May). I have used Ludlow, 645-51, where he does not conflict with these contemporary sources.

101. R. Catterall (ed.), 'Two Letters of Richard Cromwell', *AHR* 8 (1902-3), 187-8.

102. Ibid., 188-9; *Clarke Papers*, iv. 4-6 (General Council to Scottish army), 9 (Committee of Safety to Monck), 10 (reply); Baker, *Chronicle*, 662; Thurloe, vii. 669-70 (Scottish army to General Council); *Mercurius Politicus* (19-26 May) (Scottish army to Parliament).

103. CSP iii. 469 (Mordaunt to King).

104. CJ 655, 664-5, 705, 720; Thurloe, vii. 683-4 (Henry to Speaker, 15 June); Baker,

Chronicle, 662-4 (reprint of army petition); Huntingdonshire RO, Bush Acc. 731, no. 14 (Henry's out-letters).

105. The first appears in *Forty-four Quæries to the Life of Queen Dick* (15 July), the second in *Nicholas Papers*, iv. 148 ('Miles' to Nicholas).

Part Two: Chapter 2

1. The restored Parliament, notoriously, lacks diaries and also a historian. CJ 653 states the prescribed maximum number, and the highest recorded attendance appears at 683.

2. Underdown, *Pride's Purge*, and Worden, *The Rump*, supply excellent analyses of the earlier policies, composition and achievements of this Parliament.

3. William M. Lamont, *Marginal Prynne* (1963), though professing to be a critique of his writings rather than a biography, is none the less the best characterisation of this man.

4. Prynne, *A true and perfect Narrative of what was done, spoken by and between Mr. Prynne . . .* (7 May), *The true Good Old Cause rightly stated, and the False un-cased* (13 May), *The Re-Publicans* (13 May), *Mola Asinaria* (31 May), *Loyalty Banished* (16 June), and *Concordia Discors* (16 July); Annesley, *England's Confusion* (30 May); *One Sheet, or if you will A Winding Sheet for the Good Old Cause* (30 May). The Commons' vote is at CJ 646.

5. *Nicholas Papers*, iv. 134 ('Miles' to Nicholas); Ludlow, 649-50.

6. *Old Parliamentary History*, xxi. 375-6, lists ninety-one men surviving who had sat in 1653. The restored Parliament found seventy-eight apparently willing to return: CJ 653.

7. Cooper was not technically a member of this House until January 1660, as a dispute surrounding his election in 1640 had never been formally resolved. He was, however, treated as a member of the regime, and elected to its Council of State. Seven months later he took his seat in the Commons after the decision of the dispute. The latest and best life of him is K. H. D. Haley, *The First Earl of Shaftesbury* (Oxford, 1968).

8. The sole biography is William H. Dawson, *Cromwell's Understudy* (1938), but Lambert's importance is better stated in G. Heath III, 'Cromwell and Lambert', in Roots (ed.), *Cromwell: A Profile*. Woolrych, *Commonwealth to Protectorate*, confirms this view.

9. CJ 644-59, 664; Sir C. H. Firth and R. S. Rait (eds.), *Acts and Ordinances of the Interregnum* (1911), ii. 1270-1 (act for local officers), 1272-6 (act for Council); Whitelocke, *Memorials*, iv. 349. The proceedings of the Council of State survive in two minute-books, Bod. L. Rawlinson MS C179 (May-Aug.) and SP 25/79 (Aug.-Oct.), the last being calendared accurately in *CSPD*. Some of its orders and letters June-Oct. are entered in Bod. L. Rawlinson MS A134.

10. H. S(tubbe), *The Commonwealth of Israel* (16 May); *The Character or Ear-Mark of Mr. William Prynne* (17 May); (John Rogers,) *Mr. Prynne's Good Old Cause Stated and Stunted 10 years ago*; J. Streater, *A Shield Against the Parthian Dart* (22 June);

Several Reasons why Some Officers of the Army, with Many other Good People. . . . CJ 652 records Canne's appointment.

11. Josselin's Diary, 129; R. Parkinson (ed.),*The Autobiography of Henry Newcome*, Chetham Soc. xxvi (1852), i. 104.

12. Sharp, *In Contempt*, 254; Bod. L. Rawlinson MS C179, loose leaf (Council to keepers).

13. Doctor Williams's L. MS 89/3, St. Mary Woolechurch, 24, and St. Swithin's, 70.

14. PRO Assi 2/1, n.p.

15. J. H. Round, 'Colchester and the Commonwealth', *EHR* xv (1900), 569-60.

16. Hull CA, Letter 635 (Vane to corporation).

17. CJ 647-734. *Mercurius Politicus* prints nine in full. Six were published, and are among the Thomason Tracts, 669, f. 21 (32, 40, 45, 51) and in Bod. L. Wood 610 (48) and G. Pamph. 1118 (40).

18. CJ 647; Guizot, i. 370-5; Bod. L. Clarendon MS 60, f. 465 (Cooper to Hyde).

19. CJ 648-50; Barclay (ed.), *Letters*, 68 (Rawlinson to Fell). Moyer plays a significant part in Woolrych, *Commonwealth to Protectorate*.

20. CJ 670; *Mercurius Politicus* (26 May-2 June).

21. CJ 671; Corporation of London RO, Journal 41, f. 204^v.

22. *A Commonwealth and Commonwealthsmen Asserted and Vindicated* (28 June); *Twenty-seven Quæries* (6 June).

23. M. James, 'The Political Importance of the Tithes Controversy in the English Revolution', *H*, N.S. 26 (1941-2), 1-18; Reay, 'Quaker Opposition to Tithes'; Woolrych, introduction to Milton, vii. 77-82; *Long Parliament Work* (9 June); *The Humble Petition to the Parliament Against Tithes* (14 June); *The Humble Representation of . . . the County of Bedford* (16 June); (Henry Stubbe), *A Light Shining Out of Darknesse* (17 June); *The Copie of a Paper presented to the Parliament* (24 June); *The Moderate Man's Proposal to The Parliament about Tithes* (28 June); *England's Safety In The Law's Supremacy* (30 June); (James Cottrel), *Several Proposals offered . . . to . . . the Keepers of Liberties* (6 July); (John Osborne), *An Indictment Against Tithes* (18 July); William Covel, *A Declaration unto the Parliament* (1659); G(eorge) F(ox), *To The Parliament* (1659); *The Honest Design* (1659); Anthony Pearson, *The Great Case of Tithes* (1659).

24. Woolrych, introduction to *Milton*, vii. 46-57; *A Vindication of . . . Sir Henry Vane* (7 June); *Sundry Things from several Hands concerning the University of Oxford* (29 June); Covel, *A Declaration*; Thomas Collier, *The Decision and Clearing of the Great Point Now in Controversy* (1659).

25. B. Reay, 'The Quakers, 1659 and the Restoration of the Monarchy', *H* 63 (1978), 93, lists the relevant tracts.

26. Lawrence Clarkson, *Look about you*.

27. *Sundry Things from Several Hands*; *The Humble Petition of Many Inhabitants In and about the City of London* (12 May); *Twelve Quæries* (12 May); William Cole, *Several Proposals Humbly Tendered* (1659); *A Public Plea Opposed To A Private Proposal* (18 May); *A Secret Word to the Wise* (1659); *A Seasonable Question soberly proposed* (24 June).

28. James Freeze, *The Outcry And Just Appeal of the Enslaved People of England* (18 May); *A Scourge for a Den of Thieves* (June); *Long Parliament Work*; *A Vindication of the Laws of England* (10 June); William Cole, *A Rod for the Lawyers* (12 July) and *Several Proposals*; *Chaos* (18 July); Fox, *To The Parliament*.

29. Fabian Phillips, *The Pretended Perspective Glass*; (Cole,) *Several Proposals*; *Chaos* (1659).

30. Covell, *A Declaration*.

31. (Hugh Peter), *A Letter to a chief Officer of the Army* (10 May); *A Word to Purpose* (2 June); *Twenty-Seven Quæries*; *The Unhappy Marksman* (13 June); *A Pair of Spectackles* (13 June); *The Dispersed United* (14 June); *Several Resolves Prepared By The Commanding Junto* (14 June); *Truth Seekes No Corners* (14 July); *Let Me Speake Too?*

32. Prynne, *Ten Seasonable Quæries Concerning Tythes* (27 June); *A Defence and Justification of Ministers' Maintenance by Tythes* (30 June); *A Caution Against Sacrilege* (12 July).

33. *The Repugnancy and Inconsistency of the Maintenance of an Orthodox Ministry . . .* (10 June); Richard Baxter, *A Holy Commonwealth* (22 June); Samuel Clarke, *Golden Apples* (July); Robert South, *Interest Deposed and Truth Restored* (1660); Doctor Williams's L Thomas Willes, *A Word in Season* (1659).

34. *The Petition and Address of the Officers of the Army* (12 May).

35. CJ 646, 648, 659, 662, 683, 694, 700, 732; J. L. Nickalls (ed.), *The Journal of George Fox* (1952), 353; Besse, i. 531; Barclay (ed.), *Letters*, 69-70 (Benbrink, Parker, to Fell); *Nicholas Papers*, iv. 155, 157, 163 ('Miles' to Nicholas); Guizot, i. 424, 432; Steele, no. 3116.

36. CJ 655, 660, 669,675, 684, 689, 703, 737-8; Firth and Rait, *Acts and Ordinances* ii. 1286-7; Steele, no. 3109; *Nicholas Papers*, iv. 163, 165 ('Miles' to Nicholas); *To Parliament. The Humble Petition of the Sentinels. . .* (10 June).

37. CJ 654-715; Ludlow, 672; *Nicholas Papers*, iv. 163; the Revd Edward Berwick (ed.), *The Rawdon Papers* (1819), 198 (Conway to Bramhall); Firth and Rait, *Acts and Ordinances*, ii. 1299-1304; *Brief Lives*, ii. 46.

38. CJ 649-51, 670-716, 748; SP 25/127, pp. 1-100, 128, pp. 1-33 (Minutes of Army Commission); Ludlow, 660-73; *Clarke Papers*, iv. 17-20 (three news-letters to Monck); J. D. Ogilvie (ed.), *The Diary of Sir Archibald Johnston of Warriston*, Scottish History Soc., 3rd ser. 34 (1940), iii. 118; *Rawdon Papers*, 196 (Conway to Bramhall); J. R. Wardale (ed.), *Clare College Letters and Documents* (1903), 36 (Tillotson to Dillington); Firth and Davies, *passim*.

39. *CSPD* (1658-9), 357 ('De Vaux' to 'du Chastel'); G. E. Aylmer, *The State's Servants* (1973), 55, 167, 220, 257; *Mercurius Politicus* (9-16 June); J. S. Cockburn, *A History of English Assizes 1558-1714* (1972), 245; S. F. Black, thesis, pp. 231-3. Mr Black notes the significant fact that two of the judges who refused the oath to the Commonwealth had taken it in 1649, and ascribes this new reluctance to belief in the near-certainty of the Restoration. This seems, in the circumstances, an almost uncanny foresight, and it seems easier, in default of evidence, to attribute the judges' scruples to dissatisfaction with the reversal of the 'reactionary' tendencies in the later Protectorate with which these men had been identified.

40. CJ 647, 663-734; Firth and Rait, *Acts and Ordinances*, ii. 1290-8, 1308-48; Johnson, 'Buckinghamshire', 315, 'Wales', 252-3, and 'Bussy Mansell', *Morgannwg* xx (1976),9-36; Fletcher, *Sussex*, 317; Everitt, *Kent*, 309-10; Underdown, *Somerset*, 189-90; Roberts, thesis, 88-9; Cornwall RO, FS/3/47, ff. 553, 557 (Lobb to Bennet); Reay, 'The Quakers, 1659', 200-1; Capp, *Fifth Monarchy Men*, 124. The cross-section of men observed in the southern commissions seems present in the north, but we lack any detailed county study in this whole region.

41. CJ 648.

42. CJ 721-6; Bod. L. Rawlinson MS C179, p. 37; *Mercurius Politicus* (three issues, 7-28 July); *Nicholas Papers*, iv. 172; *Bloodie Newes from Enfield*; *A Relation of the Cruelties and Barbarous Murders . . .* (1659); *A Relation of the Riotous Insurrection of Divers Inhabitants of Enfield* (24 July).

43. CJ 673, 705, 732. The various blueprints are summarised and compared in Woolrych, introduction to *Milton*, vii. 101-7, and the Harringtonian group dealt with in detail in J. G. A. Pocock (ed.), *The Political Works of James Harrington* (Cambridge, 1977), 103-14.

44. Reay, 'The Quakers, 1659', 194.

45. Or so the French ambassador believed—Guizot, i. 432.

46. SP 18/203/18, 21-8 (the lists).

47. Barnard, *Ireland*, 132-3.

48. J. F. MacLear, 'Quakerism and the End of the Interregnum', *Church History* 19 (1950), 240-60; Reay, 204-5; CSP iii. 479 (Wood to Simpson); Worthington's Diary, i. 143-4 (Hartlib to Worthington); Bod. L. Tanner MS 51, ff. 73-4 (Council to Speaker); Rawlinson MS C179, f. 39; *Mercurius Politicus* (21-8 July); Wood's Life, i. 280; Alan Macfarlane, *Witchcraft in Tudor and Stuart England* (1970), 270; C. L'Estrange Ewen, *Witchcraft and Demonianism* (1933), 436; *A True Relation of the Persecutions of the people of God . . .* (1659); Roger Criup, etc., *A Voyce from Zion* (1659); Besse, *Sufferings*, i. 689; Friends' House L, Swarthmore MS iv, f. 92 (Whitehead to Fox). Undoubtedly the list of mobbings of Quakers would be much longer if their records of sufferings were all properly dated. Those which can be assigned to these months were at Holborn, Brentford, Sawbridgeworth, Liskeard, Cambridge, Arundel, Mitcham and Aylesbury.

49. *Reliquiae Baxterianae*, part ii, 180-1, 206-7; Doctor Williams's L Baxter Letters, iv, f. 231 (Baxter to Youil); the Revd R. Parkinson (ed.), *The Life of Adam Martindale*, Chetham Soc. iv (1845), 128-31; Braithwaite, *Beginnings of Quakerism*, 314-28; John Stoughton, *History of Religion in England* (1881), iii. 28-9 (Yarmouth Church Book); Susanna Parr, *Susanna's Apology Against The Elders* (May).

50. *Clarke Papers*, iv. 24-5 (news-letter to Monck); Guizot, i. 437; *Nicholas Papers*, iv. 167-8, 171; SP 77/32/270 (Nicholas to de Marces); *Clare College Letters*, 37 (Tillotson to Dillingham); *A Secret Word to the Wise* (13 June); *The Unhappy Marksman* (13 June); *A Friendly Letter of Advice to the Soldiers* (1 Aug.); *The Armie Mastered* (20 June); *The Sentinels Remonstrance* (8 June); *Twenty-four Quæries* (2 June); *Articles of High Crimes exhibited against Lt. Col. Tho. Kelsey* (28 July); Ludlow, 676-7.

51. For the details of the next two paragraphs, I have been unable to better either the sources or the interpretation of Underdown, *Royalist Conspiracy*, 235-48. The principal material is in CSP, the Clarendon and Carte MSS, and in M. Coate (ed.), *The Letter-Book of John, Viscount Mordaunt*, Camden Soc. 3rd ser. lxix (1945).

52. CSP iii. 502-4, 520 (Barwick to Hyde, and reply); Evelyn, 229; Worcester College, Oxford, Clarke MS liv, endpiece (Allestree's memoir).

53. Underdown, 239-54; CSP iii. 459-90 (Broderick, Mordaunt, to Hyde); Bod. L. Rawlinson MSS A259, pp. 1-20, and C179, pp. 5-11, 160, 224-57; Mordaunt's Letter-Book, 11-33; SP 25/98, pp. 48-92 (letters from Council).

54. This is one of the best-studied episodes of the period: R. Petty, 'The Rebellion of Sir George Booth', *JCNWAAHS* N.S. xxxiii (1939), 119-37; J. Jones, 'Booth's Rising of 1659', *BJRL* xxxix (1956-7), 416-43; N. Tucker, 'Richard Wynn and the Booth Rebellion', *Trans. Caernarfonshire Hist. Soc.* 20 (1959), 46-64; R. Dore, 'The Cheshire Rising of 1659', *Trans. Lancashire and Cheshire Antiquarian Soc.* lxix (1959), 43-69; Johnson, 'Chester', 343-9; Morrill, *Cheshire*, 300-24.

55. CJ 744-54, 760; Rawlinson MS C179, pp. 251-2, 262, 285-8; Guizot, i. 449; *Nicholas Papers*, iv. 178.

56. Underdown, 276-81; *Mercurius Politicus* (25 Aug.-1 Sept.) (bulletin from Leicester) and (8-15 Sept.) (address of Leicestershire ministers); Samuel Palmer, *The Nonconformist's Memorial* (1802-3), ii. 417; Bod. L. Clarendon MS 63, ff. 193 (Slingsby to Hyde) and 243 ('extract from a letter'); *Nicholas Papers*, iv. 171; *CSPV* xxxii. 57; Friends' House L. Barclay MS 169 (Howgill to Burroughs).

57. Martindale's Life, 136.

58. Sources as at n. 159.

59. Underdown, 288-92; CSP iii. 548 (Mordaunt to King), 570, 613-15 (Hyde to Barwick, and reply); SP 77/32/299-308 (Hyde, Nicholas, to Marces), /309 (Nicholas to Ormonde); Evelyn, *An Apology for the Royal Party* (4 Nov.); SP 25/98, pp. 193-5 (Council to militia).

60. CJ 666; Firth and Rait, *Acts and Ordinances*, ii. 1277-82 (act for Navy Commission); *Clarke Papers*, iii. 279-80 (Mountagu to Speaker), 296-8 (Mountagu to Richard); SP 78/114/273 (letter from London) and 25/79, pp. 546-7 (Council minutes); R. C. Latham and W. Matthews (eds.), *The Diary of Samuel Pepys*, i. 141; Bod. L. Clarendon MS 61, f. 303 (King to Mountagu), Carte MS 73, f. 284 (Mountagu to steward) and 30, ff. 464-6 (Hyde to Ormonde), Tanner MS 51, f. 98 (commissioners to Speaker). The biography of Mountagu is F. R. Harris, *The Life of Edward Mountagu, K.G., First Earl of Sandwich* (1912). Vol. i, ch. iv deals with this period.

61. CJ 765-80, 787-8; Firth and Rait, *Acts and Ordinances*, ii. 1347 (Sequestration Act); CCC 745-57, 3246-52; SP 25/79, pp. 519-616 (Council minutes); Johnson, 'Chester', 349; Corporation of London RO, Journal 41, f. 208; Clarendon MS 65, ff. 51 (Rumbold to Hyde), 166-7 (Moore to Hyde). Ludlow's assertion, pp. 695 6, that Fleetwood asked the House to make Lambert a general, is not endorsed by any contemporary record. Professor Davies's belief that the MPs

showed mercy in not trying Booth immediately seems mistaken: they were busy collecting evidence for a set of trials.

62. CJ 744-5; Salisbury CA, Ledge D ff. 115-16; VCH Wiltshire, v. 155-6; Jones, thesis, 195; Howell, *Newcastle*, 210; John T. Evans, *Seventeenth-Century Norwich* (Oxford, 1979), 221-2; East Suffolk RO, C6/1/6, p. 234 (Ipswich Assembly Book); CJ 721 (City petition). Despite the excellence of its records, there is no proper study of Salisbury's politics in the period.

63. Bod. L. Clarendon MSS 63, ff. 243-4 (Moore to Hyde), 330 ('London 19 Aug.'), 64, ff. 153-4 (Wright's examination), 190-1 (Woollmer to Council), Carte MS 213, f. 301 ('Political advices'); *CCC* 749 (Window's deposition); *Mercurius Politicus* (18-25 Aug.) (Taunton bulletin); Guizot, i. 467; Friends' House L. Barclay MS 169 (Howgill to Burroughs).

64. Martindale's Life, 131-41; Newcome's Autobiography, 109-13; *Reliquiae Baxterianae*, part ii, 180-1, 206-14; Johnston's Diary,134-5; Josselin's Diary, 130; *An Account of the Life and Death of Mr. Philip Henry* (1699), 42-3; Friends' House L. Barclay MS 73 (Adam to Fox) and Howard MS 8 (Hubberthorne to Fox); *Questions propounded to George Whitehead and George Fox . . . the 29th August*.

65. J(ohn) M(ilton), *Considerations touching the likeliest means . . . to remove Hirelings* (Aug.); Samuel Fisher, *To The Parliament of England* (10 Aug.); *A Few Proposals offered to the Parliament* (20 Aug.); William Gery, *Proposals for Reformation of Abuses* (28 Aug.); Henry Stubbe, *An Essay in Defence of the Good Old Cause* (Sept.); *England's Settlement* (12 Sept.); (William Sprigge), *A Modest Plea for an Equal Commonwealth* (28 Sept.); George Bishop, *Mene Tekel* (29 Sept.); *Public Intelligencer* (3-10 Oct.) (Warwickshire petition); Edward Burroughs, *To the Parliament of the Commonwealth* (16 Oct.).

66. Capp, *Fifth Monarchy Men*, 126, lists the examples.

67. Guizot, i. 474-5.

68. *A Parallel of the Spirit of the People* (?Aug.); *Politicaster* (Aug.); *Aphorisms Political* (29 Aug.); *A Model of a Democratical Government* (31 Aug.).

69. SP 30/24/22/14 (financial figures); Reece, 213, 216, App. 1, where the army is estimated to have increased from *c*.14,000 to *c*.22,000 men.

70. Bod. L. MS Dep. c. 159, ff. 73-7 (three letters from commissioners to Speaker); Bod. L. Walker MS c 11, inverted, ff. 151-40 (Leicestershire minutes).

71. Guizot, i. 467.

72. SP 25/79, pp. 520, 524-44, 590-8 (Council orders for payment); Bod. L. Carte MS 213, ff. 273-4 (Page to Ossory).

73. HMC 13th Report, iv. 234 (Rye corporation to MPs, and reply).

74. CJ 762, 770-8.

75. Ibid. 722, 744, 758, 760, 766, 775; Friends' House L. Spence MS 3, f. 59 (Fell jun. to Fell); Nedham, *Interest Will Not Lie* (17 Aug.).

76. CJ 747, 752, 769, 771, 774; Guizot, i. 478; Johnston's Diary, 134-5; *CSPD*, 207 (Nicholas to Ormonde); Carte MS 213, f. 301 ('Political advices').

77. CJ 775, 790-1; Guizot, i. 474-5; Annotated copy of *A Model of a Democratical*

Government, in Bod. L. Wood C. 13. 6. Linc. (38); Carte MS 213, ff. 364-5 (Mordaunt to King); Johnston's Diary, 138-9.

78. SP 77/32/302 (Nicholas to Marces); Guizot, i. 467; *CSPV*,xxxii.70, 74.

79. *The Army's Proposals To The Parliament* (Sept.); Baker, *Chronicle*, 676; Ludlow, 698; *Clarke Papers*, iv. 57-8 (Derby meeting to Monck),58 (G. M[abbott] to Monck).

80. CJ 784-6; Ludlow, 705; Whitelocke's *Memorials*, iv. 361; Baker, *Chronicle*, 676-8; Guizot, i. 482-4; *Clarke Papers*, iv. 56-7 (G. M[abbott] to Monck). Ludlow's charge that Fleetwood deliberately betrayed the document to Hesilrige is not, again, substantiated in the contemporary records.

81. CJ 789-90; *CSPV* xxxii. 70; Johnston's Diary, 138; Mordaunt's Letter-Book, 49; Carte MS 213, f. 365 (Mordaunt to King).

82. *The Humble Representation and Petition of the Officers . . . the 5th of October*; Johnston's Diary, 139-40; Guizot, i. 496-8; Baker, *Chronicle*, 678-9.

83. CJ 791-6; Johnston's Diary, 143-4; Thurloe, vii. 755 (the officers' letter); Ludlow, 721; Baker, *Chronicle*, 681-2.

84. *Clarke Papers*, iv. 60-1 (M[abbott] to Monck); CSP 581 (Slingsby to Hyde); Bod. L. Clarendon MS 65, ff. 60-1 ('Thomlinson' to Hyde), Carte MS 73, f. 319 (Lloyd to Mountagu); HMC 3rd Report, 88 (Champion to Potter); SP 25/79, pp. 664-5 (order of the Council of State); Ludlow, 722-6. Johnston's contemporary diary, 144, is to be preferred to Whitelocke's retrospective (and self-justificatory *Memorials*, iv. 365, where they conflict.

85. *Clarke Papers*, iv. 61-3 (M[abbot] to Monck), 63-4 (Fleetwood to Monck), 67 (officers to Monck); Johnston's Diary, 145-7; SP 25/79, pp. 668-83 (Council of State); Guizot, ii. 267-8; John Redmayne, *A True Narrative of the Proceedings in Parliament . . .* (16 Nov.), 21; Clarendon MS 65, f. 257 (Nieuport to Dutch government); Ludlow, 710-11, 727.

86. Johnston's Diary, 147-9; Ludlow, 714; *CSPD*, 255-7 (Council of State); *Clarke Papers*, iv. 67-8 (General Council to Monck); Guizot, ii. 272-3; *Mercurius Politicus* (20-7 Oct.); *A Particular Advice from the Office of Intelligence* (14-21 Oct.).

Notes to Part Two: Chapter 3

1. The most recent biography is Maurice Ashley, *General Monck* (1977). Like so many political biographies, this tends to be more illuminating upon the subject's early life and private life than upon his role in the national events for which he is chiefly remembered.

2. Thurloe, vii. 387-8.

3. Bod. L. Tanner MS 51, f. 72 (Monck to Speaker); Guizot, i. 413; CJ 680; *Clarke Papers*, iv. 22-3 (Monck to Speaker).

4. Dow, thesis, 616-17, and *Scotland*, 243-5.

5. Baker, *Chronicle*, 673 (King to Monck, and Grenville), 675; Mordaunt's Letter-Book, 59 (Barwick to King); CSP iii. 618 (Grenville to Hyde); Thomas Gumble, *The Life of General Monck* (1671), 103-9; John Price, *The Mystery and Method of His Majesties Happy Restauration* (1680), 12-31.

6. Dow, *Scotland*, 246-7.

7. Johnston's Diary, 138; Baker, *Chronicle*, 675 (clearly fraudulent); Gumble, 110-11.

8. *Clarke Papers*, iv. 58-9 (Monck to Scottish officers); Baker, *Chronicle*, 678, 682; CJ 795.

9. Baker, *Chronicle*, 685; *A Letter From a person of quality in Edinburgh* (25 Oct.); *Clarke Papers*, iv. 64-6 (Monck's order book); *Old Parliamentary History*, xxii. 4-7 (Monck to Fleetwood, Lambert, Speaker).

10. Respectively, Clarges (in Baker, *Chronicle*), Gumble, Price, and Maurice Ashley.

11. Price, *Mystery and Method*.

12. Professor Davies and (very elegantly) Professor Woolrych.

13. To which Mordaunt refers: Letter-Book, 82 (to King).

14. Reay, 'The Quakers, 1659', 210.

15. John Nicoll, *A Diary of Public Transactions* (Edinburgh, 1836), 250.

16. Price, *Mystery and Method*, 31-2.

17. Letter-Book, 65 (to King).

18. *Clarke Papers*, iv. 151-4, 227-8 (Monck to Owen, to Irish army).

19. Ibid. iv. 70-4, 77-8 (Fleetwood, Lambert, to Monck).

20. Baker, *Chronicle*, 685, 689.

21. *A Declaration of the General Council* . . . (27 Oct.); Steele, *Proclamations*, ii, no. 3133; *Mercurius Politicus* (two issues, 20 Oct.-3 Nov.); *A Particular Advice* (28 Oct.-4 Nov.); Clarendon MS 66, ff. 80-1, 143 ('Collins', 'M. F.', to Hyde); Mordaunt's Letter-Book, 80-1 (to Schomberg, Lady Mordaunt); Rawlinson MS A259, p. 138; Whitelocke, *Memorials*, iv. 369.

22. *A Declaration of the General Council*; *The Armies Vindication of this last change* (1659); *A Declaration of the Proceedings of the Parliament and Armie* (17 Oct.); *Considerations Upon the late transactions and proceedings of the Armie* (20 Oct.); *The Armies Plea* (24 Oct.); Redmayne, *A True Narrative*.

23. The Committee's warrants from 3 Nov. to 20 Dec. are in Bod. L. Rawlinson MS A259, recording a total of nine signatures. From other sources it is clear that Vane and Salway sometimes attended also.

24. Ludlow, 729-33, 744-5; Whitelock, *Memorials*, iv. 367-8; Johnston's Diary, 149-50.

25. *CSPV*, 86; Mordaunt's Letter-Book, 76, 82 (to Lunsford, King).

26. CSP, 591 (Slingsby to Hyde); Clarendon MS 66, ff. 74-5 ('Bramble'), 78-9 (Moore to Hyde), 84-6 (two anonymous letters).

27. Guizot, ii. 272; Mordaunt's Letter-Book, 76-7 (to King).

28. Johnston's Diary, 150-3; Guizot, 284; Barclay (ed.), *Letters*, 71-3 (Hubberthorne to Fell).

29. Rawlinson MS A259, p. 143; Whitelocke, iv. 373-6; Johnston's Diary, 153; Clarendon MS 66, ff. 78-9 (Moore to Hyde); R. G. Howarth (ed.), *Letters and the Second Diary of Samuel Pepys* (1932), 14-15 (Pepys to Mountagu); Black, thesis, 235-7.

30. *Clarke Papers*, 65-6 (Monck's order book), 83-4 (Berwick citizens to Monck); Baker, *Chronicle*, 687-8; *Public Intelligencer* (7-14 Nov.).

31. A. Woolrych, 'Yorkshire and the Restoration', *Yorkshire Archaeological J* 39 (1956-8), 483; HMC Leybourne-Popham MSS, 126-8 (Scrope, Robinson, to Monck).

32. Dow, *Scotland*, 253.

33. *Clarke Papers*, iv. 91-5 (two anonymous letters), 96-8 (council of war), 105-7 (Monck to Fleetwood, Lambert), 103-4, 109-10 (two reports from Monck's commissioners).

34. Ibid. 108-9 (order book); Baker, *Chronicle*, 691; Gumble, 140-1; Dow, *Scotland*, 248-53.

35. *Mercurius Britanicus*; *The Faithful Intelligencer*; Worcester College L, Oxford, *A Conference between two Souldiers* (Nov.) and *Information from some souldiers . . .* (?Nov.).

36. Woolrych, 'Yorkshire', 487-8.

37. Baker, *Chronicle*, 693.

38. Ibid. 693-4; Gumble, 151-5; *Clarke Papers*, iv. 113-15, 120-1 (three letters between Monck and gentry), 116-17 (three letters from commissioners to Monck), 117-18 (Fleetwood to Lambert), 124-5 (Lambert to Monck), 155 (Southwall to Paddon); *Public Intelligencer* (22-8 Nov.) (Newcastle bulletin).

39. *The Advice or Remonstrance of several thousands . . .* (2 Nov.).

40. *The Humble and Healing Advice of Colonel Robert Overton* (Nov.); CSPD, 293 (Grime to Hesilrige); J. Mayer (ed.), 'Inedited Letters', *Trans. Lancashire and Cheshire Hist. Soc.* N.S. 1 (1860-1), 262-73 (letters from Irish army leaders).

41. HMC 9th Report, ii. 493-4 (letter from Pyne); Doctor Williams's L, Baxter Letters 4, f. 274 (Allen to Baxter); Woolrych's introduction to *Milton*, vii. 322-34 ('A Letter to a Friend'); Fox's Journal, 358; Capp, *Fifth Monarchy Men*, 127-8.

42. Chapman sold Overton's pamphlet, while Canne wrote *The Acts and Monuments of our late Parliament* (19 Oct.) and a *Continuation* of the same (?Oct.) and printed *Complaints and Quæries upon England's Miserie* (20 Oct.), all pleas for the Parliament, but later wrote *Magna Charta* (7 Dec.), which called for unity behind a reform programme.

43. *Clarke Papers*, iv. 81-2 (ministers to Monck), 118-19 (anonymous letter), 121-4 (Owen to Monck); B. E. Howells (ed.), *A Calendar of Letters Relating to North Wales* (Cardiff, 1967), 110 (orders of militia commission).

44. Durham CL, Hunter MS 7, f. 36.

45. Prynne, *A short, legal, medicinal, useful, safe, easy Prescription . . .* (31 Oct.) and *A Brief Necessary Vindication* (7 Nov.); *A Gagg for the Quakers* (3 Nov.); Thomas Underhill, *Hell Broke Loose* (13 Nov.).

46. Reay, 'The Quakers, 1659', 209; Besse, *Sufferings*, i. 566; Somerset RO DD/SFR/8/1, pp. 29-30.

47. CCC 758-72, 3246-55, which seems to summarise the material in the PRO better than for the Civil War period. For victims' views, see *Wynn Papers*, 353 (five letters on subject) and Newcome's Autobiography, 116-17. Some property was actually granted away to government supporters see *Nicholas Papers*, iv. 206-7 (Mompesson to Nicholas).

48. Dumble, thesis, 306-11.
49. *An Alarum to Corporations* (1659); Johnson, 'Wales', 254.
50. Fox's Journal, 358; E. Peacock (ed.), *The Monckton Papers* (1884), 29 (Monckton's narrative); *Wynn Papers*, 354 (Mostyn to Wynn).
51. *Memoirs of Colonel Hutchinson*, 309-10.
52. V. Pearl, 'London's Counter-Revolution', in Aylmer (ed.), *The Interregnum*; P. S. Seaver, *The Puritan Lectureships* (Stanford, 1970), 277-80. The narratives of Gardiner and Firth trace the corporation's reactions to events during the Interregnum.
53. Ashley, *Financial and Commercial Policy*, ch. xiv; William R. Scott, *The Constitution and Finance of English, Scottish and Irish Joint-Stock Companies to 1720* (New York, 1951), i. 261-2; Norfolk RO, Norwich Mayor's Court Book 23, f. 110ᵛ.
54. S. R. Smith, 'Almost Revolutionaries: the London Apprentices during the Civil Wars', *HLQ* 42 (1978-9), 313-28.
55. *A Narrative of the Proceedings of the Committee of the Militia of London* (Nov.); *Clarke Papers*, 101-3 (anonymous letter); Guizot, 285; Corporation of London RO, Repertory 66, f. 330ᵛ; W. L. Sachse (ed.), *The Diurnal of Thomas Rugge*, Camden Soc. 3rd ser. xci (1961), 10-11.
56. *Old Parliamentary History*, xxii. 10-17 (the speeches); CSP iii. 601-2 (Phelips to Hyde); Johnston's Diary, 152; Guizot, ii. 285.
57. *CSPD*, 268 (Nicholas to Ormonde); Guizot, ii. 290; Rugge's *Diurnal*, 9-10; *Mercurius Politicus* (10-17 Nov.); Clarendon MS 66, ff. 303-4 (Moore to Hyde).
58. Haley, *Shaftesbury*, 113-16. There is no evidence that the dissident officers were ever court-martialled; they seem to have withdrawn voluntarily after suspension. Their names are appended to *The Humble Representation of some officers of the army* (1 Nov.), those of the nine members of the Council of State who opposed the Committee of Safety to their letter to Monck in *Clarke Papers*, iv. 137-9.
59. *A Parliamenter's Petition to the Armie* (1659); *Complaints and Quæries upon England's Miserie* (text dated 20 Oct.); *The Parliament's Plea* (25 Oct.); *The Declaration of the Officers of the Armie opened, examined and condemned . . .* (27 Oct.); *Twelve Seasonable Quæries* (1 Nov.); *The Humble Representation of some officers of the armie* (1 Nov.); *The Northern Quæries* (7 Nov.); *Hypocrites Unmasked* (8 Nov.); *The Armies Declaration examined and compared . . .* (8 Nov.); *The Form of the New Commissions* (8 Nov.); *A Seasonable Enquiry* (12 Nov.); *Decrees and Orders of the Committee of Safety* (12 Nov.); Bod. L. Rawlinson MS A259, pp. 145-6; Rugge's *Diurnal*, 11-12.
60. Bod. L. Tanner MS 51, f. 161 (Berners to Hobart).
61. Clarendon MS 67, f. 42 (Phelips to Hyde).
62. Ibid., ff. 34-5 (Slingsby to Hyde); *A Letter from Sir Arthur Hesilrige in Portsmouth . . .* (1659); W. D. Christie, *A Life of Sir Anthony Ashley Cooper* (1871), i. 196.
63. CSP, iii.619, 624-5 (Slingsby, Moore, to Hyde); *Clarke Papers*, 134-7 (commissioners to Monck); Guizot, ii. 296.
64. CSP, iii. 626 (Willoughby to Hyde); *Clarke Papers*, 164-7 (two anonymous letters); Guizot, ii.299-301; Rugge's *Diurnal*, 13-15; Corporation of London RO, Journal 41, f. 212; Steele, *Proclamations*, no. 3137; *To . . . the Lord Mayor, Aldermen*

and Commonalty . . . the most humble Petition and Address of divers young men (5 Dec.);
Pepys's Letters, 14-15, 17 (to Mountagu); Clarendon MS 67, f. 119 ('London' 2
Dec.); Baker, *Chronicle*, 697 (Clarges to Monck).

65. *Clarke Papers*, 126-79 (sixteen letters between Monck's army and their opponents); Gumble,177-9.

66. Clarendon MS 67, ff. 185 ('Harrison'), 270-1 ('R' to'Peter's Master'), 208 ('J. V.' to
'Jones'), 270-1 (Rumbold to King); Whitelocke, *Memorials*, iv. 378-9; *Clarke
Papers*, 186-7, 194 (anonymous letters); Guizot, ii. 304-8; *Rugge's Diurnal*,
16-17; Johnston's Diary, 155-9; *A Particular Advice from the Office of Intelligence*
(9-16 Dec.); Corporation of London RO, Repertory 66, ff. 22-3; Steele, no. 3139;
Nicholas Papers, iv. 190 (Whitley to Nicholas); *A Declaration of several of the People
called Anabaptists . . .* (12 Dec.); *The Loyal Scout* (9-16 Dec.); Clarke MS 32, f. 175ᵛ
(list of Conservators).

67. *Two Letters from Vice-Admiral John Lawson* (1659); M. H., *A Narrative of the
Proceedings of the Fleet* (1659); *CSPD*, 268 (Nicholas to Ormonde); CSP, iii. 629-30
(Broderick to Hyde); Clarendon MS 67, ff. 270-1 (Rumbold to King); Guizot, 311.

68. CSP, iii. 630-1 (Barwick to Hyde); Clarendon MS 67, ff. 246-7 (Rumbold to
King), 250-1 ('Graves'); Pepys's Letters, 18 (to Mountagu); *Rugge's Diurnal*,
17-19; Corporation of London RO, Repertory 66, f. 27, Journal 41, f. 213;
Nicholas Papers, 191-2 (Whitley to Nicholas).

69. Guizot, ii. 315-16, 318; *At a Common Council holden . . . on Tuesday the 20th of
December*; CSP, 631 (Broderick to Hyde); Johnston's Diary, 159; Steele, no. 3141;
Clarke Papers, 210, 215-17 (three anonymous letters). Whitelocke's narrative,
Memorials iv. 381-3, is not confirmed by any other source, and has an air of post-
Restoration self-exculpation about it.

70. Broderick, CSP, iii. 629-30.

71. *Public Intelligencer* (19-26 Dec.); *Weekly Post* (21-7 Dec.); CSP, iii. 634-5, 637
(Broderick to Hyde); Whitelocke, iv. 383; *Clarke Papers*, iv. 219-20 (news-letter);
Guizot, ii. 318-19.

72. *A Letter Sent from Colonel John Disbrowe* (29 Dec.).

73. HMC 11th Report, iii. 31 (Corporation to Hesilrige).

74. J. Washbourne (ed.), *Bibliotheca Gloucestrensis* (Gloucester, 1825), 429-32 (three
letters between corporation and Committee of Safety); Gloucestershire RO,
GBR/B3/3, pp. 117-21; Bristol RO, 04264 (6), p. 5; *Weekly Post* (21-7 Dec.)
(Exeter bulletin); Clarendon MS 68, ff. 167-8 (Barwick's letter).

75. Bod. L. MS Dep. c 159, ff. 87-101 (letters from Coventry, Bristol, Lyme, Stafford,
Exeter, Chester); *A Letter . . . concerning the securing of Windsor Castle* (28 Dec.);
Devon RO, Exeter Act Book 10, f.127; SP18/219/9, 11 (letters from Gloucester,
Windsor); Clarendon MS 68, ff. 107-8 (Rumbold to King); *Parliamentary Intelli-
gencer* (2-9 Jan.) (letters from Truro, King's Lynn, Hereford, Gloucester); *Weekly
Post* (3-10 Jan.) (letters from Leicester, Plymouth); *Mercurius Publicus* (12-19 Jan.)
(letter from Hereford); *Clarke Papers*, iv. 216-17 (MPs to Lytcott).

76. Bod. L. MS Dep. c 159, ff. 87, 105 (letters from Worcester, Coventry); Mordaunt's
Letter-Book, 145 (Baron to Mordaunt); SP 18/219/8 (Collins to Army

Commission), 219/10 (Burton to Hesilrige), 25/99, p. 2 (Council to Norris); Clarendon MS 68, ff. 107-8, as above; *Mercurius Publicus* (5-12 Jan.) (address of Dorset militia).

77. Guizot, ii. 318-19; *A Letter sent from Col. Will. Lockhart* (31 Dec.); Mayer (ed.), 'Inedited Letters', 278-91; Portland MSS, i. 688-9 (Irish officers to Speaker); John Bridges, Edward and Abel Warren, *A Perfect Narrative of the . . . securing of the Castle of Dublin* (1660); Barnard, *Ireland*, 133; Davies, *Restoration*, 248-9.

78. *Clarke Papers*, iv. 182-231, *passim*; HMC 7th Report, 461 (Burgoyne to Verney); Bod. L. MS Dep. c 159, f. 91 (Salmon to Currer); *Mercurius Publicus* (29 Dec. to 5 Jan.) (letter from Newcastle); Worcester College, Clarke MS 32, ff. 200ᵛ, 210 (news-letters); Peacock (ed.), *Monckton Papers*, 27-9; Woolrych, 'Yorkshire', 490-8.

79. The records for Monck's army and for Fairfax's conspiracy are consistently fuller than those for Lambert's forces. It remains unclear, for example, precisely how badly paid the latter were. All sources agree that they were badly in want, and Captain Hodgson remembered later that when he offered his services to Lambert, the general suggested that he would be most usefully employed in finding money. Yet he also recalls that he was paid £24 for himself and his men at Newcastle on 10 December: J. Horsfall Turner (ed.), *Memoirs of Captain John Hodgson* (Brighouse, 1882), 49-50. The extant sources for the end of this campaign are Guizot, ii. 327; *Clarke Papers*, iv. 223 (Speaker to Monck), 238-9 (reply), 238 (news-letter), 243 (Monck to Overton); Pepys's Diary, i. 7-8; Bod. L. MS Dep. c 159, ff. 103-9 (Wise, Carlisle garrison, Tynemouth garrison to Speaker); CJ vii. 804; Clarke MS 32, ff. 218-27ᵛ (journal of Monck's march); Brit. L. Add. MS 21425, f. 190 (Robert to Adam Baynes); SP18/219/2 (Chamberlain to Army Commission), /5 (Lilburne to Hesilrige). Given the military situation, there seems no reason to attach any political significance to Monck's initial advance into England.

80. Whitelocke, *Memorials*, iv. 385.

Part Two: Chapter 4

1. CJ 802-15; Ludlow, 814, 817; Whitelocke, iv. 384-5; Clarendon MS 68, ff. 100-1, 146 (Broderick, Morland to Hyde); Guizot, ii. 331.
2. Reece, thesis, 266-8.
3. CJ 804; *Clarke Papers*, iv. 240-1, 247-8 (Speaker to Monck, and reply).
4. CJ 805, 812, 827; CCC 772-5, 3246-55.
5. *Clarke Papers*, iv. 137-9 (Council to Monck); CJ 800-28.
6. Barclay (ed.), *Letters*, 75-9 (Billings to W. M.).
7. Reece, 268-9; CJ 805.
8. CJ 819.
9. Guizot, ii. 323; *Clarke Papers*, iv. 247-8 (Monck to Speaker); Clarendon MS 68, f. 181 (Rumbold to Hyde); HMC Leybourne-Popham MSS, 139 (Monck to Newcastle corporation, and reply).
10. J. G. Muddiman, *The King's Journalist* (1923), 84-92; Black, thesis, 239-40.

11. Dow, *Scotland*, 253-7; Barnard, *Ireland*, 133.
12. *Old Parliamentary History*, xxii. 58-62; *A Declaration of some of those people in or near London, called Anabaptists* (14 Jan.); *Anti-Quakerism* (5 Jan.); William Brownsword, *The Quaker-Jesuite* (5 Jan.); *The Quaker Disarm'd* (Jan.); John Norton, *The Heart of New England Rent* (Jan.); Thomas Danson, *The Quakers Folly* (Jan.); *The Dippers Dipp'd* (4th ed., Jan.); *Hell, with the Everlasting Torments, Asserted* (Jan.); Friends' House L, *A Journal of the Life of . . . William Caton* (1689), 57; Wood's *Life*, i. 302.
13. CJ 803-6, 826-33; Clarendon MS 68, ff. 167, 204-5 (Cooper, Rumbold, to Hyde); CSP, iii. 650 (Mordaunt to King); Guizot, 329, 331; *Memoirs of Colonel Hutchinson*, 312-14. On Morley, see Fletcher, *Sussex*, 318-19.
14. Royalists placed more stress on the latter: Clarendon MS 67, ff.250-1 ('Graves').
15. Corporation of London RO, Journal 41, ff. 216-17; Prynne, *A Brief Narrative* (26 Dec.); *Six Important Quæries* (30 Dec.), *Seven Additional Quæries* (4 Jan.), *The Privileges of Parliament* (5 Jan.), *The Case of the Old Secured, Secluded and now Exalted Members* (13 Jan.); *A Full Declaration* (30 Jan.); Guizot, ii. 320, 323-4.
16. Corporation of London RO, Journal 41, f. 218; CJ 802; Rugge's *Diurnal*, 25-9; Clarendon MS 68, ff. 100-1 (Broderick to Hyde); CSP, iii. 639, 644-6 (Rumbold, Broderick, to Hyde).
17. Nicholas, iv. 135 ('Miles' to Nicholas).
18. Seven such verses are in the Thomason collection between 31 Dec. and 26 Jan.
19. *Wynn Papers*, 354.
20. There are several references to the irregulars in *CSPD* 1659-60, 300-21 (orders and letters of Council of State).
21. Firth and Rait, *Acts and Ordinances*, ii. 1355-1403; Johnson, 'Wales', 254 and M.A. thesis, 315-16; Silcock, thesis, 296.
22. Reece, 224.
23. *Mercurius Publicus* (19-26 Jan.) (letter from Gloucester); Underdown, *Somerset*, 191-2.
24. HMC Portland MSS, i. 690 (Stephens to Speaker).
25. Clarendon MS 68, f. 175 (Wood to Hyde); *Mercurius Publicus* (19-26 Jan.) (letter from Cardiff); Friends' House L, Swarthmore MS 4, f. 219 (Gowler to Fox).
26. Coate, *Cornwall*, 307-8; *A Letter from Exeter* (14 Jan.); *Mercurius Publicus* (2 issues, 5-19 Jan.); Everitt, *Kent*, 306-8; HMC Buccleugh MSS, i. 311-12 (Exeter to Montagu); G. Davies, 'The Political Career of Sir Richard Temple', *HLQ* 4 (1940-1), 50; Clarendon MS 69, ff. 20-1, 33-4 (Barwick to Hyde); George Kitchin, *Sir Roger L'Estrange* (1913), 52-3.
27. Price, *Mystery and Method*, 80-90; *Records of the Borough of Leicester*, iv. 458-9; St. Albans Public L, Corporation Document 183 (mayor's accounts); Worcester College L, Clarke MS 32, ff. 218ᵛ-41 (journal of March).
28. Baker, *Chronicle*, 701; *Clarke Papers*, iv. 247-8 (Monck to Speaker).
29. Ludlow, 810.
30. HMC Leybourne-Popham MSS, 206-7 (Collins's narrative); Gumble, 214-16.
31. Pepys's *Diary*, i. 22; CSP, iii. 644-52 (Broderick, Mordaunt, Barwick, to Hyde).

32. These are preserved in the Thomason Tracts and SP 18/219/28-30, 37-41, or noticed in HMC Portland MSS, iii. 217 (Conway to Harley) and the Revd John Ticknell, *The History of . . . Kingston-upon-Hull* (1796), 507. Two more, which are undated and difficult to date, are in Brit. L. Stowe MS 185, ff. 148-50. The only one which seems to survive with some signatures is the Norfolk RO copy of *A Letter and Declaration of the Gentry of the County of Norfolk*, examined by Evans, *Norwich*, 223-5. There survive 794 names, but it seems very likely that some sheets have been lost, and possible, given the very large number of Norwich men, that it was the copy signed in and around the city while others were canvassed elsewhere. Certainly a real cross-section of society is represented, mixing gentry, urban magnates, ministers, freemen and freeholders, and perhaps men from other groups also.

33. Clarendon MSS 68, ff. 204-5, 69, ff. 33-4 (Rumbold, Barwick, to Hyde); Leybourne-Popham MSS, 208-9; *Clarke Papers*, iv. 249-50 (Monck to St. John); *Mercurius Publicus* (26 Jan.-2 Feb.) (letter from Dunstable).

34. *Old Parliamentary History*, xxii. 68-70. For reactions, see Mordaunt's Letter-Book, 180 (Current to Lady Mordaunt), and HMC 5th Report, 153 (Newport to Leveson).

35. Baker, *Chronicle*, 701-2; Leybourne-Popham MSS, 209-11, Ludlow, 814-15.

36. Pepys's Diary, i. 36-40; CJ 827; Ludlow, 818-19; SP 25/92, p. 46 (Monck to Council); T. H. Lister, *The Life and Administration of Edward, First Earl of Clarendon* (1837), iii. 83-4 (Wood to Hyde), 667 (Mordaunt to King); Leybourne-Popham MSS, 144-5 (Watkins to cousin); *Public Intelligencer* (30 Jan.-6 Feb.); Staffordshire RO, D868/5/508 (Thomas to John Langley).

37. Pepys, i. 44; Besse, *Sufferings*, i. 366; Barclay (ed.), *Letters*, 73-4 (Fell to sister), 75-9 (Billings to W. M.).

38. Baker, *Chronicle*, 704-6; Ludlow, 821-2, Whitelocke, *Memorials*, iv. 393-4.

39. Baker, *Chronicle*, 701-3; CSP, iii. 667 (Mordaunt to King); Leybourne-Popham MSS, 209-10, 213.

40. Pepys's Diary, i. 44.

41. Guizot, ii. 345-6.

42. Leybourne-Popham MSS, 145 (Watkins to friend); *Mercurius Publicus* (2-9 Feb.); Whitelocke, *Memorials*, iv. 394.

43. These are in the Thomason collection, Bod. L. Wood 276a, and Cornwall RO, DD/T/1762, or noticed in Rugge's *Diurnal*, 37, and *Mercurius Publicus* (2-9 Feb.). Two are undated, but from their contents seem to have been produced in the first ten days of February.

44. *CSPD*, 348-9 (letters of Council); CJ 836-8.

45. *Records of Leicester*, 459 (corporation to Monck); *Mercurius Publicus* (9-16 Feb.) (letter from Bristol); Bristol RO 04264 (6), pp. 11-12 (minute book); CJ 838; *Old Parliamentary History*, xxii. 94-7 (Barebone's petition); Pepys's Diary, i. 49.

46. SP 28/294, 334 (receivers' accounts).

47. This seems to reconcile CSP, iii. 674-5 (Barwick to Hyde); Clarendon MS 69, ff. 117-18, 126-8 (Cooper, Slingsby, Heath, to Hyde); Pepys's Diary, i. 49-52; CJ

841; Ludlow, 824-30; Baker, *Chronicle*, 706-9; Leybourne-Popham MSS, 215-20; Guizot, 345-50; Gumble, 236-50; Rugge's *Diurnal*, 39; Corporation of London RO, Repertory 67, ff. 42ᵛ-43; Christie, Life of Cooper, 207-8; *CSPV* xxxii. 118-19, Price, *Mystery and Method*, 102-3; (Roger L'Estrange), *Peace to the Nation* (14 Feb.); Brit. L. Stowe MS 185, ff. 147-9. Professor Davies's belief that the House reappointed Fleetwood Commander-in-Chief is probably a mistake derived from the repeal of the act of 6 June 1659 on 24 February.

48. Wood's Life, i. 303-4; *Mercurius Publicus* (9-16 Feb.); Rugge's *Diurnal*, 42; *CSPD*, 366 (Council to Crooke); Leybourne-Popham MSS, 153-4 (Charles Fairfax to Monck); Brit. L. Add. MS 21425, ff. 204, 208 (Robert to Adam Baynes); Aubrey, *Brief Lives*, 76.

49. *CCC*, 772-5, 3246-55; Everitt, *Kent*, 311; Leybourne-Popham MSS, 157-8 (Strode to Taunton corporation), 158 (Bovett to Monck).

50. All in Thomason tracts. For information on their origins, see *Mercurius Publicus* (9-16 Feb.) (letter from Lincoln); Leybourne-Popham MSS, 146-50 (3 letters from Yorkshire to Monck); Rugge's *Diurnal*, 40-2; Brit. L. Egerton MS 2618, f. 60 (Yorkshire gentry to Monck).

51. Leybourne-Popham MSS, 152-3 (Dublin officers to Monck); Thurloe, vii. 817-20 (Munster declaration).

52. Price, *Mystery and Method*, 103-9; CJ 842-6; Pepys's Diary, i. 55-62; Ludlow, 832-47; Baker, *Chronicle*, 709-12; *CSPD*, 358-72 (letters of Council),CSP iii. 678-9 (Monck to Hesilrige), 682 (Mordaunt to King), 688 (Wood); White-locke, 397-8; *Clarke Papers*, iv. 260-1 (Hesilrige to Monck), 261-4 (Monck to Council and Hesilrige); Leybourne-Popham MSS, 154-5 (Monck to Yorkshire gentry), 221-2 (Collins's account); Worcester College L, Clarke MS 32, f. 252ᵛ (Clarke's journal); Guizot, ii. 354-61; Gumble, 260-1; Christie's Life of Cooper, i. 211-12; Clarendon MS 69, ff. 167-8 (Howard to Hyde); *CSPV*, 121; Robert Woodrow, *The History of the Sufferings of the Church of Scotland* (Edinburgh, 1721), i. 5-6 (Sharp to Scottish clergy); *The Speech and Declaration of His Excellency the Lord General Monck* (21 Feb.).

53. Underdown, *Pride's Purge*, and Pearl, 'Oliver St John', seem to be the best authorities on this problem of identity.

54. CJ 849.

55. Payments to the ringers are common in municipal accounts, especially in the south, and occur in some of those of churchwardens.

56. Bristol RO, 04264(6), p. 14 (minute book); Leybourne-Popham MSS, 160-1 (Ellsworth to Monck); Tickell, *Hull*, 507-10.

57. Reece, thesis, 225, cites examples from Bristol, Durham, Bury St. Edmunds, Nottingham, Hereford, Yarmouth, Shrewsbury and Exeter, to which I can add Manchester (Newcome's Autobiography, 118-19). Dr Reece is surely correct in stressing the persistence of republicanism in the army in early 1660.

58. Baker, *Chronicle*, 710-11; *A Letter from General Monck and the Officers here . . .* (21 Feb.).

59. *London Apprentice's Grand Politic Informer* (27 Feb.–5 Mar.); *Public Intelligencer* (2 issues, 27 Feb.–12 Mar.).

60. CSP, iii. 693 (Broderick to Hyde); Gumble, 265; Clarendon MS 70, f. 20 (Howard to Hyde). For evidence of Ingoldsby's and Howard's royalist activities, see Mordaunt's Letter-Book, 167 ('The state of the army') and CSP, iii. 690–1 (Broderick to Hyde). Howard had been arrested on suspicion of complicity in the 1659 rising.

61. *CSPD*, 379–81 (Council to Bovett, Ceely).

62. Leybourne-Popham MSS, 160, 164–5 (Okey, Izard, Ellsworth, to Monck).

63. Baker, *Chronicle*, 712; Leybourne-Popham MSS, 157–69 (6 letters and papers concerning Rich); *Public Intelligencer* (27 Feb.–5 Mar.); HMC Portland MSS, iii. 218 (Robert to Edward Harley).

64. Baker, *Chronicle*, 713–14; CJ 865; SP 25/99, p. 229 (Council orders); Leybourne-Popham MSS, 159,163 (Charles Fairfax, Hull garrison, Overton, to Monck); *Public Intelligencer* (2 issues, 5–19 Mar.).

65. Baker, *Chronicle*, 713–14; Whitelocke, *Memorials*, iv. 403; Leybourne-Popham MSS, 156–7, 162 (lists of Lambert's supporters); Gumble, 265; HMC Portland MSS, iii. 219 (anonymous letter, 6 Mar.); CSP, iii. 698–9, 702 (Barwick to Hyde).

66. CJ 864.

67. *A Letter from Shrewsbury* (27 Feb.); *Clarke Papers*, iv. 264 (York officers to Monck); Leybourne-Popham MSS, 164–5 (Ellsworth to Monck), 165 (Tolhurst to Monck); *London Apprentice's Grand Politic Informer* (27 Feb.–5 Mar.).

68. (Henry Jessey), *The Lord's Loud Call to England* (14 Aug.), 13; Fox's Journal, 365–9; Besse, *Sufferings*, i. 742.

69. Hertfordshire RO, AH 1056–7 (Bridgewater to Halsey).

70. Rugge's *Diurnal*, 49; CSPV, 125; *A Letter sent to the Right Honourable, the Lord Mayor of the City of London by Lieutenant-Colonel Kiffin* . . . (28 Feb.); *London Apprentice's Grand Politic Informer* (27 Feb.–5 Mar.); Fox's Journal, 369; Barclay (ed.), *Letters*, 79–80 (Hubberthorne to Fell).

71. CJ 847–60; CSPV, 125, 130; Guizot, ii. 373; Rugge's *Diurnal*, 51; Corporation of London RO, Journal 41, ff. 2208-223; Pepys's Diary, i. 62.

72. Pepys, 74–7; Lister's Life of Clarendon, iii. 87–9 (Morland to Hyde); CSP, iii. 690, 693 (Dixon, Broderick, to Hyde); Bod. L. Clarendon MS 70, f. 77 (Cooper to Hyde); Guizot, ii. 372; CSPV, 125; Brit. L. Add. MS 35029, f. 7 (letter to King).

73. *The Readie and Easie Way to establish a Free Commonwealth* (3 Mar.).

74. Collected by Thomason on 10 March. Notes upon its origins appear upon the copy Bod. L. Wood 632 (42). Another republican appeal to the middle ground was *No New Parliament* (13 Mar.). Other slanders against Charles II are noted in *CSPV*, 125.

75. C. Edie, 'The Popular Idea of Monarchy on the Eve of the Stuart Restoration', *HLQ* 39 (1975–6), 344–63. Thomason collected ten royalist tracts between 21 Feb. and 16 Mar. In addition, Bod. L. Wood 276a (279) seems to be from this period.

76. These were collected in *Rats Rhymed to Death* (1660) and *Rump: or an Exact*

Collection of the Choicest Poems and Songs relating to the Late Times (1662). Twenty-one in the Thomason Tracts are dated between 21 Feb. and 16 Mar., and Bod. L. Wood 276a (269), 613 (27, 35) and 416 (50, 55, 57, 65) appear to be other examples from this time.

77. *Nicholas Papers*, iv. 198-200 (Whitley to Nicholas).
78. A. B. Worden (ed.), Edmund Ludlow, *A Voyce from the Watchtower*, Camden Soc. 4th ser. 21 (1978), 88-92; CJ 852-5; Lister's Life of Clarendon, iii. 87-9 (Morland to Hyde); *Memoirs of Colonel Hutchinson*, 314-15; Clarendon MS 70, ff. 23, 72-3 (Wood, Slingsby, to Hyde); *CSPV*, 125.
79. Buckinghamshire RO, M/11/17 (Denton to Verney, 1 Mar.).
80. CJ 854.
81. This account represents the common ground between CJ 859-67; Pepys's Diary, ii. 74-82; Baker, *Chronicle*, 716 (a badly garbled recollection); Price, *Mystery and Method*, 127-30; Lister, *Clarendon*, iii. 89-90 (Slingsby to Hyde); CSP, iii. 695-7 (Wood, Broderick, Barwick, to Hyde); Guizot, ii. 376-9; Gumble, 268-70; Rugge's *Diurnal*, 53; *CSPV*, 128-31; *Mercurius Publicus* (8-15 Mar.); *Nicholas Papers*, iv. 200-3 (Whitley to Nicholas); Buckinghamshire RO, M/11/17 (Denton to Verney, 8 Mar.); Clarendon MS 70, ff. 112-13, 122-3 (Dixon, Cooper, to Hyde); Brit. L. Add. MS 15750, f. 55 (Mowbray to Lane).
82. Firth and Rait, *Acts and Ordinances*, ii. 1425, 1459-63, 1465-9.
83. CJ 871-80; Lister, *Clarendon*, 90-1 (Morland to Hyde); Guizot, ii. 382-3; Thurloe, vii. 861 (anonymous letter); Ludlow, *A Voyce*, 98; *CSPD*, 393-4 (Downman to Nicholas). The idea of David Ogg, *England in the Reign of Charles II* (1934), i. 25-6, that Prynne saved the Act and so pushed Monck into royalism, far outruns the evidence.
84. HMC Portland MSS, iii. 218-19 (Conway to Harley).
85. Firth and Rait, *Acts and Ordinances*, ii. 1425-55. The local case-studies of its implementation are Johnson, 'Wales', 255, and M.A. thesis, 315-16; Coate, *Cornwall*, 311; Underdown, *Somerset*, 192; Morrill, *Cheshire*, 326.
86. CJ 868-80; Pepys's Diary, i. 85-9; *CSPD*, 393-4 (Downman to Nicholas); Lister's Life of Clarendon, iii. 90-1 (Morland to Hyde); Firth and Rait, *Acts and Ordinances*, ii. 1469-72; Guizot, ii. 380-1; Buckinghamshire RO, M/11/17 (letter from Sir Roger Verney, 17 Mar.); Carte MS 213, f. 667 ('political advices').
87. Pepys's Diary, i. 89; CSP iii. 700 (Broderick to Hyde); Guizot, 382; Rugge's *Diurnal*, 60; *CSPV*, 130-1; *An Exit to the Exit Tyrannus* (17 Mar.); *Newes from the Royal Exchange* (1660).
88. Underdown, *Royalist Conspiracy*, 296-304; CSP, iii. 591-673; Clarendon MSS 67, f. 66 till 69, f. 96; Mordaunt's Letter-Book, 72-180.
89. Clarendon, *History*, xvi. 137-9; CSP, iii. 674-92.
90. Mordaunt's Letter-Book, 82,95-6 (Mordaunt to King); CSP, iii.703 (Morland to King), 705, 721-2 (Slingsby, Morley, to Hyde); Arthur Collins (ed.), *Letters and Memorials of State* (1746), ii. 685-6 (Northumberland to Leicester); Pepys's Diary, i. 84, 103. The overall account of this group in this period is George R.

Abernathy, jun., *The English Presbyterians and the Stuart Restoration*, Trans. American Philosophical Soc. N.S. Part 2 (1965).

91. Mordaunt's prose style was generally as colourful as his life.
92. CSP, iii. 711-12 (Lady Mordaunt to Mordaunt), 712-14 (Lenthall to King); Clarendon MS 70, f. 175 (Lady Willoughby to Hyde).
93. Lister's Life of Clarendon, iii. 93-4 (Morland to Hyde); Clarendon MSS 70, f. 215 (Lady Willoughby to Hyde), 71, ff. 81-2 ('the whole discourse'), 107 (Barton to Hyde).
94. CJ 858; Lister's Life of Clarendon, iii. 87-91; CSP, iii. 703 (Morland to Hyde); Pepys's Diary, i. 75-7.
95. CSP, iii. 719 (King to Mountagu), 724-5 (reply); Clarendon MSS 70, f. 209, 71, ff. 101-2, 185-6 (Hatton, Braems, to Hyde); Pepys's Diary, i. 102, 110.
96. M. Coate, 'William Morice and the Restoration of Charles II', *EHR* xxxiii (1918), 367-72; Price, *Mystery and Method*, 118.
97. CSP, iii. 697 (Barwick to Hyde).
98. Baker, *Chronicle*, 717-18; Gumble, 275-8; Price, *Mystery and Method*, 133-8 and Clarendon, *History*, xvi. 165-9 agree on the details of the meeting though not upon who approached whom first. The *Chronicle* states that it took place on 18 March and that Grenville left England on the 23rd, but this is contrary to Price, Clarendon and the contemporary letters which crossed between Mordaunt and the King (CSP, iii. 706-7, 709). From these, it seems that Professor Davies was correct in postulating two meetings between 17 and 26 March. Unlike him, however, I am not convinced that Lenthall had much relevance to the matter.
99. CSP, iii. 710-11, 726-7 (Howard, Slingsby, to Hyde); Guizot, ii. 393.
100. Steele, *Proclamations*, no. 3131; CSP, iii. 529 (King to York).
101. Clarendon MS 71, ff. 362-5 is a draft declaration to this effect, apparently of this date. The reasoning is taken from Clarendon, *History*, xvi. 171-4, which may be supposed to be honest if only because of the exquisite irony of what actually happened in 1660-2.
102. The structure of events here is based on Clarendon, *History*, xvi. 171-203; Baker, *Chronicle*, 718; Price, *Mystery and Method*, 143-6; Clarendon MS 71, f. 178 (Grenville to the King). Clarendon MS 71, ff. 127-8 is a draft of the declaration, addressed to Monck, and Brit. L. Egerton MS 2542, ff. 328-9 is another with notes by Nicholas identifying the authors of the clauses.
103. e.g. Gloucestershire RO, GBR/B3/3, p. 129 (Gloucester minute book); Devon RO, Exeter Act Book 10, f. 130.
104. CSP, iii. 710-11, 715 (Howard, Robinson, to King); Clarendon MS 71, ff. 27, 83, 108-9, 156-7 (Bunce, Warwick, Barwick, Barton, to Hyde); Guizot, ii. 393, 404; *Mercurius Civicus* (19-26 Mar.); *Mercurius Publicus* (29 Mar.-5 Apr.).
105. Of these the Bod. L. preserves *Eye-Salve for the English Armie*, *The Valley of Achor* and *An Alarum to the Officers and Soldiers*.
106. Steele, no. 3174; CSP, iii. 708 (Slingsby to Hyde), 715 (Robinson to King); *Mercurius Publicus* (2 issues, 22 Mar.-5 Apr.).

107. Four such pamphlets were collected by Thomason between 3 and 23 Apr. A draft of the circular is in *Clarke Papers*, iv. 266-7.
108. Corporation of London RO, Journal 41, f. 224.
109. This follows Baker, *Chronicle*, 719, though it may be suspected that Clarges as usual plays up his own part. This account is generally compatible with, and dated by, CSP, iii. 710-11 (Howard to King); Clarendon MS 71, ff. 80, 100 (Halsall, Cooper, to Hyde); *Mercurius Publicus* (5-12 Apr.).
110. Pepys's Diary, i. 95-110; Clarendon MS 71, ff. 185-6 (Braems to Hyde); Carte MS 73, ff. 355, 399,408, 416 (letters of Lawson, Mountagu and Council); Harris, *Sandwich*, i. 176.
111. Steele, nos. 3166, 3168.
112. *CSPV* 135; *An Exact Accompt* (4 issues, 16 Mar.-13 Apr.); *Mercurius Publicus* (3 issues, 22 Mar.-12 Apr.).
113. Quoted by Rumbold to Hyde, CSP, iii. 722-3. Fears of the 'ranting royalists' are articulated by their friends in CSP, iii. 703 (Morland to King) and *Nicholas Papers*, iv. 207-8 (Nicholas to Mompesson), and by their enemies in SP 18/220/80 (Powell to Weaver).
115. HMC City of Exeter MSS, 215-16 (Council to militia commission); CSP, iii. 721 (Herne to Mordaunt); *Mercurius Publicus* (22-9 Mar.).
116. Woolrych, introduction to *Milton's Prose Works*, vii. 201-2; Griffiths, *The Fear of God and the King*; CSP, iii. 727-8 (Morley to Hyde); Clarendon MS 71, f. 174 ('TC'); *Mercurius Publicus* (29 Mar.-5 Apr.).
117. Peter Barwick, *The Life of the Reverend John Barwick* (1724), 515-27 (Hyde to Barwick).
118. Thomason collected those from Dorset, Essex, London, Hertfordshire, Shropshire and Oxfordshire between 16 and 28 Apr. Bod. L. Wood 276a (218, 220) are others from Kent and Somerset in April. The one from Worcestershire is dated 3 Mar. by Thomason, but is so similar to the others that he may have meant May. Collins, in Leybourne-Popham MSS, 228-9, insists that they were a specific response to Griffiths. They are commented upon in CSP, iii. 731 (Phelips to Hyde), but apparently in no provincial source.
119. *A Character of Charles II* (30 Apr.). Thomason collected six other tracts of this sort between 16 Mar. and this date.
120. Woolrych, introduction to *Milton*, vii. 340-88, 464-86.
121. These are studied in G. Davies, 'The General Election of 1660', *HLQ* 15 (1951-2), 211-35 and L. F. Brown, 'Religious Factors in the Convention Parliament', *EHR* xxii (1907), 52-5, to which I have added material from Everitt, *Kent*, 312-13; Fletcher, *Sussex*, 321-2; Morrill, *Cheshire*, 326; Coate, *Cornwall*, 313; Underdown, *Somerset*, 192; Silcock, thesis, 296; Holmes, *Lincolnshire*, 218; Leybourne-Popham MSS, 173 (Whetham to Monck); *Oxford Council Acts*, 255-6; HMC 11th Report, vii. 194 (Reading Corporation Diary); Surrey RO, 60/9/1 (Bletchingley poll); B. E. and K. A. Howells (eds.), *Pembrokeshire Life 1572-1843* (Pembrokeshire Record Soc., 1972), 36-41 (5 letters on Haverfordwest election); Latimer, *Annals of Bristol*, 293; HMC Portland MSS, iii. 220

(Breton to Harley); C. H. Mayo and A. M. Gould (eds.), *The Municipal Records of the Borough of Dorchester* (Exeter, 1908), 436-7; HMC Buccleugh MSS, i. 312 (Manchester to Mountagu); Fox's Journal, 369; Shakespeare's Birthplace, Stratford-upon-Avon, DR 37, Box 87 (Lee, Pichering, to Archer); Hull CA, BB6, p. 303; Bristol RO, AC/C74/11 (Ashburnham to Smyth); J. Moule (ed.), *A Descriptive Catalogue of the Charters . . . of Weymouth* (1883), 119; Pepys, 87, 99; VCH Huntingdon, ii. 29-30; Nottinghamshire RO, DD/SR/221/96/14-15 (Turner to Savile); *Exact Accompt* (30 Mar.-7 Apr.).

122. *Mercurius Aulicus*, reprinted in Dawson, *Cromwell's Understudy*, 390, tells this story in vivid detail. Rugge's *Diurnal*, 69, repeats it with different touches.

123. Steele, nos. 3178-9; Leybourne-Popham MSS, 175 (Fairfax to Monck); *Mercurius Publicus* (19-26 Apr.).

124. *Clarke Papers*, iv. 267 (Monck to army); HMC 13th Report, vi. 3-4 (Monck to Knight); *Mercurius Publicus* (5-26 Apr.); *An Exact Accompt* (13-27 Apr.); Howells (ed.), *A Calendar*, 111-12 (Caernarfonshire commissioners to gentry).

125. HMC 5th Report, 361 (seven letters of Monck and Council); *An Exact Accompt* (13-27 Apr.); *London's Diurnal* (18 Apr.-2 May); Guizot, ii. 408-12; Clarendon MS 71, ff. 242-3, 272-3 (Tomlinson, Morley, to Hyde); CSP, iii. 730-1 (Wood to Hyde); Baker, *Chronicle*, 720.

126. Ludlow, *A Voyce*, 101; *Clarke Papers*, iv. 268 (Hesilrige to Monck). Professor Davies is surely correct in being suspicious of SP 18/220/65, 70, which I consider to be the first examples of the 'forged letter' which was to be a feature of post-Restoration plot scares.

127. Lister's Life of Clarendon, iii. 93-4 (Morland to Hyde); *An Exact Accompt* (13-20 Apr.).

128. CSP, iii. 706-7 (Mordaunt to King); E. P. Shirley, *Hanley and the House of Lechmere* (1883), 30-2.

129. Diary, 91, 102-3.

130. *DNB*, 'Canne'; Muddiman, *The King's Journalist*, 112-13.

131. The horse regiments were those of Smithson, Crook, Alured, Hacker, Saunders and Hesilrige, the abortive risings were in Hertfordshire, Derbyshire, Yorkshire, Gloucestershire and Cheshire: *Mercurius Publicus* (19 Apr.-2 May); *Mercurius Civicus* (18-24 Apr.); *London's Diurnal* (25 Apr.-2 May); *An Exact Accompt* (20 Apr.-4 May); *Parliamentary Intelligencer* (16-30 Apr.); Baker, *Chronicle*, 720; Ludlow, *A Voyce*, 112; CSP, iii. 730-1 (Wood to Hyde); Leybourne-Popham MSS, 175-8 (5 letters to Monck); C. Crowder (ed.), 'Some Records mostly of the Fairfax Family', *Trans. Birmingham and Midland Institute* (1907), 31 (Fairfax to Monck); Staffordshire RO, D868/8/48a (Gower to Leveson); Derbyshire RO, 1232/M/0105 (Sheirman to Saunders).

132. This is compiled from the five newspapers cited above, plus Ludlow, 113, and CSP, iii. 734-5.

133. Dow, *Scotland*, 259-65; Barnard, *Ireland*, 133-4; Thurloe State Papers, vii. 859, 908 (Broghill to Thurloe).

134. CSP, iii. 721, 729-32 (Morley, Barwick, Mordaunt, Phelips, Willoughby, to

Hyde); Clarendon MS 72, f. 19 (Mordaunt to King); Carte MS 73, f. 406 (Thurloe to Mountagu).

135. CJ viii. 1-3; LJ ix. 35; Clarendon MS 72, ff. 19-20 (Mordaunt to King); Carte MS 214, ff. 71-2 (Weston to Ormonde); Pepys's Diary, i. 118; Maurice F. Bond (ed.), *The Diaries and Papers of Sir Edward Dering* (1976), 35; Guizot, ii. 411-17; HMC 5th Report, 206 (Langley to Leveson); Collins (ed.), *Letters and Memorials*, ii. 686 (Northumberland to Leicester); Brit. L. Add. MS 11689, f. 55 (Powell to Scudamore). Burnet's account, in his *History of My Own Time*, ed. by Osmund Airy (Oxford, 1897), Part 1, i. 160-1, is not confirmed by any contemporary source.

136. CJ 4-7; LJ 6-9; CSP, 736 (Grenville to King); Dering's Diary, 36-7.

Part Two: Chapter 5

1. Vann, *Social Development of English Quakerism*, chs. 1-2.

Part Three: Chapter 1

1. If the history of the later 1650s requires much further investigation, that of the early 1660s has been far more neglected. The general accounts are in Ogg, vol.i, and Jones, *Country and Court*. The latter is only a lively summary, and the limitations of the former were stated in the preface to this work. There are, however, a few monographs, some excellent, which have pointed the way for further research.

2. CJ viii. 14-49; LJ xi. 17-48; Edward Hyde, Earl of Clarendon, *The Life of Edward, Earl of Clarendon* (Oxford, 1836), i. 326-7; Baker, *Chronicle*, 730-4; Rugge's *Diurnal*, 79-80, 87-91; Staffordshire RO, D868/4/45a (Charlton to Leveson); HMC Le Fleming MSS, 25 (Smith to Fleming); Pepys's Diary, i. 141-58.

3. Pepys's Diary, i. 121; SP 29/4/97 (articles against Baskerville) and 7/26 (Shepley's evidence); Leybourne-Popham MSS, 182 (Fairfax to Monck); Bod. L. Carte MS 73, f. 435 (Hart to Mountagu).

4. Corporation of London RO, Journal 41, f. 231b.

5. Pepys's Diary, i. 121, 125; Fletcher, *Sussex*, 320; *CSPV* 155; *Parliamentary Intelligencer* (14-21 May); *Mercurius Publicus* (10-31 May); Wood's Life, i. 317; Evans, *Norwich*, 227; J. E. Foster (ed.), *The Diary of Samuel Newton* (Cambridge, 1870), 1; Buckinghamshire RO, M11/17 (Butterfield, 10 May); HMC Portland MSS, iii. 220-1 (Greene to Harley); VCH Leicestershire, ii. 119; Newcome's Autobiography, 120; Tickell, *Hull*, 515; Bristol RO, Ac/C64/81 (letter from Keynton); J. Horsfall Turner (ed.), *Autobiography and Diaries of Oliver Heywood* (1883), iii. 98.

6. Steele, nos. 3206, 3217, 3231, 3242; CJ 39; PRO, CRES 6/1 and 6/2, *passim*.

7. Rugge's *Diurnal*, 78-9; HMC 7th Report, 80 (Baptist petition); Jessey, *Lord's Loud Call*, 3-22; LJ 49.

8. Besse, *Sufferings*, i. 87-8, 151, 210, 671, ii. 39, 99; *For the King . . . Being a short declaration of the cruelty inflicted upon . . . Quakers . . . in Merionethshire* (n.d.); Norfolk RO, SF/95, pp. 5-9; Barclay (ed.), *Letters*, 80-2 (Hubberthorne to Fox); Berkshire RO, D/F 2 A1/1, pp. 5-6; Dorset RO, N/10/A15, pp. 1-2.

9. Ewen, *Witchcraft*, 400, and *Witch-Hunting and Witch Trials* (1929), 252-3; Macfarlane, *Witchcraft*, 270; Dorset RO, P155/CW/128 (Sherborne churchwardens' accounts); J. W. Willis-Bund (ed.), *The Diary of Henry Townshend* (Worcestershire Hist. Soc., 1915-20), 40-1; Worcestershire Hist. Soc. *Miscellany* ii (1967), 118.

10. CSP, iii. 744-5, 747-9 (Broderick to Hyde); Lister's Life of Clarendon, iii. 99-104 (Mordaunt to Hyde); Clarendon MS 72, ff.180-1, 228-9, 234, 280-1 (Coventry, Mordaunt to Hyde). The sources do not make perfectly clear how the Commons could be 'persuaded' to put Hyde's post in commission and then permit this ruling to be ignored in practice. It is presumed that the clarity of the King's views upon his return made all the difference.

11. LJ 27-50.

12. PRO, P/C 2/54, pp. 1-144. The other councillors were the Earls of Southampton, St. Albans, Lindsey, Manchester, Norwich, Berkshire and Leicester, the Marquises of Hertford and Dorchester, the Dukes of York and Gloucester, Viscount Saye and Sele, Lords Culpeper, Seymour, Wentworth and Robartes, and Sir Frederick Cornwallis, Sir Charles Berkeley and Sir George Carteret. As the royal dukes had an 'automatic' membership of the board, they have not been included in the total of royalists.

13. P/C 2/54, p. 91; Clarendon, *Life*, i. 364-70; Baker, *Chronicle*, 734; *Camden Miscellany*, ix (1895), 2 (life of Nathaniel Crew); *CSPD* (1660-1), 59-604, *passim*. The records of the law courts, Exchequer, Admiralty and other parts of the state machine give an impression of considerable continuity among lesser officials, although detailed research, of the sort carried out by Professor Aylmer for earlier periods, will be necessary to establish the precise degree. Such a study would also reveal the part played in this process by patronage, title to office and other factors.

14. P/C 2/54; W. D. Macray (ed.), *Notes which passed at Meetings of the Privy Council* (1896), 7.

15. Clarendon, *Life*, i. 370; SP 29/23/93-104 (minutes of committee?).

16. Clarendon, *Life*, i. 362-3; Bod. L. MS Eng. Hist. d. 279 (the petitions); Macray (ed.), *Notes*; LJ 54; P/C 2/54, p. 31; Lister's Life of Clarendon, ii. 19n.; Dryden, *To My Lord Chancellor* (1662).

17. CJ 21; HMC 7th Report, 79 (Keeper of Greenwich to Lords); Rugge, 93; Steele, no. 3203.

18. Dering's Diary, 44; *Parliamentary Intelligencer* (18-25 June).

19. Staffordshire RO, D868/8/53b (Gower to Leveson).

20. E. I. Carlyle, 'Clarendon and the Privy Council', *EHR* xxviii (1912), 255.

21. Ibid. 270; Brit. L. Add. MS 9311, f. 65 (constitution of board); Pepys's Diary, 191-4.

22. Black, thesis, 244-9.

23. Worcester College L. Clarke MS 53; *Parliamentary Intelligencer* (18 June-30 Aug.); *Mercurius Publicus* (28 June-19 July).

24. P/C 2/54, p. 63; Fletcher, *Sussex*, 321; Roberts, thesis, 229-30; Glanmor

Williams (ed.), *Glamorgan County History* (Cardiff, 1974), iv. 378; SP 29/14/92 (Falkland to Nicholas), 18/94 (George to Joseph Williamson); Dering's Diary, 47; *Twysden Lieutenancy Papers*, Kent Arch. Soc. x (1926), 29; NLW Add. MS 3071E; Brit. L. Add. MSS 32324, 34222, 34306, 34761 and Sloane MS 813; SP 29/19/75 (all various sets of militia papers). The Deputy-Lieutenants were chosen by the Lord-Lieutenants, but their names had to be approved 'from time to time' by the King.

25. Based upon J. R. S. Phillips, *The Justices of the Peace in Wales and Monmouthshire*, 1541-1689 (Cardiff, 1978), and the sources listed in T. Barnes and A. Hassell Smith, 'Justices of the Peace from 1558 to 1688', *BIHR* 32 (1959), 221-42, combined with all the county studies and gentry correspondence cited elsewhere. Roberts, thesis, 223-6, works out the bargaining over the Devon commission in detail.

26. *Mercurius Publicus* (1-8 Nov.).

27. Brit. L. Egerton MS 2537, f. 231 (Davy to Nicholas); SP 29/18/4 (Smith to Williamson); *CSPD* 281.

28. e.g. Kent RO, Q/SB 7/47, 68-9; Wiltshire RO, QS/OB, Mich.

29. Based upon Steele, no. 3272, and the surviving Quarter Sessions Order Books, for Durham, Surrey, Warwickshire, Dorset, Wiltshire, Caernarfonshire, Hampshire, Devon, Kent, Hertfordshire, Essex, Staffordshire, Shropshire, Cheshire, Norfolk, Suffolk and Sussex.

30. Jones, thesis, 197-8, 204; Evans, *Norwich*, 226.

31. Johnson, D.Phil. thesis, 351; L. J. Ashford, *History of High Wycombe* (1960),143; Great Yarmouth CA, Assembly Book G, f. 353; John Allen, *History of Liskeard* (1856), 244-5; HMC 11th Report, vii. 194 (Reading Corporation Diary).

32. Bath CA, Council Book 2 (14 June); Lincolnshire RO, L/1/1/1/6, p. 89 (Lincoln); *Records of the Borough of Leicester*, iv. 466-7; *Oxford Council Acts*, 258; H. Owen and J. B. Blakeway, *History of Shrewsbury* (1825), i. 479; Norfolk RO, Norwich Assembly Book, f. 210b.

33. SP 29/11/53, 14/27, 16/57, 18/60; Lincolnshire RO L/1/1/1/6, 97; Evans, *Norwich*, 229; Corporation of London RO, Journal 41, ff. 235-6; B. H. Cunnington (ed.), *Annals of Devizes* (Devizes, 1923), i.127-8; Owen and Blakeway, *Shrewsbury*, i. 481-2; P/C 2/55, p. 21.

34. SP 29/14/77 (notes on Bristol).

35. Jones, thesis, 212-18; Kent RO, Fa/AC, ff. 134-5 (Faversham assembly book); HMC 13th Report, iv. 236 (Vincent to Cinque Ports).

36. LJ 31-42.

27. HMC 1st Report, 70 (Pembroke); R. Blencowe (ed.), Campion MSS, *Sussex Arch. Collections* x (1857), 15-16 (Trinity); Thomas Baker, *History of St John's College* (Cambridge, 1869), i. 231; W. G. Searle, *History of the Queens' College* (Cambridge, 1967), 559-76; Arthur Grey and Frederick Brittain, *A History of Jesus College* (1960), 86-7; Charles H. Cooper, *Annals of Cambridge* (Cambridge, 1845), iii. 483-4; John Lamb (ed.), *Master's History of the College of Corpus Christie* (1831), 180-1; *Clare College Letters*, 39-43; Worthington's Diary, i. 202-3. It is impossible

to produce an accurate figure for the number of deprivations, and the estimate in Matthews, *Calamy Revised*, xiii, is certainly too low: eight heads of houses went, instead of his five.

38. Bod. L. MS Dep. f. 9, ff. 22-4 (Bowman's Diary).

39. F. Varley (ed.), *The Restoration Visitation of the University of Oxford*, Camden Miscellany, xviii (1948); HMC Leybourne-Popham MSS, 183-4 (Hitchcock to Commons); *Brasenose Quartercentenary Monographs* (Oxford Hist. Soc., 1909), ii. 5-7; T. Fowler, *History of Corpus Christi* (Oxford Hist. Soc., 1893), 230-2; D. Macleane, *History of Pembroke College* (Oxford Hist. Soc., 1897), 257; the Revd A. Clark, *Lincoln College* (1898), 132-3; Sidney G. Hamilton, *Hertford College* (1903), 33; John R. Magrath, *The Queen's College* (Oxford, 1921), ii. 4-32; Herbert Blakiston, *Trinity College* (1898), 149; William Carr, *University College* (1902), 121-2; F. G. Hardy, *Jesus College* (1899), 128-31; Jessey, *Lord's Loud Call*, 27-30; *Mercurius Publicus* (15-22 Nov.); Brit. L. Egerton MS 2618, f. 81 (King to Visitors).

40. White Kennet, *A Register and Chronicle Ecclesiastical and Civil* (1728), 197; VCH Cambridge, iii. 397; SP 29/14/62, 31/63, 34/8.

41. Parsloe, *TRHS* 1947.

42. Silcock, thesis, 299.

43. My sample for this consists of Staffordshire, Lancashire, Kent, Devon and Essex.

44. This was first noticed by Morrill, *Cheshire*, ch. 6 and p. 329, and seems equally true of Lancashire, Staffordshire and Kent, though not of Devon and Essex.

45. For the debates of the Convention, there survive the very slight diary of Sir Edward Dering and the good one of Seymour Bowman, which exists for the debates of 18 June to 17 August as Bod. L. MS Dep. f 9. Passages from a later part, now lost, are quoted in the *Old Parliamentary History*, vols. xxii-xxiii. Upon this J. R. Jones based his 'Political Groups and Tactics in the Convention of 1660', *HJ* vi (1962-3), 159-77, which ably demolishes the concept of a Presbyterian party but postulates that of a Court party for which I believe equally little evidence survives. Evans's thesis is less rigid in its definitions.

46. *Statutes of the Realm*, v. 226-34; CJ19-140; LJ95-148; MS Dep. f 9, ff. 1-153; Lister's Life of Clarendon, iii. 500-3 (Monck's speech); Dering's Diary, 41-3; Brit. L. Egerton MS 2537, f. 60 (De Vic to Nicholas).

47. MS Dep. f 9, ff. 1-153; Dering's Diary, 41-3; *Memoirs of Colonel Hutchinson*, 321-7; William R. Parker, *Milton* (Oxford, 1968), i. 570-1; Ruth Spalding, *The Improbable Puritan* (1975), 225-9; P/C 2/55, p. 3; Ludlow, *A Voyce*, 125-90; LJ 108-9; Rugge's *Diurnal*, 92; *Clarke Papers*, iv. 302-3 (Monck to Turner); G. F. Trevallyn Jones, *Saw-Pit Wharton* (Sydney, 1967), 167-73.

48. T. Howell (ed.), *State Trials* (1816), v. 973-1256; Nine tracts dated in Thomason collection between 10 and 15 October; Pepys, 263-9; Rugge, 116; *Mundy's Travels*, 125-6; SP 29/18/118 and 94/44 (Nicholas to Bennet, 15 and 18 Oct.).

49. CJ 117-202; LJ 205-26; *Old Parliamentary History*, xxiii. 16-58; *Statutes*, v. 288-90; Pepys's Diary, ii. 26; I. P. Earwaker, *East Cheshire* (1877), ii. 72 (news-letter); John Dart, *Westmonasterium* (n.d.), ii. 144. Pride's corpse was also sentenced, but apparently could not be found.

50. This emerges from rejected provisos to the bill, CJ 70-86, MS Dep. f 9, ff. 40-61 and Bod. L. Carte MS 81, f. 18, and private correspondence, Staffordshire RO, D260/M/F/1/6, f. 62 (Bagot to Persehouse).
51. Staffordshire RO, D868/9/10 (Charlton to Leveson).
52. Moule (ed.), Descriptive Catalogue, 83.
53. Dering's Diary, 41-2; *Memoirs of Hutchinson*, 320-1.
54. CJ 214; *Old Parliamentary History*, xxiii. 56-8.
55. Robert W. Ramsey, *Henry Cromwell* (1933), 356-67; Blomefield, *Norfolk*, xi. 364; Huntingdonshire RO, Bush Acc. 731 nos. 32-3, 75-7, 145-51 (Henry's letters and land deeds).
56. Brit. L. Add. MS 24863, f. 1 (Richard to Oxford); Ramsey, *Richard Cromwell*, 118-19.
57. LJ 108-9, 147-8.
58. A good example of this is Staffordshire RO, D260/M/F/1/6 f. 72 (deposition to Persehouse).
59. Wiltshire RO, Q/S Roll Easter 1664.
60. Such as Henry Ferrom at Ely: Cambridge UL, EDR E/45.
61. Brit. L. Egerton MS 2618, f. 58.
62. LJ 39.
63. Ibid.; Staffordshire RO, D868/3/46b (Newport to Leveson).
64. *Old Parliamentary History*, xxiii. 51-2.
65. P/C 2/54, *passim*.
66. W. G. Johnson, thesis, 72-6, 8-91.
67. *CSPV*, 159; SP 29/11/138 (complaint to King); *The Autobiography of Sir John Bramston*, Camden Soc. (1845), 117; Staffordshire RO, D868/8/10a, 9/10 (Gower to Leveson).
68. CJ 41; LJ 50; CSP iii. 747-9 (Broderick to Hyde).
69. Earl of Cardigan and Baron Freschville.
70. W. A. Shaw, *The Knights of England* (1900), ii. 225-34; G. E. Collins, *Complete Baronetage* (Exeter, 1906), iii. 25-186.
71. Compiled from P. R. Newman, *Royalist Officers in England and Wales* (1981).
72. *CSPD* (1660-1), 72, 143-5; *CTB* i. 194-421, *passim*.
73. *CSPD* 72-524, *passim*; PRO, CRES 6/21, *passim*, L/R 2/266 fs. 58; *CTB* 186-91.
74. *CTB* 181-452.
75. Ibid. xix-xx.
76. Samuel Johnson, *Lives of the English Poets* (Oxford, 1905), i. 6-14.
77. Brit. L. Egerton MS 2537, f. 279, 2542, f. 49b (Morland to Nicholas); Pepys's Diary, i. 221.
78. Peacock (ed.), *Monckton Papers*, 43-4, 76-88.
79. Maurice Ashley, *John Wildman* (1947), 156-8.
80. *Life*, i. 354.
81. Gardiner (ed.), *Oxinden and Peyton Letters*, 235-6 (Oxinden to wife); Collins (ed.), *Letters*, ii.701.

82. Ashley, *Monck*, 211; *CSPD* 137, 213, 432, 578; *CTB* 605; Gentles, 'Crown Lands', 635; Shaw, *Knights*, ii. 225-31; Pepys, i. 183-93; Ludlow, 168.

83. Hardacre, *Royalists*, 149.

84. See below.

85. B. G. Blackwood, *The Lancashire Gentry and the Great Rebellion*, Chetham Soc. 3rd ser. xxv (1978), 141-7.

86. *Statutes*, v. 207-26, 238-42; CJ 7-171; LJ 97; *Old Parliamentary History*, xxiii. 2. Some of the letters survive: HMC 3rd Report, 90, 259; Kent RO, U269/C78/2. The commission's records themselves seem to have perished.

87. HMC Kenyon MSS, 67 (Hutton to Kenyon); P/C 2/54, pp. 175-6.

88. Journal 41, ff. 240-3.

89. *Statutes*, 269-82; CJ 182-224; LJ 225-36; *Old Parliamentary History*, xxiii. 2; *CTB* viii-x.

90. CJ 176, 189.

91. Pepys's Diary, i. 259; Rugge's *Diurnal*, 111, 128; P/C 2/54, pp. 163-4; *Parliamentary Intelligencer* (1 Oct.-3 Dec.); *Mercurius Publicus* (1-22 Nov.); Blomefield, *Norfolk*, iii. 404; *CSPD* 305 (Nicholas to Bennett).

92. Guizot, ii. 422; *Parliamentary Intelligencer* (13-20 Aug.); *CSPV* 204; Clarendon MS 72, ff. 387-8 (letter from London); Brit. L. Add. MS 34306, f. 6; 34222, ff. 11-13 (militia orders).

93. LJ 172-4; *Statutes*, v. 241-2.

94. SP 29/23/71 (paper of informations).

95. Steele, no. 3296.

96. Lois G. Schwoerer, *No Standing Armies!* (1974), 79-80. I find the unsigned and undated paper cited here too flimsy a piece of evidence to be usable.

97. Charles Dalton, *English Army Lists and Commission Registers 1661-1714* (1892), i. 1-17.

98. There is now a considerable literature of excellent quality upon this; H. J. Habakkuk, 'Public Finance' and 'The Parliamentary Army and Crown Lands', *Welsh HR* 3 (1966-7), 403-26; I. Gentles, thesis 'The Sale of Crown Lands', *Ec. HR* 26 (1973), 614-35, 'The Purchasers of Northamptonshire Crown Lands', *Midland History* iii (1976), 206-32, debate with M. Kishlansky in *Ec. HR* 29 (1976), 125-35, and 'The Sale of Bishops' Lands', *EHR* xcv (1980), 573-96; I. Gentles and W. J. Shiels, *Confiscation and Restoration* (Borthwick Paper 59). Nobody has yet studied the fate of dean and chapter lands. On the settlement of 1660-1 there is J. Thirsk, 'The Restoration Land Settlement', *JMH* xxvi (1954), 315-28; W. J. Shiels, 'The Restoration and the Temporalities', *Borthwick Institute Bulletin* i (1975), 17-30; H. J. Habakkuk, 'The Land Settlement and the Restoration of Charles II', *TRHS* 5th ser. 28 (1978), 201-2; Ian Green, *The Re-Establishment of the Church of England 1660-1663* (Oxford, 1978), 100-3; Gentles and Shiels, *Confiscation and Restoration*.

99. Habakkuk, 'Land Settlement', 201.

100. Lister's Life of Clarendon, iii. 500-3.

101. *Records of Leicester*, iv. 466; CJ 41; Brit. L. Sloane MS 2717, f. 40 (petition).

102. MS Dep. f. 9, f. 31.

103. Thirsk, 317-18; Habakkuk, 'Land Settlement', 209-10, 213-14; LJ 93; CJ 72-3, 86, 113; Bod. L. MS Dep. f. 9, ff. 19, 69-73, 121-8, 139, 146.

104. Habakkuk, 211.

105. Durham UL, Cosin Letter-Book 1A, f. 66.

106. CJ 112-14.

107. Peterborough CL, MS 20, ff. 68-103 (Cosin's papers).

108. Leicestershire RO, DG11/730/4/279 (Baker to Cutler); Duppa-Isham Correspondence, 186.

109. Habakkuk, 218.

110. Rugge's *Diurnal*, 126. The records of this commission have vanished, and a reference in Guiseppi's guide to the PRO which Professor Thirsk believed to denote them in fact described other documents. However, their orders concerning Crown land were collected in CRES 6/3, and individual rulings upon Church land survive.

111. PRO, CRES 6/1-3, *passim*, L/R 1/61, 1/114, f. 258, 1/161, ff. 16-17, 2/56, 2/134, 2/266, *passim*, SP 29/16/35 (report to King); *CTB* 65, 70, 359; *Parliamentary Intelligencer* (26 Nov.-3 Dec.); Roberts, thesis, 244-5; Brit. L. Egerton MS 2542, f. 578 (paper on lands); Dorset RO, D.124, Box 233 (Strode to Strangeways) and D104/X/9-12 (Fincher papers).

112. SP 29/18/60.

113. e.g. to the Bishop of Exeter: Whiteman, thesis, 68.

114. Spalding, *Improbable Puritan*, 231-2.

115. E. Heath-Agnew, *Roundhead to Royalist* (Hereford, 1977), ch. 13.

116. Green, *Re-Establishment*, 100-4; Gentles and Shiels, 18-21; Shiels, 'The Restoration', 1-27; Gentles, 'Bishops' Lands', 594; Thirsk, 'Land Settlement', 325-6; Habakkuk, 'Land Settlement', 215; Isham (ed.), Duppa-Isham Correspondence, 188; Florence R. Goodman, *Reverend Landlords and their Tenants* (Winchester, 1930), 35; William Hutchinson, *History of the County Palatine of Durham* (Newcastle, 1787), ii. 163-6; Roberts, thesis, 248-9; Dumble, thesis; Kennett, *Register*, 376-579, *passim*; Bod. L. Rawlinson MS D1138, ff. 336-42; Bristol RO, DC/E/1/2 (register of leases).

117. CJ 178-237; LJ 194-236; *Old Parliamentary History*, xxii. 6-7; H. M. Margoliouth (ed.), *Poems and Letters of Andrew Marvell* (Oxford, 1927), ii. 2; HMC 5th Report, 145 (Terrick to Leveson).

118. Sources as at n. 116.

119. Gentles and Shiels, 26-34.

120. Thirsk, 'Land Settlement', 320-8, and 'The Sales of Royalist Land', *Ec. HR* 2nd ser. v (1952), 188-207; Habakkuk, 'Land Settlement', 214, and 'Landowners and the Civil War', *Ec. HR* 2nd ser. xviii (1965), 130-51; Blackwood, *Lancashire Gentry*, 120-47 (which compares other studies); Hardacre, *Royalists*, 151-9; Sir G. Sitwell, 'The Loyal Duke of Newcastle', *J Derbyshire Arch. and Nat. Hist. Soc.* 13 (1891), 1-8; P. Holiday, 'Land Sales and Repurchases in Yorkshire', *Northern History* v (1970), 67-92; Barry Coward, *The Stanleys*, Chetham Soc. (1983), 73-5.

121. This subject is another which has inspired excellent recent work: Bosher, *Restoration Settlement*; Sutch, *Sheldon*, Green, *Re-Establishment*; Abernathy, *English Presbyterians*; Evans, thesis, 259-60; E. A. O. Whiteman, 'The Re-Establishment of the Church of England', *TRHS* 5th ser. v (1955), 120-35, and 'The Restoration of the Church of England', in Geoffrey F. Nuttall and Owen Chadwick (eds.), *From Uniformity to Unity* (1962); A. Harold Wood, *Church Unity Without Uniformity* (1963), chs. 6-7; R. Beddard, 'The Restoration Church' in J. R. Jones (ed.), *The Restored Monarchy* (1979), 155-65. I differ in points of interpretation from all but the last (and briefest) of these, but much of my account is of course based on all, and owes a greater debt to Dr Green's work than to any other.

122. Woolrych, introduction to *Milton*, vii. 35; Baxter, *Holy Commonwealth*.

123. Morrill, 'The Church', 95; Duppa-Isham Correspondence, 187; Dr W. Pope, *The Life of . . . Seth, Lord Bishop of Salisbury* (1697), 55; the Revd J. Robertson (ed.), 'Canterbury Cathedral at the Restoration', *Archaeologia Cantiana* x (1876), 93-4; B. Williams, thesis, 91-2; the Ven. R. Burne, 'Chester Cathedral after the Restoration', *J Chester and North Wales Architectural, Arch. and Nat. Hist. Soc.* N.S. xxxix (1952), 29.

124. Morrill, 'The Church', uses those in eleven county record offices with some from parishes, being a total of 150 for the period 1637 to 1662. I have visited every county record office in England and been given transcripts of all the accounts surviving in parishes in Cheshire, Norfolk and Wiltshire by Dr Martin Crossley-Evans, to produce a sample of 306 for the period 1657-67. In using this source I must record reservations. Some counties have lodged over twenty sets in their offices, some only one or two, while urban parishes are generally much better represented than rural. My total comprises 3 per cent of the parishes of the period. Ministers, despite the instructions of the statutes, may have bought service-books instead of the churchwardens. The results can thus be taken as no more than an indication of the truth.

125. CSP iii. 722-3, 727-8, 735-6, 738 (Morley to Hyde); *Reliquiae Baxterianae*, 215-18; Barwick, *Life of Barwick*, 505-27 (letters between Barwick and Hyde); Woodrow, *Sufferings of the Church*, i. xvii-xxv (Sharp to Scottish clergy).

126. Clarendon MS 72, f. 44 (letter to Hyde); G. F. T. Jones, 'The . . . Presbyterian Party in the Convention', *EHR* 79 (1964), 307-54.

127. *Reliquiae Baxterianae*, 229-30; Bod. L. Tanner MS 49, ff. 7-10 (propositions); Woodrow, i. xxxi-ix; HMC Le Fleming MSS, 26 (Smith to Fleming); Green, 5-7; Bishop of Salisbury, *Via ad Pacem* (Oxford, 1660).

128. *Statutes*, v. 242-6.

129. Taken from the cases in A. G. Matthews, *Walker Revised* (Oxford, 1948).

130. *Calamy Revised, passim*; Richards, *Religious Developments*, Part 2, chs. 2-5; Green, 37-49; Palmer, *Nonconformist's Memorial, passim*; John H. Pruett, *The Parish Clergy under the Later Stuarts* (1978), 10-19; the Revd John Watson, *The History . . . of Halifax* (1775), 484-8; Jessup, *Twysden*, 169-76; Cox (ed.), *Derbyshire Annals*, i. 337; Newcome's Diary, xxx-xxxi; the Revd G. Ornsby (ed.), *Corre-*

spondence of John Cosin, Surtees Soc. (1872), 4–6 (Blakiston to Cosin); HMC 13th Report, iv. 343–5 (Hereford Mayor's Court); Doctor Williams's L. 89/3, St. Swithun Ward, 71-2 and Billingsgate Ward, 7; NLW Bettisfield MSS 108-9 (papers on Hanmer living); Guildhall L. 819/1 (All Hallows vestry minute). There are, inevitably, almost as many different stories of the operation of the act as there were livings affected. The summary given therefore consists of the over-simplification which seems closest to a general truth.

131. CJ 73–174; LJ 161–7; MS Dep. f 9, ff. 33-135; Dering's Diary, 46; Duppa-Isham Correspondence, 185; HMC 5th Report, 154 (Newport to Leveson).

132. Green, 22–4, 50–60, 82–97, who convincingly refutes the accounts of Bosher and Sutch; J. R. Guy, 'The Significance of indigenous clergy in the Welsh church at the restoration', *Studies in Church History* 18 (1982), 335-44.

133. Sutch's biography is as interesting but inadequate as Ramsey's of Richard Cromwell, and was severely censured by R. Beddard, 'Sheldon and Anglican Recovery', *HJ* 19 (1976), 1005–17. Sheldon's public views at the Restoration are in *David's Deliverance* (28 June).

134. *Reliquiae Baxterianae*, 242–79; Lister's Life of Clarendon, iii. 110-11 (Morley to Lauder); Clarendon MS 73, ff. 182-3, 196 (Bellings to Mountagu).

135. CJ 175–95; LJ 193–211; *Old Parliamentary History*, xxiii. 2-6, 26-31, Jones, 'Political Groups', 161, convincingly discounts the influence of an 'independent' group.

136. Beddard, 'The Restoration Church', 161-2; Bosher, 156; Staffordshire RO, D868/8/53a (Gower to Leveson).

137. *Calamy Revised*, I, 42,193,221, 259, 304,420, 461; Clarendon MS 73, ff. 218-19 (Dorset presentment); H. Jenkinson and D. Powell (eds.), *Surrey Quarter Sessions Records* (Surrey Record Soc.), xxxv. 38-9; *An Account of the Life . . . of Mr. Philip Henry* (1699),64-5; Wiltshire RO, Q/S Roll (Mich.); John Brown, *John Bunyan* (2nd ed., 1928), ch. 7; H. H. Copnall (ed.), *Nottinghamshire County Records* (Nottingham, 1915), 140.

138. Wood's Life, i. 333, 355, 366; Brit. L. Add. MS 24485, f. 27 (Chandler's memoirs).

139. SP 29/8/7, 29, 47, 105,10/22; P/C 2/54, pp. 56-7, 85, 91, 114, 147; Jessey, *Lord's Loud Call*, 24-7; G. B. Harrison (ed.), *The Church Book of Bunyan Meeting* (1928), 25; Brown, *Bunyan*, chs. 6-7; Regent's Park College Angus L, Abingdon Baptist Association Book, ff. 83-7; A. Tucker, 'The Church at Porton', *Trans. Baptist Hist. Soc.* 1 (1908), 56-61; E. B. Underhill (ed.), *Records of the Churches . . . at Fenstanton . . .* (1854), 77.

140. Richard Hubberthorne, *An Short Answer* (1660); Margaret Fell, *A Declaration and an Information* (1660); (George Bishop), *To Thee Charles Stuart* (n.d.); George Fox, *A Noble Salutation* (1660) and *A Word in the behalf of the King* (1660); SP 29/21/98-9 (declarations); *The Copies of Several Letters* (1660).

141. Fell, *A Declaration; Copies of Several Letters*; Friends' House L, Spence MS 3/56 (Fell to Parker); Clarendon, *Life*, i. 362-3; Fox's Journal, 393; Barclay (ed.), *Letters*, 82 (Hubberthorne to Fox).

142. Besse, *Sufferings*, i. 366; Fox's Journal, 383-8; P/C 2/55, p. 44; Barclay (ed.), *Letters*, 92-4 (Moore's account).

143. Friends' House L. Swarthmore MS 4, ff. 145-6 (Parker to Fox).

144. Ibid. f. 272 (Caton to Fox); Besse, *Sufferings*, i. 210; Cumbria (Kendal) RO, Kendal Indictment Book, f. 50; East Suffolk RO, B105/2/4 (Quarter Sessions minute).

145. R. S., *The Dreadful and Terrible Voice* (1660); D. B., *Yet One Warning More* (Nov. 1660); Esther Biddle, *A Warning* (1660); *An Alarm to the Priests* (1660); John Anderson, *Against Babylon* (Nov. 1660); Thomas Salthouse, *A Candle Lighted* (1660).

146. SP 29/21/107; Dorset RO, P155/130 (Sherborne churchwardens' accounts); Kent RO, U350/C2/110 (Burnett to Dering).

147. Spence MS 3/56.

148. CJ 172-4; LJ 128, 153-4, 238-9; MS Dep. f 9, ff. 67-8.

149. Friends' House L. Barclay MS 84 (Howgill to Fell).

150. Reay, thesis, 148-9; Thomas Goodaire, *A True Relation* (1660) and *A Cry of the Just* (1660); Duppa-Isham Correspondence, 185-6; Besse, *Sufferings*, i. 197, 210-11, 230, 744; Spence MS 3/2K (Bridget to Margaret Fell); Berkshire RO, D/F 2 A/1. p. 7; Cumbria (Kendal) RO, Kendal Indictment Book, f. 50.

151. C. D. Chandaman, *The English Public Revenue, 1660-1688* (1975), 11-15, 36-40, 196-202; *Statutes*, v. 181-207, 252-66, 282-7; CJ 11, 40, 48,68-103, 136-228; LJ 110, 148, 164, 214-36; *Old Parliamentary History*, xxiii. 10-22; Cobbett's *Parliamentary History* (1808), iv. 151-67; Margoliouth (ed.), Marvell's Letters, ii. 2-3, 13.

152. In addition to the comments of Hyde, Whitelocke and the Quakers, there are those in Pepys's Diary, i. 144, and Staffordshire RO, D868/4/46-7.

153. Pepys's Diary, i. 244; *CSPD* 271 (Nicholas to Bennett); SP 29/16/84 (Nicholas to Curtius); Rugge's *Diurnal*, 110; *CSPV* 198; Staffordshire RO, D868/3/54; PRO, PRO/30/53/7, f. 74 (Powys to Griffith).

154. Kennet's *Register*, 249-50 (Sandwich's Journal); SP 29/16/84.

155. The two retrospective accounts of the affair, York's (the Revd J. S. Clarke (ed.), *The Life of James II* (1816), i. 387-8) and Hyde's (*Life*, i. 371-403) are both corrected by the contemporary sources, SP 94/44 (Nicholas to Bennet, 1 Nov., 20 and 27 Dec., 3 Jan.); *CSPV* 210-12; Staffordshire RO, D868/3/59, 61, 64a (Newport to Leveson); PRO, PRO/31/3/108, ff. 1-138, 109, f. 12 (French ambassador's papers); Clarendon MS 74, ff. 126-35 (Palmer to Hyde); P/C 2/55, p. 131.

156. C. Burrage, 'The Fifth Monarchy Insurrections', *EHR* xxv (1910), 722-45; Clarendon, *Life*, i. 474-7; Baker, *Chronicle*, 756-7; *Mercurius Publicus* (3-24 Jan.); Rugge's *Diurnal*, 139-40; Clarke (ed.), *Life of James*, i. 388-91.

157. Steele, no. 3278;P/C 2/55, pp. 102-3.

158. SP 29/28/50, 56-7, 87, 99, 29/29/16, 48 (letters from local officers); *The Kingdom's Intelligencer* (14-21 Jan.); *Mercurius Publicus* (10 Jan.-14 Feb.); HMC 3rd Report, 259 (Warwickshire militia correspondence); Duppa-Isham Corre-

spondence, 190; HMC 8th Report, 439 (Mayor of Leicester to Loughborough); HMC Hastings MSS, ii. 141 (Orton to Loughborough); Brit. L. Add. MS 34306, pp. 8-9 (Derbyshire militia papers) and Add. MS 34222, pp. 16-18 (Northamptonshire militia papers); Willis-Bund (ed.), Townshend's Diary, i. 66; Owen and Blakeway, *Shrewsbury*, i. 480 (Newport to Ottley); 'Old Herbert Papers', *Montgomeryshire Collections* 20 (1886), 43-4 (Herbert to Carbery); W. J. Smith (ed.), *Herbert Correspondence* (Cardiff, 1963), 163-4 (Montgomeryshire militia correspondence); Howells (ed.), *A Calendar* (Griffith to Constable); NLW Add. MS 3071E (Caernarfonshire militia papers).

159. Reay, thesis, 190. Besse's printed records of sufferings are preserved in greater detail and with some extra cases in Friends' House L. Great Book of Sufferings (3 vols.) and Original Records of Sufferings. In addition, many other examples appear in local books of sufferings held in the record offices of Berkshire, Hampshire, Dorset, Somerset, Cornwall (two local volumes), Kent, East Suffolk, Norfolk, Lincolnshire, Staffordshire, Cheshire, Lancashire, Humberside (three local volumes) and North Yorkshire, in Newcastle CA, in Manchester Central L, and in the Friends' Meeting Houses of York and Kendal. Dr Reay has used most of these, and his figure for the recorded arrests stands, but the number of counties which lack detailed local Quaker records causes me to suspect that the actual total of committals was significantly greater.

160. *The Humble Petition . . . of Anabaptists, Inhabitants in the County of Kent* (1660-1); Thomas Crosby, *History of the English Baptists* (1736), ii. 91; Roger Hayden (ed.), *Records of a Church of Christ in Bristol* (Bristol Record Soc., 1974), 116; Brit. L. Add. MS 32324, ff. 107-9 (Wiltshire militia papers). Some court records show committees for refusing the Oath of Allegiance in excess of the number of Quaker sufferings: *Surrey Quarter Sessions Records*, xxxv. 147; Jeaffreson (ed.), *Middlesex County Records*, 311; M. J. Hood (ed.), *Portsmouth Sessions Papers* (1971), 21; Durham RO, Q/S/OB/5, pp. 82-7; Kent RO, Q/SMc/1, Epiphany; Norfolk RO, C/51/8; East Suffolk RO, B105/2/4.

161. Sources as at n. 158; *Calamy Revised*, 339; the Revd F. Colby, 'History of Great Torrington', *Report and Trans. Devon Association*, vii (1875), 154-5; E. Windeatt, 'Totnes', ibid. xxxii (1900), 417; H. Fishwick (ed.), *The Church Book of Altham*, Chetham Soc. N.S. 33 (1894), xvi-xvii.

162. *CSPV* 244.

163. *A Declaration from the Harmless and Innocent People of God* (1660-1); *The Humble Apology of some commonly called Anabaptists* (1660-1); *A Renunciation and Declaration of the Ministers of Congregational Churches* (1660-1).

164. Reay, thesis, 178-81.

165. Steele, no. 3281; P/C 2/55, pp. 108, 113, 152-3, 174, 194; NLW, Add. MS 3071E, f. 93.

166. Sources as at nn. 158-60.

167. Besse, *Sufferings*, i. 153; Wiltshire RO, Q/S Great Rolls, Easter; Kent RO, Q/SMc/1, Easter; Staffordshire RO, D3159/2/18, ff. 1-8; Norfolk RO, C/51/8,

Easter; Cumbria (Kendal) RO, Kendal Indictment Book, f. 54; Durham CL Hunter MS 9, ff. 181-2.

168. HMC Finch MSS, i. 130 (Morice to Winchelsea); Clarendon, *Life*, i. 477; Clarke (ed.), *Life of James*, 391.

169. *Reliquiae Baxterianae*, 302-5; Pepys's Diary, ii. 57; SP 29/22/83-145 (letters to provinces); Staffordshire RO, D868/4/63B (Charlton to Leveson); Clarendon MS 74, f. 297 (Hyde to Ossory); P/C 2/55, p. 178; Bramston's Autobiography, 119-20; Brit. L. Egerton MS, f. 335 (Nicholas's notes).

170. My own computation is 241 out of 488 returned by May. As the list of members given in Cobbett's Parliamentary History is not accurate, I have used contemporary broadsheets. Basil Duke Henning, *The House of Commons 1660-1690* (History of Parliament Trust, 1983) now resolves this problem, but became available just too late to be used in the present study.

171. Wharton's calculations are in Jones, *EHR* 1964, 317, supplemented by Douglas R. Lacey, *Dissent and Parliamentary Politics in England 1661-1689* (New Brunswick, 1969), apps. 2-3.

172. Henning, again, makes the study of this General Election far easier. I based my account upon Everitt, *Kent*, 319-20; Holmes, *Lincolnshire*, 221; William S. Weekes, *Clitheroe in the Seventeenth Century* (Clitheroe, 1927), 295-301; SP 29/24/9 (Escott to Williamson); Josselin's Diary, 137; *Oxford Council Acts*, 280; HMC 3rd Report, 90 (Leicester corporation to Seymour), 259 (Derby to his tenants); HMC 5th Report, 298 (Persehouse to Brooke); Staffordshire RO, D868/3/35 (Newport to Leveson), 4/102 (Thomas to John Langley); C. A. Markham and the Revd J. C. Cox (eds.), *Records of . . . Northampton* (Northampton, 1898), i. xxxiii; Northamptonshire RO, Isham MS 515 (letter from Isham); Surrey RO, 60/9/2 (Bletchingley poll); *Wynn Papers*, nos. 2288, 2294 (Bulkeley, Price, to Wynn); HMC Portland MSS, iii. 250 (Norwood to Harley); VCH Warwick, viii. 250; HMC 13th Report, iv. 236-43 (Rye corporation correspondence); Hull CA, BB6, p. 355; York CA, House Book 37, ff. 150-2; Brit. L. Add. MS 32324, ff. 74-9 (Seymour letters); Cumbria (Carlisle) RO, D/Let/2 (Potter to Curwen, and reply); E. G. Earl, *The Story of Newtown* (Carisbrooke, 1963), 9; Isle of Wight RO, 45/16b, pp. 30-3 (Newport Convocation Book); Leicestershire RO, DE/1730/4/283-7 (Barker letters); Nottinghamshire RO, DD/SR/221/96/22-4 (Turner to Savile); C. Robbins (ed.), 'Election Correspondence of Sir John Holland', *Norfolk Archaeology*, 30 (1947-52), 131-9; Bramston's Autobiography, 119-20.

173. Clarendon, *Life*, ii. 10-14; Pepys's Diary, ii. 80-7; Baker, *Chronicle*, 757-71; Staffordshire RO, D868/4/101 (Smith to Langley); Mundy's *Travels*, v. 133.

174. Payments for these occur universally through churchwardens' and municipal accounts. Details of individual urban pageants are in Wood's Life, i. 399; *Narrative of the Manner of Celebrating . . . in the City of Bath* (1661); Rugge's *Diurnal*, 179-80; J. P. Earwaker (ed.), *The Court Leet Records . . . of Manchester* (Manchester, 1887), 281-5.

175. M. H. Lee (ed.), *Diaries and Letters of Philip Henry* (1882), 84.

176. Clarendon, *Life*, i. 413-14; PRO, PRO/31/3/108/76B (French ambassador's dispatch).
177. LJ 240-4.

Part Three: Chapter 2

1. *Statutes*, v. 304-6, 308-9,315-16, 424; CJ 247-368; LJ 252-472; House of Lords RO, Committee Minutes (1661-4), pp. 8-9; Brit. L. Egerton MS 2043, ff. 8-12 (Bullen Reymes's Diary) and Add. MS 10116, ff. 202-3 (Higgens's speech); *The Funeral of the Good Old Cause* (1661); Pepys's Diary, ii. 111; HMC 5th Report, 159 (Newport to Leveson); Staffordshire RO, D868/8/17 (Gower to Leveson). Reymes's cryptic and incomplete notes are the only known source approximating to a diary of the early sessions of this Parliament.
2. *Statutes*, 315-16; CJ 395; LJ 293-314, 369-70, 382; HMC 7th Report, 159 (Newport to Leveson).
3. SP 29/39/40-7 (petitions for Council); Bod. L. MS Eng. Hist. c 184 (commission for it); Steele, no. 3329.
4. *Statutes*, v. 358-64; CJ 326-433; LJ 412-72; the Revd Edward Berwick (ed.), *The Rawdon Papers* (1819), 140-1 (Pett to Armagh); Pepys, iii. 15; HMC 12th Report, ix. 52 (Herbert to wife); Fletcher, *Sussex*, 188; A. H. Smith, 'Militia rates and militia statutes', in Peter Clark, Nicholas Tyacke, A. G. R. Smith (eds.), *The English Commonwealth 1547-1640* (1979), 109-10.
5. *Statutes*, v. 304-6, 308, 428-33; CJ 247-472; HMC Gawdy MSS, 192-3 (Holland to Gawdy).
6. P. W. Thomas, *Sir John Berkenhead* (Oxford, 1969), 212-13, 223-4; Muddiman, *King's Journalist*, 126-30.
7. P/C 2/54, pp. 87, 102, 2/55, pp. 96-7, 308, 336, 376.
8. *An Account of Injurious Proceedings against Francis Smith* (1680).
9. LJ 201-18; P/C 2/55, p. 346; *Mercurius Publicus* (30 May-6 June 1661).
10. This is to accept the prevailing literary consensus, that *Paradise Lost* was substantially written after 1660 and *The Pilgrim's Progress* conceived during Bunyan's first imprisonment.
11. Scott, *Joint-Stock Companies*, i. 263-5; Henry's Diary, 85; Steele, no.3306.
12. Chandaman, *Public Revenue*, 203; CJ 257-314; LJ 279-330; *Statutes*, v. 306-8; HMC 5th Report, 145 (Milward to Leveson); A. H. A. Hamilton (ed.), *The Note Book of Sir John Northcote* (1877), 129; *CTB* xxviii-xxxiii, 266; Jessup, *Twysden*, 157; Brit. L. Add. MS 22919, f. 159 (Cornbury to Downing); Somerset RO, DD/PH/223/118 (Southampton to JPs).
13. Chandaman, 77, 203-4; CJ 317-25, 376-85; LJ 352-8, 408-11, 474-5; *Statutes*,v. 325-48, 390-3; Brit. L. Stowe MS 304, ff. 70-1 (Temple's speech).
14. SP 29/28/1, 34/12; Evans, *Norwich*, 227-32; Tickell, *Hull*, 518-20; Gardiner (ed.), *Oxinden Letters*, 244-5 (Andrews to Oxinden); York CA, House Book 37, ff. 149-51, 155, 165; Gloucestershire RO GBR/B3/3, p. 168 (Gloucester assembly minute); Surrey RO, KB 16/7/50-5 (Kingston assembly minutes); Lincolnshire RO, L/1/1/1/6 (Lincoln Assembly minute).

15. Latimer, *Bristol*, 308-10.
16. SP 29/30/28, 35/18.
17. P/C 2/55, pp. 169, 419; SP 29/28/71, 33/51; Bath CA, Council Book 2, 27 Sept.
18. Lamont, *Prynne*, 224-8.
19. SP 44/3, p. 2; P/C 2/55, p. 407.
20. *Statutes*, v. 321-3; CJ 275-338; LJ 308-58; M. H. Nicholson (ed.), *Conway Letters* (1930), 188-9 (Finch to Conway).
21. Very general accounts of the working of the act can be found in J. Sacret, 'The Restoration Government and Municipal Corporations', *EHR* xlv (1930), 247-54, and M. Mullett, thesis, ch. 1. Local studies appear in Howell, *Newcastle*, 185-6; Jones, thesis, 220-38; Holmes, *Lincolnshire*, 223; Evans, *Norwich*, 237-8; R. Austin, 'The City of Gloucester and the Regulation of Corporations', *Trans. Bristol and Gloucestershire Arch. Soc.* 58 (1936), 257-74; Sacret, 'The Corporation Act Commissioners in Reading', *Berks, Bucks. and Oxon Arch. J* 29. 1 (1926), 18-42; P. Styles, 'The Corporation of Warwick', *Trans. Birmingham Arch. Soc.* lix (1938), 30-2 and 'The Corporation of Bewdley' in *Studies in Seventeenth Century West Midland History* (Kineton, 1978), 46-8; J. S. Davies, *A History of Southampton* (1883), 494-5; Williams (ed.), *Glamorgan County History*, iv. 308; N. Palmer, 'The Reformation of the Corporation of Cambridge', *Proceedings Cambridge Antiq. Soc.* xvii (1912-13), 76-105; T. Pape, *The Corporation of Newcastle-under-Lyme* (Manchester, 1938), 14-30; Johnson, D.Phil. thesis, 354-7; R. W. Greaves, *The Corporation of Leicester* (Oxford, 1939), 8; C. Parsloe, 'The Growth of a Borough Corporation: Newark-on-Trent', *TRHS* 4th ser. xxii (1940), 194; Earl, *Newtown*, 10; Moule, *Weymouth*, 119, and to the thirty-four cases cited there I have added seventeen from *Reliquae Baxterianae*, 376-7; SP 29/61/105, 81/78, 44/3, p. 42, 4, p. 110, 10, p. 8, P/C 2/56, pp. 151, 182, *The Kingdom's Intelligencer* (18 Aug.-1 Sept.); *Oxford Council Acts*, 293-305; HMC 3rd Report, 302 (Axbridge council minute); Rob East (ed.), *Extracts from Records . . . of Portsmouth* (1971), 168-9; B. Howard Cunningham (ed.), *Some Annals of Devizes* (Devizes, 1925), 133-4; C. Parsloe (ed.), *The Minute Book of Bedford Corporation*, Bedfordshire Hist. Record Soc. xxvi (1949), xxiii-xxxiii, 146; J. S. W. Gibson and E. R. C. Brinkworth (eds.), *Banbury Corporation Records*, Banbury Hist. Soc. 15 (1977), 211; Sir James Picton (ed.), *Liverpool Municipal Records* (Liverpool, 1883), i. 237-40; J. R. Chanter and Thomas Wainwright (eds.), *Reprint of the Barnstaple Records* (Barnstaple 1900), 230-1; Richard Holmes (ed.), *The Book of Entries of the Pontefract Corporation* (Pontefract, 1882), 77-80; J. Dennett (ed.), *Beverley Borough Records*, Yorkshire Arch. Soc. Record Ser. lxxxiv (1932), 103-4, and Brit. L. Egerton MS 2538 (Northumberland to Nicholas), and twenty-seven more from the corporation minute books and related documents of Bath, Plymouth, Shrewsbury, Stratford-upon-Avon, Colchester, Buckingham, London, Great Yarmouth, King's Lynn, York, Hull, Doncaster, Bristol, Salisbury, Coventry and Worcester (*in situ*), Bury St. Edmunds (in West Suffolk RO), Eye and Aldeburgh (in East Suffolk RO), Dorchester (in Dorset RO), Exeter (in Devon RO), Ludlow (in Shropshire RO), Faversham (in Kent RO), Northampton (in Northampton-

shire RO), Malden (in Essex RO), and Ripon (in North Yorkshire RO). This makes a total sample of seventy-eight, and more examples almost certainly survive. On the other hand, it is noteworthy that good contemporary records of Ipswich, Nottingham, Appleby and other towns pass over this episode in what seems to be a painful silence.

22. Not least R. Hutton, in *The Royalist War Effort* and an essay in Morrill (ed.), *Reactions to the English Civil War*.

23. CJ 247-306; LJ 316-30; *Statutes*, v.31-18; Pepys's Diary, iii. 19; Bod. L. Tanner MS 239, f. 19 (Holland's speech); the Revd Alexander B. Grosart (ed.), *The Complete Works of Andrew Marvell* (1875), ii. 71-2.

24. CJ 317-52, 355-6; LJ 373-81; Macray (ed.), *Notes*, 29; Brit. L. Egerton MS 2043, f. 21 (Reymes's Diary); HMC 7th Report, 155 (draft act). Clarendon himself was averse to mercy; Lister's Life of Clarendon, iii. 234-8.

25. H. G. Tibbutt, *Colonel John Okey*, Bedfordshire Hist. Soc. xxxv (1954), 130-71.

26. CJ 308, 317, 374; Dawson, *Cromwell's Understudy*, 404-5, Rowe, *Vane*, 234-41; Pepys's Diary, iii. 108, 112; Brit. L. Lansdowne MS 1236, f. 132 (King to Clarendon).

27. CJ 231-67; LJ 376; Berwick (ed.), *Rawdon Papers*, 136-9; *The Mather Papers*, Massachusetts Hist. Soc. 4th ser. viii (1868), 194; Egerton MS 2043, f. 32B.

28. CJ 288-99, 424; LJ 308-14, 438-72; *Statutes*, v. 420; Staffordshire RO, D868/3/32, 45 (Newport to Leveson).

29. CJ 272-314, 378; LJ 254, 271-379, 411; Staffordshire RO, D868/3/38; Coward, *Stanleys*, 75-6.

30. *CSPD* (1660-1), 571.

31. Brit. L. Egerton MS 2537, ff. 329-30, MS 2543, ff. 24-36 (early spy reports); SP 29/62/34 (Musgrave to Williamson).

32. W. Johnson, thesis, 102-5; Pococke (ed.), *Political Works of Harrington*, 125-6, 856-9.

33. Spalding, *Improbable Puritan*, 233-4.

34. *Diary*, iii. 225.

35. Turner (ed.), Hodgson's Memoirs, 52-8; Cox (ed.), *Derbyshire Annals*, ii. 73.

36. P/C 2/55-6; militia papers at n. 24.

37. Sir Thomas Raymond, *The Reports of Divers Special Cases Adjudged in the Courts of King's Bench, Common Pleas and Exchequer* (1696), 23; *Report of Cases Taken and Adjudged in the Court of Chancery* (3rd ed., 1796), i. 121-2, iii.5; *The Fortieth Annual Report of the Deputy Keeper of the Public Records* (1879), 127-47.

38. E. 178/7275. This is actually a copy, being f. 6 of a larger whole. It is almost certainly in fact not the result of an Exchequer Special Commission and may not be an Exchequer document at all. Neither the Commission Book (E. 221/7) nor the Agenda Book (IND/17071) nor the relevant KR file contain any clues to its identity. The LTR repertory roll was equally unhelpful, and most LTR records for the Restoration period have been destroyed. This is, perhaps, an illustration of a much larger problem of the historian of the late seventeenth century: that under the law of 1958 all documents dating from before 1660 were

declared sacrosanct, while no such safeguard exists for those from the subsequent epoch.

39. W. Johnson, thesis, 50-5; SP 44/1, p. 34 (Nicholas to Deputy-Lieutenants),29/54/7, 56/96 (papers concerning Harrington).

40. H. Helyar, 'The Arrest of Colonel William Strode', *Somerset Arch. and Nat. Hist. Soc. Proceedings* xxxvii (1891), 22-40.

41. *Statutes*, v. 380-90, 442-3; CJ 290-432; LJ 399-472; *Kingdom's Intelligencer* (16-23 June); *A List of the Officers Claiming to the Sixty Thousand Pounds* (1663); House of Lords RO, Parchment Collection Box 180 (draft bill).

42. Steele, no. 3301.

43. PRO, PRO/31/3/108, f. 98 (Mountagu to Mazarin); *CSPV* 221; *Reliquiae Baxterianae*, 277.

44. The Revd T. Ellison Gibson (ed.), *Crosby Records* (1880), 196.

45. Bod. L. MS Dep. f. 9, ff. 67-8, 115; *CSPV* 226; CJ 140.

46. LJ 276-311; Lords RO, Committee Minutes (1661-4), pp. 62-4.

47. There is no satisfactory biography of Bristol, though his wartime activities are portrayed in C. V. Wedgwood, *The King's War* (1958), and R. Hutton, 'The Structure of the Royalist Party', *HJ* 24 (1981), 553-69. At the time of going to press, however, a doctoral thesis upon him has been commenced.

48. *Old Parliamentary History*, xxii. 388-92; PRO, PRO/31/3/109, f. 19 (French ambassador's dispatch); Clarendon, *Life*, ii. 104-9.

49. Brit. L. Add. MS 14269, f. 33.

50. CSP iii. Appendix, xlvii (notes between Clarendon and King); Clarendon, *Life*, 109-11; Brit. L. Egerton MS 2071, ff. 157-8, 221-2 (French ambassador's dispatches).

51. Hamilton (ed.), *Devon Quarter Sessions*, 179; Hunt (ed.), *Townshend's Notes*, 117.

52. *CTB* xxxviii-xliv records an income of 2s. from recusancy fines in 1661-2.

53. Ornsby (ed.), *Cosin Correspondence*, 97.

54. Besse, *Sufferings*, i. 75-6, 138-9, 153, 173-4, 197-8, 255-6, 262, 307-9, 347, 366, 671-2, 746-8, 764, ii. 61-3; Kent RO, N/FQZ1, p. 27; Somerset RO, DD/SFR/8/1 f. 9.

55. J. Hall (ed.), *Memorials of the Civil War in Cheshire*, Lancashire and Cheshire Record Soc. 19 (1889), 233; R. S., *The Dreadful and Terrible Voice of God* (1660-1).

56. Crosby, *English Baptists*, ii.149-72; Hayden (ed.), *Records of a Church of Christ*, 116; HMC 3rd Report, 93 (report of Willis's arrest); Derbyshire RO, D258/29/35 (letters to Bredsall and Garssington constables); Wiltshire RO, Q/S Great Rolls, Mid. and Mich. 1661; Brit. L. Add. MS 32324, f. 108 (Wiltshire committals); Essex RO, Q/SR 390/73 and PRO/103/1, Lent 132; Jeaffreson (ed.), *Middlesex Records*, iii. 319.

57. Crosby, 161-72; *State Trials*, vi. 67-104.

58. CJ 263-305, 353; LJ 316-443; *For The King and both Houses of Parliament sitting at Westminster* (1661); Barclay (ed.), *Letters*, 99-114 (3 news-letters); Staffordshire RO, D868/3/38 (Newport to Leveson); House of Lords RO, Committee Minutes (1661-4), pp. 12-13; Bod. L. Tanner MS 338, f. 135 (Clarendon to Vice-

Chancellor); *CTB* 282 (Southampton to Deputy-Lieutenants); HMC Finch MSS, i. 173 (Nicholas to Winchelsea).

59. *Statutes*, v. 350-1; HMC 7th Report, 148 (baptist petition); Barclay (ed.), *Letters*, 99-109 (E. B.'s narrative); John Gauden, *A Discourse Concerning Public Oaths* (1662); Lords RO, Committee Minutes, 103.

60. B. Reay, 'The Authorities and Early Restoration Quakerism', *J Ecclesiastical H* 34 (1983), 75; Jeaffreson (ed.), *Middlesex Records*, 321-34; SP 29/56/91 (list of sectaries in Surrey gaol) and 62/9 (Eyre to Bennett); State Trials, vi. 202-21; Tanner MS 338, ff. 110, 133-4 (Clarendon to Vice-Chancellor, and reply); George Fox, *The Cry of the Innocent for Justice* (1662); Holmes, *Lincolnshire*, 221-2; *The Kingdom's Intelligencer* (7-14 July); *Surrey Quarter Sessions Records*, xxxvi. 65-311; Crosby, *Baptists*, 172-80; Besse, *Sufferings*, i. 139, 153-4, 175, 215, 532, 690, 749, ii. 102-8; Wiltshire RO, Q/S Great Rolls and O/B, Mich. 1662; Fox's Journal, 429-35; W. Kaye, 'Early Records of Quakers near Harrogate', *J Friends Hist. Soc.* xiv (1917), 13; Penney (ed.), *Sufferings of the Quakers in Cornwall*, 40-3; Devon RO, Q/S 1/10, 1662-3; J. Raine (ed.), *Depositions from the Castle of York*, Surtees Soc.(1861), 87-8; Berkshire RO, D/F 2 A 1/1, pp. 10-12 (book of sufferings) and A/JQ2 11, pp. 12-30 (Abingdon Quarter Sessions records); Worcestershire (Shire Hall) RO, QS/R 110/100/99-101; PRO, ASSI 2/1, ff. 78-99; Essex RO, Q/SR 394/126, 395/24, 396/124; Friends' House L. Great Book of Sufferings, vol. i. p. 84 (Bristol), Durham RO, QS/OB/5, p. 153; East Suffolk RO, B105/2/6, Mich. (sessions records).

61. Steele, no. 3367.

62. SP 19/63/70 (Quaker news-letter); Reay, thesis, 153; Richard Greenway, *An Alarm from the Holy Mountain* (1662).

63. Reay, *J Eccles H* 1983, 76, and sources cited there.

64. Source as at n. 159.

65. Reay, *J Eccles H* 1983, 76-7, and sources there.

66. Ibid. 77-8.

67. Ibid. 80-4, and sources at n. 159.

68. *The Truth Exalted in the Writings of . . . John Burnyeat* (1691), 30-1.

69. Friends' House L. Swarthmore MS 4, f. 150 (Dewsbury to Fell).

70. Fox's Journal, 437-54; Barclay (ed.), *Letters*, 119-20, 122 (Parker, Cole, to Fox); *Life of William Caton*, 78-83.

71. Shaw, *Church*, ii. 116; Shaw (ed.), *Manchester Presbyterian Classis*, 346-7, and *Bury Presbyterian Classis*, 173-4.

72. See n. 124.

73. Richards, *Religious Developments*, 402; *Calamy Revised*, 17, 402, 422, 445; Palmer (ed.), *Nonconformist's Memorial*, ii. 418; Cox (ed.), *Derbyshire Annals*, i. 336; Turner (ed.), Heywood's Autobiography, i.179-80; Wiltshire RO, Q/S Great Rolls, Ep. 1661, Ep. 1662; *Hertford Sessions Rolls*, i. 138-44; Cheshire RO, QJB 2/7, Mich. 1661; Martindale's Life, 159-63; Atkinson (ed.),*North Riding Quarter Sessions*, vi. 38; Worcestershire (Shire Hall) RO, 110/97/39; Essex RO, Q/SR 391/7 and PRO 35/102/2; Lancashire RO, QSP 282/34; Green, *Re-Establishment*, 189-92;

Kingdom's Intelligencer (24-31 Mar.); *Surrey Quarter Sessions Records*, xxxvi. 182; Cumbria (Carlisle) RO, D/LONS/L1 (warrant, 17 Mar. 1662).

74. Green, 104-14 and Tanner MSS cited there; Rev. J. Wilson, 'Some Notes from Cathedral Records', *Trans. Worcestershire Arch. Soc.* (1923-4), 118; Whiteman, thesis, 62-5 and *TRHS* 1955, 128-9; Robertson, *Archaeologia Cantiana* (1876), 93-8; Burne, *JCNWAAHS* 1952, 30-1; Goodman, *Reverend Landlords*, 7-9; Gloucester RO, D936/A 24-5 (repair bills); Bod. L. Rawlinson MS D1138, f. 15 (Exeter cathedral records); HMC Dean and Chapter of Wells MSS, 432; Willis-Bund (ed.), *Townshend's Diary*, 70; *Kingdom's Intelligencer* (31 Mar.-7 Apr.); Harwood, *Lichfield*, 56-66; the Revd A. Matthews (ed.), 'A Norfolk Dissenter's Letter', *Norfolk Archaeology* 34 (1930-2), 232; HMC Report on MSS in Various Collections vii. 62-4 (Gloucester cathedral records).

75. Green, 61-73, Peterborough CL, MS 20, ff. 68-80; Whiteman, thesis, 57-60; Dumble, thesis, 333-4; Kent RO, U2134/B3/234 (note by Banks).

76. Green, 129-35; Beddard, 'The Church', 163; Pruett, *Parish Clergy*, 19-20; Essex RO, D/ACA 55; West Sussex RO, Ep 1/10/46; Cambridge UL, EDR D/2/52; Cheshire RO, EDC 1/59/64-83; Wiltshire RO, Salisbury Court Instance Book 1661-4 and Episcopal Court Office Book 13; Norwich RO, Act/70; Cumbria (Carlisle) RO, DRC 5/2.

77. Green, 127-31; Beddard, 163; Bosher, 206-7, 235-6; Pruett, 20; P. Bignall (ed.), 'Bishop Sanderson's Ordination Book', *Trans. Lincolnshire Archit. and Arch.Soc.* ix. i (1965); Palmer, *Nonconformist's Memorial*, ii. 65-8; SP 29/4, f. 68 (Henchman to Nicholas); *Reliquiae Baxterianae*, 298-300, 374-5; Willis-Bund (ed.), *Townshend's Diary*, 78; Cheshire RO, EDC 1/59/64-83; Ornsby (ed.), *Cosin Correspondence*, 21-36; Brearley, thesis, ch. 4; the Revd H. Gee, 'The Correspondence of George Davenport', *Archaeologia Aeliana*, 3rd ser. ix (1913), 6; Burne, *JCNWAAHS* 1952, 25.

78. *Reliquiae Baxterianae*, 303-68; *An Account of the Proceedings of the Commissioners of both Persuasions* (1661); *The Grand Debate* (1661); the Revd G. Gould (ed.), *Documents Relating to the Settlement of England by the Act of Uniformity* (1862), 146-76; Brit. L. Add. MS 28053, f. 1 (Farnes to Osborne).

79. Roger L'Estrange, *State Divinity* (10 May 1661) and *The Relapsed Apostate* (14 Nov. 1661); *The Author's Letter to an Anti-Episcopal Minister* (1661); *A Lively Portrait of Our New Cavaliers* (1661).

80. 'Baxter', *His Account of the causes of his being forbidden . . . to preach* (1662); *The bishop of Worcester's letter to a friend* (1662); *Hypocrisy Unveiled* (1662); L'Estrange, *A Whipp* (1662); J. C., *Another Letter with Animadversions* (1662); *D. E. Defeated* (1662); (Edward Bagshaw), *A Second Letter unto a Person of Honour* (1662); (Sir Henry Yelverton), *A Vindication of My Lord Bishop of Worcester's Letter* (1662); Baxter, *Now or Never* (1662).

81. Thomas, *Berkenhead*, 219.

82. *Reliquiae Baxterianae*, 333.

83. Edward Cardwell (ed.), *Synodalia* (Oxford, 1842), 631-73; C. A. Swainson, *The Parliamentary History of the Act of Uniformity* (1875), 15-16; Bod. L. Tanner MS 282,

ff. 52-3 (Propositions of York Convocation); Horton Davies, *Worship and Theology in England* (Princeton, 1975), ii. 373-92; P/C 2/55, pp. 549-54.

84. *Statutes*, v. 364-70; CJ 402-24; LJ 393-450; Swainson, *Parliamentary History*, 22-46; Berwick (ed.), *Rawdon Papers*, 140-4, 160-2 (Pett to Armagh); *CSPD* (1670), 670 (Wandesford to brother); CSP iii. App. xcviii-ix (Gauden to Clarendon); SP 84/165 (De Wiquefort's letter, 31 Mar.); Spalding, *Improbable Puritan*, 235-6; Tanner MS 239, ff. 45B-6 (Holland's speech) and 282, ff. 44-7 (declaration by Convocation); Doctor Williams's L. Baxter Letters 1, f.98 (Baxter to Earle); Carte MS 81, ff. 100-5 (Wharton's speech); House of Lords RO, Committee Minutes (1661-4), pp. 117-216.

85. Clarendon, 144-50; Burnet, *History*, 341; Lister's Life of Clarendon, iii. 532-4 (Monckton's narrative); Carte MS 31, f.602; 32, f. 3 (O'Neill to Ormonde); 47, f. 359 (Nicholas to Ormonde); Clarendon MS 77, ff. 319-20, 339-40 (Sheldon, Morley, to Clarendon); Hockliffe (ed.), Josselin's Diary, 140; Peter Toon (ed.), *Correspondence of John Owen* (1970), 129-30; *Mather Papers*, 187 (O. E. to Davenport); Parkinson (ed.), Martindale's Life, 166-8; Heywood (ed.), Newcome's Diary, 101-16.

86 *Calamy Revised*, xii-xiii; Richards, *Religious Developments*, ch. 6; VCH Sussex, Essex (for parishes); Devon RO, Episcopal Record 121; Pruett, *Parish Clergy*, 23.

87. *Calamy Revised*, xii-xiii; Pruett, 23; VCH Cheshire, ii. 39.

88. Based on Green, 151-61; Whiteman, thesis, 106-10; B. Williams, thesis, 122; *Calamy Revised, passim*, and the diocesan registers and institution records of Worcester, Wells, Lincoln, and Norwich (in respective county record offices).

89. e.g., Matthews, *Norfolk Archaeology* 1930-2, 229-32; *Reliquiae Baxterianae*, 374-5.

90. Green, 165-7; Whiteman, thesis, 110-12; Pruett, 23; VCH Cheshire, ii. 40-1; B. Williams, thesis, 122.

91. *Kingdom's Intelligencer* (1 Sept.-1 Dec.).

92. All preserved in Bod. L.

93. E. R. Brinkworth (ed.), *Episcopal Visitation Book for the Archdeaconry of Buckingham*, Buckinghamshire Record Soc.(1947); Wiltshire RO, Salisbury Episcopal Visitation Returns 1662; West Sussex RO, Ep 1/22/1; Lincolnshire RO, Vj 32; Borthwick Institute, R.VI.A.27; Brearley, thesis, 31-40; Cumbria (Carlisle) RO, DR 5; Herefordshire RO, Diocesan Visitation Book 18 L17, Box 2.

94. Reports in Tanner MSS 92-217.

95. CJ285, 294, 362-79; Tanner MS 315; CSP iii. App. xcv-xcvi (Gauden to Clarendon).

96. SP 29/56-63, 44/7-9, *passim*; Carte MS 221, ff. 7-8 (Bennett to Ormonde); P/C 2/56, pp. 53-8, 185-6, 239; Dalton, *Army Lists*, 23-4; *Mather Papers*, 206 (newsletter).

97. W. Johnson, thesis, 145-53, 162-6; *State Trials*, vi. 225-74; *Kingdom's Intelligencer* (3-10 Nov., 1-15 Dec., 22-9 Dec.); SP 29/62-5, *passim*; Carte MS 31, ff. 117-18 (O'Neill to Ormonde); Friends' House L. Swarthmore MS 1, f. 44 (Huks to Fell); sources at n. 237.

98. P. Hardacre, 'Clarendon and the University of Oxford', *British J of Educational Studies* ix (1960-1), 117-31; SP 44/6, p. 6 (King to Magdalen).

99. Brian Wormald, *Clarendon* (Cambridge, 1951), part III.

100. Pepys's Diary, iii. 178; *CSPV* 184; *Mather Papers*, 201 (Newman to Davenport).

101. *Calamy Revised, passim*; Palmer, *passim*; Richards, *Religious Developments*, ch. 6.

Part Three: Chapter 3

1. *Statutes*, v.314, 401-5.

Part Four: Chapter 1

1. HMC Ormonde MSS, iii. 68 (Anglesey to Ormonde); SP 29/67/90 (Walwyn to Bennet).

2. Lamont, *Marginal Prynne*, 210-11.

3. Carte MS 32, ff. 405, 597 (O'Neill to Ormonde).

4. (John Evelyn), *A Character of England* (May 1659).

5. Rugge's *Diurnal*, 29; Brit. L. Add. MS 19253, f. 203 ('Narcisse').

6. Roger Thompson, *Unfit for Modest Ears* (1979).

7. *Diary*, i. 261.

8. John H. Wilson, *The Court Wits of the Restoration* (1967), 40-2, is the honourable exception, and cites all the references.

9. Pepys's Diary, ii. 170.

10. C. H. Hartmann, *La Belle Stuart* (1924), 33, 43.

11. Pepys's Diary, iv. 37.

12. Fidelis Morgan, *The Female Wits* (1981), ix; John H. Wilson, *All The King's Ladies* (Chicago, 1958), ch. 1; Thomas Jordan, *A Royal Arbour* (1663), 21-2; Wood's Life, i. 405-6.

13. Bray (ed.), Evelyn's Diary, 259.

14. Wood, *Life*, i. 422, 509; Samuel Butler, *Hudibras: The First Part* (1662), canto 3, lines 23-30.

15. Pepys's Diary, iii. 248, iv. 1, 19; Carte MS 32, f. 312 (O'Neill to Ormonde); Anthony, Count Hamilton, *Memoirs of Count Gramont*, ed. by Allan Fea (1906), 176-206.

16. Brian Masters, *The Mistresses of Charles II* (1979), chs. 1-3; Elizabeth Hamilton, *The Illustrious Lady* (1980), 1-40; *The Chimney's Scuffle* (1662).

17. Keith Feiling, *British Foreign Policy 1660-1672* (1930), 31-58; Edgar Prestage, *The Diplomatic Relations of Portugal with France, England and Holland 1640-1668* (Watford, 1925), 144-9; G. Belcher, 'Spain and the Anglo-Portuguese Alliance of 1661', *JBS* 15 (1975), 67-88; Clarendon, *Life*, 489-522; Lister, *Clarendon*, iii. 119-21 (Clarendon to St. Albans), 503 (declaration of marriage); Staffordshire RO, D868/3/34 (Newport to Leveson).

18. Lillian Campbell Davidson, *Catherine of Braganza* (1908), chs. I-V; Clarendon, *Life*, ii. 166-7; Pepys's Diary, iii. 87; Lister, *Clarendon*, iii. 195-7 (Mountagu, King, to Clarendon); Clarendon MS 76, ff. 248-9 (Mountagu to King); Arthur Bryant (ed.), *Letters of King Charles II* (1935), 127 (King to sister); HMC 12th

Report, ix. 52-4 (Cornbury to Lady Worcester); Townshend's Diary, i. 91; Fea (ed.), Gramont's Memoirs, 108-9; *Letters of Philip, Second Earl of Chesterfield* (1829), 122-3; Bray (ed.), Evelyn's Diary, 253; *Wynn Papers*, no. 2347 (Bodvel to Wynn).

19. Clarendon, *Life*, ii. 160-95; Pepys's Diary, iii. 146-201, 282-303; Lister, *Life of Clarendon*, 202-3 (King to Clarendon), 208-10, 221-2 (Clarendon to Ormonde); Carte MS 31, ff. 559, 602, 32, ff. 3, 10-11, 23, 25-6, 40-1 (O'Neill to Ormonde); HMC 12th Report, ix. 52-4; PRO, PRO/31/3/110, f. 470 (French ambassador's dispatch).

20. Clarendon, *Life*, ii. 252-8; Pepys's Diary, iii. 191, 237, 290, iv. 38, 99, 107; Bod. L. Ashmole MS 838, f. 80 (patent of creation); Gramont's Memoirs, 314; Brit. L. Add. MS 32324, f. 168 (letter on marriage); HMC Le Fleming MSS (Fletcher to Fleming).

21. *CSPV* 205; Lister, *Life of Clarendon*, 225-8 (Clarendon to Ormonde); Josselin's Diary, 143; Pepys's Diary, iii. 245; Clarendon MS 78, ff. 63-4 (Bagshaw's examination).

22. Clarendon, *Life*, ii. 242-52; the Revd Edward Combe (ed.), *The Sale of Dunkirk* (1728); PRO/31/3/110, f. 391; John Childs, *The Army of Charles II* (1976), 11-12; Lister, *Life of Clarendon*, iii. 497-8 (notes between Clarendon and King). No more than the Portuguese dowry was the money agreed for Dunkirk ever paid in full. Charles allowed a discount upon the later instalments to have them paid in cash; Louis declined to pay the subsidy he had promised, to support English troops in Portugal, claiming that the deal over Dunkirk included this. As a result, the actual money paid over amounted in the end to just over three-fifths of that originally agreed: C. Grose, 'The Dunkirk Money, 1662', *JMH* 5 (1933), 1-18. As Grose shows, an original potential gain to the English of nearly $£\frac{1}{2}$ million was reduced to £290,000, which sufficed to pay off only a portion of the existing public debt, though the loss of the port in itself reduced future expense.

23. Feiling, *Foreign Policy*, 43; Pepys's Diary, ii. 188; J.-J. Jusserand, *A French Ambassador at the Court of Charles II* (1892), 126.

24. Combe, ed., *Dunkirk*, 114-27 (D'Estrades to Louis); Pepys's Diary, iii. 245; Clarendon MS 78, ff. 63-4; Carte MS 32, ff. 82-3; *CSPV* 205; PRO/31/3/110, f. 391 (Battailer to Lionne).

25. Or so he told the French ambassador: Brit. L. Egerton MS 2071, pp. 273-4.

26. *CSPD* (1661-2), 244, 367, 428.

27. Salisbury, Abingdon, Norwich and Great Yarmouth.

28. Burnet, *History*, i. 169; Clarendon, *Life*, i. 420-2; Macray (ed.), *Notes*; *CSPV* 197-8.

29. Clarendon, *Life*, ii. 256-7; Pepys's Diary, ii. 142; *Rawdon Papers*, 163-5; Egerton MS 2071, f. 221; CSP, iii. App. xcvi-c (Gauden to Bristol), *CSPD* (1661-2), 373 (Gauden's election); 453 (reference of dispute to Bristol); Clarendon MS 76, ff. 176-7 (Ellesdon to Clarendon); Carte MS 32, f. 68.

30. The biography is Violet Barbour, *Henry Bennet, Earl of Arlington* (1914). His

fortunes at this period are recorded in Evelyn, *Diary*, 247; *Rawdon Papers*, 163-5; Egerton MS 2071, ff. 221-4, 344, 365; *CSPV* 203, which do not quite seem to support Mrs Barbour's belief that Bennet was given the Privy Purse to punish Clarendon for failing to support relief of Catholics.

31. Lister, *Life of Clarendon*, iii. 198-201; Carte MS 221, ff. 9-10 (Bennet to Ormonde).

32. Carte MS 32, f. 23.

33. Donald Nicholas, *Mr. Secretary Nicholas* (1955), 298-305; Clarendon, *Life*, 223-8; HMC Heathcote MSS, 54-5 (Inchiquin to Fanshaw); Lister, *Life of Clarendon*, 223-9 (Nicholas, Clarendon, to Ormonde); HMC Finch MSS, i. 22-2 (Nicholas to Winchelsea); Carte MS 32, ff. 67-8.

34. Pepys's Diary, iii. 227, 229, 290-1, 302-3; Lister, *Life of Clarendon*, iii. 223-4; Carte MS 32, ff. 82-3; *CSPV* 205, 216-17.

35. Carte MS 32, ff. 82-3, 161; 46, ff. 7-9 (O'Neill, Shaan, Bennet, to Ormonde); Combe (ed.), *Dunkirk*, 114-27 (French ambassador).

36. Cobbett, *Parliamentary History*, iv.259.

37. Pepys's Diary, iv. 5-6; *Master Edmund Calamies Leading Case* (1663); *Mercurius Politicus* (1-8 Jan.); Corporation of London RO, Mayor's Waiting Book 2, 13 Jan.; SP 28/67/39, 44/9, f. 224, 44/10, f. 28 (warrants).

38. Carte MS 221, ff. 15-16 (Bennet to Ormonde); Lister, *Life of Clarendon*, iii. 233 (Clarendon to Ormonde); *Mather Papers*, 207-10 (Hooke to Davenport); PRO/31/3/110, ff. 487-90 (French ambassador); P/C 2/56, p. 261.

39. *Mather Papers*, 107-9; O. Airy, 'Notes on the Reign of Charles II)', *British Quarterly Review* lxxvii (1880), 332-3 (Sheldon to King).

40. Lister, *Life of Clarendon*, iii. 231-3; PRO/31/3/110, ff. 456, 468, 487-90.

41. Scott, *Joint-Stock Companies*, i. 263-5; James Thorold Rogers, *A History of Agriculture and Prices in England* (Oxford, 1887), v. 272, 827.

42. *CTB* 266 (Commons to Southampton). Somerset RO, DD/PH/223/118 is an example of the resulting circular.

43. Steele, no. 3319.

44. Ibid. no. 3372; *CTB* 367-558, *passim*; Ratcliff and Johnson (eds.), Warwickshire Sessions Order Book, 225; P/C 2/56, p. 401; Essex RO, Q/SR 395/72; Stocks (ed.), Leicester Records, 486.

45. *CSPV* 180; *The Chimney's Scuffle* (1662); SP 29/57/15 (Williamson to Nicholas); Pepys's Diary, iii. 127.

46. Corporation of London RO, Remembrancia ix. 49; *CTB* 504; Jessup, *Twysden*, 157-8.

47. Clarendon, *Life*, i. 365-7; Pepys's Diary, ii. 189; Woods, *Life*, i. 465-6; *CSPV* 206. Chandaman, *Public Revenue*, seems to have proved the reality of royal extravagance during most of the reign.

48. Carte MS 32, f. 161 (Shaan to Ormonde).

49. This session is considered in D. T. Witcombe, 'The Cavalier House of Commons: the Session of 1663', *BIHR* 32 (1959), 181-91, and *Charles II and the Cavalier House of Commons 1663-1674*. These pioneering studies contain

interesting ideas, most sound, though also a few factual errors. My basic difference with Dr Witcombe is that I am more impressed by the sheer bloody-mindedness of the MPs.

50. LJ 478-9.

51. This seems to be the only possible point at which this episode, recalled in Clarendon, *Life*, ii. 204-11, could have occurred.

52. PRO/31/3/110, f. 557 (French ambassador).

53. LJ 482-90; Christie, *Shaftesbury*, i. App. lxxix-ix (the bill); *Mather Papers*, 207-10 (Hooke to Davenport).

54. This I take to be the import of the division, from the fact that one of the tellers for the minority was Thomas Clifford, on whom the government had especially relied in the Commons: Clarendon, *Life*, iii. 207.

55. CJ 436-52; Tanner MS 239, ff. 70B-71 (Holland's speech).

56. *Fair Warning* (1663); *Evangelium Armatum* (1663); Thomas Pierce, *The Primitive Rule of Reformation* (1663); *Hudibras, on Calamy's Imprisonment* (n.d.); *The Pope's Poesie* (1663); Samuel Hinde, *England's Perspective-Glass* (1663); Bishop Sanderson of Lincoln, *Reason and Judgement* (1663); Thomas Philpot, *The Creples Complaint* (1663); *Quæries upon Quæries* (1663); *Herod and Pilate Reconciled* (1663); O. Udall, *Perez Uzza* (1663); Pepys's Diary, iv. 93; Thomas, *Berkenhead*, 220-3, HMC Ormonde MSS 46-7 (Coventry to Ormonde).

57. LJ 492.

58. *Reliquiae Baxterianae*, 429-30; Lee (ed.), Henry's Diary, 129; *Mather Papers*, 207-10 (Hooke to Davenport); Heywood (ed.), Newcome's Diary, 150; Brit. L. Sloane MS 4107, ff. 16-20 (address of independents).

59. Pepys's Diary, iv. 44.

60. This was the great discovery of G. Abernathy jun., 'Clarendon and the Declaration of Indulgence', *J Ecclesiastical H* xi (1960), 64-72. I feel, however, that Professor Abernathy imposed a coherence upon his sources that they actually lack, and that the same is true to a much slighter extent of Green, *Re-Establishment*, 220-4.

61. This is the account of the contemporary sources, the French ambassador (PRO/31/3/111, ff. 55, 106) and the Venetian (*CSPV* 238), which are consistent with Clarendon's letters to Ormonde in Lister, *Life of Clarendon*, iii. 243-5. The different story told in the much later memoirs of Clarendon and York must, it seems, be disregarded.

62. CJ 452-63; LJ 495-500; Pepys's Diary, iv. 115, 123; Lister, *Life of Clarendon*, iii. 243-5; *CSPV* 241; HMC Ormonde MSS iii. 46-7; PRO/31/3/111, ff. 79, 91, 96, 106; Buckinghamshire RO, M/11/19 (Denton to Verney, 26 and 29 Mar.).

63. CJ 463-514; *Statutes*, v. 446 (Vestry Act); Lords RO, Parchment Collection, Box 13 (draft conventicle act).

64. Chandaman, 204-5; Brit. L. Harleian MSS 1223, ff. 200-46, and 1243, ff. 1726-30 (Warwick's reports); CJ 451-6.

65. V. Vale, 'Clarendon, Coventry and the Sale of Naval Offices', *Cambridge HJ* xii

(1956), 107-25, examines the problem carefully in this important area of patronage and finds little to substantiate the charge of corruption.

66. CJ 471-533; LJ 561-79; Pepys's Diary, iv. 156; SP29/90/9 (court news-letter); Carte MSS 32, ff. 390-1, 405, 597-8 and 221, ff. 44, 56 (O'Neill, Bennet, to Ormonde); Tanner MSS 47, ff. 31 (Warwick to Fanshawe), 43-9 and 47, f. 76 (correspondence and speech of Holland), and 239, ff. 47-9 (Holland's speech); *Statutes*, 453-95; *CSPV* 249; Margouliath (ed.), Marvell's Letters, ii. 35; HMC 4th Report, 329 (Chetwynd to Bagot); Latimer, *Bristol*, 321; Chandaman, 176-7.

67. Somerset RO, Q/S R 103/13. See also SP 19/68/118 for Cornwall.

68. Durham UL, Cosin Letter Book 2, f. 103 (Frewen to Cosin); SP 29/68/39 and 75/99-100 (reports from Kent); Devon RO, Exeter Q/S Rolls, Easter 1663; Palmer, *Nonconformist's Memorial*, iii. 169-70, 206; A. Matthew (ed.), 'A Censored Letter', *Trans. Congregational Hist. Soc.* ix (1824-6), 269; Berkshire RO, A/JQ2/11/30.

69. Carte MS 46, f. 51.

70. CSP iii, Ap. xlvii (King to Clarendon); Johnson, *Lives of the English Poets*, i. 139.

71. Jusserand, *French Ambassador*, 115.

72. Pepys's Diary, iv. 65; Spalding, *Improbable Puritan*, 237.

73. Pepys's Diary, iv. 249-51.

74. P/C 2/56, p. 377; *CSPD* 171.

75. *The Intelligencer* (31 Aug.).

76. Carte MS 32, f. 405.

77. HMC Ormonde MSS iii. 171 (Anglesey to Ormonde).

78. P/C 2/56, p. 402; Crosby, *English Baptists*, 180-5 (misdated 1664).

79. Sixty-seven pounds worth of which were suddenly collected in early 1663: *CTB* xxviii-xxxiv.

80. Ibid.; SP 29/90/9; Carte MS 221, f. 77; HMC 3rd Report, 92 (H. M. to Seymour); Bryant (ed.), *Letters* (King to Board of Greencloth); HMC Ormonde MSS iii. 78, 91 (Anglesey to Ormonde); HMC 15th Report, vii. 171 (Countess of Devonshire to Bruce).

81. Pepys's Diary, iv. 123, 136-8, 173; Carte MS 32, ff. 390, 477, 516.

82. His career is traced by G. Davies, 'The Political Career of Sir Richard Temple', *HLQ* iv (1940-1), 47-84; E. Gay, 'Sir Richard Temple', *HLQ* vi (1943), 255-91 and C. Roberts, 'Sir Richard Temple', *HLQ* xli (1977-8), 137-55, who between them seem to have examined all the relevant documents in the Huntington Library.

83. The story is well told between Jones, *Saw-Pit Wharton*, 197-200, and 'The Bristol Affair', *J Religious H* 5 (1968-9), 16-30, and Roberts, *HLQ* 1977-8, 140-2, to which I have added information from PRO/31/3/112, ff. 23-113; P/C 2/56, ff. 446, 525; Carte MSS 32, ff.708-9; 33, ff. 34-5; Steele, no. 3386.

84. Pepys's Diary, iv. 58, 60, 73-89; Clarendon MSS 80, ff. 73-4; 81, ff. 59-60; Tanner MS 47, ff. 68, 72, 79, 99 (news-letters); *CSPV* (1664-6), 3-11; Brit. L. Harleian MS 6011, ff. 131B-2 (Bristol to King); PRO/31/3/113, ff. 7-81, 117; Bod. L. Rawlinson MS A130, ff. 4-5 (debate in Lords); Cyril H. Hartmann, *The King My*

Brother (1954), 91-2 (King to Madame); HMC Ormonde MSS, iii. 134 (Anglesey to Ormonde).

85. The life is C. H. Hartmann, *The King's Friend* (1951). Hartmann was inclined to whitewash his subjects even more than most biographers, but the process is convincing here for Berkeley's public life, if not his private one. His peerage is recorded in Bod. L. Ashmole MS 838, f. 97.

86. The former portrait is of course C. H. Hartmann, *La Belle Stuart* (1924), who labours gallantly to counter that of Gramont's Memoirs, 119-20, 146-51, 188. Information on her in these months is in PRO/31/3/111, ff. 106-27; 112, ff. 1-199; Pepys's Diaries, iv. 37, 48, 206-38, 366-71; Carte MS 33, f. 120.

87. Pepys's Diary, iv. 339; T. Brown (ed.), *Miscellanea Aulica* (17092), 306-15 (Bennet to Ormonde, Buckingham); HMC 3rd Report, 92 (Warner to Seymour); Bryant (ed.), *Letters*, 147-9 (Charles to Madam); PRO/31/3/112, ff. 177-270; HMC Ormonde MSS, iii. 98.

88. Ornsby (ed.), *Cosin Correspondence*, 104; SP 29/70/13, 58, 78/16, 52, 81/31, 53.

89. Bod. L. MS Eng. Hist. b. 212 (Oxfordshire papers); HMC 11th Report, iv. 26 (Norfolk); HMC Le Fleming MSS, 31 (Cumberland); Brit. L. Sloane MS 813, f. 67 (Hampshire), Add. MS 34222, ff. 42B, 44 (Northamptonshire); Durham UL, Mickleton MS 31, f. 58 (Durham).

90. Carte MS 46, ff. 92, 95.

91. HMC Ormonde MSS, iii. 91.

92. The rebellion has been intensively studied piecemeal, by S. Chadwick, 'The Farnley Wood Plot', *Thoresby Soc.* xv (1909), 122-6; F. Nicholson, 'The Kaber Rigg Plot', *Trans. Cumberland and Westmorland Antiq. and Arch. Soc.* N.S. xi (1911), 212-32; The Revd H. Gee, 'A Durham and Newcastle Plot', *Archaeologia Aeliana* 3rd ser. xiv (1917), 145-56, and 'The Derwentdale Plot', *TRHS* 3rd ser. xi (1917), 127-40; C. Whiting, 'The Great Plot of 1663', *Durham University J* xxii (1920), 155-67; J. Walker, 'The Yorkshire Plot, 1663', *Yorkshire Arch. J* 31 (1932-4), 348-59; W. G. Johnson, thesis, ch. 6; Brearley, thesis, ch.3; Reay, thesis, 183-8. The full range of sources for it consists of SP 29/81-99, 44/12-16, *passim*; Add. MSS 25463, ff. 167-9 (Yorkshire evidence); 33770, ff. 1-48 (Yorkshire evidence); 34306, ff. 30-52B (Derbyshire evidence); *Newes* (22 Oct.-19 Nov.); *Intelligencer* (19 Oct.-23 Nov.); Carte MS 81, ff. 197-223 (Yorkshire and Westmorland evidence); Raine (ed.), *York Castle Depositions*, 102-17; Turner (ed.), *Hodgson's Memoirs*, 58-64; Cumbria (Carlisle) RO, D/MUS Letters, Bundles 5 and 6 (Yorkshire and Westmorland evidence).

93. *State Trials*, v. 983-5; *Newes* (14 Jan.-18 Aug.); *Intelligencer* (18 Jan.-8 Aug.); PRO, ASSI/42/1, ff. 126-7; Chadwick, *Thoresby Soc.* 1909, 125-6; HMC Heathcote MSS, 146 (news-letter); Durham UL, Mickleton MS 31, ff. 40-60.

94. Primary sources as at nn. 91 and 92.

95. Brown (ed.), *Miscellanea Aulica*, 320; HMC 11th Report, vii. 6-7 (committals); *A Narrative of the Imprisonment and Usage of Colonel John Hutchinson* (1664); *Memoirs of Colonel Hutchinson*, 340-61; *The Case and Usage of Mr. Edw. Bagshaw* (16 Mar. 1664); P/C 2/57, ff. 59, 78, 86; SP 29/92/14-15, 44/16, ff. 21-3, 84, 86.

96. *Intelligencer* (26 Oct., 9 Nov.); *Newes* (24 Dec.); SP 29/91/4 (Mascall to Froude); HMC Hastings MSS, i. 144 (Salisbury to Huntingdon).

97. SP 29/81/57, 71, 75, 96-9; HMC 3rd Report, 92-3 (3 letters to Seymour); *Calamy Revised*, 47, 196,209, 393, 431; Lee (ed.), Henry's Diary, 148-9; Stocks (ed.), Leicester Records, iv. 493-4; 'Chetwynd Papers', *Collections for a History of Staffordshire* (1942), 107-10 (3 letters to Deputy-Lieutenants); Owen and Blakeway, *Shrewsbury*, i. 485-6 (Newport to Ottley).

98. See the complaints in SP 29/79/60, 83/98.

99. SP 29/83/83, 90/38, 100, 91/7, 68, 93/23, 95/2, 98/57; Besse, *Sufferings*, i. 175, ii. 11-13; *State Trials*, v. 629-48; HMC Le Fleming MSS, 32-3; Friends' House L. Abraham MS 7 (Fox to Albemarle); Durham RO, Q/S/OB/5, ff. 1182-203; B. Quintrell (ed.), 'Proceedings of the Lancashire Justices of the Peace', *Lancashire and Cheshire Record Soc.* 121 (1981), 114; Raine (ed.), York Castle Depositions, 88, 119-20; Lancashire RO, FRM 1/39, ff. 155-6, QSP/245/23-8, 253/1 and QJ1/2, f. 119; Cumbria (Kendal) RO, Kendal Indictment Book, ff. 82, 91 and Appleby Indictment Book, Michaelmas, Hilary, Easter sessions.

100. SP 19/90/23, 92/42, 97/5; Besse, *Sufferings*, i. 92, 139, 216, 293-4, 392-3, 532, 569, 714; *Calamy Revised*, 4-5, 14, 24, 151, 176, 196, 206-7, 545; Robert Gibbs, *A Record of Local Occurrences* (Aylesbury, 1878), i. 217; Friends' House L. Swarthmore MS 4, ff. 183, 187 (Baker to Fox), 278 (Caton to Fell), and Great Book of Sufferings, i. 374; Somerset RO, DD/SFR/8/1, ff. 20-1; Warwickshire Sessions Indictments, 152-3; Wiltshire RO, Q/S Great Rolls, Easter 1664; Northamptonshire RO, QSR/1/32-3; Berkshire RO, A/JQ2/11, ff. 31-6; Surrey RO, KB 2/7/2-4; Dorset RO, Q/S Order Book 1, f. 24; Lincolnshire RO, SOC/F/13, f. 69; P/C 2/57, p. 46; Devon RO, Q/S 1/10, Easter 1664; PRO, ASSI/105/35/7; East Sussex RO, Q1/EW/3, ff. 35-43; Kent RO, Q/SMc/1, Easter 1664; Norfolk RO, Norwich Mayors' Court Book 23, f.208 and SF 95, pp. 23-31; East Suffolk RO, B105/2/6, Easter 1664; Hood (ed.), *Portsmouth Sessions Papers*, 30.

101. SP 29/81/73, 90/10, 92/83; P/C 2/56, ff. 619, 625; Besse, *Sufferings*, i. 45-50, 199-202; Hayden (ed.), *Church of Christ*, 117-18; Berkshire RO, D/F/2/A/1/1, pp. 12-15; Clarendon MS 81, ff. 182-3, 199-200 (papers on Reading arrests); Bristol RO, Q/S Minute Book, ff. 50-1; H. Cadbury (ed.), *The Swarthmore Documents in America* (1940), 69-70 (Curtis to Fox).

102. HMC 3rd Report, 92-3 (Lovett, Popham, to Seymour).

103. As evinced by the sources at n. 99.

104. LJ 582-3; J. Jones, 'Court Dependents in 1664', *BIHR* xxxiv (1961), 81-2; PRO/ 31/3/113, ff. 41, 61 (French ambassador's dispatches); Carte MS 33, f. 389 (Clarendon to Ormonde); *CSPD* (1663-4),538.

105. C. Robbins, 'The Repeal of the Triennial Act', *HLQ* 12 (1948-9), 121-40, and sources cited there; Buckinghamshire RO, M/11/19 (Denton to Verney, 25 and 31 Mar., 3 Apr., Hobart to Verney, 1 Apr.); Carte MS 81, ff. 22-4 (Wharton's speech); Leicestershire RO, DG7/Box 49/56 (Finch's speech); SP 29/96/97, 110 (Doleman to Lovelace).

106. Barclay (ed.),*Letters*, 129-31, 139; Friends' House L. Swarthmore MSS 1, f. 48

(Hookes to Fell); 4, f. 96 (Whitehead to Fox) and Spence MS 3, f. 162 (Rous to Fell).

107. *Statutes*, v. 516-20; CJ 539-66; LJ 604-21; Tanner MS 47, f. 143 (news-letter); Rawlinson MS A130, Lords' debates, 13 and 16 May; Pepys's Diary, v. 147-8; Carte MS 81, ff. 170-8 (Wharton's notes).

108. *Statutes*, v. 514-16; CJ 539-50, LJ 605-21; Tanner MS 239, ff. 69B-70 (Holland's speech).

109. *LJ* 621; Bryant (ed.), *Letters*, 156-8 (Charles to Madame).

110. SP 29/100/36-7, 77, 103/105, 112/125, 113/107; *A True, Short, Impartial Relation of the Proceedings at the Assize* (1664); *Newes* (14 July 1664-19 Jan. 1665); *Intelligencer* (15 Aug.-12 Dec. 1664); Besse, *Sufferings*, i. 24-5, 48-52, 76-7, 93, 104, 139, 155, 176, 234-5, 244-8, 263, 334, 393-406, 533, 691-3, 751, 765, ii. 17, 68-9, 109-11; *Calamy Revised*, 6, 47-8, 271-2, 444; Palmer, *Nonconformist's Memorial*, i. 114-15; Friends' House L. Barclay MS 89 (Cole to Fox) and Swarthmore MSS 1, f. 47; 3, ff. 88, 123; 4, ff. 98, 129, 179, 201; *Surrey Quarter Sessions Records*, xxxix. 188-225; *Warwickshire Sessions Indictments*, 154; Hayden, *Church of Christ*, 118-20; Bristol RO, Q/S Minute Book, ff. 55, 63; Cumbria (Carlisle) RO, D/LONS/L1 (Mittimus, 20 July 1664); Henry, *Diary*, 157; Jeaffreson (ed.), *Middlesex Records*, 340-70; Hardy (ed.), *Hertford Sessions Rolls*, i. 162-76, and *Hertford Sessions Books*, 120; Wiltshire RO, Q/S Great Rolls, Mich. 1664; Atkinson (ed.), *North Riding Sessions Records*, 78-9; Raine (ed.), York Castle Depositions, 88; Durham RO, Q/S/OB/5, pp. 210-21; Berkshire RO, A/JQ2/11, pp. 38-41; Lincolnshire RO, SOCF 13, pp. 81-2; PRO, ASSI/35/105/47-8, 106/2, 9, and ASSI/1/2/1, Hereford, Lent; East Sussex RO, Q1/EW/3, ff. 46-56; Kent RO, N/FQZ/1, pp. 29-30; Essex RO, Q/SR/402/25-6, 82-4; Corporation of London RO, Mayor's Waiting Book 3, pp. 6-130; Staffordshire RO, D3/59/2/18, f. 1B; East Suffolk RO, FK/6/2/1, p. 90 and B105/2/6; Cumbria (Kendal) RO, Kendal Indictment Book, f. 91 and Appleby Indictment Book, Midsummer 1664; Humberside RO, DD/QR/10, ff. 27-8, /24, and /25, pp. 15-16; Moule, *Weymouth*, 83; Dorset RO, Q/S Order Book 1, f. 73; Northamptonshire RO, QSR/1/37; Surrey RO, KE/2/7/5-7; Devon RO, Q/S 1/10, Epiphany 1665; Brit. L. Add. MS 27967, ff. 81-3 (Greg to Doughty); H. Fishwick (ed.), *The Church Book of Altham*, Chetham Soc. N.S. 33 (1894), xx.

111. *The History of the Life of Thomas Ellwood* (1827), 111-12; Fox's Journal, 499-502; Kent RO, U269/C307 (Newport to Berkeley, 22 Nov. 1662); Besse, *Sufferings*, i. 257; Friends' House L. Barclay MS 64 (Cole to Fox); Palmer, iii. 206.

112. Friends' House L. Great Book of Sufferings, p. 427.

113. And they recorded their meetings: Norfolk RO, SF 42-3 (Quaker registers); Norfolk Record Soc. *Miscellany* (1951) (books of gathered churches).

114. SP 29/103/110 (Carleton to Bennet).

115. Gardiner (ed.), *Oxinden Letters*, 296-300 (letters of Nichols).

116. Palmer, *Nonconformist's Memorial*, iii. 170; Friends' House L. Swarthmore MS 3, ff. 105-6 (Fisher etc. to Fox). Charles clearly did not receive Bridgeman's idea

well, for when the judge reached Hertford two weeks later he insisted upon the oath.

117. Carte MS 81, ff. 255-6 (seamen's statements); Friends' House L. Thirnbeck MS 3 (Rous to Fell); P/C 2/57, f. 314.

118. In Waiting Book 3, cited above.

119. G. Turner (ed.), 'Williamson's Spy Book', *Trans. Congregational Hist. Soc.* v (1911-12), 242-356.

120. Hayden (ed.), *Church of Christ*, 119-20; Harrison (ed.), *Bunyan Meeting*, 25-7. See also SP 29/115/40; Bod. L. Add. MS C307, f. 58.

121. Brit. L. Add. MS 24485, pp. 21-5 (Chandler's diary); Henry's Diary, 157-74; Heywood's Autobiography, 186-94; Newcome's Autobiography, i. 142; T. W. Dands, *Annals of Evangelical Nonconformity in the County of Essex* (1863), 367-8 (Stockton's diary).

122. William Sachse (ed.), *The Diary of Roger Lowe* (1938).

123. *For the King and both Houses of Parliament: Being A Declaration of the present Suffering* (1664); Swarthmore MS 1, f. 46 (Hockes to Fell).

124. See the irritation of the Mayor of Reading in Clarendon MS 81, ff. 199-200.

125. Besse, *Sufferings*, i. 199-202.

126. *Life of Ellwood*, 110-11; North Yorkshire RO, RQ/R/6/7 (message from London).

127. W. B(ayley), *An Epistle General* (1664); (William Dewsbury), *The Word of the Lord To Sion* (1664) and *The Discovery of Man's Return* (1665); George Fox, *Three General Epistles* (1664); Thomas Green, *An Epistle of Tender Love* (1664); W. S., *A Free Flowing of the Father's Love* (1664); John Crook, *A True and Faithful Testimony* (1664); W. S(mith), *The Glory of the New Covenant* (1664); George Whitehead, *This is an Epistle For The Remnant of Friends* (1665); Kent RO, N/FQZ/2, pp. 159-65; Somerset RO, DD/SFR/10/1, ff. 1-3.

128. The books of sufferings, discussed under Venner's Rising, above.

129. W. S(mith), *Joyfull Tidings* (1664).

130. P/C 2/57, pp. 226, 314 and 2/58, pp. 11, 73, 200; SP 29/105/115 (council warrant).

131. Chandaman, 23, 55, 207-9; CTB 579/647; P/C 2/57, f. 157.

132. SP 44/17, pp. 34, 62, 134-8; P/C 2/57, f. 217; West Suffolk RO, Bury St. Edmunds Assembly Book, 18 Aug. 1664.

133. SP 29/00/12 (anonymous letter); Pepys's Diary, v. 21, 41, 56, 194; E. Thompson (ed.), *Correspondence of the Family of Hatton*, Camden Soc.(1878), i. 37 (Lyttleton to Hatton); Josselin's Diary, 144; HMC Hastings MSS, ii. 148 (Salisbury to Huntingdon); PRO/31/3/113, ff. 303-40.

134. Bod. L. Add. MS C304a, ff. 156-8.

135. The returns are in Tanner MSS 130-52.

136. Tanner MS 315, ff. 66-7; Cheshire RO, EDA 2/3, ff. 20-24B.

137. CJ 549-68; HMC 7th Report, 177-8 (draft act concerning tithes).

138. Cobbett, *Parliamentary History*, iv. 309-11; Tanner MS 47, f. 201 (Hacket to Sheldon).

139. The most detailed and valuable account of English diplomacy in the 1660s remains Sir Keith Feiling, *British Foreign Policy 1660-1672* (1930), but there are additional insights of all kinds in Charles Wilson, *Profit and Power* (1957), J. R. Jones, *Britain and Europe in the Seventeenth Century* (1966); P. Rogers, *The Dutch in the Medway* (1970); R. A. Stradling, 'Spanish Conspiracy in England', *EHR* lxxxvii (1972), 269-86, and *Europe and the Decline of Spain* (1981); Herbert H. Rowen, *John De Witt* (Princeton, 1978).

140. Longleat House Coventry MS C11, f. 5 (Coventry's analysis).

141. PRO/31/3/114, f. 26.

142. There is an account in Richard Ollard's lively and accurate biography of Holmes, *Man of War* (1969), chs. vi-xi. The papers relating to the expedition are in Longleat House Coventry MS XCV and SP 29/110/87, 114/19.

143. Wilson, *Profit and Power*, 116-21.

144. PRO/31/3/113, ff. 155, 167 (Comminges to Louis).

145. Corporation of London RO, Remembrancia ix, ff. 69-74; HMC 4th Report, 229 (draft by Coventry for King); Pepys's Diary, v. 220, 231, 279; Clarendon MS 81, f. 40 (Downing to Clarendon); P/C 2/57, f. 199.

146. His biography is by John Beresford: *The Godfather of Downing Street* (1925), which is sound and useful. Feiling, 112-16, and Rowen, chs. 13, 23, add insights, as do the papers of Downing's negotiations in Brit. L. Add. MS 22920.

147. Longleat House, Coventry MS C11, f. 5.

148. CJ 548, 553; LJ 599-600.

149. Longleat House Coventry MS C11, ff. 5-7; Pepys's Diary, v. 121-61; HMC 4th Report, 229 (Coventry's draft); Thompson (ed.), *Hatton Correspondence*, 34-7 (Lyttleton to Hatton); Feiling, 83; Sir George Sitwell (ed.), *Letters of the Sitwells and Sacheverells* (Scarborough, 1900), 54 (George to Francis Sitwell); PRO/31/3/113, ff. 167, 182, 309.

150. So much is plain, though there has been no detailed study of the war since Gardiner's *History*. The finances of the republic are investigated by Habakkuk, *Ec. HR* 1962.

151. Rowen, ch. 24.

152. SP 29/98/124-99/98 (letters of Pett, Coventry); Pepys's Diary, v. 148,358; PRO/31/3/113, ff. 270-2; Longleat House Coventry MS XCV, ff. 52-3 (Rupert's instructions); PRO, SP 84/171/184-6 (Cunaeus to States General).

153. Pepys, v. 283; PRO/31/3/113, ff. 340, 421.

154. Rowen, 461-2.

155. SP 29/103/19-104/93 (letters of Pett, Rupert, Coventry, and York); PRO/31/3/113, ff. 359, 383-4, 399; SP 84/172-3 (Cunaeus and Van Gogh to Greifher or States General); National Maritime Museum, LBK 8, ff. 111-15 (Pepys to Mountagu, Coventry).

156. Corporation of London RO, Repertory 70, f. 5B and Journal 45, ff. 389B, 398, 423B.

157. CJ 567-9; LJ 624-7; Cobbett, *Parliamentary History*, iv. 306-7 (Bennet to Holles); Brit. L. Add. MS 36988, f. 88 (Paston's speech) and 32092, ff. 26-7

(Clifford to Coventry); Tanner MS 239, ff. 33B-34 (Holland's speech); *Statutes*, v. 525-52.

158. SP 29/105/92.

159. PRO/31/3/113, f. 468. For native confirmation, see East Suffolk RO, HD/36/86 (Sicklemore to bailiffs of Ipswich).

160. Carte MS 33, f. 743.

161. J. R. Tanner (ed.), *Further Correspondence of Samuel Pepys* (1929), 33-4 (Pepys to Mountagu); Clarendon MS 81, ff. 168-72 (Downing to Clarendon); Feiling, 135.

162. PRO/31/3/113, f. 493, 114, f. 29 (Ruvigny, Comminges, to Lionne).

163. Cobbett's *Parliamentary History*, iv. 308-9 (the declaration); SP 84/175, f. 188 (Van Gogh to States General, 6 March); P/C 2/58, ff. 52-3.

164. *Newes* (2-23 Mar.); *Intelligencer* (6, 27 Mar.).

165. PRO/31/3/114, f. 113 (Comminges to Lionne).

166. Bod. L. Ashmole MS 838, ff. 100-13 and Brit. L. Add. MS 4182, f. 3 (the creations); Wood's Life, ii. 7.

167. HMC Marquis of Bath MSS, ii. 147-8 (Lady Wentworth to Holles).

168. Newes (22, 29 Dec.); Sachse (ed.), Lowe's Diary, 77; J. E. Foster (ed.), *The Diary of Samuel Newton* (Cambridge, 1890), 7, 12; Tanner (ed.), *Pepys Correspondence*, 32-3 (to Mountagu); R. C. Anderson (ed.), *The Journal of Edward Mountagu, First Earl of Sandwich*, Navy Records Soc. (1929), 157-72; *The Blazing Star* (1665); W. Cooper (ed.), 'Notices of the Last Great Plague', *Archaeologia* 37 (1856), 1.

Part Four: Chapter 2

1. Bod. L. Rawlinson MS A174, f. 6 (papers on 'Loyal London').

2. SP 29/104/47 (list of ships); National Maritime Museum, LBK 8, p. 141 (Pepys to Mountagu).

3. P/C 2/57, p. 277.

4. Brit. L. Add. MS 32094, ff. 28-30 (memorandum by Coventry); Pepys's Diary, vi. 10-12.

5. P/C 2/57, p. 290; Admiral Sir Henry Richmond, *The Navy as an Instrument of Policy 1558-1727* (Cambridge, 1953), 143-4.

6. SP 29/112/124 (regulations).

7. The classic work upon this subject is Arthur W. Tedder, *The Navy of the Restoration* (Cambridge, 1916), which, though due all the honour of a pioneering study, is limited and badly in need of replacement.

8. SP 29/116/76 (list of ships); Brit. L. Add. MS 9311, ff. 20-1, 89B (navy board papers) and 36782, f. 24 (York's order); P/C 2/58, p. 30.

9. Such as in Herefordshire: Brit. L. Add. MS 11051, ff. 91-9, or Derbyshire: Sitwell (ed.), *Letters*, i. 62. See the council appealing for loans in Northamptonshire RO, Isham MS 574.

10. SP 29/103/93, 114/117 (letters of Chatham storekeeper, Middleton); Tanner (ed.), *Pepys Correspondence*, 28-45; Bod. L. Rawlinson MS A174 (contracts); P/C 2/57, pp. 275, 294; Longleat House Coventry MS xcvi, ff. 52-74 (contracts);

National Maritime Museum, LBK 8, pp. 109-11 (contracts); Brit. L. Add. MS 32094 (papers on supplies) and 36782, f. 25B (York's order).

11. HMC 9th Report, i. 267 (for Devon), 15th Report, vii. 97-8 (for Portsmouth) and Le Fleming MSS, 33 (for Westmorland); T. Hope, 'The Vice-Admiralty of Essex', *Trans. Essex Arch. Soc.* 22 (1936-40), 303; Picton (ed.), *Liverpool Municipal Records*, i. 311; P/C 2/57, 261, 294,334 and 2/58, pp. 46, 91; East Suffolk RO, HD/36/134-46; Durham UL Mickleton MS 31, ff. 45-7; *Wynn Papers*, no. 2417; Brit. L. Add. MS 18979, f. 283 (Yorkshire); NLW Penrice and Margam MS iv, f. 20 (Glamorganshire).

12. SP 29/103-18, *passim* (letters from York, Pett, Middleton, Coventry); Tanner (ed.), *Pepys Correspondence*, 32-3; P/C 2/57, p. 243; East Suffolk RO, HD/36/104, 14-7 (Ipswich correspondence); HMC Le Fleming MSS, 34; G. Thompson, 'The Bishops of Durham and the Office of Lord Lieutenant', *EHR* xl (1927), 363, 365; Foster (ed.), *Newton's Diary*, 12; PRO, ASSI/35/106/9.

13. On this see Coventry in SP 29/118/75.

14. SP 29/116/76 (layout of fleet); Tedder, *Navy*, 60; Sandwich, *Journal*, 179.

15. Sandwich, *Journal*, 180-214; SP 29/118/75-122/21 (letters from Coventry and York); Carte MS 75, f. 305 (York to Sandwich); Brit. L. Add. 10117, f. 139B (Rugge's journal).

16. Sandwich's Journal, 214-29; Newton's Diary, 12; Jusserand, *French Ambassador*, 145; Clark (ed.), *Life of James*, 407-15; Rowen, 577-9; Pepys's Diary, vi. 122-3; SP 29/122/75-123/87 (letters of Falmouth, Coventry, Burges); Carte MS 34, ff. 22-30 (Coventry to Berkeley); Temple and Anstey (eds.), *Mundy's Travels*, v. 172; Granville Penn, *Memorials of Sir William Penn* (1833), ii. 322-32; Brit. L. Add. MS 22920, f. 136 (list of captured ships); *A Second Narrative of the Signal Victory* (10 June 1665).

17. *Newes* (15 June); *Intelligencer* (10 July); Pepys's Diary, vi. 123; SP 29/124/38, 42, 49, 50 (from Norwich, Chester, Newcastle, Dartmouth); Wood, *Life*, ii. 38; HMC Le Fleming MSS, 37 (Fleming to Williamson); Jusserand, *French Ambassador*, 147. The surviving accounts of the chamberlains record the cost of the celebrations.

18. *CTB* 666.

19. Feiling, 145.

20. P/C 2/58, p. 189; Brit. L. Add. MS 4182, f. 21 (news-letter).

21. Pepys's Diary, vi. 123-4; Clarendon, *Life*, ii. 391-5, f. 42 (French envoys to Louis).

22. Rowen, 579-81; Feiling, 144; Lister, *Life of Clarendon*, ii. 344-5; SP 84/177-8 (letters of Van Gogh to Greifher and States General).

23 H. T. Colenbrander (ed.), *Bescheiden uit Vreemde Archieven omtrent de Groote Nederlansche Zeeoorlagen* ('s-Gravenhage, 1919), i. 250-7 (Sandwich's account), corrected by Sandwich's journal, 236-50; R. C. Anderson (ed.), *The Journals of Sir Thomas Allin*, Navy Records Soc. (1939-40), i. 239-41; Longleat House Coventry MSS xcv, ff. 107-57 and xxviii, ff. 78-80 (papers on Bergen affair); Pepys's Diary, vi. 195-6, 228-9; Carte MS 46, f. 197 (Arlington to Ormonde) and ·75, ff. 317, 325-6 (list of ships, Clifford to Sandwich); 'Sir Gilbert Talbot's Narrative',

Archaeologia xxii (1829), 33-48; SP 29/129/88 (Coleman to Pepys); Cyril H. Hartmann, *Clifford of the Cabal* (1937), chs. iii-iv (papers on Bergen).

24. Colenbrander (ed.), *Bescheiden*, 257-67, again corrected by Sandwich's Journal,
250-82; Anderson (ed.), Allin's Journals, i.242-51; SP 29/129/64-133/27 (letters
of Coventry, Sandwich, Rosse); Carte MSS 34, ff. 381, 389-92 (Arlington to
Ormonde); 47, f. 426 (Coventry to Ormonde); 74, f. 234 (list of ships); 75, ff. 331,
337, 348, 359, 371 (letters of Pepys, York, minutes of council of war); Brit. L.
Egerton MS 2618, f. 120 (Sandwich to Albemarle).

25. See Albemarle's letter in Carte MS 75, ff. 363-4.

26. Harris, *Sandwich*, ii, ch. ix, to which I have added material from Clarendon, *Life*,
465-82; Pepys's Diary, vi. 230-342; PRO, HCA 32/11/303-4 (examinations of
ships); SP 29/149/89-90 (report of prize officers); Brit. L. Harleian MS 7170, ff.
73-80 (report of Commons committee); Carte MS 34, ff. 452-4 (Southwell,
Broderick to Ormonde); Penn, *Memorials*, ii. 375-6 (Georges to Penn).

27. Rowen, 584-5; Carte MS 47, f. 428 (Coventry to Ormonde) and 75, ff. 375-80
(naval reports); PRO, ADM/106/11, ff. 122, 124 (Albemarle to Navy Board,
Pepys); Pepys's Diary, vi. 275-6; SP 29/135/67 (Sandwich to Arlington), 44/20, f.
89 (King to Lord-Lieutenant).

28. Of the excellent literature upon the subject, I have found the following particularly useful for the epidemic of 1665-6: J. F. D. Shrewsbury, *A History of
Bubonic Plague in the British Isles* (Cambridge, 1970); *The Plague Reconsidered*,
Local Population Studies Supplement (1977); P. Slack, 'The Disappearance of
Plague: An Alternative View', *Ec. HR* 2nd ser. 34 (1981), 469-76. On the sufferings of the capital, Walter G. Bell, *The Great Plague in London in 1665* (2nd ed.,
1951), remains full of interesting facts, though I differ from his ideas on the
behaviour of the government.

29. *Reflections on the Weekly Bills of Mortality* (1665); Shrewsbury, chs. 7-9; Slack,
469-70.

30. Shrewsbury, 461-2; Slack, 473, 475; Corporation of London RO, Remembrancia
ix, f. 74; Nathaniel Hodges, *Loimologia* (1720), 5.

31. Steele, nos. 3428, 3439; SP 44/17, p. 129 (King to navy board); Pepys's Diary, vi.
124-208, *passim*; *London's Dreadfull Visitation* (1665); C. Morris, 'Plague in
Britain' in *The Plague Reconsidered*, p. 38; Bell, 244; *Intelligencer* (5 June-24 July);
P/C 2/58, pp. 55, 135, 141, 178; Brit. L. Add. MS 4182, f. 15 (news-letter).

32. The various accounts in the Guildhall L, supplemented by *Orders Received and
Published by the Lord Mayor . . . concerning the Infection of the Plague* (1665); *The
Shutting Up Infected Houses . . . Soberly Debated* (1665); T. V(incent), *God's Terrible
Voice in the City* (1667), 31.

33. The above accounts, plus Bell, 47-9, 178-9; Corporation of London RO,
Repertory 70, ff. 153-155B; Vincent, 39, 50; Hodges, 18; William Austin, *The
Anatomie of the Pestilence* (1666), 7, 38.

34. The accounts, plus Bell, 112-13, 132-3, 197-8, 214, 220.

35. Brit. L. Add. MS 10117, f. 147 (Rugge's journal); Vincent, 34; Hodges, 8.

26. Atkinson (ed.), *North Riding Quarter Sessions Records*, 90-5; Quintrell (ed.),

Lancashire Justices of the Peace, 117; Palmer, *Nonconformist's Memorial*, i. 103-4; Essex RO, Q/SR 406/104.

37. SP 29/129/27 (Hickes to Williamson).

38. Bell, 156.

39. *The Shutting Up Infected Houses . . . Soberly Debated*; Hodges, 7; J. V., *Golgotha* (1665).

40. Pepys's Diary, vi. 186-7, 201, 268; Bray (ed.), Evelyn's Diary, 276; Howarth (ed.), *Pepys's Letters*, 24-5; the Revd Alexander Taylor (ed.), *The Works of Symon Patrick* (Oxford, 1858), ix. 584 (Patrick to Mrs Gauden); Austin, 30, 34-5; Crossley (ed.), Worthington's Diary, ii. 175.

41. G. Elliott (ed.), *Autobiography and Anecdotes by William Taswell, Camden Miscellany* ii (1853), 9; Cooper (ed.), 'Notices', *Archaeologia* 1856, 7, 9 (Allin to Fryth); Gumble, *Monck*, 415, 417; Vincent, 35, 38; Hodges, 16, 18.

42. Shrewsbury, 481, 530-5; I. Doolittle, 'The Plague in Colchester', *Trans. Essex Arch. Soc.* 3rd ser. 1-4 (1961-2), 141-2; A. Jones, 'The Great Plague in Ipswich', *Proceedings of the Suffolk Institute of Archaeology* xxviii (1958-60), 76-9; Davies, *Southampton*, 496-9; Latimer, *Bristol*, 33; J. Wilshere, 'Plague in Leicester', *Trans. Leicestershire Arch. Soc.* xliv (1968-9), 63-4; Gibbs, *Local Occurrences*, i. 221; Cooper, *Annals of Cambridge*, iii. 518; Gray and Brittain, *Jesus College*, 95; Shirley, *Hanley*, 37; Blomefield, *Norfolk*, iii. 410 (Norwich assembly order); Ashford, *High Wycombe*, 145; Brown, *Bunyan*, 173; J. Charles Cox, *The Parish Registers of England* (1910), 157, 165; HMC 2nd Report, 115 (Lover to Blythe), 6th Report, 336 (Murray to Slingsby), 11th Report, vii. 196 (Reading assembly order), 14th Report, viii. 145 (Bury assembly order); Jusserand, *French Ambassador*, 167-70; Cooper (ed.), 'Notices', 8; Palmer, *Nonconformist's Memorial*, ii. 405, iii. 314; Newton, *Diary*, 13-15; Wardale (ed.), *Clare College Letters*, 64-5, 69-71; Dennett (ed.), *Beverley Borough Records*, 136-8; Ornsby (ed.), Cosin Correspondence, 134-43; SP 29/127/33 (Carleton to Williamson), 128/32, 129/14 (Carlisle to Williamson), 134/34 (Clarke to Williamson), 134/102 (Cooley to Muddiman), and 44/17, p. 138 (King to Yarmouth bailiffs); Tanner MS 45, f. 22 (Davenport to Sancroft), 26 (Hacket to Sheldon); Brit. L. Egerton MS 2538, ff. 260-2 (Cornbury to Nicholas); Gloucestershire RO, C16/15-20, D340a (news-letters to Ducie); Buckinghamshire RO, M11/20 (Verney to father, 4 Sept., and Gardiner to Verney, 20 Sept.); Dorset RO, Q/S Order Book 1, f. 114; Norfolk RO, C/S2/2, Mids. and Mich. 1665 (Q/S Order Book); and Bradfer-Lawrence 1c (i) (Townshend to Paston, 19 June); Peterhouse L, Cambridge, Beaumont's journal, pp. 74-5.

43. Thus Shrewsbury, 534-5, dismisses the Durham cases as typhus, though the evidence is inconclusive and the strong link of the area with London through the coal trade made its infection quite possible.

44. *Londons Dreadfull Visitation*; Pepys's Diary, vi. 328, 341; Cooper (ed.), 'Notices', 18; Hodges, 27; *Newes* (9 Nov.-7 Dec.); sources at n. 210.

45. Copies of the letter survive in HMC Le Fleming MSS, 35, HMC Kenyon MSS, 75-6, and 13th Report, iv. 464-5; Brit. L. Add. MS 11049, ff. 79-80.

46. Jusserand, *French Ambassador*, 96-7.

47. Gumble, 415; Taylor (ed.), Patrick's Works, ix. 595; SP 29/128/62 (Coventry to Arlington).

48. Besse, *Sufferings*,. i. 406-7.

49. W. G. Johnson, thesis, 293-7, 342; SP 29/128/53 (Coventry to Arlington), 132/28 (Muddiman to Williamson); Brit. L. Add. MS 4182, ff. 29-43 (news-letters); Cooper (ed.), 'Notices', 8; Cornwall RO, DD/T/2003 (Bassett to Petitt); Besse, *Sufferings*, i. 407-8; *Calamy Revised*, 461; Palmer, *Nonconformist's Memorial*, ii. 255-6.

50. SP 44/20, ff. 82-3.

51. *Intelligencer* (7 Aug.-2 Oct.); *Newes* (10-24 Aug.); SP 29/128/1-133/20 (23 letters of Coventry to Arlington), 134-57 (Bettson to Arlington); HMC MSS in Various Collections, ii. 120 (Coventry to Fauconberg); *Calamy Revised*, 417; Turner (ed.), Hodgson's Memoirs, 64-5; Durham UL, Mickleton MS 31, f. 55 (Fauconberg to Cosin).

52. *Calamy Revised*, 400; SP 29/132/13 (Marley to ministers); HMC MSS in Various Collections, vii. 428 (Nottinghamshire militia papers); Durham UL, Mickleton MS 31, f. 34 (Cosin to deputies); HMC Fleming MSS, 38 (Fleming to Williamson); A. Hawkes, 'Sir Roger Bradshaigh', *Chetham Miscellany* N.S. vii (1945), 30-1.

53. Holmes, *Lincolnshire*, 224; HMC 2nd Report, 88 (Carbery to Caernarfonshire deputies) and 3rd Report, 245 (Cheshire militia papers); *Wynn Papers*, nos. 2442, 2446 (Caernarfonshire militia papers); Palmer, *Nonconformist's Memorial*, ii. 109, 124; *Calamy Revised*, 368; Henry, *Diary*, 175; Brit. L. Add. MS 41656, f. 45 (Norfolk militia papers); SP 29/132/39 (Brooke to Arlington).

54. Besse, *Sufferings*, i. 570; Bod. L. Add. MS C302, f.221 (Yelverton to Sheldon); J. Simmons (ed.), 'Some Letters from Bishop Ward of Exeter', *Devon and Cornwall Notes and Queries* xxi (1940-1), 329-31 (Ward to Sheldon).

55. Wilkins (ed.), *Concilia*, iv. 582-4 (Sheldon to bishops); Tanner MS 45, ff. 17, 21 (replies); G. Lyon Turner (ed.), *Original Records of Early Nonconformity* (1911), i. 178-84 (replies); Bod. L. Add. MS C305, f. 79 (reply); C308, ff. 32-48 (Sheldon to bishops); Durham UL Cosin Letter Book 1B, ff. 122,125 (Sheldon to Cosin).

56. The other was J. W., *A Friendly Letter to the Flying Clergy* (6 Sept. 1665). Vincent, 48, testifies to the impact of *A Pulpit*.

57. SP 29/127/136 and 129/63.

58. Bell, 225; *Calamy Revised*, 356; Palmer, *Nonconformist's Memorial*, ii. 192; Vincent, 48-50.

59. Buckinghamshire RO, M11/20 (Yate to Verney, 21 Sept.).

60. SP 29/126/11 (Coventry to Arlington); HMC Portland MSS iii. 293 (De Repos to Harley); Carte MS 34, ff. 452-3 (Southwell to Ormonde).

61. CJ 614-24; LJ 694-9; Carte MS 34, f. 468 (Broderick to Ormonde); Buckinghamshire RO, M11/20 (Hobart to Verney, 6 Dec.).

62. CJ 614-23; LJ 684-701; Carte MS 34, ff. 429, 431 (Broderick, Southwell to Ormonde) and 215, f. 214 (Broderick to Ormonde); PRO, ADM/106/3520, f. 26B (account of naval expenditure); PRO/31/3/115, f. 222 (French ambassadors to Louis); *Statutes*, v. 570-4; Pepys's Diary, vi. 270.

63. Clarendon, *Life*, iii. 1-26. Pepys's Diary, vi. 292, confirms that Downing and Coventry convinced the King of the scheme privately.

64. Pepys's Diary, vi. 275-7; Brit. L. Add. MS 32094, f. 48 (Coventry to Falmouth).

65. Pepys's Diary, vi. 276, where this news, coming as it did from Sandwich, must rank above mere court gossip. It may be compared with the news in Brit. L. Add. MS 18929, f. 283 (Brian to Lord Fairfax) that the King was considering re-founding the Council of the North by prerogative power alone.

66. CJ 617-21; *Statutes*, v. 575.

67. Sutch, *Sheldon*, 146.

68. CJ 615-21; LJ 683-700; *Statutes*, v. 576-7.

69. CJ 621-6; Carte MS 80, f. 757 (Wharton's notes).

70. Printed in C. Robbins, 'The Oxford Session', *BIHR* 21 (1946-8), 219-24.

71. *Calamy Revised*, 452.

72. Ibid., *passim*; Palmer, *Nonconformist's Memorial, passim*.

73. Simmons (ed.), 'Letters of Ward', 335-6,359-62; Rawlinson MS D1350, ff. 328-30 (declaration).

74. *Reliquiae Baxterianae*, Part 3, 13-14; Rawlinson MS D1350, f. 329 (declaration). There survive also records of two ministers who took the oath in Somerset (*Calamy Revised*, 510, 526), of eleven in Northamptonshire (Henry's Diary, 183), and of eight from Northumberland and Durham who did so (Raine [ed.], York Castle Depositions, 135-6), making the silence in other counties all the more strange.

75. *Calamy Revised*, 253; Bod. L. Add. MS c308, f. 66 (Sheldon to governor of Dover); Palmer, *Nonconformist's Memorial*, iii. 321; Fishwick (ed.), *Altham Church Book*, xx-xxi.

76. *Calamy Revised*, 57; Palmer, *Nonconformist's Memorial*, iii. 314; William Doel, *Twenty Golden Candlesticks* (Trowbridge, 1908), 22; Lee (ed.), Henry's Diary, 181.

77. *Reliquiae Baxterianae*, 14, 18; Simmons (ed.), 'Letters of Ward', 359-62.

78. Pepys's Diary, vi. 287, 292; SP 29/119/49 (Middleton to Pepys), 135/29, 57 (Gauden to Navy Board).

79. *CTB* xxviii-xxix; Chandaman, 212.

80. Pepys's Diary, vi. 11.

81. Carte MS 34, f. 484 (Broderick to Ormonde).

82. P/C 2/58, pp. 95, 111; Cooper (ed.), 'Notices', 18; F. W. Dendy (ed.), *Extracts from the Records of the Company of Hostmen of Newcastle-upon-Tyne*, Surtees Soc. (1901), 131-2; SP 29/161/47 (Forster to Williamson).

83. Steele, nos. 3422-46, *passim*.

84. Bod. L. Add. MS C308, f. 50B (Sheldon to bishops).

85. Simmons (ed.), 'Letters of Ward', 288.

86. *CTB* i. 647, 670, 723, 725.

87. HMC Kenyon MSS, 76 (Southampton and Ashley to JPs); Wiltshire RO, Q/S OB, the same letter, 30 Nov. 1665. Some justices, however, were more dutiful—see Hampshire RO, QO/4, p. 124.

88. SP 29/153/192-3 (gentry petition and reply); Clarendon MS 84, ff. 98-105

(accusations against Culpeper); Sir R. Worsley, *History of the Isle of Wight* (1781), 138-9 (Clarendon's letters).

89. *CTB* i. 688; P/C 2/59, pp. 21-2.

90. Sitwell (ed.), *Letters*, i. 62 (Sitwell to Mazine); Pepys's Diary, vi. 211; Essex RO, QSR 405/72.

91. SP 44/22, pp. 290, 324. In the end, furthermore, the privy purse actually received less than one-fortieth of the total proceeds from prizes: PRO/30/24/40/39.

92. Richard Ollard, *Pepys* (1974), 133-4.

93. And provoked an equally excellent book: Christopher Clay, *Public Finance and Private Wealth* (Oxford, 1978).

94. Clarendon, *Life*, iii. 27-32; Carte MS 34, f. 486 (Southwell to Ormonde). Southampton appears in all his feebleness and ignorance in Tanner (ed.), *Pepys Correspondence*, 41-2, 120-2 (Pepys to Coventry).

95. Brit. L. Add. MS 9311, ff. 31-2 (report among Navy Board papers); Longleat House Coventry MS xcvi, ff. 108-11 (Navy Board to York).

96. P/C 2/58-9, *passim*; Pepys's Diary, vi. 45.

97. Brit. L. Add. MS 32094, f. 28 (Coventry's notes); LJ 699.

98. Carte MS 34, f. 464 (Conway to Ormonde); HMC Portland MSS, iii. 293-4 (De Repos to Harley).

99. Pepys's Diary, vii. 8; HMC 6th Report, 336-7 (Vaus to Slingsby).

100. Wood's Life, ii. 67; HMC Portland MSS, 295-6 (De Repos to Harley).

101. Pepys's Diary, vi. 255; Tanner (ed.), *Pepys Correspondence*, 66-82 (Pepys to York, Coventry, Sandwich, Pett); Brit. L. Add. MS 32094, ff. 40-1 (Coventry's notes).

102. Feiling, 148-97; Rowen, 598-618; D. Clark, 'Edward Backwell as Royal Agent', *Ec. HR* (1938-40), 45-51; *CTB* ii. xxxiii.

103. SP 29/147/2 (draft appeal); Tanner MS 45, ff. 73, 77 (replies from bishops); the Revd A. Browne, 'Archbishop Sheldon and the Dioceses of Gloucester and Bristol', *Trans. Bristol and Gloucestershire Arch. Soc.* 61 (1939), 272-3 (Sheldon to bishops); Scott, *Joint-Stock Companies*, i. 281; Brit. L. Egerton MS 2651, f. 188 (King to Oxford); Kent RO, NR/JB, f. 26 (King to Kent commissioners); HMC 7th Report, 578 (King to Essex JPs).

104. *CTB* i. 694-725.

105. Pepys's Diary, vi. 252-5, 279; vii. 105-6; Tanner (ed.), *Pepys Correspondence*, 54-68, 93-115, 126-30 (Pepys to Albemarle, Coventry, York); Berkshire RO, Trumbull Add. MS 19/26 (Coventry's notes); Tanner MS 45, ff. 35, 41-2 (York to fleet); Brit. L. Add. MSS 9311, f. 96 (Navy Board to York) and 19399, f.99 (York to fleet); P/C 2/58, p. 338.

106. Roseveare, thesis, 45-53, App. 1; HMC 6th Report, 337 (Walsh to Slingsby).

107. SP 29/138-45, *passim* (hundreds of letters from naval officials); Tanner (ed.), *Pepys Correspondence*, 86-123, 132-40 (Pepys to Coventry, Navy Board to York); Steele, no. 3449; the Revd J. R. Powell and E. K. Timings (eds.), *The Rupert and Monck Letter-Book*, Navy Records Soc. 112 (1969), 13-48; Brit. L. Add. MSS 9311, ff. 98B-101 (Navy Board to York) and 36782, ff. 32-4B (York to fleet);

Longleat House Coventry MS xcvi, ff. 108-11 (Navy Board to York); Dorset RO, D124 Box 233 (Pley to Strangeways).

108. Longleat House Coventry MS cii, ff. 5-7; Clarendon, *Life*, ii. 465, 482-7; Pepys's Diary, vi. 323; Carte MS 34, ff. 454, 484, 512 (Broderick to Ormonde).

109. R. Shelley, 'The Division of the English Fleet in 1666', *Mariner's Mirror* xxv, pp. 178-96; Peter Fraser, *The Intelligence of the Secretaries of State* (Cambridge, 1956), ch. 4; Powell and Timings (eds.), *Letter-Book*, 200-20; Rowen, *De Witt*, 586-7; Julian S. Corbett, *England in the Mediterranean* (1904), ii. 54-8.

110. CJ ix. 12 (Albemarle's narrative); Colenbrander (ed.), *Bescheiden*, 312-401 (many English and Dutch accounts); SP 29/158/1-63 *passim* (23 letters and papers on the battle not edited by Colenbrander); Powell and Timings (eds.), *Letter-Book*, 212-60; Evelyn's Diary, 281-2; Anderson (ed.), Allin's Journals, i. 270-1; Penn, *Memorials*, ii. 388-9, 402-3; Brit. L. Harleian MS 6843, ff. 3-4 (Ayscue to King), Sloane MS 3328, ff. 12-15 and Add. MS 17484, ff. 8-9 (accounts of the battle).

111. Pepys's Diaries, vii. 150-70; Evelyn's Diary, 281; HMC Fleming MSS, 40 (Smith to Fleming); Henry's Diary, 1809; Sitwell (ed.), *Letters*, i. 76 (George to Francis Sitwell); Earwaker, *East Cheshire*, i. 115; Norfolk RO, B-L 1c (i) (Paston to wife, 7-19 June). Most of the surviving churchwardens' accounts do not distinguish between ringing for this and for the subsequent battle.

112. Rowen, 587-9; Colenbrander (ed.), *Bescheiden*, 397-410.

113. SP 44/20, pp. 108, 112-15 (King's directions) and 29/161/111-163/126, *passim* (letters concerning 22 counties); Dorset RO, D124 Box 233 (five letters, 25 June-16 July); HMC 13th Report, iv. 466-7 (3 letters on Suffolk) and MSS in Various Collections, ii. 122-3 (3 letters on Yorkshire); Dalton, *English Army Lists*, 59-62; Earwaker, *East Cheshire*, 120; Hawkes, *Chetham Miscellany* (1945), 31-2; Durham UL Mickleton MS 31, ff. 38-42.

114. Corporation of London RO, Letter-Book WW, f. 78 and Journal 46, f. 99; Lister, *Life of Clarendon*, iii. 434-5 (Clarendon to Ormonde); SP 29/158/93-5 (King to nobles); Tanner MS 45, f. 84 (Hacket to Sheldon) and 131, f. 16 (same); Browne, *Trans. Bristol and Gloucester Arch. Soc.* (1939), 274 (Sheldon to Ironside); Simmons (ed.), 'Letters of Ward', 363-4.

115. SP 29/158/72-161/132, *passim* (letters to Pepys, Coventry, and Navy Board, and related papers).

116. SP 29/159/75-164/36, *passim* (letters to Williamson, Pepys, Coventry, Arlington); PRO, ADM/106/13, ff. 165-7 (York to Navy Board); Pepys's Diary, vii. 189, 215; HMC Portland MSS, iii. 297 (De Repos to Harley); Powell and Timings (eds.), *Letter-Book*, 57-194, 262-4; Allin, *Journals*, i. 274-5; Penn, *Memorials*, 405-6 (Coventry to Penn); Brit. L. Add. MSS 9311, f. 113B (Pepys to Coventry) and 41656, f. 50 (warrant to Norfolk); P/C 2/59, pp. 69-90. Not a single press officer or pressed seaman has left a testimony: the process is seen entirely through the eyes of their superiors.

117. Colenbrander (ed.), *Bescheiden*, 411-52; Powell and Timings (eds.), *Letter-Book*, 104-13, 265-79; *Historical Memoires of . . . Prince Rupert* (1683), 44-5; Allin,

Journals, i. 277–8; R. Anderson (ed.), *Naval Operations in the Latter Part of the Year 1666*, Navy Records Soc., *Naval Miscellany*, III (1928), 5–14; Brit. L. Add. MS 17484, f. 11 (anonymous account).

118. Pepys's Diary, vii. 217; Brown (ed.), *Miscellanea Aulica*, 412 (Arlington to Ormonde); P/C 2/59, f. 92; SP 29/166/28–168/167 (letters to Williamson, Pepys, Hicke).

119. See Coventry's remarks in Pepys's Diary, vii. 225, and the King's instructions in SP 29/166/86.

120. The best account, using all sources, is in Ollard, *Man of War*, ch. xiii.

121. Powell and Timings (eds.), *Letter-Book*, 126–7; Rawlinson MS A174, f. 207 (Hayes to Pepys); Anderson (ed.), *Naval Operations*, 28.

122. Rowen, 591; SP 29/167/132–170/155, *passim* (letters of Albemarle, Rupert, Clifford, Lysle, Honeywood); Allin, *Journals*, i. 280–8, and Anderson (ed.), *Naval Operations*, 28–34; Powell and Timings (eds.), *Letter-Book*, 128–51; Brit. L. Add. MS 17484, ff. 13–15; Rawlinson MS A174, ff. 211–14 (Coventry to commanders).

123. SP 29/171/44–174/27, *passim* (letters of Rupert, Reade, Salisbury, Middleton, Allin); Powell and Timings (eds.), *Letter-Book*, 151–74; Allin, *Journals*, i. 288–95; Anderson (ed.), *Naval Operations*, 35–47; Add. MS 17484, ff. 16–18; Pepys's Diary, vi. 312.

124. Capp, *Fifth Monarchy Men*, 213; Pepys's Diary, vii. 47, 55; SP 29/160/120 (Mascall to Williamson).

125. Slack, *Ec. HR* 1981, 470–1.

126. Shrewsbury, 482–528; Doolittle, *Trans. Essex Arch. Soc.* 1961–2, 142; A. Smith, 'Plagues in Suffolk', *Notes and Queries* cxcviii (1953), 385; Jones, *Proceedings Suffolk Institute of Archaeology* (1958–60), 80–8; Blomefield, *Norfolk*, iii. 410; Davies, *Southampton*, 499; Cox, *Parish Registers*, 174; Jessup, *Twysden*, 109; Gray and Brittain, *Jesus College*, 95; Ashford, *High Wycombe*, 145; Pepys's Diary, vii. 267, 285; Evelyn's Diary, 282–3; Newton's Diary, 16; Josselin's Diary, 151–6; Cooper (ed.), 'Notices', 20–1; *The London Gazette* (22–5 Oct., 8–12 Nov.); SP 29/148/37–79/41, *passim* (Muddiman's news-letters and letters to Williamson, Arlington, Pepys and Navy Board) and 44/14, p. 89 (King to Norton); Doctor Williams's L. MS 38/208 (Dover General Baptists' Church Book); Buckinghamshire RO, M11/21 (Cary to Verney, 15 June and 23 July); Wiltshire RO, Q/S OB, Mids.-Mich.; P/C 2/58, pp. 390–1 and /59, pp. 5–125, *passim*; Kent RO, Q/SO/E1, ff. 105–16; East Suffolk RO, B105/2/7, Mids.; Norfolk RO, Mayor's Court Book 24, ff. 1–16; Hull CA, Letters 730–1; Peterhouse L. Cambridge, Beaumont's Journal, p. 83; HMC 3rd Report, 94 (Gee to Clarke); Northamptonshire RO, QSR/1/47.

127. L. Bradley, 'The Most Famous of All English Plagues', in *The Plague Reconsidered*.

128. Sources as at n. 294.

129. The very detailed account by Walter George Bell, *The Great Fire of London in 1666* (reprint, 1951) cannot be faulted, and to its sources I can add only

P. Harvey (ed.), 'A Foreign Visitor's Account of the Great Fire', *Trans. London and Middlesex Arch. Soc.* 20 (1959-61), pp. 76-87; Brit. L. Add. MS 11043, f. 117 (Sandys to Scudamore) and Cornwall RO, DD/T/2005A (John to Lewis Tremayne).

130. Steele, nos. 3470, 3473, 3477; Corporation of London RO, Journal 46, f. 20 and Repertory 71, f. 170B.

131. Bell, *Great Fire*, 218-27.

132. Carte MS 46, f. 363 (Arlington to Ormonde); Clarendon, *Life*, iii. 83-5, 96.

133. Bell, *Great Fire*, 320; Clarendon, *Life*, iii. 84-8; Steele, no. 3473; SP 29/170/121 (pamphlet); Evelyn's Diary, 288; HMC Portland MSS, iii. 298-9 (De Repos to Harley); Jeaffreson (ed.), *Middlesex Records*, iii. 384-6; Harvey (ed.), 'A Foreign Visitor's Account'; Elliott (ed.), Taswell's Autobiography, 11; 'Copy of a Letter to Sir Robert Atkyns', *Archaeologia* xix (1821), 105-9.

134. Peacock (ed.), *Monckton Papers*, 82-5 (Houlden citizens to Monckton); Wood's Life, 86-7; Quintrell (ed.), *Lancashire Justices*, 120; HMC Le Fleming MSS, 42 (Carlisle to Fleming); Raine (ed.), *York Castle Depositions*, 145-6; Hayden (ed.), *Church of Christ*, 122; Hardy (ed.), *Hertfordshire Sessions Rolls*, i. 188; Spalding, *Improbable Puritan*, 238-9; Ornsby (ed.), *Cosin Correspondence*, 155-6 (Byerly, Tempest, to Cosin); SP 29/170/152, 171/10-129, *passim* (letters from ten provincial sources).

135. *The London Gazette* (26-30 Apr.); Pepys's Diary, vii. 405.

136. Parkinson (ed.), Newcome's Autobiography, 159.

137. Bell, *Great Fire*, 191-5; HMC Portland MSS, iii. 301-2 (De Repos to Harley); Pepys's Diary, vii. 357, viii. 82-3; SP 29/175/111 (Muddiman to Mansell).

138. SP 29/163/90, 108 (Hope, Browne, to Williamson).

139. SP 29/174/109, 175/26, 43, 45, 163 (letters from Coventry, Norwich, Naneby); Evelyn's Diary, 290; Newton's Diary, 16.

140. *Diary*, vii. 286.

141. A neat outline of the whole affair is provided by Caroline A. Edie, *The Irish Cattle Bills* (1970). pp. 1-16 cover the story to this point, and there is additional information in HMC Ormonde MSS, iii. 52-8 (Coventry to Ormonde).

142. Edie, 17-22; Witcombe, *Cavalier House*, 389; Marvell's Letters, ii. 40; House of Lords RO, Committee Minutes (1664-71), pp. 90-2, and Parchment Collection, Box 13 (draft bill); Robbins, *BIHR* 1946-8, 218.

143. Clarendon, *Life*, iii. 128.

144. Pepys's Diary, vii. 337; CSPD (1660-85), 163 (George to Joseph Williamson); Roberts, thesis, 220-1.

145. Bod. L. Add. MS C302, f. 71; C. 308, f. 73B. See also the speculations about means to avoid hostility in the Commons, in Carte MSS 72, ff. 97-8; 217, f. 336.

146. Buckingham really awaits his biographer, though Hester W. Chapman, *Great Villiers* (1949), is lively and narrates his story well. Wilson, *Court Wits*, is a useful corrective to a tendency to overvalue his contribution to literature.

147. Clarendon, *Life*, iii. 133; Fea (ed.), Gramont's Memoirs, 147-51; PRO/31/3/110, ff. 487-8, 550-1.

148. Staffordshire RO, D868/3/48B, 51B (Newport, Charlton, to Leveson) and loose leaf in D868 (Talbot to Leveson, 7 Aug. 1660); Marvell's Letters, ii. 18; *CSPV* xxxiii. 172; Brit. L. Egerton MS 2071, ff.346-7 (French ambassador's dispatch).

149. To judge from the frequent references in SP 29.

150. SP 29/118/54, 83, 95 (Peterborough to Williamson); Sandwich, *Journal*, 179, 194.

151. Clayton, thesis, 1-73.

152. LJ xii. 4; CJ 625-35; Pepys's Diary, vii. 294-318; Caroline Robbins (ed.), *The Diary of John Milward, Esq.* (1938), 8-10. In Milward, we at last have a good diary of the Cavalier Commons, at precisely the moment that its proceedings become more thoroughly reported to Ormonde.

153. Pepys's Diary, vii. 309, 325; SP 29/174/85 (Clifford to Arlington).

154. Pepys's Diary, vii. 314; Evelyn's Diary, 289-90.

155. Pepys's Diary, vii. 307.

156. Edie, 23-6; Witcombe, 44; sources listed in these. I accord with Dr Witcombe's detailed narrative, but not with his impression that at this stage the Commons were deliberately delaying supply.

157. Witcombe, 46-8, and sources there. Again, I dissent from Dr Witcombe in only one point: the excise was not wholly a court project, but supported by some backbenchers.

158. CJ 627, 641-2, 649; Milward's Diary, 3, 7, 31; SP 29/177/141 (council order) and 44/20, pp. 134-5 (King to Lord-Lieutenants); LJ 21; Steele, no. 3479.

159. Edie, 37-30; Milward's Diary, 22; Haley, *Shaftesbury*, 187-91; Carte MS 35, ff. 99, 109-11, 115-17, 126, 148 (Broderick, Leigh, Gahan, Conway, to Ormonde); 46, ff. 392-402 (Arlington to Ormonde); 217, ff. 346-54 (Anglesey to Ormonde); Rawlinson MS A130, Nov. 1666; Lords RO, committee Minutes (1664-71), pp. 102-10.

160. Witcombe, 48-55 and sources there; Pepys's Diary, vii. 310-11; Marvell's Letters, 46-7; Brit. L. Add. MS 2539, f. 77 (John to Sir Edward Nicholas). I have not narrated the complex affair of the Canary patent, as I believe it to have been of far less importance than these other events.

161. Witcombe, 54-8, and sources there; *Statutes*, v. 584-622; Evelyn, *Diary*, 291; Rawlinson MS A130, Dec. 1666; Lords RO, Parchment Collection, Box 14 (Mordaunt impeachment papers).

162. J. Dewhurst, 'The Quarter Sessions Records of the County Palatine of Chester', *JCNWAAHS* N.S. xxxii (1937), 179-80. In Lancashire, constables seized the cattle and then resold them: Quintrell (ed.), *Lancashire Justices*, 122.

163. T. W. Moody, F. X. Martin, F. J. Byrne (eds.), *A New History of Ireland* (Oxford, 1978) iii. 443.

164. Reprinted in Howell (ed.), *State Trials*, vi. 807-64.

165. Carte MS 35, f. 118 (Broderick to Ormonde).

166. *CTB* i. xxviii-xxxii; Brit. L. Egerton MS 861 (accounts of prizes); Wood's Life, ii. 96; Pepys's Diary, viii. 84, 98; *London Gazette* (12-16 Apr., 14-17 May 1666); Thorold Rogers, *History of Agriculture and Prices*, v. 474.

167. There is a good example of this process at work in Hampshire RO, QO/4, p. 124.
168. SP 29/180/5, 85, 88 (letters from Bristol, King's Lynn), 181/15 (Newcastle); HMC MSS in Various Collections, ii. 381-2 (Treasury commissioners to West Riding JPs); *CTB* i. xxviii-ix; Newcome's Autobiography, 162; Herefordshire RO, Q/OS 1, f. 56; P/C 2/59, pp. 222-6, 379, 413 (references to Hereford, St. Neots, Marlborough, Hexham, North Riding, Pusey, Montgomeryshire); Lancashire RO, QSP/310/19.
169. Sources at n. 157.
170. PRO, ASSI035/108/3/28.
171. Pepys's Diary, vii. 320-1, 365, 404, viii. 6; SP 29/160/104 (anonymous letter); Berwick (ed.), *Rawdon Papers*, 227 (Conway to Armagh).
172. Chandaman, 147, 179.
173. *CTB* i. xxvii-xxxii; Brit. L. Add. MS 9311, f. 115B (naval accounts); Chester City RO, ML/412-28. This is the point which Dr Chandaman seems to miss, and which makes nonsense of the computation in Pepys's Diary, vii. 317, misattributed to Pepys himself by Dr Witcombe.
174. Pepys's Diary, vii. 331.
175. Chandaman, 147; Pepys's Diary, viii. 30; Marvell's Letters, 53; HMC 3rd Report, 245 (Southampton, Ashley, to Cheshire commissioners).
176. Tanner (ed.), *Pepys Correspondence*, 144-61; Pepys's Diary, vii. 30, 415-16, viii. 109; SP 29/180/18, 54 and 181/76 (letters to Pepys and Williamson); Tanner MS 45, f. 141 (York to Navy Board); HMC Le Fleming MSS, 44 (news-letter).
177. Pepys's Diary, vii. 349, 383-4, viii. 43; SP 29/191/43 (Skelton to Williamson).
178. Feiling, 203-4.
179. Tanner (ed.), *Pepys Correspondence*, 153-61.
180. Feiling, 210-15; Lister, *Life of Clarendon*, ii. 369-75; Pepys's Diary, viii. 61; P/C 2/59, f. 161; Carte MS 217, f. 374 (Anglesey to Ormonde); Clarendon MS 85, ff. 43-249, *passim* (letters between Clarendon and St. Albans).
181. Longleat House Coventry MS 1, f. 9; Pepys's Diary, viii. 97-8.
182. Carte MS 35, ff. 356-7 (Broderick to Ormonde).
183. HMC 7th Report, 512 (Finch to brother); SP 29/231, f. 1 (Williamson's journal).
184. Pepys's Diary, viii. 98; Carte MS 47, ff. 142, 158 (Anglesey to Ormonde); Longleat House Coventry MS xcviii, f. 166 (Coventry's notes); HMC 7th Report, 512.
185. Clarendon, *Life*, iii. 186-8; SP 29/231/78 (news-letter to Conway); Carte MS 35, f. 522 (Broderick to Ormonde).
186. Chandaman, 211-12.
187. Pepys's Diary, viii. 112, 131-2, 142-3, 201; Tanner (ed.), *Pepys Correspondence*, 162-75; SP 29/196-101, *passim* (letters to Navy Board, Pepys, Coventry); Carte MS 35, ff. 345, 378 (Broderick, Clarendon, to Ormonde); Egerton MS 2539, f. 91 (John to Sir Edward Nicholas); SP 29/231, ff. 3-17B (Williamson's journal); Brit. L. Add. MS 36782, f. 43B (York's orders).
188. Lister, *Life of Clarendon*, ii. 373-6; Feiling, 216-19.

189. SP 29/231, ff. 15-18; *London Gazette* (Apr.-May); Bryant (ed.), *Letters*, 200-1.

190. Pepys's Diary, viii. 92-3; SP 29/193/65, 113 (news-letters); Steele, no. 3486; Brit. L. Add. MS 27872, ff. 7-12 (Heydon's papers) and Egerton MS 2539, f. 91; SP 29/231, f. 1.

191. SP 29/193/86, 196/67.

192. *London Gazette* (18-22 Apr.); SP 29/231, ff. 13B-18B; Carte MS 35, f. 465 (Broderick to Ormonde); Pepys's Diary, viii. 193-5, 251-2; SP 29/102/18, 103/149 (news-letters).

193. SP 29/231, f. 21; Burnet, *History*, i. 446-7; Clarendon, *Life*, iii. 228.

194. Pepys's Diary, viii. 179, 244; Carte MS 35, f.465 (Broderick to Ormonde); Clarendon, *Life*, iii. 240-5.

195. Henry Roseveare, *The Treasury 1660-1870* (1973), 1-21, first recognised the true importance of the commission. It can be seen at work in *CTB* ii. 1-11 and through the eyes of Pepys's Diary, viii. 239-49.

196. Sources as at n. 110, plus SP 29/126/109 (Somerset gentry to Arlington), 110 (Broughton to Williamson), 127/7 and146/68 (Bradshaigh to Williamson), 134/102 (Cooley to Muddiman); Friends' House L. Great Book of Sufferings, i. 374-5; Cheshire RO, QJF/93/3/31 and EDC/10/1; Lancashire RO, FRM/1/39, ff. 156-7; Humberside RO, DD/QR/10, f. 27, /24 n.p., /25, pp. 3-16; Bristol RO, Q/S Minutes, ff. 63-6; Worcestershire (Shire Hall) RO, Q/S 110/105-9, *passim*; Norfolk RO, C/S2/2, Epiphany 1666, Norwich; North Yorkshire RO, RQ/R 13/2.

197. Worcestershire (St. Helens) RO, 898.2/1303/1, ff. 8-11; Friends' House L. Thirnbeck MS 5 (Hooker to Fell) and Swarthmore MS 1, f. 100 (Briggs to Fell); Fox's Journal, 511-12; Hayden (ed.), *Church of Christ*, 121-2; Burnyeat's Life, 36.

198. Fishwick (ed.), *Altham Church Book*, xx-xxi; Worcestershire (Shire Hall) RO, Q/S 110/109/116.

199. Examples are mentioned in HMC Hastings MSS, ii. 154 (Davys to Huntingdon); Pepys's Diary, viii. 360; HMC Le Fleming MSS, 44 (Wilson to Fleming).

200. The best description is in Ian B. Cowan, *The Scottish Covenanters* (1976), ch. 4.

201. SP 44/20, ff. 135-6 (King to Lord-Lieutenants); Pepys's Diary, vii. 395.

202. SP 29/211/17, 60, 213/90 (letters from York); Rawlinson MS D204, f. 44 (Reresby to Arlington); Raine (ed.), *York Castle Depositions*, 98.

203. SP 29/171/129, 177/80, 83, 189/2, 29, 194/44, 197/118 (letters from Kendal, Eggleston, Draycot, Yarmouth, and news-letters from London); Le Fleming MSS, 44-5 (Bellingham to Fleming); Bod. L. Add. MS C305, f. 58 (Hall to Sheldon); Quintrell (ed.), *Lancashire Justices*, 120-1; HMC 4th Report, 329 (Clarendon to Bagot) and Kenyon MSS 80 (Edward to Roger Kenyon).

204. *The Late Apology in Behalf of the Papists Reprinted and Answered* (1667); *An Abridgement or a Summary Account of all the Statute Laws* (1666); *Pyrotechnica Loyolana* (1667); *Tydings from Rome* (1667).

205. PRO/31/3/112, f. 298 (Comminges to Lionne).

206. Sources at nn. 134 and 203.

207. Fox's Journal, 502; Friends' House L. Thirnbeck MS 5 and Swarthmore MS 3, f. 159 (Howgill to Fell).
208. *A Sermon Preached before the Peers* (November 1666); W. Simon, 'Comprehension in the Age of Charles II', *Church History* 31 (1962), 440.
209. Shrewsbury, 536-7.
210. Slack, *Ec. HR* (1981).
211. Shrewsbury, 486-8; Doolittle, *Trans. Essex Arch. Soc.* 1961-2, 142-3; Jones, *Proceedings Suffolk Institute* (1958-60), 88-9.
212. Shrewsbury, 486-8.
213. E. A. Wrigley and R. S. Schofield, *The Population History of England 1541-1871* (1981), 333.
214. Hodges, *Loimologia*, 15.
215. Ibid. 28; Bell, *Great Plague*, 274; Bell, *Great Fire*, 187.
216. Doolittle, *Trans. Essex Arch. Soc.* (1961-2), 143-4.

Part Four: Chapter 3

1. *CTB* ii. xi; Chandaman, 210; *CSPV* xxxv. 144.
2. Rowen, 593-5, 625-7.
3. P. G. Rogers, *The Dutch in the Medway* (1970), is a detailed study of the raid.
4. Rogers, *Dutch in the Medway*, chs. 6-8; Carte MS 35, f. 478 (Broderick to Ormonde); 47, f. 486 (Coventry to Ormonde); Pepys's Diary, viii. 268.
5. Pepys's Diary, viii. 260, 306-11; Bryant (ed.), *Letters*, 201-2 (to Rupert); P/C 2/59, pp. 444-89; Carte MS 35, f. 484 (Broderick); Rawlinson MS D294, ff. 228-30 (notes on Chatham); SP 46/136/518-20 (notes on Thames batteries); Brit. L. Add. MS 36782, f.43B (York's orders); Dalton, *English Army Lists*, 59-84; Hunter, *South Yorkshire*, ii. 419; *Letters of Chesterfield*, 33.
6. Corporation of London RO, Repertory 72, ff. 124-46; Pepys's Diary, viii. 283, 290; Canon S. Robertson (ed.), 'Cobham Hall: Letters to the Last Duke of Lennox', *Archaeologia Cantiana* xvii (1887), 375-6; SP 29/231, f. 30B.
7. SP 44/26, ff. 11-12; Bod. L. Add. MS C308, f. 95B (Sheldon to bishops).
8. HMC MSS in Various Collections, ii. 125-6 (to Fauconberg); Rawlinson MS D204, f. 50 (Reresby to Fauconberg); Lincolnshire RO, 10 ANC 355/2 (Lindsey to Arlington).
9. Scott, *Joint-Stock Companies*, 281.
10. Colenbrander (ed.), *Bescheiden*, 587-90; PRO, AO/1/48/11-12.
11. J. R. Western, *The English Militia in the Eighteenth Century* (1965), 45-6; M. Faraday (ed.), *Herefordshire Militia Assessments of 1663*, Camden Soc. 4th ser. 10 (1972), 7.
12. *London Gazette* (13-17 June).
13. Pepys's Diary, viii. 264-5, 269; SP 29/205/63-208/111 (letters to Williamson, Hickes, Sawtell); Tanner MS 45, f. 202B (Pepys to Hobart); Josselin, *Diary*, 157; Carte MS 35, ff. 478, 522 (Broderick); Evelyn's Diary, 295-6.
14. Pepys's Diary, viii. 281.
15. Carte MS 35, f. 568 (Broderick).

16. The satirical poems, together with Waller's and the headmaster's, but not Dryden's, are reprinted in George de F. Lord (ed.), *Poems on Affairs of State* (New Haven, 1963), i. 1-152. The debate over Marvell's authorship is reviewed, and contributed to, most recently by Annabel M. Patterson, *Marvell and the Civic Crown* (Princeton, 1978), 113-67. I have used the MS sources cited by her. The prose satires Bod. L. MS Eng. Hist. c. 57. Regrettably, the *Last Instruction to a Painter*, which is perhaps the best of all these satires, has no real place in this narrative. It was composed, seemingly, in September 1667, and refers directly to the events of this year and its predecessor, but was not published till 1689 and there appears to be no reference to its impact in the sources of late 1667. Thus it has no direct relevance to the present book, which is concerned with the making and public reception of government policy.

17. Based on Dr Patterson's sources, and Pepys's Diary, viii. 313.

18. Bruce King, *Seventeenth-Century English Literature* (1982).

19. Pepys's Diary, viii. 268; W. Cooper (ed.), *Savile Correspondence*, Camden Soc. (1858), 16.

20. Clarendon, *Life*, iii. 252-60; Pepys's Diary, viii. 292-3, 332; Carte MS 35, f. 488 (Broderick); *Savile Correspondence*, 17.

21. See Broderick's letter, Carte MS 35, f.478.

22. Rogers, *Dutch in the Medway*, 136-7.

23. Pepys's Diary, viii. 295, 322; Carte MS 35, f. 502.

24. Clarendon, *Life*, iii. 279-81; Pepys's Diary, viii. 299, 302, 330-1, 342; SP 29/207/113 (Thurston to Conway); Carte MS 35, ff. 484, 502, 520k, 549 (Broderick, Carlingford); *Savile Correspondence*, 18; H. C. Foxcroft, *The Life and Letters of Sir George Savile* (1898), i. 51-2; Brit. L. Add. MS 27872, ff. 13-14 (examination); SP 29/231, ff. 32B-37. The rumour that Castlemaine obtained his release sounds like malicious gossip: Charles could hardly do otherwise.

25. Feiling, 223-5; Rowen, 629-33; Pepys's Diary, viii. 329-30.

26. *London Gazette* (20 June-29 July); SP 29/207/97-211/103, *passim* (reports to Williamson); Pepys's Diary, viii. 350-60; Colenbrander (ed.), *Bescheiden*, 564-82; Rawlinson MS A195A, ff. 264-5 (account of St. James's Day action).

27. Witcombe, 61-2, and sources cited there; Carte MS 35, f.576 (Broderick).

28. Rowen, 596-7; SP 29/212/60-215/6, *passim* (letters to Williamson).

29. Steele, nos. 3500-2.

30. Pepys's Diary, viii. 399; SP 29/215/55-216/56, *passim* (letters to Williamson).

31. Carte MS 35, f. 595 (Broderick).

32. Clarendon, *Life*, iii. 282; SP 29/231, ff. 22B, 30, 45B, 47B; P/C 2/59, p. 520; Carte MS 35, ff. 522, 624 (Broderick), 657 (Carlingford), 733 (Clarendon).

33. Clarendon, *Life*, iii. 282-94; Pepys's Diary, viii. 401-10; Lister's *Life of Clarendon*, iii. 468-70 (Arlington, Anglesey, to Ormonde); Carte MS 35, ff.682, 690, 694 (Broderick, Foster), 215, ff. 369-70 (Broderick) and 217, ff. 404-5 (Anglesey); Brit. L. Add. MS 21947, f. 141 (news-letter to Richmond); SP 29/231, ff. 50-2.

34. Carte MS 227, f.14; Pepys's Diary, viii. 413-14.

35. Clarendon, *Life*, iii. 283, 287; Lister, *Clarendon*, iii. 468; Pepys's Diary, viii. 401; Carte MS 217, f. 404; SP 29/216/19 (news-letter).
36. Carte MS 35, f. 657 (Carlingford).
37. SP 29/231, f. 293; Carte MS 35, f. 538 (Broderick).
38. Clarendon, *Life*, iii. 291; Pepys's Diary, viii. 413-15, 506-7; Foxcroft (ed.), *Savile*, i. 53-5; Howarth (ed.), *Pepys's Letters*, 29.
39. Foxcroft (ed.), *Savile*, 54-5; Morrice (ed.), Orrery State Papers, 39 (Orrery's memoir).
40. Simon, *Church History* (1962), 440; Carte MS 45, ff. 228, 232.
41. Pepys's Diary, v. 345.
42. Ibid. viii. 414-15.
43. Lister, *Clarendon*, iii. 469.
44. SP 29/231, f. 5; Brit. L. Egerton MS 2539, f. 91 (John to Sir Edward Nicholas); Fea (ed.), Gramont's Memoirs, 322-40; HMC Le Fleming MSS, 46-7 (news-letters); Margoliouth (ed.), Marvell's Letters, 297; Pepys's Diary, 120, 145, 169, 183.
45. Vol. i. 451-3.
46. Pepys's Diary, viii. 343; Clarendon, *Life*, iii. 323; Bryant (ed.), *Letters*, 203-4.
47. Steele, no. 3507.
48. Ibid. no. 3505; Carte MS 35, f. 595 (Broderick) and 47, f. 172 (Anglesey); Egerton MS 2539, f. 112; SP 29/231, f. 53.
49. SP 29/216/76 (proposals); P/C 2/59, pp. 564-86, *passim*; Pepys's Diary, viii. 424-5; Carte MS 35, f. 700 (Scott); HMC Le Fleming MSS, 53 (news-letter) and 12th Report, ix. 64 (letter from Herbert).
50. HMC 3rd Report, 94 (Gee to Clarke); Colenbrander (ed.), *Bescheiden*, 586-7 (Tyler to Pepys); Durham UL Cosin Letter Book 1B, f. 165 (Albemarle to Musgrave); SP 29/231, f. 42; CTB ii. 49, 58.
51. Tanner MS 45, f. 221 (Hacket to Sheldon); Bod. L. Add. MS C308, f. 101.
52. Simon, *Church History* (1962), 440-1; Brit. L. Egerton MS 2539, f. 13; Newcome's Autobiography, 167; SP 29/216/19 (news-letter), 133 and 217/174 (letters from Bath, Oxford); Palmer, *Nonconformist's Memorial*, i. 365.
53. Muddiman, *King's Journalist*, 172-8; Kitchin, *L'Estrange*, 147-8.
54. CTB ii. 7-92; Carte MS 35, f. 632 (Broderick); Pepys's Diary, viii. 334, 373, 378; SP 29/231, f. 67; Howarth (ed.), *Pepys's Letters*, 29-32.
55. SP 29/211/67 (council order) and 231, ff. 42, 56; Carte MS 35, f. 628 (Clifford); Pepys's Diary, viii. 398.
56. P/C 2/59, pp. 540, 557; SP 29/213/65 (plan for navy); Pepys's Diary, vii. 374, 383, 391-5; Longleat House Coventry MS xcvi, f. 267B (committee to York).
57. Pepys's Diary, viii. 397-8; Coventry MS xcvi, f. 277B (committee to York); P/C 2/59, p. 596.
58. CTB ii. 76-111; P/C 2/59, pp. 540, 553, 607; SP 29/231, f. 61.
59. For demonstrations of the falsehood of the belief, see Pepys's Diary, viii. 331 and n. 2, and CTB ii. xlix-lxvii.
60. Pepys's Diary, viii. 406, 431-4, 447; Lister, *Clarendon*, iii. 469 (Anglesey to

Ormonde); Carte MSS 35, ff. 706 (Broderick), 733 (Clarendon), 737 (Carling-ford), and 215, f. 369 (Broderick); Egerton MS 2539, f. 121.

61. Pepys's Diary, viii. 406, 431-4, 447; Carte MS 35, ff. 694 (Foster), 764 (Conway); Howarth (ed.), *Pepys's Letters*, 29-32; Brit. L. Add. MS 21947, f. 141 (news-letter to Richmond); SP 29/231, ff. 51-2.

62. Cooper (ed.), *Savile Correspondence*, 21-2; HMC Le Fleming MSS, 53 (news-letter); HMC 14th Report, ix. 370 (Bertie to Osborne).

63. Egerton MS 2539, f. 118.

64. PRO/31/3/116, ff. 96-7 (French ambassador's dispatch).

65. Clayton Roberts, 'The Impeachment of the Earl of Clarendon', *Cambridge HJ* xiii. i (1957), 4-8, and *The Growth of Responsible Government in England* (Cambridge, 1966), 158-61.

66. Witcombe, 64-5, and sources there; Pepys's Diary, viii.476-82; Gardiner (ed.), *Oxinden and Peyton Letters*, 338; Johnson, *Lives of the Poets*, i. 273-4; LJ 117-25; Carte MS 35, f. 764 (Conway); Rawlinson MS A130, 22 Oct. (Lords' debate).

67. Carte MS 35, f. 778 (Conway).

68. CJ ix. 3-8; Robbins (ed.), Milward's Diary, 86-99; Anchitell Grey, *Debates of the House of Commons* (1769), i. 1-3.

69. SP 29/231, ff. 62B-63B; P/C 2/60, pp. 10-11.

70. CJ 4-14; Pepys's Diary, viii. 483-515; Carte MSS 35, f. 779 (Broderick) and 217, f. 417 (Anglesey); Milward's Diary, 90-108; Rawlinson MS A195, f. 6 (charges before committtee); Egerton MS 2539, f. 129; SP 29/231, ff. 67-8B; Brit. L. Add. MS 36916, f. 11 (Starkey to friend).

71. Simon, *Church History* (1962), 441; P/C 2/60, p. 64.

72. Roberts, *Cambridge HJ* (1957), 12-15; Witcombe, 66-73; sources cited in these; Carte MS 46, f. 569 (Arlington); Tanner MSS 45, f. 235 (Sir John to John Hobart) and 239, ff. 78B-84B (Holland's speeches); LJ 135-52; Rawlinson MS A130, debates 12-14 Nov.; Pepys's Diary, viii. 530-44; House of Lords RO, Committee Minutes (1664-71), pp. 199-202.

73. Pepys's Diary, viii. 482, 518,532-4; Lister, *Life of Clarendon*, iii. 472 (Arlington to Ormonde); Carte MSS 35, f. 873 and 36, f. 25 (Conway); PRO/31/3/117, f. 14 (French ambassador's dispatch); Egerton MS 2539, f. 139.

74. SP 29/222/3, 223/78 (letters from Deal and Yarmouth).

75. Witcombe, 74-5, and sources there; Pepys's Diary, viii. 544; Carte MS 35, f. 873 (Conway); Evelyn's Diary, 300.

Part Four: Chapter 4

1. Pepys's Diary, iii. 237, iv. 138; Carte MS 35, ff. 126, 148, 873 and 36, f. 25 (Conway).

2. Clay, *Public Finance*, 43-5.

3. Sources at ch. 2, n. 102; Essex RO, D/ACA 55.

4. William C. Braithwaite, *The Second Period of Quakerism* (2nd edition, Cambridge 1961), 247-8; Barbour, *The Quakers*, 234-42.

5. *Calamy Revised*, 493.

6. Lambeth MS 1126.

7. VCH Lincolnshire, ii. 68.

8. Nicolson (ed.), *Conway Letters*, 243 (More to Lady Conway).

Index